A PROVISIONAL HISTORY xiii
WC - NOT NS NOR POLITICS   PROVINCE XIV ... ...TANCE XV
     — SPECIFIC GEOGRAPHICAL
WC, BRISTOL & BREXIT XVi   1, 5
WC = SOMERSET, DEVON, CO
NONCONFORMIST TRADITION   7, 286, 356
                                                    M CITY

CATHEDRALS & BBC AS WC
WC ACCENT & DIALECT NORMS, ..., .
WC ORGANS ON THE BBC 55
    — PERCY WHITLOCK
    — REGINALD FOORT 56
JIM CROW — 1838? 64
REJECTION OF MALE ALTO & OW 1895 109
BBC 112, 179, 271, 331, 349, 350, 351
'TROPES OF YOKEL HUMOUR' — WURZELS 144, 146
    — GEOGRAPHICAL SPECIFICITY 146
WC FOLK REVIVAL 147
DEVONIANS - NO MORE THAN WATCHING THE GRASS GROW 157
BLACKFACE MINSTRELSY 64, 206, 273, 287
ESCAPE FROM THE REGION 225
JOSEPH EMIDY — BLACK 237
THE INVENTION OF THE WC 254
COUNTIES 264, 267
    — CRICKET 268
WIDDECOMBE FAIR 269, 270 / SPREYTON & STICKLEPATH 269
FLORAL DANCE 270-271
WC'S OLDEST MATERIAL TRACES OF HUMAN SOCIETY 274
ZONE OF HEARSAY 275, 278
CORNISH LANGUAGE FESTIVAL PLAYS 276
    — ST. JUST 277 / ST. IVES 278
CORNWALL'S MAGNETIC PULL OVER ARTISTS 285
GOSSINGTON, AUSLEY — GLOS 286
HAS 'THE INVENTION OF THE WEST COUNTRY WORKED'? 288, 289
FISHERMEN'S FRIENDS 292
BRISTOL — CULTURAL ATTRIBUTES OF INDUSTRIAL CONURBATION 300
CLIFTON COLLEGE, 1860 & VALUING OF MUSIC 322, 323, 328
    — GAMES & CHOIR 325
J.W. ARROWSMITH 329
LISZT'S WC TOUR, 1840 345-346
'BRITON & WESTCOUNTRYMAN' 351, 352
    — BBC WEST OF ENGLAND PERFORMING GROUPS 352, 356
    — SENSE OF BELONGING VIA BBC 353-354
    — ORGANISTS & BRISTOL KEY BENEFICIARIES OF BBC PATRONAGE 354
    — ARTHUR FALLOWFIELD / RAMBLING SID RUMPO 357
'RUSTIC BLUNTNESS' 365
DARTMOUTH MAGNIFICAT (1480s) £2 374   ┌─────────┐
    — HOW OFTEN HEARD? TO WHAT EFFECT?   │ INDIRECT│
    — REMEMBERED & TALKED ABOUT 374-375?   │INFLUENCE│
    — HENRY DAVEY 1921 THURSTON DART 1840 → 1960s-70s 375 └─────────┘
    — ! ULTIMATELY THE VALUE OF WC MUSIC WILL BE WHAT WE MAKE IT!

Music in the West Country

Music in Britain, 1600–2000

ISSN 2053-3217

Series Editors:
BYRON ADAMS, RACHEL COWGILL, AND PETER HOLMAN

This series provides a forum for the best new work in the field of British music studies, placing music from the early seventeenth to the late twentieth centuries in its social, cultural, and historical contexts. Its approach is deliberately inclusive, covering immigrants and emigrants as well as native musicians, and explores Britain's musical links both within and beyond Europe. The series celebrates the vitality and diversity of music-making across Britain in whatever form it took and wherever it was found, exploring its aesthetic dimensions alongside its meaning for contemporaries, its place in the global market, and its use in the promotion of political and social agendas.

Proposal or queries should be sent in the first instance to Professors Byron Adams, Rachel Cowgill, Peter Holman, or Boydell & Brewer at the addresses shown below. All submissions will receive prompt and informed consideration.

Professor Byron Adams,
Department of Music – 061, University of California, Riverside, CA 92521–0325
email: byronadams@earthlink.net

Professor Rachel Cowgill,
Department of Music and Drama, University of Huddersfield,
Queensgate, Huddersfield, HD1 3DH
email: r.e.cowgill@hud.ac.uk

Professor Peter Holman MBE,
School of Music, University of Leeds, Leeds, LS2 9JT
email: p.k.holman@leeds.ac.uk

Boydell & Brewer, PO Box 9, Woodbridge, Suffolk, IP12 3DF
email: editorial@boydell.co.uk

Previously published volumes in this series are listed at the back of this volume.

Music in the West Country

Social and Cultural History Across an English Region

Stephen Banfield

THE BOYDELL PRESS

© Stephen Banfield 2018

All rights reserved. Except as permitted under current legislation
no part of this work may be photocopied, stored in a retrieval system,
published, performed in public, adapted, broadcast,
transmitted, recorded, or reproduced in any form or by any means,
without the prior permission of the copyright owner

The right of Stephen Banfield to be identified as
the author of this work has been asserted in accordance with
sections 77 and 78 of the Copyright, Designs and Patents Act 1988

First published 2018
The Boydell Press, Woodbridge

ISBN 978 1 78327 273 0

The Boydell Press is an imprint of Boydell & Brewer Ltd
PO Box 9, Woodbridge, Suffolk IP12 3DF, UK
and of Boydell & Brewer Inc.
668 Mt Hope Avenue, Rochester, NY 14620–2731, USA
website: www.boydellandbrewer.com

The publisher has no responsibility for the continued existence or accuracy of URLs
for external or third-party internet websites referred to in this book, and does not
guarantee that any content on such websites is, or will remain, accurate or appropriate

A CIP catalogue record for this book is available
from the British Library

This publication is printed on acid-free paper

Typeset by
Frances Hackeson Freelance Publishing Services, Brinscall

Printed and bound in Great Britain by
TJ International Ltd, Padstow, Cornwall

For Philip and Dee

Contents

List of Illustrations		viii
Preface and Acknowledgements		xi
List of Abbreviations		xviii
Author's Note		xix
1	Landscapes and Soundscapes	1
2	Musical Authority: Organs	21
3	Musical Incorporation: Bands and Choirs	64
4	Musical Livings I: The Prosopography	151
5	Musical Livings II: Individual Case Studies	209
6	Musical Capitalisation I: Events and Inventions	249
7	Musical Capitalisation II: Institutions	298
	Epilogue: The Measure of a Region	368
	Bibliography	
	Bibliographical Abbreviations	377
	1 Manuscripts, Archives, and Collections	379
	2 Regional Newspapers, Periodicals, and Series	381
	3 Internet Sites	383
	4 Films, Broadcasts, and Recordings	386
	5 Scores and Musical Editions	387
	6 Books, Articles, Dissertations, and Pamphlets	388
	Index	421

Illustrations

Illus. 2.1 Exeter Cathedral, John Loosemore's organ case of 1665. Source: author's photograph.   30

Illus. 2.2 A Scudamore organ (line drawing by G E Street and J R Robbins). Source: Baron 1858: frontispiece. © The British Library Board (shelfmark 7895.c.2).   46

Illus. 3.1 'Choristers, St Mary Church, Devon' (pen and ink sketch by John Nixon). Source: Torre Abbey, Torquay, Devon, UK / Bridgeman Images.   66

Illus. 3.2 'Royal dipping': George III bathing at Weymouth, 7 July 1789 (print by John Nixon). © Historic Royal Palaces. Photograph: Claire Collins.   78

Illus. 3.3 Thomas Hardy's plan of the Stinsford church gallery layout. Source: Dorset County Museum.   82

Illus. 3.4 The Bristol Orpheus Glee Society, collage photograph representing its jubilee concert, Victoria Rooms, Clifton, 1 Febuary 1894. Source: ASSL, DM2114/8/2. Reproduced with the kind permission of Bristol Chamber Choir (Bristol Madrigal Society).   106

Illus. 3.5 Massive Attack, 1998: Andrew Vowles (left), Robert del Naja (centre), Grant Marshall (right) (photo by Hidekazu Shimizu). Source: Everett Collection Inc/Alamy Stock Photo.   149

Illus. 4.1 Monument to Matthew Godwin, organist of Exeter Cathedral, 1587. Source: author's photograph.   156

Illus. 5.1 Thomas Gainsborough or William Jackson: Portrait of William Jackson playing the harp. © Royal Albert Memorial Museum & Art Gallery, Exeter City Council.   236

Illus. 5.2	'A musical club', Truro 1808, with Joseph Emidy (third from right). Reproduced with the kind permission of the Royal Institution of Cornwall.	238
Illus. 5.3	Advertisement for the compositions of Caleb Simper. Source: *Musical Times* lvi (1915): 122. © The British Library Board (shelfmark P.P.1945.aa).	245
Illus. 7.1	Five of Bristol's mediaeval churches. From left to right: St Nicholas, St Mary le Port, All Saints, Christ Church, St Peter. Source: author's photograph.	301
Illus. 7.2	Clifton College, Frederick Bligh Bond's Music School (right). Source: postcard, BA (BRO): 43207/19/12/76.	323
Illus. 7.3	Concert by Imrat Khan and Latif Ahmed Khan in the Great Hall, Dartington, 1970. Reproduced with the permission of the Dartington Hall Trust Archive.	334

Graph

Graph 5.1	Combined lifetime output (number of musical publications listed in British Library catalogue) of Joseph Roeckel, Jules de Sivrai (Jane Jackson), and Frederick Maker.	210

Map

Map 1.1	The west country, showing pre-1974 county boundaries. Cartographer: Catherine D'Alton.	6

Table

Table 8.1	Economic investment in sonic stimulus in the west country parish, 1366–1602.	372

Music Examples

Ex. 3.1	William Knapp, WAREHAM. Source: Knapp 1738: 18–19.	88
Ex. 3.2	R H Heath, 'It came upon the midnight clear', opening. Source: Heath 1889.	90
Ex. 3.3.	John Percival, 'The Bristol Volunteer troop', extract. Source: Percival nd: 2.	96
Ex. 5.1.	Frederick Maker: REST. Source: Barrett 1887: 268.	213
Ex. 6.1.	H Verne, 'Dear old Ilfracombe', extract. Source: Verne 1920.	259

Ex. 6.2(a) 'Midsummer Fair', melody only, stanza 1; (b) 'Widdecombe Fair', melody only, stanza 1. Sources: Sharp and Marson 1904–09: 48–9; Baring-Gould et al 1905: 32–3.   270
Ex. 6.3 The Furry Dance, first strain. Source: author's transcription, Helston, 8 May 2010.   272

The author and publishers are grateful to all the institutions and individuals listed for permission to reproduce the materials in which they hold copyright. Every effort has been made to trace the copyright holders; apologies are offered for any omission, and the publishers will be pleased to add any necessary acknowledgement in subsequent editions.

Preface and Acknowledgements

This book has been a labour of love. My affair with the region began as a young boy, when the impressive streamlined locomotives of Southern Region's West Country class, inaugurated in 1945, steamed through our town in Kent: each was named after a place in the south-west on or near the Southern network, and to me those names were pure magic – Templecombe, Bude, Okehampton, Budleigh Salterton, Yes Tor … Later we moved to Hampshire, and while the New Forest, not yet west country by my definition, was our regular playground, annual holidays began to take the family car further west. The first of these, despite being on a sodden caravan site at the rear end of Paignton, already made me a west country *aficionado*. The second, in 1966, was in an ancient cottage with pink bath-water in the middle of Bodmin Moor. By 1967 we had graduated to a prefab on a farm near Dulverton, to which we returned several times. Through much of the 1980s and '90s my parents lived in semi-retirement, first in Brushford and then in Porlock, the latter a perfect place for visits. Music was not exactly a *leitmotiv* of these experiences, except when my early music group sang a Palestrina mass liturgically one sunny Sunday morning in Luccombe parish church, or with its viols and partbooks crowded into the tiny minstrels' gallery of Chulmleigh Congregational Church to experience the wonderful acoustic. But that is perhaps the point: most of the time, music simply took its place in the scheme of things.

Three years after I moved to Bristol in 2003, I founded CHOMBEC, the Centre for the History of Music in Britain, the Empire and the Commonwealth, and proposed that it should have a threefold brief, regional, national, and transnational. Thanks to generous research leave and a research fellowship from the University, to a British Academy Small Research Grant, to the forbearance and interest of colleagues in both Music and other departments of the Faculty of Arts, and to a succession of eight-in-fifteen-days railcards from First Great Western, I was in due course able to devote an uninterrupted year to gathering the resources for a musical history of the region to which Bristol has always acted as gateway. What I did, in addition to general reading and data-gathering at my desk, was visit as many libraries as possible, some of them many times, ranging from the unique, private Morrab Library of Penzance in the west to the public libraries of Salisbury and Bournemouth in the east, most of them by public transport on a day's outing from Bristol, though Swanage, Lyme Regis, and Bideford were a challenge (duly overcome in two out of three cases), and Cornwall was tackled from our holiday cottage in Mevagissey. Naturally the county record offices were visited too, but their online catalogues allow one to do keyword searches and identify specific items in advance, whereas with the public libraries one never knew what or indeed whom one was going to encounter.

This is therefore the place to acknowledge the invaluable, often unappreciated local studies collections that even the smallest town library may boast, and their knowledgeable and willing custodians. A card index here, painstakingly compiled decades ago from the local newspapers by a team of volunteers; a privately printed pamphlet or photocopied dissertation there; a commemorative booklet produced locally, often without page numbers or date; a crumbling run of newspapers or set of town council minutes; a filing cabinet full of concert programmes and publicity materials, duly shelfmarked; a set of scrapbooks whose compiler thoughtfully deposited duplicate copies in three or four local libraries. On such visits one also overheard the range of enquiries to which the library staff were subjected and marvelled at their expertise and patience. Altogether I visited 61 libraries in the region, plus a number of museums, the record offices, and (later on) a cathedral archive.

That was in 2009–10. I am glad that I visited when I did, for such resources are perennially under threat and some have already succumbed. Exeter's wonderful Westcountry Studies Library, in which I could happily have spent the remainder of my scholarly days, has now closed. On the other hand, not having been able to revisit most of these libraries since then, I am also aware that items will have been published or deposited in the intervening years which I have missed, though I have endeavoured to keep up as much as possible with the region's scholarship through ongoing access to the British Library.

My note-taking took the form of a single database plotted on an Excel spreadsheet, which now contains just over 27,000 entries. It includes columns for place, entity, personal names, multiple keywords, year, date, observations, quotations, and various bibliographical codings, some of them retained as abbreviations in the Bibliography at the end of this book. Across a good deal of the book it is the main tool from which the narrative has been constructed, but it was laid out purely for personal use and would not lend itself to publication. It is, I believe, quite a powerful tool, but all it has done is sample. It is in no respect sufficiently exhaustive and systematic to function as a methodical transcription of the surviving record, as do, for instance, the invaluable Records of Early English Drama (*REED*) entries and the publications of the Bristol Record Society. What it enables is a picture of activity that can be scrutinised by place, trend in time, predominance of type, family involvement, and so forth. The story that it has been used to tell entails many an instance of first (or last) dated reference to a musical phenomenon, or to a person, but, again, it is important to understand that much of this information may in the long term prove inadequate: an earlier reference will be found, new evidence will show a musician's pattern of work to have differed in some respect from what has been extrapolated, a cheaper or more expensive monetary exchange or a greater number of known participants will produce a new mean, average, or calculation of strength and provision.

Let this not be misunderstood. The factual data will not, I hope, prove wrong. But some of the claims will, and I have found myself having to modify many of them after further research. Anybody who has scoured the rapidly increasing range of digitised newspapers now available online will understand this, and it is probably true to say that every named musician in the book from the earlier eighteenth century onwards would benefit from further scrutiny. Many a time I have simply had to stop because a person's or an institution's story would otherwise burgeon out of control. Not that the availability of information simply increases towards the present. Far from it: digitised newspapers fade out around 1950, and other types of primary source such as wills and accounts become progressively inaccessible as one moves through the twentieth century and into the twenty-first, making more recent prosopographical history much more difficult to construct than that for the nineteenth and earlier twentieth centuries. Questionnaires and interviews can rectify this lacuna to some extent, but it is difficult to maintain parity of critical viewpoint with too many different methodologies for different periods, and I decided in the end not to undertake them.

In every respect, therefore, *Music in the West Country* is a provisional history, opening the door for the real work to come. Nor is it a musical history of particular places, or even of types of activity. It is a paradox of what the book has aimed to portray that its account is too discontinuous to provide the former and too continuous to explain the latter, which would require much more cross-reference to data from other regions, from the metropolis, and even from other countries. If, however, it begins to encourage the generation of such histories, its job will have been done. The index has been made as comprehensive as possible so as to offer fragmented glimpses that might be turned into portraits or landscapes.

This bears a little more thought. Take Ashburton, a small but historically significant town in Devon mentioned a number of times in the text. Using the index, the reader will discover that it had a song school in the fourteenth century, possibly synonymous with its ancient grammar school, and that choral polyphony was professionally performed in the decades leading up to the Reformation in St Andrew's church, where also the organ was played until it fell into disuse under Elizabeth I, not being replaced until the later eighteenth century, when a series of musical general practitioners – Mr Sharp, William Reeve, Samuel Chapple – made their mark as paid organists, domestic teachers, and, in Chapple's case, a lively practitioner of psalmody. Reeve, who was organist not at Ashburton but at Totnes, used the district as a springboard for a London theatre career of some distinction. These pieces of information, taken together, might equally suggest two peaks in Ashburton's institutional provision of music or simply indicate particular types of source that survive or have been wholly or partially mined (parish records, musical manuscripts, and newspapers, as well as secondary studies). But there are far too many unmentioned musical topics and periods for the index to begin to represent a musical history of Ashburton.

What are readers to do about this? They can turn their attention to particular topics covered with evidence from other places in order to guess what might have been happening in some of the gaps: brass bands, Associated Board grade teachers, folk groups, or whatever. But this does not help much. Granted, the book's coverage of Okehampton, a town of comparable size on the opposite fringe of Dartmoor, has no points of overlap with that of Ashburton, consisting instead of comments on its retail provision and desire for a bandstand in the early twentieth century and its hosting of a minor rock festival in the early twenty-first. But to infer the overall history of music in Dartmoor towns from these two fragmentary treatments would be absurd. And even in writing these two paragraphs I have had to check one or two things not evident from the text itself.

Nevertheless, *Music in the West Country* does try to offer a comprehensive and reasoned framework, with detailed examples, for understanding the forces that have operated across the entire spectrum of musical activity, active and passive, within a chosen geographical entity that is not the nation state and not a political province, over a period of more than half a millennium, along with points of assessment of what has changed and what has stayed the same. Far too seldom have histories of music attempted this. Here a word about the book's organisation is in order. One single chronology would have been impossible, given the multifariousness of 'musicking' (see chapter 6) at any one time, even quite early times. Yet a study encompassing up to 700 years needs chronological thrust. This is offered on two parallel though very different fronts, in chapters 2 and 3. Chapters 4 and 5 attempt an anatomy of the musician's calling, mostly from the standpoint of the professional and of the big questions that need to be asked about how musicians function, economically and socially. Chronological change is not ignored, sometimes between one section and the next, in chapter 4, while chapter 5 turns to detailed exemplification through individual case studies. Chapter 6 is about cultural constructs, and this is where the west country does begin to feel different or special because of geographical and historical circumstance, rather than an entity destined to prove typical. The chapter is prefaced with mild reference to theory, yet it is important to stress that throughout the book, topics are expounded using the evidence of time- and place-specific data, which is why in most cases what is chronicled about any settlement beyond a certain size is likely to be spread across several or all of the seven chapters. Once chapter 6 has covered cultural ideas and motivations, chapter 7 complements them with expositions of the cultural machinery; while much of this in particular spheres at particular times might apply, *mutatis mutandis*, to any region, once again the west country can perhaps claim uniqueness, though not necessarily for the good, in how some of the machinery has played out, for example in the provision of universities, BBC broadcasting, and professional orchestral music.

I have not mentioned chapter 1. If we return for a moment to our fragmentary data, it is devoutly to be wished that what will follow the present attempt at a provisional history is more of that sterling work undertaken in local studies libraries, whether from the roots up or top-down with institutional research grants. Nothing short of exhaustive data collection for a place and a period of that place's life – and even for small villages the period would need to be quite limited – will provide the materials for the musical history every place and period deserve. Yet even once every known reference to music and musicians in, say, Chard, Crewkerne, Ilminster, and the villages encompassed by drawing a circle around these three towns has been catalogued – and it would be a big enough job doing that merely for the span of a couple of decades – we shall still only know certain things about the texture and interactions of musical experience in that area, those places, and the particular time period. What the place sounded like, from multiple standpoints, and how and why that changed over time, can never be fully reconstructed, regardless of the wealth or poverty of documentary evidence. What it *felt* like may be even less susceptible to documentary interpretation, and this is where the imagination comes in. Chapter 1 introduces the idea of soundscapes, because an author's or composer's imaginative depiction of the sounds of place, however fictional, may in the end serve as an unsurpassable historical touchstone. Authors dealing with their own time and location are naturally of the most patent value, yet alongside the data-gathering I wish to suggest that creative imagining of what is in some way remote is probably the best way in which we can continue to ponder and reconstruct past lives in their contexts. Pageants, dealt with in chapter 6, used to do this, calibrating episodes from the same place or the same fictitious or semi-fictitious person across time. Osbert Lancaster did it (see chapter 1). The song 'The Vicar of Bray' does it as a by-product of its political satire: that is, it observes change from an unchanging viewpoint, in this case that of the secure living held on to at all costs. Musical compositions and documentary film can do it. Let the imaginative treatments of west country musical history therefore begin!

Now is a good time for them to do so, for the west country may be at a turning point. The results of the referendum on Britain's membership of the EU in June 2016 showed that in the twenty-first century the region feels undervalued. Overall, it voted 'Leave' by a majority of 53 per cent, a higher figure than the national majority of just under 52 per cent. The 'Leave' vote was even greater in the former resort towns and areas, where it aggregated to 57 per cent. Apart from the Isles of Scilly, the only 'Remain' districts were university towns and their hinterlands, if one includes South Hams among the latter. Post-industrial Plymouth's and post-resort Bournemouth's substantial 'Leave' votes would probably have been greater were it not for the moderating influence of these towns' university populations. Predictably, the region's largest city, Bristol, harboured by far the largest 'Remain' vote in the west country, 62 per cent.[1]

The simplest interpretation of this result would be that most people in the region, above all in those parts of it with an ageing or isolated population, believe that things have got worse for them in the past forty years, that they deserve better, and that they have had to challenge the institutional powers that be in voting for further change. Inner London, where an overwhelming majority of 73 per cent voted 'Remain', has been making socio-economic winnings at the expense of the English regions. To a less extreme extent, Bristol has similarly sucked the life out of the further west country.

At least, that is the perception. Whether Brexit will ameliorate the equation or make it worse is difficult to predict. What cannot be denied is that unemployment and lack of productivity in many regional towns – nobody wears a suit in Torquay – and land use and the upkeep of infrastructure in many rural areas are drains on the national economy rather than contributors to it. University towns maintain some kind of economic self-sufficiency, perhaps because young graduates stay and find – or create – jobs, but even a public school and county

---

[1] Elec Comm. Percentages have been rounded to the nearest whole number.

town such as Taunton evidently does not ('Leave': 53 per cent). People in the region have felt marginalised, disempowered, or embattled by all this. They want a better balance, a greater reciprocity, the return to a time when they could take pride in their contribution. Taking a pride in their music will do no harm, and it is the aim of this book to assist in that endeavour.

Many individuals and several corporate bodies have helped in its production. Of the latter, beyond those mentioned earlier, I am profoundly grateful to *Music & Letters* for an award and to the Bernarr Rainbow Trust for a generous subvention; these covered reproduction and other costs. As for the individuals, Peter Hunter and the Milford Trust gave permission for the inclusion of unpublished material. Small queries were answered and helpful hints offered by David Allinson, Andrew Ashbee, Suzanne Aspden, Margaret Bent, the late Andrew Britton, Jeanice Brooks and her team of researchers, Iain Burnside, Hugh Cobbe, David Fallows, Anna Farthing, Lance Foy, Alain Frogley, Michael Gale, Patrick Gale, Vic Gammon, Timothy Hands, Sally Harper, Makiko Hayasaka, Clare Hickman, Mark Horton, Peter Horton, Michael Kassler, David Lasocki, Ros Lawton, Catherine Lorigan, Charles McGuire, Kenneth Mobbs, Kerry Murphy, Libby Nichol, Christopher O'Brien, Mike O'Connor, Julian Onderdonk, Christopher Page, Ian Payne, Margaret Peirson, Christopher Redwood, Stephen Roe, Jim Samson, Gavin Skinner, John Sloboda, Debra Smith, Raymond Warren, Justin Williams, Nicholas Williams, and Geoff Woolfe. Jane Bliss, Beshley Bwye-Turner, Philip Carter, Michael Daly, Sally Drage, Jerome Farrell, David Gostick, Harry Diack Johnstone, Tamaris Mucklow, David Owen Norris, Toby Parker, Deborah Sugg Ryan, Janet Snowman, and Hugh Torrens had a somewhat larger involvement. I had fruitful dialogue in the early days of mapping out the territory with colleagues at the University of Bristol: Elizabeth Archibald, Robert Bickers, James Clark, Emma Hornby, Pamela King, John Pickard, and Beth Williamson. Many librarians and archivists assisted me, from whom I must single out Angela Doughty, Jane De Gruchy, and Michael Richardson. I thank all these people, though I am bound to have forgotten some; they will, I hope, forgive me. My greatest scholarly debt, however, is to those friends, colleagues, and former students who have offered support, interest, and expertise, often over many years: Jonathan Barry, Andrew Brown, Philip Burnett, Andrew Clarke, Trevor Herbert, James Hobson, Peter Holman, Steven Martin, Nicholas Nourse, Philip Payton, Matthew Spring, Yvette Staelens, George Tatham, Nicholas Temperley, and Matthew Thomas. I have found myself thinking of them in every sentence. Finally, my partner, Oscar Martínez, has shown considerable patience throughout this book's unusually long gestation, and helped a great deal with data-gathering in the early stages. I thank him for his love and support.

London, 29 March 2017

Abbreviations

ABRSM	Associated Board of the Royal Schools of Music
AFM	American Federation of Musicians
ASCAP	American Society of Composers, Authors and Publishers
BBC	British Broadcasting Corporation
bn	bassoon
BSO	Bournemouth Symphony Orchestra
CFWI	Cornish Federation of Women's Institutes
cl	clarinet
EFDSS	English Folk Dance and Song Society
EU	European Union
fl	*floruit* (flourished)
GP	general practitioner
GWR	Great Western Railway
hn	horn
HP	hire purchase
HTV	Harlech Television
LEA	Local Education Authority
MusD	Doctor of Music
pa	per annum
RAM	Royal Academy of Music
RC	Roman Catholic
RCM	Royal College of Music
SA	Salvation Army
SATB	soprano, alto, tenor, bass
serp	serpent
tr	trumpet
TTBB	tenor, tenor, bass, bass
TUC	Trades Union Congress
WI	Women's Institute

These abbreviations cover those mentioned in the main text; for all other abbreviations please refer to the Bibliography.

Author's Note

In the interests of brevity, the references in the footnotes do not specify in which section of the Bibliography the item is to be found. It is best to look in section 6 first, then try section 3 if it is not there, though if the reference is not in author-date format and is not the issue of a newspaper, it may be in section 1. Abbreviated periodical and newspaper titles are decoded in section 2. A key to other bibliographical abbreviations will be found at the head of the Bibliography. Items only appear in the Bibliography when they have been referred to in footnotes or captions; other items, especially scores, are mentioned in the main text. Footnotes have been restricted to the ends of sentences, citations referring in order to material in the sentence in question, not necessarily at its end. Much of the time, spelling and capitalisation have been modernised. But I adopt the spelling 'quire', often used nowadays, to indicate a mixed psalmody group of singers and instrumentalists. Dates are given as found, i.e. using the Julian Calendar until 1752, but have been modernised throughout in terms of the next year beginning on 1 January. Bar numbers are counted from the first complete measure.

As for definitions and coverage, 'Duchy' and 'county' are contested terms as relating to Cornwall. While not used with any specific contradistinction in the present work, the term 'Duchy' is generally preferred, for reasons of its historic importance.[1] Counties are generally referred to in accordance with their pre-1974 identities, though it has been convenient to forget that until 1974 Bournemouth and Christchurch were in Hampshire, a county beyond the scope of this study. I use the term 'nonconformist' to denote all Protestant denominations and sects outside the Anglican church, including Methodists, Baptists, Presbyterians, Congregationalists, Unitarians, and others such as the Bible Christians. It is a moot point as to whether Quakers are best considered Protestants, but the question does not really arise. The term 'monodic' is used to mean a piece or section of music with only one vocal line, whether or not accompanied instrumentally. I may have coined the term

---

[1] Payton 2004: 78–82, 84–6.

'multitrader' for someone who earns only part of their living through music. I have very occasionally strayed over my self-appointed geographical border, discussed in chapter 1, when evidence presented itself.

Sterling currency until 1971 took the form of pounds (£), shillings (s), and pence (d). There were twelve pence in a shilling, and twenty shillings in a pound. A guinea was one pound and one shilling, £1.05 in today's denominations. A groat was four pence.

CHAPTER 1

Landscapes and Soundscapes

Around the year 1280, the music of the west country was considered something special. The Parisian music theorist Anonymous IV, writing of techniques for concluding an organum (that is, a composition in which two melodies sounded simultaneously, in this earliest phase of western art music's unusual capacity), stated that it was normal to end on the interval of a 5th or unison, except in the west country of England, where a 3rd might be heard. He actually used the word 'westcuntre' in his treatise, otherwise written in Latin. We do not know whether he meant the region of Somerset, Devon, Cornwall, Dorset, and parts of Wiltshire that has been taken to comprise the west country for the purposes of this book. If, as has been suggested, he was an Englishman influenced by Roger Bacon, who probably grew up in Somerset, he may well have done.[1] In that case, it is clear that a distinctive and perhaps admired musical practice was found there and deemed worthy of honourable note.

The west country's other venerable claim to musical fame is also mediaeval: the Sarum Rite, or Use of Sarum. This was a very different matter from the actual distinctive sounds in performance of what Anonymous IV was describing, being primarily the dissemination within most English cathedrals, and some liturgical establishments abroad, of Salisbury Cathedral's 'good constitutional practice'. True, the Use of Sarum entailed some idiosyncratic elements of musical performance practice, such as troped Kyries 'in which each phrase was sung with the words of its prosula by soloists and repeated melismatically by the choir'. But it is important to realise, as Nicholas Sandon points out, that 'Sarum chant cannot claim any great originality'. Sandon continues:

> Very little of it was peculiar to Salisbury, and although the Sarum versions of widely disseminated chants may show variance in pitch, underlay or degree of elaboration, the variants are insufficiently large, systematic or stable to

[1] Haines 2006.

constitute a recognizable dialect ... Even if it were possible to identify a sizable body of chant specifically composed at or for Salisbury, this would almost certainly not allow the identification of a local idiom; late medieval West European chant is simply not distinctive in this way.[2]

The best analogy in terms of how Salisbury's influence was manifested musically would be with the singing of a hymn nowadays to a particular tune, as decided by a combination of the authority of a hymnal, arising itself from a denominational committee's deliberations, with patterns of training on the part of clergy and organists and uptake by their congregations. Pieces of art music based on that tune would necessarily reflect the tune's liturgical currency. This is true of much English polyphony in its relation to Sarum chant, but detailed consideration of the matter lies beyond the scope of this book.

Apart from a particularly strong association of Somerset with folk music from the later nineteenth century onwards and, with a world-famous festival, that of Glastonbury, today, the region has never again merited particular musical notice. This does not mean that it lacked musical distinction, one curious example of which would be the pre-eminence of Bristol and Bath as a platform and haven for guitar virtuosi in the earlier nineteenth century and these musicians' interactions with the Bristol school of artists.[3] But the west country developed no large industrial city with a professional orchestra or music conservatoire and has supported no triennial music festival to match the resilience and influence of the Three Choirs or Leeds; even the proletarian heritage of male voice choirs and brass bands in Cornwall has been overshadowed by those of Wales and the north. Most classical music lovers readily able to identify Elgar with the Malverns and Britten with East Anglia would be hard pressed to name a west country composer, and, at the next level of connoisseurship, the English madrigal is again more associated with East Anglia than with composers and aristocratic establishments of the west. Admittedly pop music can boast the Bristol sound, but the association of Liverpool with the Beatles and a world-renowned flowering of talent outshines it a thousand to one.

There are possible reasons for this, one of them being rising Puritanism in the Jacobean period and a strong nonconformist tradition thereafter across much of the region. The west country went from being a favourite touring circuit of dramatic companies in the sixteenth century to 'one of the least rewarding' early in the seventeenth, as towns such as Barnstaple and

---

[2] Sandon 2001b: 160–1.
[3] Britton 2010: 300–1, 307–42, and passim.

Plymouth preferred to hire preachers.[4] At that period, public music-making will have been no more to these towns' tastes than shows, a disapproval that may have left some kind of a longer mark, though such an argument can never be conclusive, and historians are increasingly wary of using growing Puritanism as a 'convenient shorthand'.[5] But there are also reasons why no comprehensive history of music has yet been written for any other region of England. Vernacular music-making leaves only scattered traces, and they rarely include any real insight into how techniques, styles, and repertoires have been learnt, loved, shared, and passed on, let alone how their performances have sounded and been received. In chapter 3, it will be necessary to comment on how little we know about how popular dance musicians came into being and how their bands functioned: and this was in the twentieth century.

The lack of a regional history is brought further into relief by its converse, a relatively flourishing musicological urban industry. For a long time, historical accounts of music in a particular British town or city tended to deal with the institutional bases of church and concert hall, theatre and opera house, with perhaps a nod at schools, guilds and chantries. Sutcliffe Smith wrote about Birmingham in this way, and Farmer restricted his study of Aberdeen to an eighteenth-century concert series.[6] More recently, Trevor Fawcett has limited his coverage of Norwich – while including its county – to the eighteenth century, Susan Wollenberg hers of Oxford to the eighteenth and nineteenth centuries.[7] But even here the emphasis is mostly or exclusively on the elite tradition, as it is in Margaret Handford's history of music in Birmingham, which despatches minstrels and ballad singers along with the middle ages in the first six pages.[8] How in any case would one make a unified musical study out of the vastly different types of evidence pertaining to a cathedral and a *bhangra* producer?

What began to make different kinds of history seem possible and desirable was Reinhard Strohm's *Music in Late Medieval Bruges* of 1985, with its opening chapter 'Townscape–soundscape'. The simple ploy of associating different musical sounds in the city with different spaces opened up a musical geography that would have a place for all kinds of music, musician, and listener. Urban musical geography was implicitly political insofar as spaces were proprietorial

---

[4] MacLean 2003: 25.
[5] Fleming 2003: 98.
[6] Sutcliffe Smith 1945; Farmer 1950.
[7] Fawcett 1979; Wollenberg 2001.
[8] Handford 2006.

and dynamic, sometimes contested, and saw or rather heard various musical sounds struggling for power and representation, or even for existence, just as the people inhabiting the spaces might also be doing. Colonial contexts have proved especially fertile for this sort of study, witness David R M Irving's work on Manila and Geoffrey Baker's on Cuzco, though provincial studies of European towns and cities have also found fertile terrain following on from Strohm, as with Miguel Marín's monograph on music in eighteenth-century Jaca, Spain.[9]

To my knowledge, no town in Britain has yet been explored in this way, and even London's musical history is nowhere yet to be found in book or periodical form. There is one notable exception: *Manchester Sounds*, a more or less biennial scholarly journal which began publication in 2000. This has relied on financial support from a specifically musical charity, the Ida Carroll Trust, but it shows what can be done once that support has been secured. The title, moreover, promised full engagement with soundscape inclusivity. Yet even here, what started off as a promising blend of scholarship on blackface minstrelsy, psalmody, brass bands, folk, and the retail business (though with little or nothing on rock), as well as the usual channels of art music, has tended in later years to revert to the worn paths of this last. Bristol, meanwhile, leading city of the west country, can boast no published monograph devoted to its music, only an unpublished MA thesis; no journal; and a bibliography in *Grove* containing three items as opposed to the twenty-six for Norwich.[10]

Little wonder, then, that the trickier entity of a region lies still further off the musicological map than individual towns and cities. Roz Southey has attempted such mapping for the north-east while restricting her coverage to the eighteenth century (once again).[11] Of considerable use and encouragement for the present study is Richard McGrady's study of music and musicians in early nineteenth-century Cornwall, to which Geoffrey Self's *Music in West Cornwall: a twentieth century mirror* provides an equally helpful counterpart.[12] The position of these authors has been aided by the very remoteness and containedness of that tip of the south-west peninsula and by the perceived and asserted Celtic identity of its inhabitants, with their aspirations to function as a miniature nation in their cultural practices: after all, until the early modern period Cornwall had its own language. Cornish studies, beyond being the title of a scholarly journal in the same way as, say, *The Devon Historian*, is an academic discipline, which Devon studies or west country studies are not.

[9] Strohm 1985; Irving 2010; Baker 2008; Marín 2002.
[10] Hooper 1963; Matthews et al 2001; Temperley et al 2001.
[11] Southey 2006.
[12] McGrady 1991; Self 1997.

In contrast with this dearth of localised and regionalised studies of music, there are any number of books on the west country in general. Inevitably geared up to the tourism (including armchair tourism) that swept over it in the twentieth century and to the perceived quality of life that continues to draw people to it today, they have, one might argue, assisted in the very invention of it as a cultural entity, an invention implicitly endorsed in the use of that same phrase 'west country' by the present author. Why, then, has there been as yet no counterpart that attempts coverage of it, like those other 'west country' books, as a topographical entity but in restriction to its musical life?

Perhaps the question should be turned around: why should there be? What will it reveal? After all, there is probably no book, either, on pottery in the west country, or transport in the west country, or sport in the west country, or even monastic foundations in the west country, though there is one on its theatre, as there is also one on its emigration to Australia, while in 2009 John Payne published *The West Country: a cultural history*.[13]

The answer to these questions will be paradoxical. One of the reasons it is bound to be so is that the region as such, despite its topographical boundedness as a peninsula, can only be an arbitrary construct, all the more so in contrast with Cornwall's stronger claim to being an entity, virtually water-bound as it is because of the River Tamar, which no railway crossed until the late date of 1859. Even today, entering Cornwall by car takes one across visually exciting boundaries: the Saltash Suspension Bridge, with Brunel's Albert Bridge alongside; the climb from Tavistock followed by the plunge through the woods and up again at Gunnislake; the hoarier plunge to Greystone Bridge; or the exhilarating, barren, and seemingly endless coast road to Bude and beyond with its glimpses of the wild Atlantic and Lundy. Even the characterless A30 sounds a muted fanfare as Launceston approaches with its hilltop castle ruin. The larger peninsula boasts no such liminal features, and definitions of it have varied widely. Ronald Duncan felt that Devon and Cornwall could be combined in one study.[14] Two other books take Devon, Cornwall, and Somerset to be the west country.[15] Lewis Wilshire's *West Country Short Stories* expanded the region to Cornwall, Devon, Dorset, Wiltshire, Somerset, and Gloucestershire.[16]

There would have been something to be said for including Gloucestershire, and it is included in the UK's designated region of South West England,

---

[13] Crane 1980; Brown 1988; Payne 2009.
[14] Duncan 1966.
[15] Warren 1938; Manning-Sanders 1949.
[16] Wilshire 1949.

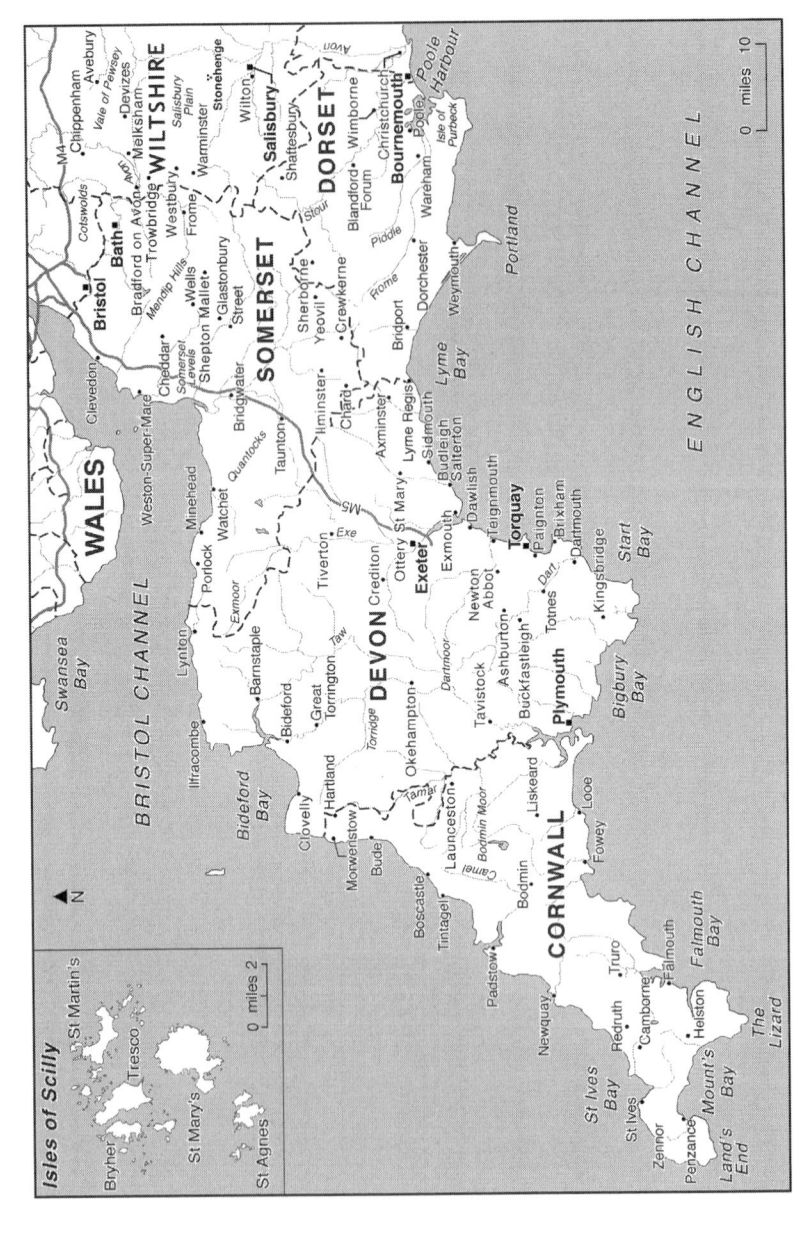

Map 1.1   The west country, showing pre-1974 county boundaries. Cartographer: Catherine D'Alton

one of the nine official regions of England and the largest in area.[17] But the musical history of Gloucestershire seemed to me so bound up with its identity as a border county and with the Three Choirs Festival that it would fit much better into a book on music in the West Midlands and the Marches, though it must not be forgotten that Bristol was part of the diocese of Worcester in the middle ages and of Gloucester for much of the nineteenth century.[18] I have ranged somewhat more narrowly: the west country for purposes of the present book is bounded by the sea, the M4 motorway, and the Hampshire Avon (Map 1.1). Thus Gloucestershire is mostly out, Wiltshire half in. This has a disadvantage to which I gave insufficient thought in choosing the geographical limits of my research: by excluding Swindon (north of the M4), I lost the opportunity of studying a nineteenth-century industrial town. But nobody thinks of Swindon as the west country, and I was more keen to highlight two important cities as entry points: Bristol and Salisbury. Gateway cities matter, socio-economically. Queen Elizabeth's 1574 progress took her no further west than Bristol, and she visited Salisbury on her way back to London via Longleat and Wilton. George III stopped off in Salisbury on his way to Weymouth in 1792 to see Wyatt's renovated cathedral and hear the new Samuel Green organ he himself had donated to it.[19] The gateway status has not always been to positive effect: Phil Johnson wrote in 1996 that 'as a staging post on the West-Country-festival circuit of the summer, Bristol has become a city of beggars for much of the year ... Many ... are junkies and there's a strong trade in heroin which affects even the outlying estates.'[20] Payne is similarly concerned with ways in, focusing on much the same territory as myself when he describes the River Wylye as 'this most enchanting and unlikely of entries into the West Country'.[21] Being enticed into the region by land from further east or north has been a significant element in many people's experience of the west country, at least since the railways arrived and probably from much earlier, for the peninsula was a favourite circuit for travelling theatre companies, with whatever music and musicians they took along, in the sixteenth century.[22] True, subduing one's way through the west country as a Roman, an Anglo-Saxon invader, John Wesley, or an eighteenth-century exciseman must have felt somewhat different. As for the railway routes, they merely capped an experience long

---

[17] Wikipedia: 'South West England'.
[18] Wikipedia: 'Diocese of Bristol'.
[19] Matthews Sal: 5; anon 1821, ii: 225.
[20] Johnson 1996: 29.
[21] Payne 2009: 14.
[22] MacLean 2003.

inscribed on the region's physiognomy. Southern Railway's lay through Salisbury to Exeter, Plymouth, and the Atlantic north coast, in competition with those of the GWR, which arrived via Chippenham, Bath, and Bristol (or Westbury). Nor should we forget Stonehenge, that ancient entry or exit point (was it that?), and alongside it the A303, another important way in but not quite passing through Salisbury and now the subject of a book.[23]

All of this is to acknowledge having made the region's boundaries not so much arbitrary as convenient to one's own purpose. Power blocs do that too, and how they define the boundaries of a region does fix specific ways of doing, organising, and paying for things within it. Music in one of the Spanish *autonomías* must be subject to all kinds of bureaucratically, financially, and politically shaping forces that help explain particular outcomes, those outcomes themselves strengthening the region's identity. But the *autonomías* were not and may not be always there, and England, for its part, has never developed strong regional government, so a top-down explanatory history of the west country or any other English region is not possible. Regional catchment areas of national institutions such as police, health, legal, and education authorities tend to overlap and shift in highly confusing ways. On the other hand, the county boundaries in the west country, while themselves subject to change, have been largely co-extensive with those of the ecclesiastical dioceses, that of Bath and Wells equating to Somerset, of Exeter to Devon, and of Salisbury to Wiltshire. (Dorset was shunted from pillar of Bristol to post of Salisbury; Cornwall separated from Exeter's jurisdiction in late 1876 when the Diocese of Truro was formed. This summary ignores the more ancient dioceses.) So one may conclude that among the strongest administrative forces in west country music have been the cathedrals, which would be true. As will be emphasised again in chapter 7, their focus as places for musical employment, performance, regulation, and consolidation has been unexampled over the 700 or so years covered by this book. The networks operating between them will surface from time to time in the narrative, mostly in terms of individuals moving around and collaborating. There is no section on cathedral music as such, but its enormously influential repertoire, liturgical principles, and patronage (including the education of its exponents), having been the subject of plenty of previous studies, emerges here repeatedly in a great variety of other contexts. So does the wider musical culture in the cathedral cities. The only musical institution remotely approaching the cathedrals in terms of regional authority has been the BBC, particularly in the postwar years, as discussed

---

[23] Fort 2012.

in chapter 7. Its western regional headquarters were in Bristol, where an outpost still remains.

Even in a hub or radiating from it, it is seldom easy to argue that music generates particularity according to place. What can be distinctive about music in the myriad towns, villages, and tracts of land which taken together are the 'country' in 'west country'? Do they all have one musical thing in common that is not quite the same in any other region, or even a definable musical identity at the county or diocese level? No. A mediaeval church tower in Somerset looks quite different from a Devon one, and the different type begins more or less as soon as you cross the border. There may be good practical reasons for this – building stone sourced from different quarries by different networks of masons; diocesan employment patterns – though I am only guessing at them, and it could have been a much less utilitarian matter of identity and fashion. Quite small variations in place can produce differences of material artefact. Speaking of the north Devon earthenware manufacturing tradition, the historian John Watkins wrote in 1792 that 'though the potteries at Barnstaple make use of the same sort of clay, yet their earthen-ware is not held in such esteem at Bristol, &c as that of Bideford' – which tells us not only that Bideford produced something special but that Bristol, the region's largest city, had to be aware of this and validated it.[24] Yet music, at least in England, seems not to work in this way, and even traditional songs, sung and passed on in the most modest of rural locations, have travelled promiscuously, despite Cecil Sharp's and Sabine Baring-Gould's attempts to give them county identities, as examined in chapter 6. Perhaps this is odd, by comparison with architecture and spoken language, for there is a west country accent and there are west country dialect words; and within these broad types there are more local differences, as with the church towers and the earthenware, not to mention the Devonian and Cornish ways of consuming a cream tea.

Instead, what will emerge throughout the following pages will be a reconstruction of many detailed musical practices and exchanges that were representative of their time and place but could, by and large, have happened and may have happened similarly or at least comparably in any other English region. Indeed, I find myself more and more interested in the idea that, *mutatis mutandis*, they may have happened similarly in other countries too. To a large extent it will be a study in what was common or normal, given the forces operating at the time: a study in prosopography, in how people went about their lives with music, and how things changed for them or did not.

---

[24] Watkins 1792: 75.

Here, then, is another element of the paradox, that the more one focuses on the geographically specific and minute – the small provincial town rather than London, the west country village rather than an East Anglian one – the more one finds that what is particular is also typical, and that data from quite another place could have been substituted to much the same argumentative effect. It becomes a matter of how music behaves, how the whole body of musical practice, of 'musicking' (see chapter 6), can be anatomised in a particular sphere or period or across them. I would argue that even districts of London, excepting perhaps the West End, would exhibit much the same phenomena as some town or village in the west country, that their music would be 'solved' using much the same equation, though with variables.

Thus the musical anatomy of any human community or geographical entity, or at least any that is subject to the familiar modes of urban and rural life as developed over many centuries in the western hemisphere and in countries subject to the patterns of western economics, begins to be glimpsed. At this point, a profoundly important study of such an anatomy needs to be mentioned: Ruth Finnegan's *The Hidden Musicians*, first published in 1989.[25] This was a comprehensive musical ethnography of the new English city of Milton Keynes, and in uncovering the extraordinary plenitude of music-making across the various 'worlds' that emerged through the author's field research, it began to make musical prosopography feel plausible. If the present work achieves a fraction of the nuanced interpretation and comprehensive coverage of Finnegan, I shall be happy. While her study deals by and large only with the present, or what was the present when she was writing it, it offers the perfect complement to many of the strands that will be traced historically below, and permits the historian of local music to glimpse where those strands may typically have ended up in our own lifetimes. Again, it is fair to assume that something very similar to how Milton Keynes was functioning musically in the 1980s would also be true of, say, Taunton or, but for its high-profile professional orchestra, the Bournemouth-Poole-Christchurch conurbation.

Were one to pursue the typical to its ultimate conclusion, however, one would end up writing a historical account of an entirely fictitious place. This Osbert Lancaster did, to wonderfully comic effect and with delicious illustrations, in his *Drayneflete Revealed* and *Progress at Pelvis Bay*.[26] The former even included the Drayneflete Carol, 'composed by an anonymous member of the community in the early fourteenth century' and already

---

[25] Finnegan 2007.
[26] Lancaster 1949; Lancaster 1936.

'the subject of twenty-one talks in the Third Programme by Professor Harpsbaum', and he laid out its three stanzas of spoof text in Gothic script and its melody in period notation.[27] Historical accounts of real places are circumscribed by the chance and partial nature of the surviving evidence, and the temptation to flesh out the evidence with supposition or methods of creative reconstruction that verge on the fictional has in general been avoided in the present study (though I have recommended it in the Preface). Nor have I at any point in the ensuing narrative attempted to take a snapshot in time of a particular village's, town's, or district's musical landscape – or soundscape. As already mentioned, Strohm did this for late mediaeval Bruges, and it could be done for many a west country location. It has in fact sometimes been done, and examples will now be offered after introducing the elements of soundscape theory.

The Canadian composer R Murray Schafer invented soundscape studies, and although he was not the first creative thinker to use the word, it was his book *The Tuning of the World*, published in 1977, that consolidated the concept.[28] His theory was startlingly simple: a soundscape may be mapped like a landscape, and the meaning of a particular soundscape will depend on two variables: the 'keynote sounds' that nobody notices because they are perceived as a natural or perennial background, and its 'soundmarks', the aural equivalent of landmarks: sounds that stand out as particular to that place. Thus again we have a general equation with local variables, variables operating in time as well as space.

Music in all its multitudinous and potentially conflicting variety is only one element in a soundscape, which will also include the noises of the natural environment (running water, birdsong, etc) and the whole range of non-musical human sounds, from speech to traffic noise. The acoustic properties of any sound vary with the landscape or streetscape – mountains cause echoes, densely built housing obscures instruments in a marching band – and thus they are part of the equation. Distance and direction matter. Clearly, then, this book, being only about music, could not have been cast as a series of soundscape studies.

But where does one draw the line? In signing off this introductory chapter with several accounts of west country soundscapes, two things will become evident. The first is that the meanings of music, especially perhaps in rural environments, may for particular individuals inhere primarily in the relation of the music in question to the other sounds that make up the soundscape.

[27] Lancaster 1949: 14.
[28] Schafer 1977.

The second is that there is no defined boundary between musical and non-musical sounds and practices, the classic case of this, hugely important as a marker of place and custom in the west country as elsewhere, being bells.

It was with regret that, surfeited with information, I decided to exclude bells as an element of this study and its database. My regret was all the stronger because Devon is more or less unique in practising call change ringing as opposed to method ringing.[29] Whether bell ringing, one of the most widespread and certainly one of the most democratic sound practices to be found in the west country over the course of four centuries or more, counts as music can be forever disputed. What cannot be disputed is that it has at times paralleled psalmody quite closely in its social complexion and independence from church authority; Vic Gammon devotes a whole chapter to it in his dissertation on popular music in rural Sussex.[30] Bells, it would seem, have formed one of the most distinctive and vividly remembered elements in the soundscape of almost any place barring the most remote – and given the transitory nature of sound, memory surely has to hold the key to a soundscape's value when the issue is not persistent and unwelcome noise.

Thomas Hardy's soundscape essay in *A Pair of Blue Eyes* (1873) takes the hour strokes of a distant church tower chime as its starting point. Awaiting a tryst, the hero establishes himself in the Endelstow churchyard, Endelstow being Hardy's name for the Cornish hamlet of St Juliot. The church clock is in Boscastle, two miles away. The meeting itself is modelled on Hardy's own courtship of his first wife.

> 'One, two, three, four, five, six, seven, eight, nine.' Stephen carefully counted the strokes, though he well knew their number beforehand. Nine o'clock ... Stephen stood at the door of the porch and listened. He could have heard the softest breathing of any person within the porch; nobody was there. He went inside the doorway, sat down upon the stone bench, and waited with a beating heart.
>
> The faint sounds heard only accented the silence. The rising and falling of the sea, far away along the coast, was the most important. A minor sound was the scurr of a distant night-hawk. Among the minutest where all were minute were the light settlement of gossamer fragments floating in the air, a toad humbly labouring along through the grass near the entrance, the crackle of a dead leaf which a worm was endeavouring to pull into the earth, a waft of air, getting nearer and nearer, and expiring at his feet under the burden of a winged seed.

---

[29] Wikipedia: 'Change ringing'.
[30] Gammon 1985: 68–103.

Among all these soft sounds came not the only soft sound he cared to hear – the footfall of Elfride.[31]

Hardy's muster of elements shows him a master of soundscape creation. His soundscape has a shape: we start not just with an instrument but with a humanly created mechanism and rhythm. The loud beating of the hour strokes has its counterpart in the intimate beating of Stephen's heart. A major sound of nature follows, then a 'minor' one (Hardy will have been aware of the musical implication), then a bouquet of four tiny elements of which two are made by vegetable, not animal nature. A moment's thought will tell us that these last four sounds, the quietest, could only have been heard by certain non-human creatures (possibly the night-hawk); thus Hardy is fusing human and non-human standpoints, to almost pantheistic effect, without actually telling us that that is what he is doing. The Boscastle clock chime places his soundscape precisely in time, as well as in the place triangulated by the two churches and the ocean. The soundscape makes both the moment (a crucial one in the protagonist's life) and the place seem unique. The sounds of the place will indeed have been unique, and although the author would need to have said a great deal more about the timbre and pitch of the bell and the sound envelope of the waves in order to prove it, it is clear that to this young visitor (Stephen, the hero), what he was hearing were vivid soundmarks, sounds that would impregnate themselves indelibly on his memory as unique to St Juliot (not least because its special inhabitant never turns up). A resident might not even have noticed them: to him or her the roar of the ocean in particular would have been a keynote sound. Thus within a soundscape, analysed in Schafer's terms, the interaction of human beings is already implicit, if the soundscape means something for a local, something else for a person who comes from elsewhere, who will respond to it accordingly. In this equation, the soundscape furthers Darwinian sexual selection.

Hardy was aware of a soundscape's socio-sexual dynamic, extraordinarily attuned as he was to the things he heard, urban as well as rural. In a notebook in 1888 he wrote that 'every echo, pit-pat, &c that makes up the general noise has behind it a motive, a prepossession, a hope, an aim, a fixed thought forward; perhaps more – a joy, a sorrow, a love, a revenge'.[32] Here, less positively than in his St Juliot episode, he implies that 'general noise' is the sum of humanity's greatest strivings, without shape or envelope. Many

---

[31] Hardy 1873, ii: 234–5.
[32] Perry 2009: 8.

soundscapes, however, *are* moulded into some kind of an aesthetic shape. Five west country examples come to mind.

The first is an actual musical composition, Richard Dering's viol fantasia with voices, *The Country Cries*, dating from the early seventeenth century.[33] As with Thomas Ravenscroft's 'Hodge Trillindle to his zweet hort Malkin', to be mentioned in chapter 6, a west country setting can be assumed because of the representation of regional speech. The music has its own, albeit loose, form, on which is superimposed a series of vocal episodes (one of them whistled rather than sung): waits announcing 'past three o'clock'; a servant telling them to begone or his mistress will fling a pisspot on their heads (she's trying to sleep, having been up all night at cards); a dialogue between a farmer and his sleepy son, the former trying to rouse the latter to go and feed the animals; the dawn chorus of birds (four species); an Easter hare hunt setting off, its participants discussing their dogs, then the hounds' barking and the running commentary (does the hare escape?); a shepherd or drover whistling to his dog; a deaf carter and his acquaintance holding a rustic conversation; a partridge hunt, calling in the dogs; a frightened boy on his way to school trying to remember his Latin; a cryer announcing a folk play in the town hall that night, with 'both a devil and a fool'; a travelling gelder of sheep and pigs; a bee-keeper trying to hive her bees by ringing a pure metal kettle (for this, the viols are instructed to play *col legno*); a party of harvesters singing a harvest song on their way to celebrate the harvest home; milkmaids singing about their own evening occupations (or the narrator describing it). It is clear that, modelled probably on Orlando Gibbons's *The Cries of London*, the music takes us through the sounds of a single day in the same place, from three o'clock in the morning to the following evening. It is less clear whether they are all observed from the same spot: a narrator's seeming intrusion, a shift as it were from direct to indirect speech in the words, in the final cameo, might suggest an observer's having moved around the streets and fields of the little town, now taking their leave. That the soundscape episodes are superimposed on a common musical form, a fantasia in duple time with contrasting sections, one of which is a triple-time episode (for the bee-keeper's folk ditty), may cause us to ask how many apparently abstract musical compositions are potential soundscapes in disguise. But as an analysis of the sociological place of music within a settlement of the time, *The Country Cries* is not particularly revealing. Singing seems to be associated with ending the day's labours, and the only other music in the soundscape is the shepherd's whistled fragment; church music and bells do not feature.

---

[33] Brett 1967: 148–57.

Two further west country soundscapes are constructed as literary, not musical accounts, one in verse, the other in prose, and they date from within a year of each other at the most, namely 1770–71. Each satirises Georgian urban society, respectively in Bristol and Bath, as a social cacophony. One of them comes from Thomas Chatterton's poem *Kew Gardens*, and here music is sociologically positioned:

> A mean assembly-room, absurdly built,
> Boasted one gorgeous lamp of copper gilt;
> With farthing candles, chandeliers of tin,
> And services of water, rum, and gin;
> There in the dull solemnity of wigs,
> The dancing bears of commerce murder jigs;
> Here dance the dowdy belles of crooked trunk,
> And often, very often, reel home drunk;
> Here dance the bucks with infinite delight,
> And club to pay the fiddlers for the night,
> While Broderip's hum-drum symphonies of flats
> Rival the harmony of midnight cats.
> What charms has music, when great Broderip sweats,
> To torture sound to what his brother sets.
> With scraps of ballad tunes, and *gude Scotch sangs*,
> Which god-like Ramsay to his bagpipe twangs;
> With tattered fragments of forgotten plays;
> With Playford's melody to Sternhold's lays,
> This pipe of science mighty Broderip comes,
> And a strange, unconnected jumble thrums.
> Rous'd to devotion in a sprightly air,
> Danc'd into piety, and jigg'd to prayer;
> A modern hornpipe's murder greets our ears,
> The heav'nly music of domestic spheres;
> The flying band in swift transition hops
> Through all the tortur'd, vile burlesque of stops.
> Sacred to sleep, in superstitious key,
> Dull, doleful diapasons die away;
> Sleep spreads his silken wings, and lull'd by sound,
> The vicar slumbers, and the snore goes round;
> Whilst Broderip at his passive organ groans
> Through all his slow variety of tones.[34]

---

[34] Chatterton 1842, ii: 355–6.

Chatterton is claiming that the sum total of Bristol's music is a tawdry clangour, and that the monopoly of it held by Edmund Broderip (*ca* 1727–79), who was organist of St James's and the Lord Mayor's Chapel and a frequent performer on the organ of the Prince's Street Assembly Room, epitomises mediocrity. The brother mentioned will have been John Broderip (1719–70), a published composer (which Edmund was not) and organist of Wells Cathedral. Edmund Broderip and Chatterton had in fact been good friends who fell out; Chatterton moved to London and in the poem seems intent on belittling the provincial soundscape, though in a satire he was bound to, and it is only fair to add that in the following lines he praises John Allen, organist of St Mary Redcliffe church.[35] Although there is a time frame in the description – Saturday night occupies the first lines, Sunday morning the last – Chatterton deliberately confuses their musical components as if to say that in their fashion and custom, sacred and secular sounds lack distinction, between as well as within them. He does, however, cover a great deal of the musical spectrum of the day: the organ, an orchestra with fiddlers, voluntaries, jigs, ballads, a hornpipe, Scots songs, bagpipe effects, symphonies (i.e. instrumental ritornelli), sprightly airs, Playford country dance tunes, and Sternhold's metrical psalm tunes. Non-musical sound is not his concern except insofar as all this music is as unedifying as caterwauling in the alleyways and snoring in church.

Tobias Smollett's description of the Bramble/Melford family's arrival in Bath in the epistolary novel *The Expedition of Humphry Clinker* (1771) almost amounts to a symphony in prose, as indeed is recognised by the long-suffering squire when, as reported by his nephew, he insists on moving lodgings:

> I wonder (added he) what sort of sonata we are to expect from this overture, in which the devil, that presides over horrid sounds, hath given us such variations of discord – The trampling of porters, the creaking and crashing of trunks, the snarling of curs, the scolding of women, the squeaking and squalling of fiddles and hautboys out of tune, the bouncing of the Irish baronet over-head, and the bursting, belching, and brattling of the French-horns in the passage (not to mention the harmonious peal that still thunders from the Abbey steeple) succeeding one another without interruption, like the different parts of the same concert, have given me such an idea of what a poor invalid has to expect in this temple, dedicated to Silence and Repose, that I shall certainly shift my quarters to-morrow.

---

[35] Lynan 2004.

This is a kind of condensed recapitulation of episodes that the nephew has already recounted in full: the squire's sister unpacking the luggage in a frenzy; her dog getting into a fight; the waits striking up in the passage below (soon silenced with money); an Irish dancing master giving a lesson in the apartment above; the Abbey bells pealing to announce a new arrival ('Mr Bullock, an eminent cow-keeper of Tottenham'); two Negro slaves playing a horn duet on the stairs; and the females of the entourage reacting dramatically to the squire's violent treatment of these last. One wonders whether Smollett invented this sequence of aural events with an actual sonata exposition in his mind. Not only does he conjure up contrasting rhythms, musical 'topics' (e.g. the bells) and timbres, he does so in the round, each one coming from a different direction, distance, and elevation (for soundscapes are generally concerned with these spatial variables): in the room, above it, behind it (the horn players), below it (the dog fight in the kitchen), immediately outside and below (the waits, possibly to the south-east), farther outside and above (the bells, to the north-west).[36]

Finally, two instances, 150 years apart, of a small town's human activities heard as a soundscape. The first includes a smellscape, and constitutes a critical contrast between the elements of industry and piety and those of idleness and luxury that have ousted them. The town is Devizes, the year 1750:

> You have turn'd the grating of your woolcombs into the scraping of Fiddles; the screeking loom into the tinckling Harpsicord; and the thumping Fulling mills into a glittering and contentious Organ. Scents of perfumes are in your churches and the odours of train oil and fermenting Urine are no more smelt amongst you. Your houses are ornamented with Bath stone wrought into Pediments, entablatures and Pillastrades; your market house (a stranger to woolpacks) is metamorphiz'd into a theatre for Balls, and Concertos, and Oratorio's.[37]

With our final example we return to a real composer, though to his prose rather than to one of his compositions. Christopher le Fleming (1908–85) grew up in Wimborne, and in the first chapter of his autobiography he conjures up the 'Sounds in a country town (c. 1910)' which he argues were all the keener to him through having been born with defective eyesight. He distinguishes nearly forty separate sounds. They are grouped according to location and distance: nearby is the horse and early motor traffic, farther away and carried in accordance with wind direction are the steam trains of

---

[36] Smollett 1771, i: 38–42.
[37] Davis 1754: 39.

two different companies. At the bottom and side of the garden are streets with various workshops and industries, and to these he adds nonconformist chapels. People in the house speak in different ways, the servants with a 'rich west country "burr"'. People in the street speak with jollity or in scolding. The Minster bells float 'serenely above' all the other sounds, and for le Fleming the quarter-jack is unquestionably music: 'Its insistence on repeating the notes C-G (Tonic-Dominant) and, by adding the lower C at the hour, taught me the most basic of all intervals in music – the octave (within which are contained all the available notes that can be used).' Bells permeate nearly all le Fleming's categories: the names of nearby villages spoken by his father (a doctor) 'rang like bells'; some carthorses' harnesses included a jingle, tuned to the liking of the farmer; a chapel bell conflicts bitonally with the singing of the nearby Salvation Army congregation; coming from the Minster are the quarters, the hour, the Sunday peal, the nightly curfew, and the death knell. Curiously, the railway soundscape with which his chapter climaxes appears to be the only one in which no bells appear.[38]

Perhaps I was wrong to have excluded bells from music in the west country, for they seem to have been responsible for a great deal of perceived uniqueness in soundscape terms. John Aubrey thought that Broadchalke possessed 'one of the tuneablest rings in Wiltshire, which hangs advantageously; the river running near the churchyard which meliorates the sound'.[39] Smollett was not the only author to remark on the Bath convention of ringing the Abbey bells for visitors (who paid for them).[40] In the mid-nineteenth century, Lord Auckland's daughter taught the swans of the Bishop's Palace in Wells to ring a bell for food, and they still do it today.[41] A reminiscence of growing up in Frome in the 1930s enumerated precisely the same bell functions emanating from the parish church as le Fleming's for Wimborne, with the addition of a hymn tune every three hours.[42] Eric Benfield, in his book on Dorset, found the electricity pylons of Blackmore Vale visually beautiful and suggested that they 'might have wind bells and harps placed on them for the delight of the ear as well'.[43] Ottery St Mary has dramatised into an annual midsummer carnival a legend that pixies tried to wreck the casting of one of its church bells in the fifteenth century.[44]

[38] Le Fleming 1982: 3–6.
[39] Olivier 1951: 20.
[40] Smith 1948: 58.
[41] Tudsbery-Turner 2002: 40.
[42] Smith 1989–90: 12.
[43] Benfield 1950: 154.
[44] Brown 1969: 282–3.

Among the region's myriad other soundmarks across time and place, a few of the more striking ones for which evidence survives can be singled out. Katherine of Aragon was kept awake by the squeaking weathercock of St Mary Major in Exeter on her way to London to marry Prince Arthur in October 1501.[45] Brockley Combe will have echoed habitually to the trumpetings of an elephant used for logging on a Backwell estate in the late Georgian period.[46] Trumpetings of a different kind greeted the RMV *Scillonian* on arrival at St Mary's in fog: until the ship was equipped with radar in the 1950s, Henry Trenwith and then his son Vic played a bugle on Peninnis Head to warn it of land.[47] Luppitt did or still does resound every day at 5am to the 'chanting ... in an ancient Indian language' of a community of Buddhist monks.[48] Padstow's Obby Oss accordion band every May Day makes for the most evocative sounds imaginable when heard at a distance from the hills above the town.[49]

The question is, how does one *value* all this wealth and diversity of sound across the region and across the ages? Dering did so by turning a soundscape into a piece of music, Smollett by imagining one, thereby transmuting negative experience into something clever and witty. Each of them was creating cultural capital out of the region's raw material. Opera composers such as George Lloyd with *Iernin* (1934), Ethel Smyth with *The Wreckers* (1904), and Inglis Gundry with *The Tinners of Cornwall* (1953) have done this too, while a (very) humble tone poem by Albert W Ketèlbey, 'In a camp of the ancient Britons', imagines one particular soundscape across time, across thousands of years in fact. It is that of Worlebury Camp above Weston-super-Mare at the time of the Roman invasion of AD 47 and in the present (1925), complete with a lurid sheet music cover showing the natives throwing rocks at a disciplined file of Romans wading through the water, a programmatic guide (supplemented by directions of encouragement in the score itself), and a scholarly note informing the reader or player that 'the Druids' music and the ancient Britons' march are founded on the authentic HYPODORIAN MODE'.[50]

My way of valuing the musical sounds of the west country in the remaining chapters of this book will be to investigate their human agency, constructing a model of it in terms of authority, incorporation, livings, and

---

[45] Orme 1986: 53.
[46] Walker and Walker 1995.
[47] StMaryMus.
[48] Smith 1990: 77.
[49] Personal visit, 1 May 2010.
[50] Personal inspection of copy in the possession of John Pickard.

the capitalisation of institutions and events. But every question leads to another, and the problem with which the Epilogue will wrestle is: how can such value be measured?

CHAPTER 2

Musical Authority: Organs

❧ Introduction

At some point in 1643, the wardens of Wimborne Minster paid 6d 'for some of the organ pipes', which they must already have taken down and put into safe keeping or had stolen while the loft remained as a seating area.[1] That same year, the Dean and Chapter of Salisbury Cathedral prudently dismantled their organ rather than have it destroyed, while the organ pipes at Warminster St Denys parish church (the 'minster') were taken out 'and hidden under a floor in the tower, lest the soldiers should spoil them, as they had done in other places'.[2] (If they were retrieved at the Restoration, it was to little effect: the organ was out of repair in 1683.[3]) These actions came none too soon, for on 9 May 1644 Parliament passed an ordinance for the removal of church organs.[4] Over the next few years, Roundhead soldiers routinely destroyed the existing organs in parish churches, as well as the cathedral organs. St Mary's, Chard, must have had one, for an 'organ loft', presumably empty, is referred to in 1659.[5] Crewkerne's organ was destroyed in 1646, as was Shepton Mallet's 'by the soldiers', the 'remains' at Crewkerne being stored by the churchwardens.[6] St Andrew's, Chippenham, sold its organ to a manor house, Lacock Abbey, probably the only organs in England to survive the Civil War and Commonwealth being those in domestic spaces.[7] At St Mary Redcliffe in Bristol, the stained glass was broken and the 'fanatics'

---

[1] Cox 1913: 199; Matthews Wim(b): 4.
[2] Matthews Sal: 1; *Harvey's Frome Almanack 1878*, quoted *WR* xi (Dec 2007): 20.
[3] Crittall 1965: 121–2.
[4] Temperley 1979, i: 79.
[5] Pulman 1875: 503–4.
[6] Dunning and Bush 1985: 31; Farbrother 1872: 64.
[7] Glennie and Woodhouse 1996: [14].

marched through the city blowing the organ pipes they had looted.[8] Most notoriously, in Exeter, the Parliamentary troops 'brake down the [cathedral] organs, and taking two or three hundred pipes with them in a most scornful and contemptuous manner went up and down the streets piping with them; and meeting with some of the choristers of the Church, whose surplices they had stolen before, and employed them to base servile offices, scoffingly told them: "Boys, we have spoiled your trade, you must go and sing hot pudding pies."'[9] What a soundscape! This will have been some time after 1645, when the cathedral organist John Lugg lost his job.[10]

Organs are important because right through to the twentieth century they formed perhaps the strongest musical signifier of authority and, until the advent of choral societies, of musical aspiration in public life. They have normally been community possessions, and for several centuries, perhaps until the later 1700s, were among the largest, most expensive, and most complex pieces of western technology – not as large, lavish, and complex in Britain as on the Continent, particularly in the Netherlands and Germany, but still comparable with a sailing ship in terms of mechanical ingenuity and intricacy on a grand scale. They represented status, especially when commissioned from a metropolitan builder, as when Bodmin's instrument arrived 'from London by sea to Fowey, by river boat to Lostwithiel, and thence by land' as early as 1529–30.[11] They could make more noise than any other human agency except gunpowder. And they made it as aural representative of the Church's authority over the community, organising the people's ragged voice into something approaching an orderly unison, exercising 'a kind of grateful violence', as one clergyman's sermon put it when a new organ in London was opened in 1696, and having a capacity to 'prevent Discord and Mistakes' and to keep voices 'up to their true pitch', as that of another maintained four years later when Bridgwater parish church's organ was inaugurated.[12]

The façade pipes in an organ case represent a minute fraction of the total number ranked behind it, and a large organ can contain many thousands of pipes varying in length from thirty-two feet to less than an inch, each one individually activated, making only one sound, and subject to engagement in a limitless number of combinations organised by mechanical contrivance.

---

[8] Turner 1949: 103.
[9] Matthews Exe: 2.
[10] ibid: 21.
[11] Orme 2010: 80.
[12] Temperley 1979, i: 101; Shuttleworth 1700: 7.

Almost no two organs are the same, and in addition to being a musical instrument an organ is an article of furniture and indeed of architecture, unique to the building that houses it, to the extent that cinema organs were built into the structure in such a way as to make them difficult to remove. Organs do move around, and, as we shall see, in the mid-nineteenth century their physical position within a parish church was almost as much a matter of national politics as had been the Puritans' opposition to them; but many a church has retained its organ case and some of the original pipework over a period of centuries. What is perhaps the finest parish organ case in the west country, that of St Peter's, Tiverton, has been in the building since the day of its dedication, 13 September 1696. The organ was commissioned, and funded by public subscription amid residual Puritan opposition, by an ambitious incumbent, Rev John Newte, who ordered it from one of the best builders in London, Christian Schmidt (nephew of 'Father' Bernard Schmidt). Possibly it was carved by Grinling Gibbons, and possibly the first ever performance of Mendelssohn's 'Wedding march' on an organ in an actual wedding was given on it in June 1847 – quite a distinction.[13]

Even the playing of an organ was a community effort insofar as until the advent of modern utilities, the organist needed to enlist a blower to pump the bellows before any sound could be made. An electric blower was expensive and many churches did not install one until the 1920s or 1930s; that for Warminster St Denys cost £367 in 1933, at a time when a new semi-detached house could be purchased for £900.[14] At Ilminster the parish church organ was still blown by two rival brothers (who had not spoken to each other for seven years) in the 1940s, and St Petroc's, Padstow, may not have had an electric blower until 1947.[15] Hydraulic power was an option explored by some churches in the nineteenth century, presumably upon the advent of mains water (though a domestic organ in Lynton was powered by a water wheel).[16] But both water and electricity could prove ruinously expensive to the parish at a time when utility bills were a novel and unpleasant shock. The former was a problem with the 1878 Willis organ at St John's, Clevedon, the latter at St John's, Frome, when the blowing went electric in 1924 (it had been hydraulic since 1882).[17] The July 1905 accounts for Sir Lewis Stucley's living of Bideford parish church include both 19s for the (human) blower and a

---

[13] Reay 1899.
[14] Personal visit, 22 April 2010.
[15] Turner 1949: 238; personal visit, 1 May 2010, though the dates on the organ itself and in the church booklet conflict.
[16] Browne 2005: 8–9.
[17] Girling 1998: 39; Norvall 1991: 43, 33–4.

water bill of £9 4s 7d for the organ 'engine', which had perhaps been installed during that year.[18]

Organ blowers were paid by the parish (sometimes by the organist, according to Browne).[19] George Palmer received 2s 8d at Barnstaple in the sixteenth century, Richard Hardwich 6d at Cheddar in 1637, though these figures indicate little until we know whether they were occasional, quarterly or annual sums. (In Tavistock, a blower was paid 1d at the inauguration of the new or repaired organ in 1538–39.)[20] In 1666 Exeter Cathedral was paying a blower 1s a day when required, which would have amounted perhaps to £3–£4 per annum if the organ was used only on Sundays and feast days. This seems comparable with the £6 3s 8d received by the Widow Hibberd in Salisbury Cathedral in 1709–10, for which she also had to oil the bells. Her successor negotiated a rate of £6 for the blowing alone, on the grounds of the physical labour the new organ required; she had perhaps given up, unequal to the struggle. Parish churches paid less – 5s per annum at Frome in the early eighteenth century, rising to £6 to a Mr Norvall or Norvill in the nineteenth; £5 to T Mortimore at Sidmouth, 1878–79; 10s in 1927 even in the Somerset hamlet of Stocklinch Ottersey.[21] S S Wesley's blower at Exeter Cathedral, named Glen, was exceedingly well paid at £20 per annum, but Wesley's textural demands on the instrument, pedals and all, were the death of him.[22] Going rates must have represented an equation of supply and demand, for there was no point in paying an organist if the blower failed to turn up, and presumably no gentleman volunteer would wish to be seen or heard pumping an organ in his shirt sleeves during divine service, any emergency arrangement thereby being ruled out. But the organ blower was surely also a targeted recipient of charity. Gender was clearly no bar (witness the Widow Hibberd), and it was a useful employment for people with learning difficulties, such as Charley Selley the sexton's son at All Saints Sidmouth (and quite possibly the brothers from Ilminster), or for people convenient to have around, such as Hugh Mawde, Salisbury Cathedral's general factotum and bell-ringer of around 1600, who also ran an alehouse in the freestanding belfry, or Wimborne Minster's blower who in the sixteenth century doubled as dog whipper.[23] The relationship between intellectually

---

[18] Watkins 1993: 211–12; *BPM* Jul 1905: 3.
[19] Browne 2005: 8.
[20] Worth 1887: 17.
[21] Edwards 1917: 3; *WellsM* Cheddar: 166; Matthews Exe: 6; Matthews Sal: 2; Norvall 1991: vii; Hutchinson 1870–80, iv: 144; Crosland 1996: 30–1.
[22] Spark 1888: 429–30.
[23] Sutton 1973: 96; Robertson 1938: 149, 162; Matthews Wim(b): 1, 3.

challenged blower and organist could be tricky, for the wind needed to be ready ahead of a music cue, and to be on the safe side Louis Parker told his blower at Sherborne School to maintain his efforts right through the service, on one occasion finding him still at it quarter of an hour after everything had finished.[24] A plaque to an organ blower is rare, though St Cuthbert's, Wells, has one, complete with a photograph of John Joseph Chamberlain (1857/58–1931), employed from 1891, looking wise, bearded, and seemingly of country stock. 'He loved his work and did it faithfully unto the end', runs the tribute, though it is not clear whether 'the end' refers to his demise or the acquisition of an electric motor, or both as cause and effect, either way round.[25]

Before the Civil War, organs had been relatively plentiful in west country churches. Exeter Cathedral possessed one in the 1280s, Wimborne Minster in 1408, Salisbury Cathedral in 1480. Glastonbury Abbey, the greatest monastic establishment in the region, was given an organ 'of incredible size' by the 51st abbot, Adam de Sodbury, some time before 1335. The first references to organists come from Exeter and Wells cathedrals, T Hop at Exeter, *ca* 1393, Walter Vageler appointed to Wells in 1416. Most other names surviving from the middle ages tend to be those of custodians (for maintenance purposes) rather than players, though the two may have been combined.[26] References to parish church organs, generally in the plural as 'a pair', though meaning one instrument, appear less frequently in the annals, but St Saviour's, Dartmouth (1433), St John the Baptist, Glastonbury (1439), St Mary's, Bridgwater (1448), St Petrock's, Exeter (1472–3), St Peter and St Paul, Barnstaple (1498), St Andrew's, Ashburton (*ca* 1510), St Peter's, Tiverton (1524), St Michael's, Chagford (1527, a cast-off from Exeter Cathedral), St Petroc's, Bodmin (1529–30), St Eustachius, Tavistock (1538–9), Holy Cross, Crediton (1539), and St Mary's, Totnes (1546), all possessed them at these dates.[27] These were wealthy places, four of them ports, Crediton with a college of priests, and organs are also mentioned in monastic establishments such as Bath Abbey, Dorchester's Franciscan Friary, and St Michael's Mount chapel.[28] But

---

[24] Graham 1888: 466.
[25] Personal visit, 13 April 2010.
[26] Orme 1978: 397; Matthews Exe: 1; Matthews Wim(a) and (b); Glastonbury LS, from Collinson's *History and Antiquities of Somerset* (1791); Bowers et al 2006: 24.
[27] Freeman 2007: 30; Bulleid 1891: 35; Woolrich nd: 1; Cox 1913: 201; Edwards 1917: 2; Hanham 1970: xvi; Curtis nd: [3]; Orme 1978: 398; Worth 1887: 17; Venn 1955: 339–40; Watkin 1917, ii: 961.
[28] Falconer 1964; Matthews Wim(a), and Cox 1913: 198–9; Clegg 1972: 66; Rowse 1941: 187.

from churchwardens' accounts there is also evidence, of which more can surely be found, of the provision of organs in modest circumstances. A study of the Somerset parish records has discovered that the villagers of Banwell had the means to install an organ (along with new pews) in 1529–35, while those of nearby Yatton, in an expression of lay piety, took fourteen years (1446–60) to build a rood screen: 'various parishioners and the stone carver, John Crosse, made trips to the parishes of Easton-in-Gordano, Bruton, and Selwood to view their rood screens'. The end product had a covered loft that housed a chapel, carvings, sixty-nine images and 'some organs'.[29] A small village such as Morebath, however, would never have possessed an organ.[30]

The Reformation turned such a riot of sound and colour into a somewhat confused noise. Monasteries would have lost their organs, presumably to parish churches and the odd manor house, when they were suppressed in 1536–39, an event which culminated in the west country on 15 November 1539 with the shameful spectacle of the elderly Abbot Whiting of Glastonbury, who had been a considerable patron of music, being dragged up the Tor on a hurdle and hanged. Chantries were abolished in 1547 when the boy Edward VI came to the throne. This had the effect of confiscating parish endowments, though it is evident that some organs continued to be repaired and some singing men continued to be paid from parish funds, at least for a while. The important feast of Corpus Christi, with its colourful parish or civic processions and often plays, was abolished in 1548.[31] The following year, in January 1549, Parliament passed the Act of Uniformity, substituting the English prayer book for the Latin service, and it came into force on Whit Sunday, 9 June. Resistance in the west country was deep and immediate, perhaps because earlier measures had been slow to take effect and the shock was more sudden. It began the following day in the Devon village of Sampford Courtenay. The Cornish soon joined in and the following month a peasant army marched on Exeter, 'demanding a reversal of the reforms. The rebellion was brutally put down by foreign mercenaries. Four thousand were killed and priests in particular were singled out for cruel treatment.'[32] With the psalms now in English doggerel and Latin plainsong outlawed, there would have been little use for organ support to the liturgy, at least until any remaining musicians worked out how to adapt the resources to their new

---

[29] French 2001: 117, 160, citing SHC D\P\ban 4/1/1, fols 53–100 and SHC D\P\yat 4/1/1.
[30] See Duffy 2001: passim.
[31] Johnston 2003: 18.
[32] Rowse 1941: 261–3; Strong 2007: 71–2.

circumstances. But a time lag such as that at Buckland Newton in Dorset, where there was still in 1550 'a pair of iron organs, weighing about 200lb, which were probably then taken down and sold', must have been typical.[33] Yet four years later the Catholic paraphernalia were back again under Mary.

In Elizabeth's reign, organs slowly withered and died, with odd exceptions such as St Edmund's and St Thomas's parish churches in Salisbury, for which Hugh Chappington built new instruments in 1567 and 1568 respectively.[34] Alan Smith thought it unlikely that in Exeter 'any organ or choir was heard in any of the [parish] churches after about 1570'.[35] Shepton Mallet appears to have sold its organ; Crediton lost its instrument in 1595 and did not get another until 1822. All that was left in Frome by 1597 were 'three small organ pipes'. At Ashburton the rood loft had already been subject to much interference and was finally taken down, along with the organ that had evidently stood upon it, in 1579–80.[36] It is difficult now to imagine the sight of a colourfully painted small organ on a parish rood loft, for the instrument almost never returned to that position except in cathedrals, where Exeter and Wells have retained it to this day. (However, John Loosemore was paid £4 for erecting an organ on the rood loft at Hartland as late as 1637–38.)[37] But in the reigns of James I and Charles I it is clear that considerable sums were spent on church furbishment, including organs that were becoming larger and must by now have attained a more independent status, in line with a growing repertoire of compositions, namely church voluntaries, playable before or after the service and before or after one of the lessons (the 'middle voluntary').[38] A west gallery became the standard position for a parish organ, though never, unlike on the Continent, for a cathedral organ. A particularly fine and extensive example of an early west gallery (though without organ) survives from 1633 at St Saviour's, Dartmouth. Lyme Regis acquired one in 1611, Uffculme in 1631, whether or not organs were placed in them.[39] Such provision was still subject to economic and, probably more important, political vagaries. Tiverton may have lost its 'great' organ in 1614 (they were still selling off pipes in 1620), but Dawlish, then a small village, had an organ in 1618, St John's, Glastonbury, was using one in 1625–26, and Warminster

---

[33] Hutchins's *History of Dorset*, 3rd edn, iii: 713, quoted G Mayo, Piddletrenthide, *SDNQ* i (1890): 151.
[34] Temperley 1979, i: 43–4; Harper 2010: 217.
[35] Smith 1967, i: 286–7.
[36] Farbrother 1872: 64; Summers 2006: 18; Norvall 1991: 2; Hanham 1970: x.
[37] Spink 1992: 44.
[38] Temperley 1979, i: 135.
[39] Roberts 1834: 207; Brooks 1988: 49.

spent large sums of money on gilding the angel on the organ case, and the pipes themselves, in 1627–29. In 1634 the Bristol city churches, all eighteen of them, were described as 'fairly beautified, richly adorned, and sweetly kept', and in most of them were 'neat, rich and melodious organs that are constantly played on', two of which were new.[40] Temperley cites further references to the repair or even inauguration of organs in the west country at this time, in 1621–22 (Launceston), the 1630s (Cheddar), 1637 (Bruton), 1639 (Sidbury), and until the late 1630s or 1640 (Hartland, St Ives, Salisbury St Martin). The region's remoteness from London delayed the effects of Puritanism.[41]

❧ After the Commonwealth

This, then, is the background to a world almost entirely devoid of organs in which the parish inhabitants and cathedral-goers of Britain woke up at the Restoration on Oak Apple Day, 29 May 1660, when Charles II entered London. What follows is a story of church provision eventually, over the next 250 years, spreading to the smallest village, but a story with chapters of quiescence or intensifications of plot that tell us much about west country culture, whether as proxy for that of the nation or by way of regional variation. Economic growth and civic responsibility drive the earlier narrative, followed by technology as barrel organs and then reed organs enter the equation in the seventy or eighty years prior to 1850. By this time, politics are greatly influencing the musical provision of parish churches as newly asserted clerical authority sweeps away west gallery bands and installs organs and organists where none were deemed necessary before. Ritualism then sweeps away the galleries themselves and repositions organs in chancels. At the same time, large organs appear in civic halls and the instrument becomes secularised. Further elements of secular culture flourishing in the earlier twentieth century produce cinema and seaside pavilion organs. Their ingenious technology challenges classically trained organists and produces a fascinating cultural crossover in which a parallel technological development, that of the electronic organ, is also implicated. Finally, in the later twentieth century, the massive decline in church-going sees a withdrawal and diversification of musical provision away from organs once again.

The cathedrals and city churches reinstated their organs first. This will have been entirely a matter of money. A pathetic entry in the accounts of

---

[40] Curtis nd: 3; Godfrey 1969: 27; Dunning 2006: 37; *WR* xi (Dec 2007): 17; Turner 1949: 102; Temperley 1979, i: 52.

[41] Temperley 1979, i: 51–2.

Exeter Cathedral for Michaelmas Quarter 1660, 'Item given a poore man for preserving 4 organ pipes ... 2s', did not hold back the Dean and Chapter from commissioning a magnificent new instrument, its case still today in position over the crossing screen, from John Loosemore, a Devon builder born in Barnstaple in 1616. A temporary instrument by him was made ready during the first half of 1661, and the main organ was completed in 1665, at an overall cost of £677 7s 10d.[42] Loosemore's organ famously contained a 20-foot double diapason for the G compass keyboard standard in England, its largest pipes grouped around the crossing pillars for all to see. They attracted a good deal of attention from the start, but did not work very well, and required octave booster pipes behind them to aid their sluggish speech. They remained in position until 1891.[43] Curiously, Loosemore's organ case contains no figure carving, unlike two Cornish ones (St Ives, where small fish swimming in and out of seaweed were deemed appropriate by the Pinwill sisters of Plymouth in 1907, and St Endellion, on which Endelienta's cow is 'discreetly memorialised').[44] But a clearer symbol of confidently re-established aural authority, of proclamatory mediation between people, establishment, and God, could hardly be found, though its interruption of an unusually unified architectural perspective from west end to east has not been to everyone's taste: Manning-Sanders objected to what seemed to her a monster with eyes peering out above the screen, and H V Morton was no more complimentary, calling the position of the case 'Exeter's anchor of ugliness' (see Illus. 2.1).[45] The organ's authority was soon tested, holding up rather better than that of the cathedral staff. William of Orange landed at Brixham on 5 November 1688, and unless a trumpet ushered in his proclamation at St Leonard's Tower in Newton Abbot later that day, among the first musical sounds of the Glorious Revolution, along with the oboes, trumpets, and kettledrums of his field musicians, will have been the pealing of the Exeter Cathedral organ four days later as he passed underneath the screen.[46] But the organist, Peter Pasmore, had fled, along with the Dean and Bishop; this was a substitute's performance.[47] Not that Pasmore could evade political commitment that easily. Two years later, 'the French fleet was menacing the coast and King William of Orange was in Ireland. The Deputy Lieutenant "desired" the Cathedral organist "to take a commission and go towards the Enemey and

[42] Matthews Exe: 2–6.
[43] ibid: 5, 13.
[44] ibid: 6; church leaflet; Endelienta.
[45] Manning-Sanders 1949: 92–3; Morton 1936: 63.
[46] Whittel 1689: 46–7.
[47] Pulman 1875: 276–7; WR iii (Dec 2005): 56; Whittel 1689: 48.

Illus. 2.1. Exeter Cathedral, John Loosemore's organ case of 1665

form a party of the Posse". This the Chapter allowed him to do and gave him "five guineas towards his expenses in his commission ... he having taken on him a commission of cornet".'[48]

---

[48] Matthews Exe: 24.

Salisbury Cathedral re-erected its Thomas Harris organ around 1661.[49] Robert Taunton must have been kept busy, for he built or rebuilt an organ for Bristol Cathedral in 1662, for St Nicholas, Bristol, in 1663, and 'a fair well tuned useful and beautiful double organ' for Wells Cathedral in 1664, this last 'at a cost of £800 or less', so comparable with Exeter's expenditure.[50] Robert Hayward of Bath was similarly occupied. His 1661 organ for Sherborne Abbey was one of the earliest Restoration instruments.[51] Wimborne Minster ordered a new organ from him in 1663, though it may have taken several years to complete or be entirely paid for.[52] What is striking over the following century is how the prosperous west country ports and industrial towns (wool, textiles) followed suit more or less according to wealth and presumably the necessity to maintain status. Newly acquired organs, as opposed to what one sometimes has to guess were reinstalled or repaired ones, appeared in Tiverton in 1696, Bridgwater in 1700, Frome in 1701, Shepton Mallet in 1709, St Mary Magdalene, Taunton, in 1710, Honiton before 1714, Minehead in 1714, Totnes in 1720, Bideford around 1728, St Andrew's, Plymouth, around 1735 (John Alcock was appointed organist in 1737), Keynsham probably before 1750, Truro in 1750, Bishops Lydeard around 1751, Chippenham in 1752, and Barnstaple (an instrument by the apparently local John Crang) in 1756-64.[53] Somehow an organ had also appeared at the Globe Inn in Exeter in 1697.[54] Frome's and Truro's parish church instruments were purchased second hand. Bristol's city churches kept pace, with organs installed in Christ Church (1707), St James and the Temple Church (both 1718), St Mary Redcliffe (1726), St Thomas (1729), and possibly St Stephen ('ante 1725?').[55] Several of these were by Renatus Harris, who subsequently retired to Bristol.[56] Bristol must have been exceptional, for in general cathedral city parishes were poorly provided for.[57] In Exeter, St Mary Arches acquired an organ in 1729 only by drawing on funds donated by the neighbouring parish of St Olave as well as

[49] Matthews Sal: 1.
[50] Boeringer 1983–89, i: 334; Jeboult 1923: 31; Bowers et al 2006: 5.
[51] Boeringer 1983–89, i: 291.
[52] Cox 1913: 199.
[53] Woolrich nd: 1; Norvall 1991: 5; Farbrother 1872: 64; Toulmin 1791: 28; Warne 1969: 135; Boeringer 1983–89, iii: 48; ibid, i: 286; Watkins 1993: 76; Gill nd: 18; Lewis 1988: 25; Boeringer 1983–89, i: 250-1; *SM*, 7 Oct 1751: 3; Glennie and Woodhouse 1996: [12]; Boeringer 1983–89, i: 97-8.
[54] Waterfield 1946: 28.
[55] Boeringer 1983–89, i: 327-37.
[56] Johnstone 2008: 106.
[57] Gregory and Chamberlain 2003: 21.

its own; no other parish church appears to have had one until 1775.[58] Bristol, then, afforded quite a soundscape to hear, just as its glittering multitude of weather-vanes on spires and pinnacles were a sight to behold as one descended steeply into the old city from St Michael's Hill.

Pipe organs have always been expensive. Wells and Exeter cathedrals incurred exceptional costs, as Salisbury must have done in 1710 when it commissioned from Renatus Harris the first four-manual organ in England.[59] But Shepton Mallet could raise £100 at a time when a curate's stipend might be £30 or less.[60] Either the instrument would be donated by the squire or the funds raised by public subscription, though Bideford's organ was provided by the Corporation along with the organist's stipend.[61] With the memory of the Civil War still fresh, fundraising could in the early days require a considerable effort of aesthetic or theological persuasion on the part of the incumbent or a clear consensus about the need to keep up with the Joneses, which must have been the case in Bristol. Rev John Newte at St Peter's, Tiverton, 'had striven for ten years to accomplish a project dear to his heart'. His argument was that 'It will Regulate the untunable Voices of the Multitude and make the Singing in the Church much more Orderly and Harmonious; / It will stir up the Affections of Men, and make them the fitter for Devotion; / It will make the whole Service of God be the more Solemn and August, and the People more Serious and Reverent'.[62] As for patronage, Sir George Amyand, one of Handel's executors, gave the Barnstaple organ.[63] Perhaps the Bridges family, again with their Handel connection, did the same for Keynsham.[64] Later, it was not uncommon for a moneyed widow or spinster to pay for the parish organ (or indeed the organist), either while living or in her will: the interpersonal skills of evangelical clergymen might reap all kinds of rewards as evangelical dogma and church politics began to produce new social *frissons*. In 1795 Gulliford Meeting House was given a barrel organ by a Miss Baring, no doubt a member of the prominent family from nearby Exmouth; a female legacy was covering William Bennett's organist's salary of £30 at St Andrew's Plymouth in 1812; two ladies called Saunders paid for the new Dicker organ in Sidmouth parish church in 1847; at the top end of the scale, in 1876–77 a Miss Chafyn Grove paid for Willis's

---

[58] Browne 2005: 14; Boeringer 1983–89, i: 275.
[59] Matthews Sal: 2.
[60] Farbrother 1872: 64; Spaeth 2003: 125.
[61] Watkins 1993: 76.
[62] Curtis nd: [2].
[63] Edwards 1917: 3–4.
[64] McGrath 1983: 4.

organ in Salisbury Cathedral, which cost £3,500.[65] Such facts reflect well on the women, badly on the male gentry: the idea had long taken root 'that an English gentleman should have nothing to do with music of any kind', with the result that 'rarely did a nobleman or a wealthy squire or merchant see fit to present his parish church with an organ', though there are some late exceptions, such as H H Wills of Bristol, who gave Clifton College its Harrison organ, built for £2,000, in 1909.[66]

Unusually, at St James's, West Teignmouth, in 1811, the new organ was owned by the organist, Joseph Parish, who had raised his own subscription for it. He was then offered ten guineas per annum for twenty years out of the church rates to play it and raise a choir.[67] The 1879 organ in Counterslip Baptist Church, Bristol, was largely given by its organist, Frederick Morgan.[68] To have been able to do this, one imagines, he must have been a successful tradesman or professional.[69] But he was also one of the editors of the *Bristol Tune-Book*, thus must have had a foot firmly in the world of professional music as well.

Anglican organists were paid. In towns across England this was a professional position, for in the seventeenth and eighteenth centuries the idea of the public amateur being eager for or persuadable into such a role was not yet established. Thus there was little point in raising money for an organ if the parish or corporation could not support someone to play it. But they could, increasingly, and it became quite common for the regional or national press to advertise an available post, which would be filled by competition involving testimonials, public audition, and interview. For young keyboard professionals, this was the only standard way of earning a living, and someone raised or trained in London, the cathedral cities or the university towns might find themselves on the stagecoach to Tavistock or Bridport, a destination in which, if successful, they could expect to spend the rest of their life, sole representative in that locality of what they wanted to think was an honourable profession. Like GPs well into recent times, they would be encouraged by assured prospects of building a decent private practice, in this case through teaching, which might double the stipend. Bideford's blandishments in 1780 included a 'ladies' school and many townspeople

---

[65] Keep 1977: 54; Pengelly 1886: 306; Hutchinson 1870–80, iv: 146; Matthews Sal: 8.
[66] Temperley 1979, i: 87; Knighton 2012: 296–7.
[67] Smith 1999b: 6.
[68] Thomas 1904: [14].
[69] Michael Richardson (personal communication, 15 Jun 2015) suggests that he could have been co-owner of W and F Morgan, stationers, of 5 Clare Street, Bristol.

desirous of learning'.[70] Within its first months of operation in 1801, the *Royal Cornwall Gazette*, printed in Falmouth but priding itself on being received in London every Monday morning, carried the following advertisement:

> Borough of Bodmin, in Cornwall
>
> Wanted, an organist, for the church, at Michaelmas next, to whom a great salary will be given. A person capable of teaching music will find the situation very advantageous, and meet with every encouragement. Respectable references for character and abilities will be required.
>
> Apply personally, or by letter (post paid) to the Town Clerk. Dated September 21, 1801.[71]

More often than not, the appointment of an organist involved some kind of Trollopian strife, and this occasion may have been no exception if William Hewitt's announcement in the *Exeter Flying Post* two weeks later that he would not be resigning his position as Bodmin's organist is anything to go by. He had been in post for twenty-two years, swiftly appointed in 1779 (to an organ built by Bryce Seede four years earlier) following a similar advertisement in the *Sherborne Mercury*, which he had then followed up with his own announcement: he would teach and tune harpsichords and spinets and teach guitar.

Hewitt's stipend had been £30.[72] This was typical for parish organists (and curates) over a 150-year period, though on the generous side, for Bideford offered only £20 in 1728, as did North Petherton, Honiton, and Poole in 1781, 1791, and 1799 respectively. Bideford had risen to £25 by 1780, the same salary as offered by Ashburton two years earlier.[73] It was still not a great deal of money, and insufficient for the expenses of a gentleman; even £40 'amounted to less than many artisans' yearly earnings'.[74] Cathedral organists might earn more: Theodore Colby, who came from London, had been appointed to Exeter in 1665 at a salary of £50 plus house, though in 1682 the salary of Bristol's organist Paul Heath, about to be dismissed for encouraging drunkenness and gambling in his house, was only £20.[75] The organist's house might be quite a grand one, as at no. 25 The Liberty, Wells, though this

---

[70] *SM*, 7 Aug 1780: 1.
[71] *RCG*, 26 Sep 1801: 2.
[72] *SM*, 8 Mar 1779: 1.
[73] Watkins 1993: 76; *SM*, 23 Apr, 1781: 1; *SM*, 5 Dec 1791: ?; PSJ extracts; *SM*, 7 Aug 1780: 1 and 23 Nov 1778: 2.
[74] Brewer 1997: 551.
[75] Matthews Exe: 23; Latimer 1900: 414.

ancient building only became 'The Organist's House' in 1866.[76] Wimborne Minster, as a Royal Peculiar in a small town, could stretch to £22 as the salary for its organist when reappointed at the Restoration (prior to discontinuance in the 1640s it had been £12).[77] Frome's initial organists, William Black (1701), James Clarke (1703), and William Clarke (1704) – or was the first of these the blower? – were paid only £6 per annum, but from the appointment of Stephen Jeffery onwards (1710) the stipend was £30, paid quarterly, an additional £10 to be made available 'in case he be then obliged to leave the sd office of an organist by reason of the non continuance of the sd organ', which suggests a parish commitment still politically rickety but also demonstrates the organ's rapidly rising cultural capital in the early eighteenth century.[78]

English organs never emulated their Continental counterparts in baroque grandeur. Their builders and players knew nothing of independent pedals or the *Werkprinzip*, the musical repertoire being accordingly very much more restricted. But the English did like mechanical contrivances. Truro's organ had a drum stop, operating semitonally adjacent low notes. Harris and Byfield's three-manual organ of 1726 for St Mary Redcliffe, Bristol, costing close on £1,000, contained not only what were probably the first integral pedals in the country, to the bottom octave of the Great (which was of full 16-foot compass), but also the first octave coupler, in addition to a swell box (a manual division enclosed within a wooden box containing louvres for *crescendi* and *diminuendi*). Abraham Jordan senior had invented the divisional Swell only in 1712, but it caught on quickly, so the activities of the Jordans, father and son, in the west country around this time – Bath, Bristol, Frome – were not necessarily responsible for its inclusion at St Mary Redcliffe.[79]

❧ *From Status Symbol to Clergyman's Friend*

The contemporary print of the St Mary Redcliffe organ with its magnificent case, standing on a specially constructed stone gallery near the west end and sporting a clock, makes it amply clear from the four perambulating and gesticulating gentlemen that an instrument such as this was an object of admiration for locals and visitors, in sound as well as sight. St Mary Redcliffe, long known as one of the grandest parish churches in the kingdom,

---

[76] BLB: 'Polydor House, Wells'; Foyle and Pevsner 2011: 690.
[77] Matthews Wim(b): 4–6, 17–18; Reeve 2000: 123, 302.
[78] Norvall 1991, v: 7–8; Alsbury 2006: 4.
[79] Boeringer 1983–89, i: 331–3; Williams 2001: 780.

was outside the mediaeval city and the first landmark reached by travellers from both London and the west country before crossing Bristol bridge. Parish organs would remain status symbols, but their more theological function, the regulation and encouragement of congregational singing, took on greater urgency during the eighteenth century as the Church of England was increasingly challenged by the popular hymnody emanating from the dissenters' meeting places, especially the Methodist ones, for it was corporate singing above all that attracted people to the nonconformist denominations, whether in the congregation or, in the nineteenth century, in increasingly co-operative, creative, competitive, and large choirs. Thus the music in Anglican parish worship gradually became an evangelical issue, and throughout the nineteenth century the clergy would stoutly exercise their principles for retaining the faithful or creating them in the rapidly expanding urban centres and seaside resorts.

Their first task was to trump the independence of the west gallery 'quires' (self-regulating groups of singers and instrumentalists, to be discussed in chapter 3) by establishing a more singular and direct line of ecclesiastical control through an organ and organist. As mentioned earlier, organs had long been positioned in west galleries, though some churches (including Tiverton and Frome as well as St Mary Redcliffe) emulated the cathedral screen position post-Restoration; west galleries continued to be erected through the earlier nineteenth century, and this was increasingly so that an organ could supplement and if necessary oust the quire. Blandford (1794), Crewkerne (1809–11), Chard (1814), Bridport (1815), and Glastonbury (St John the Baptist, 1818) offer a sufficiently congruent sequence of erections, whether of an organ on the gallery or the gallery itself, to suggest that these towns, all within the same part of the region, were following each other's lead.[80]

There was still a long way to go. Nicholas Temperley estimated that in 1801 only six parishes in Dorset contained an organ.[81] This was 2.2 per cent, a much smaller ratio than in the other areas he examined and representing one instrument per 19,000 population (though he may have missed Weymouth). Most of the organs were recent: Dorchester St Peter, 1787; Blandford, 1794 (see above); Weymouth, 1797; Poole, 1799.[82] It is quite possible that before this, the only organs in the county were those in Sherborne Abbey and Wimborne Minster, which had been there since the 1660s, plus Shaftesbury Holy Trinity

---

[80] Smith 1968: 80, 83; Andrew 1993: 15; Pulman 1875: 503; plaque in church; Bulleid 1891: 31–2.
[81] Temperley 1979, i: 112.
[82] Temperley 2009: 95; Chedzoy 2003: 27; church leaflet.

(1764).[83] Conversely, the parish quire died hard in Dorset, as Thomas Hardy's novel *Under the Greenwood Tree* and poems such as 'The choirmaster's burial' (set to music by Britten in *Winter Words*) make clear.

At the same time that market towns were erecting west galleries with keyboard organs, parsons of some country churches were investing in barrel organs to help wean their flocks away from 'the old way of singing', which had entailed the psalm tunes being droned with what might be excessive slowness, probably in a yelling chest voice, and more in heterophony than unison, because of the slides and graces indulged in by individuals. Barrel organs fixed the tempo and harmonies, though not without melodic and timbral embellishments of their own (one in Camborne even had a drum and triangle stop), and equipped with three barrels, which seems to have been the norm, containing between ten and fifteen tunes each, they offered a reasonable variety of psalmody operable by one unmusical person, if necessary the vicar himself.[84] They were an importation from the domestic sphere, where rich householders had been buying them since the 1770s. In village churches, nobody liked them, whether foisted on the congregation by squire or by vicar. The parishioners of Brampford Speke in Devon faced down both of these in turn. One William Jackson had donated a barrel organ probably in the 1830s, but 'this was not approved of in the parish, and by 1843 it had been consigned to limbo under the gallery, with the parish bier and grave-digger's tools. When Gorham was inducted in 1850, nearly all the pipes had disappeared.' What had not disappeared was the west gallery quire, and George Gorham, the new vicar, was determined to substitute another barrel organ. Unable to gain financial support for it, he purchased one himself in 1853, but an inscription on the organ about his ownership proved sufficiently contentious as to cause a brawl in the church on Easter Sunday three years later.[85] Barrel organs appeared in smaller churches throughout the first half of the nineteenth century and were not ruled out by urban parishes, as when Holy Trinity, Dorchester, resolved in 1824 'to make inquiry respecting the merits of Barrel & Finger organs'.[86] But they were less successful than reed organs.

There have been four manifestations of musical instruments built on the Chinese free reed principle, and all of them radically affected the sounds of vernacular music. These were the mouth organ, the concertina, the accordion,

---

[83] Temperley 2009: 95, citing Adams 1808: 137.
[84] Drage 2009: 170.
[85] Orme 1989: 74–5.
[86] Temperley 1971–76 (P173/C4).

and the harmonium or reed organ, and since the reeds operated without resonators, the instruments could remain small, light, and cheap. It was in the 1830s that they came onto the British market. Only the concertina was an English invention, patented by the scientist Charles Wheatstone, who was entertaining the seagulls and his picnic party with a similar invention of his, the symphonia, at Kynance Cove in Cornwall in September 1836.[87] Evidence of the popularity of the harmonium (the French version of a reed organ) dates from the 1850s and '60s. Robinson's Music Repository in Dorchester was selling specimens for 8, 10, 12, and 15 guineas in 1854 (their cheap pianos were 22 guineas), and Jones & Co of Bristol specialised in building them, from 1858 until at least the 1880s, along with metal organ pipes for the trade.[88] A rash of subscription fundraising appeared in the 1860s: at North Curry Methodist Chapel in 1860, Penryn Temperance Hall in 1861, and Redruth parish church in 1864, a purchase also being made in 1862 by Burnham Methodist Chapel (£12), by which time Corsham Baptist Church also appears to have possessed a harmonium. Tavistock Wesleyan Chapel must have been in the vanguard and in the money, for it was able to *replace* its harmonium (and orchestra) with a pipe organ in 1865, at a cost of 100 guineas, which highlights the cheapness of harmoniums.[89] In the next decade, perhaps as a result of the 1870 Education Act, whose 'payment by results' provision had incentivised class singing, elementary schools were also buying harmoniums; a fundraising concert programme survives for High Ham in 1877.[90]

By now, organs were flourishing in nonconformist churches and chapels. If for the dissenters in the seventeenth and eighteenth centuries the purity and austerity of unaccompanied singing (or, in the case of the Quakers, silence) had been at a premium, reservations about enhanced musical activity had long been overcome. Although the Methodist Conference was reluctant to authorise organs until the late 1820s, one may have appeared in Wedmore Methodist Chapel as early as 1817, preceded by a John Smith organ of 1815 in Bristol's prestigious Whitefield Tabernacle. A Penzance Methodist chapel had an organ in 1827.[91] As with the Wedmore example, chapels built with new nonconformist money increasingly contained an organ from the start,

---

[87] Brett 2008: 97.
[88] DCPRG 1985: 5; Elvin 1995: 173.
[89] SHC D\W\trnc 1/3/2; *FPWT* 10 Aug 1861: 1; Michell 1985: 44; Wrigley 1998: 38; Hird 1995: 38; Hicks 1978: 16.
[90] SHC DD\X\HRD/1.
[91] Temperley and Banfield 2010: 7; Hudson 2002: 171; Elvin 1995: 167; Julian 1988: 65.

which was also the case at Chideock Baptist Chapel in 1828.[92] Wiveliscombe Congregational Church's organ, acquired in 1829, had been used by Napoleon Bonaparte, of all people, in the Tuileries. It was built by Gray of London in 1796 and had been lent to Napoleon by Spencer Perceval, Britain's only prime minister to have been assassinated (though not for this deed).[93] Nonconformist churches in the nineteenth century were nevertheless slower to acquire organs than Anglican ones, just as they had been slower to acquire bands and choirs (see chapter 3), because the consensus of a cautious diaconate would be needed before money could be raised or spent. An instrument might be offered by one of the church's wealthier members, but there was always the fear of favour or influence expected in return. This may have been in the mind of Poole's Hill Street Baptist Church congregation, which had always sung unaccompanied, when Joseph Harman offered it a harmonium in 1871. The church meeting accepted it, but only after 'a fair trial'. (They graduated to a pipe organ within eight years.)[94] Paid directly by his congregation, a nonconformist minister might be less apt to impose his will than a parish priest fresh from Oxford or Cambridge. In the long run this probably led to less strife.

ঞ Ritualism

Strife there certainly was, often comic in retrospect but quite capable of tearing a community apart. Gorham's conflicts at Brampford Speke involved the bishop, the whole village, and even the nation where his unorthodox dogma was concerned, and went on for a decade.[95] The replacement of Huish Episcopi's church band with an organ led to such delinquency on the part of members of the former that they were hauled up in ecclesiastical court in Wells and fined, though they turned the occasion into a kind of triumph by decorating their horses with yards of blue ribbon.[96] Nor can we assume that a new organ was always played competently: it may well have disgraced a service where a good band had genuinely adorned it.[97]

Melodramas such as the following from St James's church, Taunton, were not unknown:

---

[92] Cann 2001: 48; *EPG*, 4 Oct 1828: 3.
[93] Hancock 1911: 146.
[94] Spinney 1954: [15], [23].
[95] Orme 1989.
[96] Gammon 1985: 62–3.
[97] cf ibid: 66.

[Mrs Elizabeth Chapman] filled the posts of organist and choirmistress from 1861. Unfortunately, in 1883 the churchwardens decided that she was deaf and should be replaced. Without even informing her they appointed a successor, T J Dudeney, then organist at the Temple Methodist chapel ... Despite a vestry resolution confirming Mrs Chapman in her position, the vicar demanded the organ keys from her, which she duly refused to surrender. On the following Sunday John Chapman, as sexton, let his wife into the church early that morning and she sat on the organ stool all day while Sunday lunch was passed into her through a window and Dudeney fumed impotently. Both Chapmans were hauled by the vicar before the borough magistrates for a 'riotous, violent and indecent act' but the charges were dismissed. The same performance was repeated on the next Sunday, although a constable, stationed at the back of the church to quell any demonstration, was not needed. The Archdeacon and Bishop were dragged in to save the day and advised buying Mrs Chapman off with £60 – which she promptly declined. In the event Dudeney had to return to the Temple and Mrs Chapman continued in her hard-won office until 1885. On her retirement, a public subscription raised £73 9s for her, so that she showed a profit of over £13 for her obstinacy. On her husband's death she succeeded him as female sexton and continued until her death in 1922: a truly indomitable Tauntonian.[98]

Although not the case here, ecclesiastical ritualism caused the greatest friction as the nineteenth century proceeded. The increasing militancy of the Anglican church in an era of massive population growth, industrialisation, and consequent secularisation gave rise to equally thoroughgoing changes in the texture of parish worship and the buildings that housed it. Between 1818 and the 1850s a number of new 'Commissioners' churches' were built for large congregations; they were prominent, confident statements of mission. So was St Mary's, Penzance (1832–35), not a Commissioners' church but still today the town's most visible monument along with the dome of the Market House. Standing sentinel over the harbour as it does, it was presumably intended among other things to defy the incursions of Methodism (there is a huge Wesleyan Methodist church further up Chapel Street, though it is later).[99]

The organ in Britain began to take on new burdens of significance in such a climate. Size and specification mattered, and in 1835 Henry Crabb of Exeter built for St Mary's what was at the time probably the largest organ in the peninsula west of Bristol, with ten more registers than that of Exeter Cathedral, whose organist, Sebastian Wesley, inaugurated it and

---

[98] Bush 1983: 52.
[99] Beacham and Pevsner 2014: 425–6.

helped choose the new organist. This was William Viner from St Michael's, Bath, who clearly felt it worth his while to forsake a city with a musical infrastructure second only to that of London for this last urban outpost of Duchy and indeed country, still sufficiently remote that Wesley had arrived by sea.[100] English organs were turning romantic, glorying in ever more nuanced and varied pseudo-orchestral timbres and a greater dynamic range, which eventually (though not yet in the Penzance instrument) necessitated an independent pedal division that could unleash the full panoply of Victorian sublimity in sound, whether for climactic Bach fugue entries or the noise of the deep in psalms. Worship in general was turning romantic too, as clergymen one after another subscribed to the high-church tenets of the Tractarian and Oxford movements. To use the shorthand 'ritualism' for this revolution, it meant not only the end of the west gallery quire but the end of the organ in that position, so as to concentrate all the liturgical elements and symbols of divinity and authority as much as possible towards the east end of the church, preferably in the chancel. Here a surpliced, processing choir would lead the responsive and sung congregational portions of the service and be maximally integrated into the organist's realm, or rather he or she into its realm. In short, the ideal of the cathedral service was transferred to the parish church, buildings gothicised or re-gothicised in accordance with their new mystical function. Tiles, windows, vestments, brickwork, and indeed organ pipes went polychromatic, and, as vaulted darknesses loomed, so did the sounds of the mighty organ, emanating like Wagner's orchestra at Bayreuth from mysterious, unseen sources, perhaps not deliberately but by necessity as instruments, now aspiring to 16- and 32-foot stops whose unwieldy pipes would in any case need to be hidden somewhere, were crammed into chancel aisles and side chapels, whence the sound could barely escape, and choir stalls, screens, and even rood lofts began again to encumber the interiors of parish churches.

This process took fifty years or more – much longer in some places. Nothing could be done without money, and ritualist furnishings were expensive. It was not until 1886 that the Earl and Countess of Ilchester provided the funds for a thoroughgoing 'restoration' of Abbotsbury church, which included moving both the organ and the choir from the west gallery to the chancel. The choir of twenty-four were now seated in carved oak stalls and 'all provided with cassocks and surplices which adds greatly to the dignity and solemnity of the services of the church', as a dutiful local writer pointed out.[101] In Nailsea

---

[100] PenStM leaflet; Clarke 2011; Horton 2004: 112.
[101] Cooper 1895: 22–3.

the parish church council did not even begin to argue about whither to move the west gallery organ until the 1920s (one suggestion was to split it in two on brackets either side of the west door). It continued to do so until December 1972, when it was finally decided to install it in the north chapel – the Nailsea Court Chapel, whose owner had vetoed this proposal in earlier decades. Even then a previous organist objected.[102] But the chief period for the establishment of ritualism was from the 1840s to the end of the 1880s, to judge from the proportion of entries in the database assembled for this book that deals with the installation, repositioning, rebuilding, replacing, and enlarging of organs and the activities of organists. This peaks at over 20 per cent for every decade between these dates, a figure matched at no other time since the 1750s. It was probably also the period in which the best living could be earnt as a church as opposed to cathedral musician. The scale of neo-mediaeval church-building during these decades was staggering, and all the main denominations often literally aspired to it. In Bournemouth town centre, large Gothic churches sprouted up within yards of each other – St Peter's, St Stephen's, St Michael's, Richmond Hill Congregational, Punshon Memorial Methodist, and St Andrew's Presbyterian churches. Organs and choirs followed. In the Bristol suburbs of Clifton and Redland it was similar: All Saints, Christ Church, Emmanuel, St Paul's, Tyndale Baptist, Redland Park Congregational, Victoria Methodist, and as many others again. A map of this district from 1880 identifies twenty-seven places of worship, only half of them Anglican.[103]

The flavour of respectability, 'correctness', and patronage of both the working classes and women attendant on Anglican ritualism comes across well in Joseph Leech's report for the *Bristol Times* (as 'The Church-Goer') of his Sunday visit in 1845 to the new mining village of Coalpit Heath, with its church by William Butterfield, no less:[104]

> Though the Church has been open for no more than four or five months, the great care that has been taken to render its services such as they ought to be, is very manifest in every portion, but in none more than in the musical part. The people, I am told, and indeed I could perceive, actually take a delight in it. The organ is played by a young lady, the daughter of the principal resident in the district, Mr Hewett, who has taken an interest in the good work, praiseworthy to him and fortunate for his humble neighbours; and a really effective choir of honest colliers, men and boys, now chaunt portions of the service, not from a

---

[102] Cox 2000: [31–6].
[103] Reid 1992: 56.
[104] Verey 1976: 162.

pent-up organ loft, but from their open sittings in the north aisle, with more expression than many of our town singers attempt to do. The 'Kyrie Elison' (Lord, have mercy upon us,) was remarkably well done. On the whole, I thought the chaunting better than the psalms.[105]

'Chaunting' had become a key referent, beloved of Victorian commentators. Here it would seem to indicate intoned monodic chant in liturgical responses; sometimes, for example when schoolchildren demonstrated their lessons to benefactors or inspectors, it might mean unisonal speech recitation. What it always assured was ritual and discipline, away from the (west gallery) informality and independence of the 'pent-up organ loft'. Note too the young lady organist, by now an amateur, but of impeccable social standing (and unmarried). Professional female organists were not uncommon fifty or sixty years earlier: Honiton parish church appointed Mrs Kahlen in 1787, Weymouth Mrs Delamotte when it acquired its first organ in 1797 (she also kept the post office, and was presumably a relative of the violinist Franz Lamotte, who had moved to Weymouth from Bath in 1780).[106] But as de Vries's 'industrious revolution' gave way to the breadwinner/homemaker model, they probably declined.[107] Leech also found a young female organist at Bitton, and approved of the fact that she was unpaid, commenting: 'as the phrase goes, "this is just as it ought to be"'. In Westonzoyland two decades later, Miss Mary Huxtable gave up playing the organ and running her juvenile parish choir 'whose instruction has been to her a labour of love' when she married, though this was because she was moving away – Mrs Lucette of Bridgwater was still able to play the organ at Mary's 'gay wedding' as a married woman.[108]

Ritualism produced some striking results in the west country, nowhere more than in Frome, which became a Mecca, if the word be permitted, for Anglo-Catholicism. The vicar of its parish church, St John's, from 1852 to 1886, Rev W J E Bennett, had been incumbent at the new church of St Barnabas, Pimlico, with the composer and priest Frederick Ouseley as his curate, and his high-church practices had caused the 'no popery' riots there in 1850–51 whose political fallout even involved the prime minister.[109] Pimlico was a slum, its hungry masses tinder to an inflammatory situation, and since Frome had suffered unprecedentedly severe industrial decline in

---

[105] Leech 1850: 101–2.
[106] *SM*, 29 Jan 1787: 4; Chedzoy 2003: 27; James 1990: 91–2.
[107] de Vries 2008: passim.
[108] Leech 1850: 46; *LH*, 12 Jan 1867: 5.
[109] Rainbow 1970.

the early nineteenth century and its population was 60 per cent dissenting or non-religious, Bennett's despatch there when forced to resign his Pimlico position must have seemed like asking for further trouble.[110] Strangely, such trouble never materialised – or at least, never became riotous.[111] Bennett took his reforms in easier stages, though no less radically, as a visit to St John's church today makes immediately clear, with its unique *via crucis* approach from the north and its sombre interior, both singularly out of place in this gem of a vernacular town. Inevitably, the west gallery organ had to go. It had been moved to that position in 1761 and was still considered 'one of the best toned organs in the West of England' sixty years later, but Renatus Harris's 1680 case was completely destroyed when in 1861 the instrument was repositioned yet again, into the chantry chapel of St John, and rebuilt by W G Vowles of Bristol to a design by Ouseley.[112]

Frome accepted Bennett's reforms, perhaps because against expectation he did not go over to Rome and because of his extensive welfare work. (The town's actual Roman Catholics suffered greater indignities.)[113] Elsewhere, ritualism was given a stormier reception. At St Mary Magdalene Taunton in 1865–66 it was not the surpliced choir but a marble pulpit that proved the last straw, producing a parish 'torn by dissension'. Rev Priestley Foster, who arrived at St Saviour's Dartmouth five years later, alienated his organist and congregation in turn by forbidding the one to play his instrument (the west gallery and tower were too rickety) and endeavouring to impose on the other the organ's removal to the chancel. At Lady St Mary (the parish church) in Wareham in 1878, an old rector was bypassed by an influential group of worshippers who moved the large organ bodily, without consultation or, one assumes, faculty, from the west gallery to the chancel, at which 'several people threatened to have the organ replaced and one or two "very angry people walked out of the church with their noses high in the air" when they saw what had been done'. But the change stuck, while the men of the choir robed and its women sat behind them. The charity children, as they would formerly have been known, were relegated to the vacated gallery.[114]

At its wealthiest, which tended to be in the seaside resorts and Victorian suburbs, ritualism produced some magnificent buildings, furnishings, organs, and musical practitioners. (Again, though, education and welfare

---

[110] Davie 2004: 156–7.
[111] Harding 1986: 74.
[112] Norvall 1991: 19, 21, 43; Alsbury 2006: 23.
[113] Harding 1986: 141.
[114] Bush 1983: 50; Freeman 2007: 169; Brown 2009: 14.

programmes were often the correlative, for instance at St Peter's, Plymouth.) Pride of place must go to St Stephen's, Bournemouth, which attracted Percy Whitlock in 1930, though the 1898 Hill organ was by then well past its best.[115] Another Bournemouth church, St Peter's, was one of four in what has been termed a south-west 'Catholic quadrilateral'. The others were St Peter's, Plymouth, All Saints, Clifton, and St John's, Torquay.[116] To these one might add Truro Cathedral, not exactly Anglo-Catholic but a major ecclesiological statement insofar as it was the mother church of a brand new diocese.[117] All six of these churches were exercises in pure Gothic, two of them (Truro Cathedral, St Stephen's, Bournemouth) designed by J L Pearson, one (St Peter's, Plymouth) by G H Fellowes Prynne, the rest by G E Street. Prynne was local – indeed his father was the vicar of St Peter's – but the other two architects were metropolitan.[118] The organs in question were in the main similarly commissioned from the best metropolitan builders, as emphatic statements of authority, standards, and expense. Henry Willis supplied those for Truro Cathedral (one of his finest) and St Peter's, Bournemouth, and William Hill St John's, Torquay.[119] All Saints, Clifton, and St Peter's, Plymouth, were in the only west country cities large enough to have local builders who could rise to the occasion, in this case Vowles (1874) and Hele & Co (1873); the premises of the latter were, at a slightly later date, down the street from the square in which the church stands.[120] High-profile organists were attracted apart from Whitlock – George Riseley, prior to his Bristol Cathedral appointment, and William Tregarthen to All Saints, Clifton; Bertram Luard-Selby, a fairly well-known composer, to St John's, Torquay, subsequent to his tenure at Salisbury Cathedral.[121] An additional blandishment at St John's, Torquay, was an organ with Latin stop names (such as 'Tibia Pileata Gravis') and reversed key colours, designed by the musicologist W S Rockstro, a local resident, in 1872. (He similarly made over several other organs in the vicinity.)[122] Still more colourfully, it was haunted by Luard-Selby's predecessor, Henry Ditton Newman, like Tregarthen a late Sebastian Wesley pupil. Newman died of pleurisy in 1883, a young man with a young family, after only a year or two

---

[115] Riley 2003: 47–51; Whitlock 1936.
[116] Boggis 1930: 187.
[117] Beckett and Windsor 2003.
[118] Beacham and Pevsner 2014: 658, 662; Foyle and Pevsner 2011: 319; Pevsner and Lloyd 1967: 118–19, 125; Cherry and Pevsner 1989: 107, 849.
[119] NPOR; Matthews 1989: 25.
[120] Browne 2005: 160. In fact Plymouth was not accorded city status until 1928.
[121] Banfield 2010: 356–7; Boggis 1930: 186; Brown and Stratton 1897: 365.
[122] NPOR; BMP: RCM MS 7124/11/2 (J R Goss letter to *MO*, 14 Sep 1934).

Illus. 2.2. A Scudamore organ (line drawing by G E Street and J R Robbins)

in office, having enthusiastically embarked upon what must have seemed the ultimate ritualist programme, with the 'Dies Irae' sung on Advent Sunday accompanied by cornets, trombones, and timpani to 'extremely impressive effect', a residential choir school up and running, and a book of hymn tunes in preparation.[123] The organ played by itself at his funeral, and over many decades he was heard practising or crossing from the choir school to the church, and seen standing by the organ stool or among the choir. But if Ditton Newman, his great work unfinished, was a benevolent ghost, St John's had the misfortune – or carelessness – to attract a second posthumous organist, Francis Crute, who committed suicide in 1953 and later created a feeling of 'frightful frustration and despondency' on the top floor of Montpelier House, the area of the vicarage that had housed the choir school, and in the church itself during choir or organ practice. This ghost had to be exorcised by the vicar.[124]

But the most logical expression of ritualism in organ provision was at quite the opposite end of the social scale from the wealth and fashion of Bournemouth or Torquay, and took place in the country, not in a town, in the tiny Wiltshire village of Upton Scudamore near Warminster. It was all the scheme of the rector, Rev John Baron MA, and the local blacksmith, Nelson Hall. Baron's *Scudamore Organs, or practical hints respecting organs for village churches and small chancels, on improved principles* (London, 1858) explained the idea, which, put simply, was to reinvent the mediaeval positive organ as a ritualist adjunct. Whereas a standard organ would cost £1,000, he had built one in the Upton Scudamore chancel for £40. A Scudamore organ operated on pure German principles, was blown by the organist's feet, displayed its pipes honestly *im Prospekt* in a shallow case, and placed the mechanical-action keyboard at the side or in reverse so that the organist was just another member of the choir. Compass was limited, for the organ's prime function was to serve the liturgy. Models included a St Cecilia organ, a Douglas organ (Capt Charles Douglas, who had enquired from Delhi about an organ, died in the Indian Mutiny), and a cabinet organ with doors. All the decorative details were mediaeval, with a profusion of trefoils, quatrefoils, battlements, and dogtooth. Cottage industry this may have been – the workshop was in the tithe barn – but Baron must have had considerable personal resources, since his booklet, a real period piece, was produced to a high standard with wonderful line drawings by George Edmund Street (Illus. 2.2). This was pure

---

[123] Boggis 1930: 185.
[124] *WMN*, 24 Jan 1959: 5; Farquharson-Coe 1976: 43; Brown 1982; BMP: RCM MSS 7124/1, 4, 5, 8, 9; Matthews 1989.

Puginesque idealism, the village blacksmith a winning touch. The organs sold, and some survive today, including in St Lawrence's chapel in the High Street in Warminster, but they were not well made, and Henry Willis had taken over the enterprise by 1862, when he exhibited a Scudamore organ at the second Great Exhibition.[125] Perhaps this was inevitable, but one laments the selling out of such an unexpected 'truly rural' enterprise at this period. As Baron had put it:

> London organ-builders will not make simple organs at any price ... The supply, I believe, is to be obtained by a due encouragement and improvement of indigenous talent and art; and, if necessary, by invoking foreign competition. In many districts throughout the country there is a man who has a natural passion for organ-building; some musical carpenter, or harmonious blacksmith, who might do good service if he were duly encouraged and favoured with the means of improvement.[126]

Baron, who had also taught his stable lad to play the Upton Scudamore organ, thought that every diocese should have one or two organ builders at the service of village churches, suitably trained.

❧ Romantic Sublimity

It would be wrong to give the impression that large, romantic organs only went with ritualism, for the impulse was a general one, driven by the march of musical style across Europe and the New World and by the growing secularisation of organ and choral music. Cathedral organs may have moved from screens to chancels as much because they had outgrown their old cases as for any liturgical reason, and because new technologies – pneumatic and eventually electro-pneumatic key and stop action – enabled the instrument's various divisions to be split across different spaces. Symmetrical cases above the north and south choir stalls were one possibility, reminiscent of Spain and favoured by Willis at Salisbury in 1876 in his caseless organ for the cathedral, its unpainted pipes blending visually with the marble shafts of the Early English columns.[127] At Bristol, Vowles moved the 1685 Harris case from the screen to the north side of the choir in 1860–61. Willis's 1887 Truro Cathedral organ was high up in the choir from the start.[128]

---

[125] Baron 1858; White 1903.
[126] Baron 1858: 60–1.
[127] Matthews Sal: 8–9, Illus. back cover.
[128] Briggs nd: 2, Illus. front cover.

Monster instruments conquered the flagship churches. The finest of them in the west country may well be the 1912 Harrison & Harrison organ in St Mary Redcliffe, Bristol, which by 1947 possessed no fewer than three 32-foot Pedal stops and four different string registers on the Swell.[129] Whitlock described it as 'the nearest thing to heaven I shall ever experience' when he played it in 1937.[130] Nonconformist organs in proletarian districts occasionally rivalled Anglican ones in grandeur, and needed to in order to support the lusty hymn-singing, but without the Anglicans' admittedly declining dimension of national establishment, they were in the longer term more subject to defeat by costs of upkeep, ageing congregations, and lack of a good player. In 1891 Vowles built a three-manual tracker instrument with a 'monumental' Great for Ebenezer Methodist Church in Bedminster, by then a working-class Bristol suburb. It survived until the late twentieth century. Newquay Methodist Church took the old Andover parish church organ in the early 1900s, containing eight eighteenth-century registers thought to be by Snetzler. In Penzance, Chapel Street Methodist Church's 1864 Walker was as late as 1952 turned by the Sweetland Organ Co into a beefy three-manual affair inaugurated by the well-known London organist and composer Harold Darke, summer visitor congregations no doubt still expected to fill the church to bursting for decades to come. Sweetland had built a sizable *four*-manual organ (was this unique in nonconformist annals?) for Bedford Road Methodist Church in St Ives in 1936.[131] The Roman Catholics never fostered such an organ or hymnody culture in parish circumstances, but eventually made a big splash with monastic organs at Downside Abbey near Bath (Compton, 1931) and Buckfast Abbey in Devon.[132] East Lulworth had been an exception, its 1787 castle chapel, the first Catholic church building in England since the Reformation, supporting a contemporary organ by Richard Seede and an extensive musical establishment patronised over many years by the landowners Thomas Weld, father and son, of whom the latter eventually became a cardinal.[133]

Alongside the romantic church organs, concert organs appeared in town halls and other secular public venues. Civic music in the town hall began in Birmingham, whose music festival outgrew St Philip's church and continued

---

[129] NPOR.
[130] Riley 2003: 18.
[131] Elvin 1995: 168, 163, 161, 159–60.
[132] ibid: 81–3, 142–3; Stéphan 1948: 31–2.
[133] Newman and Pevsner 1972: Illus. 81; NPOR; Matthews 1969; Rowntree 1987; Turner 2004a; Mitchell 2004. See DoHC D/WLC/MU/Boxes 1–4 and 7 for the Weld family musical *Nachlass*.

to conquer the people's hearts and pockets because it raised funds for the city hospital. Birmingham's Town Hall and Hill organ of 1834 (ownership of the latter retained by the hospital in its early years) began a movement that led most famously to the town or civic halls of Leeds, Liverpool, Manchester, Bradford, and elsewhere, including the Royal Albert Hall in London, each with its grand organ.[134] But these were booming industrial cities, and there was no direct equivalent in the west country. Clifton's Victoria Rooms of 1838–42, while perhaps hoping to emulate Birmingham – it too was a meticulously classical building – and acting from the start as Bristol's main venue for large-scale gatherings, had been built with private (Conservative Party) money, and did not see fit to acquire an organ until 1874. A fine four-manual Hill, this came from the south transept of St Paul's Cathedral in London and was inaugurated by Sebastian Wesley and Walter Parratt, the former in one of his last public engagements.[135] By then the building had been overtaken by the city centre's Colston Hall (1867), a full-size concert auditorium with a Willis organ opened by W T Best in 1870, and the opening recital in the Vic Rooms, poorly attended, elicited little enthusiasm. 'One does not wonder at this, we have so often able recitals on a fine instrument at Colston, that really I cannot see the use of another monster organ, which has almost spoilt a beautiful room', wrote one critic, though another pointed out that it contained twenty more stops than the Colston Hall organ (and cost £500 more).[136] Wesley and Parratt were cathedral musicians; Best epitomised the secular concert organist and never held a church post: an obvious illustration of uptown versus downtown culture. In the longer term, Bristol has been unlucky with its large halls and their organs, losing by fire those of the Colston Hall twice, in 1898 and 1945, of the Victoria Rooms in 1934, and of the University Great Hall in 1941. The organ in the Vic Rooms was never replaced.

It seems that no romantic organ ever appeared in any of Bath's secular public buildings; this was no doubt an indication of the city's decline as a resort. Devon remained far behind the northern industrial cities, but eventually Willis did build recital organs for the Plymouth Guildhall (1881) and Exeter's Victoria Hall (1882), the opening recital on the latter by Daniel Wood, organist of Exeter Cathedral, marred by the Artillery Volunteers' big gun drill taking place simultaneously in the room underneath. Cornwall's

---

[134] Milestone 2009: passim.
[135] Horton 2004: 302–4; Banfield 2010: 357; Little 1996: [5]; *MW*, lii (18 Apr 1874): 244.
[136] *MS* vi (2 May 1874): 296; *BM*, 2 May 1874: 7.

nineteenth-century flush of industrialisation, at home and abroad, was probably the cause of earlier results in the far west – three-manual organs in St John's Hall, Penzance (Bryceson, 1867), and the Truro Concert Room (Hill, 1868–69).[137] It would not be long before emigrant Cornish miners were helping to raise funds for massive town hall organs in South Africa and Australia as well as sending remittances home to help the cultural work there.

Riseley's recitals on the Colston Hall organ became famous, but the two west country towns seriously to market themselves for their secular organ culture were Plymouth and Bournemouth. Bournemouth only did so in 1929 when it built the Pavilion, entirely devoted to luxury, leisure, and tourism; Plymouth, as a thriving Navy port, substantiated a more civic approach earlier. But what did a civic approach imply? The secular organ had two functions: to accompany the large-scale orchestral and (especially) choral repertoire, in other words to service participating mass performers, and to educate a mass listening public with classical 'pops' otherwise assumed geographically or financially inaccessible – metropolitan opera, full symphony orchestras – while entertaining them on the basis of the short attention span and picturesque analogue. This helps makes sense of the press comment on Wood's Victoria Hall recital in Exeter: 'the introduction of some well-known operatic selections would ... have been popular and at the same time appropriate to an organ erected for orchestral purposes'.[138] The civic organ was not about music written for the organ. It was, however, about having a borough organist paid by the municipality. Plymouth's famous one was Harry Moreton (1864–1961), also organist of neighbouring St Andrew's church, where he remained in post for seventy-three years, until 1958, long after he had attempted to retire from the borough (by then city) position in 1940 (unsuccessfully, due to public outcry: he was still in post a decade later, though there was no Guildhall organ for him to play after 1941).[139] Bournemouth had a succession of borough organists of lesser or greater repute, starting with Philip Dore in 1929, including Percy Whitlock, Dore's successor in 1932, and ceasing in 1978 when the last postholder, Reginald Hamilton-White, retired.[140]

Plymouth was really proud of Moreton, locally born and educated, who must have spent an unusually full life scurrying between two city centre venues right next to each other. Having lost his son in the First World War,

---

[137] Browne 2005: 229–31.
[138] *WT*, 8 Sep 1882: 8, quoted Browne 2005: 231.
[139] Plaque in church; Plymouth Data.
[140] Ashley 2006: 67–9.

one can only imagine what he felt when both buildings, together with much of Plymouth, were flattened in the Second. When the TUC convention was held in Plymouth in 1923, the brochure announced: 'The grand hall [of the Guildhall and Municipal Buildings complex] ... will seat three thousand people, and it contains the finest organ west of London. Under the auspices of the Corporation, organ recitals are given all through the season, and popular concerts are provided in the winter.'[141] Three years later, a survey of Plymouth's musical provision asserted that 'Few men have done more to raise the standard of musical appreciation in Plymouth than Mr H Moreton, the Borough Organist, who recently gave his 2,900th recital in Plymouth Guildhall ... [where] he gives a grand organ recital ... every Thursday afternoon.'[142] Moreton's Guildhall programmes, as reported in the *Musical Times* in the 1930s, were quite serious.[143] Nor were those for St Andrew's church unambitious: a run of three weekly ones in July 1909 began with a concert of mostly short movements, including Lemare (the most popular organ composer of the day) and arrangements, but graduated to an all-French programme the following week (including the whole of Widor's 4th Symphony) and a German programme containing Bach's Fantasia and Fugue in G minor the week after that.[144] On the other hand, he arranged the music for St Andrews's Grand Eastern Market and Tamáshá, performed for three days in 1921 and consisting of six tableaux including an entrance of 'Scarabs: the dancing girls from Cairo' (his daughter Ethel was not one of them but played percussion); no doubt potboilers by Albert Ketèlbey and extracts from *Chu Chin Chow* came in handy. All in all, between the two salaries it must have been a good living (the Corporation was paying him £200 pa in 1940), though probably supplemented by teaching.[145] Whitlock's livelihood at the Pavilion and St Stephen's in Bournemouth was comparable, though his two jobs ran in parallel for only three years. He had been appointed to St Stephen's at £200 pa in 1930 and resigned the post once he could command a salary of £350 at the Pavilion, which became the case in 1935. Prior to this, Whitlock calculated his overall income at £343 for 1932–33 and £419 for 1934–35.[146]

---

[141] Plym 1923: 10.
[142] Harvey 1926: 29.
[143] See for example *MT* lxxiii (1932): 642; lxxiv (1933): 158, 259.
[144] PSAC.
[145] Plymouth Data.
[146] Riley 2003: 47, 72, 87, 89.

❦ The Organ and Secular Entertainment

It took a long time for organs to turn really frivolous. Even at the seaside, Sunday had to remain pious, and when Paignton Pier invested in an organ in the early 1880s, it was still a 'grand' one. 'Musical performances take place in the Pavilion two or three times a day in the season', a brochure proclaimed, 'and organ recitals of sacred music are given on Sunday afternoons and at other times.'[147] (Not that pier organs ever became common. When the Weston-super-Mare Grand Pier band tackled the Intermezzo from *Cavalleria rusticana* in 1911, they had to resort to a harmonium, 'frequently *grand jeux*', which attracted criticism.)[148] Even storms and scherzos were supposed to impress a deferential public with the sublimity of the melodramatic or the demonic, and it is notable that when early cinemas installed organs, they were at first to church specifications. In Plymouth, for example, when Andrews' Picture House in Union Street opened on August Bank Holiday Monday in 1910 with over 1,500 seats, it contained a 'grand organ' of the ecclesiastical type, whose purpose was 'to assist the orchestra'. The Cinedrome gained a two-manual Hele organ in 1916, opened by Aubrey Adams. The vast Palladium was a former roller-skating rink converted by a London syndicate in 1922 who thought fit to install a three-manual organ that had come from St Peter's, Croydon, probably needed if music was to compete with the corrugated iron roof 'which resounded like thunder' in heavy rain.[149] The Curzon in Clevedon, possibly the world's oldest continuously operating cinema, opened its present building in 1922, and the local organ builder Percy Daniel supplied what appears to have been a small, demure instrument positioned in a box to the audience's right of the stage; the proprietor, Victor Cox, used to play it himself while 'his stepmother, Blanche Harwood, a famous stage singer of the day, entertained the audience during the intervals'. (It actually became a church organ in the 1950s when moved to a nonconformist chapel in Winscombe.)[150]

But when Bristol's Victoria Rooms briefly functioned as the Clifton Cinema in the early 1920s – for the demand for silent cinema after the First World War was insatiable – its organ must have sounded like the shape of things to come, since the magnificent Hill specification had been thoroughly transformed (some would say ruined) in 1900 by Robert Hope-Jones, the experimental organ builder who with very heavy wind pressures and myriad

---

[147] Patterson 1952: 133.
[148] *WM*, 10 Jun 1911: 2.
[149] Hornsey 1994: 2, 9–10; Lawer 2007: 99; Gill 1979, ii: 188.
[150] Lilly 1990: 109; Girling 1998: 38.

electrical contrivances was transforming construction and style, first in Britain and then in the USA, whither he emigrated in 1903. Out went most of the upperwork and its attendant principles of scaling and sonority based on the acoustic series, in came a limited number of pipe ranks that could do multiple duty (different manuals, octave duplication) on what became known as the 'unit' principle, variations in tone colour now the province of ever more sharply differentiated and combined unison sounds of string, diapason, flute, and reed.[151] This radically reduced the number of pipes and their resonance requirements, so that quite large organs (in terms of console controls) could now be fitted into small, invisible positions in theatres, cinemas, and even churches. This of course reduced cost while expanding adaptability of function for a venue, a consideration paramount in a building such as the Bournemouth Pavilion, where no one taste or interest group could expect to command the Corporation's ear and purse. The electrical action also favoured 'traps' – a battery of percussion and sound effects. Hope-Jones eventually teamed up with Wurlitzer and the theatre or cinema organ was born. The first Wurlitzer to arrive in Britain, in 1925, went to a West Midlands cinema but since 1958 has rendered faithful service in Beer Congregational Church.[152]

The Bournemouth Pavilion organ was nevertheless something 'unique, built for special circumstances for use with the Bournemouth Municipal Orchestra', the builder's chance to create 'a true concert organ upon which all classes of music could be played'.[153] The builder was John Compton, whose work in the west country – he himself was from the East Midlands – seems to represent a period of real cachet and confidence in the region thanks to the growth of leisure and tourism. A sizable early instrument for Launceston Wesleyan Church (1909) showed him very much under the influence of Hope-Jones, with many borrowings and very little upperwork, as did his organ of the same date for Holdenhurst Road Methodist Church in Bournemouth, whose Pedal division consisted of two 32-foot stops, five 16-foot, and one 8-foot. The Bournemouth Pavilion organ came in 1929, built up in four-storey shallow chambers each side of the stage, both of them enclosed with their Swell shutters opening to the roof, which reflected the sound into the auditorium. This was utterly contrary to classical principles of organ design, but one dimension of artifice in sound relay might cancel out

---

[151] See NPOR C00925 and N03899 for the Hill and Hope-Jones specifications of the Victoria Rooms organ.
[152] Beer CCW.
[153] Ashley 2006: 72; Elvin 1995: 65.

another where radio broadcasting was concerned, and Compton's triumph as Britain's leading cinema organ builder was underlined by his instruments' broadcasting potential. The role of this medium in consolidating taste and music's association with place in the 1930s, when the BBC was awash with regular outside broadcasting slots, cannot be overestimated. The west country and a Compton instrument commandeered at least three of those slots: Downside Abbey, the Bournemouth Pavilion organ, and, for a short period at the end of Percy Whitlock's life, St Osmund's, Parkstone, a spectacular Anglo-Catholic church in a Poole suburb. Laurence Elvin cannot have been alone in his reactions to listening to two of these instruments over the air. Of the Pavilion organ he wrote:

> I shall never forget hearing a broadcast recital for the first time, through earphones in Beckenham Cottage Hospital, soon after its opening – I had just had my tonsils out and the sheer brilliance of Philip Dore's playing and the magnificence of the tone banished the soreness of throat for at least half an hour! and thereafter I listened whenever possible to broadcast recitals from the Pavilion.

He reacted equally positively to the Downside instrument with its enormous specification of 142 registers:

> The late Dom Gregory Murray's broadcast recitals revealed the great beauty of this truly remarkable organ, the effect of which I feel quite unable adequately to describe … hearing for myself a unique instrument … proved an emotional experience, which I gather has been felt by several musicians and organ builders with whom I have discussed it … After his first broadcast recital of the Compton organ, it proved so popular that a permanent radio link was installed in the Abbey and for no less than seventeen months he gave a recital weekly.[154]

Whitlock frequently broadcast on the Parkstone instrument in the last two years of his life (1944–46), and indeed the only surviving recordings of his solo playing come from that church, marking the culmination of a radio career of over 120 broadcasts, lovingly chronicled by Malcolm Riley, who notes that 'with three exceptions Whitlock broadcast exclusively on Compton instruments'. It was a career cut cruelly short by terminal weak health, and indeed his sight failed him in the middle of his final solo broadcast. His playing, while subject to the style of its period, was disciplined, rhythmically incisive, and unfussy.[155]

---

[154] Elvin 1995: 65, 82–3.
[155] Whitlock 1997, tracks 10–15; Riley 2007: 256–65; Riley 2003: 175.

Whitlock was, however, never a theatre or cinema organist in the sense then rapidly developing, and the Pavilion organ was neither a theatre nor a town hall organ but a combination of both. And unlike the Tower Ballroom, Blackpool, the Pavilion's main space was not a dance floor but an auditorium with fixed plush seating; there was a separate ballroom with its own dance band. Therefore Whitlock's performances, roughly divisible into orchestral contributions under Sir Dan Godfrey and his successors, community service functions (school concerts, stage documentaries), interludes in theatrical productions, and solo recitals, combined into a hybrid role probably as efficacious as any at that time in bringing tastes together (true also of much of Whitlock's output as a composer) but inevitably not pleasing everybody. It would be wrong to say that Whitlock was not frustrated, and he had to face criticism such as the following in 1934 from a Mrs Hicks of Boscombe:

> As a boro' organist you are a failure: why don't you use the bells & other effective stops instead of making it sound like an American organ. You have a grand instrument, learn to play it. You never get an encore as you would if you played suitable music. Wake up & get popular, & not disappoint us any longer. Yours interested in your good ability.[156]

She was not the only Bournemouth matron to bully him, for another, Gena Hutton, would soon drive him from St Stephen's.

Belligerent ratepayers were a rising breed, and perhaps real cinema organists, not paid from civic funds, instead masculinised as popular music stars like bandleaders and show singers, had it easier. It would be difficult to say who patented the type, but a pupil of Parratt, Reginald Foort, who wrote the standard book on the cinema organ, offers a convenient contrast with Whitlock in that he was the first resident organist on the Wurlitzer in the Regent Cinema, right opposite the Pavilion in Westover Road, Bournemouth. The two venues opened within a couple of months of each other in 1929. Foort, who broadcast weekly from the Regent for its first sixteen months but probably lived in London, had physical glamour and presence, evident enough from Pathé newsreel archive footage, and, like another star cinema organist, Sidney Torch, sported slicked hair and a toothbrush moustache.[157] One could never imagine Whitlock talking to camera like Foort, though Whitlock's successor at the Pavilion, Harold Coombs, would startle audience members by turning round and chatting to them while he played.[158]

[156] Riley 2003: 59, 82, 85, 88–9.
[157] Ogden 2001; George 1979: 8–9; Ashley 2006: 25; Pathé: films 1096.13, 1226.11, 1180.30.
[158] Ashley 2006: 69.

Even in 1929 the Regent was 'silent' for its first five months, until wired for sound, but in a cinema of this size the organ would never have been the sole or even the main provider of music in any case: the Regent looked to an orchestra 'of almost symphonic size' conducted by the monocled T S Clarke Brown to provide its background music.[159] The organist entertained in the intervals between films, which makes the quick establishment of an international (though 'Anglo-world') stock-in-trade of arrangements and medleys, novelty syncopation and fox-trots, easier to appreciate. On the one hand, this repertoire did develop from that of town hall organ 'pops'. On the other, it was simply the old 'miscellaneous' light concert and café format also found by this date on the bandstand, promenade, pier, and radio. Either way, Whitlock provided it at the Pavilion much as Foort will have done at the Regent, Whitlock's Variety Interlude on 4 May 1937 during the weekly run of a show being no doubt typical: a selection from *Anything Goes* (a musical he admired) plus his own 'Fox-trot'.[160] Presumably the audience talked rather than listened.

During the Depression there seems to have been a hiatus in organ provision for west country cinemas, which at this stage were 2,000-seat venues, but the Gaumont Palace in Plymouth opened with a Compton organ played by Leslie James in 1931, and Weston-super-Mare's Odeon with another in 1935 (this one is still *in situ*, sole claimant to that status beyond Leicester Square, London).[161] The 1937–38 season was one of recovery and opulence, when Salisbury's Regal opened (though it is not clear whether or not the Cathedral authorities really managed to prevent it including a neon-bedecked organ) and the inauguration of Bournemouth's Westover Cinema meant there was now a second Compton and a third entertainment organ in the same street, this one opened by yet another Reginald: Porter-Brown. A further Compton, played by Wilfrid Southworth, graced Plymouth's ABC Cinema, which opened in July 1938.[162]

The ABC's Compton contained an electronic 'Melotone' division. With church congregations falling, labour and hence maintenance costs rising, the country's industrial base declining, and technology rapidly advancing, the electronic generation of organ sound was inevitable. An electronic organ's portability was enticing, when one considers that the collapsible cinema-style

---

[159] George 1979: 8.
[160] Riley 2003: 109, 114.
[161] Wikipedia: 'Odeon Cinema, Weston-super-Mare'.
[162] Hornsey 1994: 12, 16; Richardson 1972: 30 and 1981: 6; Ashley 2006: 25, 28–9; George 1979: 9.

pipe organ with which Foort travelled around in the late 1930s weighed 20 tons.[163] Whitlock, who loved gadgetry, took a positive attitude towards the new electronic organs, attending a department store demonstration of a Hammond at Beale's in Bournemouth in November 1937 and inaugurating a suburban church installation – the shape of things to come – at St Francis of Assisi, Charminster, the following summer. (This organ was a Compton.)[164] Just as the cinema organ had created a new patent sound, so did the Hammond, as intrinsic a part of an early 1960s ballroom or *nouveau riche* living room as its décor, and by then dominating the soundscape of many a music dealer's showroom. Modernising as well as economising nonconformist churches did not hesitate to install 'electronics', particularly in this decade (for example Rosebery Park Baptist Church, Bournemouth, a relatively prosperous congregation). But there was always a sense of guilt and loss of face involved, and I remember well the shock wave that went around the Bournemouth area in about 1971 when Christchurch Priory, a church of cathedral dimensions, abandoned its ailing pipe organ and permanently installed a J J Makin instrument, of an appearance and sound that were beginning to become temporarily familiar in the larger churches when pipe organs were under repair, Makin having taken over the Compton firm.

It could be argued that the new sounds of first the cinema and then the electronic organ were part of the search for aural novelty that next produced the synthesiser and, above all, the electric guitar, both owing a fair amount, *mutatis mutandis*, to the tremulous sonorities of popular organs. What these other new instruments abandoned were the autocracy and discipline of the single player presiding at an ecclesiastical fixture – the console with pedal board. The return, after more than a century of ubiquitous organ culture, of a mixed group of instrumental and vocal musicians to church worship in Britain was a watershed. Its effect on organs has been more of marginalising than ousting them, though integration is also possible. Two contrasting examples from personal visits in 2010 illustrate the point. At Ilfracombe Baptist Chapel in the town's main street, the Vowles organ of 1891, a two-manual of mediocre design (nine of its thirteen manual registers are at 8-foot pitch, complemented by a one-stop Pedal), stands silent most of the time, used perhaps three or four times a year, mostly for weddings and funerals.[165] Percy Daniel's plaque is on it; does that firm still travel to Ilfracombe to look after it? On the rostrum in front of the instrument are

---

[163] Pathé: film 1180.30.
[164] Riley 2003: 120, 130.
[165] Personal visit, 12 July 2010, information from coffee assistant.

a grand piano and much evidence of leads, mikes, and amps. At St Mary's, Yatton, on the other hand, a proud Somerset Perpendicular church, the old Jordan organ from Bath Abbey, which arrived there to be placed on a west gallery in 1842 and was moved to the south transept thirty years later, shares a large redesigned worship space with a confident mix of elements – or rather its one surviving piece of case carving does, the rest of the instrument being newer.[166] Its attached console is at the east end of the south aisle, and in the capacious space behind the organist a set of raised choir stalls in the south aisle facing inwards evidently means business, with lamps, a generally professional look, and a well-used upright piano in front, making this a good rehearsal as well as performance space. The main worship altar is in the crossing, and the nave seating is bevelled towards it. Another, chancel altar has a further organ console next to it, presumably electronic. In the north aisle there is a grand piano.[167] Both of these churches were available for inspection because of a determined weekday schedule of community work, coffee for stray shoppers and the odd vestigial summer visitor in Ilfracombe, a veritable cathedral precinct of adjunct spaces bustling with office, nursery, and meeting activity at Yatton.

❧ Regional Distinction

The developments plotted in this chapter have occurred nationwide. What elements of the story, if any, are peculiar to the region? Where organs were concerned, Bristol's wealth and urban confidence of the early eighteenth century and Bournemouth's in the earlier twentieth have been noted. There may never have been a west country organ sound as such, but Boeringer did not hesitate to identify and describe a 'West Country School' of 'florid and idiosyncratic' cases, its most prominent preference a complex central tower with side pipes pretending to the function of pillars, though it is not always easy to see why a particular amalgam of elements occasions his labelling. Boeringer ascribes identity to a lineage of builders rather than 'local tastes':

> I think it ... likely that they [the cases] were produced by a group of builders among whom there grew up especially inventive and original traditions of case construction ... It is likely that Renatus Harris and his followers, especially Swarbrick, had something to do with the unusual resourcefulness of the group. It will be remembered that ... Renatus retired to Bristol.

---

[166] Denny 2009: 19.
[167] Personal visit, 4 May 2010.

> Earlier builders who might have established the roots of the school were the Chappingtons, the Loosemores, and some minor figures; and those who built its most characteristic cases ca. 1710–75 were the Harrises, Swarbrick, Byfield, Parsons, Crang & Hancock, the Seedes, and the John Smiths. It may eventually be possible to discover links in the form of apprenticeships, partnerships, and marriages.[168]

This takes us into the subject of chapters 4 and 5: individuals, families, and livelihoods – for organ builders have been mentioned only in passing in the present chapter. Nineteenth- and early twentieth-century west country builders certainly commandeered a healthy business in overhaul, enlargement, replacement, upkeep, and original supply of instruments, as their geographical share of a nationwide industry. They no doubt undercut metropolitan prices and appealed to church managements who preferred the builder to be close to hand for ongoing maintenance, though this probably became less of an issue as improvements in transport and postal communication enabled quarterly regional maintenance tours to be made by the metropolitan builders, who in any case often had arrangements with local ones. The regional builders tended at first to be in the cathedral cities, though Wells appears never to have had one and Salisbury to have produced primarily the eighteenth-century Charles Green and Henry Coster and A W Bryant's nineteenth-century Church Organ Co.[169] The biggest names remain Paul Micheau, Henry Crabb, H P Dicker, and possibly John Crang in Exeter; Hele & Co in Plymouth; Bryce and Richard Seede, John Smith, and W G Vowles in Bristol; George Osmond in Taunton; John Clark, William Sweetland, and Griffen and Stroud in Bath; and Percy Daniel in Clevedon.

The real question is whether, other than Crang, these became national names, inasmuch as not all 'metropolitan' builders were based in London but Rushworth and Dreaper commanded a national reputation from Liverpool, Nicholson from Worcester, Hill, Norman and Beard from Norwich, and so on. Hele and Daniel probably came closest to doing so but remained in a lower rank. Of all the west country names, only Daniel was a creative force after the Second World War. Only he was based in a resort (unless one includes Plymouth). But while his work was not particularly distinctive, the next two generations of builders, taking the story up to the present day, did accomplish something in symbiosis with the region's characteristics. It was organ design's version of the Arts and Crafts movement. An anti-industrial, retrospective approach to organ building had set in in Germany before

---

[168] Boeringer 1983–89, i: 150.
[169] Robins 1998: 59–60; Norvall 1991: 15, 21; Rhodes 1999.

the Second World War, generally thought of as the baroque revival and a major ingredient of the early music movement. The key features were the reinstatement of simple mechanical action (which meant an end to detached consoles and sprawling divisions) and a return to the *Werkprinzip* with its bright upperwork and little if any imitation of orchestral sound. Organ cases might be modern or classical – it was the sound that mattered. This emulation of Continental neoclassicism permeated Britain in the 1950s and '60s, but it was expensive to purchase a north European organ, and at first only the Oxford and Cambridge college chapels and a few other universities did so. But as the change in taste began to spread, through expanding higher education, recordings, and a level of middle-class affluence that could see provincial organists and schoolteachers purchasing their own harpsichord kit, a cottage-industry approach to organ building picked up where John Baron's complaint about London builders not providing small instruments had left off a hundred years earlier, for a classical organ should provide tonal integrity, balance, and contrast regardless of its size. Small was again beautiful. Aptness for the romantic repertoire, particularly cathedral-style service accompaniment and the support of hymn-singing, considerably impeded uptake, but since the normativity of these among the British population was rapidly declining anyway after the war, organ culture gradually returned to being a more selectively appreciated and pursued element of the good life.

Thus it was that several builders found themselves pursuing not only a musical beau-ideal but a location and *modus vivendi* to match, notably in Devon and Cornwall, counties long associated with lifestyle choice. The pioneer was Roger Yates, who removed to Bodmin as early as 1937, simply because he loved the west country. (His maintenance offices remained in Nottingham.)[170] After the war, as Elvin narrates, 'he acquired Michaelstowe Old Rectory and resumed his business in a workshop in the grounds. Many famous organ builders and organists, both English and from overseas, were visitors to his home.'[171] He became well known for his 1958 restoration of the old Bernard Smith organ in Kilkhampton parish church, which had come from Westminster Abbey in the mid-nineteenth century, and he finally acquired the imprimatur of purism with a prestigious if small commission, the organ in the Round Room at Dartington College Music School, constructed in 1969 when he was already in his sixties. Here was a specification challenging indeed (Manual 1: 8.4.2.IV; Manual 2: 4.2.1⅓.8;

---

[170] Elvin 1995: 250.
[171] ibid.

Ped 16.4.16). Its uncased action looked like a loom, appropriately enough for this seedbed of regional crafts. Here too was early evidence that British builders would wish not only to return to classical principles but to work within the paradigms of national heritage: 'This is a traditional English type of tone', an article about the new instrument commented, and Yates, in a letter to Elvin from the 1950s, had shown that he was already thinking about the implications of the English instruments he had been working on: 'the location of English organs rarely lends itself to the "block" construction needed for a good simple tracker setting out', he had written.[172] Elvin regarded Yates as 'a most remarkable man, modest in character and in the output of his work, but a truly great organ builder who was once described as "years ahead of his time"', and his legacy would seem to bear this out insofar as his last projects were taken over by two builders, William Drake of Buckfastleigh and Lance Foy of Truro, who have consolidated the idea of 'a small group of organ builders in the West Country who enjoy … working with wood and metal', though neither of them actually trained with Yates.[173]

Drake, who died in 2014, Foy, and Michael Farley of Budleigh Salterton confirm a healthy workshop basis of regional organ building today. Foy, based in Truro, is Cornish born and bred, maintains and/or has rebuilt a large proportion of Cornwall's pipe organs as well as many further afield, and is also an active organist. Drake, perhaps hoping to capitalise on the nearby Dartington experiment, staked a confident claim to west country allure when he set up his business in 1974 in and with the John Loosemore Centre, named of course after Exeter's seventeenth-century organ builder and intended to act as an educational, history, and players' workshop alongside his manufacturing operation. The outreach activities may have lasted only until the late 1980s, but the firm has continued and the Centre remains its address. The equation it cannot hope to solve is William Morris's conundrum of a century earlier: that honest craftsmanship is expensive. In the economically challenged environment of latter-day Devon, this has meant that although two-thirds of his reconstructed and restored organs are in the region, only one of his twenty-eight new ones at the time of writing had been built for a west country church (St John's, Bridgetown, Totnes, in 1983), most of the others having gone to London, to private customers, to British universities, or overseas.[174] But at least his journeyman's masterpiece, fulfilling a German apprenticeship, has remained in the peninsula, albeit in metropolitan-facing

---

[172] ibid: 251, 253, 263; *DHN*, 10 Oct 1969: page unknown.
[173] Elvin 1995: 255, 380.
[174] William Drake.

Bristol, where it is used in the Victoria Rooms by the University's students on what now remains the only traditionally oriented music degree in the west country. Farley has adopted a somewhat different approach. Apprenticed to a short-lived Exeter firm, Eustace and Aldridge, he took over some of their contracts when setting up in business on his own in 1984. Like Foy an organist himself (appointed to Ottery St Mary parish church in 1985), he has worked with Foy on at least one project, the Crang organ in Barnstaple parish church, and re-sited the Yates organ at Dartington. But he has also undertaken work that will have taken him some distance from heritage craftsmanship, such as the two electronic 32-foot registers in his large rebuild for Sidmouth parish church (1992) and the 'unit' extension principle as employed in his three-manual instrument for Dartmouth's Royal Naval College.[175]

It seems probable that the west country will continue to stand for targeted if sparse connoisseurship where organs are concerned, no longer as an adjunct to mass religion, mass employment (and hence leisure), or mass tourism, but as the occasional marker of lifestyle choice where style, money, will, and a sense of artistic community are happy enough to coincide. This clearly happened around Totnes and Dartington a generation ago, as it had happened with the artists in St Ives a generation before that. But a local labour force sustained by such an endeavour, beyond John Baron's solitary blacksmith in Upton Scudamore, was always an elusive proposition. Now perhaps it is the turn of Lyme Regis, smartened up no doubt with the help of John Fowles and Jane Austen on the small screen. A spectacularly ambitious new organ appeared in its parish church in 2009, no doubt a tribute to charismatic vision on the part of the organist, Alex Davies. But its builder is Slovenian – Anton Skrabl, fulfilling his first British commission. By June 2010 they had raised four-fifths of the £350,000 the instrument cost. With a celebrity recital series, let us hope that incoming second-home and retreat lifestyle resources will help pay off the rest.[176]

---

[175] Elvin 1995: 359–70.
[176] Personal visit, 21 Jun 2010; leaflet; flyer.

CHAPTER 3

Musical Incorporation: Bands and Choirs

✒ *Introduction*

QUEEN Victoria was crowned in Westminster Abbey on 28 June 1838. Two days later, the *Western Times* offered a town-by-town and village-by-village report on how Devon had been celebrating, or planning to celebrate, the event. Part of this liberal newspaper's purpose was to shame those places that had done nothing, for the general idea was that the local community or vicar should arrange an open-air dinner for the poor (seven to eight hundred of them in Dartmouth, for example). At Barnstaple, 'two bands of music' attended the charity schools' procession, and at the workhouse dinner 'a song composed and sung by W Russell, one of the inmates', was rendered in honour of the queen. The Brixham Band processed. At Chudleigh, 'bands from the different parishes as well as our own, playing in solemn but melodious strains to celebrate this glorious festival' began at two o'clock in the morning, and it was another eleven hours before they led off the procession from the Clifford Arms; a band was still going strong at the banquet, in due course following up the Doxology with 'Jim Crow', presumably for people to dance to, American minstrelsy by now permeating the rural west. Chulmleigh's band led the one o'clock parade through the town. In Devonport the dinner was for the schoolchildren, and the Devonport Choral Society sat on a raised platform in the middle of the tables. Exeter sported a band for the morning civic procession to the cathedral, a quartet of glee singers for the official dinner at the New London Inn, and Finnimor's band for the St Mary Steps parish parade with its 'splendid new banner'. Exmouth had 'bands parading the town', Filleigh 'a band ... in attendance'. And so on through the alphabet.[1] The revellers in some of the smaller villages, such as Littlehempston and Holcombe Burnell, for which no band is mentioned but singing or dancing is, may have been accompanied by

---

[1] Devon Celeb: 59–66; *WEPG*, 7 Jul 1838, cited Cann 2001: 116.

a lone flute or fiddle. There are upwards of nine hundred Devon place names on the *Insight Fleximap* for that county; if a third of them were represented by instrumental music, ranging from a single player to a band of (say) eight, averaging out at four, that means that 1,200 musicians were blowing, scraping, or banging in celebration of that day. Spread across the best part of four more counties, there may have been some five to six thousand instrumental musicians in the west country at the start of Victoria's reign. In a regional population estimated at about 1.2 million in 1801, we might guess that one person in two to three hundred could be called upon to play an instrument in public. Excluding women, the very young, and the very old, this would amount to more than one in a hundred active males. Has this proportion changed greatly since then?

Through technology, music in the later twentieth century was capable of becoming a more solitary occupation than it had ever been before. Until then, while it was possible to sing or play to oneself, even the gramophone or the radio was most often shared, while live performance has always implied an audience of at least one or a group of performers pleasing themselves, as madrigal and glee singers, tavern music meetings, and song-and-supper clubs have seemingly done at various periods. Yet however social in essence humanity's aptitude for making music in groups, western civilisation's bands and choirs could rarely be called spontaneous. Typologies have risen and fallen, cultural expectations, aspirations, and necessities have prompted association in one manner or another, money has changed hands for specific if not always explicit purposes, and the actual music has taken forms that reflected these elements. An opposite and equal force to spontaneity has been discipline or uniformity not just of musical effort (implicit in the notion of a good corporate performance) but also of dress, whether formal or, at the other extreme, deliberately demotic – the surpliced church choir, the military or brass band, the concert party, the rock group, the waits, the charity children, the choral society. Have the appearances as well as the sounds of these bands and choirs all in some way or another symbolised the cohesiveness of society, reflecting now the associational freedom of personal liberty, now the eschatology of heavenly praise and reward, now the defence or triumph of the nation or the combat of sin, now the city's law and order, now the community's responsibilities to the poor?

The oldest and best model for bands and choirs was always the Old Testament, and even the humble quire of St Marychurch, Devon, has hung a large depiction of King David playing the harp on the rear wall of its gallery in John Nixon's sketch of around 1812 (Illus. 3.1). Joshua brought down the walls of Jericho with seven ramshorn trumpets; seraphim calling 'Holy, holy, holy' to each other may have been chanting or singing it, as did a large choir

Illus. 3.1 'Choristers, St Mary Church, Devon' (pen and ink sketch by John Nixon)

in Solomon's Temple; Psalm 150 exhorts the people, and indeed animals ('every thing that hath breath'), to praise God with trumpet, psaltery (or lute), harp, timbrel, strings, organ (or pipe), cymbals (both loud and 'high'), dance, and voice.[2] Instrumentalists carved around 1500 can be found around the south porch of St Bartholomew's parish church, Crewkerne, but whether they represent 'a heavenly orchestra to greet the faithful as they enter the church' is debatable, since they include a bagpiper. They may bear a more promising relation to the minstrels, somewhat eroded but still clearly visible, on the heavily decorated exterior of St Mary's, Launceston, a church consecrated in 1524, and musicians carved on wooden bench ends in the same period, the west country's best known being a fiddler and bagpiper at Altarnun, not far from Launceston.[3] Imponderable, though, is the gap between iconographic or textual typology, representing rank upon rank of angels or humans singing or playing, and reality. Lorigan draws attention to a speech given by King David in the Cornish *Ordinalia* play cycle from the late fourteenth

[2] Smith 2001a: 768.
[3] Andrew 1993: 9; Turner 1949: 166; Lorigan 2009: 80, 84–5; Stally and Woods nd.

century which 'contains an extensive list of musicians and instruments[:] Blow minstrels and drums, / three hundred harpers, and trumpeters, / dulcimer, fiddle, viol, and psaltery, [cythol crowd fylh ha savtry] / shawm, zithers, and kettle-drums, / organs, also cymbals, / recorders and hurdy-gurdy' – but this simply mimics the Bible, and it cannot be known how many instrumentalists, and of what sort, actually played out the performance, though Richard Rastall thinks that it should be taken literally where possible, bar the three hundred harps.[4] Again, 'choir' is both an architectural part of a cathedral, abbey, or collegiate church and an organised body of singers performing a service in it, but in late mediaeval and early modern England the latter were mostly clergy whose numbers and functions were various, musical consolidation being only part of the liturgical picture.

Musical consolidation is nevertheless the history to be sought, in terms of patronage, significance, and efficacy. What made its mark, why, and how? As with organs, patchy evidence from before the Restoration admits of no firm picture, though size, extent, and growth are generally the indicative measures of what a community thought important and of how we prefer – and in the *Ordinalia*, how they preferred – to picture mediaeval achievement and identity. A band of pipers still matters to the Cornish, featuring prominently in Penzance's current midsummer festival of Golowan:

> Between the children's groups come the big bands – the Scottish pipers in their full highland regalia, the Falmouth Marine band in their own tartan with waistcoats in contrast to the long-sleeved jackets of the Scotsmen, the Golowan Band. There is music to last a whole midsummer's day through. And finally comes Bagas Degol – Feast Day band in Cornish. They perform in a wide variety of settings and dress, but for Mazey Day they have opted for the formal and the tartan. The basic line-up is one that will be familiar to anyone who has ever attended a Celtic folk music event in Brittany or Galicia (Spain) – the bagpipe, woodwind (in the case of Bagas Degol, usually a clarinet), the side-drum ... for other events, the clarinet may become saxophone or guitar, the drum a variety of percussion, and the pipes Scottish bagpipe or Galician gaita. Bagas Degol are smart and professional, highly respected far beyond Cornwall ... but in Penzance they are on home ground.[5]

Music aplenty is the counterpart to the need for a crowd, happy if not noisy, without which a festivity would not be festive, and 550 years earlier, beyond the Celtic fringe, Bridgwater had also been celebrating with pipers, on Corpus Christi, when its common bailiff presented his Michaelmas account:

---

[4] Lorigan 2009: 79; Rastall 2001a: 316.
[5] Payne 2009: 210–12.

'the pipers of Ash Priors' were paid 1s 4d in 1449, which seems a bargain compared with the cost of the (single?) piper's cloak seven years later (7s 9d), though why Ash Priors in particular, a village the other side of Taunton, was able to supply these instrumentalists, how many there were, and whether they played bagpipes or other outdoor wind instruments is unanswerable.[6] To search for regional identity remains tempting. The churches of Altarnun, Bradock, Davidstow, St Columb Major, and St Austell, as well as Tavistock over the border in Devon, all vaunt carvings of the Cornish bagpipes that nevertheless remain a Celtic 'fact or fiction'.[7] But then so do three churches in a particular part of Somerset that might be taken to include Ash Priors: Crewkerne, already mentioned, plus Curry Rivel and North Perrott.[8] Was there a local culture of piping in that area too?

Waits

When in 1494 Bridgwater's Corpus Christi procession was attended by royalty in the shape of the king's mother, as well as the mayor of Bristol, the Earl of Arundel, and others, the king's minstrels provided the music. This show of retinue – one visualises banners, livery, uniformity – must have made civic officials envious, determined to emulate it. A band of waits was the answer. Waits were civic minstrels, permanently employed by a town, and they flourished from the late fifteenth century until overtaken by the military finances and indeed music of the Napoleonic period. (Bristol's waits survived until the Municipal Corporations Act of 1835.)[9] Launceston's minstrels were flourishing earlier, if the Bishop of Exeter's forty-day indulgence of 1440 was heeded, granted as it would be to 'all who were truly penitent and ... gave ... free alms to the support of the confraternity of minstrels of St Mary Magdalene at Launceston'. He proclaimed this because, 'supposedly, on a visitation to Launceston, at the top of the long ascent from Polson Bridge and Ridgegrove he heard the minstrels and said *'tis the angels singing!* It has been called Angel Hill ever since.'[10] Bodmin paid its waits in 1503–04 (4s) and again in 1519–20; Poole made plentiful payments to minstrels in the early sixteenth century but most of them seem to have been visiting with theatrical players, these peripatetic musicians adding a further series of unknowns to

---

[6] Dilks 1948: 55, 93.
[7] Lorigan 2009: 80, 83; Wikipedia: 'Davidstow'; personal visit, 13 Jun 2011; Woodhouse 1994. Bradock is also known as Braddock, Bradoc, and Broadoak.
[8] Turner 1949: 166.
[9] Rastall 2001b; Woodfill 1953: 33–53, 74–108; Latimer 1893: 239.
[10] Joyce and Newlyn 1999: 582; O'Connor 2007: 43.

the historical equation.[11] In addition, Poole in 1515–17 paid a piper to go about the town 'for the whole year ... in the mornings and the evenings'; in 1516 the payment was made 'to Cornyssh for the minstrel'. Was this the piper's own name? *Was* he Cornish?[12] (Poole has retained its public spirit, mounting a First Festival of Busking alongside its Festival of Running in June 2011.)[13]

Exeter's waits are very well documented, though the earliest references may have been to a solitary, casually employed minstrel or watchman.[14] As early as 1362–63, annual payments of 26s 8d were being made to a wait, first John Beare, then Peter Bylewyne, then for the best part of a decade Thomas [the] Wayte, then John Eget 'and his fellows' (there were three waits in 1405–06 and 1427–28), which suggests that the earlier payees had also split the money. Eget was still being paid in 1398–99, but later accounts specify that the money was 'for their robes', which leads one to wonder whether they had a day job.[15] A hundred and fifty years later any day job would have exhausted them, for they were up round the town 'with their noises and melodies' at 3am five days a week throughout the winter, or at least in the run-up to Christmas, in addition to their numerous mayoral duties every Sunday and Monday and on special occasions. This exercise and the strong pair of lungs needed for blowing windcap reed instruments may have stood them in good stead when one of them was deputed to chalk 'white crosses over the doors where the plague was' in 1590–91.[16] In the later sixteenth century they were still being paid 26s 8d, split now between four people (6s 8d each) and specified as wages. Their livery included a silver collar, for which they had to pay surety: these collars and the waits' badges were extremely valuable (two Bristol badges from 1683 survive[17]). In 1575 the instruments that the city had purchased for the Exeter waits comprised a double curtal, a lysarden or lizard (a serpentine tenor cornett), a treble and two tenor hautboys, a cornett, and a set of four recorders. This more than covered four-part 'soft' and 'loud' scorings.[18] A sum of £5 was set aside for a new double curtal in 1602.[19] Unanticipated instrument expenditure must have occurred after a notorious occasion twenty-nine years later when the waits found themselves in a fight

---

[11] Joyce and Newlyn 1999: 470, 472; Hays and McGee 1999: 42, 238–41.
[12] Hays and McGee 1999: 239.
[13] PFB 2011.
[14] Rastall 1968, i: 217–18.
[15] Wasson 1986: 346–65.
[16] ibid: 172.
[17] Bridge 1928: illustrated between 76 and 77.
[18] Wasson 1986: 166–72.
[19] ibid: 177–8.

with some drunken citizens at two o'clock in the morning and the cornett and one of the tenor hautboys got broken, Henry Gale being berated about the head with a fragment of the latter.[20]

Plymouth already had waits in 1496–97, the town paying for their gowns and in 1524 a handout for their midsummer night watch, an explosive occasion involving wildfire.[21] George Starling doubled as chief wait and parish clerk, paid separately for each office, from 1582 to 1607, his musicians earning considerably more than Exeter's, a total of £4 per annum (£1 each if they were four). Again Plymouth's civic pride shines through, and Guy Parsloe drew attention to it in *The English Country Town*:

> In 1589–91, after years of agitation and the passing of a special act of parliament, Plymouth carried the River Meavy into the town ... When this work was finished, on 24th April 1591, the occasion was marked by a ceremonial feast. Four trumpeters were sent at the mayor's command; bread, wine, and other provisions were despatched; there were payments for guns and powder, and for a dinner.[22]

A man called Cole was the town drummer, and enlisted other drummers for May Day celebrations each year: two in 1595, plus five trumpeters (six in 1599). The town possessed at least three drums.[23] As a port of embarkation for the New World, Plymouth was an exciting place in the age of exploration. The great Plymouth privateers had their own musicians – anything up to a dozen, it would seem – on board ship, and the antiphony of Sir Richard Hawkins's departure on 12 June 1593 will have been a tremendously invigorating occasion:

> I set sail ... about three of the clock in the afternoon ... and all put in order, I loosed near the shore to give my farewell to all the inhabitants of the town, whereof the most part were gathered together upon the Hoe to show their grateful correspondency to the love and zeal which I, my father and predecessors have ever borne to that place, as to our natural and mother town. And first with my noise of trumpets, after with my waits, and then with my other music, and lastly with the artillery of my ships, I made the best signification I could of a kind farewell. This they answered with the waits of the town and the ordinance of the shore, and with shouting of voices, which with the fair evening and silence of the night were heard a great distance off.[24]

---

[20] Draisey 1996: 64.
[21] Wasson 1986: 213, 221.
[22] Parsloe 1952: 107.
[23] Wasson 1986: 250–7.
[24] ibid: 254–5, spelling and punctuation modernised.

Had Percy Whitlock read this glorious description? The trumpet calls and modal sea-breeze figuration of the Toccata finale to his *Plymouth Suite* (1937) perfectly capture the soundscape and the ideological confidence underlying it – but also something of the endeavour's severity, for Hawkins would land himself in Spanish gaols for eight years before he could return home. Similarly, Sir Francis Drake's musicians – eleven of them, plus another eight on John Hawkins's ships, not to mention the sixteen trumpeters – were given a send-off with 'hue and cry' by the town on 28 August 1595 on the occasion of his last, disastrous voyage.[25] Six years earlier, Drake's voyage to Portugal had been scarcely more successful, and for this we know that he hired the Norwich waits and that of the six players, only two returned.[26]

There were well-developed networks between the waits of different towns. Lorigan has traced the personal connections between John Richards, a musician of St Austell (*fl* 1619), and John Gadgecombe of Fowey, who became an Exeter wait in 1639–40 and may have moved on to Plymouth.[27] Samuel John, another Cornish musician, joined the Exeter waits at the same time as Gadgecombe.[28] Both the Bath and Bristol waits were paid by Bath in 1568–69, the Bristol ones 'against my Lord of Pembroke's coming'.[29] In 1595–96 the waits of both Bath and Plymouth were paid 2s for some unspecified appearance in Exeter, and eventually the Plymouth waits felt they had lost out to Exeter's, which will have been what occasioned their petition to the mayor, probably of 1638–39, arguing for a restitution of the £10 salary and perquisites 'near totally taken away' since the great days of their institution 'by that never to be forgotten knight Sir Francis Drake'. This was complete nonsense, and effected nothing, but Exeter's waits had indeed enjoyed a rise in salary to £10 in 1602. However, this now had to cover financial outlay previously itemised separately by the city (and already amounting to nearly £6 in 1562–63 when there were only three of them): the costs of their keeping 'two boys trained up in music' as potential successors (one of their number, John Medland, charged with doing this), of instrument maintenance and strings, of purchasing 'a set of viols and other instruments', and possibly of clothing.[30] Their operation was becoming increasingly professionalised, which may have meant increasingly subject to market forces. The number of

---

[25] Woodfield 1995: 13–15.
[26] Bridge 1928: 84–5, Woodfill 1953: 86–7 with slightly different figures; Woodfield 1995: 15.
[27] Lorigan 2009: 123.
[28] Wasson 1986: 204.
[29] Stokes 1996: 10.
[30] Wasson 1986: 150, 178, 275–6, 451.

waits in Exeter rose to five in the early seventeenth century but then dropped again to three before stabilising at four.[31]

Waits travelled around, possibly to accompany plays and certainly progresses. Two minstrels from Exeter were paid a modest sum by the town of Barnstaple in 1454–55 and again in 1470–71. Waits appearing in Tavistock in 1573–74 could have been the town's own or those of nearby Plymouth.[32] The Bristol waits perhaps travelled more than other west country ones, appearing in Bridgwater in 1495–96, Plymouth in 1561–62, both Plymouth and Dartmouth in 1565–66, again in Bridgwater in 1567 and 1571 and Plymouth in 1568–69, Totnes in 1569–70, and Barnstaple in 1574–75. Nor did they confine themselves to the region: they played in Chelmsford in 1562, Southampton in 1582, and on two separate occasions in Nottingham in 1587. In 1613–15 they turned up twice in Carlisle.[33]

In other respects, as summarised by Pilkinton, the operation of the Bristol waits was comparable to that of Plymouth's and Exeter's. Four civic minstrels occur in the records from 1391–92 but are called waits only from 1508–09, around the time Thomas White, a harper, becomes the first named one. They are paid £29s 8d, unless this is a scribal error for the standard 26s 8d each of them earned annually in the early modern period. In the mid-sixteenth century they lived together in a house in Tucker Street, though in the early seventeenth at least one of them, William Johnson, had a family, his son joining in 1619 as a fifth paid player (of the sackbut), the system by now apparently being the same as Exeter's, of having apprentices 'trained up'.[34] An innkeeper called Thomas Rancock had taken on four apprentices within the space of little more than a year as early as 1549–50, and each of them was to be given a viol, three of them a loud and a soft shawm, one of them a recorder, and two of them a rebec.[35] If Rancock was not one of the official waits, this was carefully targeted private enterprise, furnishing him (depending on what he himself played) with contrasting string and wind ensembles; one should perhaps not rule out the possibility that they were for use on board ship, though Goodman preferred to picture Rancock and his wife 'building up a little three-piece pop group for their four-ale bar'.[36] The first apprentice was indentured for seven years, the others for ten (perhaps he

[31] ibid: 425–31.
[32] Worth 1887: 30.
[33] Wasson 1986: 338, 341, 45, 62–3, 65–6, 235–7, 239, 280–1; Pilkinton 1997: 42; Chambers 1923, ii: 140; Stokes 1996: 49, 502; Woodfill 1953: 105, 107.
[34] Pilkinton 1997: xli–xliii, 111; Latimer 1900: 70.
[35] Pilkinton 1997: 256–7.
[36] Goodman 1974: 12.

realised that training was going to take longer than originally anticipated), and they came from as far afield as Yorkshire and south Devon. Did his innkeeper's credentials furnish him with such networking skills?

William Johnson trained other apprentices, and must be credited along with eight less prominent Bristol musicians with maintaining and passing on formal musical culture beyond the Church. Their knowledge and resources must have encompassed the materialities of instruments and printed and manuscript music, how to teach notation and performance, and how to network with other centres and their leading musicians. How much of this would also have applied to the town's trumpeters and drummers, again in evidence comparably to Plymouth's, is difficult to say.[37] Wells also had waits, paid £2 until 1618, when public expenditure cuts reduced their support to the livery only plus some kind of benefit, perhaps licence to busk house-to-house, at Christmas. In 1624–25 they consisted of two men, John Nash and Henry Loxton, plus four boys. Again the sustainability of their networks and training is underlined, for Loxton's son (also Henry) went to Exeter looking for work as a musician in 1634, a letter signed by the mayor in his pocket, and another Wells musician, Richard Heale, replaced the deceased Medland in Exeter in 1640–41, taking his two boys with him. As Wells declined, which it clearly did relative to other towns, these networks were crucial.[38]

However visible their establishment, the actual music performed by the waits remains elusive. No notated sources of potential repertoire particular to the region survive, with one exception, a somewhat gauche tune entitled 'Bristol waits' in the first edition of John Playford's *Apollo's Banquet* (ca 1669).[39] For the most part they will have played in the earlier period music in three-, in the later period in four-part harmony, its complexity limited by public taste and by what the musicians could safely memorise if they were not to be obscured behind music stands or a lectern at ceremonial events. The simpler pieces in Henry VIII's Book were probably typical: Henry's own 'Pastime with good company' and Cornish's 'Blow thy horn, hunter' remain relatively well known, partly because they are largely homophonic and serve well for proclamatory purposes.[40] But when the waits played viols, we have to imagine them seated, concentrating on the notation of the intricate, rich dance and fantasia repertoire of the period, for they were highly skilled

---

[37] Pilkinton 1997: xli–xliii.
[38] Stokes 1996: 379, 381, 503.
[39] Spink 1992: 8; Playford 1669, no. 85.
[40] BL Add MS 31922 – see Stevens 1969: 10–11, 29 for modern editions of these pieces.

musicians. Thomas Morley, for his part, dedicated his *First Book of Consort Lessons* (1599) to the London waits via their patrons, the mayor and aldermen of London, and it consists of arrangements of dances (mostly pavans and galliards), marches, and popular songs, though this was indoor and possibly background music.[41]

Perambulating besieged cities during the Civil War will have been a dangerous business, even if any money remained for payment, which it clearly did at Bristol in 1647, when the waits acquired new liveries for Christmas.[42] Waits operated during the Commonwealth, thereby representing an important element of musical continuity lacking in the sacred sphere, even if not everywhere, for Bridge claims that at Exeter they had to be reconstituted in 1660 'after many years sequestration'.[43] The Bath waits were performing at a sufficiently high standard in 1668 to have impressed Samuel Pepys on his visit to the city, when he found their music 'extraordinary good as ever I heard at London almost, or anywhere', and paid them 5s for their pains.[44]

Bands of Music After the Restoration

What happened thereafter to the tradition of professional instrumentalists, primarily wind players, blends, if only partially, with the main outlines of the history of classical music. All things fashionable took their cue from London and the Restoration Court, the latter newly modelled on those of Italy and above all France, where Charles II had passed his exile. In Paris and Versailles, Jean-Baptiste Lully had more or less invented the orchestra, combining regimented bodies of stringed instruments (of the violin family) with cohorts of wind and brass. As we have seen, waits might play viols, and could provide the wind. But violins were a different proposition altogether, representing the conspicuous aristocratic and then public consumption of supreme virtuosity imported from the Continent. Perhaps nevertheless it was the domestic currency of the viol that explains why leisured gentlemen should subsequently have taken up the violin as an amateur pursuit, no doubt as gratifying to conquer as swordsmanship in an age of ruffles and duels. Claver Morris, a physician of Wells, is a good early example of the new type of gentleman amateur, who might be compared with a late example of the old type, another physician, the surgeon Edward Anne of Devizes. At

---

[41] Woodfill 1953: 45.
[42] Latimer 1900: 219.
[43] Spink 1992: 8; Bridge 1928: 74.
[44] Smith 1948: 47.

Anne's death in 1687 he left 'three pairs of organs, two virginals and one chest of viols', witness to a private and domestic sound world.[45] By contrast, Morris, well known because of the survival of his meticulous records from 1684 to 1726 and indeed of his splendid house of around 1700 at no. 19 The Liberty, played the violin and organised and participated in a lively musical programme in the city as well as networking with other musical gentry in Keynsham and Kelston (both near Bath).[46] While not necessarily public in the sense later understood, this was a more extrovert musical culture.

Although the nobility and gentry had patronised music, including the latest music from overseas, in their country houses (see below, chapter 4), Restoration music-making of a genteel provincial kind quite suddenly became visible and corporate in the towns. Wells itself may have been stagnating, but the economically driven 'urban renaissance' examined by Borsay and others is evident today in the wealth of classically designed houses and streets, Queen Anne, Georgian, or earlier, in many of its surrounding towns, including Blandford, Bradford on Avon, Bridgwater, Chippenham, Frome, Poole, and Trowbridge, as well as the other west country cathedral cities and Bath.[47] (Bath was at once exceptional and paradigmatic.)

As with organs, a forty-year near silence about bands and secular musicians at the Restoration then quickly blossoms into fascinating regional evidence for this new culture, which crudely speaking consisted in the main of gentlemanly amateurs or cathedral musicians for the string playing plus civic and military personnel – the waits plus immigrant soldiers – for the winds. The regional amateur orchestra was thereby born, a British invention according to Peter Holman.[48] Its vehicle was the provincial music club, one of its spin-offs the gradual establishment of the provincial music teacher, descendant of the private country-house tutor but now a freelance musician teaching a genteel technical accomplishment to all who cared to pay, be it in the form of keyboard, plucked string, or violin lessons. (It is interesting to note that the physician Claver Morris's daughter Betty was having violin lessons in Wells in the 1720s: already, the ability to pay was outweighing expectations of role.[49])

Musical players thus became an adjunct not to civic or aristocratic authority but to a publicly visible lifestyle of free association. Mandeville, an

---

[45] Haycock 2001: 282.
[46] Hobhouse 1934; Johnstone 2008; *SDNQ* Morris; Foyle and Pevsner 2011: 690–1.
[47] Borsay 1989; Chevill 1993: 1–2.
[48] Holman 2000: 3–4; Cowgill and Holman 2007: 5.
[49] Johnstone 2008: 98.

early apologist for consumerism, saw sociability as a progressive virtue, 'a process of learning over time' which gained ground most quickly in 'great cities or considerable towns'.[50] Bath's sociability was carefully and brilliantly modelled by Beau Nash from the early eighteenth century – so carefully that rather than bring the city's waits indoors from the Bowling Green, where they played for dances, he may have taken the precaution of replacing or supplementing them with musicians from London in 1706 or thereabouts to form the Pump Room Orchestra, which 300 years later could boast of being the oldest continuously operating band in Britain, and to accompany balls in the new Assembly Room of 1708.[51] Salisbury had some kind of a music club before this, for Thomas Naish junior, sub-dean of the cathedral and rector of St Edmund's, preached to the Society of Lovers of Musick on 22 November 1700, St Cecilia's Day, assuring his listeners that music brings the human passions 'into harmony and order'.[52] The invocation of harmony in both its technical and figurative sense would furnish the approved resonance of any participatory musical gathering, as well as many an eating, dancing, and drinking assembly – insofar as one can separate out these occasions – for the next 150 years and more. Music clubs soon sprang up in other towns. That of Wells is mentioned below, and was in existence by 1704.[53] Exeter had a music society by 1738 as well as a fair amount of concert activity earlier, and Crewkerne had or founded a music club in 1748, meeting at the Nag's Head on 23 November for its annual feast under the direction of its steward, W Stiby.[54] Not to be outdone, the Dorset village of Evershot raised some kind of a music club meeting in the church and the King's Arms in January 1753.[55] By the mid-eighteenth century, many leisured associations involving music at least incidentally were being established, such as the Bear Club in Devizes, founded in 1756, which met at the inn of that name every Tuesday night and at least by 1816 had songs and glees after its annual dinner in August.[56] Doubtless the Bristol branch of the Society of Ancient Britons, inaugurated in 1754 with an eye to the '"revival of that ancient feast" of St David's', also involved music.[57]

[50] de Vries 2008: 64, quoting John Robertson.
[51] Hyman and Hyman 2011: 3–4; James 1987: 127–9, 380–2; Young 1968: 66ff; Fawcett 2001: 132; *Time*, 17 Apr 1939: 55.
[52] Slatter 1965: 4, 42–3; Spaeth 2003: 131.
[53] Chevill 1993: 7, 10–11.
[54] Dunning and Bush 1985: 9; *SM*, 14 Nov 1748: 3; Chevill 1993: 111.
[55] *SM*, 8 Jan 1753: 3.
[56] Haycock 1991: 62–5 and 2001: 284.
[57] Dresser and Fleming 2007: 67.

Songs and glees were in such cases probably unaccompanied singing, but music clubs needed instrumental ensembles. The Bristol waits were dismissed by the Corporation in 1686 but their records begin again in 1690, and among the names from around 1700 – John Legg, possibly chief, Richard Tomkins, Charles Wedmore, Andrew Norwood – there soon appear German ones: John Friedrich Dinglestadt, Augustus Spittle or Spittel.[58] Both were probably exchanging a military career in Germany for a mixed one in Britain, and both played trumpet and oboe, as well as bassoon in Dinglestadt's case and violin and perhaps other instruments in Spittle's. Dinglestadt played for Claver Morris in 1718 and 1720, Spittle at the Wells Music Club St Cecilia's Day celebration of 1721.[59] And here we have early evidence of the civil and military patronage of music working hand in hand. Military officers were beginning to sponsor their own bands, and throughout the second half of the eighteenth century there is plentiful evidence of a band, which by 1800 might comprise two oboes or clarinets, two horns, two bassoons, and drums or cymbals, being attached to a regiment serving anywhere in the British Empire. Evidence at home is perhaps harder to come by, but we know that Spittle played with 'General Evans's Hoboys' – five of them on at least one occasion – when the 4th Dragoons (later Hussars) were posted to Wells in 1723–24, and that he, or possibly his son, was active in Salisbury as late as 1746.[60] Even when the military was not involved, it is clear that waits might drive professional music-making in the provinces, insofar as the Exeter waits Francis Wellington and Shadrach Radford took benefit concerts in the 1720s.[61]

Early concert life will be pursued further in chapter 7. What is difficult to pin down in the present context is the emergence of the notion of a fixed ensemble beyond the waits, given what to later expectations appear to have been admirably flexible relationships between wind and string expertise, civil and military establishments, amateurs and professionals, and, where music clubs and concert programmes were concerned, vocal and instrumental items. Several of these boundaries long remained porous, which undoubtedly helped musical growth, and by 1776, in a bastion of privilege and resource such as the Salisbury Cathedral close, an orchestra of 22 could be assembled for a subscription series, combining cathedral professionals, local amateurs

---

[58] Latimer 1900: 441; Barry 2010a.
[59] Johnstone 2008: 101, 103.
[60] ibid: 104, 112–13; Barry 2010a; Chevill 1993: 244.
[61] Chevill 1993: 114–18.

Illus. 3.2 'Royal dipping': George III bathing at Weymouth, 7 July 1789 (print by John Nixon)

such as the lawyer John Marsh, and possibly military personnel – certainly there were military officers in the audience.[62]

But somewhere along the way 'a band of music' became a term of reference, something that could be hired or borrowed or displayed for purposes such as the coronation celebrations with which this chapter commenced. We have seen that the Pump Room band was formed in Bath at the very beginning of the eighteenth century, but it was not until the 1750s that the term began to be regularly used, normally implying a wind, often a militia band. What is clear is that those not under military command (and pay) very soon got the hang of organising themselves and making themselves available as a group, probably quite a new thing to be doing by free association. A 'band of music' attended the procession to church of the Colyton Female Friendly Society on 7 June 1775.[63] But what did they play?

---

[62] Robins 1998: 145.
[63] *SM*, 29 May 1775: 2.

The question of repertoire partially resolves itself from 1789 onwards. This was the year of George III's recovery from his first bout of porphyria and of his first convalescent trip to Weymouth for sea bathing. It was also the year of the French Revolution, news of which (the storming of the Bastille) reached him while staying in the town. From that moment onwards, the one piece of music any band had to be able to play, and probably the most frequently heard tune in Britain beyond parish worship, was 'God save the King', which had made its initial mark in London's Drury Lane theatre when the nation was threatened by the Jacobite army in September 1745.[64] (Its very first provincial performance may have been in Bath, little more than a month later, when it was played at Mrs Wiltshire's Assembly Rooms in honour of George II's birthday.[65]) John Nixon's wonderful caricature of the King's initial venture into the sea at Weymouth on 7 July 1789, published in London the following week, shows an oboist, a horn player, a seasick trumpeter, a bassoonist, and a naked boy with a saltbox, all up to their knees in the water, by the side of the feeble monarch being lowered into the sea from his pedimented bathing machine by a buxom female (Illus. 3.2). This was satirical licence, for the band was actually in a neighbouring bathing machine.[66] Nor was Weymouth itself devoid of satire, for that same summer, a notorious celebrity, Mary Wells, 'stalked the king at Weymouth by hiring a yacht and following his boat, all the while seated on a gun and singing "God save the King"'. She was 'a comedienne and mimic' whose lover, the journalist Edward Topham, had declared her insane.[67]

It is by no means certain that George III would have brought his own musicians with him from London, thus we return to the question of local organisation. Tradition has it that the men, including 'fiddlers' according to Fanny Burney, who was with the royal entourage in Weymouth, were from the band of the Dorset Rangers, but this cannot be right, since the Rangers were not formed until 1794. There was, however, an early band in Dorset: John Mahon, Britain's pre-eminent clarinettist, testified in 1809 as having been bandmaster of the Dorset regiment; this will have been the 'fine' Dorset Militia band that John Marsh heard playing in Salisbury Cathedral close in 1778.[68] Alternatively, the Weymouth bandsmen could have come from Bath, where there was a ready pool of professionals used to turning their hands to

---

[64] Colley 1992: 43–4; Scholes 1954: 9.
[65] Scholes 1954: 31.
[66] Chedzoy 2003: 31; Haslam 1996: 195.
[67] Clarke 2009: 28.
[68] *ST*, 6 Sep 1919: 12; Herbert and Barlow 2013: 135; Robins 1998: 180.

anything and in whose newspapers coaches to Weymouth were increasingly being advertised. Or they could have contained or consisted of enterprising multitraders, perhaps church-based.

𝄞 Parish Psalmody and Carols

St Mary's, Weymouth, did have instrumentalists at the time of George III's first visit to the town. We are thus reminded that in Georgian England, a music club or assembly room was not the only place where a mixed ensemble of voices and instruments might be found: the gallery of a parish church or meeting house was another.[69] The singing came before the playing, however, and it would be a mistake to think of this now increasingly revered vernacular heritage primarily as a matter of church bands. Nevertheless, let us deal with the bands first.

Bands to accompany psalmody in churches and chapels that had not yet acquired an organ – that is, mostly poor or rural ones – developed in the last quarter of the eighteenth century, and it was a trend that, as we have seen in chapter 2, burgeoned to such an extent and such uncontrollable effect that the clergy eventually stamped it out. (Carols are included in this section because neighbourhood carolling became one of the mainstays of psalmody bands after they had been ousted from the Church, and because the psalmody style survived much later in local carols than in other forms of music.[70]) Instruments other than the organ had been associated in some way with cathedrals, for choristers were taught viols in the sixteenth and earlier seventeenth centuries: Exeter's choirboys are recorded as playing them as early as 1550. They were apparently heard in the cathedral in combination with organ and voices in 'melodious and heavenly harmony, able to ravish the … ears' of a visiting Norwich lieutenant in 1634, though evidence for their liturgical use is otherwise lacking. Exeter Cathedral also used sackbuts and cornetts both before the Civil War and after the Restoration, though if their purpose was to strengthen the choir's voices in standard liturgical contexts, they are unlikely to have been played from the minstrels' gallery still surviving halfway along the nave.[71] There is also evidence for the use of sackbuts in the cathedral, and of viols in the choristers' school house, at Salisbury.[72] Something of this culture must have percolated through to

---

[69] Evans 1969: 69–70; Pulman 1875: 305; Bulleid 1891: 36; Chedzoy 2003: 27.
[70] Gammon 1985: 57.
[71] Matthews Exe: 2.
[72] Payne 2003: 375, 380–1.

parish churches as well, for the large west gallery dated 1631 in St Saviour's, Dartmouth, was also called a minstrels' gallery, and Bishops Lydeard church had a 'bass' out of repair in 1694. But not until the 1760s do clear records of parish provision of instruments emerge.[73] Blandford bought a bass viol for £1 7s by subscription in 1764; thirty-two parishioners contributed, including nine women.[74] Sir John Hugh Smyth, as effective squire, contributed towards the cost of a bass viol (meaning, by this date, cello) for Pucklechurch in the 1770s.[75] A similar instrument was refurbished by James Toby for Sidmouth in 1773, with purchase of strings thereafter reimbursed by the churchwardens. Sidmouth also used a clarinet and had an oboe in 1786, the oboe's reed provided by Will Turner.[76] Redruth's psalm-singing was accompanied by fiddle, serpent, and double bass at some point after the church was rebuilt with a choir gallery across the tower arch in 1768.[77] Harpford parish church bought a bass viol for £2 10s in 1781, and acquired an oboe soon afterwards. Crewkerne bought or refurbished a tenor violin (viola) for £1 11s in 1782. St John the Baptist, Glastonbury, spent 5s on 'reeds for the singers' in 1785 but also 2s 6d on a new pitchpipe in 1789, which might mean that the instruments were unsuccessful or not always used. These, then, were the years in which the fashion for church bands, their members almost invariably male, arose.[78]

By then, amateur parish psalmodists had in many places been singing in parts for some decades or even generations, usually at the west end of the church in a designated area or a gallery. (Charles Cox could remember the entire congregation turning round to face west when the clerk announced the hymns at Luccombe parish church in the 1840s or '50s.[79]) Like change ringing of the bells, such singing required a good deal of practice. As a determined, even obsessive social activity it appealed to youth, as will be demonstrated much later in this chapter, and was stimulated by the visits and publications of itinerant singing masters, a matter to be discussed in chapter 4.

In this, the west country will have been no more than typical of rural practice. Yet as the epitome of music with a local habitation and a name, psalmody has made the region feel distinctive. On several fronts it could claim to be. First, today's closely protected community ownership of carols

---

[73] Hill 1942: 13; SHC DD\GS\4\26.
[74] Temperley 1971–76 (P167/CW1).
[75] Toby Parker, personal communication, 10 Aug 2010.
[76] Hutchinson 1870–80, iv: 145–6.
[77] Michell 1985: 42.
[78] Drage 2009: 73.
[79] Cox 1913: 206.

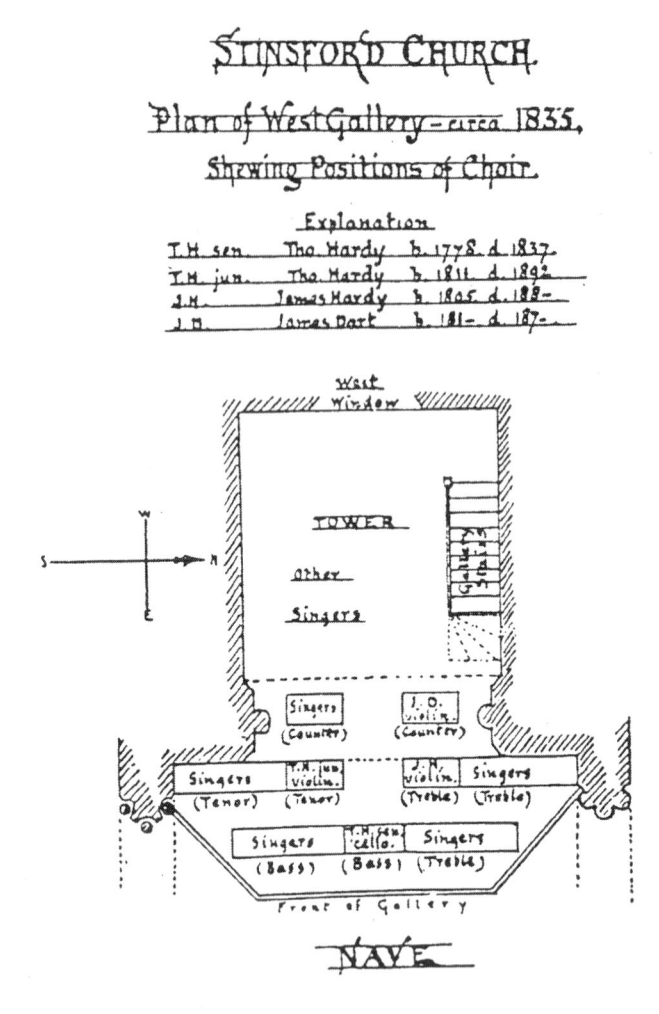

Illus. 3.3 Thomas Hardy's plan of the Stinsford church gallery layout

in 'fuging tune' psalmody style in individual villages such as Porlock on Exmoor and Odcombe near Yeovil, and the perpetuation of a carol tradition in areas of Cornwall, including Padstow and Redruth, might suggest a certain regional pre-eminence in terms of the purity or authenticity associated with cultural isolation, though we need to be aware that many of today's guardians of regional heritage, such as the researchers and members of amateur quires who have become psalmody's experts, are likely to be 'incomers', a phenomenon to be discussed in chapter 6.[80] Second, Thomas Hardy's veneration and literary treatment of the psalmody at his own family's church, Stinsford ('Mellstock' in his works), which it is important to remember he did not recall personally, since the quire was disbanded when he was one year old, has made the phenomenon much better known latterly than it would otherwise have been, and therefore particularly associated in the public mind with the rural south-west.[81] Hardy even drew a detailed plan of the Stinsford ensemble's physical layout in the west tower gallery (Illus. 3.3). The 'tenor man' of 'The choirmaster's burial' was Hardy's father, playing his viola with the tenor singers, or his violin with them an octave higher. Was the band unusual in consisting only of strings? Third, church bands were long thought to have died out later in the west country than anywhere else in England, and may have been particularly cherished in out-of-the-way spots. Buckland Filleigh was actually paying its quire to 'keep up the singing' in 1823; Dorset still had bands at the very end of the nineteenth century, and with the exception of Essex and his own thoroughly researched county of Sussex, MacDermott drew up a longer list of bands for Dorset than for anywhere else.[82]

The local habitation and name of psalmody turned literal when psalm tunes began to be identified toponymically. At the outset they were named after cathedral cities, yet by 1594 there was already a GLASTONBURY.[83] From the eighteenth and early nineteenth centuries come WAREHAM and ASHBURTON, mentioned below, Isaac Tucker's DEVIZES (a favourite of the Stinsford quire, according to Hardy), TIVERTON, and many others.[84] William Knapp invoked a veritable gazetteer of place names from his part of Dorset – CORFE MULLEN, LONGFLEET, HAMPRESTON, and SANDWICH (meaning Swanage), to name four.[85] There were at least three tunes called ST AUSTELL.[86] The *Bristol Tune-Book* of 1863, an old-fashioned enterprise giving tunes alone for the simpler metres and one or two stanzas of accompanying text for the rarer, contained names bestowed by their regional composers such as ST MARY REDCLIFFE (Cornelius Bryan), a new BRISTOL (Edward Hodges), CHARMOUTH (E B Fripp, member of a politically prominent Bristol family),

---

[80] VC: 'Cornish carolling'; Banfield 2015: 74; Patten 2016: 4.
[81] Hands 1992 and 2000.
[82] Drage 2009: 55; Galpin 1893 and 1906; MacDermott 1948: 67–71.
[83] Temperley 1979, i: 68–9.
[84] Hands 2000: 196.
[85] Temperley 2009: 163–4.
[86] Woodhouse 1997: 67.

and LOSTWITHIEL (a most interesting tune by James Turle).[87] Turle had left his native west country for London – Westminster Abbey, no less – in 1817 while still in his teens, and Hodges spent most of his career in the USA, so it is possible that the exile's nostalgia was already beginning to inform the region's identity when it came to the naming of tunes. It can certainly inform the hearing and the singing of them, as this author discovered when listening to a young Indian organist practising Cyril Taylor's ABBOTS LEIGH (named after the village in which he resided while working for the BBC in Bristol) in St Andrew's Anglican cathedral, Singapore.[88]

West galleries were probably not often constructed purely for the convenience and delectation of adult amateur singers, let alone bands. Some that had housed organs survived from before the Civil War, and if in later times the parish could afford an organ and again wanted one, that is where it would most often be placed, as we have seen in chapter 2. With or without an organ, in the seventeenth and eighteenth centuries and the first half of the nineteenth, the west gallery might seat a grammar school master and his pupils, as at Crewkerne in 1662, or the charity school children, both constituencies tasked with disciplined monodic singing as an exemplary element of the congregation.[89] At Box in 1717 this element had swelled to 160 musically literate young singers, including the charity children.[90]

When a west gallery, tiered seating at the west end, or a special pew somewhere in the church was erected for a group of adult church singers, it was often paid for by themselves or by their fundraising efforts, simply because all other pew space was already owned or rented by individuals and families. As early as 1699, the village of Clapton-in-Gordano near Bristol boasted a Society of Singers who paid for a 'pew' – it must have been a whole set of choir stalls – to be erected for their sole use 'for ever', their number comprising four basses (including the rector), five tenors, two countertenors, four unspecified male voices, and four female trebles, namely Mrs Rachel Hollyman, Rachel Hollyman (perhaps her daughter), Mary Cuff of Weston[-in-Gordano?], and Sarah Hardwick. Two of the men came from Wiltshire, another, plus a non-singing female donor, from Bristol, so perhaps the Society got together only or additionally for special occasions.[91] In 1741 the young men of St Benedict's, Glastonbury, were given a felled elm tree in

---

[87] Latimer 1887: 244.
[88] Personal visit, 17 Jul 2004.
[89] Dunning and Bush 1985: 31.
[90] Spaeth 2003: 137; Drage 2000: 173 and 2009: 48–9, 50.
[91] SHC D\P\C.in g 2/1/1; see also Drage 2009: 79.

Northover from which to fashion their own singing gallery provided they haul it the mile or so to their church without 'horse, bullock, wheel or engine' (they took it but cheated).[92] The church gallery of Stone, north of Bristol, was repaired or rebuilt in the mid-eighteenth century 'by the singers'.[93] Here began the spirit of independence that later so vexed the clergy, many of them suspicious from the start of singing societies' propensity to exercise their hobby in gatherings separate from worship and beyond the confines of the parish, for, like bell ringers, neighbouring groups visited each other's turf.[94]

It will be evident from the foregoing pages that the west country boasts a fine psalmody repertoire that such singers enthusiastically explored. They were Anglican at first but later included nonconformists, and nonconformist churches eventually introduced bands as well: that of the rebuilt Wellington Baptist Church in 1833 consisted of two flutes, cello, double bass, and serpent.[95] Psalmodists learnt their repertoire with the help of the resident or an itinerant singing master. It was published and later copied into manuscript part books, scores, and instrumentalists' all-purpose tune books which are still being rediscovered. These manuscripts sometimes contain unpublished original compositions by local practitioners, and although one has to be wary of claiming this before all concordances are known, their value in the documentation of local, often rural usage is exceptional, reason enough for them to have been taken so to heart by psalmody revivalists. The Ashburton manuscripts of the early nineteenth century are cases in point.[96] The town's blind organist, Samuel Chapple (1775–1833), was no unlettered rustic but a sophisticated and exceptionally lively professional composer. He published his liturgical compositions, *Six Anthems in Score* (ca 1815), in London, though they are dedicated to the Ashburton choir, and the same is true of two further sets of anthems and psalms published during his lifetime. Several works drawn from his output were republished in London well after his death.[97] But they also circulated during his lifetime in manuscripts such as the Ashburton ones, which will have been compiled by members of his own choir (or quire). One of the Ashburton volumes binds up Chapple's first and second printed collections, which it follows with a variety of other pieces, including more of his own. Another again includes published anthems by

---

[92] Money 2010, ii: 488.
[93] Leech 1850: 125.
[94] Spaeth 2003: 139.
[95] Drage 2009: 200.
[96] DeHC 2141A/PZ1–4.
[97] Tamaris Mucklow, personal communication, 21 Aug 2015; ChoralWiki: 'Samuel Chapple'; BL Cat.

him, copied out in manuscript.[98] His music is also found in the Otterton and Cruwys Morchard psalmody manuscripts (and even in one from the Isle of Man), and his florid hymn tune ASHBURTON, not known from his own publications, was included in *A Collection of Tunes* by Thomas Hawkes of Williton, a massive Methodist compilation published in Watchet in 1833.[99]

William Knapp of Poole, discussed further in chapter 4, was the west country's pre-eminent composer of psalmody (*A Set of New Psalm Tunes* [Poole, 1738]; *Anthems for Christmas Day* [London, 1744]; *New Church Melody* [London, 1753]). His hymn tune WAREHAM is still well known, though not with its original layout and harmonies. Poole also boasted Joseph Stephenson (*Church Harmony Sacred to Devotion* [London, 1757]; *The Musical Companion ... for the use of country choirs* [London, 1771]), clerk of Poole's Unitarian chapel and thus not strictly speaking a parish psalmodist. Other practitioners within the region who published psalmody volumes included Benjamin Milgrove, organist of the Countess of Huntingdon's proprietary chapel in Bath (*Sixteen Hymns* [Bath, 3 books, 1768–81]), John Broderip of Wells (*Portions of Psalms ... adapted to fifty tunes* [Bath, 1798]), Cornelius Bryan of Bristol (*A Collection of Psalm Tunes ... interspersed with original compositions* [London, 1830]), William Bennett of Combeinteignhead, possibly father of the Plymouth organist of the same name (*A New Set of Psalm Tunes and Anthems* [Exeter, ca 1782]), William Gifford of South Petherton (*Twelve New Psalm Tunes* [London, ca 1805]), the weaver Thomas Shoel of Montacute, who was also a poet (seven sets of psalm tunes, 1800–25), John Smith of Market Lavington (*A Set of Services, Anthems and Psalm Tunes for country choirs all entirely new* [London, 3 books, 1746–55]),[100] another blind organist, R Partridge of Kennerleigh in Devon (*Sacred Music* [London, 1835]), the obscure Shadrach Chapman of Draycott near Wells (*Sacred Music* [London, 1838]), William Harvey, presumably of Melksham (*The Melksham Harmony* [London, ca 1800]), and a late exponent, Henry Bennett junior of Lyme Regis (*The Lyme Regis Psalmody*, ca 1845).[101]

There were many other parochial composers within the region, including some who appear never to have published a volume of their music, though the greater surprise is how many did, Chapman including in his preface letters regarding his long battle to find someone who would take it on. With

---

[98] ChoralWiki: 'Samuel Chapple'.
[99] DeHC 2423A/PR12 and 2075M/Z1–3; ChoralWiki: 'Samuel Chapple'; ChoralWiki: 'O God of peace and pardoning love (Samuel Chapple)'.
[100] Market Lavington is in Wiltshire, not in Hampshire as repeatedly stated in Temperley 1979 and Temperley and Drage 2007.
[101] HTI; Humphries and Smith 1970: passim; Powell 2008: 21–4.

the exception of William Bennett, and of Knapp and Shoel in their earlier editions, they all published in London or Bath, and they included organists of cathedrals and important urban churches (Broderip, Milgrove, and Bryan).[102] These organists cannot really be thought of in a separate category, and Temperley's distinction between urban psalmody with organ and rural without is not easy to sustain, for example where Ashburton is concerned. (Ashburton had an organ from at least 1778; admittedly there is no evidence of its use in the psalmody manuscripts.[103]) Not all the music in the published volumes was necessarily composed by their eponymous producers unless that is specifically avowed. Most of the publications eschew a separate keyboard part, even in long monodic solos, though there are exceptions and figured bass is occasionally found. As for the manuscript compilations, they can be quite large, running to hundreds of pages and items; such are *Music for Church Use by John Williams Sampford Brett 1805*, the psalmody book of Rev Thomas Bartlett of Swanage (terminated in 1839), and the enormous Dunster volume initiated by William Jenkins in 1799.[104] Page openings of three nineteenth-century Cornish tune books, one having belonged to Hannibal Lugg Lyne of St Mawgan, the other two to Thomas Prisk of Illogan, are illustrated by Harry Woodhouse in his book on church and chapel bands in Cornwall.[105] These books lasted a lifetime or more and, like the family Bible's genealogical notes, were added to continually.

As can be seen above, psalmody was produced over a long period, during which its musical idiom changed much less than might have been expected. A hundred years after the death of Handel, the bluff 'Georgian survival' style of rhythmic block harmony and short-winded contrapuntal imitation associated above all with that composer's 'Hallelujah' Chorus continued to serve and appeal. It did so in the multi-section 'set pieces' (nonconformist) and anthems (Anglican); strophic hymn and psalm tunes might also include 'fuging' elements (not always strictly imitative) while purveying a melody which was suave or florid (often, like WAREHAM, in triple metre) and at the same time still showing rough traces of pre-tonal harmony and part-writing. Knapp's original arrangement of WAREHAM (Ex. 3.1) is a case in point, though without any fuging. A blatant chain of consecutive 5ths occurs between the tenor and treble, and then tenor and bass, three, four, and five

---

[102] Temperley 1979, i: 181, where the date of 1736 is given for Knapp's first edition, probably in error; BL Cat.
[103] *SM*, 23 Nov 1778: 2.
[104] SHC DD\X\WMS; USSC; SHC A\CZR/1.
[105] Woodhouse 1997: 68.

Ex. 3.1 William Knapp, WAREHAM

bars before the end. True, most of these would become unobjectionable consecutive 4ths were the tune transferred to the upper octave and the treble to the lower, which frequently happened; but then other 5ths would appear (for example in bar 1). The harmony, meanwhile, does not always accord with fully tonal inflection, several instances of F or F sharp moving upwards by step to G proving awkward. The first one, in bars 1–2, produces a destabilising interrupted cadence too early in the piece. That in bars 5–6 is mollified if the F is sharpened (as occurs authorially two bars later), but one doubts whether this was Knapp's intention; if it was not, the effect, including the consecutive 5ths, is bracing. The effect in bars 9–10, complete with another consecutive 5th, is positively mediaeval, because the F wants to be the 7th of a dominant function, given that the next chord is the tonic, and is not allowed to be. Overall, the tune and the almost time-warped idiom that its treatment represents are an artisanal survival of the most sturdy kind, perennially poised for us today between quaint and current (for the voice-leading can be heard renascent in contemporary folk music), innocent and knowing.

It is tempting to conclude that right up to the end of the nineteenth century where Cornish and Exmoor carols were concerned, it was as though not just Mozart and Beethoven had never existed, let alone Chopin and Wagner, but Thomas Moore's *Irish Melodies* as well. Yet this is an exaggeration, and even syncopation begins to be found after Moody and Sankey had swept Britain with their gospel music. Some old favourites have turned out to be American.[106] The Redruth region's Methodist production of carols in the second half of the nineteenth century offers a test bed of ingredients. On the one hand, this repertoire displays a potentially stultifying sameness between one tune and another. Carols in F major occur again and again, as Geoffrey Self has pointed out, and Self identifies among the distinguishing features of 'the Redruth carol' 'a chordal statement of the first line', repetition of subsequent lines, often with a reduced-voice texture in line 2 or 3, and 'very basic voice-leading and imitation' in the last line.[107] One could go further and point out the paucity of modulation, which is to the dominant, normally at the end of the second line, or entirely lacking, and the font of basic Handelian rhythms seemingly shared by all the carols. The words are equally formulaic. Yet Thomas Merritt's carols, which 'follow this pattern closely', manage at the same time to be more than alive melodically, as two fine examples reproduced in their musical entirety by Susan Skinner demonstrate and as Malcolm Arnold discovered when he lived in Cornwall in the 1960s and resurrected Merritt's music in a concert in Truro Cathedral.[108] Merritt was

[106] Wilson 2012: 12.
[107] Self 1997: 30–1.
[108] Skinner 2013: 84, 86.

Ex. 3.2 R H Heath, 'It came upon the midnight clear', opening

largely self-taught as a musician; his father was a miner.[109] R H Heath, born in Torquay, was organist at Redruth's Wesleyan Chapel and probably the town's leading musician when Merritt presided at the harmonium in its Bible Christian Chapel.[110] (Merritt later became organist at two Illogan Highway Methodist churches as well as forming and accompanying a choral society in that village, barely a mile distant from Redruth, though by this time Heath, older and more ambitious, had emigrated to South Africa, becoming organist of churches in Johannesburg and elsewhere as well as an organ teacher at Johannesburg's South African College of Music.[111]) Heath's melodic gift was equal to Merritt's, though it will have been acquired through more extensive musical channels and was exercised to different effect, for his carols refer to a much broader range of styles. The melodic repetition in the first two lines of his hauntingly attractive 'It came upon the midnight clear' (Ex. 3.2), an inspiration charged with conveying 'that glorious song of old', could not have been written without the example of Mendelssohn and his period; nor could his static tenor part, starkly different from older artisanal ones still itching to convey the tune. Elsewhere, Heath writes melodies with elements from Irish folk music or draws on the heritage of 'national' song, as when echoing 'The *Golden Vanity*' in his 'High let us swell'.

The fact is that, not least because different musical impulses and hugely differing creative abilities and educational training did coexist in this repertoire, a critical anatomy of it will remain elusive. Temperley laid down strong taxonomic guidelines in *The Music of the English Parish Church*, but

---

[109] Self 1997: 31–2.
[110] ibid: 29; *RCG*, 21 Feb 1889: 5; *WB*, 22 Aug 1889: 10 and 26 Sep 1889: 5.
[111] *WB*, 9 Jan 1902: 5 and 22 May 1902: 5; *CRT*, 23 Apr 1908: 4; Self 1997: 29–30; Wolpowitz 1982.

taking the very long view, including local carols up to and beyond the end of the nineteenth century, and basing inclusion on the status of reception, heritage, and local identity, rather than distinctions of historical production, are approaches that make the further task daunting. One postpones it because of the impossibility of declaring any particular item of no musical value when it may remain a village favourite, loved through long familiarity. (I am thinking of some of the Porlock carols.) But a comprehensive definition and assessment of the vernacular psalmody repertoire of the eighteenth and nineteenth centuries as received up to the present day will in the end be necessary and fascinating.

One element of the problem, invoked above in referring to the repertoire's stylistic conservatism, is what used to be called making allowances. The *Musical World* was eager enough to do this when Chapman's volume was published:

> MUSICAL GENIUS. - A labouring man, named Shadrack [sic] Chapman, who resides at Draycott, near Wells, in Somersetshire, who has nothing but his wages as an agricultural day labourer to subsist on, and who has never received the smallest instruction in music, has composed a series of anthems, psalm tunes, and sacred pieces of music, arranged for one, three, and four voices, several of which contain merit of the highest order. The author of these works is self-taught by perseverance; and surmounting the most incredible difficulties, he has acquired a perfect knowledge of the rules of harmony, thorough bass, fugue, and counterpoint. This knowledge may rather be called practical than theoretical, as it has been acquired by finding out the rules by which the masters have written, from a perusal of their music, and not from the study of works of instruction. Amongst the pieces composed by Chapman are several fugues, that for grammatical accuracy might have done credit to the old masters. The poor man has been taken by the hand by a benevolent clergyman, who is publishing several of his works by subscription, at a small charge. Chapman plays no instrument; but so accurate is his ear that he can correctly call every note, including the flats and sharps, as they are sounded.[112]

At the same time we must never forget that psalmody died out not just because the clergy hated the musicians' autonomy, but because it could be an embarrassment for parishioners to have to sit or stand through. Any number of satirical engravings convey its roughness, and as transferred to Australia in the early nineteenth century it evoked 'an assemblage of hogs' in the view of one exasperated writer to the *Sydney Gazette*.[113] We need to be aware

---

[112] *MW* x (1838): 91.
[113] *Sydney Gazette*, 23 Dec 1824: 4.

that its tuning seems not to have been unduly criticised, and may well have been exquisitely adjusted in ways only possible when performers have played and sung together in extreme intimacy over long periods. This is as true of barbershop today as it probably was of psalmody then. What refined taste will have objected to were the elements now identified as a folk or popular vocal delivery: screwed-up facial features, nasality, hard-edged tone, mobile vowels and elaborate transients, chest-voice yelling, falsetto hooting, and sheer loudness.[114] Reformers wanted something 'sweeter'.[115] Then there was the serpent. Even Woodhouse, a present-day enthusiast and exponent, stresses its 'defective' nature and extreme difficulty of playing. He points out that 'nobody today really knows what the serpent sounded like in the hands of a virtuoso player', which is not strictly true, for Phil Humphries of the Mellstock Band achieves amazing results, affirming the instrument's unique compatibility with the sound of a lower male voice.[116] Humphries, however, is probably the exception that proves the rule of what it sounded like in the hands of a bungling performer.

Military Bands

The connection between church bands and military bands remains largely indefinable, but Lomas presents persuasive evidence that it was certainly there, church bands arising from bands of the auxiliary forces or *vice versa* and sometimes sharing personnel, patronage, and instruments.[117] From the time of the Seven Years' War, whose conclusion with the Treaty of Paris and Britain's acquisition of Canada in 1763 ushered in a period of growth of empire and of military activity overseas, county towns increasingly amassed, recruited, and drilled professional regiments of soldiery. Their musicians in the west country were brought together and trained in Exeter, Taunton, Salisbury, Dorchester, Truro, or Bristol prior to serving in India, North America, the Caribbean, Australia, and, by 1800, South Africa. Thus the 62nd Foot, formed in Exeter in 1756 and later to become the 1st Battalion, Wiltshire Regiment, were in Quebec under Wolfe, in Ireland 1761–62, in Dominica, in the American War of Independence under Burgoyne, then back home in Trowbridge; in Ireland, in Halifax (Nova Scotia) for service in Jamaica and San Domingo in the 1790s, then fighting Napoleon in Egypt, and all over

---

[114] Gammon 1985: 27–9, and 2006: paras 19–31. See also Drage 2009: 275–7.
[115] Gammon 1985: 50.
[116] Woodhouse 1997: 41; Mellstock: samples.
[117] Lomas 1990, i: 65–71. See also Drage 2009: 36–7, 72–3.

the British world in the nineteenth century.[118] Such regiments might pass through Plymouth, where notaries must have done a brisk trade with those hastily recruited: the will of John Gilbert, 'musician in the 22nd Regiment of Foot now lying in Marlborough Square in Plymouth Dock', survives, dated 30 May 1786.[119] In Plymouth the Royal Marines also developed a band, formed in 1767 and sixty years later clearly a classy ensemble, for its bandmaster was a Mr Stockham, 'late of Almack's', Almack's being the premier dance venue in London.[120]

In tandem with the consolidation and expansion of the regular army's regiments, militia units for part-time home service were formed. A third development was the volunteer divisions that came into being during the 1790s when Britain was at war with France and every small community had to be ready and trained for imminent invasion. Volunteer forces would only be disbanded after the defeat of Napoleon at Waterloo in 1815. These three types of service unit each had music, which at least in the regulars and militia consisted of two kinds of musician. Fifers and drummers were field musicians, professional soldiers who went into action conveying signals and marching or 'signature' tunes. They suffered high casualties. The military wind band was a group of adjunct professional musicians employed for ceremonial and entertainment purposes.

The soundscape of quite small places must have come alive with military music as soldiers marched through, were quartered or drilled, or their musicians lent their services to local events, always done with the permission of the division's commanding officer, which was rarely refused. As a lad, the violinist John Davy 'was entranced on hearing the fifes of a military detachment quartered at Crediton; and when a soldier lent him one he soon learnt to play tunes tolerably well'.[121] This will have been around 1773, by which time a stirring, binary-form tune such as 'The Wiltshire march' will have been familiar from several publications for more than a decade. Later, in the Napoleonic period, Blandford racecourse became a military training centre, and the town must have heard as well as seen uniformed musicians, though no positive evidence of military music there seems to be forthcoming.[122]

[118] Gibson 1969: [iv].
[119] NA online: wills.
[120] Royal Marines Band Service; Smith 1999b: 10.
[121] Venn 1955: 407.
[122] Smith 1968: 22.

The smaller the place and the more closely related its military activity to field manoeuvres, the more likely the soundscape is to have consisted only of fifes and drums. The addition of a wind band was seen as a desirable development while remaining vulnerable to fluctuating patronage and interest. In 1766 the Wiltshire Militia were purchasing accessories for drummers and fifers, but within three years they set up a wind band and appointed a London musician, J A Buckner, possibly a German immigrant, to act as bandmaster. The band consisted of pairs of bassoons and horns and three clarinets.[123] The Somerset Militia had established a band by 1777, there was a good one in Bodmin the same year, the South Devon Militia possessed one in the early nineteenth century when John Distin, born in Plympton in 1798, played in it as a boy trumpeter, and the band of the 1st Devon Militia, based in Exeter, in 1805–06 contained clarinets, a serpent and/or a trombone, and a turbaned performer (probably a black percussionist).[124] Yet William Shepherd, who enlisted with the 1st Devon Militia in 1853, claimed that a band was not formed (under bandmaster Pinney, one of a family of musicians active around Exeter) until 'about the middle of March 1854. Previous to this it was fife and drums.'[125] The earlier one had ceased to function, probably after 1825 amid the economic distress of that decade. The same will have been true of the band of the Earl of Devon at Powderham Castle, which brings us back to the starting point of this chapter, for it was revived in 1838 for the coronation celebrations. The *Western Times* furnished a description well conveying the strength of association of bands with the patriotism of 1793–1815:

> The Powderham band is a resurrection of the old regimental band of the Exminster Hundred volunteer regiment. These martial musicals had long been registered with the forgotten past. Their musical instruments buried beneath the silent accumulations of dusty years, were no longer associated with the tuneful spirit of the present day, but like musty armour hanging on old walls, bore mute evidence of the martial music that had excited heroic souls to action in the Exminster hundred when Buonaparte threatened to invade that peaceful region. Never since the skeleton review of Buonaparte's army on the plains of Moscow has there been such a re-animation. We understand that these resuscitated veterans will henceforth play on the parade at Starcross every Wednesday evening.[126]

---

[123] Lomas 1990, ii: 2, citing WHC 9/[1]/[3]/[1]/[1].
[124] Lomas 1990, i: 38–9, 71; Wormleighton 1996: 208; Walrond 1897: 235, 241.
[125] Shepherd 1907: 1.
[126] Devon Celeb: 63.

(Starcross had become a minor estuary resort.)

When a harmonic band did come into being, the military was *creating* musicians, which it has continued to do, for it was willing to train them from scratch, as we know from Buckner's methods with the Wiltshire Militia: he 'seems to have tried his men out on different instruments before deciding upon which part they had to play. It also appears that he would have given up with one of the bassoonists had it not been for the man's great desire to learn.'[127] Music, like a brightly coloured uniform, was an enormous draw to recruitment, as demonstrated by one Bristol observer in 1805:

> A recruiting party proceeded nearly at my pace, with fifteen lads whom they escorted, with the honours of war, to the branching of the road, two miles and a half from Bristol; where they were committed to the care of three soldiers; and the martial musick, with the *fine* gentlemen bedecked with ribands, returned to the city to ensnare others.
>
> The drums and fifes roused the inhabitants of Bedminster, and brought them to their doors.[128]

Of course professional stiffening would always help, as it continues to help many an amateur orchestra today, and half of the twelve members of the Bristol Volunteer Band in 1797 were professional musicians: John Percival, Joseph Stansbury, Andrew Winpenny Waite, David Williams, Joseph Sturge, and William Fryer. The remainder were artisans and tradespeople, most likely a carpenter, a watchmaker, a shoemaker, a warehouse keeper, a butcher or cork-cutter, and a sign painter.[129] The professionals included leading local figures. Percival composed their march, Stansbury, a violinist, was leading the Bristol Theatre Royal orchestra 30 years later, Williams was organist of All Saints and had taught Samuel Wesley, and Sturge, probably from a wait family, was a music seller operating at 28 Park Street.[130]

Here we have actual music to assist in recreating the soundscape. James Matthews, a leading Bath music seller, composed 'The new Somersetshire march' on 11 October 1797. Josiah Ashley's 'Royal Dorsetshire march' was 'perform'd before their Majesties at Weymouth. Composed ... for that Occasion' in 1797, and is scored for two clarinets, two horns, two trumpets, and optional bassoon.[131] J Tebay's 'Bath Volunteers' march' was published

---

[127] Lomas 1990, i: 55–7.
[128] Malcolm 1807, quoted Beeson 2009: 215.
[129] Lomas 1990, i: 57–61.
[130] Concert handbill, 10 Dec 1829; Barry 2010a; Barry 2010b: 143, 145; Humphries and Smith 1970: 303.
[131] BL Cat; Herbert 2010.

Ex. 3.3 John Percival, 'The Bristol Volunteer troop', extract

around 1800. Percival's march, 'The Bristol Volunteer troop', published in London at about the same time, may well also date from 1797, for this was the year of maximum defence panic as all Europe except Britain fell to Napoleon and the French were specifically intent on invading Bristol (though they got no further than Fishguard).[132] The music is orchestrated for pairs of clarinets, horns, and bassoons, with the addition of serpent (as double bass) and trumpet, and was provided with a piano reduction and optional parts for two flutes, which suggests ready take-up in the domestic sphere. All this is fully typical of the military scoring of the period, clarinets (often more than two in a band) having clearly ousted oboes by this date, perhaps as quick tuition by a bandmaster on an easier instrument replaced long apprenticeship with the waits as the skilling method.[133] The jaunty one-in-a-bar triple metre of 'The Bristol Volunteer troop' offers just the right flavour of redcoat bravado and might equally accompany a heavy march tread or a tripping country dance (Ex. 3.3).

The rise in social temperature afforded at the period of the French wars by the military and its accomplishments and the latter's association with Germany from the eighteenth century onwards are well illustrated by Chedzoy's portrait of Weymouth in the summer of 1804:

> German officers soon became popular in Weymouth society. Many were good dancers, and because of this were invited to local balls. Some were able to dance the waltz, which had only just arrived in England and was considered rather daring. Twenty-one year old Elizabeth Ham, then living in Weymouth, noted in her diary that 'The officers of the German Legion used to amuse us greatly with their ... vain efforts to try to induce us to try a waltz. This was the first we had ever seen of this kind of dance, nothing but country dances were then in vogue.'
>
> In addition to their dancing skills, the Germans were often good musicians and singers, and willing to perform for their hosts. It soon became customary to ask them to play or sing ... the gallant bearing of these German troops excited general admiration, as did their musical abilities. Each regiment had its own band, which played while the men sang and marched along the roads. Their uniforms were dashing and colourful.[134]

The waltz was indeed novel, and not yet of settled orthography, for in 1800 the *Bath Chronicle* carried an advertisement from a local violinist, J Cellars, 'who, *inter alia*, could play the "Walths" in the Germanic manner'.[135]

Volunteer bands and field musicians were kept busy at various points during the Napoleonic conflict by news of peace in 1801 and again in 1814,

---

[132] Humphries and Smith 1970: 332; James 1987: 805–10.
[133] Murray 2001: 686; Lomas 1990, i: 79.
[134] Chedzoy 2003: 66–7.
[135] Fawcett 1988: 48.

by the King's jubilee in October 1810, and by various other reminders that life was continuing despite the wars. It would have been impossible for any local resident to be unaware of international developments when Camborne responded thus to the news of peace with France reaching this remote town around 10pm on a Sunday night (4 October 1801): 'The bells were immediately set a ringing, drums beating, fifes playing through the streets, the Volunteers rose from out their beds and arrived on the place of rendezvous, as did a great number of the inhabitants, where they sung "God save the King," &c &c the bells ringing and drums beating the greatest part of the night.' Not content with that, the volunteers wrote and sang a large number of new verses for the national anthem, printed in full in the *Royal Cornwall Gazette*.[136] The following morning, in Truro, 'A little before ten o'clock, the whole of the people employed at the carpet manufactory of Messrs Martyn and Turner, walked in regular procession through the town, accompanied by a band of music, to the grateful and heartfelt satisfaction of the spectators' – did the firm therefore have its own band? The *Gazette* reported general rejoicing in the Cornish towns, songs sung in pubs, bells rung, and community dancing. Polperro set up illuminations, 'a thing never done there within the memory of man', and all involved repaired to the Ship Inn for supper with toasts and 'some excellent loyal songs'. On the 16th, Wynn's Hotel in Falmouth hosted a concert and ball at which the Royal Cornwall Militia joined forces with the gentlemen of the Falmouth Harmonic Society. Early the following month at Devonport (it was still called Dock then), the procession, manoeuvres, and choral efforts (in national songs) of 4,000 naval dockyard workers witnessed by an estimated 30,000 spectators were claimed to be 'without exception, the grandest national spectacle ever exhibited in any country in the world', an exaggeration no doubt aimed at the French liberty festivals of the previous decade. 'The bands and drums of the regiments in garrison attended on the occasions, and played several marches in a grand style during the march. There were near 500 flags and banners emblematical of peace, the fine arts, and different trades, beautifully executed.'[137]

Curiously, when a lasting peace did finally arrive with victory at Waterloo in June 1815, immediate celebrations may have been more muted; the populace had been through it all a year before, and the weather did not help, when in the middle of a large subscription dinner for the poor in a field with a 'band of music' near Wedmore, 'down came the rain in torrents on the dinner table. Surrounded by at least 800 persons it was indeed most woefully unfortunate',

---

[136] *RCG*, 17 Oct 1801: 3.
[137] ibid; *RCG*, 10 Oct 1801: 3, 24 Oct 1801: 3, 10 Oct 1801: 2, 14 Nov 1801: 3.

as a local diarist, Ann White, recorded.[138] But to hear the popular actor James Woulds singing Charles Cummins's arrangement of 'The white cockade' in the Bath and Bristol Theatres Royal will have been stirring enough, with its refrain 'So master Boney now, now, now / Is off without beat of the row, row, row, / In dastard haste lo! sore dismay'd / He trembles and flies from the "White Cockade".' There was plenty of row the following month when Boney appeared in Torbay and then in Plymouth Sound. Parties of boating females, their hands over their ears as cannon fired, swooned at the sight of the lone figure peering from the top deck of the *Bellerophon* on his way to St Helena. Were the vast, over-excited crowds in Jules Girardet's painting cheering or jeering him? – such a small difference.[139] The Plymouth waits were possibly defunct by then, unable to augment the din as they had done for Drake and Hawkins on the same spot 220 years earlier.

✒ *Bands for Social Dancing*

Civilian freedoms restored, the military cadence rapidly transformed itself into a new social dance, the quadrille (though *Loder's Collection of Dances, for 1814 ... as danced ... in BATH* already looks much like a quadrille sequence). Truro advertised its first quadrille ball in 1818.[140] Choreographically a complex set of square manoeuvres for four couples, fraught enough for the unwary, the quadrille was musically speaking a sequence of five multi-section tunes played to the same beat (but varying time signatures) more or less without a break. 'The Clifton quadrilles', third set, by William Wrenn, 'Professor of the Flute & Leader of the Quadrille Band at the Assembly Rooms Clifton', published in the early 1820s, pound their way through four such tunes before emerging triumphant with 'The much admired Air / Fall of Paris' for a finale, truly with something of the last movement of Beethoven's Seventh Symphony about it.[141] At this date, professional continuity emerges, for quadrille bands were beginning to be run by named freelance musicians as a going concern, advertised and hired out. In local terms, and in a manner not applicable to the waltz, the quadrille was the first of the dance crazes to create a genre not just of leisure but of corporate identification, amateur or professional, on the part of latter-day minstrels, who formed quadrille bands

---

[138] Hudson 2002: 198.
[139] Jules Girardet: 'Napoleon on the *Bellerophon* in Plymouth Sound, 1815', PCMAG.
[140] McGrady 1991: 68.
[141] See Thomas 2009b for further information about Wrenn.

just as they would later form jazz bands, swing bands, jug bands, skiffle groups, rock bands, and punk bands. Many men, but few women, must have spent all their free time playing in them, encouraging and enlisting their friends and educating their sons and nephews to take up an instrument and join in when the moment was ripe. They still do.

The quadrille, with its undemanding but infectious walking step, retained currency right through the nineteenth century, its regional references thick with the odour of local music-making. A quadrille band attended Sir Digory Forrest's 'splendid Ball and supper at his elegant mansion in Exmouth' on 2 February 1826.[142] South Devon was developing its seaside resorts at this time, and we find the Exonian Quadrille Band advertising in 1830, Mr Melhuish leading the Dawlish Quadrille Band in 1836, Attwater's Quadrille Band engaged for a private concert at the Prince de Ponthieu's residence in Exmouth in 1842, and the ubiquitous Mr Stockham running a quadrille band in Plymouth in 1844–45. Two attempts at forming the Torquay Quadrille Band were made, in 1853 and 1854, the first of them by H P Sorge and a Mr Webber.[143]

The semiotics of quadrille titles were distinctive, celebrating the local with a pride which even then must have raised a smile at assumed French graces, such a temptation after the peace, when around 1830 John Upjohn of Weymouth published at his music warehouse in that town *The Yeomanry Cavalry Quadrilles*. They contained 'La Dorchester', 'La Bridport', 'La Shaftesbury', 'La Sherborne', and 'La Sturminster Newton', climaxing with 'La Blandford, Poole[,] Wareham et Wimborne / Yeomanry Waltz'. This was merely taking its cue from Spagnoletti's 'La Dorset', first figure of the 'Lancers quadrilles' popular from 1817 but itself a much older tune.[144] Wrenn had dedicated his 'Clifton quadrilles' to local 'ladies of distinction' (Lady Vaughan, Mrs Barber, Miss Curzon, and Mrs Yerbary), though a romantic 'young lady (of Clifton)' preferred to title her own set, 'The Talisman', after the characters and a location in Walter Scott's 1825 Crusade novel of that name, concluding with 'Saladin'. In the 1840s and '50s, Bertram von der Mark, who with his wife ran the grandly named Bristol Conservatoire of Music, turned out a stream of titled dance music including 'The Bristol quadrilles' (for Free Port Day, 1848) and the 'Rifle Brigade quadrilles', dedicated to 'the officers

---

[142] *Alf*, 7 Feb 1826, cited Cann 1977: 16.
[143] *EFP*, 13 Jun 1830: 4; *EPG*, 9 Oct 1836, cited *DLHGN* May 2009: 2; *EFP*, 3 Feb 1842, cited Cann and Bush 1967: 421; *EPG*, 21 Sep 1844: 2, 6 Sep 1845: 3; *EFP*, 4 Aug 1853: 3, 16 Nov 1854: 4, both indexed EFPSCI.
[144] Lamb 2001; Woolfe 2007: 11, 21.

of the Rifle Brigade, at Horfield'. Quite why Mrs M Yates's 'Ilfracombe quadrilles', with their pleasant cover lithograph of Ilfracombe harbour and chapel with cliffs behind, were published in New York around 1835, rather than in London or more locally, remains a mystery.[145] And what applied to quadrilles also applied to waltzes. Samuel Summerhayes of Taunton published the 'Nynehead Court waltzes' in 1847, to give just one example. No doubt he wanted to advertise patronage by the gentry in this minor country house near Wellington which was showing unusual enterprise in its garden layout around the same date.[146]

With his Dorset place names Upjohn was attempting to corner a county market. But he suffered for his pains:

> Sir, A report having been industriously circulated to the effect that my Quadrille Band, when at Yeovil, on the 16th December, conducted themselves in so disorderly a manner, that had it not been for their faces they would not have been recognized, in justice to the members of it, I deem it necessary to make the following statement to the public, and which I beg the favor of insertion in your valuable journal.
>
> Before going to Yeovil, I gave Mr Trehern to understand we could not play in the Orchestra, it being so long that the performers at one extreme could not hear those at the other, and in other respects, totally unfit for a Quadrille Band. On my arrival there, however, I found there was no other convenience provided for us, but that a Piano-forte was placed at one extremity of it, which gave me but a partial view of the company, with scarce room to sit, and the worst possible situation for a leader; nor was this all, for during the whole evening we were much annoyed by strangers, intruding themselves into the Orchestra, by means of a trap door, who at times equally prevented the different performers from using their instruments. I several times endeavoured to clear it, but could not succeed, until assisted by Mr Trehern. I then placed the double bass performer on the trap door to keep it down, but to my great surprise he was several times lifted completely up to the ceiling. Now I ask, was it possible for any set of performers to go through difficult pieces, with any degree of credit to themselves, under such disadvantages; in whose vindication I need only refer to those before whom they have so often had the honor of performing, and with whom their character as a Quadrille Band has been long established. One of the stewards, no doubt will recollect that towards the close of the evening, I addressed him, stating the disadvantages under which we have laboured. – Since the above has taken place I have been deprived of an engagement, which had been entered into, in the usual way,

---

[145] Copies respectively in ASSL: DM58, BL, IlfM.
[146] BL Cat; Mowl and Mako 2010: 174, 195.

between Mr Hilliar and myself, for the Ball, at Sherborne, on the 9th instant. Not that I complain so much of the person's having the engagement, as I do of his conduct, in endeavouring to fulfil that engagement by bribing over my band; but I feel great pleasure in saying that, with one dishonourable exception, they all refused his overtures, through gratitude for the pains I have so many years taken with them – thus establishing them as the only trained Quadrille Band in the county.[147]

We can piece together something of bands' and band-leaders' profiles. Upjohn, this account demonstrates, led from the piano, and his band included a double bass. Attwater was a violinist, capable also of mounting a genteel public concert in Exmouth. A William Melhuish was a music dealer and teacher in Torquay in 1862 – if not the Dawlish man, then possibly his son or nephew. Sorge was already known in Torquay as a band-leader. Webber was probably not Thomas Nichols Webber, organist at Ottery St Mary and then Axminster, who lived to be ninety-one, but one of the other musical Webbers in Devon at that period.[148] One of the Summerhayes family, probably John (organist of Crewkerne parish church), Robert, or Samuel (dealers in Taunton), had a quadrille band that was engaged for a Masonic Ball in Yeovil in 1852.[149]

The anonymous 'band of music' was becoming commodified. This never happened to church bands, though they did sometimes play at secular events and expected to make a bit of money doing the rounds of the houses of the gentry and farmers at Christmas. But, as has been suggested, military bands, both professional and voluntary, were very much a civil asset and, whoever paid for the instruments, their custody became increasingly a matter of community care, as did their players by way of metonymic extension. Thus the notion of the village or town band arose. There was a Crewkerne Town Band in 1843, and between the mid-nineteenth century and the present most towns have formed one at some point, though not necessarily retained it: Wareham in or before 1858, St Mary's, Isles of Scilly, in 1876 (it disbanded in 1950), Moretonhampstead in 1878 (if its appeal for funds was successful), and so on. Town bands spotted giving concerts indoors or outdoors in 2010 included those of Sherborne, Portishead, and Chippenham, the last in a summer series of three in John Coles Park.

---

[147] *SJ*, 8 Jan 1835: 3.
[148] *EFP*, 3 Feb 1842, cited Cann and Bush 1967: 421–2; *EFP*, 4 Nov 1852: 3; *EFP*, 26 Sep 1830 as indexed EFPSCI; HaHa 1862: 262, 547; *WT*, 30 Jan 1888: 2; *Cambridge Independent Press*, 23 Jun 1905: 2.
[149] Pulman 1875: 317; SDeB [:83]; *ST*, 14 Feb 1852: 8.

Modbury, a large village in southernmost Devon, formed a band in July 1838 – one wonders whether it had shamed itself into doing so by a poor showing at the coronation festivities the previous month – and its surviving archive tells us something about its constitution and dynamics. The instruments were supplied, resisting attempts at haggling, by Thomas Stockham, a dealer of Stonehouse (Plymouth) and quite likely the Mr Stockham already encountered.[150] The funds had been raised by parish subscription under a trust chaired by the vicar, though there is no evidence that the band was to play in church. Stockham seems to have supplied about eight instruments, some of them signed out with an advance from players no doubt aiming at owning them through a kind of hire purchase. Yet the band was considerably bigger than this, consisting of five clarinets, two octave flutes, one or two trumpets and a keyed bugle, a French horn, a bass horn and bass trombone, a serpent, and drums, so perhaps some of the instruments and players had been present previously, although uniformity of pitch could not have been guaranteed. It was of course all male, and three players were double-handers, David Tiddy on serpent and trumpet, Robert Boon and Gilbert Taylor both on clarinet and trumpet (or keyed bugle in Taylor's case). Two families supplied two players each, John and Robert Boon and George and William Flashman. The terms were strict: in addition to being responsible for their instruments, each player had to 'provide himself with a Music Book and copy therein any music provided by the Committee but shall not retain the same [i.e. a circulating score or rented parts] longer than necessary, to the end that the other musicians may have the like opportunity with all convenient dispatch'.[151]

No sooner had the Modbury band been inaugurated than it broke up in strife, irreconcilable differences between Robert Cove and James Dore being such that half the players left, intent on forming their own ensemble along with one newcomer. The instruments were recalled, and we do not know what happened to them. One senses a social dynamic in transition between the demotic west gallery tradition and the new paternalism that aimed at an 'improving' uniformity vested in the musical authority of a bandmaster. What better ways to inculcate that uniformity than literally, through clothes, and harmonically, by concentrating the ensemble on a matched 'family' of instruments manufactured to the same pitch standard, timbral specification, and valved mode of chromatic tonal production? By the 1840s Adolphe Sax

---

[150] Lomas (1990, i: 275) confuses this town with Stonehouse in Gloucestershire.
[151] DeHC Z7/box 19(7).

and others were producing such families of instruments, and the brass band as we know it took root.

❧ Not Psalmody: Other Singing Groups

The urge towards uniformity under the eye of authority or community approval had already been long apparent where singers were concerned, and it can be traced from the charity children through to the manifestations of social compliance and 'improvement' in the nineteenth century such as massed Sunday school cohorts, burgeoning choral societies and temperance choirs, and quite simply classes of elementary schoolchildren. By the later nineteenth century all these constituencies were singing, and, as will be remarked in chapter 7, it appeared, to the dismay of cultural arbiters, that the only people in England who were not were the upper classes.

If, then, organised amateur singing has long been a hallmark of the British, not least in Cornwall, whose current cultural identity owes a good deal to its male voice choirs, it was not always thus. Temperley states categorically that 'the first recorded congregational singing in an English church was at St Antholin, London, on 21 September 1559'.[152] Before this, it is possible that adult volunteers were included in pre-Reformation parish choirs, either as lay amateurs who had received training in polyphony most probably as child choristers, or as priests without notational skills who helped to sustain a long-note *cantus firmus* surrounded by professionals on the polyphony when a complex piece of composed music was performed.[153] But mass singing for pleasure, beyond whatever personal inspiration the old way of singing may have afforded its participants in the liturgy, belongs to a much later age.

How much later? What was happening vocally as the Victorian age approached? One's general sense is of groups of singers becoming ever larger. Yet we must recall Box parish church's 160 youths singing from notation in 1717, and note that even the modest village of Clapton-in-Gordano apparently mustered nineteen church singers in 1699. Some psalmody choirs in Lancashire in the early eighteenth century numbered between forty and fifty singers, and it has been argued that the 'untunable Voices of the Multitude' in Rev Newte's church in Tiverton in 1696 were his choir, not the unrehearsed congregation.[154] Even tiny Clovelly had twenty-three singers plus two instrumentalists in its quire in the early nineteenth century. This

---

[152] Temperley 1979, i: 43.
[153] ibid: 10; Bowers 2004: 838.
[154] Drage 2009: 86–9.

represented 3.5 per cent of the village's 1801 population.[155] It is perhaps another indication that a musical participation rate of 1 in 100, 1 in 50, or even more is a not unfeasible expectation, *mutatis mutandis*, over the centuries in any community (see also chapter 7). Clovelly's musicians included 'three masons, a farmer who came "to Church about once in a quarter of a year", another with a "good voice" and his son, a bass who was "very nosey in Voice", a shoemaker, a carpenter, a labourer, a carrier's son, a ploughman's son, an innkeeper, a sempstress, two daughters of one of the masons and his niece, a butcher's daughter, a shopkeeper's daughter, a carpenter's daughter, and a groom's wife'.[156]

This was social inclusivity extending to gender. Meanwhile, the culture of homosociality that had produced the coffee houses undoubtedly continued to flourish in its musical manifestations into the nineteenth century and beyond. Such manifestations were primarily those of the glee or catch club, whether it performed in private, in inns, or in concert venues as (or with) a 'harmonic society' or musical association of more heterogeneous dimensions. The (gentlemen's) Harmonic Society of Exeter was formed in 1829 with thirty to forty singing members, and in 1844 the 'gentlemen' of the Barnstaple Harmonic Society were assisting at a concert in that town's Assembly Rooms.[157] Quite often three or four male musicians, amateur, professional, or a mixture of both, would sing together a concerted item or two in a miscellaneous concert, sometimes doubling as instrumentalists elsewhere on the programme and quite likely including the town's (or cathedral's) organist and whoever was the impresario of the moment. This can still happen today. In Georgian times, glees could also include women's solo voices, apt to be drawn on when a professional female singer or actress was on the bill or a musical family was providing the personnel. The *Miscellaneous Collection of Vocal Music*, op 9 (1791) by John Broderip's son Robert, includes three-voice glees apparently for two treble-register voices and bass. (Robert Broderip also edited *A Collection of Duets, Rotas, Canons, Catches and Glees*, dedicated 'To the members of the Bristol Catch Club, and the Cecilian Society' and published in 1795. He was organist of St Michael's and the Lord Mayor's Chapel in Bristol and a prolific composer.) However, the top line in the Bath Harmonic Society's glee-singing was taken by boys, and this was also true of madrigal societies.[158]

---

[155] VBT.
[156] Drage 2009: 89–90.
[157] *EFP*, 29 Jan 1829: 2; *NDJ*, 22 Aug 1844: 2.
[158] Kollmann 1812: 140.

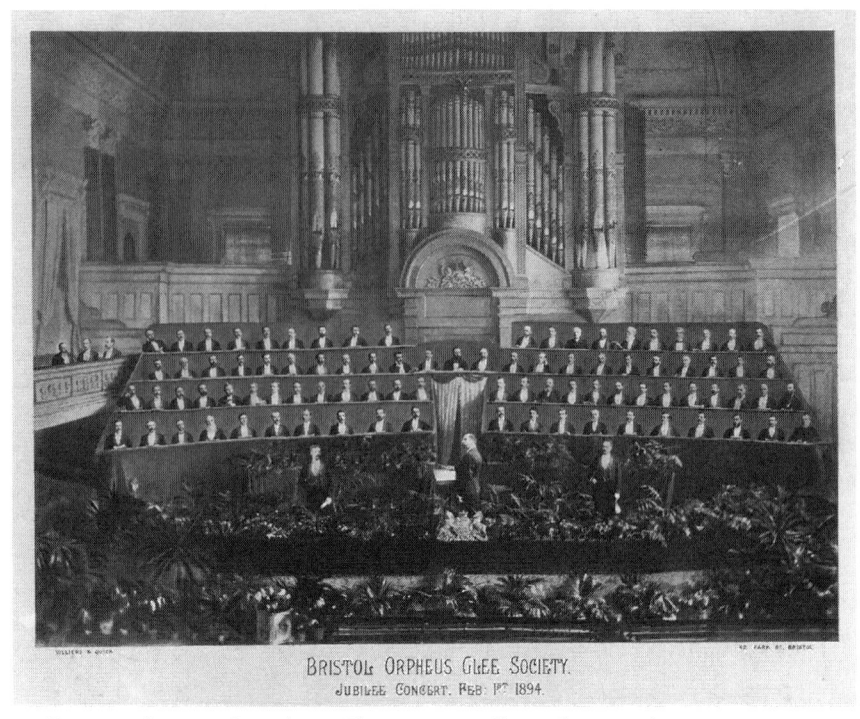

Illus. 3.4 The Bristol Orpheus Glee Society, collage photograph representing its jubilee concert, Victoria Rooms, Clifton, 1 Febuary 1894

The terminology of associations for vocal and/or instrumental music is confusing in the later eighteenth century and for a good deal of the nineteenth, as Sally Drage has recognised.[159] But there was no mistaking a glee or a catch club as the epitome of male sociability made audible. These began in cathedral cities, modelled on male music-making in London, Oxford, and Cambridge, and will have consisted largely of the clergy and lay clerks; thus we find the Bristol Catch Club established by 1774 and the Salisbury Catch Club by 1776.[160] The Devon Glee Club followed much later, in 1821, starting life as the Devon and Exeter Catch and Glee Club and progressively shortening its name, perhaps partly because catches, often bawdy, were by then felt to run counter to the growing culture of respectability, though they

---

[159] Drage 2009: 283.
[160] Robins 2006: 90, 96.

had begun being toned down much earlier.[161] (The last newspaper report of its activities with 'Catch' in the title was on 11 March 1824, though catches were still being sung in 1837. The last report overall was in 1843.[162]) Catch and glee clubs were highly self-satisfied entities, their members making sure that the meetings were reported in the local press in the manner of balls and association dinners.

'Glee' in a male voice choir's title continued to resonate: in Devon we find the Honiton Glee Club in existence in 1849, the Topsham Glee Club in 1850, the Ottery Glee Club in 1860, and the Torrington Glee Union in 1862.[163] In general these will have been larger choirs in smaller places, though the Clifton Glee Singers toured their region as a solo male voice quartet from 1896 (three of them were Bristol Cathedral lay clerks).[164] The Bristol Orpheus Glee Society, initiated 'when in 1844 ten singers visited each other's houses and sang glees for their own pleasure', was directed for its first thirty-two years by its founder, T H Crook, and then for two years by Alfred Stone until his death at the age of thirty-six in 1878. It became a force to be reckoned with, adding 'Royal' to its title after its third conductor, George Riseley, had engineered a command performance in 1895. As the collage photograph of its jubilee concert in the Victoria Rooms in 1894 shows, by then it consisted of about ninety earnest gentlemen (Illus. 3.4).[165] The repertoire of such choirs had travelled far from its earlier staple of catches and simple strophic odes and elegies, and Walford Davies's 'The sturdy rock', which won the Bristol society's prize in 1894, is a most complex piece. It includes an alto part. Classy printed programmes of the Weston-super-Mare Orpheus Glee Society, again with male altos, survive until 1931.[166] The only chronological outlier identified is the Stockton Glee Choir of 2004 – but this was the participatory audience of a fundraising concert for the village in the Wylye Valley, unaware of its identity until after the interval, when the organist Michael Thomas got them going.[167] The Stockton Glee Choir was not the only unusual manifestation of social harmony in that bucolic part of Wiltshire, for in the early eighteenth century the remote Fovant Hut, high on the treeless ridgeway, had been the venue for a supposed music club run by Henry Goode, 'the Gentleman

---

[161] Hobson 2015: 157 and 2010: 278.
[162] *EFP*, 11 Mar 1824: 4, 6 Apr 1837: 3, and 2 Feb 1843: 3.
[163] *EFP*, 22 Nov 1849: 8, 14 Mar 1850: 8, 18 Jan 1860: 7, and 19 Mar 1862: 7, all indexed EFPSCI.
[164] NSLS, Mogg's Band Cuttings Book, 'Bands' file in cabinet (A/BWG/4/98/3).
[165] *RT*, 25 Dec 1936: 40; Brown and Stratton 1897: 397; Gugan 2006, i: 15–16.
[166] NSLS.
[167] *WR* i (Dec 2005): 9–11.

Poacher of Cranborne Chase'. It seems clear that the carefully laid out instruments and music books were, as in *The Ladykillers*, merely a front, in this case for his associates' ensnarement and partition of venison.[168]

A more serious counterpart to the glee club was the madrigal society. Its original constituency was the same: lay clerks and a variety of gentlemen with enough leisure and education to consider themselves connoisseurs of participational singing, their musical bent in this case being antiquarian. Given that the Madrigal Society in London had been founded as early as 1744, it may seem strange that its provincial emulation had to wait so long, for not until 1825 was the Devon Madrigal Society inaugurated; the Bristol Madrigal Society followed in 1837.[169] Here a treble line was essential, and it was supplied by the cathedral choristers of Exeter and Bristol respectively, which meant that a madrigal society could only flourish if the master of the choristers was involved. Many of the members of these two groups were also glee singers, and will thus already have known each other for years when they decided to start a new type of choir. Indeed, 'Devon Madrigal Society meetings always took place on the night following the meeting of the Devon Glee Club', and 'the membership of the two Devon societies was formed of the same core of people', while the staging for the Bristol Orpheus Glee Society's concert pictured in Illustration 3.4 actually belonged to the Bristol Madrigal Society, which used it for its Ladies' Nights.[170]

The Devon Madrigal Society lasted only until 1839, its unsustainability symptomatic of the relative decline of Exeter at that period. The Bristol Madrigal Society, which survives today as the Bristol Chamber Choir, having changed its name in 1988, has been no less indicative of its home town's curious standing, proud, complacent, and impervious to cultural competitiveness long after it ceased to be Britain's second city. This mindset did produce real distinction, embodied in the Society's venue, the Victoria Rooms, where on the increasingly fashionable Ladies' Nights (when women attended but did not sing) the row of carriages would stretch most of the way up to Clifton Village, and in the one composer of genius produced by England's madrigal revival: Robert Lucas Pearsall. The majority of Pearsall's madrigals were written for the Bristol Madrigal Society, although the composer, moneyed and not a professional musician, lived abroad much of the time. One or two of them, above all 'Lay a garland' (1840), are among

---

[168] Olivier 1951: 271.
[169] Hobson 2015: 2, 9–10, 25, 122, 135, 138–50.
[170] ibid: 33; Gugan 2006, i: 15–16.

the most perfect short pieces of music of the nineteenth century from any country.[171]

With the exception of Bristol's Æolian Male Voice Choir, inaugurated in January 1894 and really a glee club, west country bodies with 'Male Voice Choir' in their title seem to date from the twentieth century or at the earliest from the last half-decade of the nineteenth.[172] 'Glee' had perhaps by now gone the way of 'catch' as unduly frivolous. Plymouth's Orpheus Society, founded as a male group in 1906 by David Parkes, used none of these terminologies. Like the Bristol Orpheus Glee Society, it became a highly resourceful institution, which after adding a ladies' section in 1922 numbered over three hundred voices. Such a body could afford to share its platform with stars, even if they performed separately – a smart ploy resulting in the appearance in Plymouth's Drill Hall of Pachmann, Melba, Suggia, Kreisler, and others, for the Society actually floated an entire international celebrity subscription series in 1926–27 and 1927–28, if not without difficulties. In March 1927 it hired Beecham and the full London Symphony Orchestra for a serious programme, though it contributed only three short interludes itself, presumably unaccompanied or with piano.[173] The Mousehole Male Voice Choir and no doubt other leading Cornish ones have similarly engaged solo performers of the calibre of Felicity Lott and Benjamin Luxon.[174]

The corollary to a choir divisible into men's and ladies' sections was the demise of the male alto. Except in cathedrals, this had become an endangered species by 1900, male voice choirs consisting solely of tenor and bass parts, normally two of each with the upper bass part often termed baritone. Welsh choirs were established in this formation by the 1880s.[175] The definitive rejection of the male alto and the sudden rise of the TTBB choir in England, slightly later than in Wales, may have had something to do with the trial of Oscar Wilde in 1895, which overnight bred frantic and lasting insecurities about masculinity, though pundits had seen this change coming for a long time with the emulation of German male choruses, which lacked altos, the invention of the British (female) contralto, and greater female participation in secular choral music in general.[176] Now the tenor voice took on a heroic function in amateur choral singing, despite the 'physiognomies

---

[171] Gugan 2006, v, passim; Hunt 1977: 112–19; Byard 1966: [5].
[172] *WDP*, 23 Jan 1894: 3.
[173] Harvey 1926: 11–12, 31; *WMN*, 17 Mar 1927: 5, 24 Sep 1927: 11 and 17 Mar 1928: 5; *C*, 6 Oct 1926: 1.
[174] Williams nd: 23–5.
[175] Skinner 2013: 67.
[176] Wiltshire 1993: 70–80.

strained apparently almost to apoplexy' that in the opinion of the *Musical Times* accompanied its textural predominance on the Continent.[177] One wonders whether in Cornwall this apotheosis of the tenor and the rise of the male voice choirs were a way of compensating for its fishermen's loss of occupation and status when their industry declined precipitately, their frustration reaching the point of considerable violence in Newlyn in 1896 – though evidence of occupational malaise in Mousehole in 1909, the year its male voice choir was founded, is indecisive.[178] The virile role model provided by Enrico Caruso, the world's first recording superstar, was certainly not irrelevant, his one and only public concert in the west country taking place in Plymouth in that same year of 1909.[179]

Already in 1602 Carew had found Cornwall notable for its 'three mens songs, cunningly contrived for the ditty, and pleasantly for the note', but a century and a half of Methodist hymn-singing will have been what rendered the latter-day Cornishman so susceptible to harmonic participation in song – Mousehole Male Voice Choir's young members around 1945 were 'taught to read music and sing as part of the experience from the two chapels in the village'.[180] The Marazion Apollo Male Choir was founded in 1904, Mousehole Male Voice Choir, as mentioned above, in 1909, the Newlyn Male Choir in 1921.[181] All from Mount's Bay, these are among the oldest Cornish male voice choirs that became fully established, though those of St Agnes (1902) and Goldsithney and District (1903), the latter conducted by a Welshman, Mr Rees, predated them.[182] Two of the three singled out above have continued to flourish, but it must have been a shock to many when the Newlyn choir disbanded seven years short of its centenary, due to 'dwindling members' (down to thirteen).[183] The Mousehole choir's website states that it 'is very fortunate to have many working men in their membership, younger than the average choir'; but still there are more white and bald heads than not in the accompanying photograph.[184] In its early years much of the membership was teenage, and from sequences of photographs one sees the average age quite suddenly rising in the 1950s and '60s, when full-time career prospects, scarce

---

[177] ibid: 75.
[178] Payton 2004: 222–4; Williams nd: 19–20.
[179] Williams nd: 8; *EPG*, 9 Aug 1909: 2.
[180] Lorigan 2009: 125; Williams nd: 50.
[181] Marazion AMC; Williams nd and Balls nd: passim.
[182] Skinner 2013: 65, 91–3.
[183] BBCN, 13 Mar 2014.
[184] Mousehole MVC.

in Cornwall, were becoming irresistible elsewhere to the many young people who emigrated to 'England'.[185]

Twenty-one Cornish male voice choirs were listed in the Male Choir International Index (MCII) in 2006. (There is also a Cornish Federation of Male Voice Choirs, founded in 1983, which in 2006 listed a further eleven choirs.) The MCII's figure of twenty-one represented just under 10 per cent of the nation's total, i.e. greatly exceeding Cornwall's percentage of the British population. Wales had 33 per cent, but since its population is six times that of Cornwall, its participation rate was only half as great, Cornwall's representing roughly 1 in 200 of the gender cohort if the average choir size was forty.[186] One wonders whether Cornwall's extraordinarily high rate of participation in recent years has been due to the region's desirability as a place to retire, i.e. because so many members have ample leisure as incomers. Most of the twenty-one choirs were attached to maritime locations or areas where mining used to take place, though only one of them, the Polperro Fishermen's Choir (an outlier in several respects), specified an occupation, and if a concert given by the Mevagissey Male Choir around this time was anything to go by, its members were not the village's fishermen but largely retired incomers.[187]

Yet Port Isaac's Fishermen's (the name now changed to Fisherman's) Friends are no youngsters, and their oldest member, Peter Rowe (now retired from singing), is in his late seventies.[188] A male shanty group of ten or eleven singers, they have achieved runaway musical success on the basis of what seems like a very traditional multitrade portfolio (see chapter 4) centred on the little village and its harbour and amounting to two occupations per person on average. According to the sleeve note of their 2002 CD, two brothers were fishermen, and Peter Rowe had been one; two men were coastguards; one worked in the boatyard, having been a farmer; carpenter, electrician, builder, potter, postmaster, and owner of a gardening business were also represented. Seven of their personnel were or had been part-time lifeboat crew or launchers.[189] The Mousehole Male Voice Choir lost a member, Nigel Brockman, in the Penlee Lifeboat disaster of December 1981, and we are reminded that a village with a lifeboat simply has to pull together in an emergency.[190] The Fisherman's Friends also lost one of

---

[185] Williams nd: 50 and passim; Skinner 2013: 283–4, 292–303.
[186] MCII; CFMVC.
[187] Personal observation; Skinner 2013: 193–6.
[188] FF.
[189] FF 2002.
[190] Williams nd: 10.

their number, and their promoter, in a theatre accident in 2013 but carried on.[191] There can be no arguing with the effects of such unity, mutuality, and trust on musical ensemble. The Fisherman's Friends' harmonic tuning is superb, and at the sustained peak of committed performance on these local fronts the distinction between amateur and professional has ceased to have any meaning in terms of standard. Here, perhaps, is another long-term continuity if one considers the gentleman dilettante of the eighteenth century. Broadcasting recognised such excellence (see chapter 7), and radio relays feature prominently in the Mousehole choir's history.[192] They will have put the village, with its quaint name, on the map for hundreds if not thousands of tourists.

It would be interesting to know whether any of the Fisherman's Friends have been members of one of the male voice choirs of Cornwall, for their folk act feels and sounds quite different from the classical one that propelled the male voice choir movement. Yet both types of group, or a portion of the latter, might bond by rehearsing in the pub. (How this squared in the past with the Methodist background of the Mousehole singers is unexplained.)[193] The real difference resides in the exhibition of cultural authority underlying groups trained by a conductor or teacher, for such bodies remain in a state of pupillage and institutional, quasi-military conformity that can be traced back to the charity children and Sunday school training. Choral societies and male and female voice choirs are outgrowths of these, and their group semiotics, most obvious in the uniform they wear when performing (a distinctive blazer and tie for most of the male voice choirs), are a world apart from those of a folk group. The Fisherman's Friends dress variously as working men with tough outdoor jobs: the music is something that happens in connection with these, their clothes tell us.

The ultimate model for the disciplined, uniformed choir, as suggested at the start of this chapter, was always the Bible's angelic hosts, and we need to remember that it was Christian sacred music that the charity children sang, Sunday school children were taught, and until quite recently the entire body of pupils in any school perforce joined in every day in morning assembly. William Blake's famous description of the London charity children's annual service in St Paul's Cathedral in his poem 'Holy Thursday' likened their sound to 'a mighty wind' before adding the angelic simile: 'or like harmonious thunderings the seats of heaven among'; on a smaller scale, many

---

[191] *Mail* online, 2 Aug 2013.
[192] Williams nd: passim.
[193] ibid: 58.

a west country parish church from the eighteenth century onwards, and virtually every plebeian schoolroom by the end of the nineteenth, will have resonated with this sound when classes of children were singing. One can easily imagine the procession (itself silent, one presumes) up Frome's main street from its Bluecoat School by the river to St John's church, where in the course of time a monument in the north transept would record endowments by the Stevens brothers, John and Richard, respectively for ten extra charity boys and 'towards the improvement of its choir', meaning the church's choir of charity children. Clergymen generally preferred the unadorned unison of the charity children's psalm-singing to the raucous polyphony of a quire, Richard Eastcott of Exeter holding it up as a model in which 'no voice … [was] to be distinctly heard above the rest'.[194]

It was this tonal uniformity that choral societies eventually emulated, Eastcott again encouraging it with appeal to the London charity children's annual service: 'If it should be advanced, that it is impossible, to regulate a great number of mixed voices, and to keep them within proper bounds, so as to produce an even and pleasing volume of sound, I answer that this effect is annually produced by the greatest part of five thousand *charity children* singing together, at their general assembly at *St Paul's*.'[195] Until a voluntary robed chancel choir could be raised, charity children's choirs must have had increasingly wide currency in parish churches. In 1831 Benjamin Daw was appointed at All Saints Dorchester to regulate an unruly quire, and without jettisoning its instruments he brought in boys not from an endowed charitable foundation but from the local National School: Anglican church attendance was in fact a condition of National School enrolment, and it led to a late rash of gallery-building around this time.[196] How the schoolchildren actually may have learnt their music is illustrated in Richard White's unpublished reminiscences. In Mells around 1839 it was not simply by rote: 'We were … taught singing by Hullah's Sol-fa system that was then introduced. There was a large black-board plain on one side with ruled lines for music on the other. On this board we had to do a deal of copying by chalk of the tunes of the Hymns we afterwards sang. We had to do this sometimes from memory. A more practical way of teaching there could not be.'[197] Joseph Leech, in his Sunday peregrinations around Bristol's hinterland in the 1840s, wrote appreciatively of the schoolchildren he found singing parts of the

[194] Eastcott 1793: 180.
[195] ibid: 176.
[196] Temperley 1971–76 (P35/VE1); Patten 2016: 4.
[197] White 1903.

parish service in Dundry, Horfield, Pensford (girls only), Wrington, Chew Magna, and Yatton; at St John's, Glastonbury there was only the organ, much to his disappointment.[198] At Whitchurch the schoolchildren sat together but dared not compete with a bumptious quire: 'In Miss Whippie's gallery, close by, amongst the little human pipes of the parish children, there are some forty or fifty far better musical instruments than that spoiled, clamorous, and monopolizing clarionet, if they would only set them to work; but they seemed to me not to open their mouths', wrote Leech.[199]

The rise of the Sunday school further spread the phenomenon of the musically audible, uniformly disciplined child, to the point at which it seems that almost the entire juvenile population of a town must have been musically active. Statistics for the nineteenth century make the high participation rates of later adult choirs, especially in nonconformist areas, immediately comprehensible. From very early beginnings in the Congregational Church in 1774, predating Robert Raikes's Sunday school in Gloucester by six years, Tiverton's Sunday school registration in 1845 amounted to 53 per cent of the town's youth, with 11 per cent attending the Congregational Sunday school. Figures extrapolated from newspaper reports of Falmouth's Sunday school anniversary treats in 1861 suggest that 'by then virtually all of the town's children must have been involved. Of these, as many as 83 per cent would appear to have been attending the nonconformist churches. And they were all singing.'[200] What they were singing was not always specified beyond 'select' pieces; when it was, it was hymns.[201] Many of the children may have been taught tonic sol-fa, re-utilised in some cases as an adult skill for the purposes of participation in church and community choirs.[202]

Choral societies were similarly inclined towards emulating angels, insofar as they took their more ambitious repertoire from that of the cathedral festivals or 'music meetings': oratorios, sacred cantatas, and ceremonial anthems, with secular cantatas gradually added. One soon concludes that the bastions of male sociability could be stormed by amateur female singers only in the name of religion. Prior to the accession of Queen Victoria, there is no evidence of active female participation in any west country harmonic society, which was therefore essentially a glee club or orchestra (also all male, of course), or both. (Harmonic societies are discussed further in chapter 7.)

[198] Leech 1850: 196, 226, 131–4, 152, 221, 41.
[199] ibid: 218.
[200] Banfield 2015: 74–5.
[201] *FPWT*, 29 Jun 1861: 1, 13 Jul 1861: 1, 20 Jul 1861: 1, and 27 Jul 1861: 1.
[202] Skinner 2013: 72.

But when *sacred* harmonic societies began to be instigated in the wake of London's, founded in 1832, it was almost certainly with adult female voices on the soprano line and perhaps the alto as well. The Wellington, Taunton, and Torrington Sacred Harmonic Societies, the first two active in 1843, the last in 1856, will have adopted the London society's precedent.[203] Whether they were at this period capable of tackling entire oratorios remains doubtful, however.

Wellington's choir may have consisted only of women, its concerts no more than the usual miscellany within which they sang a few items. In the twentieth century, women's choirs paralleled male voice choirs to a certain extent, but gained one distinct advantage over them after the Women's Institute, founded in Canada in 1897, took hold in Britain, which happened during the First World War: for the WI brought the resources of a national constitution and organisation to the running of isolated groups, learning to run groups indeed being part of the point of the WI. This meant that there were mechanisms and incentives for small, limited choirs to gather together and raise the bar for special occasions. Music was part of the WI from the very start, and the Cornish Federation of Women's Institutes (CFWI) was founded as early as 1918.[204] Not long after this, Ilva Thomas composed her 'Cornishwomen's clan song' 'The women of Cornwall', with words by her father, a newspaper editor, and dedicated it to the Women's Institutes of Cornwall.[205] Later, from 1950 onwards, Truro Cathedral hosted CFWI carol festivals, while the S[omerset]FWI mounted *Merrie England* – a pageant, or the light opera? – as its contribution to the Festival of Britain in 1951.[206] Also in 1950, several choirs from the region, including those of Treviscoe/Trethosa, Devoran, and St Austell in Cornwall and Yatton in Somerset, won county and area performance competitions to join in the massed-voice premiere of Vaughan Williams's WI cantata *Folk Songs of the Four Seasons* at the Royal Albert Hall in London.[207] In 1976 the Cornwall County Music Adviser, Henry Mills, composed a CFWI cantata, *Cornish Portraits*, premiered in Newquay accompanied by a brass quintet, apparently of male youths.[208]

Returning to the mid-nineteenth century, little by little the model of the amateur mixed-voice choir capable of singing large-scale works and sustaining an entire programme became established, as Novello made those

---

[203] *SCH*, 28 Oct 1843: 4 and 18 Nov 1843: 4; *EFP*, 21 Aug 1856: 8, indexed EFPSCI.
[204] Robinson 2011: 15.
[205] Copy in the possession of the author.
[206] Donnelly 1978: 25; Taunton 1951: 57.
[207] Donnelly 1978: 25; Nicholas 1991: 7 (with wrong date).
[208] Donnelly 1978: 24–5.

works available in cheap editions with modern clefs and piano reduction, both elements crucial for the rehearsal of singers who would need to be taught their parts through note repetition, whether or not they had learnt to read staff notation. Sol-fa was an alternative notation, easier than staff notation for those with no access to an instrument, but not one that obviated a long, repetitive learning process. The rehearsal, as much as the performance, was where the conductor came in, and where the element of 'improving' discipline overtook the ethos of mutual delight and sociability that had propelled both psalmody and glee-singing. With this massive shift the modern choral society was born. Devonport was quite early in possessing, in 1838, a group called a choral society: only Exeter (1817), Bristol (1835), and Tavistock (1837) currently furnish earlier references from the region, while the fashion was clearly beginning to spread, with similar references to Trowbridge appearing in 1839, Exmouth in 1844, Honiton in 1848, Torquay in 1851, Barnstaple in 1858, and so on.[209] We are reminded that the oldest continuously operating musical journal in the world began in 1844 as *The Musical Times and Singing Class Circular*, reflecting or helping to create this fashion. Note the 'class' – this was education, betterment, as the use of the word 'pupils' makes clear in this newspaper report of a concert on 29 December 1859: 'The Hayle Choral Society has only been a short time in existence, and great credit is due to the conductor, Mr J H Nunn, for bringing on his pupils to appear in so short a time before the public.'[210] Sidmouth Choral Society was founded in 1872 on a similar basis, giving no concerts at first.[211] Musical education for all was not universally approved of: 'one lady of important social position' in Barnstaple accused John Edwards of being 'a leveller of society' with his choral society.[212] The idea of a class of singers being educated in practical music makes sense of some of a choral society's continuing elements – the subscription, the insistence on weekly attendance, the authoritarian drill.[213] Witnessing the near-military discipline inculcated in adult singers by a new-style choirmaster came as a shock to some: 'I was almost frightened … at the change from Mr Shaw's voice when singing – where it is mellifluent, and when correcting or instructing his pupils, – where it becomes so harsh

---

[209] *EFP*, 25 Dec 1817: 4, 17 Aug 1837: 3, 6 Apr 1848: 3, and 2 Oct 1851: 2, all indexed EFPSCI; Edwards 2002: 37; Lansdown 1997: 26; *WEPG*, 1 Jun 1844, cited Cann 2001: 140; Edwards 1917: 8.
[210] *WMN*, 5 Jan 1860: 2.
[211] Sutton 1973: 101.
[212] Edwards 1917: 8.
[213] Skinner 2013: 71–4.

and loud that it seemed as if he were drilling an awkward squad of wild Irishmen', wrote Falmouth's gossip columnist of a singing class in 1861.[214]

The year before his Hayle debut, John Nunn had founded the Penzance Choral Society, and here he included orchestral players whom he trained and for whom he arranged for instruments to be made available.[215] This reminds us of how little could be taken for granted by way of musical resources in a town of modest size at that time, and among the Penzance choir's many tribulations in its earlier years were having to help pay for an expensive organ in their performance venue, and indeed the inadequacy of all available venues in the town.[216] Speaking generally, notwithstanding the depredations of two world wars, especially on the availability of personnel, practical obstacles receded and cultural facilitation increased into the second half of the twentieth century, thanks to mundane but vital adjuncts such as heating, lighting, communication by telephone, photocopying, private cars, and government grants. But then, after a hundred years of the 'decency' and 'improvement' made audible and visible in a community's classical music choirs, came the revolution in popular taste.

To turn this phenomenon around, it may seem curious that types of musical organisation such as choral societies and brass bands, dating from an earlier period of unprecedentedly rapid social change, should continue in existence today (the Penzance Choral Society has lasted nearly 160 years), when so much else of the socio-economic fabric and technological infrastructure established in the earlier years of Victoria's reign has again changed beyond recognition. Even the men of our orchestras, amateur or professional, continue to wear early Victorian clothes, though this is true for weddings as well. Something makes us hold on to these symbols of cultural permanence, orderliness, and security, just as we have continued to hold on to the Mendelssohn Wedding March ever since Tiverton tried it out in 1847. But sustaining an oratorio choir, which needs an orchestra and professional soloists as well as a balanced vocal ensemble, has never been easy. The Penzance choir all but disbanded three or four times, and at its lowest point was down to one tenor in a residual group of about twenty singers. In each case it was rescued by a charismatic and determined conductor.[217] Such musical leaders simply cannot stop themselves: in a stable democracy they seem culturally programmed to galvanise or re-galvanise whole communities. Not

---

[214] *FPWT*, 3 Aug 1861: 1.
[215] Walker 2008: 17–18.
[216] ibid: 6, 14, 16–19, 21.
[217] ibid: 29–30, 37–9, 45–9.

all choral societies endure. Truro's first one was established in 1849, but its second did not materialise until 1962, formed from a series of separate choirs from Truro and other towns so that Elgar's *The Dream of Gerontius* could have its belated Cornish premiere.[218] As early as 1834, John Loder seems to have trained up a Bath Choral Society of amateurs practising 'at hours stolen from repose after the toiling labours of the day', but it did not last, and over the years a bewildering variety of named and renamed choirs and orchestras has come and gone in the city (as has the Festival Chorus).[219] The business model is always an uphill struggle, and Trevor Walker concludes his history of the Penzance Choral Society with four bullet points (!) illustrating the difficulties, namely: legal restrictions of access to under-sixteen (and now under-eighteen?) teenagers in an era when singing in schools has declined precipitately and choirs have aged; difficulties in recruiting working women, compounding the perennial tenor problem; the audience problem when live classical music is 'a minority interest' (and when the Cornish weather is so fickle); and the reduced capacity of halls due to red tape (fire regulations, insurance).[220]

Brass Bands and Other Types of Band in the Later Nineteenth Century

The earliest brass band found in southern England by Lomas was the St Austell Amateur Brass Band, playing in public by the end of November 1837. (This marginally predates the better-known Cyfarthfa Band of South Wales; not to be forgotten is that John Distin's family brass quintet was performing in Bristol at exactly the same time.)[221] Nearby St Blazey followed suit a few months later, reaching an 'almost astonishing' proficiency in a short time.[222] At this period the instruments were probably not valved. Tiverton, still an industrial town, had a brass band by 1845, its instruments paid for by the players themselves. It was much respected, so much so that a summer promenade concert series was mooted, the only drawback being the lack of a promenade.[223] Blandford's 'cornopean' band (indicating valved cornets as opposed to keyed bugles and natural trumpets) was in existence by 1848

---

[218] Hedges 2002: 1, 11, 24–5.
[219] Clarke 2007: 25–6, 29–54, 55.
[220] Walker 2008: 60.
[221] Lomas 1990, i: 434, citing *WB*, 1 Dec 1837: 2; *BM*, 25 Nov 1837: 2.
[222] Lomas 1990, i: 431, citing *WB*, 20 Apr 1838: 3.
[223] *EFP*, 19 Jun 1845: 3.

and was described as 'famous' when stationed nightly outside the Antelope Hotel in Dorchester in 1854 during what will have been the Dorset Militia's annual training period, when it supported the band.[224] The spread of valved instruments to the lower pitch regions is implied by the names of the St Austell Sax Horn Band, Pascoe's Sax-Tuba Band, the Falmouth Sax-Tuba Band, the Miners Sax-Tuba Band, and the Truro Amateur Sax-Tuba Band, all from the 1850s.[225]

Famous the Blandford band certainly was, for it took first place in an Enderby Jackson band contest in Exeter in 1861, and two years later won his 'National' at the Crystal Palace in London, returning home to a heroes' welcome, even if the ensemble paying tribute (or the journalist) only knew one tune:

> The Rifle Corps ... mustered strong in the Market-place ... and preceded by the drums and fifes, marched to the Railway Station, where numbers of spectators were already gathered. After a few minutes the clanging bell and the shrill whistle of the engine announced the arrival of the train, and the order, 'Present arms,' being given, the band struck up 'See the conquering hero comes,' and three hearty British cheers welcomed home the winning men ... On reaching the town the street windows, balconies, &c, were crowded with spectators, and a most hearty and enthusiastic reception was given by them. Three cheers were first given, then three cheers more, and then the band woke up the echoes again with 'See the conquering hero comes,' and the bells rang out a merry peal, while the waving of handkerchiefs by the ladies at the windows, and the shouts of the assemblage were continuous ... A second cordial reception awaited Mr Eyers at his hotel, the smoking-room of which was crowded with gentlemen, among whom was Mr Henry Distin, who loudly cheered the bandmaster.[226]

Their trophies on this occasion included £30 cash, a cup, two instruments, and a banner. Robert Eyers, the bandmaster, was a local publican who later became mayor of Blandford – hardly a downtrodden proletarian, since by 1875 he was running the Crown and the Greyhound, a wine business, an agency for the Somerset and Dorset Railway, and the town's inland revenue office.[227] Nor would the increasingly unindustrial west country play much of a distinguished role in competitive banding at the national level: it seems

---

[224] Lomas 1990, i: 437; DCPRG 1985: 58 (see also Lomas 1990, i: 569); *DCC*, 18 May 1854: 4.
[225] Lomas 1990, i: 368, 387, citing *WB*, 3 Dec 1852: 5, 11 Aug 1854: 5, 4 Jan 1856: 5, 3 Nov 1854: 5, 8 Apr 1853: 8.
[226] Herbert 2000: 327; *SWJ*, 1 Aug 1863: 7.
[227] Kelly *Hampshire, Wiltshire and Dorset* 1875: 760, 762.

that no other brass band from the region won prizes at the Finals of an 'Open' or 'National' until 1974-76, when the Stanshawe Band of Bristol conducted by Walter Hargreaves thrice came second in one or the other of these competitions; as the Sun Life Band it went on to win the Open in 1990.[228] Camborne Town Band came fourth in the 'National' in 1977, achieving this position again in 1982.[229]

The uniformity of brass grew alongside the working-class reach of bands, but regimental bands of the regular army have always retained a mixture of woodwind and brass instruments, a combination normally implied by the term 'military band', and from the foundation of Kneller Hall (the Royal Military School of Music) in 1857, professional army musicians were trained to play two instruments, which might be strings as well as wind, on the 'double-handed' principle. This adaptability has served many a theatre, seaside, circus, or municipal band well, is still enshrined in the West End and on Broadway where 'reed' scoring is for players of more than one instrument, and has meant that a municipal band such as Bournemouth's could develop over time into a symphony orchestra.

In Britain in the latter half of the nineteenth century, following the general demise of the church bands, four types of band in addition to the commodified 'scratch' or regular quadrille and theatre ensembles were found in increasing numbers. These were town bands, dealt with above, works and associational bands, Salvation Army bands, and the new army volunteer bands.

Factory or mine bands, presumed working-class insofar as constituting the actual workers, may have been in evidence as early as 1801 (see Truro, above), and were firmly visible by 1867-68, when Samuel Bowen's annual treat for his Nailsea Glassworks employees included their parading through the village accompanied by two brass bands from the works.[230] Tavistock hosted the Devon Great Consols Miners' Band in the 1860s, and there will have been similar entities in Cornwall.[231] The link between brass bands and industry has never been lost. Appledore has a shipyard, and the town band plays for launchings (it 'had to work extremely hard to become proficient in the rendering of the Cuban national anthem' when a dredger was launched for a Cuban owner).[232] In some respects works bands must have been set up

---

[228] Lomas 1990, i: 761 (see also 727-39); Herbert 2000: 328-53.
[229] Mansell 2005: 151, 157.
[230] Thomas 1993: 82.
[231] Woodcock 2010: 93.
[232] Appledore nd: 15.

to counteract the earlier enlistment of musicians in demonstrations *against* employers or proletarian oppression, of which there is colourful evidence from the Trowbridge Chartists. At a Trowbridge Working Men's Association outdoor meeting in August 1838, the Trowbridge band was engaged to play in a specially erected gallery behind the platform. 'The utmost harmony and good order prevailed' among the 800 attending, but it was not to last. A march of 3,000 Chartists through the town three months later, again accompanied by a band as well as the flags and banners of which it functioned very much as the aural equivalent, was a prelude to stormier scenes in nearby Devizes, where on 22 March 1839 three Trowbridge weavers attempted a stump speech from a waggon in the marketplace. A band was present; they were routed and warned by the constable not to come again. But they did come again, this time in a formal march from Trowbridge, joined also by Bradford men, on 1 April, Easter Monday. It had begun with music in the streets of Trowbridge at 7.30am and a band ('a drum, clarionets and other instruments') for the muster outside the Queen's Arms around ten o'clock. The Chartists entered Devizes '6 or 8 abreast, each person decorated with a green ribbon, the band playing "Oh, dear, what can the matter be?"', this tune deliciously associated with insubordination in other places too.[233] The Tories had a mob of drunkards and boys ready for them. It advanced on the waggon with 'rough music' comprising two dozen tin horns blown to drown out the speakers, ordered in advance from a local shopkeeper by a rabble-rouser. (They probably came in handy again on May Day.) Taking possession of the banners, this mob mercilessly bludgeoned the demonstrators, who fled for their lives. 'The musicians went first', according to a pathetic comment at the leaders' trial in Salisbury the following year.[234] Devizes was no stranger to rough music: it had accompanied the burning of a Jew in effigy at the repeal of the Jewish Naturalization Act in 1754.[235]

Prudent they may have been on this occasion, but musicians in Trowbridge were political. Two of them, Noah Crook and William Collier, were sufficiently committed to the left-wing cause to subscribe to Feargus O'Connor's National Land Scheme in 1846, and the Trowbridge Choral Society helped raise funds for the Chartists arrested in Devizes. But Henry Righton, a local 'professor of music' and son of the organist of Trowbridge parish church, was clearly Tory. Called as a witness at the 1840 trial, he was cross-examined by one of the defendants, Carrier, for not being able to

---

[233] Lomas 1990, i: 233.
[234] Lansdown 1997: 10–31.
[235] *SM*, 7 Jan 1754: 1.

identify the tune played by the band at one of the meetings. 'Call yourself a professor?' was the tenor of the taunt.[236]

By the end of the nineteenth century, the demonstration of workers' solidarity through marching accompanied by a band had become a much more familiar concept, as when John Berry & Sons' textile workers in Buckfastleigh struck, were replaced by seventy to eighty workers from Ashburton, and marched in protest to Ashburton with the support of the (Plymouth?) Gasworkers' Brass Band.[237] This was in early 1892, and may have been an orderly occasion, but it comes as a shock to realise how violent could be the popular reaction to such a musical demonstration even in the high Victorian years. The Salvation Army, borrowing recruiting-party techniques and vocabulary from the military, seems to have incurred universal opprobrium for its brass bands (which almost from the beginning contained women) when they first appeared on the streets of English towns, desecrating the Sabbath and affronting respectability with its popular choruses; it must have done much to demolish the bastion of musical good taste along with the fortress of sin, acting as a vanguard for the onslaught of Tin Pan Alley and jazz.[238] Still called the Christian Missioners, the movement appears to have had its first band formed by members of the Fry family in Salisbury in 1878.[239] By 1883 there may have been four hundred Salvation Army bands in Britain, but they had to fight every inch of the way. In Paignton their march to the sea front was shadowed by a 'Skeleton Army' of young toughs, the Skeleton Army being an organised opposition group possibly inaugurated at Weston-super-Mare in 1882, where it disrupted a Salvation Army processional and broke some instruments on 23 March. In Crediton, hooligans had countered the SA's 'invasion' in 1881, and later, 'when ... someone presented them with a big drum, it became something to be fought for and defended'. All hopes of an outdoor focus for the Army's first mission week in Taunton in April 1883 were dashed when 'Happy Harry' and his band were received with rotten eggs and ripe oranges; and persecution and prosecutions are recorded in Torquay as late as 1887.[240] In these instances, notions of respectability seem to have applied neither to the band's status nor to the behaviour of the populace. But people get used to change, and the sound and sight of a Salvation Army band quickly went from being something threatening to something viewed

---

[236] Lansdown 1997: 26–9, 47.
[237] Porter 1984: 71; *WT*, 11 Jan 1892: 2.
[238] Lomas 1990, i: 361; Herbert 2000: 196–7.
[239] Lomas 1990, i: 357.
[240] Patterson 1952: 138; *The Times*, 5 Apr 1882: 8; Venn 1955: 368–9; Bush 1983: 53; Penwill 1953: 42.

and heard with affection, part of the heritage. Yeovil's SA Band participated in the town's celebrations to mark the end of the Second World War in 1945, when the residents also burnt an effigy of Hitler in a huge bonfire on Summerhouse Hill. More mellow associations, of seagulls, putting greens, and the smell of seaweed, will have attended many an aural recollection of the SA's holiday presence in west country seaside resorts, be it a band on the beach opposite Brunswick House in Clevedon, on the Wharf in St Ives on Easter Monday in the 1920s (courtesy of the Penzance and Mousehole Corps), or at Plymouth during the annual SA convention in the 1970s, an occasion painted by local celebrity artist Beryl Cook. ('I copied the musical instruments from the magazines [the *War Cry*], but had to leave out quite a few pieces of them, they were so complicated.')[241]

As for volunteer bands, their second wave occurred after 1859, once the British government moved to acknowledge the growing presence of rifle volunteer corps – 'Saturday night soldiers' as they were sometimes referred to and the 'Territorials' as they became – across the country following the Indian Mutiny and at a time of renewed distrust of France. Their bands were an important, expensively equipped, and sizable part of the whole movement – often well over a third of all volunteers at a muster were bandsmen, some practised in rifle drill, some not – and might comprise brass or fifes and drums.[242] When the 17th Devon or Dart Vale Rifle Volunteers marched to Totnes Guildhall to be sworn in by the mayor on 27 March 1860, they already had a fife and drum band. Much newspaper discussion ensued about whether it should exchange fifes for piccolos, 'Fifer' and 'Flauto' putting their respective cases. But the important thing to note is that the band was still not a regular part of the unit but an assortment of the town's musicians, and they expected to be paid. A rifle match at Newton Abbot in early October, joined also by the Dartmouth Artillery Corps and their band, was the occasion of a grievance and triggered this letter to the *Totnes Times*:

> Gentlemen, – Some misunderstanding having arisen on the pay the Band was to have for the late trip to Newton, we the undersigned, members of the Band, beg respectfully to state for your consideration the sum per day we shall expect at any future time we may be wanted: – G R Stone, 5s; H C Veale, 2s 6d; S[amuel] Prowse, 2s 6d; W Kellow, 2s 6d; A Richards, 2s; N Fogwill, 2s; and for Bartlett, Johns, and Parkhouse, 1s each, exclusive of travelling expenses and provisions. When employed in the town we do not charge for rations. We will

---

[241] Yeovil VE/VJ 2005: [6], [12]; *SIT*, 17 Apr 1925: 4; Lumbard 1998: 74; Cook 1982: [34–5].
[242] Lomas 1990, i: 535.

give our time as usual for playing to and from drill and for practice. We also wish it to be understood that we are to have the use of the piccolos, drums, &c, for any (non-political) engagement we may choose to accept, the Band to be answerable for any damage or loss that may occur when on such engagement.

We beg to remain, Gentlemen, Your obedient Servants ... Totnes, October 13th, 1860.

Unsatisfied by the 17th Devon committee's response, by the end of November the band had withdrawn its services and broken up, Stone as bandmaster having already formed the Totnes and Bridgetown Fife and Drum Subscription Band instead. Presumably he thought there was better money to be made by his men and boys – the shilling recipients above were probably boys – on a freelance basis.[243]

The friction at Totnes was not isolated and may have been indicative of a shift in musicians' status in such places in the final third of the nineteenth century.[244] The general picture at this time, clear enough, is of local fundraising, by the bands themselves or more likely well-wishers' subscription efforts, for the acquisition of uniforms and brass instruments. Bampton was discussing such matters in relation to the band of the Devon Rifle Volunteers 11th Battalion in 1868–69, Crediton raising money for volunteer band instruments through a 'fancy fair' at Penton House in or around 1876, *noblesse* presumably obliging as it had always done. And once a band was up and running, it in turn could then help to raise funds – for 'the widows and orphans of Railway servants' in the case of the Nailsea Volunteers' annual charity concert in 1883.[245] Just as the independence of the church bands was finally crushed, it is therefore possible that the informal secular union of local jobbing musicians to hire themselves out as opportunity arose was eroded by the rise of the patronised amateur, at least in the arena of parades and civic celebrations. A good bandmaster would remain at a premium and must have been paid, to judge from the frequency of proud and approving mention in local newspaper reports, but his charges lost their musicianly leverage as uniformity in all senses triumphed. Educational changes will also have reinforced this shift, as boys ceased to be the formal or casual extra pair of hands to an artisanal jobber, music working like many another trade here, and got involved in banding instead through peer and community pressure as an 'improving' leisure pursuit ('rational recreation' was the catchphrase), as such unpaid. This hypothesis needs further testing,

---

[243] Peach 1987: 5, 20, 37–9.
[244] See Lomas 1990, i: 557.
[245] DeHCSCI 2547M/SS24/44–57; Venn 1955: 106; Milton 1993: 6.

however, for although something similar is visible in the growth of local choral societies and works choirs, parish church choirboys by contrast *were* paid (at Bideford through the Choir and Altar Fund), having been recruited by various means – the vicar visiting the local school to find the best talent and reward it, the headmaster guaranteeing a constant supply because he was also a churchwarden, or the organist descending on the Scout Cub hut one Thursday evening, as happened respectively in Backwell, Allington (Bridport), and Devizes.[246]

Like the masculinity of the moustache and the helmet, civic and volunteer band culture probably peaked (as it were) in the imperialistic and patriotic years leading up to the First World War, and from the 1860s onwards countless archive photographs testify to these signifiers in combination. Having increased from a norm of nine to twelve players at the Exeter contest of 1861, a band of around eighteen to twenty male musicians seems to have been the aim; this number can be seen in photographs of the Tresco Band (Isles of Scilly, 1875–80), the Chard Volunteer Band (June 1882), Chard's Perry Street Works Band, and the Wells Brush Works Band (*ca* 1900).[247] Larger forces might be achieved by a school (Taunton School's fife and drum band, *ca* 1865) or a major military unit such as the Somerset Light Infantry, Band of the 3rd Battalion (about thirty-seven players in 1900), smaller by a modest community (fourteen in the Swanage Town Band, 1890s), though even the Uffculme Band managed fifteen men (Whit Monday 1909). Salvation Army bands were probably smaller (ten, all male, in the Highbridge SA Band *ca* 1905). Wareham Town Band numbered twenty-five men in 1908, and it is worth noting that the band publishers Wright and Round had been proclaiming a full band to consist of twenty-four valved brass players plus drums as early as 1889.[248] The actual norm was certainly brass, two to four percussion, and a bandmaster, but still included the odd clarinet or flute, with a more extensive woodwind component in the biggest ensembles. Not all men sported a uniform, or uniformity might descend no further than the cap or helmet. The average age was young, the band might include boys, and it often contained more than one family member, to judge from illustrations and programmes in which players' names were identified – four members of the Ware family, one of them the bandmaster, plus two Godwins are among

---

[246] *BPM*, Jan 1905: vi, Jul 1905: 3; Brain 1995: 17; Hill 2007: 27; Leech 1995: 29.
[247] Lomas 1990, i: 693–9 (cf 701–5); StMaryMus; Gosling and Huddy 1992: 76; Howell 1989: 92.
[248] Bush 1983: 74; NSLS 'Bands' file in cabinet (A/BWG/4/98/3); Legg 1983: 96; Payne 1988: 105; Maslen 1988: 114; Ladle 1994: [illus] 81; Lomas 1990, i: 713.

the twenty men of the Clevedon Silver Band in a splendid photo from 1912.[249] At the turn of the century, some community bands were mutating into salon orchestras or simply continuing the quadrille band tradition: the nineteen members of the Ilfracombe Town Band in a photograph from 1906 include six violinists (one of them a boy) and a double bass player, though apparently no cellist, at least three woodwind players, and two women without instruments, probably pianists or harpists.[250]

In parallel harmony with this amateur soundscape ran the immigrant professionals, their foreign credentials real or assumed. Until 1914 put an abrupt stop to the allure of pan-European mobility, the seaside resorts in particular were awash with them, and even the young Gustav Holst earnt his seasonal living as a faux-Viennese trombonist, though not in the peninsula beyond Bath. Groups such as the 'Tyrolese Minstrels' and 'the celebrated Hungarian singers' appearing 'in the National Costume of the country' had been touring Devon as early as the 1820s and '30s, but it was from the 1870s onwards that no seaside pavilion was complete without an Italian or Hungarian band, German bands being considered too mainstream to warrant identification as such.[251] That their members were in many cases demobbed conscripts (conditions inapplicable to the British at this time) is attested and seems likely enough following the unification of Italy and of Germany after the Franco-Prussian War.[252] Weston's Italian Band was giving fashionable promenade concerts under Signor Ulrico in 1871; Bournemouth and Torquay each had a Royal Italian Band of some pretension and longevity; Bideford sported a Hungarian Military Season Band in 1902, while Blue Hungarian Bands (or the same one) were to be found at the Kursaal on Ilfracombe Pier the following year and on Weston-super-Mare's Old Pier under bandmaster Hubner in 1911.[253]

Loved as characters or hated as martinets, the resorts' bandmasters and conductors were colourful, resilient figures and as autocratic as hoteliers. Signor E Bertini of the Bournemouth Corporation Military Band may quickly have lost out in the early 1890s to Dan Godfrey, who transcended the type, but Herr Willy

---

[249] Lilly 1990: 96.
[250] Bartlett 1995: 43.
[251] *EFP* 5 Nov 1829: 2, Cann 1977: 30 and Christie and Grant 2005: 75; Cann and Bush 1967: 385.
[252] Watkins 1914: 10.
[253] *WSMG*, 14 Oct 1922 in NSLS Bands; Watkins 1914: 10, Street and Carpenter 1993: 10–11, Barber 1980: 2, Devon Celeb: 47, 72–4, TTC Min 5541–3 and TTC Min: xxvii–xxviii (1911); Christie and Grant 2005: 68, 71; Bartlett 1995: 72; *WM*, 10 Jun: s2 [*recte* 4?].

Goetze and his Weston-super-Mare Grand Pier band had the local press exactly where they wanted it at the beginning of his season's engagement in 1911:

> [Goetze is] a typical product of musical Vienna. He is intense and emotional in method, and has an artistically directed mind and attuned ear for the production of colourful result, whether in delicate nuance or broad effect. Above all, he possesses a forceful insistence which guarantees a ready response to his aim from the Band. The latter consists of twenty members, and their disposition in instrumental force leaves little to desire ... the Grand Pier management have engaged a really high-class band, and one that, once settled down, may be relied on to do splendid work.

With an estimated 42,000 day trippers descending on Weston at the start of the season that Whit Monday, and with no fewer than four pier establishments, the Grand, the Old, Knightstone, and one on an extension of the Island, each requiring live music, the resort music business could not fail.[254] It was, however, perennially contentious where ratepayers' money was concerned. Take the bandstand as a civic amenity. Torquay's proposals for a band enclosure that would have been built out into the harbour raised municipal temperatures to boiling point between the wars.[255] Exmouth's plans for replacing its old bandstand occupied the local press for well over ten years from 1992, with headlines such as 'new bandstand plans strike sour note', 'brakes on plan for bandstand after discovery of sewer', 'still no home for town's bandstand', 'after all, no bandstand', 'oh yes it is – bandstand is now going ahead', and 'bandstand is in sight at last'; a personal visit in 2010 confirmed a postmodern equivalent of a traditional bandstand, the Performance Stage, now standing in the Manor Gardens.[256] As for Okehampton, which did once consider itself a 'moorland health resort', it was keen to commemorate the coronation of George V in 1911 with the erection of a bandstand in Simmons Park, until someone pointed out that the town had no band. The structure went ahead anyway.[257]

---

[254] Watkins 1914: 10, 62, Street and Carpenter 1993: 12; *WM*, 10 Jun: 1, 2.

[255] Morgan 1991, i: 113, ii: 305–9.

[256] *EL*, 16 Apr 1992: 14; *EH*, 17 Nov 1995: 9; *EJ*, 25 Jan 1996: 17, 7 Mar 1996: 9; *EH*, 9 May 1997: 3, 5 Dec 1997: 7, 13 Feb 1998: 5, 27 Feb 1998: 3, 12 Jun 1998: 7, 26 Jun 1998: 3; *EJ*, 3 Jun 1999: 5, 19 Aug 1999: 5, 28 Oct 1999: 12, 27 Jan 2000: 3, 10 Feb 2000: 7, 18 Feb 2000: 1, 23 Mar 2000: 3, 26 Oct 2000: 13; *EH*, 27 Oct 2000: 1, 3; *EJ*, 2 Nov 2000: 1, 15 Feb 2001: 19; *EH*, 9 Mar 2001: 5; *EJ*, 15 Aug 2002: 3, 5 Dec 2002: 6 (all ExmLSCI).

[257] *OGA*, 18 Feb 1911: 2, 21 Feb 1911: 3, 13 May 1911: 2, 32 May 1911: 2, 10 Jun 1911: np, 5 Aug 1911: 2, 30 Sep 1911: 3.

The Twentieth Century: Changes in Musical Practice

Yet as already suggested, bands reflect individual liberties, community temperatures, and changing fashions where choirs do not. Fears as early as 1885 that young dancers' decorum on Paignton Pier might not hold out against the observed excesses of lads and lasses in northern resorts, who were 'hugging each other cheek by jowl as they whirled frantically in the valse and polka', gave way to far greater shocks when the generation too young to have served in the First World War seemed to lose all inhibitions in the social dances of the 1920s.[258]

How this was reflected in changes in musical practice is curiously difficult to plot, for a fundamental shift from the public and civic back to the private seems to have pertained where bands are concerned. Brass bands and salon orchestras gave way to dance bands; bandmasters became bandleaders; syncopated rhythms begat new textures, instrumentation, and approaches to tempo and expression; new channels of communication brought bands together and made their availability known (though *The Era* was still full of advertisements for bands wanting musicians and musicians wanting engagements); different types of financial agreement, not obviously visible now, must have kept bands afloat and enticed players. How did all this happen, in terms of the actual musicians? We do not know, though that there was a paradigm shift in terms of training, emulation, and social transmission we can be certain, its upshot lasting until today. We still understand very little about how band musicians learn, develop, and organise their livelihoods, certainly at the sub-national level.

Informal communication was key, helped by two new types of business, the car repairer and the electrical shop (sometimes combined). Two bandleaders in Portishead, probably from the 1920s and 1930s, illustrate the point. Kerwin 'Jack' Tuckwell 'had a small workshop opposite the Plough Inn. He repaired cars and anything of a mechanical nature. He also ran a small dance band which performed in the Band Stand at Battery Point on Saturday evenings and special holidays … if Jack was busy repairing a car, he would have a quick wash, put a clean stiff front on to cover the grease on his shirt and rush to Battery Point.' Arthur Picton came from a family that had run the post office since 1865; he also 'ran a small dance band called "We Three"; Arthur, Harry and Charlie Davies. They played for dancing in the Federation Hut opposite Wesley House. Two of Arthur's favourite songs were "I pushed her through the window", and "It's a handy little thing to

---

[258] Patterson 1952: 136.

have about you". A first class, funny entertainer. He ended his days in Australia.' Note the association of music with community wit and feeling, each band remembered for a signature tune, funny or sentimental (Tuckwell's was 'Red sails in the sunset').[259]

Gramophones were certainly sold by music dealers: Stephen Nicholas of Redruth, one of the region's carol composers, 'was probably the first local trader to sell gramophones: his Saturday night record concerts were a feature of that time' (the early 1900s), and Duck, Son and Pinker's Royal Promenade branch in Clifton, 'a few doors from the Victoria Rooms', was offloading 'Pathephones, gramophones, Zonophones, &c ... 1000 discs to be cleared at cost price ... 2000 music rolls to be cleared, from 6d to 2/6' to visiting Westonians in 1911.[260] But T Day and Sons of the Arcade, Okehampton, selling gramophones, phonographs, and disc machines in 1910–11, advertised themselves as 'motor and general engineers, cycle manufacturers, &c' (they built the Oketon Cycle, whatever that was). Similarly, Glover's of Tregenna Hill, St Ives, called itself 'Cycle & Gramophone Stores'.[261] The medium of cultural exchange for musical sounds was now not a 'professor' embodying authority, especially over females, but a mechanic or shop assistant with a cocked ear. This was surely an overlapping transition layered by class as well as gender. In Clevedon, 'Jimmy' Joint's business, where according to one reminiscence 'Dad and his brothers' – men, note – bought their gramophone records, was in Chapel Hill in the workers' part of town, and later became an electrical shop, as did Mr Dark's music shop underneath the Curzon Cinema. Uptown, in Hill Road, a venerable sequence of music, piano, and book dealerships in various combinations had long been established and managed to survive the onslaught of technology. One of them, Seeley's, is still trading.[262]

Radio strengthened the idea that music was a consumer novelty and came out of a machine – a machine within a machine in the case of car radios. By 1925, radios were being offered for sale, installation, and in one case demonstration in a public hall, by the Carbis Bay Motor Garage, Warren and Ninnes, and Blewett's Garages of St Ives, where the St Ives Jazz Band was also flourishing, its busy spring schedule of the Easter Dance (16 April), Drill Hall dances every Saturday evening (e.g. 18 April), and the Conservative

---

[259] Joslin 1987: 42, 44–6. H Montague's 'A handy little thing to have about you' was published in 1900, Hugh Williams's 'Red sails in the sunset' with lyrics by Jimmy Kennedy in 1935.
[260] Quick 2000: 10; *WM*, 10 Jun 1911: s2.
[261] *OGA*, 24 Dec 1910: 2, 1 Apr 1911: 4; *SIT*, 3 Apr 1925: 6.
[262] Lilly 1999 and 2002: passim.

Association Dance (23 April) causing one to wonder whether its members had day jobs or this was part of a multitrade living.[263] Jazz had come in very suddenly at the end of the First World War: 'the American musical and singing band Jazzbo' was performing at the Bristol Empire in April 1918, advertised as 'the coming craze', there were tut-tuttings in the press by December, and the Plymouth Guildhall announced a 'jazz band from Keith House, London' as the special attraction at its fancy dress ball on 28 January 1919.[264] Regional jazz bands will have taken a little longer to form. Dance and jazz bands soon began to broadcast (live, of course) from pretentious venues, especially those at the seaside, the musicians' mystique no doubt just as much enhanced by invisibility and distance as was the resort hotels' business by clients' determination to see and hear them in person. Bournemouth, the closest west country resort to London, attained a musical glamour in the 1920s and '30s that it has long since lost. For many years between the wars, Alex Wainwright presided at the Royal Bath Hotel's ballroom and broadcast from there; he 'had the habit of strolling among the dancers during waltzes, playing his violin while bathed in a spotlight'. Guest residencies included Harry Roy's Lyricals – was Roy himself with them? Sergei Rachmaninov is supposed to have crossed the road to the Royal Bath following his afternoon concert at the Pavilion on 13 March 1934 'and sat in the lounge [one source says the dining room] to hear what type of music the British people were listening to', but this will have been the Geraldo salon orchestra led by violinist Montague Birch, who became conductor of the Municipal Orchestra during the Second World War after Richard Austin's resignation.[265] At the time of the opening of the Pavilion in 1929, crossing the road in another direction took one to the Westover Ballroom where Percy Pearce and his suspiciously generic-sounding London Dance Band were in residence. An early feature in the Pavilion auditorium was an evening concert by 'Herman Darewski (Himself) and His Band' while his Pavilians, 'the dance band with the compelling rhythm', were a fixture in its ballroom, the well-known Darewski being musical director of the Winter Gardens, Blackpool, at the time.[266] Then there were the department stores – Plummer Roddis, Bobby's, Beale's. 'Each had a trio, quartet, or more, playing for morning coffee, lunch and afternoon tea', and although these were hardly dance bands, they did broadcast, while the roof garden restaurant at Plummer Roddis was opened

---

[263] *SIT*, 3 Apr 1925: 7, 9, 12; 10 Apr: 10; 17 Apr: 7.
[264] *WDP*, 22 Apr 1918: 1; *WMN*, 15 Jan 1919: 3.
[265] George 1979: 9, 11; Ashley 2006: 26–7.
[266] Ashley 2006: 11–12.

by Ivor Novello in the 1930s. Bright's Restaurant featured an orchestra led by Jack Greenstone in 1934, Alfred Jupp was another popular salon violinist and began his career there, and at one point before the war the young Mantovani could be found playing in a small ensemble in a café on Westover Road.[267]

This plethora of violinists reminds us that social dancing and background musical entertainment between the wars were not all about swing, saxophones, and fast cars. In fact the rise of ballroom dancing required massed strings for waltzes and other elements of the repertoire, and there may well have been a greater number of 'literate' (notationally educated) string players in Britain then than at any other time, all of them having undergone extensive and gruelling formal training in their instrument. Ernest G Oram's Orchestra posing in 1922 on the Grand Pier, Weston-super-Mare, where it played each night in the ballroom, was what we would now call a chamber orchestra, though probably not a good one – 'fourth-rate' would be typical, according to the 1967 reminiscences of Alfred Corum, a Weston pier violinist between the wars.[268] But even Percy Cook's Grand Pier Orchestra of 1947, looking every bit the big band with conducting bandleader, draped music desks, and amplified female vocalist in a photographic vignette on the front cover of J G Brenner's 'The Grand Pier song', has what appear to be violinists doubling on saxophone.[269]

Perhaps the influx of American servicemen in the Second World War did the most to loosen up social behaviour and modernise popular music and dance. Thousands of them descended on certain parts of the west country, especially between late 1943 and June 1944 in the run-up to D-Day. In uniform, their military bands were of the finest: 'Guildhall to-night. American Forces Military Band (28 performers), bandmaster Mr R L Higgins, will give a band concert', announced a poster in St Ives, 17 December 1943.[270] Out of uniform, they shared the latest recordings in the pub, the village hall, and the bedroom, and suddenly a populace was letting itself go. In Wedmore church schoolroom, 'dances were often held ... and the Americans used to come. Bill Lukins took the front and top off the piano, and played as loudly as he could. The Americans taught everybody to jitterbug, throwing the girls over their shoulders.'[271] Jitterbugging was all the rage in St Ives as well, where 'the many local dances were extremely popular ... many popular bands played

---

[267] George 1979: 10–12; Ashley 2006: 29.
[268] *WM*, 8 Sep 1967 in NSLS Bands.
[269] Poole 2009: 32–3.
[270] Lever and Jeyes 2005: 44.
[271] Hudson 2002: 227.

here including "The Rhythm Arcadians", Jimmy Rickard and sometimes an American Army Band. Tickets were 2/- for civilians and 1/6d for the forces.'[272] Americans completely swamped the South Hams countryside in Devon as Slapton Sands became a practice beach for the Normandy landings.[273] Then, suddenly, they were all gone. Over nine hundred had perished there in the disastrous Operation Tiger in April; many more died in Normandy. How many gramophone records were left behind with sweethearts, to be picked up and musically emulated by younger brothers deprived of male role models?

It remains infuriatingly difficult to quantify such changes in local practice. But long before the war, Parsloe had noted the Americanisation of provincial taste:

> There is one [country town] I know where the town band plays on Saturday nights in a garden by the river, and boys and girls dance together under the trees. The tunes were made in Chicago, and the dances began in the negro south – for folk-dancing belongs to garden suburbs. But the spirit of the dancers is as English as their faces. The old men sit round, banging the rhythm out on the earth with their sticks; the hills fling back the tune … the old houses listen in the darkness to the saxophones that have replaced the fiddles, to jazz that has ousted the country tunes, to the new-fashioned shuffle.[274]

But here Parsloe possibly elides a brass or military band with a dance band. It would seem that they remained separate in motivation, instrumentation, style, and purpose. They were, however, proximate, for the Yeovil VE-Day celebrations included marching Boys' Brigade and Girls' Brigade bands in addition to the SA Band mentioned above, but were capped by Bill Kelly and His Band, 'relayed through amplifiers on a National Fire Service van'. Kelly's will have been the sound people remembered: 'Hour by hour the crowd thickened … On and on the band played[;] on and on the dancers danced. Midnight struck. The band had played non-stop since the early evening. They played until they could play no more … The band went home, but the crowd didn't. From nowhere appeared accordions and hundreds at a time gathered round the single minstrel.' The civic formality of a marching band would similarly give way to the demotic release of a dance band in many a carnival, as in Ottery St Mary two years later, whose Silver Band along with Sidmouth Town Band took part in the torchlight procession but were followed by Percy Hill and His Band playing for the dance at the Institute, which continued

---

[272] Lever and Jeyes 2005: 44.
[273] Oswald 1988: 109–11.
[274] Parsloe 1932: 194.

until 1am and cost 2s 6d.[275] One imagines Percy Hill being paid, the Silver Band not; Percy Hill engaged by word-of-mouth reputation, the Silver Band by official consensus; possibly Hill being phoned up by a different member of the carnival committee from the negotiator with the Silver Band. Did any musicians play in both?

A sample of Plymouth dance bands throws up the Raleigh Dance Orchestra of the 1930s, the Paramount Dance Band founded by the proprietor of the dance hall of that name in 1937 or 1938, the proleptic Victory Revellers Dance Band of 1943 onwards (with accordion again, in a husband-and-wife team), and George Day and His Band of the 1950s. The White Notes Dance Band raises the curtain a little on formal genesis (and formal demise). It originated in the 4th Plymouth Boys' Brigade in early 1944, having been founded for the annual parents' night by four of the boys, one of whom, the drummer Gordon Tope, acted as manager aged eighteen, no doubt commandeering his parents' phone for long stretches. (Surely the spread of dance bands would have been impossible without the spread of the domestic telephone.) By 1945, playing for a Victory Dance, they had grown from four to seven – two saxes, two accordions, string bass, drums, plus Pauline Levy on piano, who had taken over from the Boys' Brigade's Bill Worth. Much in demand at that time for Victory street parties, 'we'd play the top tunes of the day – It's Only a Paper Moon, We'll Gather Lilacs, and Alice Blue Gown. Our signature tune was Cherokee' – of which only the one English song, Novello's 'We'll gather lilacs', was brand new, the others, all American, dating respectively from 1933, 1919, and (as a swing standard) 1938–39. The following year their name was changed to Jock West and His Music, in the late 1940s they enjoyed a successful Saturday night and Bank Holiday residency at the Yealmpton Hotel out on the moors, for a while (until posted away) they added the services of a couple of Royal Marine bandsmen, and then in 1952 they broke up for two typical reasons, change of fashion and personal circumstances. By their own testimony, country and western was taking over, and their manager's civil defence job took him to Bath. Eight years was a good stint, but the liberties of youth are age-limited, or were then.[276]

There was indeed, from the late 1940s, a reaction to the cosmopolitan slickness of American swing. As country and western or rhythm 'n' blues this reaction was itself American, aided in the USA by the broadcasters' boycott of ASCAP songs, closely followed as it had been by a two-year-long recording strike of AFM members, which provided openings for regional and 'race'

---

[275] Yeovil VE/VJ 2005: [6], quoted *WG*; handbill, Devon Celeb: 38.
[276] Robinson 1999a and b, 2004.

recordings.[277] But as a folk revival in Britain it was an indigenous political shift, promoted by the BBC in welfare-state consciousness of workers' culture and balladry. It seems to have coincided with the first major expansion of the university student population, at least in Bristol (whither one of the members of Jock West and His Music departed as an undergraduate in 1947).[278] Bristol University's undergraduate numbers trebled to three thousand (a third of them women) between 1945 and 1959, and from 1949 the institution could boast some form of folk dance club or society, the catalyst being a new physical education lecturer, Jack Williams, who had discovered the English Folk Dance and Song Society at teacher training college. The Bristol University Morris and Long-Swords Men were founded by Williams in 1951. That same year the Inter-Varsity Folk-Dance Festival began in Leeds, and Bristol's Students' Union, at that time occupying the Vic Rooms, hosted it in 1957. Williams can be seen in the photo of 'a square dance at the Victoria Rooms in the spring of 1952 with "Nibs" Matthews and the Haymakers [which] attracted 430 enthusiastic dancers'. Oxford University had perhaps set the example, and first among the reasons given in a *Cherwell* interview by Tom Fletcher for the setting up of its Cecil Sharp Club in 1947 was that 'people are becoming sick of the regularity of the Saturday-night "hop"'. Folk dance had emerged from Parsloe's garden suburbs, though the odour of compost and flowerpots would continue to stick to it.[279]

Insofar as folk dance, morris dance, and step dance are display dances, it may still have taken the ensuing fad for American square dance to turn this element of the second folk revival (the first will be examined in chapter 6) into mass participation. But at this point a nagging doubt surfaces: had not something comparable been going on all along in west country villages, country houses, ballrooms, and city taverns? As early as 1735, Bristol's thirty-seven taverns in Marsh Street alone, 'reputedly in Irish hands … were notorious for their "music, dancing, rioting, drunkenness and profane swearing"'.[280] The Irish have always been an immigrant presence in the west country, and it may be that with their large and distressed numbers in Devon in the earlier seventeenth century they were beginning to take up fiddling at that time as an alternative or a supplement to parish relief.[281] But what about the English?

[277] Wikipedia: 'ASCAP boycott', '1942–44 musicians' strike'.
[278] Robinson 1999a.
[279] Cottle and Sherborne 1959: 43; Skinner 2011; Nourse 2008: 8–9.
[280] BA (BRO) 04343(5), quoted Dresser and Fleming 2007: 77.
[281] Worth 1887: 43–4.

A fiddle, no different from a violin, is patently not a band, though for a period of nearly three hundred years (and long before that in its mediaeval guise) it formed the minimum and for many purposes sufficient musical requirement for the job that a band has always done: accompanying group bodily movement, in this case social dancing. James Barnard advertised precisely that service in Sidmouth in 1836.[282] But the fiddle did more than that, playing also in the church bands. As such it provides the best signifier, and a wonderfully unifying one, for what would otherwise falsely seem a set of separate and dichotomous musickings.

What secular music did a fiddle play? Why was the fiddler's elbow a byword for animation? The short answer is that the instrument and its bowing set the pace and established the articulation and genial catchiness of the jigging, tripping – 'prancing', Thomas Hardy called it in his poem 'The fiddler' – and (in the step dance) flashy footwork of country dancing, to use the term broadly and generically, and that only when this impulse was, it seems, genuinely foregone for the swing and syncopation of American dances did the fiddle lose its currency, as Parsloe rightly observed.[283] Thus with one exception the author's database contains no reference to the fiddle between 1897 and 1972. On 21 January 1897, a church tea and evening concert were held, with the customary solos, duets, piano accompaniments, recitations, spinsters, and vicars, in the remote Mead Barn, last building before a crashing sea and 350-foot cliff in the parish of Welcombe on the north Devon–Cornish border. A dance followed, 'to the strains of a violin in the skilful hands of Mr Fred Tape of Coombe, Morwenstowe'.[284] Perhaps he walked the three and three-quarter miles from his equally remote and beautiful coastal hamlet, late testament to an ability and social facility both taken for granted and sought after. Only a reference to German prisoners of war in Dorchester Barracks in 1914 playing on their 'concertinas and fiddles' comes between this and the deliberate recovery of a tradition in the Dartington Institute of Traditional Arts with its recordings of Devon fiddle music played by Fred Pidgeon of Stockland, Pidgeon's photograph gracing the pages of a 1972 Dartington publication.[285] Clearly continuity survived in pockets, as exemplified by the Biddick family and associates of Boscastle and Tintagel, Cyril Biddick and William Hockin photographed with concertina

---

[282] Sutton 1973: 81.
[283] Hardy 1930: 231.
[284] *HC*, Feb 1897: 3.
[285] Draper 2001: 91; Dartington 1972 [np].

and fiddle at some point in the earlier twentieth century and recorded by the BBC in 1943.[286] But survival was all it was.

Those prisoners of war were observed by Thomas Hardy, and two years later Hardy wrote his poem 'To my father's violin', an instrument silent since its owner's death in 1892, though Hardy did later play it again.[287] The poet's father, stonemason by trade, had been a Dorset village fiddler for dances and, as already discussed, in the church band. In the poem Hardy acknowledges both media, seeing them as complementary, however strongly contrasted, and according them one stanza each. After describing psalmody 'In the gallery west the nave', the poet turns to country dancing:

> And, too, what merry tunes
> He would bow at nights or noons
> That chanced to find him bent to lute a measure,
> When he made you speak his heart
> As in dream,
> Without book or music-chart,
> On some theme
> Elusive as a jack-o'-lanthorn's gleam,
> And the psalm of duty shelved for trill of pleasure.

The role of the country fiddler is carefully denoted here. He is an amateur, only engaged for a social dance ('a measure', archaic usage) when he feels like it ('bent') or the occasion arises ('chanced'); his eyes are probably closed ('As in dream'), in that withdrawn, inward stance of the folk musician; he is playing by ear, Hardy wishes us to believe, perhaps varying the melody each time so that it never seems to have a fixed identity ('some theme / Elusive'); the tunes' purpose and effect are quite simply 'pleasure' (not arousal or desire, though these ensue in 'The fiddler').[288]

Hardy's father may have fiddled from memory, but he also compiled his own manuscript tune book of ninety-seven dance melodies, and with his brother and father was regularly invited by the vicar to Stinsford House to form a quartet of some kind. This is congruent with the fact that the contents of surviving fiddle (or occasionally flute) tune books from the west country and elsewhere present a smooth continuum between 'classical', commercially popular, and traditional melodies, between old and new, English and foreign, and in some cases between regionally unique and broadly standard material. They are, quite simply, individual manifestations of a national (to some

---

[286] Davey 2009: 49, 51.
[287] Brocklebank 1977: [1–2].
[288] Hardy 1930: 423–4.

extent international) repertoire and social practice, a practice that cut across classes, economies, demographics, and formal and informal occasions. The fiddle, whether or not harmonically supported, was the sound motor for it all, though the portable free-reed instruments, accordion and concertina, quickly adopted the same role because similarly agile of accent, phrasing, and the sudden 'lift' in articulation that is such an irresistible if indescribable part of the country dance impulse. (The poet Hardy's father gave him an accordion at the age of four. This will have been around 1844, still fairly early for rural dissemination of this invention of the previous decade.[289])

Thus in Bath in the later eighteenth century a fiddler for social dance might be an orchestral player (Francis Fleming, 1715–78), a French gentlewoman, or an Irish dancing master; in Lympstone in 1822 a young female pianist sitting out the Tuesday quadrille might offer to play the music so as to snobbishly oust the lone fiddler (or to supplement his insufficiently audible efforts?); from playing at the annual fair in Mells, an itinerant fiddler (no fair was complete without one) might eventually make his fortune as a sheep dealer; John Bennett in Lyme Regis, who fiddled for dancing in the Assembly Rooms and for psalmody in the parish church, could be described at his wedding in 1788 as 'cordwainer and musician'; in Par in the early nineteenth century, the harpist and probable fiddler John Old might piece together at least a partial living from doing the rounds of nearby country houses whose young family members required dance instruction; and 'Old' Marsh in Glastonbury forty years later might combine the 'incongruous' occupations of parish fiddler and gravedigger.[290] Like those of Hardy in the Dorset chalkland and William Winter in the Quantocks, the manuscript tune book of John Old survives. From Cornwall, so do those of John Giddy of Kea, playing for social dances in Truro *ca* 1730–50, William Allen of St Ives (covering *ca* 1815–58), Michael Harris of St Dennis (flute, 1858, a psalmody band part but including two reels), and books pertaining to Prideaux Place in Padstow (1788–96) and the Buller family of Morval House near Looe (probably 1770).[291] The survival of as many as seventeen manuscript music books from Widecombe further demonstrates the synergy between fiddling and psalmody. Two of them are

---

[289] Brocklebank 1977: [1].
[290] Fawcett 1988: 33–8, 48 (citing *BC*, 1 Jan 1784); James 1987: 605ff; Cann 2001: 27–8, citing *WEPG*, 30 Nov 1822; White 1903; Powell 2008: 11; O'Connor 2007: 40; Bulleid 1891: 42.
[291] Woolfe 2007; O'Connor 2002, 2005, 2006, 2007; Davey and O'Connor 2006; Davey 2009.

fiddle tune books, the remainder band scores, mostly of church repertoire. The same hands compiled both types.[292]

In the tune books, jigs, reels, waltzes, quadrilles, schottisches, polkas, hornpipes, and marches jogged or wafted along in 6/8, 3/4, 4/4, or 2/4, all except the waltzes to a stepping beat and all to periodic tonal tunes (plus the odd vestigially modal one) whose standard phraseology, cadence, and harmonic underpinnings easily outweighed the changes in fashion nevertheless perceptible (and datable) in some of the rhythmic details and melodic contours. Parlour ballads, opera and oratorio arias, blackface minstrelsy, and music-hall tunes also feature in the tune books, along with the odd hymn or psalm tune. They were commonplace books, their cumulative format between two covers found in today's practice only in the photo album or recipe scrapbook. Some tunes developed a patina of age, others fell out of use. Yet a melody such as 'The dashing white sergeant' (it is in the Hardy tune book) remained current for the best part of 150 years, and was still part of the juvenile soundscape of the author's generation, played almost daily for country dancing on the junior school's gramophone or radio at the same moment that rock 'n' roll was conquering the record player or transistor radio in the older brother's bedroom.

❧ Rock and Its Others

The overall idiom and generic function of rock – amplified guitar (but also voice) and drumkit rather than fiddle, and a mindset of sociability stemming from pounding beat rather than tripping pulse – may survive just as long, still today's musical *lingua franca* and showing no sign of obsolescence after more than half a century of currency across region, nation, and western hemisphere.[293] As already stated, it is not easy to pinpoint its moments of entry and their social and educational workings. If we return for a moment to the Plymouth White Notes Dance Band, it becomes clear that with light-touch institutional provision and resourcing from the adult community, which might amount to no more than the availability of the church house for meetings or the tower loft for change ringing, youngsters, especially males, have in any century since at least the late middle ages capitalised on their propensity to bond and achieve something as a group that satisfies their adolescent energies, develops their powers, makes a local difference, sits often on a knife-edge between artistry and delinquency, and is age-limited. Here

---

[292] Woods 2009: [1]; WGMA.
[293] Middleton 1995: 79.

is John Cannon writing about the village youths' activities in West Lydford, Somerset, in 1702, when he was an eighteen-year-old ploughboy:

> Amongst all these scandalous companions & idle practices, I growing of a better understanding began to shake it off & betake myself to a more manly exercise which pleased my father & friends more better. For now myself, my brother, my uncle's son William, Nathaniel Withers & Parker & one or two more we had associated with us, began to learn to sing in the Church, & also the art of ringing, which as it were comendable, so it was encouraged by our friends, fathers, & masters, and there were sett nights for our assembling together. And yet after these exercises were over, we commonly went into the churchhouse where lived one Robert Parfet, being our master at ringing, & so sit up late & sometimes all night at cards, both sexes in several companies, that in short time this house became a publick talk, & was called a gaming house & bruited about besides for other scandalous practices being encouraged by the occupiers thereof. This created ill will with our friends who often advised & admonished, reproved & chastised us & their servants too for so scandalously misspending their time. This took with me & my companions so effectually that suddenly after, we followed no other diversions but ringing as long as we kept together in our own parish. Always after we had rung a peal or two, we with a general consent, dispersed and went each to his respective vocation, by which such alteration we ingratiated ourselves into the favour & affection of our parents or masters, that they never refused us the time nor money to prosecute our innocent recreations.
>
> Thus continuing closely together like a small but united corporation or body, till some died, some married & removed, I being at last removed as shall be declared hereafter, we went & came undisturbed, & would admit of none to join with us to encrease our number, but one Ambrose Fframpton & that upon particular occasions, & where ever we went we behaved circumspectly & without the least injury to any ... & for this our good behaviour, we obtained a good esteem, favour & love of strangers from abroad.[294]

As with the White Notes, the band, in this case of singers and then bell-ringers, the former trained by an itinerant singing master, lasted until members moved away or got married, though having death added to the reasons for dispersal pulls one up short.

How many rock or folk groups similarly started in a church youth club, the Scouts, or the Boys' Brigade, not forgetting the Salvation Army? These will have been not the least of places in which the latest record purchases could be listened to and reactions, based on the close listening of fresh ears, shared

---

[294] Money 2010, i: 41–2.

and developed. The Dorset folk group the Yetties met in the Yetminster Scouts, turning professional in 1967, acquiring an international reputation, and retiring in 2011. Bob Common was one of this band of four males until 1979, while his wife Pam, Dublin-born, set up the all-girl Yetminster Irish Dancers in 1972: segregation of the adolescent sexes even in a small village clearly fired creative combustion.[295] The SA, which was not segregated, and the Boys' Brigade continued to offer hands-on musical experience at a time 'in the mid–50s [when] there were precious few teach-yourself books, and household budgets would not normally allow the provision of professional tuition': a time when school music teachers would scarcely countenance (do they ever?) helping what 'all the young pupils really wanted to do', namely 'belt out some skiffle on a guitar or drum-kit'.[296] Sometimes a more aggressive facilitation has taken effect, as with Yvette Staelens's Young Women's Band Project in Chard, 'Girls Rock ON!'[297]

Skiffle was short-lived but will have accounted decisively for the turn to the guitar among British youth.[298] It reminds us that rock 'n' roll was as much a bottom-up phenomenon as Britain's emergent obsession with DIY, and helps emphasise that documentation at the local level is the best way of providing the materials for its cultural history. Sowden has done this for Devon and Somerset, Moody and Nash for Salisbury, Kent for Cornwall.[299] Yet the triggering of motivation and skills and the community's transition from one accepted norm of entertainment to another can be neither explained nor traced without awareness of the workings of the market and the media. Thus whereas a trumpet or saxophone or, to mild astonishment, a bassoon appearing in a local rock band line-up may be explained by community continuity (the bassoon in the Pathfinders from Salisbury), the suddenly ubiquitous electric guitar and drumkit cannot.[300] Something changed, very big and very wholesale.

The *Bristol Evening Post*'s reaction to such change in a cartoon caption of 1956 was that of timeless shock: 'Today, we are faced with a type of music that reaches deep down into the ancient savagery of the African forests, and its rhythmic and insistent throb recalls the primaeval urges of ju-ju and devil worship.' This was no different from how the waltz had been greeted 150 years earlier, or perhaps even the 'new way of singing', as Cannon described

---

[295] Yetties 1986; Wikipedia: 'The Yetties'; Fashion 1989.
[296] Sowden 2003: 11.
[297] Staelens 2002.
[298] Nicholas Nourse, comment to the author.
[299] Sowden 2002, 2003, 2004; Moody and Nash 2007; Kent 2007a.
[300] Sowden 2003: 27; Moody and Nash 2007: 131.

it, in the eighteenth century.[301] In 1959, the bands engaged for various new year's dances in Taunton and Bridgwater were as yet showing no obvious sign of co-opting rock, and the use of the word 'orchestra' in three out of four of those mentioned – Reg Dyer's Orchestra, Dick Clarke and His Band, the Tone Ballroom Orchestra, and the Les Pusey Orchestra – speaks for itself, implying sections or strings. Three years later, the nomenclature of Brian Blackmore's Band, engaged for the Malt Shovel Inn Cricket Club Dance in Spaxton Village Hall, might or might not imply something different, Blackmore perhaps the 'lead' guitar and/or vocalist of the new form of double-handedness, minstrels who sang and played, each on a different instrument.[302] More obvious across these years is how the metropolitan entertainment industry drove and reflected change, for at the Taunton Gaumont on 4 January 1959 were Chris Barber and his band, top-notch cosmopolitan jazz, whereas on 27 January 1962 John Smith's management was providing the 'Rhythm Group THE BARONS' along with Bert Weedon and the Temperance Seven, any rock element in this case part of an updated variety format. Rock or pop within family entertainment was one thing, and it included star singer appearances in the front-rank professional pantomimes of the region, though these will have been largely limited to those of the Bristol Hippodrome and the Bournemouth and Torquay Pavilions until Plymouth got its new Theatre Royal in 1982. A rock concert was quite another, in the archetypally sour and reactionary view of the Taunton press covering early 1962:

> Teenage idol Billy Fury will not be coming to Taunton on Friday, 30th March. He was booked to top the bill in 'The Big Show of 1962', but his place is being taken by ... actor John Leyton[, who] jumped on the 'rock' band wagon a few months ago and managed two 'hit' records. This presumably qualifies him to top the bill in this particular show.
> Also in the show is Eden Kane, who, like most of the other performers in this entertainment, has been to the town before ... This 'turn again' principle, which seems to form the basis of most 'rock' shows, would be all right if the performers produced a different act with each visit. But when the only difference is the addition of their latest 'hit' the act wears a bit thin after the second or third visit.[303]

The reviewer was right in pointing out how the consumption of rock was entirely beholden to the workings of the music industry. That industry was run in the UK overwhelmingly from London, and provincial representation

---

[301] *BEP*, cited Dresser and Fleming 2007: 142; Money 2010, ii: 379.
[302] *SCH*, 3 Jan 1959: 6–7, 10 Jan 1959: 6–7, 20 Jan 1962: 5.
[303] *SCH*, 3 Jan 1959: 5, 13 Jan 1962: 8.

in the weekly trade journal *Melody Maker* at this time was extremely sparse. From the west country, one lone dance band, the Gordon Baker Orchestra from Bristol, appeared in the classified ads and one business, Peter Russell of Plymouth, in the section 'Your Record Dealer' in the issue of 2 January 1960. At the end of the following year, Minns of Bournemouth was the only west country instrument dealer placing a box advertisement (for guitars, drumkits, and amplifiers).[304]

These businesses were in the three largest west country conurbations, but a fruitful equation of talent, fashion, and opportunity might arise anywhere that conditions of support pertained. Up to a point these conditions were probably still middle-class in the welfare-state Britain of the 1950s and '60s – a bedroom of one's own, a living room that parents could vacate for band practice, not just a record player but a guitar or amplifier as Christmas present, a white-collar job with sufficient leisure and pay to buy an old van and take it on the road. But that class was broad and reasonably porous, though it would be good to ascertain how many groups were formed from boys attending 'secondary moderns' as opposed to grammar schools. In accounts such as Sowden's, it is striking how often the school and the church youth club provided the nexus, along with Bill Greenhalgh's music shop in Fore Street, Exeter, in his volume on that area. Sadly, it is also striking how many young musicians from and in the region were killed in car crashes while driving long distances home from gigs in the days prior to easy and acceptable hotel accommodation in Britain, prior to seatbelt and alcohol laws, and prior to at least a few decent roads. In 1974 Adge Cutler, founder of the Wurzels, died at a roundabout in Chepstow after a concert, aged forty-three. The most famous of such casualties, the American rock star Eddie Cochran, however, was being driven when his car hit a lamp-post opposite some 1930s houses in a Chippenham suburb in April 1960. Visiting by chance at the fiftieth anniversary, I found bouquets propped up against a garden fence at this spot.

Clearly, in their earlier days pop and rock were not in themselves urban youth culture in the sense we now understand it, let alone urban subculture, that holy grail of musical authenticity ever since New Orleans created jazz and Buenos Aires the tango. Was it the demographic changes of ethnic immigration and youth mobility and the socio-economic revolution of consumer choice that turned them into something bohemian? For it is clear that on a curve between the 1960s and the 1990s, a west country town's guidebook attractions went from being golf clubs, churches, bowling greens,

[304] *MM*, 2 Jan 1960: 12, 14, 16 Dec 1961: 30.

parks, and hotels to restaurants and cafes, folk clubs, gay clubs, and rock, rave, and hip-hop venues, and that they ceased to be aimed at the older members of a family. The younger ones now had the leisure and the money, and the cultural authority for ways of spending them. The cultural equation that for three hundred years had seen music oil the wheels of voluntary association in glee clubs, Freemasonry, and all manner of charitable and mutual organisations now broke down into a series of self-identifications with music as a matter of individual freedom, personal choice being as important a tenet as the electoral vote. In a global age, the music venue, the restaurant, and the urban ghetto are the sounds, tastes, and topographies of democracy.

It should not surprise us that Bristol, with its intricate three-dimensional geography of uptown and downtown neighbourhoods, its long history as a port city, and its gateway status, should have bred a 'sound' of lasting capitalisation. It is not simply a matter of immigrant communities and a strong and early African-Caribbean presence, for the brand could in fact be thought of as at least two triumphing sounds or tribal 'scenes', folk and trip hop, if the former takes in the rural hinterland.[305] It might, however, be a matter of marginalised places, Adge Cutler coming from unglamorous Nailsea and trip hop (the Bristol sound) from run-down St Paul's parish in Bristol city.

Any relationship between these two musics would involve a hazardous and recalcitrant critique, for who would risk a comparison of the Wurzels and Massive Attack, beyond the obvious contrast of the good humour, alcoholic cheer, and major tonalities of the one and the deadly seriousness, narcotic melancholia, and predominantly minor–3rd modes of the other?[306] Yet Phil Johnson's account of the Bristol sound tackles the mystery of subculture's emergence using precisely these co-ordinates:

> Trying to find reasons for the sudden growth of a new musical culture in Bristol is a difficult business. You could, admittedly, draw a line between Acker Bilk (from nearby Pensford), Adge Cutler and the Wurzels and Massive Attack or Tricky, but it would be a very blurred one. The move from cider to spliff as the drug of choice would also have to be accommodated, though Massive have met the Wurzels and talk admiringly of their alleged appetite for stimulants in the old days. There's not even an equivalent to Liverpool's beat boom to bridge the gap; the Avon must have been the only major river in

---

[305] Jones 2009 and Johnson 1996: passim.
[306] Wurzels TW nd; MAC 2006.

Britain not to have a sound named after it and ... Russ Conway was probably the last Bristolian prior to Massive Attack to see any sustained chart action.[307]

In acceptance of Johnson's blurred line, it becomes less evident that popular success in music in welfare-state Britain can be binarised into folk and rock. At this point, Bilk (1929–2014) and Conway (1925–2000) exact further consideration, with a third Bristol star of the second half of the twentieth century, Fred Wedlock (1942–2010), added in for good measure.

What they, the Wurzels, and the Bristol sound (pre-eminently Massive Attack, Portishead, and Tricky) all have in common are two things. First, their fame consisted in recorded hits – singles or albums – and was thus directly dependent on the talent-spotting and promotion of the music industry, which entailed branding and the identification of some unique element, aural but, in the age of television and then pop video, visual as well. A good deal of the earlier branding was taken over from the variety tradition: tropes of yokel humour in the case of the Wurzels, who made great play with the idea of Bristol as some kind of sump for rural types (as in 'I wish I were back on the farm'), a more suburban and updated comedy in Wedlock's guitar-accompanied songs, jazz-band nostalgia with a hint of the bohemian (bowler hat, striped waistcoat) behind Bilk and his clarinet, and cocktail-lounge suavity for the handsome but shy Russ Conway, whose TV producers told him to smile at the viewers at bar 16 of whatever piece he was playing and whose effect on his female and gay male ones was devastating.[308] Conway (real name Trevor Stanford) peaked first, with two No. 1 British singles hits in 1959, his signature tune 'Side saddle' plus 'Roulette', 'Side saddle' remaining in position for four weeks. Bilk's 'Stranger on the shore' for solo clarinet and instrumental accompaniment followed in 1961–62, reaching only No. 2 in Britain but No. 1 in the USA. The following decade saw the Wurzels' 'The combine harvester', a *contrafactum* of the American singer Melanie's *risqué* song about roller skates, 'Brand new key', at No. 1 in Britain in 1976. Wedlock's 'The oldest swinger in town' reached No. 6 in Britain in 1981. It is less easy to pin numerical fame on subcultural trip hop, but Massive Attack's 'Unfinished sympathy' 'has frequently been described as one of the best songs of all time' (meaning the time of recorded western popular music).[309]

---

[307] Johnson 1996: 45.
[308] YouTube: 'Un-edited version – Adge Cutler and the Wurzels "Back on the farm"'; Russ Conway obituary, *Daily Telegraph*, 17 Nov 2000: 2, 31.
[309] Wikipedia: 'Lists of UK Singles Chart number ones', 'List of *Billboard* Hot 100 number-one singles of 1962', 'Bristol underground scene'.

Second, these five manifestations of popular success, they and their confreres supreme musicians all, owed nothing or very little to the institutional training paths of music. Most of them were working class and had irregular early careers. Bilk, born in what was by then a declining mining community (Pensford), worked in Wills's tobacco factory in Bristol, Cutler in Nailsea's cider factory, though both did other jobs over time. Bilk's first clarinet was borrowed and did not even have a reed until a friend fashioned a makeshift one. Conway grew up in what is now a comfortable-looking house in Southville to a father who was a clerk, but appears to have been an unruly youth who spent three years in institutional care ('Borstal'), though reliable biographical information on his childhood seems difficult to come by. Both Bilk and Conway, of an age to be called up for national service, honed their musical skills during spare time in the armed forces, Bilk in the Royal Engineers, Conway in the Royal Navy, where he was decorated, and afterwards in the merchant service. Wedlock, of a younger generation and probably a more secure background (his father ran a Bristol city pub), went to university, though not to study music, and became a teacher. The exception to this self-made musical status was yet again boyhood participation in the church choir or at least its establishment: Wedlock was a chorister at St Mary Redcliffe, Conway won a scholarship to Bristol Cathedral School. Conway, Cutler, Wedlock, and presumably Bilk had Bristol or north Somerset accents, but Robert del Naja, the leading force behind Massive Attack, does not, for his father (another publican) was an immigrant from Naples and del Naja was sent to a Roman Catholic school, where it would have been trained out of him, but as a denizen of inner-city Bristol his demotic credentials have been defined by geographical solidarity and bohemian activity, one assumes never encompassing a 'respectable' career aspiration, if he ever 'worked' at all. Like his world-famous Bristol contemporary Banksy, who acknowledges his influence, del Naja began as a graffiti artist, one of the four manifestations of hip-hop. Tricky, meanwhile, brought up a black boy in a poor white suburb, Knowle West (and Bristol's poor white suburbs have become notorious), like Conway spent time detained at Her Majesty's pleasure.[310]

Conway should be credited with the first Bristol sound – did he invent it during his long lonely hours in Borstal? – for what he discovered was brilliant. He took the elements of stride piano, with its rich texture in the tenor register that includes both the binding 10th above the bass and the

---

[310] Wikipedia: 'Acker Bilk', 'Russ Conway', 'Adge Cutler', 'Robert del Naja', 'Tricky (musician)', 'Fred Wedlock'; Blue plaques; *Guardian* online, 13 Jun 2008.

full weak-beat 'pah' chord of the 'oompah' formula, and realigned the 10th rhythmically so that the one for the next beat is caught by the thumb at the very end of the preceding weak beat on the hand's way back down to the bass, with the advantage that the bass is then precisely on the beat. This 'back-tenth' was not entirely unknown in earlier pianists such as Fats Waller, but direct influence seems unlikely: Conway did it faster, without swing, and in a different context. It accounts for the unique richness and catchiness of his honky-tonk style; it is counterintuitive, formidably difficult for already formed pianists to master, and requires steely nerve, perfect rhythmic control, and masterly pedalling.[311]

Yet Conway was still mainstream culture; nor did he have a band, or make his career attached to Bristol, unlike Bilk, whose success was consolidated with his Bristol Paramount Jazz Band, albeit operating from London. By contrast, the Wurzels' reference points could not have been more local, with songs such as 'Pill Pill', 'Sunny Weston-super-Mare', 'Virtuet industrial' (a satire on Bristol's motto), 'Down in Nempnett Thrubwell', 'When the Common Market comes to Stanton Drew', 'The Shepton Mallet matador', 'Rock around the A38', and so on, with a holiday outlier in 'Mevagissey'.[312] One obvious reason for this geographical specificity will have been that for the most part it paralleled the particularity and seclusion of the venues in which the songs were heard, village halls and pubs. If you wanted to hear Robin Teague's Blue Vinney Folk Band in the summer of 1974, for example, you went to the Anchor Inn in the tiny hamlet of Seatown in Dorset, where they were playing three times a week within sound of the dragging shingle.[313]

Subculture returned music from the nationwide dimensions of the variety equation, stronger than ever in the age of television, to complete personal identification with a local venue. Was this because subculture was synonymous with resistance to authority and its manifestations had to be hidden away – because it was 'underground', literally so in the case of the west country's most important locale, the Dug Out Club in Bristol? Wary though Ruth Finnegan was of sociologists' apotheosis of subculture in music, the term can still be made to resonate, if sometimes away from their favourite concerns.[314] The back bar of an English pub, while hardly invisible, had for centuries been a model for subculture, be it the gathering place for smugglers or retired pirates *à la Treasure Island* or simply the room

---

[311] Thomson 2010.
[312] Wurzels TW nd, tracks 1–6, 10–11.
[313] Teague 2008: 98–9.
[314] Finnegan 2007: 121–3.

where the male community's more bawdy traditional songs would be heard, well away from the vicar's earshot. In repressive political regimes, cabaret provided the formula for forbidden musical satire, just as in Prohibition USA the speakeasy associated jazz with alcohol. A port city pub neighbourhood would be a locus for prostitution, while long after legalisation a gay club would provide safe and stimulating dancing behind a black-painted closed door with a tiny wicket. As for what eventually became the biggest rock venue in the south-west, the Cornwall Coliseum at Carlyon Bay (demolished in 2015), its emphasis on heavy metal could hardly be called subcultural when commercialised in such a context, but what one imagines was negotiated on its adjacent beach at night, be it drugs or sex, might be.[315] Subculture in clear opposition to societal norms would at its height embody itself in the rave venues and traveller festivals of the 1980s, often arranged on the grapevine to circumvent police intervention; Cornish ones have been well covered by Alan Kent, as has the later techno and house music of north Cornwall's surfing subculture by Philip Hayward.[316] If we turn back to the liberated 1960s, in Bristol and other cities subcultural music had organised itself as jazz, folk, or rock in 'dives' that the parents of their young *habitués* will have deplored as dens of narcotic iniquity, whether or not they really were. Such identification with transgression was sufficient in itself to make the music exciting, and even today a comedy club hosts stand-up humour a little too sharp for mainstream environments and a crucial element of both the songs and the spoken repartee that characterised artists like Fred Wedlock.

But just as with Harlem in the 1930s, it was probably no accident that Bristol spent its subcultural money exactly 'where the underworld meets the elite', on the borderland of downtown and Clifton, for the Dug Out was at 54 Park Row, on the edge of the University precinct, right opposite what is now a symbol of civic respectability, the Merchant Venturers Building, and only a few yards from the little statue of Nipper the HMV dog. At the other end of Clifton and of subculture's musical spectrum was the Bristol Troubadour in Waterloo Street, a folk club ('the most famous and influential … outside London') which flourished between 1966 and 1971.[317] Such venues benefit from or produce musical figureheads. Cyril Tawney (1930–2005), often viewed as the father of the west country folk revival, turned the Plymouth Folk Song Club into the West of England Folk Centre. This was in January 1965, and Tawney's manifesto hardly reads like subculture: 'Apart

---

[315] Wikipedia: 'Cornwall Coliseum'; Kent 2007a: 230–2.
[316] Kent 2007a: 233; Hayward 2009.
[317] Anderson 2012.

from Cecil Sharp House in London ... the Plymouth Folk Centre will be the only one of its kind in England, a place which will accommodate folk singing, folk dancing, films, lectures, instructional courses, and many other similar activities related to folk culture, as well as housing eventually a library and record collection together with an archive of field recordings to be undertaken by the Centre itself'. It struggled, and it is not clear how long it survived.[318] The Bristol Troubadour's leading light, Ian Anderson, who founded the folk record company Village Thing, based in Clifton, was testifying to subculture's inevitable tendency to become something else with time when interviewed about his intended move away from Bristol in 1972:

> He explained that he needed to live within contact of a constant flow of music. Bristol was no longer providing this and he would hate to return to living in London. The ideal compromise was to live near enough to the capital to benefit from its musical assets without being involved in its bustle. 'We've got ourselves lumbered with being a West Country record company [Village Thing], which we've never set out to be', he explained. 'It just so happens that there's been more good artists living in the West Country than anywhere else for a while.'[319]

Eight years later, St Paul's erupted with the first of a spate of race riots in the UK when another subcultural venue, though not a musical one, the aptly named Black and White Café, was raided for drugs. By the end of the 1970s it was essential for white youths of any subcultural pretension to show solidarity with blacks, regardless of how violent such a venue might actually be (this one, raided more often than any other UK premises, was eventually demolished in 2004), and regardless of the fact that only two white youths took part in the St Paul's riot.[320] At that same time the Dug Out was flourishing, prior to being itself closed by the disgruntled traders of Park Street in 1986. Opinions differ as to whether the races really mixed there, but they certainly wanted to be seen together, and its musical programme was a vital ingredient in the complex network of bands, sound systems, and individuals that formed and re-formed in subcultural Bristol – Thomas Götz's *Stadt und Sound* contains a mind-boggling but indispensable graphic diagram of this web – eventually to reach global fame with Massive Attack, Portishead, Reprazent (these three a 'holy trinity' according to Peter Webb), and Tricky.[321] At least one commentator has been keen to emblematise Massive

---

[318] PFSFSC: Plymouth Folk Song Club, letters to members, Jan and Aug 1965.
[319] Means 1972.
[320] Johnson 1996: 40–4; Wikipedia: 'Black and White Café'.
[321] Johnson 1996: 48–59; Götz 2006: 49; Webb 2007: 52.

Illus. 3.5 Massive Attack, 1998: Andrew Vowles (left), Robert del Naja (centre), Grant Marshall (right). Photo by Hidekazu Shimizu.

Attack's racial mix: 'There's a satisfying visual rhyme in the appearances of Massive Attack. Grant Marshall (Daddy G, or G for short) is very tall and very dark; Robert Del Naja (3D, D, Delge) is small, white and blonde. And ... like the product of some strange union between the other two, is the medium-tall, light-brown Andrew Vowles (Mushroom).'[322] (Illus. 3.5.)

This leaves consideration of the Bristol sound's musical blend. It has been called 'sad hip hop ... not provocative ... not rebellious ... not about protest ... just very down-to-earth', though this undervalues the sheer weirdness of the Bristol Channel towns – Portishead, Clevedon, Weston-super-Mare,

[322] Johnson 1996: 90.

Watchet, Minehead, Lynton, Ilfracombe – as social and architectural archaeology, a group of places whose upstream *fons et origo* lent its name to the second of the trip hop bands, its members Geoff Barrow, who grew up in Portishead, Beth Gibbons as vocalist, and Adrian Utley. 'Isn't it just like you British', the American record producer Guy Eckstine commented to Phil Johnson, 'to take something so essentially happy and upbeat as hip-hop, and make it all damp and foggy, like Portishead'.[323] *Musique noire* might be a suitable descriptor, and film music, especially for strings, has certainly been a strong ingredient in trip hop's aural identity, along with subdued rapping, cool reggae-influenced rhythms, a sparse and original placement of *objets trouvés* as sampling, female vocals in an anorexic head voice, minor-key soul harmonies, and a notably strong bass. (The stranded bass G sharps in Massive Attack's 'Live with me' [2006] are masterly.)[324] Whether, consciously or subconsciously, the Bristol sound reflects the city's awareness of a 200-year decline, its greater, guiltier awareness of the slave trade that gave it its earlier prosperity, or its peculiarly melancholic building style of grey and purple sandstone would be impossible to determine. No more easy to tease out is the Bristol sound's ongoing relation to local culture. The concept 'glocalisation' would seem to apply, not in the sense of a global brand adapted to place (McDonald's recipes adjusted in acknowledgement of local food traditions), but in the opposite sense, as posited by the sociologist Roland Robertson: local production or groundedness with global reach, something of a philosopher's stone for the arts in all ages.[325] Yet as early as 1996, Johnson could point to complaints that the trip hop stars and their bands rarely if ever played in Bristol.[326] One is reminded of Robert Pearsall, composing 'Lay a garland' in Karlsruhe for the Bristol Madrigal Society but with no intention of returning to live in his native city.[327] If 'Live with me', with American guest vocalist Terry Callier, proves as perfect and emotionally durable a piece of music as 'Lay a garland', as well it may, the west country will be foolish not to claim it and the band for its own.

---

[323] Götz 2006: 25; Johnson 1996: 151–4, 157.
[324] MAC 2006, track 14.
[325] Götz 2006: 19.
[326] Johnson 1996: 27–8.
[327] Hunt 1977: 26–7.

CHAPTER 4

Musical Livings I: The Prosopography

✽ Introduction

AT WHITSUN 1610 a minstrel from Nailsea, John Stretting or Streating, was booked to play at Clevedon, five miles away, the next settlement of any size across the north Somerset levels. Clevedon's festivities must have been continuing through the week, for he left home on the Tuesday and was not expected back until the next day or the day after. Unfortunately for his wife Grace, he had forgotten his 'box of strings', and, returning with another man late on the Tuesday night to retrieve it, found a half undressed interloper in the house. The wife was sent packing to her father and money changed hands to appease the offended husband.[1]

No doubt he was reluctant to include songs about cuckolds in his repertoire thereafter, for the affair got abroad. But we cannot be sure that he sang in any case. In fact we know precious little about him. Did he play the harp, lute, or fiddle? Where would he have got his strings from? How much would the Clevedon parishioners have paid him, and what exactly would he have contributed to the Whitsun ale? Was he part of a band, or alone? *Was* he booked, or did he just turn up as a busker? If the former – for there is evidence of high demand for and planned acquisition of musicians' services – how far ahead would he have been secured, by whom, and by what method of communication? Could he read? Did he keep an engagement diary? Was he a trained musician, and did that mean that he was literate in music notation? What else did he do, or was this his full-time occupation? Did he keep his box of strings in his instrument case? If not, it seems less likely that he had genuinely forgotten such a crucial item of luggage and more possible that, already suspicious, he did it on purpose and made sure he had a witness to hand.

---

[1] Stokes 1996: 176, 915.

It is not just time that has obscured our knowledge of Stretting's livelihood and performance practice; as already indicated in chapter 3, we might ask many of the same questions about a twentieth-century band musician without expecting to find easy answers. Informal musical culture leaves only scattered biographical, economic, and administrative traces. Yet the secular musical culture of which Stretting was part was by no means entirely informal, and we can in fact begin to answer some of the questions curiosity poses about the background to one early modern citizen's cameo role in regional history. Data is not lacking; it is the scholarship that has been in short supply, as John Stevens already noted in 1961 when he raised many of these same questions in an essay on 'Professional musicians' and was able to pronounce on quite a few of them.[2] Stevens apart, musicologists have probably been discouraged by the lumping together of 'herbalists, charlatans, minstrels, jugglers, and tumblers' in one chapter of Jusserand's *English Wayfaring Life in the Middle Ages* or by Frank Harrison's much later assertion, in a book boldly entitled *Music in Medieval Britain*, that since 'nothing identifiable as minstrel music has survived', the history of minstrelsy 'belongs to the study of social life and customs rather than of actual music'.[3] Harrison, to whom 'actual music' meant surviving notated repertoire, accordingly dealt only with sacred music and its institutions. True, the practising musician would love to know what Stretting performed and what it sounded like but cannot begin to find out. Today's music historian barks up a different tree, however, and can hope to dislodge a number of squirrels.

James Stokes interprets Stretting's absence as one of more than a week, covering two Tuesdays. Unless he was including a number of towns and villages in a single tour, this seems unlikely, for the church ale, most commonly held at Whitsun, represented the peak of an annual parish festivity season which, although by Stretting's time much subject to post-Reformation decline and discontinuation, still lasted traditionally from Easter until midsummer. With the possible exception of Christmas and new year, no period in the calendar had greater call for secular musicians, and a church ale must have been as unthinkable without music as a bride-ale, namely a wedding reception, today. With every parish dancing, drinking, and fundraising in the churchyard or church house during the same extended weekend, where were all the musicians to come from? Clevedon's call on Stretting on Tuesday and Wednesday probably means that he had

---

[2] Stevens 1961: 296–328.
[3] Jusserand 1905: 177–218; Harrison 1963: xiii–xiv. Rastall 1968 remains the most sustained treatment of secular music in England in the middle ages.

been somewhere more important, that is, lucrative, on Sunday and Monday. Musical demand must have far outstripped supply for Whitsun ales.

It should not surprise us, therefore, that thanks above all to *Records of Early English Drama*, the names of 250 or more secular musicians (i.e. not in church employment) in the west country are known from the mid-fourteenth century to 1642. Their unnamed peers based in the region must amount to several times this number from records of parish and borough payments alone, and musicians attached to troupes of travelling actors, to ships, and to visiting nobility and royalty swell the total a great deal further, though incalculably. This makes it difficult to argue that hearing paid-for music, instrumental probably even more than vocal, was a rare thing for the late mediaeval or early modern dweller in the region, though it may still be true that sacred music of the parish liturgy remained 'the only regular, formal musical experience for perhaps half the population of England', as Temperley claims.[4]

Clearly, there were livings to be made. But how many, where, of how much money, and on what terms of sustainability? In the remainder of this chapter, the starting point will be the careers that secular musicians have had to create for themselves in a variety of times and places, although the patronage of the Church will enter the equation from time to time, to be further explored institutionally in chapter 7.

The best framework for answering the above questions is in terms of how musicians sought what little security they could hope for – for, as Woodfill pointed out, 'Few musicians have steady jobs bringing them reasonably adequate and dependable incomes; in sixteenth and seventeenth century England this aristocracy included chiefly members of the King's Musick, some waits, and servants in the households of noblemen and gentlemen.'[5] The first of these categories was inapplicable in the west country, and, as we shall see, the third appears not to have been prominent. With this in mind, the quest for security can be said to have been against four odds. There was the high level of seasonable fluctuation in demand; secular musicians were of dubious and confined status and especially in a period of violent political and religious change could all too frequently find themselves on the wrong side of the law; they were as subject to bad health, accident, and natural disaster as the rest of the population; and they had to compete for finite resources. In counteracting these disadvantages, secular musicians adopted six strategies, often using several in combination. First, they could seek permanent

---

[4] Temperley 1979, i: xvii.
[5] Woodfill 1953: 3.

patronage, from the nobility or from civic authorities. Second, they could take the career path of qualification, in the early modern period that of apprenticing themselves to a master in a particular borough, a process which would on redemption make them freemen of that place with all the privileges entailed. Third, they could build up a freelance portfolio and practise as broadly as possible within their art, for example by combining performing and teaching with instrument making and composition, or by combining sacred employment of one kind with secular of another. Fourth, they could make music only a part of their livelihood, combining it with some other trade or occupation or keeping it as a pastime generating supplementary income and/or status. Fifth, they might consolidate a family business or tradition, thereby formalising the networks that were in any case crucial to a successful living. And sixth, they could choose where to live, which might amount to fixing on a place where the demand might be steady and supply was non-existent, to moving to a key city or to the metropolis, or, conversely, to wandering the region or beyond. Since most of these conditions and lifeways continued to apply well beyond the middle ages and early modern era and may to a certain recognisable extent still be applicable even today, they will be examined in turn.

Before this is done, the vagaries of a secular musical living must not be overstated. Already in the middle ages there were plenty of musicians who successfully pursued their occupation for a lengthy period in the same place, and indeed the same job, without known interruption. In the early fifteenth century, John Lynde was one of the Exeter waits for twenty years or more, from 1415 or earlier to 1435 or after.[6] Again in Exeter, a trumpeter, no doubt Spanish or Italian in origin and probably called Alfonso – they never did get the name right – was called upon and paid by the borough for his services on sundry occasions from 1402 until at least 1430.[7] Waits who served thirty years or more include John Dawe or Dow (Exeter, 1427–64 or longer), Robert Beaumont (Exeter, 1467–97 or longer), William Johnson (Bristol, 1596–1627 or longer), and John Medland (Exeter, 1602 or earlier to 1640) – and if in some of these cases one allows for the possibility that a son or nephew of the same name took over without being referred to as such, that merely demonstrates another mode of continuity.[8] The strength and societal importance of institutional patronage in the sacred sphere makes somewhat less noteworthy the fact that church musicians remained in

---

[6] Wasson 1986: 360, 371.
[7] ibid: 353–67.
[8] ibid: 365–77, 377–87, 178–204; Pilkinton 1997: 261–6.

position for just as long or longer. To take two cathedral organists, John Lugg was at Exeter from 1603 until the post was discontinued in the mid-1640s, and Giles Tomkins at Salisbury from 1630 until his death in 1667, managing to remain in the choristers' house right through the Commonwealth period of discontinued choral services.[9] John Silver the younger was organist of Wimborne Minster from 1664 until his death thirty years later.[10] In later times, those organists toughened rather than overwhelmed by the damp and draught in their places of employment might serve more than half a century in the same post, as did Harry Moreton in Plymouth, mentioned in chapter 2. Thomas Hyde was at Sherborne Abbey from 1776 to 1838, James Parfitt, blind from infancy, at Shepton Mallet parish church from 1800 or 1801 to 1856, Matthew Clemens at Fore St Methodist Church, Redruth, from 1887 to 1940; George Barrett remained at Holy Trinity, Hotwells, and Herbert Worth at St Mary's, Totnes, respectively for fifty-two and fifty-one years in the nineteenth century and Janet Hardwick Head at St Mary's, Yatton, for over sixty years in the twentieth. John Davis Corfe was organist of Bristol Cathedral from 1825 until his death in 1876, though he could not beat the record of his father Arthur Thomas Corfe at Salisbury Cathedral, where he was organist from 1804 to 1863.[11] Perkins, father and son, notched up seventy-eight consecutive years at Wells Cathedral (1781–1859).[12] Bath Abbey required only two successive organists in almost a century, between 1839 and 1933: James Kendrick Pyne (fifty-three years) followed by Albert Edward New (forty-three years, including a two-year overlap). Lay clerks singing for a half-century might seem a more alarming proposition, but it did happen. Another member of the Barrett family of Bristol, Slater, was in the cathedral choir for over fifty years, as possibly was Thomas Trimnell, described as 'the oldest lay clerk', though they had retired him on a pension some years before his death in 1865.[13] Joseph Potter at Exeter was still singing 'a weak bass' aged over seventy in the 1830s (and had never seen the sea until the younger lay clerks took him to Exmouth).[14]

---

[9] Bowers et al 2006: 24–5; Payne 2004; Matthews Sal: 16.
[10] Matthews and Spink 2001.
[11] George Tatham, personal communication; plaque in church; Michell 1985: 113; Brown and Stratton 1897: 31; plaque in church; plaque on organ; Matthews 2001b: 464.
[12] Bowers et al 2006: 34–6.
[13] Brown and Stratton 1897: 30–1, 417.
[14] Spark 1888: 431–3.

Illus. 4.1 Monument to Matthew Godwin, organist of Exeter Cathedral, 1587

Staying put may in many cases have indicated a life of steadfastness or quiescence against a background of little change (or, conversely, great change), but not always. Richard Henman held the post of organist of Exeter Cathedral for forty-seven years from 1694 despite admonishment within a year of taking up office and frequent recurrence thereof on later occasions for absence and bad language (he was the penultimate in an unbroken succession of six dubious incumbents of the Exeter position).[15] Elway Bevin survived more than fifty years as organist of Bristol Cathedral from his appointment in 1585, only to be dismissed in 1637 or 1638, not for being a Catholic spy as used to be maintained, but for incapacity. It must have been an unpleasant three or four years for all concerned if it took that long to get rid of him after Archbishop Laud's Bristol visitation of 1634 had pinpointed his old age and

[15] Matthews Exe: 24; Shaw 1991: 110–13.

the cathedral's declining musical standards.[16] On a different front entirely, a troublesome family of fiddlers from Holt near Wimborne named Bright alias Lucas was being hauled up in front of the authorities for this or that misdemeanour, such as playing on Sunday or in service time, in 1591 and continued to be thirty years later.[17]

Young and presumably ambitious musicians did often move around before settling down, as they have continued to do. Bevin was a vicar choral at Wells Cathedral for six years prior to his Bristol appointment, and the prodigious teenager Matthew Godwin, 'a pious, gentle, and clever youth' who nevertheless had influential relatives in both places, was organist of Canterbury Cathedral before moving on to Exeter, where he survived only two years, dying at the age of seventeen and a half in 1587 and occasioning in the cathedral what is probably the first monument to a musician in England. There he kneels among music books and (his?) instruments: organ, lute, cittern, cornett, and trumpet (Illus. 4.1).[18] But clearly the default position, in a society infinitely more closed than ours and remaining so in many respects up to and through much of the nineteenth century, was to stay where one was. However difficult we may find it to inhabit such a mindset now, it becomes easier to understand when the risks and rewards of a musical livelihood in the west country, as indeed in any English region, are more fully explored.

❧ *Patronage*

The west country has seldom been noted for lavish patronage of the arts. The author Ronald Duncan, Britten's librettist for *The Rape of Lucretia* in 1946 and therefore fully aware of what patronage in that most expensive of art forms, opera, could achieve in a moment of national confidence, lived in Devon and suggested that nature's bounty there had made spiritual striving unnecessary: 'many Devonians appear to do no more than watch the grass grow … And why is it they so seldom sing? Is it that they are so spoiled by nature that they are bored by her? They tolerate this good fortune rather like a man who, married to a beautiful wife, is both faithful and indifferent' – a complacency nevertheless difficult to square with the spirit of the great Devon adventurers Drake, Hawkins, Grenville, and Raleigh, who did indeed patronise

---

[16] Brown and Stratton 1897: 45; Barlow 2004; Bettey 2007: 58–70.
[17] Hays and McGee 1999: 283–7, 363.
[18] Hooper 2001: 497; Matthews Exe: 22; Cherry and Pevsner 1989: 383; Woodfill 1953: between 48 and 49; Little 1983: 39.

shipboard musicians, as we have seen.[19] Be that as it may, of the thirty-six English renaissance composers who either published a volume of madrigals or contributed to Morley's *Triumphs of Oriana*, only one of them was based in the west country, where no aristocratic estate matched the employment of John Wilbye, George Kirbye, Henry Youll, and Edward Johnson in rural Suffolk. This was John Holmes, lay vicar and master of the choristers (but not organist) at Salisbury Cathedral from 1621 until his death in 1629 and composer of the solitary 'Thus Bonny-boots the birthday celebrated'.[20] Nor does consideration of published books of lute songs alter the picture (though instrumental music does, as mentioned below). At that time, making one's mark as a secular composer based in the provinces without such patronage was virtually impossible, as the sycophantic dedication pages of madrigalists' volumes amply demonstrate.

Evidence of what one might call petty patronage of individuals is not hard to find. In the past two hundred years, investment in musical people by way of calculated risk has frequently taken the form of sponsorship of their education and training, such as when the opera singer Fanny Moody, who came from a modest though musical family in Redruth, attracted the patronage of Mrs Basset of Tehidy, who not only paid for her metropolitan lessons with Charlotte Sainton-Dolby but made sure to take her 'to various "at homes" in London', which was equally important.[21] (Basset was the widow of one of Cornwall's biggest landowners, and it was the Harley Street salon of Lady Morell Mackenzie that afforded Moody her breakthrough.[22]) A different branch of the Basset family, that of Watermouth Castle in north Devon, offers one of countless instances in which the name and good offices of the local gentry were lent to good musical causes such as the foundation and running of a local choral society (in this case Barnstaple's), by chairing committees, appearing on letterheads and programmes, pulling strings, and making the odd donation in kind or in money as required.[23] This probably still happens.

Prior to the nineteenth century, performing musicians were simply servants, and in the early modern period many of the west country aristocracy and some of its wealthier citizens will have kept one. In 1477-78, William Greville was described as 'Lord FitzWarin's minstrel' when he

---

[19] Duncan 1966: 22.
[20] le Huray and Morehen 2001: 644; Payne 2003; the count of composers is taken from Sternfeld and Greer 1967.
[21] Michell 1985: 165.
[22] Graves 1958: 558.
[23] Edwards 1917: 9–10.

performed in Barnstaple, FitzWarin, the 2nd earl, being Fulk Bourchier, from the ancient north Devon family of that name.[24] Greville turns up repeatedly in the Barnstaple records, and probably lived there. He was a harper, and since he had his own servant, John Magge, separately paid by the Barnstaple civic authorities, he was no doubt blind, as many harpers were.[25] When a minstrel did travel, 'awareness that … travelling players were playing a role in an elaborate patronage system' will have made both the receiving towns and the sending aristocrats of such minstrels eager for liveried visibility and the accomplishment of gracious exchange.[26] One never knew when a town or indeed a lord might need protection. Even if Greville was not locally domiciled, 130 years later William Moore, described as 'lute servant' of Sir Amos Bampfield and Sir John Acland, surely was, in order for him to be able to make the transition to Exeter town wait at the agreement of both parties, replacing a deceased member.[27] When it comes to the merchant class it is fully likely that their household musician(s) would remain on hand. The listing of an old pair of virginals, two citterns, and a rebec or violin in 'the servants chamber' of the late Richard Brace of Bristol in 1642 suggests that he could afford to keep a musician as one of his domestic servants. Brace was a physician.[28]

In all this, however, it is difficult to know how peripatetic 'kept' musicians were and how much of an occupation their music was (for many of them will have had other domestic duties as their and their employers' primary concern). Was there any really grand patronage, definable as the determination to create artistic monumentality in music, in the west country? Its apparent dearth cannot be the whole truth, yet Walter Woodfill warned many decades ago of the general lack of evidence, nationwide, for permanently retained professional musicians in noble households: John Wilbye was possibly an almost unique exception in his time.[29] Several country estates in the west nevertheless bear investigation. First, the young Sir Richard Champernowne kept a fine consort, it is assumed at Modbury in Devon, and it was even rumoured that he had castrated boy trebles in order to preserve their voices; he certainly traded boy singers with his cousin Sir Robert Cecil. So fine was his band, indeed, that when he declined to lend

---

[24] Wasson 1986: 343.
[25] ibid: 340.
[26] Hays and McGee 1999: 42, quoting Blackstone 1988: 118.
[27] Wasson 1986: 180–1.
[28] Pilkinton 1997: lxi, 246.
[29] Woodfill 1953: 59–70.

its services to Queen Elizabeth I she exacted her revenge by ruining him.[30] Whether the lutenist Antony Holborne was party to any of this we cannot tell: the dedication of his book of dances *Pavans, Galliads, Almains* (1599) might imply that he was Champernowne's teacher and had been resident at Modbury.[31] Second, Sir Philip Sidney's sister Mary, a fine musician and well-known poet, was married to the 2nd earl of Pembroke, Henry Herbert, and lived at Wilton House, where she cultivated a hugely productive and important literary salon.[32] Her son William, the 3rd earl, was no less significant a patron of the arts, including music, to judge from the large number of publications dedicated to him, Tomkins and Dowland among their composers; moreover, he was a favourite of James I, who visited Wilton several times, as did Charles I.[33] It seems implausible that Wilton House lacked some kind of a resident musical establishment. Certainly one violinist later pre-eminent in London, Davis Mell, son of a violinist in Pembroke's employment, was born at Wilton, and it has been suggested that the young Henry Lawes was patronised by Pembroke at Wilton House, as was his younger brother William by Edward Seymour, earl of Hertford, probably in Seymour's house, Amesbury Abbey, a few miles north of Salisbury, where the master to whom Lawes was apprenticed, John Cooper ('Coprario'), was composer in residence.[34]

The tiny and long-decayed town of Wilton, its River Nadder spanned by the famous covered bridge in Wilton House's grounds, lies on an idyllic valley axis, with the village of Dinton, where Henry and possibly William Lawes were born, several miles to the west and Salisbury, where the Lawes brothers may have been choristers, a shorter distance to the east. Between Wilton and Salisbury is Bemerton, where Pembroke's non-aristocratic relation, the poet George Herbert, was rector from 1630 until his death in 1633. Pursuing a musical livelihood of a different sort, an amateur one (he was a lutenist, viol player, and singer), Herbert walked into Salisbury twice a week for cathedral evensong, after which he made music there with friends who no doubt included the cathedral lay vicars all too soon singing at his funeral in Bemerton.[35] This was musical patronage at one remove, the clerical living having been arranged through the King by Pembroke or his brother, who

---

[30] Waterfield 1946: 26; Holman 1993: 128.
[31] Spring 2001: 108; Price 1981: 173–4; Harwood 2004: 591.
[32] Hannay 2004: 709.
[33] Stater 2004: 740–3.
[34] Holman 2001b; Spink 2004b: 772; Pinto 2004: 778; Spink 2000: 4; Field 2001: 408; Lefkowitz 1960: 1–7.
[35] Payne 2003: 382–3.

got not quite the social equation they would have expected. On one occasion Herbert arrived for a musical session in a dishevelled state, having helped 'a poor man, with a poorer horse' on his way to Salisbury, but discountenanced the musicians' raised eyebrows with a defence of both his act and his art when he said, 'And now, let's tune our instruments.'[36] George Herbert was too late to have known William and Henry Lawes and the composer John Holmes at Salisbury, but quite likely made music with John's son Thomas, the Lawes's father Thomas, a singing man from Dinder, Somerset, who remained in the cathedral establishment for nearly forty years, and with Thomas Lawes junior, a Salisbury lay vicar who took his father's place when the latter was promoted to vicar choral.[37] William Madge was another Salisbury viol player at this time.[38]

George Herbert has come as close to Anglican sainthood as is possible, a model of the pastoral ideal in both its clerical and its rural sense, and thereby the epitome of the local. He offers a wry contrast with his distant kinsman behind the long wall of the Wilton estate, where the nurturing of local talent, as at Amesbury, gave nothing directly back to the community but whisked the Lawes brothers off to Court in London. It is important nevertheless to recognise that the triangulation of estate, Court, and obscure parish and a broader notion of retirement 'from Court to cottage' were already something of a social and literary topic in Herbert's time and thus emblematically conceived even while being acted out.[39]

At a different level from the destinies of the Lawes brothers, there is no doubt that local or regional musicians were given work on the great country estates, as our third example may indicate. This is Longleat, seat of the Thynnes and the first of the great Elizabethan 'prodigy houses'.[40] It may have taken decades for seigneurial preoccupation with the vast building works of the 1570s and 1580s to give way to the pursuit of music, but by the years 1605–10 Sir Thomas Thynne was buying a bass viol and song books, a lute, and a violin with livery for its performer, a man called Jake. There were also a resident trumpeter, a man called King paid to be trained up locally in fiddling by one Peter Wylie, and in 1612 the six-month residency of a lute teacher, Mr

---

[36] Wilcox 2004: 680–1; Smith et al 2001: 401.
[37] Spink 2000: 1–3; Robertson 1938: 167–71; Payne 2003: passim.
[38] Payne 2003: 383.
[39] See the self-personifications of Sir Henry Lee, Queen Elizabeth's champion, in lute-song texts set to music by John Dowland, 'His golden locks Time hath to silver turned' and 'Far from triumphing Court and wonted glory', reprinted in Sternfeld and Greer 1967: 464, 506.
[40] Pevsner and Cherry 1975: 308.

Wood. A lot of lute teaching took place at Longleat, and Wood remained there for a number of years, Lady Thynne his enthusiastic and generous pupil in 1617 when she gave him £10 for his tuition, a considerable sum. He must have been well connected, for he also hired John Daniel to teach family members, probably in London as Price speculates, though Daniel was born not far away, at Wellow, and may have married in the next village. It is quite possible that Wood was the John Wood from Dunster apprenticed for nine years to Geoffrey Hellier in Bristol in 1594, and that he knew Daniel from the region, though Daniel was a generation older. If so, Wood's employment beyond the city of his professional training might appear to be typical, for very few of the Bristol apprentices in music of this period feature in the city's subsequent annals.[41]

Lute teachers, closeted in ladies' boudoirs and no doubt privy to all manner of confidences whispered as the strings were fingered, represent a special kind of social permeability at this period, as would singing and piano teachers – and tuners – amid the country-house denizens of later ages. There was a lute teacher in Wells in 1607, William Tidderleigh, who arrived at the home of the schoolmaster William Evans to give Evans's daughter one of her lessons and was in receipt of some of the scurrilous verses circulating in the town, which he showed to Evans.[42] But attractive though this picture of musicians flitting in and out of the lives of their patrons may be, with the aristocratic estate it is the sense of seclusion and separation that remains uppermost, notwithstanding Bruce Smith's brilliant and persuasive reconstruction of an early modern soundscape that it shared with the village and countryside on those same terms of permeability, in this case aural.[43]

To give a fourth and later example of country-house patronage, the most intense isolation must have been that of the young Muzio Clementi on Peter Beckford's estate at Stepleton House in Iwerne, near Blandford. It seems extraordinary that this major European musician, the young Mozart's chief rival as a pianist, should have spent most of his teenage years (1766–74) closeted in rural Dorset without remotely developing the credentials to be considered a west country musician. He appears not even to have had a teacher there, though it is difficult to see how he can have graduated directly to a leading role in London's concert and theatre life – he naturally removed to the metropolis as soon as he was at liberty to do so – without having gained considerable orchestral experience while in Dorset, something

---

[41] Price 1981: 129–31; Greer 2004: 69; Pilkinton 1997: 261.
[42] Stokes 1996: 295.
[43] Smith 1999b: 71–83.

of which we have absolutely no record.[44] Here is a real geographical puzzle. On 14 July 1773, Johann Christian Bach was within four miles of Stepleton House, giving a concert in association with the Blandford races as one of a highly distinguished set of metropolitan performers.[45] Did they meet? Perhaps not, though Clementi's isolated circumstances should probably be taken with a pinch of salt, for Beckford would have been in London for many an occasion and no doubt took his young protégé with him at times. Nevertheless, Stepleton's archival silence reminds us that music's relationship to place, horse-racing concerts aside, could not yet begin to compete with that of sport, Beckford no doubt enjoying a genuine symbiosis with the local environment in his capacity as the first monographer of fox hunting and an expert on dog kennels.[46] Even Mozart, aged eight, and his father may have come and gone at nearby Fonthill, a year or so before Clementi arrived at Stepleton, without anybody local noticing.

Artistic patronage such as Peter Beckford's tasks the region with something different from local benefit. John Caldwell prefers to restrict the use of the term to financial investment through 'employment, or other assistance ... such as to afford a musician the leisure to compose works of permanent value', and would no doubt be happy in the case of Clementi to substitute for composition the attainment of performing virtuosity of European significance.[47] Not that composition should be excluded in Clementi's case: his six op 1 piano sonatas, presumably written at Stepleton and dedicated to Beckford, must be among the most wholeheartedly up-to-date embodiments of the classical style to be found in England at that time, original and attractive within their modest, presumably targeted limitations. All in all, music-lovers have much to thank Beckford for; but little if any of the culture's added value flowed back into Dorset. Not that any of it flowed back into Jamaica either, whose black slaves were the ultimate source of Beckford's wealth and Clementi's success.

Scarcely at a remove from music, it should not be forgotten, though it has been, that one of the biggest names in the Romantic movement in literature lived in the west country under aristocratic patronage: Tom Moore, he of the *Irish Melodies*. Probably because he was Irish, Catholic, and all too naturally gifted a musician (being a guitarist did not help), he has conveniently slipped through the net of regional recognition, though his influence on romantic

---

[44] anon 1820: 309–10; Plantinga and Tyson 2001: 39–40.
[45] Matthews 1967: 703.
[46] Southern 1925.
[47] Caldwell 1991: 347–8.

music as well as poetry, from popular song and folksong to grand opera, was immeasurable.[48] For thirty-five years, apart from a three-year period abroad on the run from debt, he lived at Sloperton Cottage in Bromham, Wiltshire, patronised by Lord Lansdowne of nearby Bowood House. He died at Sloperton.[49]

The west country's proudest and most organic example of grand musical patronage was James Harris (1709–80), who exercised his munificence not from an isolated country seat but in the heart of Salisbury, for he lived in Malmesbury House in the close, where Handel stayed and was present at a concert in 1739, held in the room above St Ann's Gate attached to the house.[50] Harris, who compiled the text for *L'allegro, il penseroso ed il moderato* which was then fashioned by Charles Jennens into Handel's libretto, was a classic enlightened dilettante and a classic English Handelian of Italianate taste.[51] This did not prevent him from furthering glees and catches in concerts and soirées or from applying a new architectural fashion, Rococo Gothick, to his library's features.[52] But with his good taste, a quality which he himself expounded in one of his several published treatises as well as his own musical compositions, came a patrician, monopolising approach to musical performance that built up the Salisbury Festival from its earlier St Cecilia celebrations and enabled the city's subscription concert series to flourish more securely, perhaps, than in any English city beyond London, and this did not go uncontested.[53] Rather like William Jackson, to be discussed in chapter 5, Harris has suffered from negative comment in high places: Samuel Johnson called him 'a prig and a bad prig', and this may well have minimised our historical appreciation of him as well as misrepresented what by other testimony appears to have been a highly agreeable nature.[54] Nevertheless, the distance of class between aristocratic amateurs and musical professionals was more than once exacerbated in Salisbury by Harris's attitude towards dancing-master violinists. He clearly made John Tewkesbury nervous.[55] Another one, Mr Burgat, was a difficult character, and rather than mollify him after a disagreement, in 1776 Harris dismissed him from his orchestra

[48] Britton 2010: 127–8.
[49] Carnall 2004; Warrack 2001.
[50] Probyn 1991: 208–38; Olivier 1951: 181; Burrows and Dunhill 2002: xxvii, 76, 84, 86.
[51] Dunhill 2004: 431.
[52] Robins 2006: 104, 125; Pevsner and Cherry 1975: 426.
[53] Driscoll 2008: 188–204.
[54] Dunhill 2004: 431.
[55] Robins 1998: 152–3.

(which Harris led from the keyboard). The result was that Burgat pointedly started his own subscription series, in which 'he shew'd his resentment by his extreme liberality to the lower class of performers whom he now treated at his concerts to Madeira etc remarking that at Mr Harris's concerts they got nothing but beer', as clear an example of class tension as could be sought.[56] Burgat soon failed and moved on to Winchester, but the damage was done. Salisbury's music, including the Festival, fell apart 'within weeks of Harris's death', when Joseph Corfe and John Parry started rival concert series, doomed as all provincial rivalries are to spreading their catchment too thinly.[57] It is, however, only fair to add that the city had in any case lost three of its most prominent musicians at almost the same time, John Tewkesbury and the cathedral organist John Stephens also dying in the latter part of 1780, its musical life being in no position to carry on as normal.[58]

Harris remains exceptional, very much an Enlightenment, eighteenth-century phenomenon, and it might be argued that his monopoly over Salisbury music would not have lasted in any case into a more commercially-minded era. In the nineteenth century the local benefits of musical patronage by the gentry remained in general insignificant, once one moves beyond the provision of community bands and church organs. Sebastian Wesley may have written two sets of organ pieces for Lady Acland at Killerton in Devon and visited the family and the house on various occasions in the 1830s, but one somehow does not expect the Aclands to have recognised that here was England's finest contemporary composer, that he was producing his best work at Exeter, in the shape of a number of large-scale anthems, and that they themselves might keep him there by transferring him to the sphere of private patronage (for his cathedral posts always turned sour). There was simply no model for such a possibility; as Peter Horton points out, Wesley's strength of assocation with the Aclands 'meant nothing in the context of his employment'.[59] Later in the century, with the development of rail transport, it was easy enough for top professional musicians to be hired for a country-house entertainment – but they would 'come down' from London for the purpose. This was the case with a new year play and 'musical fantasy' at the Amphora Theatre of Ugbrooke House, Chudleigh, in 1899. Lord and Lady Clifford and their guests acted in it but took care to secure professional lighting and scenery, and a librettist (the actress Aimée Lowther) and musical

---

[56] ibid: 151, quoting John Marsh.
[57] Driscoll 2008: 199–207.
[58] Robins 1998: 222, 224–5.
[59] Horton 1993; Horton 2004: 121, 312.

director (Stanley Hawley) from the metropolis.[60] Again, when William Henry Laverton, a rich mill owner, bought Leighton House in Westbury (Wilts) in 1888 and installed a theatre in the grounds, reached by a bridge over the Warminster road, he engaged artists such as Melba, Caruso, and Dan Leno to perform there privately.[61] But in terms of local benefit, what Westbury got from Laverton was a swimming pool, not an opera house with composer attached, which would have been unthinkable, however much Rutland Boughton might dream of it for Glastonbury. The indoor pool, apparently the only remaining Victorian one, is no less out of proportion and character with the tiny town than an opera house would have been.[62] As for the theatre, its building may well survive, but Leighton House is now a Ministry of Defence dog depot. Once again, kennels have overtaken music.

❧ Qualification

In place of contractual patronage, or hand in hand with it, musicians have sought qualification and recognition by organising and regulating their calling. There appears to have been no equivalent of London's Company of Musicians in the west country, and so the freelance musician based in the region (as opposed to travelling there in the livery of a nobleman's company of players or minstrels) was much more isolated.[63] It was possible to acquire local authority permission to travel as an independent minstrel, but only within the county: a late sixteenth-century licence from the Dorset Justices of the Peace survives, permitting W C and his son H C from parish G 'to wander and go abroad with their instruments using their trade of minstrelsy, playing or singing through and in all places within the said county only, behaving themselves orderly and using their said licence according to the said statute, which licence is to endure the space of one whole year after the date hereof'. They got the licence because they were known to be of 'good and honest behaviour'.[64]

A formal apprenticeship was the foundational machinery for secular and much sacred musicianship until the nineteenth century, indeed well into the twentieth where some teenage organists were concerned, especially if they had been choristers, for with suitable aptitude they could be apprenticed to

---

[60] Steven Martin, personal communication, 7 Feb 2011, based on materials in ExeLWSL.
[61] Flight nd: 72.
[62] Personal visit, 28 Sep 2009.
[63] Woodfill 1953: 3–32, 110.
[64] Hays and McGee 1999: 118–19.

the local cathedral organist when their voice broke. In Bristol, for example, Thomas Tallis Trimnell (1827–97), who eventually made a name for himself in New Zealand, and George Riseley (1845–1932), having been choristers in the cathedral about twenty years apart, were both subsequently apprenticed to its organist John Davis Corfe – though in the nineteenth century the word 'apprenticed' gave way to 'articled' in this context, no doubt because of the desperate drive on the part of musical practitioners in Britain to transform their trade into a gentlemanly profession, for lawyers had articled clerks.[65] Riseley went on to become Corfe's successor.[66] Note, however, that cathedral choristers would generally be sent out of the choir to be apprenticed to a non-musical trade when their voices broke. This happened to James Coombs at Salisbury, apprenticed to a printer in 1784 at a premium of £20 paid by the cathedral chapter; he landed on his feet when, shortly after becoming organist of Chippenham parish church in 1789, he married a printer's widow. This led to an active and successful life in Chippenham as performer, composer, printer, and bookseller, while he rose to become High Bailiff of the town.[67]

Apprenticeship was recognised as a career path for a son by families from a wide range of towns and villages across the region – and on occasions for a daughter too, for Elizabeth Phillips, a local girl, was apprenticed to the Bristol wait William Johnson in July 1598.[68] Of the forty-eight musical apprentices taken on in Bristol between 1532, when the surviving registers begin, and 1643, over half of them (twenty-seven) came from Bristol itself or the immediately surrounding villages, but that still leaves fourteen coming from the rest of the region, as far away as Dunster (as we have seen), Carhampton, and Diptford in Devon, though apparently not from Cornwall. The remaining seven came from even further away, including Stafford, Billericay in Essex, and Finghall in Yorkshire.[69] Bristol was clearly a centre for musical training, increasingly so from the 1580s with what appears to have been an influx of new masters in that decade. If all the apprentices stayed in Bristol after they had gained their freedom, and with a conservative estimate of lifespan, this could have given a total of over twenty-five secular musicians practising in the city into the 1600s. But very few Bristol apprentices' names subsequently appear as masters taking their own apprentices, at least not by 1642, so a

---

[65] Brown and Stratton 1897: 346, 417.
[66] Bell nd: 8; Edwards 2002: 39–42.
[67] Kent 2007b: 163–71.
[68] Pilkinton 1997: 262.
[69] Pilkinton 1997: 146, 256–68, 289–90; Goodman 1974.

strong implication is that they either went elsewhere, as we have speculated John Wood may have done, or that their main occupation as freeman was something other than music.

Bristol's most famous musical apprentice from the period did indeed move on almost immediately. This was William Child, born in Bristol and apprenticed to the cathedral lay clerk Thomas Prince in 1620 for eight years. Child became lay clerk and then organist at St George's Chapel, Windsor, in 1630, living on there into his nineties as a Chapel Royal musician as well, distinguished as England's leading composer of the early Restoration period. He amassed sufficient wealth that he could be generous with charitable donations in his later years, though it is not clear that any of them came in Bristol's direction, and none of his music can be dated to his time in Bristol.[70]

No such semblance of professional growth as mentioned above appears at the same time in other places (for example Exeter, where the records of musicians are most consistent over a long period), so not too much should be read into it. Nor were the largest cities the only places to train: there were masters and apprentices in much smaller settlements. John Webbe of Blagdon was a carpenter and a minstrel, and he had an apprentice, Roger Lockestone, in 1574. William Keele from Bridport took on Thomas Maniford for an unspecified number of years in 1610, to 'teach and inform his said apprentice in the art and mystery of music, with gentle usage and moderate correction', the last two phrases conjuring up a respect for the discipline and for people touching to read of in the heart of Dorset. Six years later, in strong contrast to this vision of a provincial idyll, Thomas Coombes of Trudoxhill, Nunney (near Frome), was training up Robert Gunnell but absconded through insolvency, selling the bass viol that Gunnell, his father languishing in the almshouse in Wells, had had to equip himself with.[71]

The two obvious types of apprenticeship were for instrumental performance and instrument making, though cathedral 'singing men' – lay clerks, as we would call them now, distinguished in earlier times from ordained vicars choral – also took apprentices, not least because in many cases they had more than the one trade. Performers might be trained up in several instruments over a period of anything up to ten years (fourteen in one case) and then, sensibly, given whichever instrument they had proved most adept at playing when they completed the apprenticeship, as was the case with William Johnson's apprentice John Hayward, a boy from

---

[70] Spink 2004a.
[71] Stokes 1996: 881; Hays and McGee 1999: 154; Stokes 1996: 186–8.

Bedminster indentured in 1625–26.[72] Thomas Rancock's apprentices of 1549–50, on the other hand, were clearly expected to play both wind and stringed instruments (see p.72). Whether the waits (for example) made their own instruments is not known, though it seems more likely that their skills stopped short at repairs. Certainly there was more than one specialist instrument maker in Bristol in the early seventeenth century. John Collyer and his father Giles, John Burch, and William Levasher (or Lavasher) and his relative Thomas all made instruments – we do not know which ones, though William Levasher was probably a luthier – and took apprentices.[73] More prominent is Isaac Bryne (Brian), who made virginals between 1609, when he was admitted to the liberties of the city, and some time after 1643, when he took his son Humphrey as an apprentice for seven years, having had four other apprentices in the intervening decades.[74] Sixteen pairs of virginals turn up in Bristol wills and inventories during this period and in its aftermath, and none beforehand; perhaps Brian created a local fashion, while simply reflecting a national one. Apparently none of his instruments survive.[75]

Nowhere was the need for a critical mass of urban population as apparent as in the specialised field of instrument making, for apart from organs and with perhaps only two other exceptions, Bristol alone in the region supported this skill and its market to a recognisable extent. Elsewhere in the west country, the only 'secular' musical instrument makers known to us prior to the eighteenth century were also organ builders: Charles Rewallin and John Loosemore, both active in Exeter and both known to have constructed virginals.[76] Thus they had the patronage of the Church to fall back on, in Loosemore's case as clerk of works for Exeter Cathedral, a position which may have superseded instrument making as his living. Conversely, it may have been precisely during the Commonwealth, when the Church ceased to patronise music, that Loosemore turned to making instruments for the secular market instead, since his one surviving pair of virginals, possibly commissioned for Tawstock Court and now in the Victoria and Albert Museum, is dated 1655.[77] Two of Rewallin's virginals are extant, one in the Museum of Somerset in Taunton Castle (1675), the other in the Royal Albert Memorial Museum in Exeter (1679).[78]

---

[72] Pilkinton 1997: 265–6.
[73] ibid: 263–5; Lasocki 1992: 112.
[74] Pilkinton 1997: 263, 265–7, 298; Goodman 1974: 11.
[75] Pilkinton 1997: passim; Goodman 1974: 12–14; Martin 2003, i: 301.
[76] Boalch 1956: 137–8.
[77] Martin 2003, i: 307; Matthews Exe: 4–5; Loosemore 2006; V&A.
[78] Martin 2003, i: 309, 313–14.

The exceptions mentioned in the previous paragraph were, first, John Hill MacCann, a nineteenth-century concertina maker in Plymouth who patented the Duet concertina, and, second, Benjamin Banks of Salisbury (1727–95).[79] Along with William Forster, Banks became Britain's leading maker of violins in the second half of the eighteenth century, though not of international stature – it was still a Stainer violin, not a Banks or a Forster, that the young Samuel Wesley coveted.[80] Forster, it will be noted, left Cumberland for London at the age of twenty in 1759, whereas Banks managed to rise to pre-eminence while remaining in Salisbury. It would be good, though perhaps not possible, to prove that he achieved this as part of an urban symbiosis between himself, James Harris as grand patron, the Salisbury Festival, and the cathedral establishment. Whether the uniquely organic geography of Salisbury ('New Sarum') as a planned cathedral city, with surely the most beautiful and spacious cathedral close in the country, somehow guaranteed this at a particular moment of Enlightenment wealth and expansiveness, who knows?[81] Banks, apprenticed as instrument maker to his uncle William Huttoft, was already warranting his instruments 'as good as in London' in his first *Salisbury Journal* advertisement, dating from 1757.[82] He sold sheet music too from the premises at 17–19 Catherine Street, and played violin alongside John Marsh in many a Salisbury concert, in some of which his daughter Ann sang, while at least one other of his ten children, James, was a cathedral chorister, and a younger daughter also sang in public.[83] Banks was evidently well connected in London, and owned property in Hammersmith, while Ann went on to marry the son of the London music publisher Thomas Cahusac.[84] But Henry and James Banks, who carried on their father's business, eventually sold it to Alexander Lucas, another Salisbury dealer (and father of the London violinist Charles Lucas). They then moved to Liverpool and set up there.[85] We may infer that Salisbury, which had failed to industrialise, was by the early nineteenth century in no position to compete with the rapidly growing northern and midland cities as a base for specialised skills and manufacture. What one would really like to know, however, is whether the brothers ever considered moving to Bristol, so

[79] MacCann; Brown and Stratton 1897: 258.
[80] Barry 2010b: 153.
[81] Robins 1998: 143.
[82] Cooper 1989: 11, 26, 28.
[83] Robins 1998: 273.
[84] Cooper 1989: 23, 26, 29; Robins 1998: 144–5.
[85] Cooper 1989: 42, 44.

much closer geographically, but recognised that it too was falling behind the industrialising north.

࿐ *Trade and Enterprise*

Notwithstanding a region's relative decline, it is the case that on less ambitious fronts of the musical economy than instrument making, as the population of England grew, so did the viability of musical trades and livings in towns previously too small to have sustained them. The increase in middle-class wealth and the spread of leisured consumption were no doubt an additional factor in the level of demand, though we must always try to answer the question: how much music does a community need and how much will it pay for? – for there may be more of a constant here than one would at first guess, and we shall return to this consideration. The other question, however, is: what enhances the consumer's cultural capital most, in a provincial context? – and here the gradual but steady improvements in road transport make it clear that the *shop* was the thing, stocking expensive and desirable metropolitan goods. The picture of 'Madame' Fribsby in Thackeray's *Pendennis*, running a milliner's shop in tiny Ottery St Mary in the 1830s and impressing her provincial customers with her atrocious French, is irresistible. It is not clear that anyone buys anything, though Fribsby is probably needed for sartorial advice, alterations, and accessories. But the entrance of the rector's wife 'to inspect her monthly book of fashions just arrived from London' legitimates the place as a site of small-town gossip.[86]

Thus, similarly, the music dealer comes on the scene, and from a certain period, with probably few exceptions, will have refurbished instruments as an adjunct to selling them as well as sheet music and services such as lessons, tunings, and repairs. Here was one freelance portfolio, to turn to our third form of security. Another, increasingly, was that of the music teacher, where again a conduit to the world beyond the locality, in this case a place of qualification and status, was implied when teachers began to be called 'professor'. We shall take each of these portfolios in turn.

The earliest music dealers, as one might expect, tended to be booksellers dabbling in psalmody or new hits from the London stage. The first two that have come to light in the west country, John March in Exeter and Mr Leake (probably James) in Bath, were both active in the 1720s, both advertising songs by Henry Carey, London's leading composer of what would today be called musicals, though Leake also acted as publishing agent for songs by the

---

[86] Thackeray 1848–50: 184–8, 988.

local composer Thomas Chilcot when printed in London in 1744.[87] As for the psalmody, the *Set of New Psalm-Tunes* composed by William Knapp, parish clerk of Poole, and published in 1738, to give one example, was 'sold by him in Poole; Mr George Torbuck in Wimborne ... Mr Gould in Dorchester ... Messrs John and Joshua Cook in Sherborne ... Mrs Chauklin in Taunton ... [and] Mr Hurst Glover in Blandford'. One doubts whether all of these people ran full-time businesses or displayed publications in shop windows, but John Cook had been active in Sherborne since 1713 and in 1740 promised a subscription to John Broderip's *New Set of Anthems*, presumably in order to sell copies on. (Broderip was at that time organist of Minehead parish church, prior to his appointment at Wells Cathedral the following year; it may have taken a further seven years to get the anthems into print.) Cook appears also to have had an outlet in Yeovil in 1740. Whether another of Broderip's promised subscribers, 'Mr Axford, ironmonger, Bridgwater', also intended to sell the anthems in his shop cannot be known.[88] Some booksellers printed music. William Pine, printer, of Wine Street, Bristol, was in business for half a century from 1753, and must have made a lot of money out of the third and fourth editions (1770 and 1773) of John Wesley's *Select Hymns with Tunes Annexed: designed chiefly for the use of the people called Methodists*, one of a large number of hymnals whose sales financed the Wesley brothers' lifelong preaching mission in the second half of the eighteenth century, many of them published by Pine.[89]

Gradually the music dealers developed their own separate sphere, aligned as suggested above with other musical artefacts and processes of consumption rather than with books. But there remained exceptions to this, newspaper proprietors among them. Benjamin Collins, Salisbury's first music dealer (from 1737 or earlier), was proprietor of the *Salisbury Journal*.[90] John Heard, publisher, bookseller, and music dealer of Truro, founded Cornwall's second newspaper, the liberal *West Briton*, in 1810; later in the century, Heard & Sons branched out in the unexpected direction of organ building, still active in it as late as 1920.[91] Heard must surely take some of the credit for the centrality of music to Cornwall's culture.

Bristol was not particularly forward in the provision of music sellers, its first known one being Richard Haynes Plomer, active in 1745 and dying

---

[87] Humphries and Smith 1970: 225, 151.
[88] ibid: 113; *SM* 12 Aug 1740: 4; Matthews 2001a: 417; Lynan 2004.
[89] Humphries and Smith 1970: 379; COPAC; Leaver 2010: 45, 50.
[90] Humphries and Smith 1970: 112; Cooper 1989: 26.
[91] *WB*, 20 Jul 1810; Barton 1970: 9; PenStM leaflet; Elvin 1995: 382.

three years later.[92] By 1775, however, it boasted five dealers, who combined their occupation with those of teacher and stationer (William Attwood), making or selling toys (Charles and Isabella Crump; Thomas Woodward), publican (William Glendoning of the Bell, 15 Pithay), and goldsmith and cutler (Thomas Naish). Woodward, also a cutler, and the Crumps probably sold instruments only, and these could have been musical boxes.[93] But 'music seller' should indicate that the others sold sheet music.

Until overtaken by the seaside resorts, Bath was always the west country's, indeed the nation's, Mecca for conspicuous consumption, and it is no surprise that early signs of the music emporium are found there. By 1782, James and Walter Lintern had set up as 'musical instrument makers, music sellers and publishers' in Abbey Yard.[94] By 1792 a second dealer was in business, James Mathews, and he too published music, including his own compositions. He had a 'music warehouse' in the High Street, as, a little later (*ca* 1798), did John Ashley in Wade's Passage, this nomenclature implying great spaces and stock, as, even more, did the term 'repository', a usage traced to 1785 by the *OED* and in my west country researches to 1810 in Truro, where Tregoning's Repository, which advertised only once in the *West Briton*, would surely have come into competition with that of John Heard.[95] Tycho Pilbrow, who was also a keyboard performer, was calling his Exeter dealership a musical repository in 1813; the music warehouse of Thomas Howell, father and son (the son another composer), at 12 and then 13 Clare Street was an enduring Bristol institution; and by the 1830s the music emporium, again called repository or warehouse, was an essential adjunct to a seaside resort (Upjohn & Drake, Weymouth, *ca* 1830; John Nicks, Exmouth, 1834).[96]

A music repository was a convenient place for any musician to establish a proprietorial presence and availability to be engaged for other purposes such as teaching and performance. Thus, prior to the greater specialisations and gentrifications of the later nineteenth century, it is no surprise to find leading individuals and families running one, as did John David Loder and his cousin Andrew in Bath from about 1813. If you could claim accreditation, as did the Loders, 'to her late Majesty [Queen Charlotte, wife of George III] and their royal highnesses The Princesses', so much the better. The Loders

---

[92] Barry 2010a.
[93] ibid; Humphries and Smith 1970: 241; Sketchley 1775: 3, 22, 36, 69, 109.
[94] Humphries and Smith 1970: 213.
[95] Bath 1792: 20; Humphries and Smith 1970: 54; *WB*, 20 Jul 1810: 1.
[96] *EFP*, 26 Aug 1813: 4, indexed EFPSCI; Humphries and Smith 1970: 188 and Banfield 2006: 44–6; BL Cat (Upjohn: *The Yeomanry Cavalry Quadrilles*); Cann 2001: 90.

gave private concerts at their business premises.[97] But the essential allure of the music warehouse, coming as it did at a time when the expanding British Empire and in particular the East India Company were stimulating the display, availability, and abundance of lavish, colourful, or exotic goods, resided in the pianoforte. As the rate and cheapness of production of this instrument rapidly increased, thanks above all to John Broadwood of London, the more essential it became that a young lady acquire a suitable model for her parental home, with periodic tunings guaranteed, a suitable teacher for her lessons, and suitable songs and pieces to play on it, perhaps with an accompanying part for any talented young male violinist or flautist willing to oblige as he stood behind her. In the early seventeenth century the virginals, along with the lute and cittern, had consolidated a fashion for female amateur accomplishment in music at a bourgeois level that continued with the harpsichord and spinet throughout the eighteenth, and references to these keyboard instruments being owned and played by or taught to west country women are easy to come by, for example with Sara Fowens (1609), Katherine Bowcher (1614), and Mrs Grace Mosley (1682), all in Bristol, and Miss Margaret Buller at Morval House in Cornwall (1676) and Mrs Mary Cox in Salisbury (1707).[98] But it was the piano that swept the board, in time coming virtually to define bourgeois acquisitiveness.

One can trace something of the piano's progress by locality. Following its 'London debut as a solo instrument' (as opposed to novelty) by J C Bach in 1768, it took some kind of early hold in south Devon.[99] The six sonatas 'for the harpsichord or piano forte', op 1, by Rev Richard Eastcott were already available in Exeter in 1772, and seven years later Mr Sharp of Ashburton, a pupil of Nelme Rogers in Bristol, was advertising that he taught the fortepiano as well as the harpsichord.[100] William Churchill, a Dartmouth organist and composer, specified the piano as an alternative to the harpsichord when his *Three Lessons*, op 3, were published in London in 1791 (or possibly 1788).[101] In Salisbury, John Marsh had his first encounter with a piano in 1776, when it was played by a Miss Mary Hancock and he accompanied on his violin, though the Harris family had heard the instrument at a private concert in the city eight years earlier.[102] Bath saw a Mr Markodt (*recte* J Markordt?) playing J C Bach publicly on the piano in 1777, and it was in Bath ten years

---

[97] Clarke 2011: 37–8.
[98] Pilkinton 1997: 170, 200; Lorigan 2009: 124; Slatter 1965: 4, 58.
[99] Ehrlich 1990: 13.
[100] BL Cat; *SM*, 30 Nov 1772: 3 and 10 May 1779: 1.
[101] *EFP*, 27 Jan 1791: 3, indexed EFPSCI; BL Cat.
[102] Robins 1998: 146; Burrows and Dunhill 2002: 509.

later that Charles Dibdin developed his one-man 'cabaret' shows, in which he accompanied himself on the piano, giving the first of them there in March 1787.[103] William Jeboult (1758–1817), an organist trained under Robert Parry at Wells Cathedral, was teaching harpsichord, piano, and guitar in North Petherton and Wells in 1781 and also tuned instruments.[104] The greater weight and tension of piano strings by comparison with those of a harpsichord already made self-tuning difficult, it would seem. But perhaps there were not yet any pianos in the mansions of Somerset, for when he moved in 1783 or early 1784 to Taunton (which the Jeboult family proceeded to dominate culturally for the next century and a half), he advertised tuition only on the harpsichord and guitar.[105] Yet, as Loesser speculates, Peter Beckford's Dorset mansion at Stepleton may have housed a piano if Beckford acquired one in London for Clementi during his sequestration there, which seems likely given the idiom of Clementi's op 1 sonatas.[106] References to pianos in Bristol begin only in 1782, when Thomas Howell was selling music playable on the piano and Thomas Naish was auctioning off actual instruments along with many other effects, probably to stave off bankruptcy.[107] As for Plymouth, William Bennett (1767–1827), appointed organist at St Andrew's in 1793, 'is said to have been the first to introduce grand pianofortes' into the town – which would figure, if as is claimed he had been a pupil of Bach.[108]

As George Dodd noted in 1843, nothing clinched the commercial dominance of London over the regions more than the spread of the piano.[109] By contrast with violins and, up to a point, organs, there would never be a major manufacturer of pianos in the west country. The early speculative market must have been tempting to London entrepreneurs, for one of them, a maker and a tuner, was advertising in the *Sherborne Mercury* as being on tour in the west country in 1800, and twenty-five years later it was a tuner from one of the leading London makers that the Exeter dealer Pilbrow promised would visit Barnstaple quarterly. Later in 1800, the *Mercury* advertised a London showroom that was running a complicated magazine subscription scheme, at the end of which one gained a free piano. We know that the family instrument so keenly practised on in Trowbridge in 1822 by the boy Isaac Pitman, who later invented Pitman's shorthand, was a Broadwood, revered

[103] *SM*, 30 Jun 1777: 2; Nourse 2012: 184.
[104] Bush 1983: 11; *SM*, 7 May 1781: 3.
[105] Bush 1983: 11.
[106] Loesser 1990: 223.
[107] *FFBJ*, 23 Mar 1782: 2 and 31 Aug 1782: 2.
[108] *TDA* 1846.
[109] Ehrlich 1990: 34.

by him to the extent that he quietly saved up 5s to put in the Baptist church collection box for its value.[110]

As the nineteenth century progressed, music dealerships became more and more synonymous with piano warehouses, the instruments' ever-increasing size and weight necessitating the quasi-industrial paraphernalia of cavernous premises and teams of removers with their equipment. Whether in concert programmes, on the lid of a piano or, as pre-war photos of Plymouth demonstrate, on the side of a city centre building, the most visible names in local musical provision became those of the great piano dealers – Moon in Plymouth, Minns in Bournemouth, Mickleburgh in Bristol, Duck, Son and Pinker in Bath, Paish in Torquay.[111] Their catchment is clear enough from this 1910 advertisement for Moon in the *Okehampton Gazette and Advertiser*: 'This winter you will require a piano or an organ. Your piano may require tuning or repairs. Moon & Sons, Plymouth, are the pianoforte makers of the west. Pianos or organs may be seen and prices obtained of our local representative, A Shepherd, 19 New Road, Okehampton.'[112] They were not the only music dealers in town, of course. In 1862 Exeter had six, Plymouth eight, and Torquay six music shops. Smaller towns such as Exmouth, Chippenham, Clevedon, and Bideford boasted, respectively, three in 1862, two in 1877–79, two in the 1880s, and three in 1890.[113] But the expansion of the biggest dealerships put them in a different league. Moon had branches in Barnstaple and other towns in Devon and Cornwall, presumably catering for the industrial brass band culture of the china clay area when it opened one in Bugle. At the end of the nineteenth century the firm was promoting concert tours to the far west of the nation's top singers such as Clara Butt and Edward Lloyd, and handled Caruso's visit to the west country.[114] Paish also developed subsidiary branches (as did Duck, Son and Pinker) and promoted concerts by international artists. Much later, Minns had by the 1970s expanded to thirteen branches along the south coast and even to London, with outlets at the Brent Cross Shopping Centre, Selfridges, and Harrods – a rare musical

---

[110] *SM*, 25 Aug 1800: 4 and 22 Dec 1800: 1; *NDJ*, 24 Jun 1825: 1; Montague-Smith 2004: 3–4.
[111] Plymouth Data; HaHa 1862: 685, 693; PCMAG; Devon Celeb: 72–4; DeHC 4827B/A1–5 and Z1.
[112] *OGA*, 24 Dec 1910: 4.
[113] HaHa 1862: 68, 666, 684–5, 693, 547; HaHa 1862: 143; Spinke 1877–79; Kelly *Somerset* 1883, 1889; Bideford 1890: 11, 17, 25.
[114] NDRO B858/1/4; Plymouth Data; *RCG*, 25 Oct 1900: 8, 1 Nov 1900: 2; *EPG*, 9 Aug 1909: 2.

invasion of the metropolis from a west country base.[115] Thus fortunes waxed, but eventually they waned. Duck, Son and Pinker, an unforgettable adjunct to Pulteney Bridge from as early as 1848, flourished for a long time before finally closing in 2011.[116] Moon never really recovered from the wartime bombing of Plymouth. Minns now operates as Intermusic from a business park in the hinterland of Poole. Mickleburgh may have fared best, currently with a shop in Bath in addition to its 1903 Bristol premises in Stokes Croft, always something of a musicians' quarter and only yards from where Charles and Samuel Wesley were born.[117] Overall, a culture that had seen pianos inaugurate the hire purchase system in the mid-nineteenth century shifted decisively to one in which the piano was no longer the next most expensive family purchase after the house. The car showroom replaced the piano repository.

The *Bristol Mercury* for 5 July 1890 contains fifty-five references to pianos – one per 4,000 population, as it were. Surprisingly, Bournemouth and Poole's combined 1891 population of around 60,000 produced no more than ten in the *Bournemouth Guardian* of 5 July 1890. (That would be one per 6,000 population.)[118] Piano consumption will have peaked in the subsequent two decades but, as early as 1810, Tregoning in Truro was 'lending' pianos at 10s 6d a month. This was still a great deal of money for, say, an organist earning perhaps no more than £50–£60 per annum from mixed sources, and, if manageable at all by anyone below the status of gentry, would have felt like a young professional's hefty mortgage today. (That same year, sailors in Plymouth were rioting at the increase of a theatre pit ticket from 2s to 2s 6d.)[119] The point, though, must be that more and more people were determined to make it manageable as consumer goods spead downmarket. Thus it is easy to see how the demand for a return on the investment grew, and the piano became the hirer's property at the end of a rental period. The affordability of a family piano came about only slowly over the earlier Victorian period, as historians have stressed, but the hire purchase system was widespread in the west country by the 1870s, to judge from advertisements by William Masland in Clevedon ('may be purchased, if desired, by instalments extending over a period of years') and John Whitby & Son in Bridgwater ('supplied at

---

[115] *EM* vii (1979): 147; anon 1975: 51–3.
[116] *BC*, 7 Apr 2011: 2; Manns 1948.
[117] Intermusic; Mickleburgh; Brown 1994.
[118] VBT; *BM*, 5 Jul 1890; *BG*, 5 Jul 1890.
[119] *WB*, 20 July 1810: 1 and 30 Nov 1810: 2.

low prices, for cash, for hire, or on the three years' system of payment if preferred').[120]

The surviving archive of the Torquay dealer Paish & Co affords us a window on the piano business in a seaside resort about the same size as Bournemouth in 1891, though longer established and growing less rapidly.[121] An undated brochure, which to judge from the stack of banjos at the bottom of the stairs dates from 1900 or thereabouts, pictures a cluttered sales parlour with, if not exactly a sweeping, at least a prominent staircase, plus two showrooms fairly stuffed with pianos, the majority of them low uprights of the 'cottage' or 'pianette' variety, clearly the bulk of Paish's market. A cottage piano by an unprestigious maker had a cost price of around £15 but a list price of twice that amount, actually selling for some figure between the two depending on how long it had been in stock and other factors. From stock listed respectively in 1904, 1912, and 1925, three consolidated samples give figures and demographics for sales to seventy-two customers altogether (not including those whose second-hand pianos people bought).

In the period 1904–15, one quarter of the fifty-six instruments sold from the two samples were disposed of through hire purchase agreements. It was not only the lower end of the market that availed itself of HP, for, taking three grands out of the equation, because they were in an entirely different league of expense, the average HP purchase price from this sample was £38, whereas the outright payment average was £34. No doubt the HP mark-up accounts for the difference and £34 was the real average value of a piano purchase in Torquay at this period. Widespread snobbery about HP prevented neither a clergyman, Rev Tilley, from buying in 1904 a Bord pianette (purchase price £22 10s, cost price £15 8s, in stock since August 1899) nor Mr J C Reade from Chelston from buying in 1909 a fancy and expensive instrument, namely a Bechstein 'mediaeval' model (purchase price £75 12s, list price 85 guineas, cost price £50, in stock since February 1899), on the three-year system. Note that the Bechstein had taken a decade to sell.

Ehrlich states that one in six pianos sold in Britain by 1914 was German.[122] In Torquay, the figure appears to have been upwards of one in five (22 per cent) – hardly surprising in a resort whose pre-war presiding bandsmen included Stanislaus Wurm, Karl Kaps, and Basil Hindenberg, Julian Kandt petitioning unsuccessfully to join them.[123] Allowing for a little guesswork

---

[120] Ehrlich 1990: 9–10; Morris 1872; *WSFP*, 1 Mar 1879: 2.
[121] DeHC 4827B/A1–5, Z1.
[122] Ehrlich 1990: 88.
[123] *WT*, 14 Mar 1905: 6; TTC Mins 5089, 8280, and 8879.

concerning unidentifiable makers, 58 per cent of sales from the sampled stock up to 1914 were of English pianos, though the figure rose to 67 per cent overall because of the war, for not a single German piano from this sample was sold thereafter. Seven French pianos were sold, five of them Bords and the other two Pleyels. One Steinway Model 1 represents the sole American sale, interestingly at a low mark-up (22 per cent) and well below list price. Women accounted for 40 per cent of Paish's piano-buying customers. Most of them were married, purchasing, one imagines, on a husband's account, or for boarding houses if they were separated, widowed, or military wives. A number of the women, and the clergyman, stressed their gentility in giving the names of their houses – Edgehill, Bay View, Hyperion, Beeches, Ocean View – for perish the thought that they should live in a street with numbered houses. The men were either less concerned about this or more readily identifiable without an address. Twenty-three of the seventy-two customers, roughly one-third, were living in Torquay or its constituent villages, and another thirteen in adjacent Paignton. The remainder were from the Devon villages and more distant towns such as Kingsbridge, with one or two from Exeter and Devonport and one from Ilminster in Somerset. Nobody, it seems, made an impulsive holiday purchase to be shipped to another part of the country entirely; no doubt carriage charges and the importance of a local maintenance contract ruled this out. (Delivery costs, prior to postwar inflation, averaged just under 18s when incurred – 2.6 per cent of the average purchase price.)

Only one of the sampled customers can be positively identified. Dr Rhodes of Preston was Harold Rhodes, organist of St John's, Torquay, and soon to become well known as a national broadcaster after he moved to the posts of Coventry Cathedral and then Winchester Cathedral; in 1925 he bought for £93 9s a second-hand Marshall piano previously owned by Dr McGregor of Livermead, the next suburb but one along Torbay from Preston. Another customer was Professor Vecsey, purchasing a fairly cheap second-hand Krause piano on 1 April 1905. The boy violinist Franz von Vecsey appeared in Exeter in December 1905, and Paish & Co promoted his reappearance there two years later, though it is difficult to see how all these facts might be interrelated. Perhaps, then, the 'professor' was not the violinist's father or guardian but the salon orchestra conductor Armand Vecsey, in a residency or on vacation from London.[124]

---

[124] Kelly *Devonshire* 1923: 912, 1206, and 1926: 966, 1268; Ah; *WT*, 8 Dec 1905: 5; *EPG*, 30 Dec 1907: 1; Vecsey 1931: 131, 142.

It is difficult to generalise about mark-ups, which varied enormously according to the customer, the condition and status of the instrument (some were second-hand, some had been in stock for several years), and the condition of the business – there seems to have been a concerted effort to get rid of old stock in 1904, a year of particularly high HP business. But a 50 per cent mark-up on cost price was common. Very striking is the huge mark-up applying to a number of sales in the 1915–25 period, when business was slower and many pianos remained unsold. It averaged 79 per cent. Times were getting hard for the piano market, which was now having to target particular purchasers and their susceptibilities much more aggressively, in other words having to aim for higher profit margins amid lower turnover. Of the four pianos from the stock samples that sold for over £100 – and they averaged £164 – three were player pianos, sold in 1912 and 1925. The remaining one, cheapest of the four by some margin, was a Schiedmayer grand.

Clearly mechanical music was overtaking self-made music as a consumer priority, though one has to factor in the durability of the pianos sold at the beginning of the century, which from this reputable dealer may have been quite high, for one sees almost no customers making repeat purchases. And so Paish's business found itself shifting significantly to wirelesses, gramophones, and radio-gramophones, the latter prominently advertised in a poster, probably from the late 1920s, as costing up to £150 (with HP available), twice the price of a decent upright piano at that date.[125] The sites of cultural capital were shifting rapidly. They would shift further after the Second World War, when musical exchange, following a period in which electric organs flooded the showrooms, became the inexorable province of youth, thereby transforming itself into subcultural capital. The smartest music businesses, such as Minns, went with this trend – or perhaps they were the dealers least embedded in the traditional values and networks of a literate musical community. (It is known that Leslie Fudge, the last director of Duck, Son and Pinker, bankrolled the business personally prior to its final collapse, because he cared for what it represented.[126]) But if Minns, like so many specialist shops in other fields, also had to leave the high street eventually, it will have been for changes in consumer marketing that have affected much besides music, even if the hoodie in the guitar shop was earlier than the anorak in the model shop in preferring the back street or the railways arches as his cavern of resort.

[125] DeHC, 4827B/A1, loose insert.
[126] *BC*, 7 Apr 2011: 2.

✒ The Music Professor

Like the music dealer, the freelance music teacher also came and went, but in two distinct chronologies. First there was the period of the itinerant singing master, a phase in English musical culture about which little is known but which entailed the ousting of the florid, improvisatory 'old way of singing' in country parish churches through the employment of a visiting professional or semi-professional who would teach a parish congregation, or more frequently just a group of young male volunteers (though they sometimes included 'maidens'), to sing the psalms from musical notation, i.e. in harmonic settings by published composers who often included themselves. This was a popular movement of the late seventeenth and earlier eighteenth centuries, attested to by two leading literary figures, Addison and Pope, who stereotyped them in 1711 and 1727 respectively. Addison's fictitious squire Sir Roger de Coverley patronised genteel psalmody in his parish by employing 'an itinerant singing-master, who goes about the country for that purpose, to instruct them rightly in the tunes of the psalms; upon which they now very much value themselves'. Pope, supposedly with John Gay as co-author, was more satirical: he described 'London singing masters sent into every parish, like unto excisemen', his target the unwarranted self-satisfaction of parishioners about standards.[127]

Not all singing masters were from London, for there were clearly regional networks, and it seems unlikely that the 2s spent on a singing master by the far-west parish of St Ives in 1698 would have been for a metropolitan visitor. Hartland parish, equally remote, paid 6s to 'Bideford men for singing' in 1696–97, and, forty years later, when the taught psalmody movement may have been reaching its zenith, Knapp rustled up as many as nine subscribers to his *Set of New Psalm-Tunes* described as singing masters, at least some of whom must surely have been based in Dorset and the surrounding counties. None of their names can be identified for sure in any other context, which renders them yet more shadowy, but several share a surname with other subscribers, suggesting a local family, and Stephen Hooper may well have been 'Hooper the Singing Master' who joined with the gallery choir at Sunday service in Castle Cary parish church in 1769.[128] Knapp himself seems to have taught choirs in his part of Dorset.[129]

The most detailed west country evidence we have for such teachers is from the scrivener John Cannon (1684–1743), encountered in the previous

---

[127] Temperley 1979, i: 141–7.
[128] Temperley 2001c: 473.
[129] Temperley 1979, i: 145, 180–1; Knapp 1738; Temperley 2001a.

chapter as a teenager participating in his tiny Somerset village in a group of church singers and bell ringers that behaved rather loosely until shamed into becoming more responsible (which did not prevent one of Cannon's young cronies dying in a bell ringing accident). Later, as a typical parent, he disapproved of his own youthful enjoyments, and forbad his daughter to sing in the West Lydford choir 'because mixed singing was the first step to debauchery'. In this case he was right, for a new incarnation of the West Lydford choir in 1724 under Simon Harvey, perhaps another itinerant master, had led to goings-on after the choir's feast whereby some 'females got their bellies enlarged, by which means they obtained husbands sooner than they expected'. In 1736–39 singers in one of the two Glastonbury parishes, of which Cannon by now seems to have been clerk, were being taught by a master called Charles Evans (from Wales?), at the expense of the parish authorities, and in February 1738 Evans took the Glastonbury choir to perform evensong in Mere church, where they 'sang the Magnificat & Nunc dimittis with other anthems & psalms, having been billeted like soldiers at several of the inhabitants' houses for a dinner'. Their hosts were the Mere singers, possibly another of Evans's groups, though Mere is a good twenty miles from Glastonbury. Later they all got thoroughly drunk, the minister included. Cannon's son was among them, accompanied by Cannon himself, who seems to have protested a little too much about the activity for which he clearly still had some fondness. In November of that same year, Cannon helped Evans draw up the announcement of a district competition for the 'new way of singing' in Glastonbury, for voices in consort in two, three, or four parts, with a 'valuable piece of plate' as prize. After various delays it took place at the George Inn on Shrove Tuesday 1739 and yet again ended in drunken disarray. By now Evans himself had got a local girl pregnant and Cannon was called upon to draw up an agreement that mollified the offended parties and hushed it up. Finally, in 1740–41, almost thirty of the West Lydford youth were being musically instructed by Nathaniel Parker of Kingsdon, who received £7 from the parish rates for a year's tuition on two evenings a week. Late enrolment cost a singer 2s 6d, each absence ('failure') 2d, and discontinuation 5s. On such a bi-weekly basis Parker can hardly have managed more than three or four village choirs at a time, but combining these with other piecemeal occupations, musical or non-musical, will have given him an income not too far behind that of a town organist who was also doing some teaching. The Lydford singers performed at Somerton in 1742; Somerton, the Lydfords, Kingsdon, and perhaps Glastonbury would have made for a manageable teaching circuit, and nearby Walton could have been part of it, for it was employing a singing master in 1740.[130]

Itinerant singing masters were still serving the quire of Buckland Filleigh in north Devon as late as 1820, but by then the typical music teacher was the music 'professor' of a quite different role.[131] The professor was of fixed habitation and flourished after the piano had become a family accomplishment *de rigueur* and before the nationwide institutionalisation of civil education embraced music provision, both for professionals in the form of music conservatoires and for amateurs and as pre-professional training in local and private schools. Although there was an amateur market for singing and violin lessons, the piano accounted for the vast majority of individual teaching, as indicated by the proportions of entrants for the Associated Board (ABRSM) examinations in 1910: nationwide, from a total number of 4,180 entrants, 3,550 (85 per cent) were pianists, with only 415 violinists (10 per cent) and 152 singers (3.5 per cent). (The remaining 1.5 per cent were mainly organists and cellists.)[132] The precocity of Britain's piano culture at one end of the nineteenth century combined, at the other, with its development of unmediated music education for individuals in the form of the Associated Board and Trinity College examination system, guaranteed demand for teachers of music, who fuelled it through their determination as practitioners to rise from the level of servants and tradespeople to that of gentlemen and ladies – to become a profession. For they took pains to create their own mystique, as George Bernard Shaw never tired of pointing out, which they did through the fetishisation of music 'theory' – mostly what we would now call rudiments, harmony, and counterpoint – and of paper qualifications for both teachers and pupils.[133]

Bristol and all points west were a receiving, not a sending culture where teachers were concerned, for prior to the proliferation of universities in the mid-twentieth century there was never a nationally sanctioned music college or tertiary department in the west country: such private initiatives as appeared fleetingly will be discussed in chapter 7. Yet even metropolitan institutions that could do the sending appeared very late, for the Royal Academy of Music (RAM), founded in 1822 and admitting tiny numbers of students, limped along ineffectually through most of the nineteenth century

---

[130] Money 2010, i: xliv, 41–2, 74, 179, and ii: 281, 329–30, 361, 377, 379, 383, 471–2, 500, 531; Dunning 2006: 210.
[131] Drage 2009: 55.
[132] Wright 2013: 77.
[133] ibid: 34–9; Laurence 1981: passim, especially ii: 98–9, 898–900, 960–4.

without a shadow of the authority and standardising influence of the Paris or Leipzig conservatoire. It was not until 1875 that Trinity College of Music commenced operation in the recognisable form of a national training centre, followed by the Guildhall School of Music and Drama in 1880 and colleges in Manchester, Birmingham, and Glasgow before the end of the century. Nor did what we would now think of as a first degree in music exist in the universities, where it appeared by and large only after the Second World War. What made the real difference was the founding of the Royal College of Music (RCM) in 1883. From that point onwards, and with the fortunes of the RAM revived too, a flood of teachers qualified in music was unleashed on the market, more of them women than men.[134]

Until then, the skills of most music teachers must have continued to be learnt through family training or apprenticeship (and as we have already seen, this often meant both), though some teachers were experienced professionals who had retired to the area, Venanzio Rauzzini (1746–1810), the star castrato who spent his last two decades and more in Bath, being the best known of these.[135] Before the era of paper qualifications, it is understandable therefore that an incoming musician would announce who had taught him or her when advertising for custom, personal lineage becoming the overriding initial factor in market advantage, which to a great extent is still true today. We have already seen Sharp of Ashburton advertising in 1779 that he had studied with Nelme Rogers in Bristol. Rogers was organist of St Mary Redcliffe, thus not far behind a cathedral organist in status; nevertheless, Sharp could not match the credentials of William Reeve, who two years later in Ashburton was announcing singing and harpischord lessons privately and in schools as a pupil of Benjamin Cooke in London (he had been appointed organist at Totnes and later became famous as a West End theatre composer).[136] Into the next century, Samuel Rootham, first member of the family to settle in Bristol when appointed lay clerk at the cathedral, announced himself 'to the gentry and inhabitants of Bristol and Clifton' as 'late pupil of Dr Walmisley' in a prominent advertisement for piano and voice lessons and schoolteaching placed in the *Bristol Mercury* in 1851.[137] Perhaps this raised sufficient custom, for he never advertised again, but in terms of ongoing lineage his brother Daniel, who soon joined him in the Bristol Cathedral choir, would outshine

---

[134] Wright 2013: 30–1, 39, 44.
[135] James 1990.
[136] Wikipedia: 'St Mary Redcliffe'; *SM*, 13 Aug 1781: 1; Troost 2001.
[137] *BM*, 29 Mar 1851: 5.

him, producing two star vocal pupils, Clara Butt and Eva Turner, both eventually knighted.[138]

The most sought-after female teachers, meanwhile, were those who had studied with a male virtuoso. Cecilia Summerhayes was a member of the Taunton musical family and highly active in the west country in the mid-nineteenth century as a pianist. She could lay claim to both Hallé and Thalberg as her teachers.[139] Whether they were her route to the top violinists of the time is not known, but she must have been a fine accompanist, for she was already playing for Prosper Sainton at a concert in Taunton in 1857, and the following year, supposedly still only sixteen years old (though actually eighteen), she made a successful London debut accompanying Henry Blagrove. During 1859 she taught in both the metropolis and Taunton, and must have become something of a star, billed as leading pianist for the 1859 Three Choirs Festival alongside artists of the calibre of Clara Novello, Charlotte Dolby, Thérèse Tietjens, and Sims Reeves. Between her London engagements and frequent reappearances in Taunton in the early 1860s, Birmingham took her to its heart, as evidently did one of its citizens in particular, the chemistry professor Alfred Anderson of Queen's College, for she married him in 1864 and was settled in Edgbaston in 1866, still teaching but of course no longer at liberty to appear on the professional concert platform. Two of their young children died in 1870, one in Taunton and one in London, and Cecilia eventually returned to Taunton as a teacher in 1879.[140]

Talent, luck, and her family networks must all have helped Summerhayes, but the London kick-start was crucial, as Thomas Henry Davis, organist of Wells Cathedral, made absolutely clear to another female pianist of local roots (her father was vicar of Theale) with professional aspirations fifty years later. Joan Singleton was returning from Leipzig, where she had been studying with Robert Teichmüller, and living at home while acting as organist for Wookey parish church. Davis advised that the 'only thing ... was to have a friend ... give an "At Home" in her drawing-room in London' (this was 1908). There was no point in wasting money on a provincial debut: 'As regards playing in the school-room at Wells, you must not think of it. It would be madness', and no route for a professional pianist, which he must have thought her capable of being or at least determined to be, for he

[138] Dobson 1995: 9; Tooley 2004: 613.
[139] Bush 1983: 21–2, 79; *SM*, 23 Nov 1858: 4.
[140] *TC*, 16 Sep 1857: 1; *MW* xxxvi (1858): 325; Census 1841, 1851; *SM*, 14 Dec 1858: 5; *TC*, 2 Mar 1859: 9; *The Times*, 24 Nov 1859: 14; *TC*, 7 Sep 1859: 2; *Birmingham Gazette*, 3 Sep 1864: 5 and 27 Oct 1866: 4; *TC*, 12 Jan 1870: 4 and 11 May 1870: 4; *SCG*, 28 Dec 1878: 1.

discouraged thoughts of settling down locally to earn her musical living: 'the teaching in the county is not good, I mean as regards fees obtainable[,] and would become hard work if you depended on it entirely'. She followed Davis's advice, and like Summerhayes developed a dual urban base: London and Edinburgh. It is interesting that neither she nor Davis appears to have considered Bristol sufficiently professional for this purpose. Women pianists from Clifton had made their name within an economic partnership of de Vries's old-fashioned 'industrious' type, namely a musical marriage: Jane Jackson will be considered below, and Clara Meller, a generation older than Singleton, had similarly studied in Leipzig but remained there, marrying the musicologist Hermann Kretzschmar.[141]

The sobriquet 'professor of music' first appears in our annals around 1820. A Devon teacher, John Newcombe, called himself that in 1817, and a plaque to a rare musical endowment at Warminster St Denys commemorating a music 'professor', Roger Townsend, who died ninety years earlier, is dated 1820. At the opening of the new Gray organ in Holy Cross, Crediton, in 1822, Mr Jones, the local organist, 'modestly stood down "so that a regular bred professor might preside at it"', such wording beginning to speak volumes. Far-away Helston had a music professor, Roger Faning, by 1823. North Devon directory entries for 'professors and teachers' in 1830 listed three in Barnstaple, where the only other person in this category was a French teacher – so music was *the* private living. Even though Bideford had a French teacher and a dancing mistress but no-one teaching music, this private enterprise is still 50 per cent musical when split between the two towns.[142]

Already in 1792 the *New Bath Directory* listed seven music teachers, including Rauzzini. Three of them were women. Exeter's seven in 1816 were all men; it being a cathedral city might be expected to have explained this, but in fact none of the seven doubled as a lay clerk, even though three of the lay clerks had another occupation. By 1827, Exeter's greatly increased number of fifteen music teachers did include three women. Not too much emphasis should be placed on these statistics, for a different Exeter directory three years later listed only eight music teachers, and it seems unlikely that the other seven had in reality all disappeared. Clearly numbers were rising in general, for an 1850 directory lists as many as thirty-two, four of them (12.5 per cent) women.[143] Plymouth, Stonehouse, and Devonport's music

---

[141] Slaytor 2013: 37–8; Brown and Stratton 1897: 279.
[142] DeHCSCI 53/6 Box 104; personal visit, 22 Apr 2010; Venn 1955: 340; Pigot 1823: 186; Pigot 1830: 50.
[143] *EPJ* 1816 and 1827 and EFPSCI; Pigot 1830: 74; White 1850: 170.

teachers numbered ten in 1830 and seventeen in 1862, with again roughly 12 per cent of them women in the latter year. But by 1932, three of the six music teachers on the music selection committee for the competitive festival of the British Music Society's Plymouth centre were women, and this considerable feminisation of the occupation is borne out elsewhere.[144] Salisbury's seven identified music teachers in 1897 already included four women (57 per cent), and of the twenty-four listed in *Kelly's Directory of Salisbury* for 1939, of whom eighteen were in the city itself, as many as eighteen (75 per cent) were female, fourteen of these spinsters.[145] The male death toll of the First World War, not least in this military city, will have been partly responsible for the unmarried parade of Gladyses, Ivys, Elsies, and Nellies (they really were called that), but the growth of the music colleges' intake and the success of their external and diploma examination systems are the greatest witness to what was also an increasingly surburbanised phenomenon, for ribbon development had done its work: nine of the teachers lived on main roads out of the city or village or a through road in a new estate. One can just imagine their gloomy Tudorbethan houses, the bus stop outside, the small child alighting with music case, and the mothballed examiner with his cup of tea in the front room. (In fact this picture conflates two images; teachers were not at that time permitted to be the ABRSM honorary local representatives who hosted visiting examiners.)

One is thus tempted to view these Salisbury teachers as a rather sad phenomenon, matching David Wright's perception of the 'poor generic image of local women music teachers, of cheap lessons and no real musical authority'.[146] This would be unfair. Glades Smith, who in 1933 was conducting madrigals in George Herbert's garden in the presence of John Masefield, Sir Henry Newbolt, and the Earl of Pembroke, was probably a force to be reckoned with. Una Swayne-Hall led the St Edmund's parish church orchestra and was generally active as a violinist, as was Edna Moore, who led the Salisbury Musical Society orchestra. Alfred Candler was the pianist in The Serenaders Concert Party. Elsie Graham had her own light opera society. Thomas A Tunmore was a Salisbury Cathedral lay clerk.[147] The names of Sydney H Lovett, Ivy Tapper, and Antony and Fiona Brown crop up in various musical contexts. True, the fourteen remaining

---

[144] Pigot 1830: 110, 118; HaHa 1862: 693, 710, 751, 757; Plym 1932: 2.
[145] Salisbury 1897–98: 186; Kelly *Salisbury* 1939: 11, 346.
[146] Wright 2013: 143 (see also 225–6).
[147] *WWJ*, 9 Jun 1933: 8; *WG*, 11 Jan 1935: 12; *WWJ*, 1 Jan 1932: 8; *WTTA*, 24 Jan 1931: 4; *WG*, 8 Dec 1933: 4; *WWJ*, 21 Apr 1933: 7.

teachers, all but two of them female, may have had very little wider musical involvement in their community. Aligning Bridgwater's ten music teachers of 1938 with references in the digitised Taunton newspapers for the period produces similarly mixed results. It is the four church organists (C E Hobbs, W H Phillips, G A Thompson, and May Wood) plus the husband of one of them (Fred Wood) who make most of the local running, though Miss Eves and Miss Jeffcoat, having teamed up to run the Bridgwater Studio of Music and Dramatic Art, are also in evidence on a broader front. But of B Durston, Miss G Garland, and Miss Doris Reed there is nothing else to be seen.[148]

The provincial teacher, however ripe for caricature, could accomplish much, and one of the west country ones, Annie O Warburton, MusDoc, LRAM, ARCM, became a household name. Near the beginning of my field research, I enjoyed an excellent lunch at Bridgwater's Tudor Restaurant, where the barlady remembered her thrill as a schoolgirl cellist at having been chosen for the Bridgwater Youth Orchestra's tour of Germany in the 1960s. To her, Warburton, who conducted it, was a very spinsterly lady with her hair bound back – clearly the Imogen Holst type.[149] (Another witness says that she was short, with bad eyesight, and bent over a miniature score gave the impression that she was conducting over her head.) In fact Warburton was married, her husband Robert H Hawkins being the education officer for Somerset, and they were incomers, for in 1946 Warburton retired as music mistress of Manchester High School for Girls. Living in Burnham-on-Sea, she then became music mistress of Bridgwater Grammar School for Girls and conductor from 1947 of the twenty-strong Bridgwater String Orchestra.[150] However, Warburton is remembered more widely not for all this but for her books *Harmony, Melody Writing and Analysis, Score Reading, Form and History, Read, Sing and Play, Analyses of Musical Classics, Basic Music Knowledge,* and *Graded Aural Tests*, all published by Longmans in London between 1952 and 1971, following an earlier incarnation of the harmony textbook dating from 1938. What she had done was corner the rising GCE 'O' level market after the war, and substantial royalties it must have brought her. Longmans frequently republished the books, and two of them were taken over by Cambridge University Press as late as 1995.[151] Not necessarily a name recalled with affection, hers will take a long time to forget. Academics and critics of the 1990s still found it worthwhile to lay into

---

[148] *MT*: passim; *BA* 1938; *TC*: passim.
[149] Personal information, 10 Sep 2009.
[150] *TC*, 22 Mar 1947: 3.
[151] BL Cat.

'the Annie O Warburton school of music criticism' and into her confidence about melodic 'nonsense', while her dubious classification of the saxophone occasioned a lengthy blog in 2004 and her books were still on a teachers' training bibliography in Tanzania in 2012.[152]

❦ Families

James Boeringer was quoted in chapter 2 as pointing out how apprenticeships, business partnerships, and marriages will have given rise to regional continuities. (The common pattern of the male apprentice marrying the master's daughter frequently entailed all three of these relationships.) Organ builders, Boeringer's concern, offer at least the possibility of one exceptionally long line of practice. John Loosemore learnt his trade from his father, Samuel, who may have been apprenticed to one of the Chappington family of organ builders (Richard, Hugh, John, and Ralph, active 1536–1620). Loosemore's daughter married his assistant John Shearme. They had no surviving children, and since Shearme died in 1686, he cannot have provided any direct link with the next notable organ builder from north Devon, John Crang, whose earliest known work dates from 1745 but who 'is traditionally said to have been apprenticed to the Loosemore family'.[153] One suspects wishful thinking, here and elsewhere, having insisted on a regional lineage because it would reflect a desirable continuity of vernacular values and wholesomeness of locally sourced craft. Yet one has to acknowledge the overwhelming sense of monopoly and singularity that such a trade represented in any particular place, right up to the end of the nineteenth century and beyond in smaller communities, for a musical living had to be jealously guarded, as Ehrlich makes abundantly clear in his history of the music profession in Britain.[154] In a society where there were all kinds of reasons, legal, economic, and social, why only one person could do business and why, conversely, they had to remain where they were, it could be argued that for occupations and skills as specialised as the various musical ones were, the onus must be on proving the absence of a lineage or network rather than the opposite. If in the case of Crang there really was a connection with Loosemore, that would give a 'family' tree stretching forward from 1536 for nearly three hundred years, for John Crang's business partner in London, James Hancock, married Crang's sister, and their son James Crang Hancock carried on the family business

---

[152] Thomas 1996: 20; Green 1988: 48–9; Warburton blog; Butimba.
[153] Loosemore 2006; Matthews Exe: 7; Wickens 2001.
[154] Ehrlich 1985: 10, 19.

until about 1820 at least. Curiously, he moved back to the west country that his uncle had relinquished for London, and was operating from a workshop in lower Clifton in 1800.[155] Another extended line, passing from Thomas Dallam through the Harrises, Swarbrick, the Byfields, Richard Bridge, and the Englands, is not as long as this and was centred on the west country (Bristol) only for a few years in the early eighteenth century, though examples of the work of most of these builders can be found somewhere in the region, with moments of concentration.

Here the essence of a family advantage will have resided in security of capital and stock; flexible labour force; secret knowledge; capacity for after-sales service of a product known for its longevity; and trademark publicity. Organ builders need a sizable workshop, whether or not attached to the family house, and they work with what in the past will have been very expensive metals, as well as an extraordinarily wide variety of other hardware, much of it bulky. (The lengths to which jewellery manufacturers had to go to prevent employees from smuggling out gold dust are well demonstrated in the Birmingham Museum of the Jewellery Quarter. Family trust and interest would obviate these.) At times they need to call upon two, three, or four people for a team operation, at others to leave a reliable person in charge while visiting another town or region. All kinds of knowledge gained through experience and imparted on the job are entailed, especially in the voicing and scaling of pipes. Extensive travel is involved in the ongoing maintenance contracts that follow both from this secret knowledge and from the durability of an instrument, which will often have been saved up for over a period of years and expected to serve for decades if not centuries. The county directories and guide books of the eighteenth and earlier nineteenth centuries always mention the cathedral or parish church organ, if there is one, in the introduction to a town, as something to be seen and heard, and although the builder's name is rarely stated, quality assurance in terms of a named brand will have followed indirectly from this publicity.

The family advantage for performers has varied over time. In the twentieth-century revival of traditional music, it has in a number of striking instances made for a marked control of product, production, and ideology: the Kennedy family in Britain, the Seeger family in the USA, and on a more modest front Seth Lakeman and his two brothers in west Devon and the Davey family in Cornwall come to mind, this last coming to prominence in the later 1970s with their group Bucca, comprised of not three but four brothers, the Lakemans, from Buckland Monachorum, in 1994 with the

---

[155] Wickens 2001.

album *Three Piece Suite*.[156] More generally, travelling troupes of players naturally benefit from the variety of roles a spouse, children, and perhaps even their grandparents can provide without the need to hire labour, and this will have applied to some minstrels, even though the lone minstrel may be thought equally typical. As early as 1225 in Frome we find Alice and her husband, a minstrel, accommodating two other minstrels in their house, and in Barnstaple Thomas Greville's wife received a payment of 4d in 1462–63 for some function in connection with the minstrels, Greville himself probably being a relative of William Greville the blind harper already encountered.[157] Husband-and-wife minstrel teams such as John and Mabel Hobby, prosecuted with others for playing for dancing on the sabbath in Bath in 1607, sound vaguely disreputable, for one assumes that they travelled around, there being no female waits as respectable role models.[158] The poor minstrel couple survived at least into the nineteenth century, to judge from illustrations such as Robert Cruikshank's of the rowdy Buff Club at the Pig and Whistle, Bath. A broken-down soldier playing the fiddle is accompanied on the drum by a woman who is presumably his wife, common-law or otherwise, and the action centre-stage is not a country dance but a fight between two females.[159]

Whether or not also involved with the business, the wait's or instrument maker's wife was clearly the homemaker when their boy might be inducted or apprenticed into the waits' group, as happened with perhaps as many as four generations of Bussells, possibly including brothers, in Exeter in the sixteenth and seventeenth centuries, with William Johnson's son in Bristol in 1619, and at various times with other wait families.[160] Nor did it suit the Bristol secular musicians to operate as widowers. Johnson's apprentices were fed by three different wives in succession, Matilda, Margaret, and Alice, those of Nicholas Holden the trumpeter by two, Elizabeth and (again) Matilda.[161]

The rise of concert life added its own terms to the equation, as illustrated by a number of musical families in Bath. Here the Herschels, the Linleys, the Ashes, and the Loders all make for fruitful case studies, to be furthered in chapter 5, though one might add plenty of others – Kenneth James identified thirteen musical families operating in Bath in the eighteenth century, to which Andrew Clarke has added three more in the early nineteenth.[162] There

---

[156] Kent 2007a: 217–20; Wikipedia: 'Seth Lakeman'.
[157] Stokes 1996: 500; Wasson 1986: 339.
[158] Stokes 1996: 20.
[159] Nourse 2012: 80.
[160] Wasson 1986: 152–3, 178, 190, 198, 414–15, 418, 423; Pilkinton 1997: 201–11.
[161] Pilkinton 1997: 261–6, 258–61.
[162] James 1987: 453–965; Clarke 2011: 23–5.

were of course marriages between them; conversely, the number increases if one includes brother-sister pairs such as the Taylors and, at a pinch, the Storaces.[163] Not that families were everything: it was a person incapable of producing one, Rauzzini, who brought more musical capital into Bath than anyone else. But the professional musical family may have been the best enabler of careers for women in particular. Bath's roster of such families produced two outstanding metropolitan pianists in the nineteenth century, Lucy Anderson (Queen Victoria's teacher) and Kate Loder.[164] William Pryce Aylward of Salisbury (ca 1810–90) not only had Salisbury's three parish church appointments (St Thomas's, St Edmund's, and St Martin's) sewn up between himself and two of his sons, but became mayor of the city and also produced two daughters employed as singers in London and another active in Salisbury, as well as one who died young and a further son who played cello in the top London ensembles.[165]

Concert life was a musical concomitant to the urban consumer culture that had developed steadily throughout the eighteenth century, and it gave entrepreneurial families a geographical freedom of movement unknown to earlier generations. They were at liberty to raise subscriptions wherever sufficient performers could be enlisted and patrons be expected, though they would need to have established some kind of a teaching base, dealership, organist's post, or non-musical occupation in the locality first. The rewards might be great, but so were the risks, and bankruptcy continually dogged musicians' annals until a series of laws passed between 1825 and 1869 permitted them to operate through limited liability companies. Before that, a musical trader's bankruptcy was among the most frequent announcements in the press. The greater the stock-in-trade element of the business, the more likely his bankruptcy, it would seem, to judge from the bankruptcies of instrument makers and of dealers. Paul Micheau (Exeter, 1817), Joseph Parish (Teignmouth, 1818), Charles and John Bailey (Exeter and Exmouth, 1816, 1820, and 1822), Stephen Marsh (Bristol, 1833), and Josiah Jones (Bridgwater, 1841) exemplify the former, John Cole and John Ashley (Bath, 1814), William Bennett (Plymouth, 1814), Thomas Mason (Exeter, 1816), Thomas Rowe (Plymouth, 1819), Andrew Loder (Bath, 1827), Henry West (Bath, 1837), Frederick Crouch (Plymouth, 1840), James Montrie (Bristol, 1844), Bertram von der Mark (Bristol, 1853), James Ling (Taunton, 1856), and one of the Vinnicombe brothers (Exeter, 1869) the latter. Several of these men

---

[163] James 1987: 981–7, 997–1003.
[164] Temperley 2016: 31, 103–4; Ellsworth 2016; Brown and Stratton 1897: 10.
[165] Brown and Stratton 1897: 19.

were petitioning for release from debtors' prison, where they would have languished for fourteen days.[166] Society could be callous in such matters, and even without bankruptcy a court case might cost a trader dearly, as it did Joseph Anelli in Clifton in 1833 when sued by another dealer, presumably for some element of unfair competition.[167] Henry Burgum (1739–89), pewterer of Bristol and one of Thomas Chatterton's patrons, was a colourful concert impresario who was seen by many, including Thomas Linley senior, as having got his comeuppance when he eventually went bankrupt in 1783.[168] Linley was smarter, as well as luckier, as will be seen in chapter 5.

❧ Diversification, Mobility and Escape

Families can be oppressive. A standard British trope in the eighteenth and nineteenth centuries was the son who went to sea to prove himself or, conversely, to obviate the need to prove himself within the family calling, which could become an overcrowded marketplace. Without knowing their precise motives, we see the pattern in Thomas Linley's son Samuel and, beyond the region, in Charles Burney's son James, who accompanied Captain Cook on his second voyage and returned home in the company of a noble savage, Omai from the Society Islands.[169] Sam Linley died after contracting a fever at sea; as Black points out, he would have died anyway, for his ship went down with all hands on her next voyage.[170]

But long before the age of the virtuoso and its attendant culture of emulation, it had been common enough for musicians to have another occupation, most commonly retaining music as an economic insurance within an ongoing portfolio. A well-known instance was Palestrina's pursuit of the fur trade, through his second wife's business, alongside church music. If such combinations of employment or enterprise are to the twenty-first-century mind curious to contemplate, they may have seemed perfectly normal to earlier types of breadwinner, especially in post-Reformation England, where they were more common than in Palestrina's Rome, with its

---

[166] *EFP*, 20 Nov 1817: 4, 23 Apr 1818: 1, 21 Sep 1820: 1, 14 Feb 1822: 1, 30 May 1833: 3, 25 Feb 1841: 3, 9 Jun 1814: 1, 3 Nov 1814: 1, 27 Oct 1814: 4, 21 Nov 1816: 1, 18 Mar 1819: 1, 22 Mar 1827: 3, 5 Jan 1837: 3, 2 Jan 1840: 3, 26 Dec 1844: 3, 18 Sep 1856: 8, and 29 Nov 1865: 1, all indexed EFPSCI; *LG*, 5 Aug 1853: 2162; Cann 2001: 7–8; Wikipedia: 'History of bankruptcy law'; Vinnicombe.
[167] Britton 2010: 247–9.
[168] Chappell 1992; Barry 1985: 194–5; Barry 2010b: 151.
[169] Irving 2005.
[170] Black 1926: 119–20.

largely celibate church musicians. It is also the case that vicars choral had always been businessmen, thus lay musicians had an obvious role model.[171]

Lay clerks and singing men had lively portfolios. Their dynamic of diversity worked in two directions during the course of the sixteenth century, for the fashion for choral polyphony in monasteries, chapels, and wealthy parish churches before the Reformation increasingly necessitated the buying in of expert lay singers (hence the occupation 'singing man'), which the wholesale termination of ecclesiastical musicians' posts through religious and political upheaval then proceeded to reverse. Many a highly trained musician must have had to seek an alternative source of income during the turbulent mid-century years, which is probably putting it mildly. What, for example, happened to James Renynger, Glastonbury Abbey's last master of the choristers, appointed in 1534? We know that he petitioned for a pension after the dissolution of the abbey in 1539 – this is why his contract survives, for it was presented as evidence of tenure.[172] But it seems likely that he will have had to find some other livelihood. On the other hand, Thomas Rayne was still living on a pension in his 'shelled corner house' in Tywardreath seven years after the dissolution of his priory.[173] Furthermore, it is clear that there remained a lively freelance market for ecclesiastical singing men in London at least until the 1570s, and something similar obtained provincially on a smaller scale, for example at St Edmund's, Salisbury.[174]

The appointment of Thomas Rayne as clerk to the chapel of Tywardreath Priory in 1522 furnishes a well-documented example of a singing man bought in by a religious house. In addition to singing, playing the organ, and training up boys (though only two) in the performance of polyphony, he had to shave the prior every week, so at least he had his barber's skill to fall back on, it being a common one among musicians.[175] Robert Perry, married singing man of Bristol, took a musical apprentice, William Symons, in 1588 'only to sing and play on the virginals'; so he was quite a specialised musician. Nevertheless, at the time of his death in 1597 he had considerable business interests in knitted woollens, selling them through an agent in London and employing knitters in St Peter's parish, probably poor people, for in his will he left small bequests not only to them but to the remaining paupers.[176] Cathedral lay clerks, never

---

[171] Hampson 2012.
[172] Watkin 1950; Stokes 1996: 127–8.
[173] Orme 1990: 278–9.
[174] Cox 1913: 207–9.
[175] Orme 1990; Orme 2010: 292; Lorigan 2009: 125, citing Michael Fleming; Bowers 2007: 31–2, 36.
[176] Goodman 1974: 10; NA online: wills.

well paid, exhibited a variety of other occupations in the nineteenth century. Thomas Trimnell (Bristol) was a saddle-tree maker; at Exeter, John Hake sold clerical robes, and John Risdon was a bookseller in the High Street.[177]

Nor should it be forgotten that the materialities of music have always entailed complex networks of supply and symbiosis with artisanal expertise in non-musical areas. Until the era of electrical and then electronic technology, printing, publishing, and bookselling perennially hovered on the one side of musical trade, as on the other did toy and cabinet making and the manufacture of non-musical instruments such as barometers. The Hicks family of Bristol (and London), active in cabinet making prior to their involvement with organs and pianos, became so strongly associated in the earlier nineteenth century with the manufacture of street barrel organs and barrel pianos that they were long credited with the invention of the latter around 1805, although the real origins of the barrel piano seem to have been in Italy.[178]

Minstrels and players sometimes had other business. A man called Twigges was hawking his seasonal interludes around Cornwall in the 1570s possibly as a spy, in order to sniff out recusants, including Francis Tregian, father of the musical copyist; it has been suggested that the Protestant Arundells were his paymasters.[179] Above board, musical multitraders in the west country have included Reynold Prickett (tailor and minstrel, Pensford, between 1581 and 1611), Nicholas Holden (surgeon and trumpeter, Bristol, 1589), Thomas Peters (shoemaker and drummer, Wells, 1607), John Temple (joiner and fiddler, Winsham, 1635), two Jewish eighteenth-century musicians in Bath, Thomas Pinto and Emanuel Siprutini (respectively purveyor of Venetian eye-salve and violinist, and wine merchant and cellist), William Bayton (nurse and organist, Bristol, 1775), Mr Boyter (organist of St Thomas's and landlord of the Three Lions Inn, Salisbury, 1778), Peter Daniel (bookseller and organist, Frome, 1790s), Mrs Delamotte (postmistress and organist, Weymouth, 1797), Taverner Wilkey (victualler and musician, Bath, died 1793 – he had been a Bristol wait), and J Rio (linen draper and organist, Chard, 1799).[180] After this came a colourful assortment of nineteenth-

---

[177] Hobson 2012: 48; *EPJ* 1796, Universal 1799, iii: 13, 20 and *Alf*, 6 Jun 1815: 3; *EPJ* 1816 and 1822 and Pigot 1830: 70.
[178] Nourse 2014.
[179] Lorigan 2009: 97, 130–1.
[180] Stokes 1996: 205; Pilkinton 1997: 260; Stokes 1996: 298–302; ibid: 98, 501; Brown and Samuel 1986: 153 and James 1987: 879–83, 969; Sketchley 1775: 6; Robins 1998: 189; SDeB [3: 136]; Chedzoy 2003: 27; NA online: wills and Barry 2010a; Universal 1799, ii: 547.

century ones: J J Trathan of Falmouth, also a 'collector of minerals' in 1823; Bennett Swaffield, the pioneering choirmaster of St Austell, who in 1830 was Inspector of Corn Returns for the district (which can hardly have increased his popularity); W E Bennett of Langport, who doubled as a chemist in 1867; John Lovegrove of Clevedon, also dressing hair and selling perfumes in 1875 and adding a beer agency to his portfolio in the early 1880s; and two music dealers of Chippenham, A Taylor and Jacob Buckland, who respectively took photographs and sold seeds in the late 1870s.[181] Joseph Robinson of Weymouth left his 'Music and Fancy business' to his wife when he made his will in 1889; he also tuned instruments and taught.[182] J W Williams of Williton may have been a grocer, but the cocoa flutes he was selling in 1879 along with violins and clarinets were real musical instruments, cocoa being the hardwood of which they were made.[183] A versatile musician of Ilminster, John Holbrook, ran a pub called the Harmony Restored.[184] Various instrument makers were also joiners or carpenters or built other kinds of machinery, James Clarke of Frome (1658–1728), watchmaker, organist, and organ builder, being a typical example; but few of these will have been as creative as John Smith, last member of the Seede family of Bristol organ builders, who also built Bristol's first steamboat, designed a life-saving rocket apparatus for coastguards, and produced a road cleansing machine.[185] Karl Eulenstein played and taught the guitar in nineteenth-century Bath and travelled as a virtuoso but also put his immigrant status to excellent use when in his later years he published a successful series of German grammar and language books for the English and an English primer for Germans.[186] A more dubious utilisation of a musician's other skill was that of George Gay, psalmodist and stonemason from Corsham, who committed suicide by cutting his throat with his own mallet and chisel in 1833.[187]

Sadly, in none of the above cases is there additional data or comment that would tell us the balance of their occupations and income streams, though we do know that Eulenstein turned to language pedagogy from 'a lull in [music] teaching in the early 1840s'.[188] One sometimes gets the

---

[181] Pigot 1823: 183; McGrady 1991: 106; *LH*, 5 Jan 1867: 8; Kelly *Somerset* 1875 and 1883; Spinke 1877–79.
[182] BA (BRO) 40142/2.
[183] *WSFP*, 1 Mar 1879: 4.
[184] Mrs Annie Martin, cited *SCH*, 3 Jan 1959: 4.
[185] Norvall 1991: v, 7; Elvin 1995: 164–5, quoting Bristol 1883.
[186] Britton 2010: 251.
[187] Brown and Stratton 1897: 158.
[188] Britton 2010: 251.

impression that music will have been a modest but steady if seasonable earner, and probably an unpaid pursuit as well, while trading in something else responded to fashion or was speculative. But non-musical, industrial labour could be just as seasonal. The Leicester hosiery manufacturer (and important amateur musician) William Gardiner (1770–1853) recounted that some of his laid-off workers, all carefree young bachelors, 'formed the project of going into the south of England in the character of beggars'; singing a song in the streets of Exeter about their hungry wives and children, they 'collected £2 17s 6d in one day ... they had a good hot supper every night'.[189] And there were amateur musicians who started with a steady day job and then managed to turn professional, having built up a practice. The organist of Truro parish church, Charles William Hempel, was in a position to give up his position as a bank clerk in 1809, not something to have been undertaken lightly, especially since he had just got married.[190] The reliability of musical exchange will have been far less assured, however, when a person decided to jettison their interpersonal networks and move elsewhere. Beyond letters of recommendation, all they were then taking with them were their talent and their experience. Vulnerable but probably viable will have been the Wells waits who relocated to Exeter, as narrated in chapter 3.

Migration is an important element in a prosopographical story whose elements of stasis are easily exaggerated. Musical migration into the region has been touched upon at various points, as with the German band musicians and Irish fiddlers of the 'long' nineteenth century, to whom can be added the Italian buskers and organ grinders. There was a whole street of these in Bristol in 1891, still close to where St James's Fair had been held, and one of them, a survivor of Garibaldi's campaigns who spoke little English, would ply his trade as far afield as Truro as late as the 1920s.[191] The seasonal migration of London professionals to Bath in the eighteenth century and to the seaside resorts in the nineteenth and twentieth is implicit in various elements of the region's musical structure already accounted for, and touring virtuosi will be dealt with in chapter 6. Long preceding this culture of consumption, the regular influx of musicians with noblemen's travelling players will be recalled. Not to be forgotten, however, are the musicians already settled in the region who sometimes took time out to tour. We have encountered the Bristol waits doing this, but not yet the group of regional professionals who on various occasions in the mid-eighteenth century may well have gone

---

[189] Palmer 1996: 99, quoting Gardiner 1838–53, ii: 586–7.
[190] McGrady 1991: 74, 117–22.
[191] Dresser and Fleming 2007: 123; Radford 1965: 28.

on a short concertising holiday entirely for their own amusement, though one hopes to their pecuniary advantage as well. In August 1743, October 1752, April 1753, and September 1764 the record shows 'several of the best Hands from Salisbury and elsewhere' (Bath, Bristol, Exeter) turning up in Sherborne, and in 1743 in Shaftesbury as well, to play what must have been their favourite repertoire, some of it quite up to date, for in addition to plenty of Handel, in 1764 horn concertos by Abel and J C Bach, a song by Tenducci, and pieces by Sammartini and Pasquali feature.[192] Witness to the strength of associational networks, these concerts show top regional players and singers apparently jumping at the opportunity to get together in relatively out-of-the-way spots. William Biddlecombe (trumpeter), Thomas Norris and Joseph Corfe (tenors, Salisbury), and Mr Phillips (oboist, Bath) all participated in this philharmonic feast on one occasion or more, as did the local fixers John Tewkesbury (violinist and dancing master, Wincanton, who had earlier been the leader of Bath's regular orchestra) and William Thompson (organist, Sherborne Abbey). At least, one assumes that Thompson, who sold the tickets, will have played too. Elected in 1741, was it he who organised the first concert and began the tradition?[193] A similar equation, probably involving some of the same people, played itself out in Devizes between 1743 and 1750.[194]

Migration out of the region might be subdivided into the departure of those moving on through promotion or ambition and the migration of the failed. It is too facile to say that the former went to London and the latter went abroad. Nor is it easy to pin down failure: many young musicians will have tried their luck elsewhere, or tried a different calling, through a sense of adventure, impatience, social claustrophobia, or romantic unhappiness. (Any of these might have applied to Sam Linley.) In an era of great financial insecurity and social change such as the earlier decades of the nineteenth century, ambition might be a matter of doing whatever it would take to circumvent failure rather than an aptitude for competitiveness or a drive for power *per se*. Edward Hodges was a Bristol organist and composer of nonconformist origins who emigrated to New York via Toronto in 1838. His biographer sums up the equation as Hodges must have calculated it: 'St James' Cathedral in Toronto was taking delivery of a new English-built organ that summer and had offered him the post of organist. Prior experiences had shown him that no corresponding offer from a large parish or collegiate

---

[192] *SM*, 9 Aug 1743: 4, 9 Oct 1752: 3, 30 Oct 1752: 3, 9 Apr 1753: 3 and 10 Sep 1764: 2.
[193] Burrows and Dunhill 2002: 32, 112, 328–9, 1143, 1181; James 1987: 1008–10; *EFP*, 27 Mar 1767: 1; WHCSCI 2944/110; George Tatham, personal communication.
[194] Chevill 1993: 141–2.

church or cathedral in England was ever likely to come his way.'[195] With his Cambridge MusD, he had been shortlisted for the post at St George's Chapel, Windsor, but lost out to George Elvey, who was only nineteen. Lack of preferment drove him abroad, very quickly out of the welcoming arms of Toronto and into those of Trinity Church, New York, where he established Anglican musical conventions that led the continent. But a quarter of a century later he retired back to Bristol, to find John Davis Corfe still at his cathedral organist's post.[196] Around 1800, from an infinitely smaller settlement, Walton near Street, James Everdell, son of a local musician, had also emigrated to New York, where he became a music teacher.[197] Aaron Upjohn Hayter, born in Gillingham in 1799 and a Salisbury Cathedral chorister from the age of six, went to New York as organist of Grace Church in 1835, soon moving on to Trinity Church in Boston, a city in which he also made his mark as conductor of the Handel and Haydn Society. His father, Samuel Hayter, had been organist of Mere parish church, and the son, unlike Hodges, occupied a cathedral post (Hereford) prior to emigration.[198]

To elaborate on the triangulation of province, metropolis, and overseas territory already implict in the career of Hodges, a study taking nineteenth-century Bristol as the exemplar identifies relatively little musical migration between the British regions but plenty of relocation to London and emigration to the 'British world' overseas, including the USA. Of around seventy-five genteel (as opposed to proletarian) musicians born between *ca* 1760 and 1880, the largest single cohort was still the group of twenty-one whose entire careers were spent in Bristol, having mostly been born and bred there. Ten musicians settled in Bristol having already been established elsewhere, but more than three times this number moved in the opposite direction, leaving a musical living or amateur presence in Bristol for one somewhere else – only seven or eight to other provincial parts of Britain (two of these remaining in the west country) but fifteen to London and eleven abroad, in every case to somewhere within the formal or informal British world. A few people figure in more than one category, some could not be firmly assigned, and the British-world emigrants swell to thirteen if one includes those from wider parts of Somerset. The figures would benefit from being expanded

---

[195] Ogasapian 1994: 93.
[196] Banfield 2006: 32–3, 37–40.
[197] Dunning 2006: 200.
[198] Brown and Stratton 1897: 192.

and finessed (for example, to take separate account of places of study).[199] The brain drain to London and its environs was well under way by the early seventeenth century, when, in addition to William Child, John Levasher, son of the Bristol instrument maker Thomas, headed towards the big city, where he is found performing in James Shirley's masque *The Triumph of Peace* as one of the musicians of the Cockpit Theatre in 1634. Levashers settled in the Quantock village of Stogursey as Huguenot refugees; whether this included any of the musicians in the family is not known, though they seem to have come from Paris. If it did, John and one or more of his forbears represent the recurrent phenomenon of double migration: to regional gateway, then to the metropolis.[200]

The outgoing figures for Bristol are probably typical, and data concerning musicians' mobility assembled by the author across the west country as a whole over a broader timescale tends to confirm them, though with London having more of an edge over foreign destinations (fifty-one emigrants indexed for the period from the 1750s to 1914, as opposed to ninety-five persons bound for London). Bristol's incoming figures cannot be representative of the entire region, however, for the simple reason that west country seaside resorts such as Weston-super-Mare and Bournemouth grew from nothing at the beginning of the nineteenth century into sizable centres of population by the time of the First World War. Organists, bandsmen, and teachers migrated into these settlements on the basis of sector job creation, a happy circumstance which with relatively minor exceptions (public school and eventually state school and university posts) did not occur elsewhere.

The draining of regional creative talent by the metropolis would appear to be a perennial fact of British life, though the available data for musicians shows variation by decade and period. But there is no doubt about overall economic decline in the west country as a further backdrop to this. Money was ceasing to be made in Frome and the Wiltshire textile towns in the early nineteenth century as industry triumphed in the north, William Cobbett noting the irony in Frome in 1826 of licensed 'weavers from the North, *singing about the towns ballads of Distress!*', as though Frome were not in even greater distress and in no position to support them.[201] In the same period, the cultural economy of Bath was declining as the fashionable deserted it for Brighton and other newer resorts. Exeter and Salisbury, like most cathedral cities, were failing to industrialise. Cornwall's prosperity collapsed in the

---

[199] Banfield 2010.
[200] Lefkowitz 1965: 48; Lasocki 1983, i: 294, ii: 762; Lasocki 1992.
[201] Cobbett 1967: 341.

1860s when the copper mines could no longer compete with those of South America, Plymouth's after the Second World War with cutbacks in the Royal Navy, and that of the seaside resorts in the 1960s as people began to fly abroad for their holidays. Wells had declined far earlier than the nineteenth century. Bristol declined in relative terms, through slower industrial growth than that of the northern cities and a port too far upriver, its main rival Liverpool having overtaken it in size of population by 1801.

No fewer than three sons of the barrel piano manufacturer Joseph Hicks senior moved to London from Bristol after their father died in 1844 (two of them subsequently emigrated).[202] Clarke has shown how the Loders' centre of gravity weakened as members found better livings elsewhere. John David and Kate Loder were drawn firmly into London's musical life as performers and teachers, Kate's metropolitan establishment as a pianist after studying there contrasting with Cecilia Summerhayes's adoption of Birmingham and return to Taunton fifteen or so years later. For all the opprobrium that has been heaped upon the early decades of the institution, one wonders whether the establishment in 1822 of the Royal Academy of Music, where both Kate and John David Loder later taught, sent out a positive signal about London as a fulcrum for English-born musicians alongside the constant influx of foreign virtuosi; if so, Nash's Regent Street and the Philharmonic Society project strengthened the signal, as we are only now beginning to understand.[203] For in the 1820s, '30s, and '40s, seventeen west country musicians are recorded as having established themselves in the metropolis, by contrast with only eight known to have emigrated in this period. On the other hand, Edward Loder, ambitious for English composition, found his best job as musical director in a Manchester theatre, and George Loder junior did emigrate in the 1830s.[204]

Another way of viewing emigration, analysed by Philip Payton in his study of the west country's most distinctive migratory cohort, the Cornish, is as a variable equation of 'push' and 'pull' factors.[205] The most extreme example of 'push' was transportation for crime. Several musical convicts transported to Australia from the west country have been identified. Henry Honey, the 21-year-old musician son of a Plymouth piano tuner of the same name living in King St, was the most spectacular of them. In July 1835, many British newspapers carried the story of how he had killed his young wife by cutting her throat. But he was shaving at the time of the confrontation,

---

[202] Nourse 2014.
[203] Langley 2013.
[204] Clarke 2011: passim; Temperley 2001b.
[205] Payton 2005: 12 and passim.

and the jury of the Devon Assizes returned a verdict of manslaughter, not murder; his own life was thus spared. He was transported for life to New South Wales, but this violent and drunken character seems to have left no musical mark on Australia.[206]

Three and a half years earlier, Henry James Witton had been convicted of obtaining musical instruments under false pretences at the Bristol Quarter Sessions and transported for seven years. He made good in Tasmania, only to be rearrested for forgery, but eventually settled down to a musician's portfolio of dealership, teaching, performing, and composing in all of Australia's major cities except Perth, dying in 1875. He claimed to be a pupil of the RAM but it seems more likely that this was only by proxy, if (say) he was the brother of the oboist J Witton who had been admitted in 1825, two or more Wittons being prominent British oboists of the 1820s and '30s.[207] But wind instrument expert he certainly was: he displayed a box of clarinet reeds and apparently a flute of his own manufacture at the London International Exhibition of 1862.[208] Quite what Witton had been doing in Bristol, other than stealing musical instruments, is anybody's guess, but these were unsettled times, for Bristol was rioting in October 1831, so it was a restive place for any subaltern musician to be. Seven years after Witton, a shoemaker and amateur musician from Bath, Samuel Woods (an alias), was transported to Tasmania and came to an altogether stickier end, hanged in Melbourne Gaol in 1864 as violent accomplice to a murderer. 'He was very fond of singing, and previous to his condemnation copied a lot of music. He also used to play the harmonium in the Gaol. His music-book he gave to the senior warder.'[209] A third convict, John Charles Tapp, 'a respectable-looking young man' convicted of forging a cheque at the Taunton Assizes in 1847, aged twenty-two like Witton and sentenced to fourteen years' transportation, claims infinitely more sympathy than Woods and probably typifies the desperation of his class in the Frome area in the 'hungry forties'. He came from Stoke St Michael, and the previous year he or a near relative had been attempting to lease out Ham grist mill near the next village, Coleford. Already a Methodist, one imagines, Tapp had to endure four years in a prison hulk before joining one of the last shipments of convicts to Tasmania, where he lost no time in attaching himself to the Wesleyan Sunday School in Hobart, gained a conditional pardon in 1854,

---

[206] Pigot 1830: 112; *EFP*, 6 Aug 1835: 2; Australharmony.
[207] *BM*, 14 Feb 1832: 3; Australharmony; Kathy Adamson and Janet Snowman, personal communications, Jan 2014.
[208] Exhibition Catalogue 1862: 145; Waterhouse 1993: 433.
[209] Australharmony; *The Mercury* (Hobart), 8 Aug 1864: 2.

became known as a Hobart organist, and published *Tasmanian Sacred Melodies* in 1855. He held various administrative posts at the Port Arthur prison and died in the same year as Witton, 1875.[210] Judging from *Tasmanian Sacred Melodies*, which comprise set pieces in the best Methodist tradition (i.e. hymns of multiple musical sections with instrumental 'symphonies') plus a number of chants, Tapp was a composer of real if unlettered vitality lost to the west country.[211]

Few emigrant musicians before the late nineteenth century will have gone abroad with a correspondingly strong 'pull': a job awaiting them. Hodges was exceptional, the more so in leaving direct from Bristol. Patronage via London was a later and commoner route, as in the case of Ernest Slater, born in Taunton, who after studying at the RAM became assistant organist of Exeter Cathedral in 1881 but two years later left again for London, where for another two years he was organist of Lambeth parish church. This building could not be closer to the residence of the Archbishop of Canterbury, who will have consulted Sir John Stainer, organist of St Paul's Cathedral, about the best musical incumbent for Calcutta Cathedral. Stainer 'selected' Slater, and off he went.[212]

Without such patronage, youth, adaptability, and an open mind as to eventual outcome were the best ingredients for survival. A sense of adventure may have driven some, but as the growing culture of financial remittance shows, so in many cases did a sense of responsibility towards the family. The building of whole streets in Redruth was supposedly financed by Cornish miners' remittances.[213] It is difficult to judge when adventurers were being irresponsible and when they were being quite the opposite. George Loder's father had died aged thirty-nine in 1829, leaving three children with no mother. The family network must have helped support them, but the emigration of the eldest, George, to New York at the age of twenty in 1836 seems likely to have been premised partly on the responsibility either to cease being a burden to his Bath relatives or to make a good living abroad and send money home at a time when his younger sister Kate was still only eleven years old. He proved a true upholder of the Loders' musical authority: where his uncle had led the orchestra of the Philharmonic Society, he in time became one of the conductors of the New York Philharmonic, in which capacity he directed the first American performance of Beethoven's 9th

---

[210] *Stamford Mercury*, 9 Apr 1847: 4; *TC*, 25 Mar 1846: 1; Australharmony.
[211] NLA, digitally available.
[212] Brown and Stratton 1897: 376.
[213] Payton 2005: 94, 351–3, 365.

Symphony.[214] But while he was adventurous enough subsequently to follow the gold rushes to San Francisco (1852) and then to Australia (1855), his colourful memoirs furnishing one of the classic accounts of hauling pianos up and down mountainsides, he also took pains to warn would-be emigrants of the equation:

> I cannot too strongly beg all young men who, in England or elsewhere, are in possession of a certain employment, if even a bare living, with a prospect of advancement, to weigh well the *pros* and *cons* before they place themselves in the sad position in which thousands of men of talent, energy, and education are now suffering in the colonies. Success in the new land is quite a lottery, and for one who has been enabled to obtain respectable employment, at least twenty suffer almost from starvation.[215]

After more than twenty years abroad, Loder was back in Britain when he wrote this; but keeping up with the professional rat-race in London was no easy matter either, and he returned to Australia in 1862, only to die in Adelaide six years later 'on a lonely bed in the hospital, with no relation near to close his death-glazed eyes, or drop a kindly tear over his pillow', having lost two wives to disease on his various travels.[216]

Whether actually taking one's shovel and going digging, or seizing the opportunity of a ready-made audience starved of feminine beauty and 'good' music (the latter applying to George Loder), the sense of excitement and personal opportunity offered by the mid-century gold rushes of California and Victoria, Australia, and the later attractions of diamonds in South Africa and more gold there and in the Yukon, created a 'pull' of an extremity difficult to imagine now. Charles Summers, from a family of stonemasons in Charlton Mackrell, Somerset, emigrated to Victoria in 1852 and was soon working the goldfields in sibling company. Settled and successful as a sculptor in Melbourne, he cast in one piece the bronze Burke and Wills memorial, received £4,000 for it, and perhaps on the back of this induced his musician brother Joseph, who was still in England, to join him there in 1865. Joseph (1839–1917) should not have needed to emigrate, for he had recently been appointed organist of a new, large church, Holy Trinity, in what at the time must have been the west country's fastest-growing town, Weston-super-Mare. But emigrate he did, and remained in Australia in a somewhat combative

---

[214] Clarke 2011: 59–74, 100.
[215] Loder 1858: 564.
[216] *Ballarat Star*, 25 Jul 1868: 2; Loder 1858: 487, 499.

variety of official musical capacities, ecclesiastical and educational.[217] Austin Turner (1823–1901), probably the son of George Turner, Bristol music teacher and founder member of the Bristol Madrigal Society, went to Australia in 1854 (from Lincoln, where he was a vicar choral, not directly from Bristol) and in late 1857 settled in Ballarat, just before its population of gold diggers peaked. He wasted no time in founding the Ballarat Philharmonic a few months later, and remained the town's leading musician for the following quarter-century.[218] Like so many of Bristol's musicians, he had been a chorister at the cathedral, and so had Austin Phillips (ca 1805–51), another of the Bristol Madrigal Society's founder members, whose emigration was, however, as strong a 'push' as Summers's and Turner's later 'pulls' must have been, since Phillips, organist of St Michael's church, was declared bankrupt in late 1837, not long after attending the first meeting of the Bristol Madrigal Society. Having cleared his debts, he made a fresh start in the USA the following year, composing on the voyage out on Brunel's SS *Great Western* the song 'Farewell awhile my native isle' with words by fellow traveller John Wilson, a copy of which they threw overboard 'for behoof of all Lovers of Song'. Later published in Bristol (though presumably not from the waterborne copy), the sheet music includes a fine engraving of the ship.[219]

Many west country emigrants were musical amateurs, their accomplishment of added value but not essential for survival. Payton mentions several of these among the Cornish, including Alfred Nicholls, a miner from near Redruth whose musical skills helped him gain a wife in the Upper Peninsula, Michigan, and 'Fiddler Jim' Richards from Perranporth, one of the contributors to *Christmas Welcome: a choice collection of Cornish carols*, published at Moonta, South Australia, in 1893.[220] In the 1870s, an Exeter medical man, Clarence Visick, chose (one assumes) the balmy climate of Málaga in Spain in which to tend to the health of the expatriate community and keep up his amateur musical skills, which he did as organist of the Anglican church there for thirty-nine years.[221] Other emigrants were only children or young teenagers and accordingly only latent musicians at the time of their departure with or without their family. Conversely, the vast majority of assisted emigrants in the nineteenth century were agricultural

---

[217] Brown 1988: 167–70; Summers 1910: 5–6; Brown and Stratton 1897: 401; Stevens 1976.
[218] Hobson 2012: 48; Brown and Stratton 1897: 419–20; Wikipedia: 'Ballarat'; Doggett 2006, i: 204, 206, 212–14, and passim.
[219] Hobson 2012: 48; Hobson 2008.
[220] Payton 2005: 151–3, 288–9.
[221] St George's Church, Málaga, wall plaque: personal visit, 17 May 2015.

workers, domestics, or artisans (or said they were), though the odd teacher appears in the records; it is therefore a tribute to the new land that it gave their offspring his or her opportunity in music.[222] The USA and Canada were best placed to do this, as the example of two Cornishmen from mining dynasties demonstrates. Richard Jose (1862–1941), from Lanner, emigrated after his father's death in 1876, going in search of an uncle in Nevada, though not as the mere child he would later claim to have been when he falsified his birth date to 1869. In Reno he apprenticed himself to a blacksmith, but it was blackface that later called him, and he became a leading minstrelsy performer and one of America's earliest popular recording artists. A high tenor rather than the countertenor he is often described as, he somehow managed to extend a chest register right up to e″, the c#″ apex pitch on his recording of Theodore Morse's 'Dear old girl' constituting an extraordinary but unforced and wholly convincing sound, complete with residual Cornish accent.[223] Jose's near contemporary James Opie Brokenshire from Redruth (1865–1938; later spelt Brockenshire) also left for the New World in his teens, in 1883 or 1884. Plenty of other Brokenshires, a family including earlier literate musicians, had already emigrated or would do so, turning up in North and South America, Australia, and New Zealand in the peculiarly Cornish cohort of expert miners abroad. James Opie Brokenshire enlisted in the US Army as a bandsman in the 7th Cavalry Regiment (Custer's Cavalry) and subsequently enjoyed a prominent military career, in charge of federal army music purchases almost until his death.[224]

Another young emigrant, this time from Chudleigh Knighton in Devon, William Luscombe Searell (1853–1907; later spelt Searelle) was taken by his parents to Christchurch, New Zealand as a child aged eight, along with his numerous siblings. His father had worked the mill at Bellamarsh Barton – there is a farm called Luscombe some way up a side valley – and was no doubt, like Tapp, in urgent need of a better living, which he seems to have found in the same trade in Christchurch, where there is a street named after him. Luscombe's music came from his mother, a trained amateur of higher social standing than his father, and he bucked a respectable education and strict, churchy upbringing to conform to the cosmopolitan theatre type. He enjoyed a colourful and raffish career spanning the composition and production of operettas on three continents, in New Zealand, Australia,

---

[222] Payton 2005: 75–7.
[223] Debus 2006: 18–19; Minstrelsy 2006, tracks 17–18 [17]; Gracyk 2006; Payton 2005: 334–5.
[224] Free BMD; Rehrig 2013; *RCG*, 21 Jan 1815: 2; Payton 2005: 61–2, 121, 307, 391.

South Africa, London, and the USA, and eventually teamed up with Ella Wheeler Wilcox for a biblical opera, *Mizpah*, produced in San Francisco.[225]

Quite often it was one or more sons who went first, the father or whole family eventually following. Viner, after twenty-four years at St Mary's Penzance, ended his days in Massachusetts, emigrating in 1859 at the age of sixty-nine to join his son Frederick, who had been there since 1851. A family organ-building business was duly established in New England between two or three of the sons, one of whom later relocated to Buffalo.[226] W C Peters (1805–66) emigrated from Woodbury, Devon, somewhere between the ages of fifteen and twenty – the sources conflict – and built up a large music publishing empire in the eastern United States, known for its Stephen Foster imprints and the first issue of 'Jim Crow'. His elder brother had preceded him to North America and his father followed; perhaps both father and son were militia musicians and emigrated after their skills became redundant with the peace, for W C Peters is said to have been in a Canadian military band around 1823 before entering the USA, and apparently his father was also a bandmaster and also in Canada. Roman Catholic, and with W C Peters settling in Cincinnati, they may well have been of German descent. (The father, William S Peters, went on to found a Utopian colony in Texas.)[227] From Tavistock at the other end of Devon, William Robjohn (1843–1920) left with his family for New York in 1858 aged fifteen and, his voice evidently not yet broken, became a chorister at Trinity Church under Hodges' successor; later he was assistant organist there, and composed under the pseudonym Caryl Florio. His father, also William, was emigrating to join brother Thomas in the organ-building trade, Thomas having been apprenticed to Gray in London prior to his own emigration many years earlier, in or before 1834.[228]

Not to be forgotten amid all this New World enterprise, however, is its opposite: west country amateur occupation in music so rooted in place and company that we have not thought to ask whether it survived transplantation. John England of Hambridge, Somerset, then aged thirty-seven or thirty-eight, sparked off the first English folksong revival when he sang 'The seeds of love' within earshot of Cecil Sharp, probably on 22 August 1903, while

---

[225] Wikipedia: 'Luscombe Searelle'; Greenaway 2007; Pinner 2011. Malan 1986 contains such puzzlingly different details that one suspects their invention by Searelle himself.

[226] Clarke 2011: 54–7.

[227] Wetzel 2001 and 1983: 27–9; Wade.

[228] Osborne 2013; Ogasapian 1994: 112–13, 120; Pinel 2006.

mowing the vicar's lawn. Eight years later he emigrated with his family to Saskatchewan. Did he still sing it there? Did they notice?[229]

---

[229] *WG*, 24 Mar 1911: 4; Bearman and Staelens 2006; Karpeles 1967: 32.

CHAPTER 5

Musical Livings II: Individual Case Studies

ଈ *Three Bristol Portfolios*

THE LATE Andrew Britton made a study of three guitarists active in Bristol and Bath in the period of the Spanish guitar's greatest popularity, the 1820s to the 1840s, which casts a great deal of light not only on the portfolios of two immigrant virtuosi, Karl (Charles) Eulenstein and Giuseppe (Joseph) Anelli, and one member of a home-grown musical family, Stephen Pratten, but by extension on the typical conditions of a musical living at this time.[1] Three Bristol teacher-musicians from later in the nineteenth century provide comparable material amid changing conditions. Two of them, Joseph Leopold Roeckel (1838–1923) and Jane Jackson (1834–1907), were a married couple. They operated from a secular base in wealthy Clifton, and both used pen names. Jackson was one of the two musical daughters of Bristol's most important artist, Samuel Jackson (himself a fine pianist and a guitarist closely connected with the subjects of Britton's study), her younger sister Ada becoming a leading local singer.[2] Jackson published all her compositions under the name Jules de Sivrai. Roeckel's pen name, frequently used in his earlier years, was Edouard Dorn, though there has to remain some margin for doubt here, since Dorn is given a separate identity and different birth date in certain catalogue entries, at least one of which extends the known output alarmingly.[3] The third figure was Frederick Charles Maker (1844–1927), organist and choirmaster of the fashionable Redland Park Congregational Church in an adjoining suburb. His church, bombed in December 1940, subject in that state of a fine John Piper oil painting, and then rebuilt, is still a thriving concern.

---

[1] Britton 2010: 229–73, 347–50; BA (BRO) 15399.
[2] Greenacre and Stoddard 1988: 85–90.
[3] Pazdírek nd, [iv]: 380–3.

210 MUSIC IN THE WEST COUNTRY

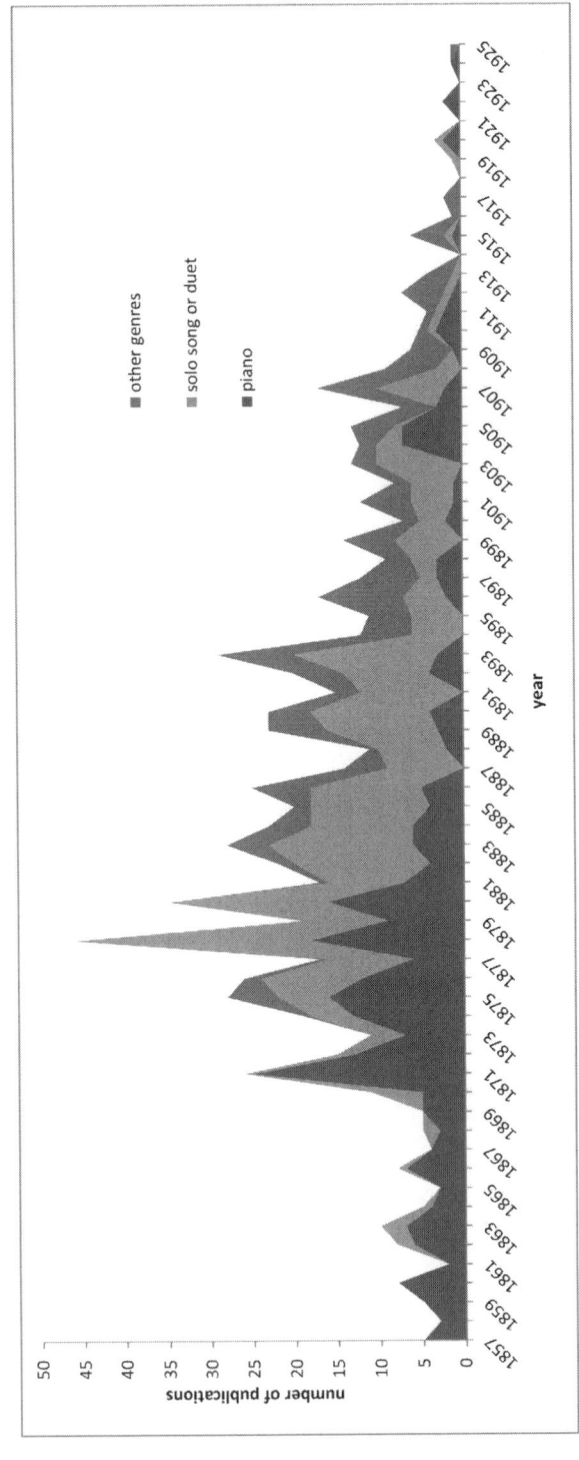

Graph 5.1 Combined lifetime output (number of musical publications listed in British Library catalogue) of Joseph Roeckel, Jules de Sivrai (Jane Jackson), and Frederick Maker

All three of them must have earned part of their living from teaching and performing, but it is the size of their output as composers and arrangers that attracts remark, for between them, and assuming Dorn to have been Roeckel, they must have seen 1,000 or more publications through the press in their lifetimes. Of the 820 or so that are in the British Library, about 75 per cent are by Roeckel, whose most popular piece, the balletic piano miniature 'Air du Dauphin' (dedicated to George Riseley), was published in nine versions, and who in 1871, one of his peak years, was turning out more than one elaborated medley of a famous opera per month, as well as other things.[4] This was while his wife was quarrying the same repertoire for virtuoso piano fantasias, for example on themes from *L'Elisir d'amore*, in the expectation that her friend Arabella Goddard would play them on the concert platforms of London and the Empire (which she did, as far away as Australia and New Zealand).[5] Roeckel's note-spinning of this sort was pure hackwork; quite how Jackson viewed hers is less easy to ascertain. There will certainly have been a pride in their freelance solvency, which in the census of the same year saw them living comfortably with two servants.[6]

They could spin their notes because of the advent of cheap printing, pioneered above all by Vincent and J Alfred Novello.[7] The compositions of our provincial trio (Graph 5.1), published in London or overseas, confirm the market conditions and therefore the chief possibilities of a living for a musician – teacher, performer, composer – outside the Church, the military, and the theatre in Britain at this period. Both husband and wife were supplying large amounts of piano music in the 1860s, '70s and '80s. But since the overall market did not seem to expand – or was it that they were receiving ongoing royalties and needed to publish less new material? – the volume of piano music fell as the demand for popular songs and ballads rose. This demand was created or at least fiercely fuelled by publishers, John Boosey setting a trend with his popular ballad concerts at St James's Hall in London in the mid-1860s.[8] Not many of Roeckel's songs were published by Boosey, but he wrote skilfully for the ballad concerts' matinee idol, the tenor Sims Reeves, for example in 'I cannot say goodbye', with words by John Oxenford.[9]

---

[4] BL Cat, though this is not exhaustive.
[5] *Brisbane Courier*, 12 Jul 1873: 1, *Nelson Evening Mail*, 6 Nov 1874: 2, and many later references via Trove and Papers Past; see also *The Times*, 13 Jan 1877: 1.
[6] Census 1871.
[7] Hughes 2001: 215; Cooper 2003: 11–13, 70–6, 79–82.
[8] CPH, 'Ballad concerts', gives the date 1864; Krummel 1981: 54 has 1866; Boosey 1931: 15 states that they began in 1867.
[9] NLA, digitally available.

It may be that Roeckel's relationship with his publishers and hence with the market was a more businesslike, masculine affair than Jackson's with Goddard, and she accordingly dropped out of the running, never publishing many songs. Meanwhile, Maker entered the scene in the 1880s largely with anthems, and one suspects that the expanding market here was primarily for nonconformist church choirs, though new Anglican churches in the suburbs and ritualised ones in the towns and villages will have increased demand as well. Roeckel also published a few anthems in the late 1890s and after, but as part of a generally more diversified and smaller output from this period onwards – in other words, a more selective one. In addition to a number of salon publications for violin and piano (was there a growing market for café music?), Roeckel tried his hand at cantatas both sacred and secular, at partsongs, and at the odd light work for the stage, though in most of these categories he restricted himself to educational and children's music, another area of increased demand perhaps as a delayed result of the 1870 Education Act but doubtless due to other social developments as well. It seems odd, however, that Maker published nothing for the organ.

All three composers have been forgotten, and one might leave where it lies the utter disjunction between a buoyant provincial living and posterity, were it not for three observations. First, Maker has not in fact been entirely forgotten, but lives on in his tune REST (also called ELTON), associated with the hymn 'Dear Lord and Father of mankind' in the USA in preference to Parry's REPTON, though neither tune was written for these words. No better example of Victorian taste than REST will be found (Ex. 5.1), with its semitonal chromatic inflections in the melody (two of them in the first line alone), its yearning augmented triad and whole-tone sonority underpinning the melodic apex in line 3 (particularly well fitted to 'the strain and stress' in stanza 4), and its use of the diminished 7th as both the second and penultimate chord of the tune. Thoroughly feminised, such sentiment was soon outlawed in the end-of-century nationalist programmes for art and its infrastructures, and already in 1888 Parry's tune was negating similar diminished 7ths that might have been expected, putting a stern dominant bass in the place of one and a *Tristan* chord of another. The nonconformist churches in Britain and the Protestant denominations of the USA were much less subject to such cultural manoeuvring than the established Church of England, and for REST's survival we can thank them.

Second, it is less easy than for Roeckel to measure the difference that Jackson made through her compositions alone. The feminine sphere of musical activity and influence was driven by private, personal components with fewer of their public counterparts than entailed by the man's world of publications, business meetings, boards, committees, recommendations,

Ex. 5.1 Frederick Maker: REST

and appointments, and although women were beginning to infiltrate these spheres, they were not Jackson's primary habitat. Yet her *Musical Times* obituary – a great deal longer than her husband's eventual one-liner – saw it as important to quote at length from a local one that had appeared in the *Bristol Mirror*. Even if Joseph Roeckel were its author (and he wasted no time in remarrying, doing so the following year), its testimony would be difficult to dismiss:

> Her goodness of heart and the generosity of her nature were shown in multifarious ways, and although some of her acts of devotion and benevolence were known, hundreds were secretly done. It is quite impossible even to remember the very numerous concerts she organized to assist those of her kindred and others in distress. The writer can call to memory many instances where her thoughtful kindness and generosity brought relief to sorrowful

hearts. She founded the Teachers' Provident Association in 1885. Perhaps one of the most notable instances of her goodness is [the violinist] Miss Marie Hall. Everyone is acquainted with the early life of the brilliant little artist. It was one of poverty and of drudgery, and of gaining a pittance by playing in the streets. Mainly through the instrumentality of Mrs Roeckel the child was rescued and brought to the notice of Mr P Napier Miles, who placed her under accomplished masters. How she has profited by the tuition she received everyone knows. Surely of Mrs Roeckel it may fittingly be said she rests from her labours and her works follow her.[10]

One place, therefore, where her good works followed her was back into musical composition, for Vaughan Williams's *The Lark Ascending* was written for Hall in 1914 and first performed by her in Shirehampton, the village on the edge of Bristol where Jackson herself had been buried a few years earlier. With *The Lark Ascending* having been voted Britain's favourite piece of classical music and 'Dear Lord and Father of mankind' its second favourite hymn in recent years, musical history begins to inhabit unlikely dwellings.[11]

Our third observation must be to marvel at an oblivion that Joseph Roeckel so little deserves. He had an extraordinarily distinguished musical pedigree, as the press was proud to note on his first appearance as a pianist in Clifton aged twenty-three in 1861: 'Mr Joseph Roeckel, a young *pianiste*, residing in Bath, then played Beethoven's Sonata in F, in a manner which spoke well for his future career. He comes, we learn, indeed, from a fine musical stock. His father, a singer, was the close friend of the great master whose work he himself essayed, and whose opera of *Fidelio* was written for him, and he is a nephew of the renowned Hummel.'[12] The tenor Joseph Röckel had indeed been the first Florestan in the revised version of Beethoven's *Fidelio*, and his sister Elisabeth, another well-known singer who at one time was considered to have been the dedicatee of Beethoven's 'Für Elise', had married Johann Nepomuk Hummel. Röckel senior taught Henriette Sontag and as a director was later responsible for pioneering seasons of German opera in Paris and London, the London one conducted by Hummel, and in retirement he settled as a teacher in York, though eventually he returned to Germany, where he died in his late eighties.[13] Joseph Leopold, born when his father was in his mid-fifties, must have been something of an afterthought, for his

[10] Free BMD; *MT* xlviii (1907): 670.
[11] Wikipedia: 'Dear Lord and Father of mankind', '*The Lark Ascending*'.
[12] *BM*, 21 Sep 1861: 2.
[13] Barclay Squire 2001; Wikipedia: 'Elisabeth Röckel'.

eldest brothers were nearly a generation his senior. He may have had little contact with August (1814–76), which would have been just as well when the latter, who was director of music at the Dresden opera house, manned the revolutionary barricades in 1849, encouraging Wagner to do the same, and when the enterprise failed found that a price was on the heads of them both. August Röckel was in fact sentenced to death, though this was commuted to thirteen years' imprisonment. Wagner fled Germany.[14]

Another elder brother of Joseph Leopold, the pianist and composer Edouard (1816–99), was active in both Germany and England as a young man and probably wise to have settled in 1848 as far away from political turmoil as possible, namely in Bath, where he subsisted as another of our freelance teacher-performers. There was yet another brother, Alfred, a French military veteran and chevalier of the Légion d'Honneur and various other orders, who died in 1862, Joseph Leopold having visited him in France four years previously.[15] More mysterious is the Armand Roeckel who was active as a pianist in Cork, Ireland, in the first half of the 1850s, and described as being 'from the Conservatoire de Musique, Paris', sometimes with a Madame Roeckel, also from Paris, sharing the platform as singer.[16] At a concert in 1854 he stormed off the stage in mid-accompaniment of another female singer, Mrs Eiffe, and in April 1855 'Mons J Roeckel' first appears in Cork, as a conductor.[17] What seems to have happened is that the eighteen-year-old Joseph was being inducted into a living by his relative Armand, who did not intend to remain there, though the *Cork Examiner* never drew attention to the fact that there were at this point two musically presiding Roeckels. Perhaps Armand bribed it not to, for after mid-May 1855 he simply disappears from the notices. Whether or not fleeing from Madame Roeckel or from creditors (or indeed from Mrs Eiffe), soon he was on his way to Australia, where he was active in Sydney throughout 1856 and the following year published 'The Australian polka mazurka' for piano (none other than his 'Souvenir de Cork' under a new title) plus one or two other works, apparently returning to France, where a son was born in 1863.[18] Armand may have been a fifth brother, or perhaps the son of one of the eldest brothers, who could quite easily have been older than Joseph himself. Joseph, for his part, evidently tried his hand in London and perhaps elsewhere before himself settling in

---

[14] Banfield 2006: 46–9.
[15] *CE*, 25 Jun 1858: 3 and 11 Apr 1862: 3.
[16] *CE*, 14 Oct 1853: 2.
[17] *CE*, 26 Jul 1854: 2 and 23 Apr 1855: 2.
[18] *The Empire*, 2 Jan 1856: 1, *Sydney Morning Herald*, 9 Sep 1857: 6, and other refs; NLA, digitally available; *CE*, 26 May 1863: 2; Australharmony.

Cork in early 1857, where he too was always known as 'Monsieur' Roeckel and described as coming from the Paris Conservatoire.[19] There seems little doubt that Joseph really had trained or at least sojourned in Paris, even though early *Grove* entries, compiled while he was still alive and drawn on ever since, made no mention of this. It would help explain the French titles of about fifty of his piano pieces, including most of those published in the 1850s, '60s and '70s, a propensity going well beyond fashion. Perhaps he lodged with or was brought up by Alfred during their father's later London years. But here, almost like a French farce, another singing Madame Roeckel enters the scene, and the young Joseph evidently turns as deft an operator as Armand, preparing an exit for himself 'on account of his health' (which would keep him alive almost as long as his father).[20] From 1859 to 1863 he divided his time between Cork and Bath, cultivating the fashionable Bath and Clifton markets with the help of Edward (as he now was), with whom he gave a two-piano performance on one occasion, on others appearing in concert with artists as famous as Pauline Viardot, Thérèse Tietjens, and Luigi Arditi.[21] The farewell concert in Cork of 'Mons and Madame Joseph Roeckel' in June 1863 would seem to leave the situation quite unambiguous, for we hear no more of her (or indeed of him for the following seven months).[22] Probably they had never actually been married and their ways parted at this point, Joseph, for Bristol purposes, conveniently losing whatever French accent he had inherited or cultivated, not to mention all reference to Paris and Cork in his instructions to Barclay Squire for *Grove*, Madame Roeckel keeping the child Nina and returning with her to her native land (the duet of mother and daughter in the farewell concert was entitled 'Le retour en France').[23] Did Jane Jackson, whom Roeckel married the following year when he consolidated his position in Bristol, know of their existence? Regardless of whether she did or not, the chain of speculation accords nicely with what the lace curtains and sash windows of Clifton could so conveniently hide, but even more with Roeckel's voluminous output, if this was partly a matter of having to support estranged dependants by keeping up the publications and keeping them popular. At least by 1874 Nina was off his hands and conveniently far away, for in that year the singer Christiana Roeckel, 'daughter of Joseph Roeckel, the musical composer' and also known as Jeanne Rekel, married in New Caledonia, of all

[19] *CE*, 3 Jul 1857: 2, 15 Jan 1858: 2, and other refs.
[20] *CE*, 26 May 1863: 2.
[21] *BC*, 15 Nov 1860: 4, 6 Jan 1859: 4 and 11 Apr 1861: 4.
[22] *CE*, 2 Jun 1863: 2.
[23] *CE*, 4 Jun 1863: 2.

places. Or had the newspapers muddled up the Roeckels? One article stated that her father, M Rekel, accompanied her for the purpose. It is even possible that he did: the continual references in the *Bristol Mercury* to Roeckel's public appearances and activities, and indeed to those of Jackson, cease completely between September 1873 and October 1877.[24] 'Mr Roeckel should write an autobiography', the *Musical Times* declared in 1912.[25] But he never did.

How much it was Roeckel's courtship of Jackson that tamed him would be impossible to guess at this distance. It is worth noting that as late as January 1864, following a concert in Clifton, he returned to Paris, priming the salons and making sure to be announced there with a lion's reputation as a keyboard player.[26] So perhaps it was a close thing that he did finally settle in Bristol. The possible trip to New Caledonia aside, his mature career hardly seems to match his promise and credentials, though he clearly retained dignity and authority right through to the turn of the twentieth century, when in 1903 his blessing was invoked for the founding of the ambitious Bristol Music Club, which proceeded to make him one of its first honorary members.[27]

Yet another trail of interest and distinction on the part of Roeckel has similarly gone unremarked. At some point in his early Bristol years he met Fred Weatherly, still at that time an Oxford undergraduate and living during the vacations with his parents in Portishead. As we shall see in chapter 6, Weatherly more or less invented the musical celebration of the west country through his popular ballad lyrics. What has never been recognised, except by Weatherly himself, is that it was Roeckel who first taught him how to do it. In Weatherly's autobiography Roeckel warranted one of the twelve illustrations, a fine studio photograph of him complementing those of Ellen Terry, Henry Irving, and others of similar fame. In the text, Weatherly stated that his first ever song lyric, written in 1868 at the age of nineteen or twenty, was 'A message o'er the sea', which Roeckel proceeded to set to music, though the song was apparently not published until about 1895. Weatherly went on to pay generous tribute to his older friend, who set eighty or more of his lyrics to music over the period of half a century:

> It was at his suggestion and with help and guidance from him – a man not only of great musical skill but of a refined literary taste – that I took to writing songs. It was he who directed my reading and told me of the great German song writers – Heine, Uhland, Wilhelm Müller … It was he who first taught

---

[24] *The Argus* (Melbourne), 29 Aug 1874: 7 and 25 Nov 1874: 1.
[25] *MT* liii (1912): 175.
[26] *L'Orchestre*, 16 Jan 1864: [2].
[27] Dobson 1995: 3–4.

me the musical requirements of song. My work for him was followed by work for Molloy and Michael Maybrick (known as a composer by the name of Stephen Adams), and none of the many other friends who have set my songs will be surprised that I speak of those three as my first, best and dearest in the world of music.[28]

Molloy ('Love's old sweet song') and Maybrick ('The holy city') have retained some household currency; Roeckel, sadly, has not, and in the end must be judged as having lacked their genius for popular melody. But his west country songs deserve to be remembered, and will be in chapter 6.

More Families: Bath and Its Environs

Joseph Roeckel's place in what one might call the Bristol musical workshop was also the equivalent of a branch of the family business, this one straddling not just regional towns (Bristol, Bath, York) but whole countries. Indeed, one is almost tempted to suspect that any member of the Roeckel family felt free to publish under the name Edouard Dorn when for whatever contractual or personal reason it suited them. Would there be any known precedents for this? The Roeckel brothers and/or cousins and nephews represent more or less the last generations in which, for musicians, the family was coterminous with the trade in countless instances, though Ruth Finnegan's work on Milton Keynes emphasises again and again how music still runs in families.[29] Since what the Roeckels represented was a social equation that had operated for many centuries and was one of the most important drivers of the regional musical economy, it is not surprising that a dozen or so of the most significant west country family dynasties and networks have already been mentioned in one context or another. Others will now be discussed.

The Linleys of Bath remain the acme of the west country musical family. William Linley, father of Thomas Linley the elder, was not a musician, and not from Bath, but a carpenter from Badminton in Gloucestershire who apprenticed or at least attached his son to Thomas Chilcot, organist of Bath Abbey; the notice and patronage of the Duke of Beaufort, whose seat was and remains at Badminton, may have been instrumental in all this, as has been surmised.[30] Thomas Linley's greatest assets were his musicality, his looks, and his wife Mary Johnson, it being perhaps the combination of the second and third of these that lent him his drive and authority, for Mary was a

---

[28] Weatherly 1926: 70–1, 94.
[29] Finnegan 2007: 54, 308–11, and passim.
[30] Personal conversation with Andrew Brown, 2013.

formidable woman, later wardrobe mistress of Drury Lane Theatre when her husband was its proprietor, and she lived to be ninety-one, having borne him twelve children along the way, several of them vivacious beauties. Thomas and Mary were married in 1752, and the production of children began immediately. Clementina Black sums up the ensuing economic equation:

> It is a fair inference that, as late as twelve years after their marriage, the Linleys were still struggling. At a later date they became not merely prosperous, but wealthy, and in the spring of 1772 were living in one of the fine new houses in the Crescent, now called Royal Crescent ... Up to 1767 or thereabouts the expenses of the household must have been heavy and the father the only breadwinner. By the end of the year 1765 there were six children, the eldest of whom was but a little over eleven years old ... After the first dozen years of family life, however, the children, instead of impoverishing their parents, began to enrich them, and before another half-dozen years were over the earnings of Elizabeth alone were sufficient to have supported the whole household in affluence, while Tom and Mary, although not commanding payments so large as hers, were successful and prosperous public performers.[31]

Elizabeth, expertly and determinedly taught by her father, became between the ages of fifteen and nineteen the leading English soprano, and it was calculated by the *Bath Chronicle* that in those four years she had made nearly £10,000 for him. Has any west country musician ever earnt more in the region? He kept it all, which shocked Black in 1911 (but then she was a feminist, labour agitator, and suffragette).[32] It was a matter of cashing it in while he could, for although Elizabeth's succession of problematic suitors, the duels between them, and her elopement with Sheridan merely fuelled what today would be a top media profile for her and her family, they also put an end to this source of income when she retired from the concert platform on her marriage to Sheridan in 1773, on her husband's orders. She remained involved behind the scenes when Sheridan and her father took over Drury Lane, where her younger sister Mary, 'Handsome, but *nothing* near her sister' according to Fanny Burney, sang in the oratorio seasons until she too married in 1780.[33] The family music business had further human resources: Maria, the eighth child, also sang professionally, William was a London theatre composer (and writer), and Thomas junior became England's white hope of compositional talent, a hope thwarted when he drowned at the age of twenty-two.

---

[31] Black 1926: 13–16.
[32] Aspden 2004: 927; Black 1926: 16–17; Wikipedia: 'Clementina Black'.
[33] Aspden 2004: 929.

All the singing daughters were dead before the age of forty, and Samuel, another son, also died young. Their father's severity of demeanour thus had ample personal cause, but he had always been ruthless, discomfiting colleagues through rivalry and exclusion, manoeuvrings suffered by Herschel and Francis Fleming in Bath and Herschel in Bristol, as recent accounts such as Aspden's make clear.[34]

Yet every musical household at this time, rather as in the ongoing sagas of our age's TV soap operas, must have enjoyed liveliness, bustle, spontaneity, and artistic sociability that could at any moment take some difficult turn through internecine conflict, external competition, or ill fortune. One perennially nagging issue, evident enough in the Linley family, was how to reconcile heart, hearth, and purse when it came to marriage. Another was the sustainability of a provincial base, a question particularly acute for the musicians of Bath and Bristol in the later eighteenth and earlier nineteenth centuries because of their position along a corridor of season and fashion that brought patrons from London but also led back there – if death did not intervene (both Elizabeth and Mary Linley died at the Hotwells, Clifton's spa). Even the Wesley family, with one eye on music as the boys' occupation but with the other on the flourishing and expanding culture of Methodism, relocated from Bristol to London in the 1770s. So did the Linleys. Thus it is difficult to class the Wesley sons and Thomas Linley junior as west country composers, although Charles Wesley did spend a good deal of time in Bath in later life, writing the odd glee for the Bath Harmonic Society, and his brother Samuel returned to Bristol on two notable occasions towards the end of his career, to play the organ at St Mary Redcliffe and elsewhere in the city in 1829 and to give a series of lectures the following year.[35]

All these themes play out in the Herschel, Ashe, and Loder families, strikingly various as were their musical origins prior to convergence on Bath. The oboist and composer William Herschel and the leading flautist Andrew Ashe owed their musical training to the military: Herschel in the Hanoverian foot guards, which he quitted for England after their severe defeat at Hastenbeck in 1757; Ashe, who was Irish, through his formal adoption by Colonel Bentinck, with whom he was stationed in Menorca and Holland, following enrolment in the Royal Military Academy at Woolwich as a boy, these events taking place in the 1760s and '70s.[36] Herschel flourished in London and then in the north of England but could not turn down the

[34] ibid: 927.
[35] Nightingale 2010: 237–8; Olleson 2003: 203–9; Banfield 2006: 31.
[36] Thomas 2009a: 16–20.

position of organist at Bath's new Octagon Chapel in 1766. Three musical brothers, Jacob, Dietrich, and Alexander, had joined him in Bath by the end of the decade, though two of them moved on. The female resource in Herschel's economic enterprise had to be created by him: in 1772 he fetched his sister Caroline from Hanover and proceeded to make a singer out of her:

> Her brother gave her two singing lessons daily, sometimes three, as well as teaching her English and arithmetic, and she had coaching from a dancing-mistress to give her the stage presence required for oratorios. Before long she was appearing at Bath or Bristol as many as five nights a week, singing leading soprano parts in works such as *Messiah*, *Samson*, and *Judas Maccabaeus*. The transformation wrought by William was dramatic: only a short while before, Caroline had been qualified to work only as a housemaid.[37]

This family partnership developed in ways that neither brother nor sister can have anticipated. William's interest in astronomy led to his discovery of Uranus, from his back garden in Bath in 1781, and a position as Court astronomer, away from Bath and away from music. (He built his enormous telescope in Slough, Buckinghamshire, where it was visible from Windsor Castle and easily visited by the King.) Caroline, while forever subservient to her brother's career, assisting in his observations and following him to Datchet, near Slough, nevertheless became a celebrated astronomer in her own right, dying (back in Hanover) at the age of ninety-seven, having been awarded a gold medal for science by Alexander von Humboldt on her ninety-sixth birthday.[38]

The Herschels left Bath in 1782, at which date the Linleys were already in London. From 1780 until his death in 1810, Rauzzini directed the Bath concerts, and then Ashe took over, following a concert career first as violinist and then as flautist in Dublin and subsequently London, where he was engaged as first flute in Salomon's Haydn premieres in the 1790s. (Ashe claimed that it was he who dubbed Haydn's Symphony no. 94 'The Surprise', to the composer's pleasure.)[39] He was already well known in Bath, for he had featured repeatedly in Rauzzini's concerts in the 1790s, seems to have lived there until 1802, and had even been the one to introduce Haydn to Rauzzini; he was also impresario for at least one Bristol series (1798-99) and for concerts in Cheltenham.[40] In 1810 Ashe moved back to Bath from London, but his Bath concerts were at first in direct competition with those of the

---

[37] Hoskin 2004: 823.
[38] ibid: 824-5.
[39] Baldwin and Wilson 2004: 118; James 1990: 92; Thomas 2008: 14 and 2009a: 33.
[40] James 1987: 453-6.

wonderfully named Gesualdo Lanza, who engaged John David Loder to lead his series at the Lower Assembly Rooms, Ashe presiding at the Upper. Ashe won the struggle for a public, and Lanza's series was not completed, but later competition, this time with Robert Greethead's subscription series in Bristol in 1820, was more pernicious.[41]

Ashe's wife was another prominent singer, an occasional Rauzzini pupil named Mary Comer, and here there was no question of her retiring from the concert platform after they married in 1799. They ran their business as a joint venture, augmented in due course by two children, Gertrude, a harpist, and Honoria, a pianist (there were twelve children altogether).[42] Ashe's father-in-law was clerk of the Kensington proprietary chapel in Bath, and Kenneth James states that Mary had been apprenticed to the Bath singing teacher Mrs Wingrove; it would be interesting to know whether this was a formal indenture, but there is no reason to believe that it was not. The intricacy and ubiquity of the family networks at this period are easily demonstrated by noting that Mary was also taught by Mrs Wingrove's sister, Mrs Miles, and surely must have been related not only to the Misses Comer who ran, respectively, a dancing academy and a music teaching establishment in early nineteenth-century Bath but also to the John Comer (1800–88) who for a number of years directed the performing bodies in Taunton.[43] Her father promoted at least one concert in his chapel, in 1809, at which William Viner played the organ.[44]

Andrew Ashe, 'the first great professional English flute player' and a founder member of the (London) Philharmonic Society, was a real musical pioneer, though, a party trick of multiphonics notwithstanding, he seems not to have kept up with developments on his instrument or felt the need to set down the foundations of his technique, two imperatives of the nineteenth-century virtuoso.[45] However, it is difficult to conclude whether he furnishes an example of how this level of drive and creativity could be sustained only by the metropolis, or whether entrepreneurial failure might be expected anywhere and it was best to have irons in the provincial fire as well as in London. Either way, his west country subscription enterprises eventually failed, and he lost a great deal of money on them before giving up on Bath and Bristol in the earlier 1820s and retiring to Ireland.[46] Ashe's own view was

[41] Clarke 2011: 34; Thomas 2009a: 55–8; see also Kollmann 1812: 135–7.
[42] Gertrude's first given name was also Mary.
[43] James 1987: 456–9; Clarke 2011: 104; Bush 1983: 28.
[44] Clarke 2011: 48.
[45] Thomas 2008: 15 and 2009a: 48–9.
[46] Thomas 2008: 14.

that Bath was declining: it was set to 'become a quiet second Worcester'; but perhaps he took heart when Greethead went bankrupt.[47]

As for the musical Loders, there were nineteen of them across three generations, including seven women. Seven more female performers married a Loder, most of them continuing to perform, some under their maiden name, others as Loders. The musical dynasty's origins were closer to those of the Linleys than those of the Herschels and Ashe, for Loader is a Dorset name and it was probably one of the kinsmen of Joseph Loader, quire singer of Holwell in 1789, who in the later eighteenth century relocated to Bath.[48] There, Andrew Loder I (1728–70) seems not to have been an active musician but fathered the two musical fountainheads of the family, Andrew Loder II (1751–1806) and John Loder (1757–95). Of the children of these two, the most musically significant were Andrew Loder III (1785–1838) and John David Loder (1788–1846), while another, George Loder senior (1794–1829), produced two of the three third-generation musicians of consequence. These were George Loder II (1816–68), the colourful character already encountered, and his sister Kate (1825–1904). The third significant musician of this generation was not only a performer like the others but a composer of importance, indeed possibly the best English opera composer of the nineteenth century: Edward James Loder (1809–65).[49]

Three or more of the Loders intermarried with other musical dynasties. John married Bathsheba Cantelo (alias Richards, it would seem), and the second husband of their daughter Ann was John Henry Distin from Plympton. She had borne his four sons, and the couple formed their famous family brass quintet three years after being enabled at last to marry in 1829 on the death of Ann's first husband. George Loder senior married Mary Cook, seemingly from another family of Bath musicians if related to various Cookes, one of whom was apprenticed to John David Loder.[50]

For twenty or thirty years in the early nineteenth century it was difficult to find a major concert in Bath or Bristol, or a festival performance in Exeter, Salisbury, or Truro, that did not involve a Loder. The same was true of smaller towns such as Chippenham and Melksham.[51] As often as not the event or series was led from the violin by John David, frequently with Andrew or Mrs George Loder singing. Furthermore, after Ann married

---

[47] Clarke 2011: 18; *BM*, 15 Mar 1824: 1.
[48] Temperley 1971–76 (P186/VE2).
[49] Clarke 2011: 100.
[50] Eliason and Farrar 2001: 381; Mitroulia and Myers 2011: 1, 16; Clarke 2011: 35, 59; James 1987: 515–30, 551–5.
[51] Kent 2007b: 173; *BC*, 17 Jul 1817: 3, 7 Aug 1817: 3, and 14 Aug 1817: 3.

Distin she remained musically active, accompanying the family ensemble on the piano in Scotland, where her husband was a bandmaster, and then on tour in Britain and abroad.[52] The touring family troupe of concert musicians was a new economic outlet, drawing on the latest enhancements of transport and advertising (an engraving of the Distin quintet appeared in the *Illustrated London News* of 14 December 1844).[53] Parading, as it were, private music-making for the love of it (amateur, family) in public (professional, company), it betokened a bourgeois rectitude whose paradoxical equation was thoroughly squared by the Victorians, and Ann Loder must take her place in having helped set its pattern, though not from a west country base. With this development the travelling minstrel family reappeared, now the paragon of 'rational recreation' rather than the bugbear of the law.

Although the musical family, as already suggested, ceased in most areas of activity to be a standard economic unit in England in the later nineteenth century, a latter-day manifestation of it to trump the Loders, with thirty or more performing members, came to pass in the same region, at Croscombe near Wells, and was filmed in an HTV West documentary, *Harmony at Parsonage Farm*, in 1976.[54] This was the Bevan family. Roger and Maurice Bevan were two musical brothers of an Anglican clergyman, but Roger married a Catholic, Cecilia Baldock, and converted. The couple began producing their fifteen children (the penultimate one, Bridget, was stillborn), Roger was appointed director of music at Downside School in 1953, and the Bevan Family Choir became well known in the 1970s.[55] A parallel with the Linleys is in certain respects strong, for this family has also produced two female opera stars, Sophie and Mary Bevan, though as grandchildren, not children, of the founding musician, who was again a figure of some discipline while his wife, not part of the musical competition, was one of forthright views, as the documentary makes clear. The film accordingly interrogates tensions, but very different from the eighteenth century was the family's absence of eventual earning power to compensate for the hardships of raising a large brood, in this case on one salary, the Croscombe smallholding surrounding the rambling old house they were helped to buy in 1965 necessitating an infinitely more modest and informal lifestyle than that of the Linleys in the Royal Crescent.[56] One element that modern film-making

---

[52] Mitroulia and Myers 2011: 1–2.
[53] It is reproduced in Eliason and Farrar 2001: 381.
[54] Bevan family 1976; Bevan 1995: 126.
[55] Thicknesse 2012.
[56] Bevan 1984: 182–4 and 1995: 122–4.

could bring out was how naturally the musicality developed in such a close family environment, the choral singing reaching an apparently effortless professional standard through domestic participation. It was not, however, quite that simple, and instrumental lessons still had to be paid for, as did higher education at least for the children's children, when it had ceased to be free and supported by one's LEA in England. Nor, riding the crest of a wave after the documentary and various concert tours, did many of the children *want* to be in a professional family choir, a matter over which they would have had little or no control in earlier times.[57]

Of the twenty-four Bevan performers listed in a family concert programme in Bath in 2013, some have been active in London and elsewhere, but a number have remained in or returned to Somerset.[58] Rachel and Anthony teach music at Downside, Rupert runs choirs in Bradford on Avon and at St John's RC Church, Bath, Michael has studied music at Bristol University, and the metropolitan operatic careers of Sophie, Mary, and Ben are nicely counterpoised by another cultural extremity of which Roger Bevan would have firmly disapproved, the rock band Rocketeer, in which Hugh, Benny, Tom, and Francis played at the Glastonbury Festival in 2008.[59] One wonders whether their performance on the John Peel Stage was audible from Parsonage Farm, only two and a half miles away.

❧ *Metropolitan Distinction*

Escape from the region has been the perennial concomitant of talent, ambition, and opportunity, as already intimated. Two examples, from the later Georgian period when the attractions of London appear to have been greater than ever before or since, demonstrate the musical performer's potential – and pitfalls – in the consumer market. In this era the West End was surely growing faster than almost any other residential area of Europe, and the theatres were sufficiently implicated in the real estate development that they have continued to be attached to its name, first used in 1807.[60] Our two musicians, Charles Incledon (1762/63–1826) and John Davy (1763–1824), born within a year of one other, both made their living in the West End theatres, and specifically at Covent Garden, from 1790.[61] At least, we are told

---

[57] Bevan 1984: 191–2 and 1995: 126–7.
[58] Bevan 2013.
[59] ibid.
[60] *SOED*, ii: 2529.
[61] Rosselli 2004; Fiske 2001a.

that Davy moved to London then, though he was still mounting concerts in the west country, with James Paddon in Exeter and on his own in Exmouth, throughout and beyond the first half of the 1790s, and is described by Eastcott in 1793, Doane in 1794, and a local directory in 1796 as residing in Exeter.[62] At Covent Garden, Incledon became the nation's leading tenor while the humbler Davy played violin in the orchestra and composed a great deal of theatre music.

Davy and Incledon were close friends in London, and an 1838 memoir of Incledon stated that it was he who got Davy the Covent Garden job.[63] The impression it wanted to give was that these two west country lads stuck together in the city: 'whenever he [Incledon] had any difficult music to study … they locked themselves up in a room with two bottles of wine, and never quitted it till Incledon was perfect in his task, which was not the work of much time'. They had probably first associated as boys in Exeter, for both served under William Jackson in the cathedral, Incledon as a chorister from the age of eight, Davy apprenticed from the age of twelve. Indeed it was for a revival of Jackson's 'hit musical' *The Lord of the Manor* of 1780 that Davy composed an interpolated song, 'Silent tears', and dedicated it 'to his friend Chas Incledon' when printed in 1812.[64] Incledon and Davy did a summer tour together in 1802, staging a song and piano show called *Variety, or Something New*.[65]

Incledon's career march on the metropolis, like that of the rebel leader of 1497, had started from almost as far away in the south-west mainland as it was possible to be: St Keverne in the Lizard, where his father was a surgeon.[66] Davy's journey was geographically smaller but socially greater, for he was born illegitimate in Upton Hellions, near Crediton, and brought up by his blacksmith uncle. His early musical experience was thoroughly rustic: the blacksmith played cello in the church band, the young boy heard the chimes of Crediton church and purloined some horseshoes from a neighbouring forge to create a makeshift glockenspiel on which he could imitate them. As usual, it was the rector who knew what to do with such raw talent, assisting in its development in this case because he himself had a harpsichord, which

---

[62] *EFP*, 4 Feb 1790: 3, 21 Oct 1790: 2, 7 Mar 1793: 3, 5 Feb 1795: 3, 6 Aug 1795: 3, 23 Jun 1796: 3, all indexed EFPSCI; Cann and Bush 1967: 56, 63; Eastcott 1793: 99; Doane 1794: 18; *EPJ* 1796.
[63] Hook 1838: 218.
[64] *Morning Chronicle*, 28 Oct 1812: 3.
[65] Hook 1838: 219; various newspaper announcements (Leeds, Chester, Bury St Edmunds, etc).
[66] Hook 1838: 216; Payton 2004: 107–10.

Davy soon mastered, and then placing it in a more urban setting via Richard Eastcott, one of Jackson's vicars choral and a prominent writer on music, who eased the route to Jackson himself.[67]

Neither musician earned sufficient or managed his earnings wisely enough to end his days in financial security; thus another story of failure to become a gentleman eventuates. Incledon, who retired to Brighton after his voice began to fail, at least provided a £50 annuity for his wife, but suffered late money troubles, perhaps surmounted before his death if it is true that his estate amounted to £8,000.[68] Roger Fiske rated Davy's compositional abilities very highly, closing his book *English Theatre Music in the Eighteenth Century* with excerpts from the overture to Davy's comic opera *What a Blunder!* of 1800 in order to remind British readers yet one more time of the results of underinvesting in native talent, for which, as so often, the metropolis, not the provinces, was to be blamed.[69] In the harp sonata published around 1805, Davy devised themes 'developed with a power shown by no other English composer of the time'. But he could not find the way – which would have been through hard-as-nails dealings and self-promotion – to turn his composer's quality into a composer's reputation. Collaborative hackwork increasingly ensued, 'and as he lost heart his own contribution lapsed into near nonsense'.[70] He took to drink, sustained a long illness, died in poverty, and was buried at the expense of two tradesmen, one of them a native of Crediton.[71]

That the obituaries mentioned the charitable 'native of Crediton' indicates the trope at which they were keen to hint in respect of Davy: that provincial talent should perhaps have stayed where it was. Half a century earlier, the poet Thomas Chatterton had provided the romantic model for the local genius whose precipitate relocation to the metropolis proves fatal – though one posthumous Devon commentator on Davy took the opposite line to expecting him to have starved in a London garret, by suggesting that there was no excuse for 'musical prodigies falling into disasters ... in the midst of a large, music-loving population'.[72] Davy was seen after his death as having lacked the character to follow through his creative drive: he was 'provokingly reserved', dying 'of neglect ... in silent misery'; 'naturally indolent', with 'an habitual improvidence'; abusive of the professional charity that sustained

[67] Eastcott 1793: 95–9.
[68] Rosselli 2004: 228; Hook 1838: 228.
[69] Fiske 1973: 583–4.
[70] Fiske 2001a: 82.
[71] Warrack 2004.
[72] Badcock 1837: 340.

his final years; 'a man of mild, amiable, and unassuming manners' who 'had once a passion for the stage, and actually made his *debut* as a tragic hero at Exeter' – following a chimera, it was implied (and it was Zanga the villain, not Alonso, he had played in Edward Young's *The Revenge*).[73] He was paid well for 'The Bay of Biscay' (£100) – supposedly a sea shanty Incledon had given him – but failed to capitalise on such success. 'Poor *Davy!*' they exclaimed.[74]

But then they said 'Poor Incledon' as well.[75] Whether or not Davy's descent was in some way due to underlying lack of social confidence and solid upbringing, or they wanted it to have been, even Incledon never entirely escaped from imputations of having remained something of a bumpkin, the fellow lucky enough to find fame and (evanescent) fortune but with his unsophisticated origins still showing. He was criticised for his vanity, 'want of cultivation', and 'slovenly acting'. He never lost his west country accent, and Byron took delight in imitating it.[76] The fact that he had run away to sea as a lad did not help, though to that he owed the irresistible image of the singing tar when he performed 'The storm' and 'Black-eyed Susan'. Of course, all these things may have increased the affection in which he was held; but they correspondingly created a glass ceiling.

One posthumous account of Davy states that it was against the advice of his friends that he had gone to London, and in the face of having been appointed Jackson's successor as organist of Exeter Cathedral.[77] This last fact cannot be right, for Davy was well established in the metropolis long before Jackson died in post. Yet it need not prevent us from wondering whether of Jackson's two pupils Paddon and Davy, Davy was promised the succession as the more talented man (though he was also older). In the event it was James Paddon who followed Jackson at the cathedral, and Paddon who lived a sober and productive enough life to repay whatever debt he owed Jackson by publishing an edition of his works. But he was also sufficiently faceless that Betty Matthews could find out nothing about him.[78]

---

[73] ibid; anon 1824a; anon 1824b: 281; anon 1824c; Radford 1950: 266.
[74] Badcock 1837: 340.
[75] W R 1829: 567.
[76] Baldwin and Wilson 2001; W R 1829: 567, 569.
[77] anon 1824a.
[78] Matthews Exe: 26.

❧ William Jackson

This brings us to Jackson himself, who had lived in London for two years as a teenager, as he wrote to Davy in a letter in which he mused upon the latter's theatrical success and productiveness. Was he drawing attention to these circumstances in subliminal envy of not having had the courage to make the leap himself? Or was it a coded warning, proud and secure as he was in having for once proved that a provincial name in music could be made and sustained? For Jackson's achievement was extraordinary, and has not been properly recognised.

His grandfather, descended from a line of Devon farmers, was an Exeter serge maker whose son, a grocer, 'soon dissipated his little fortune' and became a functionary of some kind, as Jackson's invaluable autobiography tells us.[79] (One source says that he was master of the Exeter workhouse.)[80] Jackson himself thus received a good education though no inheritance. 'Grocer' was not, however, the humble station it may seem, and will have implied a specialist merchant.[81] In fact it would be difficult to imagine anyone in the eighteenth century matching more closely than William Jackson the archetype of Britain's rising middle classes, for this was clearly a money-making family, if at times that meant money-losing, and Jackson's letters to his son Tom bandy about large sums by way of advice on shares and investments.[82] But because of his father's straitened circumstances, which cut short his studies in London with John Travers, Jackson developed the thrift and pride of the self-made man:

> Under eighteen I was obliged to practice my profession for a subsistence. My first year produced so little that the most severe economy could not prevent my having a debt of a few pounds – the next year discharged it, and from thence to the present moment, I never owed a shilling but have ever paid my bills as soon as delivered. I was early possessed with the idea that a debtor was the most miserable situation in life, and to prevent being so, was determined never to spend any money until I had not only earned it, but had it in my pocket.[83]

Nor was he bashful about the amassing of material means, and one of his published essays (they appeared as *Thirty Letters* to an imaginary correspondent) salutes the wealthy ('every man should endeavour to be rich')

---

[79] Jackson 1802: 58.
[80] Jackson 1971: 273.
[81] ibid.
[82] Jackson 1783–1802: 114–15, 117, 125–9.
[83] Jackson 1802: 60.

and even the miser, who, 'knowing that he has it in his power to procure everything', 'is as well satisfied as if the thing itself was in his possession'.[84]

One has to conclude that, however he managed to do it, and even if he overstated his father's material reduction, it was possible in the mid-eighteenth century, starting from a zero base, to make a stable and increasing living as a provincial music teacher, for this undoubtedly is what Jackson accomplished, with that crucial asset of his liberal education (not an apprenticeship) and with presumably equal measures of determination and, where health in particular was concerned, luck. He successfully amplified his credentials to those of a gentleman, and, unlike Elgar, did so without marrying above himself, his wife Mary Bartlett, a milliner, being 'a sober, virtuous, good woman ... as totally unfit for her husband as he was for her'.[85] By whatever means of assiduity, patronage (of which there is no surviving record), and interpersonal skill, he entered the circle of Linley and Gainsborough in Bath (for Jackson was a serious painter as well as a composer) and maintained connections both in that city and in London, visiting the latter annually, the former twice a year.[86] Completing the gentlemanly status about which British musicians would continue to feel insecure for another century or more, he even undertook a Grand Tour, setting off from Exeter one summer morning in 1785 with his lawyer friend James White, bound for France, the Alps, and Turin. He wanted to see mountains, as a landscape painter at this date undoubtably would.[87]

To combine all this with becoming a cathedral organist and producing a West End hit 'musical' (*The Lord of the Manor*, 1780) would seem to have been unprecedented, indeed unique, and however one eventually weighs up Jackson as a successful provincial musician – for there is a debit side as well – it is clear that Bristol and Salisbury could lay claim to no such thing. To Exeter, therefore, goes the distinction of having produced a west country musician with a national reputation continuing to operate and be resourced from a provincial base. And what was culturally consolidated in and from Exeter in the eighteenth century and into the nineteenth makes the city's later decline all the sadder. Jackson was not the city's only painter, for William Gandy, who died in 1729, was sufficiently eminent to have been known to and praised by Reynolds (it was Jackson himself who reported this).[88] Nor

---

[84] Jackson 1795: 6.
[85] Jackson 1802: 62.
[86] Jackson 1783–1802: 129, 133.
[87] ibid: 77.
[88] Jackson 1882: 623.

was Jackson its only belletristic musician, for Richard Eastcott, already mentioned several times, published one of the leading musical treatises of its time in Britain, his *Sketches of the Origin, Progress and Effects of Music* of 1793. Jackson, having somehow *bought* the cathedral organistship from his restless predecessor, Richard Langdon, in 1777 (by which time he had already been making his musical living in Exeter for nearly thirty years and publishing his compositions for the greater part of that period), proceeded to reform the lacklustre choir: 'it is now (1801) and has been for many years, the first in the kingdom', he confidently asserted.[89] This must have laid at least some abiding foundations for Sebastian Wesley's later achievements, Exeter being Wesley's most productive appointment, and probably for Sir John Leman Rogers's Devon Madrigal Society.[90] As cathedral organist, Jackson was also finally in a position to develop Exeter's concert life, taking over Langdon's winter series and at least for a while (six seasons) consolidating a fine orchestra, 'the second band out of London – that at Bath being the first'.[91] Like most other concert impresarios at this period, he soon had to cut his losses, but again in the earlier nineteenth century it was Exeter where with Wesley's short-lived music club and Kellow Pye's concert series we find Beethoven symphonies being performed.[92]

Jackson's son William became an East India Company employee and made his fortune in India and Macao before returning to Devon to marry into the Baring(-Gould) family of Exmouth and set up in business with them.[93] His father turned architect and designed him a fine house, Cowley Place, on a gorgeous riverside location just outside Exeter; it still stands, and is praised by Pevsner.[94] A younger son, Thomas, was given an Oxford education and gained a fellowship at his college (Exeter) before he too went abroad, becoming *chargé d'affaires* at Turin (his father's destination on the 1785 trip) and later a leading diplomat, possibly even a government spy, in Trieste, Rome, and Vienna, where Jackson's descendants still live.[95] By any reckoning this was an impressive family achievement given the composer's start; and Jackson himself remained comfortably off until his death at the age of seventy-three, at which he left £10,000.[96]

---

[89] Jackson 1802: 69.
[90] Hobson 2012: 33, 37–44, 52–3.
[91] Jackson 1802: 70.
[92] Horton 2004: 123.
[93] Jackson 1971: 278–82.
[94] Jackson 1783–1802: 124–5; map ref SX907957; Cherry and Pevsner 1989: 293.
[95] Jackson 1971: 282–8, 304.
[96] Williamson 2004: 534.

Was Jackson above all things a shrewd operator? As a youngster in London he had inveigled his way into Handel's presence, turning pages for him at a rehearsal for *Judas Maccabeus*.[97] Later, the appearance on his published title pages of the suffix 'of Exeter' might be argued as evidence of spin, though there really was, as Jackson claimed, a William Jackson of Oxford with whom he might otherwise have been confused, and in any case the soubriquet was closer to being the liability of a provincial give-away than the fillip of pseudo-seigneurial snobbery.[98] If it did show pride in his place of origin and residence, this was probably natural, genuine, and innocent. One thing is clear: that he wanted to be a man of letters and not just a musician. He numbered among his acquaintances Gainsborough, Reynolds, Goldsmith, Herschel, Charles and Fanny Burney, J C Bach, Abel, Charles Jennens, the Linleys, Sheridan, General Burgoyne (who wrote the playscript of *The Lord of the Manor*), John Wolcot ('Peter Pindar'), Southey, and the Exeter poet John Bampfylde.[99] At one time he considered making his living as a painter rather than a musician, and, although advised against it by Gainsborough, was in the same breath assured that he would be able to make £500 or £600 a year.[100] In the end he must have found ways of approaching these sums through his musical and literary activities. He presumably made money from *The Lord of the Manor* when it ran for twenty-six nights at Drury Lane, and he built up a popular reputation as a composer of songs, canzonets, and elegies, which were at the remunerative end of the sheet music market. In the nineteenth century, when the taste for English 'airs' had changed to a fashion for Italian *bel canto*, he could be lamented as a superseded national songwriter in the same breath as Arne, Storace, Linley, Shield, Dibdin – and Davy.[101] He produced Davy and Paddon, and nurtured Incledon. Altogether this was quite some achievement. One would not dream of including Charles Burney in the above list of purveyors of national melody, yet what Burney did stand for, the intellectual musician, was also Jackson's rightful province, and it is difficult to think of anyone in his period who fulfilled this function other than Burney, Jackson, and Herschel. Jackson's own account of an evening spent with Herschel in Windsor admiring his enormous new telescope and hearing about his amazing discoveries – alas, it was an overcast night – makes

---

[97] Jackson 1802: 60.
[98] Matthews 1985: 80; Highfill et al 1973–93, viii: 124.
[99] Jackson 1783–1802: 114, 116; Jackson 1802: 54, 59, 65, 66, 67, 68, 70; Jackson 1882; Jackson 1971: 292–3, 311–23.
[100] Gainsborough 1882: 719.
[101] W R 1829: 568.

delightful reading.[102] So do many of his essays and his treatise on *The Four Ages*, and the prefaces to his published compositions.[103] And if much of his speculation sits on a knife-edge between profundity and naivety, one would say exactly the same of Herschel, producing his utterly fanciful theories alongside world-changing observations. This, though it was very soon to change, was how the age was, and Jackson's music needs to be approached in the same spirit, by accepting an unconstrained aesthetic that mixes learned craft, commonsense or popular feeling, and artificial sensibility.

Yet none of this squares with Jackson's posthumous standing, which has been not just modest but feeble. He is the subject of no scholarly dissertation, no critical edition, no book, and very few articles. None of his melodies became a national song, outlasting its moment, in the manner of Boyce's 'Heart of oak', Arne's 'Rule, Britannia!', Dibdin's 'Tom Bowling', Hook's 'The lass of Richmond Hill', Shield's 'The *Arethusa*', Horn's 'Cherry ripe', and Davy's 'The Bay of Biscay' – though one might say the same of Stephen Storace and Samuel Arnold. His name is still known, but only for 'Jackson in F', a set of workaday canticles – deliberately so, along the lines of what Hindemith would later term *Gebrauchsmusik* – that does his individuality no favours. This, as astutely identified by Richard McGrady in his *New Grove* article, furnished the moiety of Jackson's nemesis. The remainder, as McGrady again points out, came from his biggest mistake: to have picked a quarrel with Burney.[104]

Burney and Jackson were too alike. Born four years apart in the provinces (Burney was from Shrewsbury), each had a lasting career relationship with both London and a region – Burney took an organist's post in King's Lynn for nine years – and both, as already suggested, brought the music profession in England firmly into the sphere of the gentlemanly and the intellectual (though it failed to stay there). Each man was therefore some kind of a native model, and, subtracting Herschel, who as a foreigner corresponded to a different equation, each might be viewed as the only representative of what the English gentleman musician should aspire to be and do.[105] In other words, they were rivals. Burney was the progressive, Jackson the conservative: Burney furthering the conquest of contemporary Continental and specifically Italian taste, Jackson beginning to dig himself in to what he saw as the waning tradition of plain English values, above all in melody.

---

[102] Jackson 1783–1802: 116.
[103] Jackson 1798.
[104] McGrady 2001b: 725.
[105] Grant 2001: 642.

Jackson criticised Burney's magisterial *History* for its downgrading of English music, and Burney lashed out against Jackson's *Observations on the Present State of Music in London* (1791).[106]

Much might be said about what was at bottom an uneasy friendship, but the point is to consider what it tells us about Jackson the provincial. Jackson must have known that he was on the losing side, that he was merely stirring with an inflammatory pamphlet – the copy belonging to the Chapter Coffee House in Paternoster Row survives – and that he would change nothing through his rejection of Haydn's modernity and, increasingly, of Handel's veneration as being both inimical to English interests. (He was right about the monumentalisation of Handel but hopelessly wrong about Haydn.)[107] It is as though he were finally taking a stand against metropolitan stakes, protesting that they were simply rising too high. Perhaps every age has its version of this, for Roger North's musical protests of 100 years earlier were not very different, and ours today about the London property prices and financial climate exhibit comparable defensiveness.[108] Burney, however, was clearly sensitive about the accusations, or he would not have returned to his criticism of Jackson years after the latter's death. Did he feel that in his ambitiousness he himself had sold out, and that there was therefore some justice in Jackson's claims? Was he more disappointed as a composer than Jackson, recognising Jackson's greater achievement (which it was) in this activity? If so, he may have found Jackson smug, in that he had settled for something more comfortable and convenient than the ongoing competition at the highest levels of risk and ambition that Burney's position in London, and above all his *History*, undoubtedly represented.

Those who know what they have had to invest in, risk, and forego for ambition commonly turn on those who from a more secure and less demanding position fail to support or applaud them. Burney's annoyance with Jackson is understandable. For his part, Jackson undoubtedly had, or developed, a chip on his shoulder. In reality he had made his choice, pursued his love of the west country and decided on a balance between what talent and ambition might – should? – have exacted of him and what would afford a secure and comfortable life without too many challenges he might fail. *The Lord of the Manor* was an unusual, perhaps unique achievement for a provincially based composer, but to follow it up, London was not going to come to him: he would have to go there, and for the fish to have made the leap

---

[106] Williamson 1996/97: 39–42.
[107] Jackson 1791: 16–17, 19–20, 26–32.
[108] Wilson 1959: 11–12.

into the biggest pool of all at the age of fifty would have been a risky, perhaps foolhardy thing to do, especially since he had only come into possession of the Exeter Cathedral organistship three years earlier. But he felt he should have accomplished more, and late in life began making excuses.

Commenting on *The Lord of the Manor*, he wrote in his autobiography, 'I never made the least pretension to be a violent ephemeral favourite, my ambition was to win the public attention by slow approaches, and then to retain it', but in the same breath explained why this could not happen: continuing success in musical comedy was always contingent upon casts and stars and upon lavish promotion. The creator of the French character part in *The Lord of the Manor* had soon died, and for *The Metamorphosis* of 1783 Jackson failed to ask 'one single person to attend the performance', with the result that 'of course it was not attended at all, not even the first night; so that it came into the world weak & soon died of a consumption' (which has happened to countless musicals since).[109]

But choices are made for reasons, and Jackson in his autobiography, which almost pathologically enumerates the causes as he sees them for the limitations of his success, repeatedly stresses his eyesight as a source of social misunderstanding in others: 'my short-sight preventing me from the interchange of little attentions and civilities by which the general connections of life are carried on, and my abstraction from company "working together for my ruin" I have been for many years ... hated for being supposed a character perfectly the reverse of the truth' – in other words, he was not in reality antisocial.[110] True, some people did take him to be, and one wonders whether he had a psychological difficulty in recognising faces, the condition now known as prosopagnosia. Another possibility is suggested by the portrait, supposedly by Gainsborough but now sometimes thought to be by Jackson himself, of him playing the harp. In it he appears positively wall-eyed (Illus. 5.1), though Fanny Burney found him 'very handsome'.[111] If his references to shortsightedness were a euphemism for this condition, his discomfort in demanding social situations and fear that others would avoid him or misconstrue his demeanour would be fully understandable. Self-absorption or over-compensation may have taken any number of turns and forms in Jackson's exchanges, including those of critical aggression and vanity, which were what Burney accused him of.

---

[109] Jackson 1802: 70–1.
[110] ibid: 68.
[111] Baker 1978: 60–1; Asfour and Williamson 1996/97; cited Shaw 1991: 115.

Illus. 5.1 Thomas Gainsborough or William Jackson: Portrait of William Jackson playing the harp

Whereas Jackson's last years may have been spent in what he thought of as obscurity, they were not unadventurous, and, perhaps no longer in a position to 'twang upon Mrs Jackson', as Gainsborough had saucily put it, in his late sixties he fathered an illegitimate child on the daughter of an Exeter clergyman.[112] This set local tongues wagging, and it may well have been what caused Coleridge, whose deceased father had been vicar of Ottery St Mary and who attended the Society of Exeter Gentlemen which Jackson had helped to found in 1792, to refer to Jackson as 'out of all doubt a bad man'.[113] Southey also judged him harshly, claiming that 'nobody likes Jackson'.[114] But one cannot help regretting that that appears still to be true.

❧ *Regional Distinction*

In striking contrast with Davy and Incledon, the careers of two other professional west country musicians of uncommon distinction took the opposite trajectory, with adventure left firmly behind them when they settled in the region to enjoy a long, domesticated, and unusually productive living there. These were Joseph Emidy (*ca* 1775–1835), of Falmouth and Truro, and Sir Dan Godfrey (1868–1939), of Bournemouth.

We shall never know Emidy's full story. Released into freedom, he stepped off the Royal Navy frigate HMS *Indefatigable* onto the Falmouth quayside on 28 February 1799 after the best part of four years at sea as ship's fiddler, during which time his vessel, under the distinguished command of Admiral Pellew, had captured, disabled, or sunk scores of enemy ships, including the *Droits d'homme* in 1797. (C S Forester's fictional Midshipman Hornblower was also on the *Indefatigable* during Emidy's time under Pellew.)[115] Emidy was black, but this did not stand in the way of his setting up as Cornwall's leading literate musician in the secular field (he was never involved with church music), based first in Falmouth and moving in or after 1812 to Truro, where he remained for the rest of his life. In Falmouth he married a Cornishwoman, Jennifer Hutchins, and they produced six children. One of these was Thomas, who for many years ran a quadrille band in Cornwall. Other descendants, including a circus bandmaster, emigrated to the USA.[116]

Emidy must have been highly trained. He led orchestras and chamber groups on all possible occasions, public and private (see Illus. 5.2), taught violin, viola, cello, flute, and English and Spanish guitar (but not keyboard, it seems), tuned harps and pianos, and regulated the latter 'according to the directions of Messrs Broadwood and Sons, in any part of the county'.[117]

---

[112] Gainsborough 1882: 719; Jackson 1971: 294–300.
[113] Griggs 1956–71, i: 539.
[114] Williamson 1996/97: 42; Curry 1965, i: 202.
[115] McGrady 1991: 21–36; Wikipedia: 'HMS *Indefatigable* (1784)'.
[116] McGrady 1991: 41, 148; Emidy 2000; Rose nd.
[117] *WB*, 1 Dec 1820, cited McGrady 1991: 40–1; *RCG*, 25 Sep 1813: 3.

Illus. 5.2 'A musical club', Truro 1808, with Joseph Emidy (third from right)

He was a keen composer, and we know that he wrote one or more violin concertos, a horn concerto, chamber music, variations for piano, and a set of symphonies. But not a scrap of his music survives, the saddest testimony to its loss perhaps the following notice:

> We learn that Mr EMIDY is about to publish by subscription a set of Sinfonias for a full band. As the celebrated Mr SALOMON *the leader of the Grand Concerts in Hanover Square*, has spoken very highly of their merit we doubt not but that the lovers of music in this neighbourhood will soon enable Mr E to send the Manuscripts to the engraver, as he numbers already amongst his subscribers, several titled personages and other *diletanti* [sic] of science and judgment.[118]

Where did he learn such accomplishment? Other than his ship's official records and the frequent newspaper notices, no written account of him dates from his lifetime, and on his tombstone in Kenwyn churchyard he is described as 'a native of Portugal / which country he quitted about forty years

---

[118] *RCG*, 15 Jun 1811: 3; McGrady 2001a.

since', Lisbon also given as his place of birth in the *Indefatigable*'s muster book.[119] Given that he was said to have been playing second violin in one of the Lisbon theatre orchestras when he joined the *Indefatigable*, the likeliest surmise would be that he grew up in Lisbon and was expertly educated there in music. Slave blood, via Brazil, he most certainly would have possessed, given his colour. But as to whether this was from a previous generation or bespoke his personal origins, we have only the account of his friend and patron James Silk Buckingham to go on, published twenty years after his death and quite likely embellished by fancy, his own or Emidy's (for Emidy himself may not have known where he was born and how his upbringing began). Thus Buckingham's story of Emidy's having been born in Guinea, sold by Portuguese traders into slavery in Brazil 'when quite a boy', taken to Lisbon by his master, and then 'supplied with a violin and a teacher' for three or four years may or may not be true, though it does seem odd that an enslaved past was not mentioned on the gravestone, erected less than a year after the momentous event of Emancipation in British territories.[120] The other element to be questioned is the trope of the lone press-ganged innocent, spotted bowing vigorously in the Lisbon orchestra by Pellew while his ship was in for repairs and mugged outside the stage door after the performance, violin and all. Emidy embarked as a landsman on the ship along with two others, and they may well have sold their services as a band for a mess ball – which implies that Emidy was already an experienced freelancer in Lisbon – only to find themselves on the high seas with no means of escape. Yes, this must have been impressment or deceit of some kind, even if Emidy, who was paid for his duties in the Navy, was not averse to taking a short voyage.[121] The point is not automatically to sentimentalise Emidy when we would not do so for Incledon, whose period in the Navy, possibly longer than Emidy's, was similarly enforced, if we are to believe the account of his oboist friend W T Parke. Parke claimed that 'the son of one of the dignitaries of the church [in Exeter] having committed an offence which the evidence of Incledon might have proved, he was taken on board a ship-of-war to the West Indies' and obliged to remain in the Service until the affair, be it sodomy or whatever, had blown over.[122]

What really matters is to be able to assess whether Emidy made the most of his talents, which would mean that Truro in the end was the right place

---

[119] McGrady 1991: 1, 29.
[120] ibid: 15–16.
[121] ibid: 26–7, 29–30, 36.
[122] Parke 1830, ii: 248.

for him, or whether they remained thwarted. Buckingham, to his great credit, tried hard, on a trip to London around 1807, to interest Salomon in Emidy's compositions – how Jackson would have disapproved of this approach to Haydn's London impresario! – and 'at the shop of Mr Betts' two of the symphonies, a quartet, and a quintet were duly tried out. Salomon was impressed and thought Emidy should try for a concert in London, but others partaking of the occasion felt 'that his colour would be so much against him, that there would be great risk of failure: and that it would be a pity to take him from a sphere in which he was now making a handsome livelihood and enjoying a high reputation, on the risk of so uncertain a speculation'. John Davy (who could even have been among the players), take note.[123]

Alas, unless the music itself turns up, we shall never be able to judge for ourselves. The Londoners, who raised a subscription for him, may have been right, although the remark about his colour is hardly borne out when we recall that the mixed-race violinist and composer George Bridgetower, already internationally known, was rising particularly high in the musical ranks of the metropolis in the very same year of 1807.[124] If they were wrong, and deprived British musical history of a significant symphonist, then the Royal Navy is first to be blamed for depriving Portugal of one.

Dan Godfrey's colourful past had been a matter of choice, when in 1891 as a young band conductor of twenty-five he was invited to tour South Africa as music director for an opera company which was to open the Standard Theatre in Johannesburg, then at the height of its gold rush and still a wild place.[125] Godfrey came from a family of famous bandmasters – there are eight of them in *Grove* – but fell foul of what must have been recent regulations by having been educated at the RCM rather than Kneller Hall, which had not impeded his forbears' taking up army bandmasterships but prevented him from doing so.[126] There were plenty of other 'military' (i.e. mixed) bands to conduct, and their cross-fertilisation with theatre and resort orchestras was increasingly fecund, but Godfrey's salaried municipal position in Bournemouth, where he was first contracted in 1893 and which he developed as an extraordinary power base for himself and his growing orchestra of similarly salaried performers, was a new national development.

What this meant for Bournemouth and the west country will be discussed in chapter 7. What it meant for Godfrey was consolidating a model of

---

[123] McGrady 1991: 144–6.
[124] Squire and Golby 2004: 597.
[125] Godfrey 1924: 50–67.
[126] ibid: 45.

reverse migration. No longer was it necessary for British musicians of talent, promise, and ambition to go abroad or sink or swim in London (though they continued to do both). Here was a regional town, not even a city, offering a secure and settled livelihood to professional classical musicians as permanent patronage, and on an all-year-round basis, not just 'like the swallow, peculiar to summer'.[127] On the one hand their band was the revival and magnification for the modern age of the wait tradition. On the other, and a factor of sharper cultural import, it was the closest Britain had yet come to the pattern of court orchestras and municipal opera houses in Germany. Godfrey must have recognised his moment and, like all successful conductors a relentlessly hard-working martinet, determined to capitalise on it.

If he had not done so, the soporific pines of Bournemouth would have killed him with boredom. They were no match for the excitement of Johannesburg, where on one occasion Godfrey looked in on a member of his company at his hotel room only to find him dead on the floor, his skull split open by an axe. On another, having undertaken body-building before he went abroad, Godfrey was equal to the personal combat challenge necessitated by having rashly taken sides in an interval discussion at the theatre bar. It seems somehow apt that it was at a boxing entertainment to musical accompaniment in London, Godfrey himself not untouched in the pit when an upstart challenger (probably Jack Ellis) fell through the ropes, that the mayor of Bournemouth thought of attracting a member of the well-known family to his ambitious resort. This was actually in March 1891, several months before Godfrey embarked for South Africa, so Bournemouth Corporation took its time to issue the invitation, which was found by Dan languishing in his father's in-tray in January 1893.[128]

Godfrey remained in Bournemouth for the rest of his life, and in post until he reached the council's retirement age of sixty-five, this last an all too novel and desirable attainment for a professional musician. (In fact he stayed on a little longer while they found his successor.)[129] As to why, as a leading conductor, he was devoted to Bournemouth for so long, it may again have been a matter of preferred balance between security and ambition, and, whether or not he recognised the fact, the equation did in his case produce something unique: the only professional musician, it would seem, ever to have been knighted for services based in the west country.

---

[127] ibid: 285.
[128] *Morning Post*, 9 Mar 1891: 2; Godfrey 1924: 47, 72; Lloyd 1995: 16.
[129] Lloyd 1995: 196–204.

Not that the honour occurred naturally to those in power. It would never have materialised (in 1922) without formidable lobbying by Dame Ethel Smyth, and she targeted British composers rather than regional worthies for support.[130] Quite why Godfrey increasingly chose new British music as his niche market or brand is not clear, unless it simply followed from his determination to attract artists as well as audiences to Bournemouth for his pioneering performances and festivals, and it would have cost too much and, after the First World War, resulted in too many disappointments and complications to focus on Continental composers. But choose it he did, and the results, in numerical terms at least, were staggering: 'the Bournemouth Symphony Concerts, which, at the end of December, 1923, reached a total of 1,635', wrote Hadley Watkins, introducing an appendix to Godfrey's memoirs, 'have been given with unbroken continuity since their inception in October, 1895. This list contains a total of 642 different works by British composers, of which 153 were *actual first performances*.' There are 161 composers in the list, most of them at the time still or recently active. At least twelve of them were women, and Godfrey gave a concert entirely of British women's compositions in 1927.[131]

It is only fair to say that today the majority of these 161 composers are obscure and that many of their works are not even extant. Of these, one most regrets the loss of Bertini's *Bournemouth* Symphony, whose finale depicted the proceedings of the town's notoriously cantankerous council.[132] Some of the composers whose music Godfrey played were, by the law of averages, from the region, including the nineteen-year-old George Lloyd from St Ives and the Plymouth organist Harold Lake, who both had works performed in 1933.[133] Some, increasingly as time went on, came from elsewhere and let their imaginations run riot along the lines of Bournemouth or the west country as a holiday or festival destination, for in due course Godfrey found himself conducting Adam Carse's *Winton* Suite – if this refers to the rather dreary Bournemouth suburb – and symphonic poems with conceptions such as Susan Spain-Dunk's *Stonehenge* and, surely one of the most unusual classical music titles, *A Stag's Morning Prayer at Dartmoor* by Alexis Gunning, father of the composer of the famous Martini ad.[134] Some, like Bertini, were local, Craigie Ross a female piano teacher who played many concertos with the

---

[130] ibid: 140–2, 146–51.
[131] Godfrey 1924: 296–305; Lloyd 1995: 173.
[132] Lloyd 1995: 87.
[133] ibid: 197–8.
[134] ibid: 180, 187, 198.

orchestra, Arthur Wood for a while its second flautist.[135] Wood's later fame was metropolitan and nationwide, as a theatre conductor and composer of *The Archers*' signature tune. Thomas Arthur Burton, organist of St Peter's and then Holy Trinity in Bournemouth, had nearly thirty of his works performed by Godfrey and the Municipal Orchestra, including, as Stephen Lloyd writes, 'six overtures, ten orchestral suites, a scena ... for soprano and orchestra, two symphonic poems, a set of *Variations on an American Air*, a *Capriccio drammatico* for piano and orchestra, a violin concerto, and four symphonies'. An opera and an oratorio had been given elsewhere in Bournemouth. Lloyd adds, however, that 'most of his works achieved only a single performance there'.[136] There must have been something of the trainspotter in Godfrey for him to have wanted to keep amassing unfamiliar compositions like this without a plan for their consolidation, though there were British works that he followed up tenaciously, most notably Vaughan Williams's *A London Symphony*, which he performed twenty-five times and recorded.[137] And it is important to add that the opportunities he offered those who inevitably have fallen by the wayside in large numbers were by no means disproportionate to his exposure of the nation's senior composers such as Parry, Stanford, and Mackenzie and encouragement of its junior ones, including Holst, Vaughan Williams, and Coleridge-Taylor.

This was all done on ratepayers' money, and after the first few seasons Godfrey and the orchestral players became permanent and full-time employees of the Corporation, which will have explained the constant carping, in the press and in person, about municipal priorities, procedures, working conditions, salaries, and value. The interminable machinery for accountability of the present day may not have been in place then, but the mindsets that gave rise to it certainly were, and Lloyd gives ample examples of pettiness and its opposite, high-handedness (to which Godfrey himself was partial), exercised in the universal assumption that what the ratepayers had put in should be returned to them by Bournemouth's visitors, i.e. that the Winter Gardens and their concerts should not make a loss. They tended to compute this as a direct equation rather than consider the indirect benefits of Bournemouth's classy reputation.

As a direct equation, the orchestra did make an overall accumulated loss of £5,443 10s 5d over the first twenty-one years, up to 1914. Additionally, the municipality invested £2,500 in the purchase of its music and also bought

---

[135] ibid: 26–7, 44.
[136] ibid: 27; Torrens 2015.
[137] Lloyd 1995: 115.

percussion instruments.[138] Against this, many must have taken pride in the secure livings it offered the players and their conductor, who almost at the start became the Corporation's entertainment director, booking everything from ventriloquists to performing dogs for the Winter Gardens as well as organising his band's appearances and programmes.[139] His musicians' salaries were always controversial, whether Godfrey raised the issue or others did.[140] Their conditions were strict, and they were not permitted to take any other paid engagements. Nor did the orchestra tour, until relatively late in its life under Godfrey when it visited Wales and just touched another part of the west country at Weston-super-Mare. Godfrey looked after his men well, however, and chose them with sufficient care that he only ever had to dismiss four in a period of over forty years. In other words, he had brought between thirty and fifty top-quality professional musicians to live and work permanently in the west country at any one time.[141] Many of them stayed for a long period and brought up their families in Bournemouth. One of them, the horn player Alfonso Trevisone, had even been a member of Bertini's Royal Italian Band, probably as an immigrant, and, although not in Godfrey's band in its earliest days, proceeded to outlast him in the Bournemouth Municipal Orchestra.[142]

❧ Success and the Compositional Idiom

Once the Bournemouth Pavilion had opened in 1929, the borough was employing two executive musicians, not one, for when Philip Dore moved on, Percy Whitlock was in charge of its organ where Godfrey continued to direct the municipal orchestra and its players, at a good salary of £1,325. (Whitlock, as we have seen, earnt something less than a third of this, from multiple sources.) The Pavilion also had a general manager, and altogether must be seen as a critical and perhaps unparalleled example of municipal patronage in Britain, costly, on an economic knife-edge throughout the Depression years, and thoroughly modern, not least in its profile as a broadcasting venue. Godfrey, close to retirement, lost some of his autonomy when the orchestra moved there, but the Pavilion clearly suited Whitlock, who found his overall *métier* as composer, music journalist, and organ performer (including

---

[138] Watkins 1914: 63.
[139] Lloyd 1995: 25–6, 48, 147–8.
[140] ibid: 131–2.
[141] ibid: 48, 214, 220–3; Barber 1980: 10–11; Godfrey 1924: 98–102.
[142] Lloyd 1995: 18, 220–3; Watkins 1914: 11; *Mercury* 1 (1948): 50.

OVER SIX MILLION COPIES OF CALEB SIMPER'S
Compositions in Church Music now sold.
WORLD-WIDE POPULARITY. FAVOURITES EVERYWHERE.
Free Specimens of the first three Anthems to Organists from
Caleb Simper, "Kilbirnie," Barnstaple.

NEW EASTER ANTHEMS, Etc.
COMPOSED BY CALEB SIMPER.

*WORTHY IS THE LAMB .. .. New 4d.
    Powerful, vigorous and interesting Choruses, and a beautiful and
        expressive Soprano or Tenor Solo.
*And the Third Day rise again .. ..18th Edition 3d.
    Bright, jubilant and most impressive.
NOW IS CHRIST RISEN. (Norman Stewart.) New   6th 1000   2d.
*I will praise the Name of God. New last year ..   10th 1000   4d.
    One of the most fascinating and attractive anthems.
*Arise from the Dead. A great favourite   ..   .. 11th 1000   3d.
*Awake up, my Glory. Very popular ..   ..   ..33rd Edition   4d.
*Now is come Salvation ..   .. 10th 1000   3d.
*He is not here, but is risen   ..   .. 13th 1000   3d.
*Christ being raised   ..   .. 15th 1000   4d.
*Let us keep the Feast   ..   .. 11th 1000   4d.
*We will rejoice   ..   .. 19th 1000   3d.
*The Lord is risen indeed ..   .. 14th 1000   4d.
*He hath done wonders ..   .. 18th 1000   3d.
Easy Holy Communion Service in A flat   .. 11th Edition   4d.
    Very devotional, melodious and complete.
Benedicite in G, together with other Canticles and Kyries.
    No. 6, Kilbirnie Edition   ..   ..   .. 10th 1000   2d.
Benedicite in E flat. An effective shortened setting. No. 11.
    Kilbirnie Edition. Verses for Boys only and Men only. 7th 1000   2d.
*Benedicite, No. 8. Three shortened settings, complete. 8th 1000   2d.
Benedicite in C. Varied Chant setting   ..   .. 3rd 1000   2d.
Magnificat and Nunc Dimittis in G (Novello & Co., Ltd.)   4d.
    By ROLAND C. SIMPER, F.R.C.O., L.R.A.M. A very effective
    setting with most effective modulations.
*The Story of the Crucifixion   ..   ..   .. 4th 1000   6d.
    Words separately, 7s. per 100. Written by the Rev. THOMAS BLACK-
    BURN, B.A., Rector of Woodville, Adelaide, South Australia. For Holy
    Week and Good Friday. Can be sung by any average choir. Time,
    about 20 minutes. Solos for Soprano, Tenor, and Bass, with Quartets
    and Choruses. Already much appreciated. "I like the music well."
    "It just meets our need." "Much admired by my parishioners."
    "Most beautiful," &c.
NEW VOLUNTARY BOOKS. Nos. 9 and 10. 1s. 6d. each. Written
on Two Staves. Over 200 Editions of this useful and wonderfully
popular series now sold. Also issued in Two Gilt-Lettered Cloth
Volumes (85 Voluntaries in each), 5s. each Volume.
*NEW NO. 22 ANNIVERSARY SELECTION. Complete, 2d. Words
only, 3s. 6d. per 100. Quantities on liberal terms. A charming set of
Eight Children's Festival Hymns and Tunes. Three of the Hymns
specially written by Caleb Simper.
*New War Hymn, O LORD OF HOSTS   ..   ..   1d.
    For Intercession Services and ordinary use. The refrain is, "Thou
    who makest wars to cease, Grant us soon a lasting peace." Words only,
    1s. 6d. per 100.
        Those marked * are also issued in Tonic Sol-fa.
London : WEEKES & Co., 14, Hanover Street, Regent Street, W.
Canada : ANGLO-CANADIAN M.P.A. Ltd., 144, Victoria St., Toronto.
Chicago, U.S.A. : CLAYTON F. SUMMY Co., 62-66, E. Van Buren Street.

Illus. 5.3 Advertisement for the compositions of Caleb Simper

national broadcaster) from within its civic embrace, achieving considerable distinction with his music of the 'lighter straight' kind, as one BBC memo put it.[143] What composers such as Butterworth, Gurney, and Warlock had done for the art song, Whitlock achieved for the organ, developing an attractive and eclectic idiom of exquisite craftsmanship in the detail, of memorability in the turn of phrase and sentiment, of Englishness in the semiotic awareness, and of ambition in the generic and structural confidence that emerged when appropriate, as in the organ sonata and organ symphony, of 1936 and 1937 respectively and both now clearly recognisable as the leading British works in their field. Thus to Bournemouth goes the accolade of double musical distinction.

Nevertheless, this chapter must end with an organ (and choral) composer whose efficacy and reputation not only, like Whitlock's, have been underplayed by the musical establishment – witness Whitlock's scandalously brief article in *Grove*, only redressed by the *ODNB* – but were positively suppressed by it.[144] Although it has been understandably reluctant to advertise the fact, Barnstaple was home to not one but two execrated Victorian composers. George Tolhurst, composer of what Percy Scholes described as the worst oratorio ever composed, *Ruth* (1864), in a fit of reverse migration from Australia returned to his native England and spent his final years in Barnstaple, where he was reduced to playing the piano in its music-hall bill of 'two hours' uninterrupted fun!'.[145] But our subject here is Caleb Simper (1856–1942). He was born to proletarian, nonconformist parents in Barford St Martin near Wilton, his father Alfred, himself the son of a labourer, a boot and shoemaker, his mother the daughter of a dairyman. Alfred was an amateur violinist, one presumes musically literate rather than a 'folk' fiddler, for he played in the Salisbury Musical Society. Caleb married an Australian in Wilton and took a job managing a music shop in Worcester, more or less next door to that of the Elgar brothers. Although Simper, a handsome man, was also a church organist and choirmaster, his aspirations in those directions were seemingly modest, and his genius, as he rapidly discovered, lay in composing easy anthems and voluntaries for organ or harmonium.[146] Only months after he had taken over Copplestone's music warehouse in Barnstaple with a Worcester colleague, John White, in 1891, he was able to relinquish his position in the business and 'retire' to the town aged

---

[143] Lloyd 1995: 182–7; Riley 2003: 89–140; Hayasaka 2016.
[144] Riley 2004.
[145] Scholes 1947, i: 95–7; *NDJ*, 15 Apr 1875: 1.
[146] Clegg nd and 2006: 107–12.

thirty-four with his wife and children because his compositions had taken off so spectacularly.[147] In his field this was possibly unprecedented prior to John Rutter, though Simper did also take up another organist's position, at Emmanuel Church in Barnstaple, and did teach from home.[148]

By 1915 the London publisher Weekes was able to advertise in the *Musical Times*, with not much exaggeration, that over six million copies of Simper's church compositions had been sold, and that their popularity was worldwide (Illus. 5.3). Indeed it was. Simper must have had training, or trained himself, in the rudiments of music, for he fully absorbed decorum and 'correctness' of technique, which for the later Victorians rested at bottom on the classical mannerisms of Mozart as filtered through Gounod, while at the same time through some distant metamorphosis of the demotic psalmody impulse managing to keep them forthright, basic, and completely innocent. The whole style, and apparently his personality, emanated compliance, and the clergy loved it. Taste-making musicians increasingly hated it, and did all they could to discredit such success, Vaughan Williams joking about Simper's name (and that of the equally popular J H Maunder), *Grove* ignoring him completely, which it continues to do, as did Henry Edwards in his article on the history of music in Barnstaple.[149] Perhaps this hardly mattered to Simper, who carried on posting off free samples of anthems to organists from his house, 'Kilbirnie', at 34 Ashleigh Road, Barnstaple. At his death he left £19,232, about forty-five times Whitlock's annual income of a few years earlier and today worth about three quarters of a million.[150]

'Sung throughout the Civilised World', the *Musical Times* claimed of Simper's church music in 1903.[151] It is an inspiring tribute to the imperviousness of materialities and taste to critical opinion that the music of this modest west country musician still is thus sung. His very ordinariness gave him the common touch, those relentlessly four-square phrases reassuring anybody that they might have thought them up, which must be precisely what continues to appeal. At the time of writing there are 180 broadcasts of his music on YouTube. These are performances, overwhelmingly amateur, given over the past few years by church choirs and organists in at least a dozen lands: the USA, Canada, Australia, India (particularly there), Singapore, Holland, Sweden, Wales, Ulster, Qatar, and even La Réunion, though there is

---

[147] *NDJ*, 28 May 1891: 5 and 29 Oct 1891: 5.
[148] *NDJ*, 12 Nov 1891: 4.
[149] Edwards 1917.
[150] *The Times*, 23 Oct 1942: 7.
[151] *MT* xliv (1903): 273.

curiously little from England. 'Kilburnie' (as currently spelt) still stands, now a care home, but the burghers of Barnstaple have not thought to put a plaque on it. They should.

CHAPTER 6

Musical Capitalisation I: Events and Inventions

❦ *A Song and Some Theory*

IN CHAPTER 3 a poem by Thomas Hardy about instrumental playing was quoted and discussed. Another Hardy poem, 'Her song', presented below in its entirety, is about singing.

> I sang that song on Sunday,
>   To witch an idle while,
> I sang that song on Monday,
>   As fittest to beguile:
> I sang it as the year outwore,
>   And the new slid in;
> I thought not what might shape before
>   Another would begin.
>
> I sang that song in summer,
>   All unforeknowingly,
> To him as a new-comer
>   From regions strange to me:
> I sang it when in afteryears
>   The shades stretched out,
> And paths were faint; and flocking fears
>   Brought cup-eyed care and doubt.
>
> Sings he that song on Sundays
>   In some dim land afar,
> On Saturdays, or Mondays,
>   As when the evening star
> Glimpsed in upon his bending face,
>   And my hanging hair,
> And time untouched me with a trace
>   Of soul-smart or despair?

This poem's protagonist, like all of Hardy's heroines a Wessex or west country woman, is undoubtedly rural, if part of the man's attraction was that he came from a different region. Hardy therefore wants us to think of her song as a folksong, with three functions specified in turn in the first six lines: it is sung at leisure, at work, and at feasting. She sings the song on Sunday because in a rural community there is nothing else to do on a Sunday, and by 1850 half the population of England was no longer going to church. (Nevertheless, the first line is intended to shock: one should not sing a secular song on the Sabbath.) She doubtless sings the song on Monday while she does the washing, though there is also the implication, returning in the final stanza, that it was on Monday that the song undid her, when she beguiled somebody with it. Then she sings it at a New Year's Eve party.

She will probably have learnt the song from her mother, who quite likely underwent a similar life and may still be working and singing alongside her, and, although no child is mentioned, there would not have been such dreadful 'cup-eyed care and doubt' without one, and it is probably to the child that she is passing on the song during the second half of stanza 2. But the fatal function of the song was the fourth one, mentioned above, when it was performed not for village entertainment or to ease the rigours of laundry or turnip-hoeing, but to entice or entrap her man erotically. Music is responsible for her downfall.

Perhaps by stanza 3 her child has grown up and gone away and she is on her own with no further role and therefore is no longer singing. Does her child still sing the song? Does her man? This is the question of heritage raised at the start of stanza 3 and indeed, briefly, at the end of chapter 4. What happened to rural children in later nineteenth-century England was that they went to find work in the towns. My own great-grandfather was a blacksmith in Devon who migrated to London as a young man and stayed there. He probably left his rural songs behind and filled his head with music-hall jingles (certainly beloved of my grandmother's family), and who could blame him? Where rural life survived was in the settler colonies, and Hardy seems to be suggesting, or hoping, as does the protagonist, that some link with place and earlier time somehow remains in the isolation of the outback or frontier, even if the man is now singing the song to another woman (note that little phrase 'as when').

The poem is therefore about song as both possession and exchange across time and space, and the ambiguities of this. The diurnal repetitions and wearings-down of time are hauntingly expressed in the repeated 'Sunday' and 'Monday' (zoomed out to plurals in stanza 3). 'Saturday' is sneaked into stanza 3, the magic of a first meeting at a Saturday night dance perhaps the prelude to Monday's seduction. Not just the weeks but the years are beginning to pass at the end of stanza 1, and it is only in the middle of the second year that the man appears on the scene, and even then their union, or at least the course of it, is not yet predicted or planned. That happens over the following years – many of them. By the time of the present he has long deserted her, for he is now in 'some dim land afar'.

We might think of the abandoned girl as Fanny Robin (the poem, therefore, about Sergeant Troy). She is a woman who has been left in her proletarian place, not just without her lover but with no news – no means of leverage, therefore – and, above all, no material resources: hence the 'cup-eyed care', a powerful phrase, and, worse still, 'despair', the last word of the poem. All she has to show for it are her song and the memories it brings with it: the song that caused the trouble in the first place but whose enshrining capability, the 'untouching' of time through recall, makes the whole thing unregrettable.

One could put an entirely different interpretation on the scenario of 'Her song', starting from the fact that the 'new-comer / From regions strange to me' more obviously fits the meeting of Hardy and his first wife Emma Gifford than that between Robin and Troy. This has to be admitted. Nevertheless, song in this poem usefully symbolises the transmission and transformation of culture and, more than that, through its prosopographical efficacy also shows itself to be their essence. What we are given, however, is only the half of it, for folksong is words plus tune; you cannot have one without the other. Yet we are never told what this particular song is like, musically speaking, or what it is about, semantically: that is not the point. Furthermore, given that every other line in stanza 1 and half that number in stanza 2 begin with the first person singular, it is striking that Hardy calls it not 'My song' but 'Her song': it is already being heard and passed on by somebody else, in this case the poet. For the poet, 'Her song' becomes 'My song', and what he gives us might almost as well be the original song text – a song singing about itself. But the whole poem is in the girl's speech, so *she* is already singing a song about a song. Hardy is writing a song about a song about a song, to which the composer John Ireland added a fourth layer when he composed a musical setting of Hardy's poem three years after it had appeared in print in 1922 in *Late Lyrics and Earlier*. What he contributed was an art song for solo voice and piano pretending to be the musical manifestation of that song about a song about a song, as though it were what Hardy heard in his mind. *We* only hear it, of course, when a real woman sings Ireland's song in concert, thus adding a fifth layer and bringing the whole thing full circle to actual performance, short-cutting the layers of narration and distancing (which are themselves symbolic) to pretend to have given us the girl's song itself, since the first word the woman on the concert platform sings is 'I'. Sure enough, Ireland does make the setting sound like a folksong, complete with its two-bar melodic introduction, and keeps an essential ambiguity of mode between dorian on G and dorian on D. At the same time, he fully betrays the observing townsman's sophistication, as if he were on holiday, hearing or collecting the song from the product of a quaintly alien lifestyle encountered in passing, when near the end of his setting he momentarily stills the cycle-of-5ths harmonies, as inexorable as the ravages of time on the girl's life, dissolving them into a tritonal dominant substitution (D^{b7} plus G^7) that triggers the 'untouching' of time – one of those wonderful invented Hardy words – and allows us privileged passage over the entire landscape of biography and social process. As a musical gambit this is far from folksong, though it may remind us of the parallels between fractured lives in rural Dorset and those in the black American south that gave rise to jazz.

Although he was not a folksong collector, Ireland had been on holiday in Dorset in 1923, touring by car with a young lover or would-be lover, Arthur Miller, who to judge from the number of compositions Ireland dedicated to him will have been quite the equal of 'Her song''s 'he' as the projection of vital experience shared and passed on.[1] Ireland's eight Hardy settings for voice and piano followed in 1925–26. He already knew the region, and had composed one 'impression' of it, his symphonic rhapsody *Mai-Dun*, an orchestral piece 'about' Maiden Castle, England's largest prehistoric hill fort, in 1920–21. (Ireland was not the only composer to make a musical setting of 'Her song'. Another is by Christopher le Fleming, where it appears in his cantata *Six Country Songs* of 1963.[2])

'Her song', and John Ireland with his setting of the poem as art music, can both be called upon to represent two rather strongly contrasting ways of theorising music in the west country. The first way is implicit in the point made above about us not knowing the anatomy and content of 'her song'. Here, music is not something that is but something one does; a verb, not a noun; a process of sound exchange, not a reification of sounds. It was in something approaching anthropological desperation that the late Christopher Small found the way of helping us to grasp this essence, by coining the term *musicking*.[3] It means *doing* music, the performance and cultural interaction of music, not just by the players and singers but by the listeners, the patrons, the roadies, the impresarios, the composers, the publishers, the instrument makers, and the sacred and secular authorities. Musicking is the ritual set of relationships that these people and their roles set up, sustain, clarify, or

---

[1] Richards 2000: 153 and Plates 10–12.
[2] le Fleming 1982: 194.
[3] Small 1995.

destroy, and all human beings are and always have been involved in them. It is quite clear how 'Her song' is about process and progress through a life and its relationships with other lives, the song itself, or rather the performance, the *musicking* of it, changing those lives and giving them meaning and pattern. And John Ireland setting 'Her song' to music and publishing it was also an example of musicking. A very particular relationship with a place, a time, a person, and a culture lay behind something he did, behind deciding to make an artistic manifesto out of them all, deciding, that is, to identify with the poem, its author, the folksong movement, the celebration of west country landscapes, and so on.

Why was Small so insistent on the activity of musicking? I believe it was because music is in perennial struggle between this ritual agency and our perhaps equally fundamental desires to *capitalise* on it. This is the second way of theorising music in the west country: as symbolic or cultural capital, borrowing the concept from the French sociologist Pierre Bourdieu.[4] Here, music freezes again, into an attitude, a thing staked out, a possession invested with exchange value, a guarded or cherished identity or even a fortune. Indeed, 'her song' was the girl's fortune in Hardy's poem, giving her identity the capital it needed to find a mate and accomplishing that task for both good (the cherished value of her erotic experience) and ill (her desertion). Ireland's setting of the poem helped stake out his identity as an artistic man of his time and place – going on holiday to the west country, responding to its landscapes, imbuing them with hints of the satisfaction of secret desires, and finding a market for all these things in consumers of like mind or training, who would buy his songs on publication, perform them, teach them to their students, pay to go to a concert hall and listen to them, or consider part of their radio licence fee value for money when they came up in the *Radio Times*. Music here becomes an element of the symbolic capital with which we invest our lives, part of who we think we are and what we want to accomplish with that identity.

There is a third, possibly deeper theory of how music might be embedded in time and place, and that is as a sound object in the memory. It is quite possible that the woman in 'Her song' had the song going through her head only, and it was not sung out loud on most of the occasions to which the poem refers (though it would be difficult to see how this could apply when she sang it 'to him', unless it was as a spell, which in rural culture is a quite possible interpretation). Music heard only in the head, or only remembered, is one of the medium's most potent dimensions, for it is desire to hear a particular

---

[4] Bourdieu 1984.

sequence of musical sounds again that makes musical form work, from hymn or strophic song to symphony. The memory of a soundscape and the memory of a landscape are not so very different in the mind, and together they form a 'pull' to a place, a time, and an event. They can develop into the full machinery of geographical and social nostalgia, but they can also be directed towards an imagined future, as when undertaking a pilgrimage to a place or event never before experienced. Certainly this theory of musical operation is not at odds with the other two, for in pursuing our lives and our identities we all want to capitalise on it – to have been there, done that – while at the same time we accept that such *motivation*, which is the brain's production of formulations based on memory and desire, has its active counterpart in the musicking with which we engage as social process.

Let musicking, capitalization, and memorialisation be the three identifiable modes of myth-making pertaining to the events and institutions of music in the west country – for musicking constructs myths, just like the other two agencies, insofar as enjoying patterned but non-semantically coded noise is all that musical performance actually consists of. The purpose of seeing how these cultural engines have propelled myths is to understand and appreciate some of the ways in which the west country, immemorially tasked like the other regions with being tributary to the metropolis and nation, has fought back and attempted to draw cultural power, which as capital is economic power, unto itself.

The Invention of the West Country

The most powerful myth has been the invention of the west country itself, and this, at last, is where the region can claim to have developed some kind of edge over other provincial areas, which for many of the foregoing purposes of this study can be seen as interchangeable with the west country or even arbitrary in their geographical enumeration, like so many police forces or health authorities. The notion of the western areas of Britain, or indeed the western areas of other countries such as the USA and now China, needing to be subdued and become tributary goes far back in history. Perhaps the west always wants to be wild and peripheral. As seen right at the beginning of this book, the middle ages already had their ideas about the west country, a phrase which nevertheless through into the early modern period might mean any of the western areas of Britain, or indeed Wessex, a much broader region not really including Cornwall. But more often than not it was the south-west peninsula that was assumed, and in the nineteenth century this region began to create for itself a sense of specialisation in its relation to the metropolis and nation. An economic dimension to this arrived with improved transport links – 'steam shipping made western Cornwall a part of London's hinterland district around 1838 for the supply of early vegetables' – and this favourability of climate combined with the great extent of coast and the excitement of a not too inconvenient remoteness then set their seal on the region's identity as a health and leisure destination.[5] Somewhere in the wake of this, the idea of the west country as the place of good living, heritage values, and beauty of landscape and vernacular building ensued. On holiday or in retirement there, one needed something to buy into, something to write home about, including a human host to idealise, scrutinize, or criticise. A good part of the cultural capital of the west country, then, has consisted in the celebration of what might be called its socio-geographical particularities, alongside the promotion of its folklore. These two vectors have, in the twentieth and twenty-first centuries, combined with the region's share of national institutions such as cathedrals, universities, and bureaucratic agencies to produce and limit whatever musical impetus the west country might hope to safeguard and invest in for the future. The folklore and socio-geographical particularity will be examined in this chapter, the region's share of national institutions in the next.

Until the Romantics began to idealise inaccessible scenery, the west country was more likely to be satirised than celebrated in music. In Thomas Ravenscroft's 'Hodge Trillindle to his zweet hort Malkin' from his *Briefe Discourse* of 1614, in effect a miniscule opera or cantata of three numbers (with a fourth by John Bennet), its two characters are slow-witted but decent yokels who sing, in an almost unintelligibly thick west country accent, such phrases as 'Thon, Roger, zweare / Yo wool be virmer thon yo weare … Zo, Roger, zweare an oape' in the song headed 'Their goncluzion *(Dhurd bart)*'.[6] Two centuries later, John Parry was composing the songs and writing the spoken dialogue for a Drury Lane farce entitled *High Notions, or A Trip to Exmouth* (1819), which on its first night played as an afterpiece to Kean's *Othello*.[7]

The previous year, the poet John Keats had made a trip not to Exmouth but to nearby Teignmouth to help look after his dying brother Tom, who was sojourning there for the obvious health reasons. He arrived in March, and to begin with it rained incessantly, which did not prevent him from composing, within the first three days, 'The Devon maid', with its mixture of sexual

---

[5] Bellich 2009: 441.
[6] Morehen and Mateer 2012: 157–63.
[7] *The Times*, 11 Feb 1819: 2.

fantasy and satire of such rustic longings.[8] It has been set to music scores of times, though possibly not before 1881, when Catherine Wyatt published her setting.[9] Keats took his first line from a traditional ballad.

The poet had not been in Teignmouth a month before its music dealer, the Joseph Parish encountered in two previous chapters, went bankrupt. The background to this was curious. Parish's brother Benjamin had been charged with an 'unnatural crime' (presumably homosexuality) but under oath sought to incriminate five more Teignmouth men. They were acquitted, and one of them, the baker James Martin, won a subsequent action for damages of £100 against Joseph, who was in some way defending or responsible for his brother.[10] This and the inevitable loss of business must have been more than Joseph could afford, and his bankruptcy swiftly followed, though it did not prevent his ten-year-old son Eli from making his first significant concert appearance as a harpist that same year, in Totnes. Eli would become in due course 'Teignmouth's most distinguished son', the leading virtuoso harpist of his generation, admired for his pioneering techniques by Berlioz and others, and a prolific composer. He changed his name to Elias Parish Alvars and after a period teaching in Dawlish moved to the Continent, eventually settling in Vienna.[11] Not much is known about him, and Brown and Stratton's categorical statement, 'Jewish by parentage', has not been convincingly followed up.[12] Nor does his only opera, *The Legend of Teignmouth*, survive beyond its overture, even if it was composed, though there is a complete symphony in manuscript and a number of concertos that have now been recorded, testimony to his engagement with the larger forms.[13] Parish Alvars is mentioned here because, romantic that he was, with *The Legend of Teignmouth* he was proposing one of the first musical celebrations of the west country in a century that would begin to generate many more. Alas, we cannot even be sure to which legend the opera refers. The poet Letitia Elizabeth Landon had published a poem of that title in 1834, about 'Sir Francis' and his betrothed, dead by the time of his return from sea, while the better-known story of the avaricious parson and his clerk, led into the sea by the Devil to form the rocks of those names, was printed in 1848 but would have been known to the composer long before. A sense of the

---

[8] Mackenzie 2006.
[9] BL Cat.
[10] Smith 1999b: 7; *EFP*, 12 Mar 1818: 4, 26 Mar 1818: 1, and 9 Apr 1818: 3.
[11] Smith 1999b: 3, 6; Griffiths 2001; Pigot 1830: 65.
[12] Brown and Stratton 1897: 308; see also JCR-UK, though it simply adds confusion.
[13] Sacchi 1999: 166, 176.

daredevil in the overture to *The Legend of Teignmouth* makes the latter story more likely as the opera's plot.

Not many operas refer to the west country in their titles, and Parish Alvars may have been genuinely homesick, for he wrote a song entitled 'Heimweh' ('Homesickness') and tried resettling in England in 1842, only to go abroad again where the opportunities were greater. True, his musical 'topics' (compositional signposts whose meanings were understood or felt by the public) were to some extent generic marketing ploys, but he was also capable of the languishing or militant harmonic precipitation being developed by his close contemporary Chopin (they died the same year) as the expression of the unspeakable yearnings of exile in terms of musical subjectivity.

A generation later, that subjectivity and its musical expression began to become a cultural commonplace, building itself around the perceived particularity of an individual location and an individual person's particular and happy (or nurturing) time invested in it. There were premonitions of such a sensibility in 1845 when William Spark, S S Wesley's musical apprentice at Exeter whom he had taken with him to Leeds in 1842, published a song there, 'The vallies [sic] of Devon'. Worthwhile not least for the exquisite miniature of Torquay lithographed on the front cover, the song itself decorous though not uninteresting, its three-verse strophic form reveals a longing not just for the topography of the county but in the third stanza for the inevitable female inhabitant, thus harking back to Keats. Spark's feeling for Devon was clearly genuine, for he returned there that same year as organist of St Peter's, Tiverton, though he was off northwards again in 1847 and Leeds eventually drew him back permanently.[14]

Consolidation of the musical celebration of the west country began much later, in the 1870s, in a place it would long remain: Clovelly. This, one must assume, was at a moment when an unusually isolated, north-facing cliff village had ceased to be hostile to aliens while ridden with potentially violent crime (smuggling), and now felt cosy and quaint. Perhaps this was not least because with the rural depression of the decade its inhabitants were moving away, leaving premises vacant, or having to take in visitors, thereby creating an open settlement for the first time – though it is easy to underestimate how remote Cornwall and north Devon still were in the later nineteenth century, and how much it cost to get there.[15] The first musical souvenir of Clovelly was a song composed by John Old, 'Dreamy Clovelly', published in London in 1873. Old does not quite know how to develop his topic, for the long,

---

[14] *EPG*, 10 May 1845: 3 and 16 Jan 1847: 3.
[15] See Braggs and Harris 2006: 29–31.

rambling verse section in 6/8 time, straying from E flat into G flat major (he likes his modulations), wants to be a Chopin barcarolle or ballade, missing the simplicity of rustic feeling that by contrast brings bathos to the 3/4 waltz refrain with its truly dreadful words: 'Dreamy Clovelly, / Charming, / Fairy, / Ne'er have I met with so lovely a spot; / Scene of Enchantment, / Dreamy, / Fairy, / Once seen, Clovelly, never forgot.' Virginia Gabriel's song 'Clovelly', which followed in 1875, is a different matter altogether, more in 'The sands of Dee' mode with its ballad narrative of a fisherman who must go to sea in defiance of a grim weather forecast because his children have nothing to eat. This was closer to proletarian reality (both Cornish mining and fishing were in crisis by that date),[16] and found a tense D minor 6/8 framework with plenty of Neapolitan harmony as its musical concomitant, though hope that God will spare the fisherman brings a relative major conclusion.

H Verne (one of the fifty pseudonyms for Charles Rawlings, most of them French) took a different tack again in his 'Clovelly: a song of Devon' of 1905, durable enough to have been republished in 1930. He sacralises the place in a hymn-like setting in E flat that begins on the low dominant, thus aimed at the lugubrious English contralto voice that 'Miss Margaret Cooper' must have possessed. Each stanza ends with 'Adieu ... Adieu' after stating that the protagonist will never go back there, without specifying why. Nostalgia for the west as a glimpse of heaven, a kind of lost chord, subsequently foregone for no good reason, is in full flood. Yet Verne could do other west country tropes as well, and he or his London publisher was smart enough to issue 'Clovelly', together with two other songs about north Devon, 'Dear old Ilfracombe' and 'Watersmeet', in partnership with the music dealer John T White of Barnstaple, Bideford, and Ilfracombe, Simper's ex-business partner encountered in the previous chapter. Marketed as *Verne's Souvenir Songs of Devon*, 'received with extraordinary enthusiasm at Ilfracombe Band Concerts', the back cover of 'Dear old Ilfracombe' also advertises three other 'famous west country songs' by another composer, G H Stone, to a variety of cultural topics: 'The western land' ('the favourite patriotic song'), 'Down 'ome by Kirton town' ('Dialect Song – Sung at all West Country gatherings'), and 'Dear county in the west' ('A charming melody set to good words'), rounding them off with 'Widdecombe Fair' ('Sung everywhere').

By this date, the place-specific content of musical merchandise might be no more meaningful than a name on a mug or a T-shirt today. Percy W Keen's 'Clovelly' of 1905 is simply a waltz for piano. After the war it was the new popular market for catchy or dance-hall numbers that cashed in

---

[16] Payton 2004: 218–19, 223.

Ex. 6.1 H Verne, 'Dear old Ilfracombe', extract

on the name with L Silberman's song 'Down in Clovelly' of 1924, Richard Elton's 'Quaint Clovelly' of 1925, and Julian Wright's 'Clovelly' of 1938. But plenty of songs from the later nineteenth century onwards do achieve an effective coalescence of topics in the music and the words. Verne's 'Dear old

Ilfracombe', for which he also wrote the words, is one such. The protagonist is the Squire of Brendon, who has lost his way after a day's hunting, which sets up the cultural motifs of the Exmoor Stag Hunt (one of the most famous in Britain), a remote and picturesque place (Brendon), and social stability in a rural setting (the squire). A Devon maid, once again encountered on a country path, gives the squire directions with her 'sweet voice', presumably in a lilting west country accent though not represented in dialect. This forms the refrain (Ex. 6.1), which draws on musical elements from two types of national song of the seventeenth and eighteenth centuries, the drinking and the patriotic. The characteristically multisyllabic Devon place-names 'Chambercombe' and 'Ilfracombe' are enumerated over their dominant pedal with musical repetition of a 'house-that-Jack-built' type, as though the list were to become longer and longer and a test for inebriated cronies, as with the names of the people on the horse in 'Widdecombe Fair' (to retain White's spelling). Emotional expansion and the patriotic dimension come with the top F and sturdy Handelian harmonies onto a dominant cadence at the line 'Grandest spot in the world it be': topographical rootedness in its natural, almost religious perfection, we are to understand. But this is immediately followed by a miniature pastoral, anchoring that rootedness in artisanal humility – 'cottages', fishermen, 'folk', a tonic pedal, diatonic 10ths, and a leading note that falls 'primitively' rather than rise. Lest this last should seem threateningly 'other', the cosiness of the song's title phrase is then affirmed and circumscribed with the downward octave F, landing at the word 'old' on a sonorous first inversion as reassuring as a Devon scone. Some effort is then made in the remaining two stanzas to assure a respectable, family audience, at which this and all other west country songs of the period will have been aimed, that the squire's intentions were honourable: he marries the fisher maid and accompanies her, now the lady, when she goes to visit her old friends 'below'.

Verne's 'Clovelly' and 'Dear old Ilfracombe' represent two types of commercial response to west country topography, the religiose and the good humoured. The former, in a kind of Victorian outgrowth of the fatality of the Border ballads, naturally encompassed the potentially tragic lot of downtrodden communities, especially the fishermen, miners, and emigrants of Cornwall, platitudinising them as late as 1921 in 'There's a quaint Cornish village' by B Carton and Edward Andrews, a particularly maudlin specimen of the genre. Winifred Vaughan's 'Pearl of the west (My Cornish haven)', with words by Roland Merry, similarly associates Cornwall's remoteness and seclusion with death, though in this case death as desire: 'And so when life is past, / There I would lie at last', the protagonist avows, to a semitonally inflected sequence reminiscent of the hymn 'Great is Thy faithfulness' (though the song was written first) if not quite of Isolde's *Liebestod*, of which its Celtic topic is a very humble relation. Perhaps such songs had picked up something from the Cornish love of funerals, itself closely associated with the Methodists and their hymns, though a broader, immemorial cultural resonance of humans electing 'to set their ultimate haven somewhere in the West', as Henry Warren put it, was also at work.[17]

But 'Pearl of the west' is also a stirring march, and proprietorial affection for the west country became increasingly associated with having a good or a healthy time there. Roeckel had set a breezy tone with 'The skippers of St Ives' in 1875, an early fruit of his collaboration with Weatherly, which like Verne's 'Dear old Ilfracombe' harnesses various national and folksong topics to humorous indulgence in gentle misogyny, doing so in a tale about wives who gossip for a thousand years. ''Twas on a Monday morning', the words begin, and the tune is soon echoing 'Annie Laurie', while the drinking element appears with a switch from 4/4 to 6/8 metre and 'Say, boys!' among its refrain tags. Rollicking anthems to the region burgeoned with the rise of leisure and vacation opportunities, and one of John Ireland's Hardy songs is a setting of the poem 'Great things', again by implication a male drinking song, hymning Dorset 'cyder', imbibed on a 'spin' down to Weymouth, dancing, and girls. 'Great things' takes the opposite viewpoint to the religious: 'Joy-jaunts' and 'impassioned flings' will have been worth it when 'One' calls, be it God or the Devil.

But well before the twentieth century, bravado had already been brought into partnership with west country living. In 1853, Morwenstow's eccentric vicar and poet, Rev Robert Hawker, published a hunting ballad of the 'John Peel' variety about the eighteenth-century squire 'Arscott of Tetcott', Tetcott being a village on the Devon–Cornwall border between Launceston and Holsworthy in the same general swathe of upland countryside that later hosted the 'sporting parson' Rev Jack Russell, after whom the breed of dog is named. Hawker's poem ends triumphantly, as though it were an account of the day's sport sung at the hunt supper, but for a version of it with a tune, which had been collected in Tetcott itself as a folksong by Sabine Baring-Gould, one has to turn to Baring-Gould's *Songs and Ballads of the West* (1889–91), where the minor-key song ends with the hunters gone to their doom, as with Teignmouth's Parson and Clerk.[18] Hawker had a genius for rousing ballads, and his 'Cornish emigrant's song', its ambiguous stance analysed by Payton in some detail, was published in 1908 in a musical setting

---

[17] Berry 1949: 228–30; Payton 2004: 203–5; Warren 1938: 1.
[18] Baring-Gould and Sheppard 1889–91; SBG 'Arscott of Tetcott'.

for solo voice and piano by James Richard Dear which the well-known baritone Harry Plunket Greene used to sing, as indeed he sang Battison Haynes's 'Off to Philadelphia', which the poem resembles generically.[19] In Dear's song we hear the musical *élan* of the west country man who will go out to conquer the world with his repeated 'We are going, we are going, / To North Americay'. It was a small step from such expansive sentiments to bolting onto the imperialism of Victorian and Edwardian Britain a renewed association of the west country with Drake, Raleigh, and what we would now call Elizabethan piracy. This was done with great popular success in Charles Kingsley's novel *Westward Ho!* (1855), which even spawned a rather desperate holiday resort. (John Old dedicated 'Dreamy Clovelly' to Kingsley and quoted the author's description of the fishing village in an epigraph heading the music.) The musical equivalent of *Westward Ho!*'s cultural coinage was minted in 1905 with Edward German's song 'Glorious Devon', to words by Harold Boulton. Here patriotism is personified by the county, and no-one could possibly have done it better; 'Devon's the fount of the bravest blood / That braces England's breed', as Boulton asserts, though not without the humour of partisan exaggeration, while German's music revels in stirring cycles of 5ths, diatonic solidity guaranteeing the element of sacralisation, and just enough of a country-dance topic to keep the feet tripping on local soil.

Glorious Devon, and the whole of the west country, became suddenly more accessible in the 1920s. 'This is the record of a motor-car journey round England', declared H V Morton's *In Search of England*, which went through twenty-three editions in nine years subsequent to publication in 1927, in its very first sentence. Morton devoted half the book to exploration south-west of London, the best direction in which to set off if wishing to postpone an encounter with the industrial cities while experiencing something more than flat land. Between the two world wars, following the sobering experience of the First, the west country, and Devon in particular, was tasked with absorbing a good deal of the topographical subjectivity that earlier generations could project onto the nation as a whole when 'pushed' or 'pulled' abroad with a view to peopling the world with the British or policing it by them. It would be too glib to suggest that the charabanc and the family car took the place of the destroyer as the vehicle of conquest. But certainly the west country bore a disproportionate share of invasion by 'the hideous *faux bonhomie* of the hiker ... singing obsolete sea chanties with the aid of the *Week-End Book* ... and astounding the local garage proprietor by slapping

---

[19] Payton 2005: 58–9.

him on the back', as Constant Lambert memorably put it in *Music Ho!*[20] A series of song anthologies published by Boosey for George V's jubilee in 1935 covered the lands of the thistle, shamrock, and rose (omitting the leek), and three of the songs in *The Rose Jubilee Song Book* were about the west country, none of the other five specifying a region. They comprised 'Glorious Devon' and two songs by Wilfrid Sanderson, 'Up from Somerset' (to words by Weatherly) and 'Drake goes west'. All three of these numbers included militaristic content, sentiment already needing to be banked against further war, but they could at the same time be read as blandishments towards tourist investment in the region of healthy living and sturdy inhabitants, as could a much wider variety of musical effusion, much of it no doubt conceived and most of it published in London.

The same combination of patriotism and romanticism could be found in Herbert Oliver's *Songs of the Devon Moors* (1912), with lyrics by the prolific Edward Teschemacher. As if to prove the point about its being a synthetic metropolitan production, the back matter advertised song cycles by the same team devoted to other places: *Songs of Merrie England*, *Songs of the Northern Hills*, *Songs of Old London*, *Songs of the Orient*, and *Three Persian Songs*. After the First World War such song cycles were joined and increasingly superseded by the instrumental suite, each of whose movements in some way depicted a particular location within the county chosen for the work's title, by analogy with the picture postcard showing four or five views and the pictorial lettercard which flourished in the same era. (*Songs of the Devon Moors* actually had a photograph of some Dartmoor boulders pasted onto the front cover.) Julius Harrison seems to have inaugurated the topographical suite with his *Worcestershire Suite* of 1917 for orchestra; his *Cornish Holiday Sketches* for strings followed in 1938. Percy Whitlock's *Plymouth Suite* for organ (1939) was mentioned in an earlier chapter; other west country suites include Ernest Markham's *Rivers of Devon Suite* for piano (1929), Eldridge Newman's *In Dorset*, a suite for orchestra (1931), Alfred Hale's *Cornish Suite for Small Orchestra* (1936), York Bowen's *Somerset Suite* for piano or organ (1940), and Raymond Sutton's *Wiltshire Downs*, a suite for piano (1949), between them covering all five of our counties.[21]

The aural celebrations of the west country dealt with so far could all be described as light music, which peaked between the First and Second World Wars and for one or two decades following the latter. In fostering a cultural allegiance not just at the national or regional but at the county

---

[20] Lambert 1948: 125.
[21] O'Toole 2011: 6.

level, the suites mentioned above take their place alongside a number of non-musical phenomena. One of them will have been important because it opened the way to a county identity for what was then called the 'common man': the restructuring into 'county regiments' of the British army infantry in the Childers Reforms of 1881.[22] Cricket and sports such as hunting had long been organised for amateurs, i.e. gentlemen of means, by county, and other inducements to good living followed suit. Cars appeared: Austin manufactured the Somerset, the Dorset, and the Devon versions of their A40 model in the late 1940s and early 1950s. But above all it was a matter of guide books for independent travellers. Here the Pevsner architecture guides have perpetuated a county gazetteer format already familiar from Arthur Mee's *The King's England* and other series such as the Penguin and Shell touring guides, while the Robert Hale topographical companions of the immediate postwar period were similarly apportioned by county.[23] Music suggesting the cheerful exploration of a county continued to be produced so long as there was an expanding market of people for whom such exploration remained a novelty and badge of affluence.

❧ The Invention of Folk Music

Folksong has also been culturally aggregated by county. Why is this, and how does it fit into the institutionalisation of the west country as so far analysed?

There was no such thing as folklore until 1846, when an influential antiquary, William Thoms, who three years later would also found the journal *Notes and Queries*, pseudonymously proposed the use of the term to supersede what until then had been known as the study and collection of 'popular antiquities'.[24] Folksongs, as a translation of the German term *Volkslieder*, there had already been. But this further embedding by Thoms of the romanticising formulation of the 'folk', and possibly also its distancing from the 'popular' as the latter's commercial connotations and reach rapidly gathered pace, were key cultural moves that would have an enormous effect on perceptions of the south-west peninsula when followed up by later cultural arbiters. If one invented west country was to be that of a holiday playground with euphoric living and an abundance of manly enterprise, another would be in some respects the opposite, that of a remote and backward agricultural

---

[22] Parker 2016: 307.
[23] ibid: 344–7.
[24] Alford 1952: 1; *Athenaeum* 982 (22 Aug 1846): 862–3.

region where age-old traditions, including stores of tunes, had survived, unaffected by modern developments.

The two inventions were linked, and it was as a man on vacation that Cecil Sharp, who like most musicians of his time earned the bulk of his living by teaching, and did so in a boys' prep school, paid the visits to his friend Rev Charles Marson, vicar of Hambridge in Somerset, that would result in his collecting over 1,000 songs, orally transmitted, largely from three rural areas of the county.[25] Dave Harker points out that there was 'not a male agricultural labourer' among the most trusted and prolific of his 350 singers, many of whom were women, though this is tendentious insofar as other scholarship has demonstrated beyond doubt that most of Sharp's singers were working class.[26] Harker's thorough deconstruction of Sharp's amazing project, a project which changed the cultural configuration of music in England for ever, and within three years (1904–07) at that, was nonetheless important and necessary, and while there is no need to repeat the exercise here, within the regional context certain elements of the folksong myth can still benefit from additional light being cast on them.[27]

John England, already mentioned at the end of chapter 4, was Marson's gardener, and it was in response to Sharp's having questioned Marson by letter about possible folksingers in his neighbourhood that Marson must have set up England's lawn-mowing performance of 'The seeds of love'. The literal *quid pro quo* was a pipeful of tobacco.[28] England exacts further investigation. A handsome man with a keen gaze, he was still in his thirties and thus in no way a vindication of Sharp's theory that only old people cherished the songs because a cultural break had been created by those born after 1840.[29] Indeed he was a collector himself, as any singer in demand has to be, for he had heard 'The seeds of love' while working on the land in Dorset. It is quite possible that he too had transcribed it in musical notation, since he had been a member of the Hambridge parish church choir – a surpliced choir, at that – and would probably have learnt to read music; indeed, Marson had first heard him sing the tune, unaccompanied only because they could find no printed source, with one of the women of Hambridge choir at the annual choir supper.[30] England was parish clerk and sexton.[31] He may well have

---

[25] Heaney 2004: 4–5; Harker 1985: 189–91.
[26] Harker 1985: 191.
[27] ibid: 172–210.
[28] Heaney 2004: 5.
[29] Bearman and Staelens 2006; Sharp 1907: 119–20.
[30] Marson 1904: xiv.
[31] *TC*, 16 Oct 1895: 6; *WG*, 24 Mar 1911: 4.

been the same John England who led the Hambridge and Westport Band, or at least a near relative of that John England, and although England was a common enough surname in the area, it being that of the mother of two of Sharp's other singers, this patronymic nexus serves to remind us that the strands of village music were surely more interwoven, as musicking and as manifestations of musical capital and commodification, than Marson and Sharp would all too soon persuade their readers to believe.[32] The first casualty of their reifying urge was any documentation of what else the village balladeers sang and what proportion, focus, and purpose within their repertoire traditional songs represented. We do know that they prized the music-hall songs immediately dismissed by Sharp, but for anything like representation of the whole picture one has to turn to instrumental tune books compiled in manuscript, of course within a notated tradition and of course earlier. These contain a very broad range of material, and their popular hits from minstrelsy and opera were up-to-date.

On the other hand, attempts to link practitioners of early nineteenth-century Somerset psalmody with families that later continued singing traditional songs have not so far been conclusive or particularly encouraging, although a heartfelt ballad on the clerical ousting of psalmody clearly went the rounds of Devon and was known elsewhere in England. Baring-Gould included it in *Songs and Ballads of the West* as 'Brixham town', its tune replete with Handelian strains, while a one-stanza version from North Tawton to a cruder version of the melody runs as follows:

> North Tawton men are rare
> In singing, I declare.
> None with them can compare
> > In Harmonie.
> There is a man of might,
> Who strives both day and night,
> To put down singing quite,
> > Which shall not be.

This link notwithstanding, the demise of psalmody strongly suggests a new breed of genteel musician (and audience) having replaced its practitioners.[33] From this socially pessimistic viewpoint, we might posit at least three mutually exclusive types of Victorian village musician, in Somerset and elsewhere: the progressive organist or chancel choir member; the progressively silenced

---

[32] *TC*, 1 Jun 1892: 6 and 5 Jun 1895: 6; Bearman and Staelens 2006.
[33] Bwye-Turner 2010: 40–4; Baring-Gould et al 1905: 18–19; SBG 'Brixham town'; Full English SBG 1/1/56.

gallery quire practitioner; and the balladeer. Class certainly played into such separation as there really was, and the comprehensive five-fold tiering of rural status depicted by Hardy in *The Woodlanders*, with Marty South at the bottom, seems confirmed when one reads the biography of Emma Overd, one of Sharp's leading singers, though Overd was temperamentally quite the opposite of the shy South. Father and husband were agricultural labourers; mother died when she was eight; three of her nine children died before adulthood; worked at willow peeling as a cottage industry; lived in a hamlet and subsequently in a 'bad' street in Langport; aged sixty-five, made a crude exhibition of Sharp outside the pub with her cronies when he first approached her; shared a huge repertoire, dramatically performed; and could finally afford her 'weekly indulgence of beer' when old age pensions were introduced in 1909.[34] This was a musical life quite different from any of those depicted in the previous two chapters. Folksong was after all a thing apart.

Still, Sharp would probably not have spurned an invitation to conduct John England's band, and that would have weakened the class barrier; what strengthened it again, and fuelled the myth of a genre's rescue operation through publication and use in education, was that he and his fellow collectors could not conceive of becoming singers themselves. They were, for the purpose, gentlemen scholars, not executants. It was acceptable for an Oxbridge dean to transmit a west country ghost story along with the port in the senior common room during a power cut, but would have been unthinkable for him to sing an unaccompanied narrative ballad under those same circumstances.[35]

To what extent, then, English folksong was one of pre-war Britain's invented traditions remains debatable. But the invention of its county identity, a perception particularly strong in the south-west because Somerset became Sharp's focus, is not in doubt. Here he did achieve something mythical, and time and again when mentioning to others my work on the history of music in the west country, their response, when not blank puzzlement, was to assume folk music as its focus. Scholars of traditional tunes and ballad narratives stress the extent to which the artefacts travel and know no county or even national boundaries. A L Lloyd compared a lullaby in Baring-Gould's *Songs and Ballads of the West* with one from Asturias, Spain.[36] Maud Karpeles pointed out that the preposition in Sharp's key publication of 1904–09, the five-volume *Folk Songs from Somerset*, was not *of* (which one could argue

---

[34] Bearman 2004.
[35] Rowse 1949.
[36] Lloyd 1969: 175–8.

merely served to draw attention to his collection as a tourist's souvenir, like clotted cream from Devon or a postcard from Cornwall).[37] Marson, mindful perhaps that 'Brixham town' was known elsewhere as 'Wrexham town', was careful to emphasise that even a song with a title such as 'Bruton town' was 'not necessarily native'.[38]

Sharp and Marson wanted the monument to be folksongs *for* Somerset. Introducing them educationally into the Hambridge village school, which Sharp did, meant that the pupils' parents also began to take repossession of what their own parents had rejected, for Sharp a happy by-product of his main ideological aim, quite possibly prompted in the first place by Marson, which was through school education to purge his industrial nation of commercial popular song, much of it American, and render the English spirit pure and somehow rural again.[39] That this was one equivalent in sound of many another thrust in English social and cultural history of the period, such as the garden city movement and Arts and Crafts architecture, hardly needs stressing. What does have to be emphasised is that Sharp, reliant on his teaching income like all musical general practitioners, dreamed of a more creatively satisfying living, particularly after he resigned from the Hampstead Conservatoire in 1905 following a dispute. He retained his Ludgrove post, but beyond that 'his income was henceforth derived largely from lecturing and publishing on folk-music'.[40]

Appealing to the county constituency was an obvious way of securing a place for his product. The collector of those 'popular antiquities' that suddenly became folklore had typically been a landed gentleman or his sacred adjunct, the parish incumbent, and while their responsibilities were towards their villagers, their social life beyond entertaining at the vicarage or on the estate centred on the town, above all the county town, which in Devon and Wiltshire was also the Anglican see.[41] Here, in Georgian society, the assizes, races, balls, and music festivals were held, administration and its documentation were centred, regiments and volunteer corps were based, public services such as hospitals were established, and the marriage market was concentrated (county cricket came later).

---

[37] Karpeles 1973: 78.
[38] Marson 1904: xii.
[39] Sharp 1907: 120, 135.
[40] Heaney 2004: 6.
[41] Salisbury was in some respects Wiltshire's county town, though Devizes and the eponymous Wilton also exercised elements of that function, which has now migrated to Trowbridge, while the County Record Office is now in Chippenham.

Sharp could not suddenly become a squire like Sabine Baring-Gould at Lewtrenchard near the Devon–Cornwall border, the latter's *Songs and Ballads of the West*, collected 'from the mouths of the people', representing the eighteenth- and nineteenth-century model of heritage conservation based on social responsibility and landed privilege within the locality. Nor could Marson. But Sharp was swift to collaborate with Baring-Gould in the latter's heavily revised second edition of 1905, which he must strongly have influenced, its title and subtitle changed to avoid the word 'ballad' but include 'folk', two counties (Devon and Cornwall) now specified, its essay on the tunes by Sheppard omitted, its most obviously tonal songs (those with a midway dominant modulation) rejected, and its scholarly presentation standardised. He was equally swift to ground his publications and look for patronage at the county level. So was Marson, many of whose ideas appear to stem from Baring-Gould, though the traffic became two-way.[42] Both the five volumes of *Folk Songs from Somerset*, closely based on the four of *Songs and Ballads of the West* in being a cumulative series in one numbered sequence, and Sharp's *English Folk-Song: some conclusions* (1907) were co-published by a London firm and Barnicott and Pearce of Taunton, which had already issued a clerical tract by Marson and *Songs of Somerset* by J H Stephenson (1898), the latter 'songs' only in the conventional sense of poetic effusions. *Folk Songs from Somerset* was published as a connoisseur's item, in spacious format on cream paper and with the full scholarly apparatus of a critical edition, including an introduction, which in the first series terminated in notes on performance practice, and a critical commentary on each item and its sources at the back of each volume.

Nor was Sharp above praising his adopted county at the expense of its neighbour, and when Joseph Cornelius from Shepton Beauchamp in Somerset sang him a variant of 'Widdecombe Fair' as 'Midsummer Fair', he was keen to acclaim that its melody was 'older than the Devonshire tune and … has more character and a better rhythm'.[43] Sharp was probably right about seniority of tune (see Ex. 6.2), though probably wrong in thinking that 'Widdecombe Fair' was a later nineteenth-century corruption, for Uncle Tom Cobley, a 'genial old bachelor' who lived in the parish of Spreyton, died in the 1790s (all the other named characters came from Sticklepath).[44] Beyond this, his judgement was coloured by dislike of the *bonhomie* of 'Widdecombe Fair', whose endurance to this day as popular materiality reproduced on the spot

---

[42] Compare Baring-Gould 1891, Marson 1904, and Baring-Gould 1905a.
[43] Sharp and Marson 1904–9, ii (1905): 73.
[44] Baring-Gould 1905b: 6.

Ex. 6.2 a) 'Midsummer Fair', melody only, stanza 1;
b) 'Widdecombe Fair', melody only, stanza 1

(a) Tom Pearce, Tom Pearce, lend me the grey mare, An-to-be-lone, a-lal-lee-lal-lee, That I may go ride to some Mid-sum-mer Fair, To my oor, bag boor, bag nig-ger, bag wal-ler and ban-ta-ba-loo.

(b) "Tom Pearce, Tom Pearce, lend me your grey mare, All a-long, down a-long, out a-long, lee. For I want for to go to Wid-de-combe Fair, Wi' Bill Brewer, Jan Stewer, Peter Gurney, Peter Davy, Dan'l Whiddon, Harry Hawk, old Un-cle Tom Cob-ley and all. Old Un-cle Tom Cob-ley and all.'

in postcard, colouring book, or musical box would have been anathema to him. Yet the real 'folk' are surely those who over the generations have passed through Widecombe on holiday, bought the postcard, and remembered the song. We have all done that.

A few years after Sharp, another west country visitor accomplished what Sharp never managed to achieve: to turn one of its traditional musical artefacts into an enduring popular hit on the basis of a locality – and how many other English towns can boast of this? Katie Moss, a young professional musician from Acton, London, was present in Helston for Flora Day 1911 (held that year on 6 May because 8 May, a Monday, was market day), and on the train home began to sketch out her song, for which she wrote her own words, 'The floral dance'. As published that same year and recorded in 1912 by the Australian baritone Peter Dawson, who later recorded many another celebratory west country song, such as 'Glorious Devon', it became an immediate and lasting success, surely now one of the best-known compositions by a woman, and helped bring what to some extent had been the languishing rites of Helston back to life, as did BBC outside broadcasts of Flora Day from 1935 onwards. Now 'a quaint old Cornish town' was not only an evocative locution but a familiar melodic phrase too. From the 1960s, the comedian Ken Dodd has spoofed Moss's song in his media act; the melody lurks intertextually in the Wurzels' 'The Charlton Mackrell Jug Band'; in 1975 the West End stage show version of *Dad's Army* used it as its 'Choir practice' Act I finale, Ian Lavender as Pike bringing the house down with 'I could only stand and stare, / For I had no boy girl with me', to conductor Mainwaring's expostulation 'Stupid boy!'; and then in 1977 an updated musical arrangement by Derek Broadbent, played by his Brighouse and Rastrick Brass Band, soared to no. 2 in the UK hit singles chart with the help of disc jockey Terry Wogan, who recorded his own solo version of it, reinstating Moss's words, the following year.[45] Broadbent's arrangement featured in the film *Brassed Off* (1996), and even the Helston Town Band has been known to play it.[46]

Moss has been castigated for playing fast and loose with a traditional artefact, and serious literature on the Furry Dance and on Cornwall's May festivals barely acknowledges her.[47] To what extent her invocation of non-brass instruments (violin, cello, flute, clarinet, bassoon), fast tempo for the dance tune, reference to dancers kissing, and clear indication of bystanders joining in indicate evolving performance practice over more than a century is difficult to know. Baring-Gould called the tune a hornpipe,[48] but today's Furry Dance, played by brass and percussion only (the Helston Town Band split into two large sections, at the front of the procession and much further back), has a slow tempo and almost hieratic phrasing (Ex. 6.3); demeanour is formal, and participation is certainly not for all comers. Marshall, in an exhaustive study, points out Moss's falsification of the tune

---

[45] All these manifestations except the full version of Ken Dodd's can be found on YouTube.
[46] Marshall 2003: 65.
[47] Newton 1978: 4, 20; Cunnack nd; Jones 2006: 42–101.
[48] Baring-Gould 1899: 243.

by introducing a melodic sequence and the impossibility of there ever having been a cello in the band, while acknowledging that no other instrument name would have fitted her lyrics at that point.[49] But she must be acclaimed for having taken an approach to capitalising on a traditional artefact utterly different from that of the antiquarian collector. What she did instead was become the anthropological observer-participant, albeit only for a day. Nowadays, the result would be a documentary screen media product with half its sounds generically overdubbed in the studio; Moss wrote the entire experience, sights, actions, and soundscape, into six pages of popular sheet music that utterly caught the public's imagination. They did so because they perfectly represent the position of any willing and curious visitor to an alien yet alluring custom, to that mixture of the unusual and the attractive that tourism trades on. (She cleverly transfers the idea of curiosity to the band with its 'curious tone'.) The visitor remains an outsider – hence the *sotto voce* commentary tending towards a voiceover monotone, an interior registering of the sights and sounds – and is in danger of growing offhand at her lack of knowledge of how the culture works ('Whether they knew one another I care not, / Whether they cared at all, I know not') until the invitation to join in arrives in the shape of a friend who can become her dance partner. Then she understands what it is all about, and so do we.

The idea was essentially that of the symphonic soundscape, developed by composers such as Gershwin (*An American in Paris*) and Debussy (*Ibéria*), with the one big difference of words, which made the narrative explicit in a manner long exploited in nineteenth-century popular songs such as Sullivan's 'The lost chord'. Moss is not a symphonist, and a three-strophe ballad is what eventuates, each stanza containing sections A (the singer's rising monotone accompanied by rising and then falling diatonic 10ths of the sisters-and-his-cousins-and-his-aunts variety, to build anticipation), B (heady falling chromatic triads for the first aural signals carried on a 'gentle breeze', the first full view of the intoxicating dance, and finally the thrilled recognition of an approaching dance partner), and C, the tune of the band

Ex. 6.3 The Furry Dance, first strain, Helston, 8 May 2010

[49] Marshall 2003: 20.

itself overlaid on the monotonal chanting of the singer's perceptions. The A section has a dominant pivot at each appearance, but the lack of a larger-scale key change prevents any real development in storytelling register, which is the song's ultimate limitation as a musical soundscape. But the gradual approach of the band, its melody lost on the breeze for a couple of bars at the words 'Far away, as in a trance', the bustling sound and then the sight as she gets closer to what is going on, and finally the tune openly perceived, *forte*, 'rhythm well marked', and repeated *fortissimo* in its full glory with no verbal commentary as though its overwhelming presence now fills the totality of sense, are all well handled.

Festival Culture in Cornwall

The earliest printed description of the Furry Dance dates from 1790, though it was clearly well established by then, and seems similar to the notorious 'long dances' found in the streets of Wells in the spring of 1607 and possibly to the Salisbury city parishes' Whit Week 'dancing days', on record between 1478 and 1624.[50] Every year, a week earlier than Helston's festivities, Padstow's Obby Oss 'Day song' (or 'Morning song') resounds through its streets played by the massed accordions that lend it an excitingly primitive aura. Like the Furry Dance, however, it is probably a social dance tune or in this case perhaps a drinking song from no earlier than the Georgian or Restoration period, and the accordions and the top-hatted, jigging master of ceremonies with his 'bones' offer more of a parallel with blackface minstrelsy. These are elements that were not yet present in 1932, as a Pathé newsreel demonstrates, and both the Padstow and the Helston dance music seem to have slowed down since earlier in the twentieth century.[51] But the ceremonial occasions in both Padstow and Helston also sport a secondary musical ritual whose tune, along with its words, is probably much older than the main item. Padstow's is a periodic interruption or trope of the 'Day song', Helston's the 'Hal an Tow'.[52] Both refer to St George, Padstow's in the words, Helston's in costume play, with the dragon, St Michael, and the Devil being also involved in the latter.[53]

---

[50] Jones 2006: 67–8; Stokes 2003: 37, 48; Douglas 1996: passim, and 2003: 71–4.
[51] YouTube: 'Padstow "Hobby Hoss" (1932)'.
[52] Padstow's nomenclature is confused; some earlier accounts (see Jones 2006: 38–9) call the trope the 'Day song'.
[53] See Jones 2006: 30–2, 38–9 for the music; YouTube: 'Hal an Tow Hellys Helston 2015'.

That old music and an old ritual survive and flourish as something that once a year seems quite natural – and the hearty performance of the Hal an Tow song by local girls (young and old), the verve of Padstow's accordion band, and the Helston Town Band's proud formality make it abundantly clear that they do – should not really surprise us. Consumer culture in the northern hemisphere still succumbs for a month or more every midwinter to fuging textures, baroque major-key sequences, soaring descants, and reassuringly twee tonal jingles, in its obligatory and inescapable diet of Christmas carols, at a time when the signifiers of contemporary musical sound have in all other respects and at all other seasons moved far away from these to modal, rock-based, or minor-key topics. As if to emphasise the point by contrast, Glastonbury, legendary site of Christianity's most ancient appearance in Britain as well as an archaeologically factual repository of pre-Roman culture in the form of its lake villages, has at the opposite solstice developed the nation's most gigantic music festival, and done so on the basis of modern youth and pop culture.

It has tended to be said of rural, agricultural societies that every third day was a festival. This seems to have been true of England in the 200-year period of its Perpendicular Gothic architecture starting roughly in the mid-fourteenth century and climaxing in the early sixteenth, as the dates attached to Ronald Hutton's detailed description of England's ritual year – or rather half-year, for most of the feasts occurred between Christmas and midsummer – indicate.[54] Insofar as this densely festive and densely regulated culture was organised and celebrated at the level of the parish, it was an accommodation between the rhythm of the Church's year and that of pagan tradition whether Celtic, Roman, Anglo-Saxon, Danish, or some mixture of these. A festival or 'holy day', like our modern weekend, was both repetitiously normal and special, a manifestation of 'that union of change and permanence which we call Rhythm' as Laurence Whistler notes, quoting C S Lewis's Screwtape,[55] and another aspect of the accommodation of the exceptional to the regular and *vice versa*.

Festival culture and its music, so special yet in this case literally everpresent, adheres to some of the west country's very oldest material traces of human society, the stone circles at St Buryan (Merry Maidens) and Boskednan (Nine Maidens), both in western Cornwall, at Stanton Drew, near Bristol, and on Bodmin Moor (the Hurlers), plus the Nine Maidens stone row, again in Cornwall, near St Columb Major. In every case, humans

---

[54] Hutton 1994.
[55] Whistler 1947: 17–18.

were turned to stone for dancing (or hurling) on the Sabbath, while larger stones some way off from the circle or the row are supposed to be the fiddlers or pipers who managed to escape a short distance before being overtaken by a similar fate. (At Stanton Drew it was the bride and groom of an overrunning Saturday wedding who started escaping, the fiddler being the Devil.)[56] However anachronistically, these legends remind us that music for a festival has always been in the minds of rural west country people, and this returns us to the questions of chapter 4 about how it could suddenly become expertly available for special occasions and what were the implications of it as a skilled undercurrent the rest of the time – that is, about its institutional and economic infrastructure, about its circulation of capital within the culture. For there is no doubt that if there was a holiday every third day, there was music too. Hutton mentions music on almost every page. Equally pervasive is reference to money, in a see-saw pattern of payments into and out of the parish accounts (which is where most of the evidence of festive activity comes from) – into, when a church ale, play enactment, or procession raised substantial funds for upkeep of the parish fabric, out of, when people, including musicians, needed to be paid for providing something special and obligatory.[57] *How* special may have been relative to the size of the financial contribution, and we shall return to this as a measure of distinction in the Epilogue.

For hundreds of years the Church was the prime enabler and regulator of this cultural economy, in a strict or more extended sense. Its bells provided all parish markers in time. Festival culture as a marker of place, however, is the idea that can most fruitfully be calibrated and that lends the west country historic distinction. Bells again offer a way in. 'The bell tower', Alain Corbin states, 'prescribed an auditory space that corresponded to a particular notion of territoriality, one obsessed with mutual acquaintance. The bell reinforced divisions between an inside and an outside.' Corbin summarises the French ethnographer Marcel Maget's identification of 'a set of concentric circles containing a zone of mutual acquaintance, a zone of marriage alliances, a zone of leisure activities, and a *zone of hearsay* that define social acquaintance in rural societies', adding that 'the range of a bell should be analyzed in very much the same terms'.[58] So, perhaps, should the range and reach of music, not in as strictly acoustic a manner as the bell, but in terms of how far

---

[56] Warren 1938: 92; Turner 1949: 17–18; Wikipedia: 'The Hurlers', 'Nine Maidens stone row'.
[57] Hutton 1994.
[58] Corbin 1998: 95–6.

people's social and economic attachment to music would take them or bring it. For what is the compulsion to attend a concert or to approach the distant, wind-borne sounds of a fair or a festival but the musical operation of the zone of hearsay? People will pay to experience at first hand something they have overheard or heard about.

Cornwall provides the best examples of music forming part of the magnetic attraction of place in the west country. In the fifteenth and sixteenth centuries, there flourished a tradition of festival plays comparable with the miracle cycles of York, Wakefield, Chester, and elsewhere, except that they were written and performed in the Cornish language. The *Ordinalia*, Cornwall's extant three-day cycle of complete plays made up of separate episodes, will have been a production for the feast of Corpus Christi, falling on the second Thursday after Whitsun, and a festival officially recognised by the Church from 1264 and widely promoted from 1311, the latter milestone no doubt accounting for its growth thereafter, which seems to have occurred earlier in the west country than elsewhere in England.[59] Other Cornish texts surviving in whole or in part are a fifteenth-century play about the life of St Meriasek, *Beunans Meriasek*, assumed to belong to Camborne, the only parish with that dedication, a recently discovered *Beunans Ke* (*Life of St Kea*),[60] and a much later, incomplete *Creacion* cycle.

None of this artistic creativity was the work of unlettered rustics, and the *Ordinalia* are generally believed to have been written by a cleric at Glasney collegiate church on the southern edge of Penryn, 'the "most flourishing and richest institution in Cornwall" up to the Dissolution', of which scarcely a stone survives. Glasney must have established something of a west country blueprint for place as the crucible of cultural capital:

> The [Glasney] church was a likely place for entertainments and attracted residents as no other establishment in Cornwall could. For many rectors, living in rural parishes was a lonely life ... So attracted to Glasney were they that in 1372 Bishop Brantingham 'wrote to the Provost of the College complaining that some rectors absented themselves from their parishes and resided in the College' ... Bishop Grandisson chastised Glasney in his 1360 prohibition ... threatening excommunication, against 'silly and harmful pastimes', holiday entertainments, and plays.[61]

Perhaps some of those absentee clerics took the festival plays with them when forced back to their parishes. The question then arises as to how they put

---

[59] Johnston 2003: 15.
[60] Payton 2004: 98.
[61] Joyce and Newlyn 1999: 392, quoting Henderson 1964: 157; ibid.

together the personnel required for the plays' performance (which according to Carew was not from memory but by rote from a prompter who followed the actor around, though this may have been a late degeneration).[62] More to our purpose here, how did they provide some simulacrum of the music indicated in the text or implied, at the very least in the form of sound effects, at various moments of physical theatre? On occasions the references to music become a matter of expertise and resource almost to the point of showing off, as already mentioned in chapter 3 and further indicated by the closing speech of the *Ordinalia*'s 'Death of Pilate' episode, spoken by a character, Tulfric, who was clearly both a compelling humorist and part of a harmonic trio of demons:

> Yah, kiss my rear!
> For its end is out
> Very long behind me.
> Beelzebub and Satan,
> You sing a great drone bass,
> And I will sing a fine treble.[63]

Were these three professional minstrels, drafted in to play opposite the other characters? Or were actors who were amateur musicians as capable as church choristers and singing men of improvising counterpoint of the faburden kind?[64]

Cornwall developed outdoor sites for parish play performances such as are not found elsewhere in Britain. There is one such *plain-an-gwary* ('playing place') right by the main square in St Just, in the form of a small circular amphitheatre with banked seating all round, and possible identifications of more than thirty others across the Duchy are listed in *REED*, which is nevertheless careful to point out that some of them may have been used for games such as hurling, not necessarily for plays.[65] Production values were enterprising, to judge from the remains of a trench and pit in one such playing place, enabling surprise entries from the ground, as necessitated when Pilate's dead body melodramatically refuses to stay in the earth.[66] The lists of expenses found in the St Ives borough accounts of 1571–72 indicate something comparable, the plays by then having become a firmly civic venture, as Corpus Christi processions in parishes always were, and as the

---

[62] Carew 1602: 71v; Payton 2004: 135.
[63] Cawley 1956: 263.
[64] See Rastall 2001a: 314, 322, and chapter 7, below.
[65] Joyce and Newlyn 1999: 559–63.
[66] ibid: 405–6.

Semana Santa processions still are in Spain.[67] Wages for pipers are included in the St Ives account, and pipers are instructed to generate the dancing at the end of the play in the closing speech of whichever character concludes a particular day's drama, be he King Solomon, the Earl of Vannes, or Noah.[68]

The 'zone of hearsay' for a Cornish play must have been extensive. Carew states that 'the country people flock from all sides, many miles off, to hear & see it: for they have therein, devils and devices, to delight as well the eye as the ear'.[69] The St Ives play of 1572 went on for six days, and with the sales of drink and side attractions as well as entry fees took a total of £16 16s 8d, a very substantial sum. Expenditure on props, staging, and costumes amounted to only £2 1s 9d, and the unspecified wages of the pipers cannot have reduced the large profit margin by too much.[70] How many people attended? The fact that takings built up sharply to day 3 and, apart from an equally sharp dip on day 4, tailed off gradually towards day 6 suggests that people came from afar, some not managing to arrive until the festivities had been going for a day or two, others having to be on their way home before the end. The figures could also indicate that hearsay that it was happening reached them at a distance on or after day 1, they took a day or so to get there, and then drifted off after witnessing a day or more's play. Without knowing the price of admittance we cannot be sure of audience numbers, but if each person paid a penny for entrance, which was the cost of attending a London open-air theatre as a groundling, then they peaked at over a thousand on day 3, with a total of 3,560 'bums on seats', to use modern parlance, over the six days.[71]

St Ives was a borough of maybe a thousand inhabitants or more in the later sixteenth century, but the playing places of the tiny villages of Ruan Minor and Ruan Major, on bare, windswept common land above the cliffs of the Lizard peninsula, must have made for even more striking gatherings of people when they hosted plays; Manning-Sanders was surely close to the mark in imagining 'the huge watching crowds, with their sleeping booths and tents … ringed round by the harsh grandeur of moors and cliffs, and girdled by the ever-restless, ever-reverberating ocean'.[72] Rowena Cade's Minack Theatre, inaugurated in 1932 as an open-air amphitheatre on a cliff ledge above Porthcurno, has recaptured something of Cornwall's pre-modern festival spirit, though Gilbert and Sullivan – *The Pirates of Penzance* is inescapable

[67] ibid: 513–14.
[68] ibid: 590–2.
[69] Carew 1602: 71v.
[70] Joyce and Newlyn 1999: 513–14.
[71] Burnett 1969: 95.
[72] Joyce and Newlyn 1999: 394; Manning-Sanders 1949: 47.

at this longitude – can hardly match the particular mixture of transcendence and rough humour that a Cornish miracle play must have conveyed.[73] John Wesley, however, tapped directly into whatever was collectively recalled of the tradition in the eighteenth century when he attracted huge numbers of miners to Gwennap Pit, a circular amphitheatre on the hills above Redruth, for his preaching, while the evangelical camp meeting, held in the open air in remote spots well away from towns in the anglophone Old and New Worlds in the nineteenth century, must be thought of as answering people's ongoing urge to be taken out of themselves emotionally in a combination of numerous company and isolated location experienced nowhere else in their lives. Hearing music, participating in dancing and bodily movement, and, in the case of the Methodists, singing *en masse* in such places were experiences never to be forgotten. Wesley himself found at Gwennap in 1775 that 'no music is to be heard upon earth comparable to the sound of many thousand voices when they are all harmoniously joined together singing "praises to God and the Lamb"'.[74] The present-day evangelical Christians who gather in their thousands for 'Spring Harvest' every Easter at the Butlins holiday camp in Minehead (admittedly not in Cornwall), and indeed every Whitsun at Gwennap Pit, now owned and administered by the Methodist Church, must feel something similar.[75]

Baring-Gould noted in 1899 that Cornwall's livelihood had changed from an industrial economy producing one form of metal, mined tin and copper, to one earning another, the coins of visitors.[76] For the past 100–150 years, these people, a mass of individuals attracted seasonally or permanently to the peninsula, have had to carry the burden of festivals in place of a population increasingly making its money, finding its employment, outside the Duchy, whether in Bristol, London, or abroad. This is one of the paradoxes of Cornwall (and to a lesser extent of the west country as a whole) identified in the very first paragraph of Payton's history of the county, that between the incomer's haven of peace and tranquillity and the native's 'struggle to make ends meet in a low-wage economy', and it applies as strongly to music as to anything else.[77] Indeed, it has been suggested that Padstow's self-assertive May Day and 'darkie day' festival sounds help to claim back territory from the incomer or tourist as the 'other'.[78]

---

[73] Crane 1980: 191–4.
[74] Smith 1892: 5.
[75] GP.
[76] Baring-Gould 1899: 66.
[77] Payton 2004: 1.
[78] Davey 2006: 236.

Until the era of folk and pop, there were two models of music festival in Britain. One, that of the Three Choirs, founded in the early eighteenth century, stemmed from cathedral cities and had as its annual or triennial purpose large-scale charitable fundraising, typically for a city or county hospital, and always bought in from the metropolis its vocal stars (often world leaders) and the bulk of its orchestra: that was a large part of the attraction. The other, dating from the late nineteenth century, was educational, an annual competition of soloists and choirs, many of them children, testing their prowess among their peers by the standards of a metropolitan judge, generally a well-known demagogue for whom it was an important part of his (occasionally her) income. In both cases the choruses and the audience would be local, 'county' at farthest. Cornwall has struggled to maintain such festivals, and the relevant chapter in Geoffrey Self's monograph on classical music in west Cornwall is by and large a catalogue of unsustainability.[79]

The Salisbury Festival, as already implied in chapter 4, had set an ambitious west country precedent in the later eighteenth century, and in fact Cornwall was ahead of Devon in responding to it, for Truro, as yet without a cathedral, attempted to establish a triennial festival in 1806, repeating the venture in 1809, whereas Exeter did not mount its first until 1813. Truro also hosted a festival, its third, in 1813, a year in which there was clearly a co-ordination of dates between Salisbury (18–20 August), Exeter (23–27 August), and Truro (31 August to 2 September). This was probably down to Angelica Catalani, the opera star, who shouldered the entire financial risk of such festivals herself and pocketed the proceeds after donating 20 per cent to charity.[80] She was the main draw at all three of these, trailing John David Loder in her wake, who led the second violins at Salisbury and the orchestra as a whole at Exeter and Truro.[81] But despite being 'attended by almost all the gentry in the county', the 1813 Truro festival was its last in this format for nearly 150 years.[82] County Music Adviser Henry Mills revived the triennial endeavour in 1962, and again it managed three meetings (1962, 1965, and 1968) before running out of steam.[83] 'The problem of the balance between the costs of a professional orchestra [the Bournemouth Symphony Orchestra] and soloists on the one hand, and the capacity of a Truro audience to pay for them on the other, was never to be entirely solved in the remaining years of the century', writes Self,

---

[79] Self 1997: 59–69.
[80] Drummond 2011: 204.
[81] Self 1997: 63; *EFP*, 15 Jul, 12 Aug 1813; *RCG*, 14 Aug 1813; McGrady 1991: 59; *EFP*, 11 Aug 1814.
[82] Barton 1970: 45–6; Self 1997: 63; McGrady 1991: 48–61.
[83] Hedges 2002: 9.

for this festival's successor, the Three Spires Festival, which commenced in 1981, a permanent festival chorus lending it new added value, again could not solve this particular financial equation (again the orchestra being the BSO, though not invariably).[84] It became diluted as 'a Celebration of the Arts in Cornwall', diversified its venues, and went into liquidation in the late 1990s, though an independent offshoot, the Three Spires Singers, has survived.[85]

Smaller classical music festivals have taken the form of holiday ventures. One of Britain's leading composers, Michael Tippett, of Cornish ancestry, took up residence in St Ives for the period of the Coronation in 1953, having helped organise a week-long festival in a town already bursting with permanent creativity in the visual and plastic arts, headed by that of the sculptor Barbara Hepworth. Hepworth's friend, the composer Priaulx Rainier, St Ives's only musician in the circle, was also a close friend of Tippett. This was five years after Britten had founded the Aldeburgh Festival at the English coastline's opposite extremity. But Britten lived in Aldeburgh, and Tippett, only visiting St Ives, did not consolidate the initiative. Nor did Rainier, who did live there.[86] An even smaller settlement, Mylor, attracted an annual early music festival in the 1960s, organised by a full-time resident of the Duchy, Ian Graham-Jones, who was on the staff of the Cornwall Rural Music School. Graham-Jones left the area for other employment in 1971; the St Mylor Festival nevertheless continued, a series of guest directors distinguishing it throughout the 1970s.[87] But – another hazard – it outgrew its model and venue and gave way to the Three Spires Festival. Smaller still, the tiny Prussia Cove has since 1972 seen an astonishing influx of musical talent once a year with its International Musicians' Seminar, created by the Hungarian violinist Sándor Végh. The craggy Austro-Hungarian performance tradition of Brahms – the shamblingly terrifying Végh must have seemed like the master reincarnate – lives on thanks to west Cornwall's equally craggy cliffs, which inspired Végh to locate his annual high-pressure masterclass there along the lines of a professional retreat, now directed by the cellist Steven Isserlis. Its co-founder Hilary Tunstall-Behrens says little about how it was funded but acknowledges that with a series of filmed masterclasses and a television documentary in 1979, the latter the first BBC production ever to permit commercial credits, 'Marks & Spencers had given the IMS a major sponsorship'. The Seminar has in turn given Cornwall fourteen professional

---

[84] Self 1997: 66–7.
[85] ibid: 67–8.
[86] ibid: 63; Opie 1988: 42.
[87] Self 1997: 64–5.

concerts a year in a variety of venues such as mediaeval churches and country houses, and the audience turns up to most of them not knowing which works it will hear.[88]

Competitive music festivals must frequently have seemed the painful opposite of such starry professionalism. Cornwall's annual one began in 1910 and has against considerable odds survived to the present day, held now in the capacious Truro Methodist Church. The feminisation of music education exemplified in chapter 4 by Salisbury's freelance music teachers found its aggressive counterpart here and elsewhere in the country at the hands of powerful women who were determined to better a broad range of children and adults by actively involving them with 'good' music, which in the earlier twentieth century meant classical music and folksong, on the basis of emulation. The Associated Board and Trinity exam systems were already doing this on an individual basis, and it made sense to counterbalance them with something more corporate, though at the risk of the obsession with quantified results that British education never seems able to avoid for long. Cornwall's competitive festival was started by Lady Mary Trefusis, the Lady Mary Lygon of Elgar's 13th *Enigma* variation who had by now married into the Cornish gentry. It was in many respects no different from those in other parts of the west country, of which Wiltshire inaugurated its meeting the following year, Plymouth in 1914, and Devon (at Exeter) in 1920, though mid-Somerset's festival had been going since 1903 or earlier.[89] Competitive festivals really belong within discussion of educational institutions, but Cornwall's exceptionalism warrants mention of its county festival here for two reasons. One is that built into the enterprise, so far from the metropolis and the large industrial and cultural centres, was a submission to cultural cringe every time some martinet of an adjudicator from up-country was paid handsomely to flatter, insult, or patronise the county's cap-doffing musical amateurs. 'You can sing jolly well down here', exclaimed Edward Bairstow, organist of York Minster, in 1924, while Hugh Roberton was remembered as 'witty and kind', Julius Harrison as 'very tough'.[90] The other reason is that the formidable dynamic of the festival's founder, who 'had very strong views on what a festival should be', was redoubled after her death in 1927 by that of her joint successors, who were two of Cornwall's musical legends.[91]

---

[88] Tunstall-Behrens 2007: 30–1, 35; International Musicians' Seminar.
[89] *SMR* xx (1911): 17; Harvey 1926: 27; *MH* 869 (Aug 1920): 382; *SMR* xi (1902): 121.
[90] Self 1997: 61.
[91] ibid: 58–61.

The sisters Evelyn and Maisie Radford, eccentric spinsters with not a little of Hinge and Bracket about them, had grown up on Roborough Down on the western edge of Dartmoor, but Cornwall, geographically so near, was still imbued with the magic of the 'other' when they spent childhood holidays at Porthoustock and Porthgwarra. Evelyn, a pianist, studied classics at Cambridge, Maisie the violin in Berlin, and on their return they could have settled into a desultory professional existence in London based at their parents' house there, were it not for the fact that their mother had in 1912 bought a cottage for their use in St Anthony in Roseland.[92] After the First World War, 'on that golden afternoon ... rowing on the river up the Carrick Roads to buy plums, we finally decided not to go back to London but to stay in Cornwall and make our music there'.[93] This was a classic instance, at a classic postwar moment, of quality of life colouring career decisions and influencing musical results. But the Radfords also believed that the specialness of place was important not only as a setting for music as a special art but for triggering creative vision: 'Often on a holiday on the top of a mountain pass, in that wonderful moment of release and achievement when the whole distance is revealed stretching far away fold upon fold, and the foreground with its small obstructions seems forgotten, we would suddenly decide, "Let us do this."'[94] Wordsworth would have understood, and it makes one wonder how many important musical decisions or plans may have been hatched in the west country in recent centuries, ever since it became a cultural destination.

How good was their music-making? Reginald Jacques was 'not easily forgiven' when he criticised Evelyn's accompaniment skills, though as opera translators the sisters have been found 'accurate, elegant and singable'.[95] But it seems almost indelicate to ask the question, and some kind of theory of critical relativity needs to be devised so that the answer can take into account the facts of their idyllic and unique power base. St Anthony in Roseland, famously discovered by Morton in *In Search of England* around the same time, was the perfect place from which to mythologise themselves. In their early days, from a population supposedly of ten they formed a choir of nine for the Penzance Festival; they would row across the water to take rehearsals in St Mawes, whose choir they had formed when a builder up a ladder had shouted 'How about starting a choral society?'; they could reach Falmouth for rehearsals by ferry in a few minutes, whereas dropping off musicians after

---

[92] Radford 1965: 13–18.
[93] ibid: 20.
[94] ibid: 21.
[95] Self 1997: 62; Campbell 1992.

rehearsals all around the Fal inlets by car would take hours.[96] They were not the only enterprising opera producers in unlikely parts of Britain at this time, but the fact remains that with their Falmouth Opera Singers they gave the first English performances of Gluck's *La Cythère assiégée* (1950) and Mozart's *Idomeneo* (1937), the first English revival since 1840 of Mozart's *La clemenza di Tito* (1930), the first English stage performances of Rossini's *Moses in Egypt* (1953) and three of Handel's oratorios, the first performances in English of several other historically important operas, and the world premiere of Philip Cannon's opera *Morvoren* (1964), based on the legend of the Mermaid of Zennor. And they took both *La clemenza di Tito* and *Idomeneo* to London.[97]

In the title of their memoir, the Radfords dubbed their enterprises 'musical adventures', and most professionals and all amateurs would nowadays consider this both the ideal spirit of classical music-making and one difficult to attain amid the pressures of metropolitan life. Many musicians have sought that spirit in the conditions of a working vacation or retreat, and not to be forgotten are the self-governing orchestras with choir formed by music students while back home for the college and university holidays. In the heyday of student privilege (increasing numbers; free tuition, hence employment-free vacations for many), Bournemouth had a particularly fine one of these, *Gli amici della musica*, which flourished from around 1970 until 2000. St Mary's Arts Festival in Penzance was similarly drawing on the vacation presence of its home-grown music students in the 1990s.[98] The pinnacle of musical adventure in Cornwall has to be the St Endellion Festival, which also began as a vacation meeting of college friends when in 1958 the incumbent of the parish's magnificent, isolated late mediaeval church, Roger Gaunt, who was musical, invited a number of them to help him restore the derelict rectory. Gradually an orchestra and choir materialised, the summer festival was joined by an Easter one, and an ensemble formed for one of those occasions achieved permanence as the Endellion String Quartet, since 1992 in residence at the University of Cambridge. When the conductor Richard Hickox, who had been participating in the festivals, took over as artistic director in 1975, extraordinary things would be achieved for no pay by top professionals among the continuing amateurs until his untimely death in 2008. If Mozart operatic premieres in Falmouth had seemed unlikely in the 1930s, triumphant concert performances of Britten's *Peter Grimes* and even Wagner's *Die Walküre* in this windswept spot with not even a surrounding

---

[96] Radford 1965: 47–8, 56–8.
[97] Radford 1965: 102–3; Campbell 1992.
[98] Self 1997: 68.

village to support it have been more so, owing who knows what to the spirit of place established so many centuries earlier by the patient and inspired saint and her cow, in a land that, like Hickox himself, with his 'beaming, boyish face', never quite lost its innocence. Hickox, whose passion for surfing could be indulged both here on the north Cornish coast and in Sydney, when he became musical director of Opera Australia, undoubtedly found in St Endellion his spiritual home. He 'responded to long phrases in music – his was not a small tight beat but a large expressive wave – just the kind he longed to catch in the surf'. He bought a cottage next to the church, and he is buried in the churchyard, as closely identified with it thenceforth as Sir John Betjeman with neighbouring St Enodoc.[99] Can any other county boast of such a magnetic pull over artists?

❧ Evaluating Mass Events

For every fifty visitors seeking out Betjeman's grave, there will be perhaps one who knows about that of Hickox, for classical music matters to few people now, whereas with Betjeman new poetry continued to reach an enormous readership. But classical music still represents significant, possibly increased cultural capital for its adherents, so its standing cannot be quantified by one measure alone, any more than for other types of music. Cornwall itself multiplies that capital for all those who, as the phrase goes, buy into it in some way or other. The sense that cultural attraction is, at bottom, power is perfectly expressed by D H Lawrence, who understood the equation early on in Cornwall's cultural revival, in Zennor in 1916. In *Kangaroo* (1923) he writes of one of his characters: 'He loved the place so much ... If only I can stay till the foxgloves come ... Then it was the heather – would he see the heather? And then the primroses in the hollow down to the sea.'[100] The visitor is like a spouse who desires unconditional, unilateral possession: he cannot bear the thought that the entity has any business of its own which he cannot control through his presence, emotional reactions, and capitalisation of experience. Creative artists, including composers, are driven by this desire when they set up a locality as a place to which they will return again and again, or which they will simply take over: there is marital violence in the idea. The violated partner is the unnoticed or indifferent indigenous population and its concerns, so deprived in the case of Cornwall that in 1921–22, more or

---

[99] ibid: 63–4; Adams 1986: 39–40; St Endellion Festivals: 'History', 'Richard Hickox' (including Varcoe nd); Millington 2008.
[100] quoted Payton 2004: 253.

less at the time of the Radfords' first 'adventures', with scarcely a mine still working, Camborne police station had to be transformed into an emergency clothing centre.[101]

If Cornish festivals are thus to be understood as the imposition of an alien will, it is a view that needs both amplifying and moderating through consideration of other event profiles in other places. Insofar as mass events have needed some kind of an empowered host and an organising principle, they belong to institutional history. Yet the second Glastonbury Festival, sole prerogative of a lone farmer, Michael Eavis, would seem to represent contemporary society's ability to be brought together on a massive scale with few if any of these attributes. Although uniquely large and uniquely sustained, it heads a bewildering proliferation of events found on today's media calendars of the region. *The Big Issue: South West* for 5–11 July 2010 listed the following festivals taking place between July and early October that year, most of them in the period of the school holidays from mid-July to the end of August: Aeon Festival at Shobrooke Park, Crediton; Bath Folk Festival; Buddhafield Festival in Taunton; Camp Bestival at Lulworth Castle; Chagstock in Okehampton; a Farm Festival at Gilcombe Farm, Bruton; Galhampton's Party in the Park; Gaunts House Summer Gathering in Wimborne; a gypsy festival at Gossington, Dursley; Hamswell Festival at Hamswell Farm near Bath; Ivy Live in Ivybridge; Quest and the South Devon Festival, both on the Newton Abbot Racecourse; Sidmouth Folk Week; the Swanage Jazz Festival; the Two Moors Festival on Exmoor and Dartmoor; Watchet Music Festival at Parsonage Farm; Whiteford Festival in Stoke Climsland; and Womad in Charlton Park, Wiltshire. Some of these gatherings will have been of national importance, the well-established Sidmouth Folk Week showcasing the genre's leading artists including Bellowhead, Eliza Carthy, June Tabor, and Blowzabella. Others were taking a largely subaltern approach, the Aeon Festival promising a 'three-day bash' with 'emerging artists, unsigned gems, along with some of the finest DJs'.[102] One assumes that music will have been a feature of most if not all of them, and in *The Big Issue*, perpetuating an assumed alliance between counterculture and the fight against oppression, music means folk, rock, or world. The actual alliance between counterculture and landed tradition offers a delicious irony when both farms and aristocratic estates feature prominently in the list. It is not just at Worthy Farm, Pilton, site of the current Glastonbury Festival, that music and land usage in a post-agricultural society go hand-in-hand.

---

[101] Payton 2004: 239–40.
[102] *Big Issue: South West*, 5–11 Jul 2010: 4, 11–14, back cover.

There was at least one festival somewhere in the region for every remaining month of that same year, even chilly March sporting a modest event at Weston-in-Gordano, while the winter months were good for competitive concentration and Christmas saw not only a plethora of Festivals of Nine Lessons and Carols, a format invented by Bishop Edward Benson for Truro Cathedral in 1880 based on pre-Reformation liturgical practice in another context, but also Padstow's controversial 'darkie days' with their blackface 'guizing'.[103] One is perhaps surprised at the amount of (broadly) classical music: the Taunton and Somerset Music and Drama Festival, one of the competitive ones, in November, and its sequel of five finalists for the Taunton Young Musician of the Year award in January; Brass at the Octagon, presumably again competitive (the first item at 09.30 am), in Yeovil in February; the Sherborne Abbey Festival in late April and early May, featuring the internationally known Tallis Scholars alongside a local miscellany; the Bath International Music Festival from late May through to early June; the Shaldon Festival in June; a follow-up Glastonbury event in St John's Church in July, opened by the star organist Carlo Curley.[104] Bath even attempted an organ builder festival, dedicated to Sweetland, in September.[105] Beyond this, youth and flowers seem to have been prominent themes, the former exemplified by the South Somerset Youth Choir performing at the Hinton St George Festival in June and the West Wiltshire Youth Orchestra, Young Singers, and Junior Wind at the Wiltshire Music Centre in Bradford on Avon in July, the latter by the Ilminster Flower Festival in June ('a floral experience in music' in the parish church) and one at Kilkhampton parish church in August, its choir sponsoring one of the displays.[106] Two more folk festivals within the region were those of Chippenham (late May) and Wimborne (June), while Chippenham's April rock 'n' roll weekend, a tribute to Eddie Cochran, had a peculiar poignancy on the fiftieth anniversary of his death.[107] In Weston-super-Mare's T4 on the Beach (4 July), 'Britain's biggest

---

[103] Personal visit, 15 Mar 2010; Williams 1979: 74; *RCG*, 24 Dec 1880: 4; Davey 2006.
[104] Taunton Library, personal visit, 23 Jun 2010; TAPA Diary; *CM* 108 (Feb 2010): 6; Sherborne Abbey Festival leaflet; Bath International Music Festival brochure; Shaldon Festival flyer; St John's Glastonbury, personal visit, 27 Apr 2010.
[105] Andrew Clarke, personal communication, 26 May 2010.
[106] Hinton St George Festival leaflet; Wiltshire Music Centre brochure; Crewkerne parish church, poster; Kilkhampton parish church, personal visit, 22 Aug 2010.
[107] Chippenham Folk Festival brochure; personal knowledge; King 2010: 32.

beach party', the demotic end of rock was represented in an environment once again long deprived of its original respectability, a point made with international impact five years later with Banksy's *Dismaland*, also held in this saddest of all west country ex-resorts.[108] The Frome Festival (July) and the St Ives September Festival of 2010 were probably typical of the cultural eclecticism of our day, politically correct but difficult to interpret with anything approaching profundity. St Ives achieved an impressive mix of regional and international pre-eminence: the Fishermen's Friends, the Mousehole Male Voice Choir, Donovan (sold out three months in advance), Paco Peña, Courtney Pine, and others, the main venue being the Guildhall.[109]

What is the audience constituency for these festivals? Have surveys been undertaken? The other question that would be worth framing and answering is whether the region has more than an average number and range of such events; in other words, whether the invention of the west country worked. That would necessitate detailed comparison with another region, a worthwhile project.

Then there are the pageants. Pageants were devised by towns in early modern England for a very privileged incomer indeed: the visiting monarch. No expense could be spared, and music was included along with interminable odes and noisy sporting displays or mock battles, sight and sound combining in all of these to enforce the message of tribute and largesse. When Edward IV visited Bristol in the first year of his reign, on 9 September 1461, he was entertained at Temple Cross by St George fighting the dragon, at whose slaying 'there was a great melody of angels' (probably choristers).[110] 'Great melody and singing' also greeted Henry VII in Bristol on his first provincial progress in May 1486.[111] Nearly a hundred years later, Elizabeth I's royal progress to Bristol of 14–21 August 1574, a major occasion in the city's history and the one on which she supposedly called St Mary Redcliffe the fairest church in England, entailed the singing of a ditty from *Paradise of Dainty Devices* by Richard Edwards, the Court poet and composer by then dead but still popular. He had been born in Somerset, so he conveniently represented the delicate balance between regional pride and deference to the centre that, as Francis Wardell has shown, had to be struck on such an occasion.[112] The tune for another of Edwards's verses, 'In going to my naked bed', would

---

[108] *Metro*, Bristol edition, 1 Apr 2010: 48; Wikipedia: 'Dismaland'.
[109] Frome Festival brochure; St Ives, personal visit, 23 Jun 2010.
[110] Pilkinton 1997: 8.
[111] ibid: 11.
[112] Wardell 2011: 111–12.

easily have fitted this ditty too, and its elaboration in the Mulliner Book shows how it could have been arranged by the waits' consort.[113] She was also greeted by a 'solemn song' sung by orphans at St John's Gate on her way out of the town.[114] For James I's visit to Wells in 1613 with his Queen, Anne of Denmark (who also visited Bristol on that occasion), a complex processional pageant was mounted with enactments or displays by each trade, and at the very least the cordwainers' morris dance must have included music.[115]

After this, the word 'pageant' is scarcely found as a descriptive term for nearly three hundred years, and its reappearance strongly suggests yet another facet to the construction of the west country for the cultural purposes of the twentieth century and beyond. If Cecil Sharp disclosed its secret songs and the observer-participant artists framed its peopled landscapes in their creative works and festivals, the heritage movement would capitalise on its history, in a wholesale cultural impulse now as pervasive as ever after more than a century of it. This capitalisation did not begin with the Sherborne Pageant, for a repertoire of safeguarded sites for visitors (Tintagel for King Arthur, Buckland Abbey and Plymouth Hoe for Drake, and so on) was already evident. (The Old Post Office in Tintagel was among the first buildings acquired by the National Trust, in 1903.) But the *performance* of a town's history, done by its very inhabitants, was something a good deal more than the availability of an object for passive consumption: as an act of reflexivity it could immediately rebut concerns about imposed culture. From 12 to 16 June 1905 Louis Napoleon Parker achieved this for Sherborne with a cast of eight hundred, a total audience of thirty thousand, and the ruined castle as a backdrop, and he went on to be pageant master for a host of similar celebrations in other English towns and cities, making a new career of it (it was effectively his third), though never again in the west country, whither he nevertheless retired around 1924, dying in Bishopsteignton twenty years later at the age of ninety-one.[116]

If Parker's cantata *Silvia* of 1880 is anything to go by, he was a really terrible composer. But like almost all composers, he was never going to earn his living through that art, and the fact that unlike many in his position he was willing to have a go at something else instead, and went on to make a great success of it, causes one to admire him. He had gone to Dorset in 1873 as a graduating student of the Royal Academy of Music, standing in for the piano

---

[113] ibid: 109–10; Smith 2001b: 902; Caldwell 2011: 119–20.
[114] Pilkinton 1997: 91.
[115] *WellsM* 1 (Mar 1854): 2–4; Pilkinton 1997: 173–95.
[116] Ensor and Banerji 2004.

teacher at Sherborne School on the advice of his principal, William Sterndale Bennett, whose son James was director of music there. Taking over from James Bennett in 1877, he raised musical standards and left nineteen years later not for a more prestigious musical position but to become a dramatist in London.[117] One reason for this curious move was that he was going deaf, another a 'temporary but disastrous decline of Sherborne School', to which he testified more than once.[118] Although this eagerness to explain his reasons for leaving might suggest a cover-up, *persona non grata* he could not long have been, for he was back as town impresario nine years later on a scale never before seen in Britain.

Like many national impulses in the decades before the First World War, pageant-making was a way of competing with Germany. Parker stated that at Sherborne his ambition had been not only 'to produce a folk-play similar to those which used to be represented at Coventry and Chester' (and in Cornwall, he might have added) but to emulate those 'represented now at Worms and Rothenburg, and in many other towns and villages on the Continent'.[119] Pageants are difficult to evaluate musically, but a seventeen-minute silent film of the Sherborne Pageant survives, to which some passages of the original music, composed by Parker, Archibald F Tester, and F C S Carey, have been fitted in good modern performances by the Sherborne Chamber Choir under Paul Ellis and the Sherborne Town Band. They sound surprisingly effective, and there is no reason to believe that Parker's local performers let him down musically, any more than they did with their acting, dancing, and fighting, all of which look convincing in the film.[120] Whatever Parker's musical limitations, he was by this stage of his career an experienced West End creator and director and knew what worked; it was Sherborne's unique luck that he was also the local man. Elsewhere, a local musician might or might not be up to the job of producing the music. Bath in 1909 was able to command new music by Sir Charles Stanford (a choric ode) for its pageant, and Bridgwater in 1927 commissioned a substantial score, now lost, from the young Percy Whitlock, at that time still based in his native Medway towns.[121] As time went on, actual music from the period being depicted may have come at more of a premium. When Bristol was privileged in 1924 to present its history nationally at the Pageant of Empire in the new Wembley

---

[117] ibid; Parker 1894: 102.
[118] Ensor and Banerji 2004; Parker 1918: 24; Parker 1928: 127.
[119] anon 1904–05: 36.
[120] Tester et al 1905; YouTube: 'Sherborne Pageant'; Sherborne Pageant.
[121] Swift and Elliott 2009; Riley 2003: 38–9.

Stadium, having first done so locally in the grounds of Ashton Court, its cathedral organist, Hubert Hunt, who conducted the orchestra, assembled most of the score from period repertoire, though he composed the 'Bristol Pageant hymn' (to words by Weatherly).[122]

Glastonbury staged a pageant for the future Queen Mary in the Abbey grounds in 1909, and thirteen years later Alice Buckton, a local worthy of no little determination, managed to get another silent film made. It was of Glastonbury history and included 'a lavish parade through the town' and 'period costumes for the historical sketches [that] were magnificent', though Sherborne's had been pretty good too.[123] The Radford sisters' first enterprise in Cornwall was actually a pageant, which they wrote themselves, at St Mawes Castle; one would like to think it was subtle and sensitive, introducing Henry VIII to the piano as the King 'dreamily wondered what the music of the future would be'. They claimed that a Women's Institute pageant in Falmouth, inspired by a pageant at Bradstone in Devon, was what emboldened them to attempt opera, though this chronology seems faulty, for they began producing opera in 1923 and the Bradstone Pageant was not until 1929.[124] The printed libretto of *Scenes from the Life of Drake* held in the Plymouth Drill Hall in October 1923 includes references to music and dance but no indications of what was used or created.[125] Nor do we know about the music for the Bideford Bridge Trust's pageant, involving several hundred townspeople dressed as historical characters, mounted in 1925 to celebrate the widening of the historic bridge.[126] Fundraising for the National Trust at Tintagel in 1930 spawned a pageant that Melissa Hardie, not without reason, fears 'must have been straight out of the pages of Just William, or an Angela Thirkell novel'. Gramophone records provided some of the music, with loudspeakers all too visible, and the singing did not avoid criticism.[127] Bournemouth, meanwhile, had concocted its *Pageant of the Months* in May 1913, performed by schoolchildren apparently accompanied by the Municipal Orchestra, and staged a *Pageant of Wessex History* in 1935, almost the last event to be held in the old Winter Gardens before their demolition.[128] By this time pageant mania, straddling the Great War as though it had never occurred, was long past its peak. One is left with limited curiosity as to

---

[122] Bristol 1924.
[123] Payne 2009: 86; Benham 2006: 162.
[124] Radford 1965: 21–4, 102; *WMN*, 20 Jul 1926: 3 and 1 Aug 1929: 6.
[125] Richards 1923.
[126] Christie and Grant 2005: 8.
[127] Hardie 1992: 19.
[128] Watkins 1914: 53; Ashley 2006: 28.

what it may have accomplished musically, but with the hope that the young Whitlock, later to prove uniquely skilled in fusing musical connoisseurship with good-humoured approachability, managed to produce for Bridgwater the best musical content there could possibly have been within the pageant formula, a formula which Riley's account of his contribution helps clarify:

> The local paper announced that 'He has been given a free hand in undertaking the work, which is intended for performance by soloists, chorus, orchestra and probably dancers.' The Prologue, which consisted of four numbers, was described as 'a kind of imaginative fantasy introducing sea and river sprites battling for possession. They were calmed by the Archangel Michael, under whose protection a man, woman and child came to settle with the Spirit of the Bridge keeping the sea and river in their lawful places.' The *Bristol Times and Mirror* referred to the special music as having 'a charm and dignity admirably suited to such an event', and the *Bridgwater Mercury* referred to Whitlock as 'a rising young English composer'. Unfortunately the whole of this substantial score (which involved a military band and strings) is lost, apart from a solitary song-sheet, a setting for unison voices of the sturdy and stirring Song of the Bridgwater Men.[129]

If any place could be guaranteed to defeat attempts at encapsulating a long chronology within some artistic framework, it would be Glastonbury. What are we to make of this mean and ungainly town with its prehistoric lake villages, its legends of Joseph of Arimathea, King Arthur and the Holy Grail, its shocking Reformation history now represented by the gaping hole at its centre where the abbey once stood, its spectacular Tor linked on countless speculative maps by straight lines to this or that other spiritual site, and the consequent New Age clutter of its unprepossessing streets? Wearyall Hill with its beribboned Thorn feels unique, yet the view from it is of sprawling council and trading estates, red brick and sheet metal far outweighing mellow stone. Moving on to nearby Street reveals an even less attractive town, now little more than a series of large car parks for its 'outlet' shopping village. One hails the Clark shoe company's employment enterprise while despairing of any cultural branding to match it, either here or in Glastonbury. St Ives has long squared its fishing and Methodist heritage with both 'Riviera' tourism and artisanal artistic production, and must be accounted a sustained success in these terms. Lyme Regis seems to be following suit, thanks to Jane Austen and John Fowles. Port Isaac, miraculously, has witnessed a local male voice group, the Fishermen's Friends, shot to contemporary stardom. Glastonbury,

---

[129] Riley 2003: 38–9, quoting *Chatham, Rochester and Gillingham Observer*, 11 Feb 1927.

or rather Pilton, once a year has its unspeakably muddy fields, its hundreds of thousands of dishevelled youngsters, its disruption of roads and rail services for many miles around, and its open-air stages covered with miles of trailing cables. Perhaps these represent the apogee of English liberty, and a nation gets not only the politicians but the festival it deserves. Is this where it was all leading, from the *Ordinalia* onwards through the charitable oratorio performances of the cathedral towns and the stage-fright of miserable children paraded in front of some crusty metropolitan adjudicator for the economic enhancement of their competitive teachers?

This is unfair to the Glastonbury Festival. It celebrates the unreliable English weather as a matter of refreshing honesty when that must have similarly dampened seven out of ten occasions in an otherwise idealised past, *Ordinalia* and all. It brings money and at least seasonal employment into a depressed region, and with the loss of incentive for agricultural production represents a creative use of large tracts of land. Both stars and audiences have got to know the region and set up there, whether or not as a direct result or borrowing from a more general resonance that has accrued, a resonance probably felt as far away as Bristol and Bath, both now cities in which many university students wish to remain on graduating. (Peter Gabriel's studio at Box and the conductor Charles Hazlewood's near Glastonbury itself both partake of this resonance.)[130] It reveals as a *fait accompli* that yesterday's counterculture is today's main stream of musical consumption by the not-so-young as well as the young. It is democracy in sound, and it makes a profit – considerable funds go to charity – though not always as large a one as might have been expected.[131]

But the present Glastonbury Festival is its second, and it is the first that now seems the phenomenon that its time and place deserved. All the ingredients and problems identified in the foregoing discussion of west country festivals came together here: outsiders and incomers imposing their vision, the summer school as incubator of performance, the local children roped in willy-nilly, the stubborn belief in homespun as superior to commercial fabric, the mystique of a spiritual freedom or depth drawn from the locality constantly threatening to descend into bathos, the perception nevertheless that something exceptional had been achieved in terms of performance standard or authenticity, the vulnerability to circumstance (in Glastonbury's case disruption by both the First World War and its instigator's irregular

---

[130] Frame 1999: 198; Real World Studios.
[131] *Guardian* online, 9 Oct 2014; *Telegraph* online, 10 Oct 2015.

love life), the lack of a suitable venue and the growing but impossible need to create one, and above all the economic unsustainability.

It is a fascinating story, best read in Michael Hurd's fine account.[132] Elements can only be pinpointed here. Richard Wagner had swept Europe with his revival of the festival spirit of ancient Greece when in 1876 he instituted his shrine for music drama of the future (its exemplars composed by himself, words and all) at Bayreuth, an attractive small town in Bavaria answering perfectly to the growing requirements of a national heartland. The Bayreuth Festival was to be experienced as spiritual pilgrimage, walks in the wooded hills and homework on the relevant plot, libretto, or index of musical themes forming the day's preparation for a performance beginning at 4pm each day with leisurely breaks for meals between the acts. A tetralogy of music dramas (they were not called operas) could thus be experienced over four or more days without external distraction or accumulating tiredness. This was music for the people, the specially constructed amphitheatre (sensibly not open-air) ensuring that no-one went to be seen but that instead they simply concentrated on the sound and spectacle delivered in a darkened auditorium, the blackout a novelty at the time. It was a magnificent idea and it worked, although the egalitarian ideal that Wagner's erstwhile anarchism had envisioned was quickly forgotten in the convergence every year of the intellectual elite of Europe, creating what has remained the hottest ticket in the world, and in the festival's gargantuan appetite for patronage, be it from Ludwig II or fundraising in European capitals by Wagner and top performers.

Good socialist that he was, George Bernard Shaw soon called for an English equivalent, a true national theatre, proposed by him for Richmond Hill, that would encourage English creative genius to flourish and would fund it when it did. What he had not bargained for was the self-styled genius emerging first, supporting conditions somehow to follow, and this is the equation that Rutland Boughton (1878–1960) naively insisted on attempting to solve. What Shaw really thought of Boughton is impossible to know now, but once again the cultural imperative before the war to emulate Germany, and after the war to prove its hegemonic idioms superseded, left him no option, once he had ceased to be a professional music critic, but to support what those in an increasing number of quarters were inclining to accept as the real thing.

Boughton's mindset was towards the new, as the new was understood in an Arts and Crafts context – simplicity of design owing nothing to academic or

---

[132] Hurd 1962; see also Benham 2006: 169–88.

cosmopolitan accretion, the remaking of the past from fresh angles (with new materials or ethnic influences), the artisanal democracy of production. Much of what he believed in was truly revolutionary in this way: his refusal to divide voices into high and low; his extensive use of that British tradition (albeit a recent one), the amateur mixed chorus, but as dancers and decor as well as singers (the 'human scenery' as celebrated and sometimes misunderstood); sparseness and abstraction of production; and what we would now call a workshop ethos. It is important to remember that his kindred spirit Reginald Buckley (appropriated as his librettist) envisaged a new town, Letchworth, not an old one, as the location in which all this might be pioneered, and that Boughton's ideas had matured in Birmingham, not in some post-agricultural environment, though he nevertheless favoured a rural artistic co-operative for his venture and would eventually come to live in a commune on the land. But since Boughton's and Buckley's primary ambition was to consolidate a cycle of Arthurian music dramas, Boughton going one better than Wagner with a total of five, and since sooner or later somebody had to come up with some material resources, when a house was made available in Glastonbury there was no resisting that town as their base, regardless of its complete lack of musical distinction and capital infrastructure.

In time, Roger Clark of Street become Boughton's Ludwig II, paying him £2 per week to remain in Glastonbury year round and develop his festival, and generally helping to put the endeavour on a regular financial footing.[133] But the Arthurian element was in the end a red herring. Curiously, there are no enduring English musical monuments to Arthurian romance beyond Purcell's semi-opera. Boughton's inspiration tailed off, and his last two music dramas have never even been performed. The true fruits of the Glastonbury Festival were his revivals of Gluck; his own *Alkestis*; his nativity opera *Bethlehem*, first performed in the Crispin Hall, Street, spin-offs including the *Little Plays of St Francis* by Laurence Housman (who took up residence in Street) and Clarence Raybould's exploration of Japanese nō drama in *The Sumida River*, decades before Britten's and with a libretto by Marie Stopes (of all people); and above all Boughton's metropolitan success with *The Immortal Hour*, which in the early 1920s, following a makeshift premiere in Glastonbury only days after war was declared in 1914, managed what almost no other English opera has ever achieved, a nightly commercial run in London. The festival's west country touchstone was Boughton's operatic setting of Thomas Hardy's late play *The Queen of Cornwall*, whose premiere in 1924 Hardy and his wife attended, along with T E Lawrence in habitual

[133] Hurd 1962: 51, 73–5.

incognito; the grandeur of King Arthur would remain incompatible with the frankly dismaying limitations of the Glastonbury Assembly Rooms. (No festival performance ever rose to an orchestra: a grand piano was the accompaniment.)

It was mercenary Bournemouth, about as distant from the spirit of Celtic mysticism as could be imagined, that thanks to Dan Godfrey and his orchestra had the resources and the will to test Boughton's inspiration against regular professional conditions. There *The Immortal Hour* would receive its first performance with orchestra in January 1915. A Margaret Morris summer school for dance in Bournemouth in the summer of 1913 had culminated in portions of *The Birth of Arthur* being produced on stage in the Winter Gardens, and on that occasion the *Daily News* commented:

The men form square and sing

> Dark and stark and strong
> Tintagel Castle stands

while the women advance and retreat with tossing arms, telling in verse of 'the splash and the surge of the sea on the rocks of Tintagel' ... I found the music and dancing gave just the necessary direction to the imaginative faculty. Whether the human scenery should be allowed to remain on the stage during the dialogue is, however, another matter. Four-square Tintagel narrowly escaped the comic, and flapping of the young lady billows' hands when Igraine mentioned 'the white wave-crests how fair' was a little too near the detested realism.[134]

Just William again raises its head. Boughton never managed to avoid Wardour Street English (nobody in real life calls a wave 'fair') or musical fustian, and when the chorus in Boughton's 'Faery song' from *The Immortal Hour* enunciates the line 'They laugh and they sing and are terrible', we may be inclined to agree with it. Yet Shaw's testimony cannot be overlooked. Of the Glastonbury performance of Gluck's *Iphigenia in Tauris* at Easter 1916 he wrote that 'some of the freshness and excellence of the performance were due to the fact that there was no conductor ... There was fortunately no scenery and no opera house; in short, no nonsense; but there was a Shrine of Diana and sufficient decoration by Miss Walshe's screens and curtains to create much more illusion in the big schoolroom than I have ever been able to feel in Covent Garden.'[135]

---

[134] *Daily News*, 28 Aug 1913: 5.
[135] *The Nation*, 6 May 1916, quoted Hurd 1962: 60.

The design and costumes of Boughton's partner Christina Walshe may in the end have been the most robustly original element of the Glastonbury experiment, and it is perhaps significant that she wished to measure herself by cosmopolitan standards when after splitting up from Boughton she went to Paris, 'studying Cubism and other kinds of shapemaking' as he expressed it.[136] He was content to continue ploughing his own provincial furrow, and although one applauds the regional will that for a while he drew out – both Charles Marson and the Bristol entrepreneur Philip Napier Miles backed the first Glastonbury appeal, and Boughton's Glastonbury Festival Players took to touring the peninsula on a co-operative basis[137] – it is sadly the case that he laid no permanent foundations for a west country identity in music or for a festival culture to match the region's developing leisure profile. Few if any of the thousands of visitors who today seek something musically unique in and around Glastonbury will notice the blue plaque in the passageway to the Assembly Rooms. Yet it was not that the vision was wrong. Benjamin Britten's Aldeburgh Festival would soon enough generate the community masterpiece to knock all west country pageants, droopy music dramas, and mystery plays mounted in remote locations into a cocked hat: *Noyes Fludde* of 1957. Among all the incomers and their projects surveyed in this chapter, only Tippett might have stolen a march on this, for the simple reason that only he was a good enough composer. Now, in the twenty-first century, it is far too late to dream of music regaining its imagined capacity to round everybody up through a single charismatic figure. Such investment of cultural capital now attaches itself – still using a foreign term – to chefs, not maestros. What Tippett chose, for whatever reason, not to add to the already impressive array of impositions on St Ives, Rick Stein has added to those on Padstow. Something else will in its turn supersede this latest chimera of fusing exceptional experience with exceptional place, but it will not be west country music.

---

[136] Hurd 1962: 77.
[137] ibid: 46, 76.

CHAPTER 7

Musical Capitalisation II: Institutions

ঌ *An Institutional Peak? Sacred Polyphony Before the Reformation*

MUSIC, even folksinging, only happens with institutional support. Performers need to learn, to teach, to join together, and to network, acquiring or exchanging artefacts as well as experience. Audiences need gathering places and occasions, agreement as to how and when these should be activated, and frameworks within which they are willing to pay with their money or with their effort to hear music, doing so to a set of shared and understood values that render the experience worthwhile for them. Beyond private patronage and individual enterprise, the institutions facilitating and regulating these equations have been the Church, the military and civil authorities, educational establishments, and the entertainment industry. They have sustained music in places where one worships, where one prepares to fight or consolidate one's citizenship, where one learns, and where one enjoys oneself. The music may be subsidiary to some other institutional function (a church service, a march, a civic procession, a ball, a show), or may be an end in itself, as with concerts, musical interludes in theatres, and singing in pubs. This chapter will examine the Church, educational establishments, and entertainment networks (including broadcasting) as institutional providers. The military and civil authorities have already been considered in the context of bands in chapter 3, although the development of municipal orchestras requires separate treatment here, providing as it does the touchstone for the aspirations and limitations of regional musical culture in the case of the Bournemouth Symphony Orchestra.

By far the most pervasive musical institution in any English region, over a period of hundreds of years, has been the Church. Greatly disrupted as its musical provision was at the Reformation, and again during the Civil War and Commonwealth, its provision of cathedrals was never entirely lost, indeed was enhanced when the Augustinian abbey in Bristol was suppressed and its church became the city's 'new foundation' cathedral. (Bath Abbey was the new name for what had already been a monastic cathedral, Bath Priory. The other three mediaeval cathedrals in the west country, Exeter, Salisbury, and Wells, were 'secular', i.e. they lacked a community of monks.) Until relatively recent times, and with important exceptions, this provision offered easily the most important focus for musical employment, education, and performance that could be expected. To some extent this is still true today in Exeter, Salisbury, and Truro, diocesan centres in which it is scarcely possible to imagine the cathedral's role as a monumental presence and venue being upstaged by any auditorium or arts centre, however much cathedral patronage may have declined relative to opportunities outside its orbit.

To demonstrate cathedral patronage as a motor for musical provision in any particular city, with a return on the investment (it would be hoped) of musical creativity and excellence, has not been a direct concern of this book except in chapter 2, but it is worth considering here for a moment. If we take Exeter in the early decades of the seventeenth century, a period which probably represented one of its musical peaks, we find the following professional musicians being paid for, within the cathedral and beyond it. As already mentioned, John Lugg was cathedral organist from 1603 until the mid-1640s. He was a reasonably prolific composer of vocal cathedral music and organ voluntaries, three of which 'are the best examples of this peculiarly English genre written before the Civil War'.[1] For most of this same period, Orlando Gibbons's brother Edward was master of the choristers, a separate post, and he too is known as a composer of cathedral music, though very few pieces have survived. At least from time to time, both Lugg and Gibbons had deputies, officially appointed – Peter Chambers, Greenwood Randell, Thomas Gale, and others, who one guesses may have been apprentices or singing men.[2] These musicians worked with as many as six basses and six countertenors, 'the rest as seems fit', if the ordinances are to be believed in terms of how many men were actually being paid to sing.[3] In addition to these fourteen or more professionals, there were the four waits, paid by the city Corporation, who in 1601–02 were Aldred and John Bussell, Humphrey Doddridge, and John Medland; Medland trained up boy apprentices.[4] As mentioned in chapter 4, the Bampfield and/or Acland families kept a lutenist, William Moore, who in time became one of the waits. Then there were the choristers. Around 1618, Hugh Facy was trained up to become a secondary

[1] Steele 2001: 287.
[2] Harper 2001: 835; Matthews Exe: 21–2.
[3] ExeterVC: 4.
[4] Wasson 1986: 178.

(an adolescent singing man), a useful organist, and a skilful composer before he left Exeter, possibly to go abroad.[5] Matthew Locke, a chorister from around 1630 and subsequently a secondary who carved his name on the organ screen, represented an even more handsome return on musical investment.[6] Again as mentioned earlier, the choristers were taught to play viols, which appear to have been used in the cathedral on certain occasions, as were sackbuts and cornetts, of which the cathedral ordered a set in 1637.[7] The choristers were also paid by the mayor for doing something in 1606, and in addition to them and the waits, the city was used to paying for drummers and trumpeters on Midsummer's Eve, Thomas and Radford Gill being presumably kept in employment for when they were needed, apparently as members of the local militia (the Exeter Trainband).[8] Then there was the Chappington family of organ builders, whom we should probably assume had a resident base in Exeter. That amounts to around two dozen musical livings at least, excluding the choristers, in a city ranking perhaps sixth in the country with its possible population of around 9,000: roughly one adult professional musician for every 400 inhabitants, not far from the proportion 250 years later in Bath, which had 'probably ... the highest ratio of musicians to population of any major English town'.[9] It made for a rich, stable organism, much but by no means all of it sustained by the cathedral, whose productivity in the form of compositions would take its place within the national legacy.

Something of the same conspectus might be constructed for Salisbury at the same period, and Truro has certainly provided the most ambitious musical focus for Cornwall, all told, in the period since it became a cathedral city. The west country's other three cathedral cities have played a different role, however. Bristol developed the cultural attributes of an industrial conurbation, most importantly a large concert hall (two, actually), a proliferation of theatres, a zoo, and in the twentieth century a university, though, as already pointed out, never a recognised conservatoire. The city's expansion brought with it wealth invested in new suburban places of worship, nonconformist and Jewish as well as Anglican, a factor not to be forgotten. Bath's role as Britain's leading spa made it into a kind of cultural microcosm of London, punching greatly above its weight in concert life, theatre, and to a lesser extent education, though since the city's relative decline as a

---

[5] Jeans 2001.
[6] Holman 2001a: 44; Thompson 2004: 231.
[7] Matthews Exe: 2.
[8] Wasson 1986: 179–92; Wylie 1916: 83.
[9] Wikipedia: 'List of towns and cities in England by historical population'; Rowse 1950: 221–2; Russell 2000: 235–6.

Illus. 7.1 Five of Bristol's mediaeval churches. From left to right: St Nicholas, St Mary le Port, All Saints, Christ Church, St Peter

resort in the early nineteenth century the Abbey has probably become more prominent in Bath's musical culture. Wells failed to develop at all in post-mediaeval times, and remains a tiny town whose cathedral resources therefore far outweigh anything else it can muster musically, though it also hosts one of England's four specialist music schools.

Cathedral music was not a monopoly, however, and the focus of this section is to move beyond it. Before the Reformation, Bristol's All Saints, at the central crossroads of the mediaeval city, developed a musical culture equal to almost any, though it was a small parish and by no means the city's richest (see Illus. 7.1)[10] What this meant was the capacity for singing 'pricksong', that is, fifteenth- and early sixteenth-century polyphony in up to five, or even more, simultaneously harmonised vocal parts, each with a high degree of melodic independence, as composed by the most highly trained individuals to a set of sophisticated principles forming the basis of all the subsequent achievements of western art music. The singers and copyists of

---

[10] Burgess and Wathey 2000: 34–5.

this repertoire had to be no less highly trained, and were by and large the same people, part of a tight, efficient, and, it would seem, mobile network. Whether or not the performers were non-clerical part-time singing men, like the slightly later Robert Perry referred to in chapter 4, secular clergy, or members of monastic orders, they had to have had this extensive training, some of which they would have acquired as boy choristers.

All Saints' ability to pay for polyphony stemmed from the bequests of Thomas Halleway and his wife Joan, their wills proved in 1453.[11] As Clive Burgess and Andrew Wathey point out, 'England's wealthier classes were, in all probability, more generous towards the Church in the century or more preceding the Reformation than at any time since', and this generosity patronised music.[12] Thomas's will provided for 'six chaplains present at the obsequies on the day of his death, and for Dirige and Mass solemnly with music (cum nota) daily for four weeks following his death, in the same church'; they were paid 6s 8d each, a little less than 3d per performance.[13] As the years went on, 'priests' were paid to be present annually in the Halleways' chantry for their year's mind. Nine were paid 4d each in 1482, ten in 1489, eleven in 1490, fourteen in 1497, and fifteen in 1500, though ten remained the norm thereafter, declining to six, seven, or eight until chantries were abolished in 1547.[14] It is difficult to believe that such a large number of men were needed unless they were singing. Further chantry bequests that specifically referred to singing were those of John and Edith Chancellor in 1466, John Snygge in 1495, John Penke the younger in 1498, William Leke in 1516, Henry, John, and Alice Chester in 1519 (the prayers with 'descanting tones'), and Joan Pernaunt in 1534.[15] At the very least, accumulated funding of this sort enabled one chantry priest, David Dowell, aged fifty-three, to have been employed to sing in the church 'for ever', 'having no other living', as we know from the certificate issued at the dissolution. In other words, he was full-time at All Saints. His annual salary had been £5 13s 4d, a great deal more than the £1 6s 8d each of the Bristol waits was earning, as we have seen, later in the century.[16] And in 1530 someone called Goodman, apparently a musician, had been paid wages of 33s 4d a quarter – £6 13s 4d a year, an

---

[11] Burgess 2004: 71–89, 94–5.
[12] Burgess and Wathey 2000: 8.
[13] BA (BRO) P.AS/D/NA/45/217; Burgess 2004: 17.
[14] Burgess 2004: 167–215ff.
[15] BA (BRO) P.AS/D/CS/B/6/Bristol Deed 234, and P.AS/D/HS/C/11 a,b/291,296; Burgess 2004: 40, 41, 51, 53, 58.
[16] Burgess 2004: 356.

even greater sum, though still modest compared with the £11 15s an Exeter Cathedral vicar choral would have been earning by the 1540s.[17]

What was one full-time musician doing in a parish church, and what were Dowell, Goodman, and all these other people singing? A summary anatomy of pre-Reformation church music performance practice and its funding in England is incumbent.[18] In the fourteenth, fifteenth, and earlier sixteenth centuries there were three types of vocal music employed in the liturgy: plainsong, note-against-note counterpoint improvised or notated around plainsong (called 'faburden', 'discant', or 'counter'),[19] and the intricately composed repertoire of polyphony, with its voice parts all written out across the openings of one large lectern copy (a choirbook), rather like those of a piano duet today, or, towards the end of the period, in separate partbooks, each held and read only by the singer(s) of that particular part. The difficulty is knowing which of these types was meant by 'with music (cum nota)' or 'per notam'; one wants it to have been polyphony, and it probably was.[20] Plainsong, however, continued to serve most musical occasions and circumstances, including the celebration of mass in a cathedral or (if there was any music at all) a parish church on ordinary days in the Church's calendar, plus the various services (the 'Office') taking place every day and half the night in the main performance space, the chancel or 'choir', of a monastery or convent. In the case of a monastic house, all the monks or nuns, anything up to ninety of the former or fifty or more of the latter, would join in the plainsong: 'the community *was* the choir'.[21] In a secular cathedral such as Salisbury or Wells, the minor ordained clergy (those of long standing being priests, the younger or newer ones deacons or subdeacons) substituting for the endowed canons, and thus called vicars choral, were responsible for this plainsong performance, and there were over fifty of them in each place; until the mid-fifteenth century they were expected to know the entire liturgical repertoire off by heart.

Thus strength in numbers might simply mean more people singing plainsong in unison. Or additional funding for a liturgical purpose or occasion might permit the employment of one musical priest singing plainsong where otherwise the text would only have been spoken. The more priests praying for the salvation of your soul, and doing so with music, the

---

[17] Burgess 2000: 360; Orme 1980: xviii–xix.
[18] The following account draws pervasively on Bowers 1975 and 2007.
[19] Bowers 2007: 33, footnote 64.
[20] Temperley 1979, i: 8.
[21] Bowers 1975: 1006.

more efficacious the intercession would be. But there was also the question of special and important services: cyclic observances beyond the personal obsequies sung in individuals' chantries. Here, as with the personal obsequies, music was at a premium, and these observances fell into two types. One comprised services sung regularly – daily, weekly – outside the choir, typically in a Lady Chapel: this practice, and the musical demands associated with it, grew throughout the later middle ages. The other type was the still familiar pattern of services associated with festal occasions: Christmas, Lent, Holy Week and Easter, Corpus Christi, patronal saints' days, and so on.

Before the Reformation, we can be fairly sure that polyphony was only associated with special places or special occasions as outlined above. The special places might be a chantry chapel, a cathedral's or monastery's Lady Chapel, or a college or royal chapel. Not all of the special occasions were necessarily liturgical, and the surviving west country carols, in two and three parts and dating from the mid- or later fifteenth century, of (William?) Child, possibly rector of West Lydford, Thomas Philips, chorister and later vicar choral of Salisbury Cathedral, and the Exeter musicians John Truelove and Richard Smert may never have been heard in church.[22] It perhaps makes more sense to think of them as performed, after careful rehearsal, at some joyful feast in a location such as the hall of the vicars choral (a building surviving to this day in the case of Wells), though All Saints, Bristol, did pay one John Beech 5s for 'pricking' five carol books – that is, making partbook copies – in 1524–25.[23]

Fully composed polyphony, then, was for important functions and particular ecclesiastical locations. The question next arises of who sang it, and how they learnt to do so. It was a male art, but there is little if any evidence that boy choristers sang polyphony before the later fifteenth century, if one excludes discant. Choristers did not in fact do all that much: like the charity children of later centuries, they were educationally supported by endowments and made visible and aural on liturgical occasions in return. There were almonry schools in monasteries and song schools attached to bishops' palaces, colleges of priests, and cathedrals, and perhaps to some ordinary parish churches. There the boys were taught Latin and music sufficiently well that they could sing plainsong (perhaps only two or three boys in unison), individually read out loud and understand lessons in liturgical services, exercise ancillary ritual functions in processions and at altars, and proceed in at least some cases straight to university, for cathedral song schools ran

---

[22] Stevens 1952; Greer 2001a, b, c, and d; Simkins 1939: 25.
[23] Burgess 2000: 304.

parallel to grammar schools: they were not preparatory to them, though Nicholas Orme finds it necessary to finesse this statement for Exeter.[24] How many of the boys were thereby destined to become clergy, for whom monodic music (plainsong) would play its part, would be difficult to say, and training for a clerical career cannot have been the simple point, though it was undoubtedly a route and a cycle within the provision.[25] In monasteries, choristers only took part in Lady Chapel observances, not appearing in the main choir. The function of choristers was partly decorative. Instructing the boys was a lowly task for a priest, not a career position, and will not have garnered much musical satisfaction beyond that attached to a successful rendering of three-part faburden, a chorister or two on the plainsong, one or two more duplicating it a 4th higher, and the instructor supplying the 'false bass' mostly a 3rd below it. It is possible that the two small slates inscribed with fragments of mensural music now in Wells Museum are remnants of some robust teaching or learning method for this kind of modest function, which will have continued into the fifteenth and sixteenth centuries, slate being a cheap and readily available material.[26]

Beyond this, we have to imagine three or four adult male soloists tackling the more complex composed polyphony, doing so with a considerable amount of rehearsal (the notation could be very obscure) and for important occasions only. As a recondite art, perhaps deliberately so in order to protect musicians' status, it might be expected to have flourished best in a tight-knit community where the skills were for ever on hand.[27] Yet there is little evidence that monastic houses remained in the forefront of such practice after the mid-fourteenth century, and quite the opposite condition, that of mobile and flexible access to developing techniques, practitioners, and repertoire, seems to have governed polyphonic emulation: it was the dynamic places, newly founded or reorganised, that rolled out its usage.[28] Monasteries were content to be left behind, or had to catch up, and the same was true of cathedrals, especially Salisbury, insofar as their statutes made any change of practice cumbersome to finance and enact.[29]

From the earlier fifteenth century onwards, what happened was that creative confidence on the part of composers and singers together with lavish endowments on the part of rich merchants, bishops, aristocracy, and royalty

---

[24] Orme 2013: 7, 10–11, 12–13.
[25] ibid: 17–19.
[26] Blezzard 1979.
[27] Rastall 1996: 302.
[28] Bowers 1975: 4068.
[29] ibid: 5018, 5020–1, 6070, 6094–5.

gradually expanded the range of musical texture in polyphonic composition, and with it the number of performers on each part. A true bass and a boy treble part (sometimes with a boy mezzo or 'mean' below it) were added to what had been a norm of three adult male parts of which two circled round each other in tenor/baritone range and the third sang somewhat higher with falsetto where necessary. With this increased range, modern notions of 'SATB' texture in four or more comparably behaving and interacting parts emerged, each part sung ideally by more than one person, balanced against the others in strength and tone, and occupying its own registral space unless there were, say, two tenor parts or treble parts.

Mensural notation was gradually simplified, but choirboys now had to master it, for they became an integral, increasingly necessary, and increasingly numerous part of the 'choir' of voices. (The most lavish new foundations of the later fourteenth and earlier fifteenth centuries, Eton, King's, New and Winchester Colleges, were all endowed with sixteen choristers; the Chapel Royal also had sixteen in the later middle ages, while Exeter Cathedral's numbers settled at fourteen.)[30] A larger number of expert singers, adult and juvenile, was required, as was a greater degree of authoritative co-ordination of the musical forces: hence the developing position(s) of organist and master of the choristers, soon the most desirable type of musical post in the land. There was money to pay these 'profession-conscious' musicians, and in the eighty or so years before the radicalisation of the liturgy in the later 1540s a whole new career path of 'singing man' developed, the key thing being that he need no longer be a priest.[31] This meant that neither was he a vicar choral, but a lay vicar or lay clerk, though Watkins Shaw states that Salisbury Cathedral was admitting laymen into its statutory body of vicars choral by the late fifteenth century.[32] The singing man could sell his services to a cathedral, either just for singing or for playing the organ, acquiring and writing the polyphony, and instructing the choristers as well, or sell them to a monastery, a collegiate church, or a parish church.

This numerical increase in the circulation of skill needs hypothesising. One can imagine that the wealth poured into college foundations of the later fourteenth and earlier fifteenth centuries – the important west country ones were Crantock, Crediton, Glasney, Ottery, Westbury-on-Trym, and Wimborne – produced or at least sustained a growing number of musically literate clergy within the conditions that would exploit and develop their

---

[30] ibid: 4011Bff; Orme 2013: 2.
[31] Orme 1978: 405.
[32] Shaw 1991: 257.

creative ambitions, much as the Cornish *Ordinalia* probably emerged from those same conditions. These men wrote and performed music that demanded greater numbers of choristers with greater skill, and they taught them. This greater number of choristers, now educated in an increasingly specialist musical manner, thus less equipped to go on to university and become priests, may have been the overriding factor creating the lay 'singing man', trained from youth to be musically expert and versatile and to live partly or wholly by such skill.

What remains is the question of whether the profession of the polyphonic singing man, priest or no (and there is evidence that more priests learnt polyphony too, in the later pre-Reformation years), was largely a freelance one or whether full-time or part-time salaried positions were the thing. Where town churches are concerned, it is difficult to be sure, because most of the financial indications that survive are from churchwardens' accounts, and these only deal with extras, the payments for special occasions. Thus their instances of musical outlay are quite likely to include payments for polyphony, but without knowing the names of those paid and without the survival of other types of account, for example those of guilds, it is impossible to tell whether the persons concerned were being paid a bonus for a particularly time-consuming or challenging task over and above their regular remit of employment in the same institution, or whether they were drafted in from a freelance market solely for the occasion. One is inclined to guess that the latter was increasingly the case as polyphonic emulation spread, and that particularly enterprising or skilled singing men learnt to act as 'fixers', whether or not from a salaried position of their own. If this was the case, then regional networks were the thing. And of course a part-time salary in one institution would imply freelance engagement by others, unless the balance of a living were made up through non-musical employment or business enterprise, which as we have already seen undoubtedly happened. One further complication is that parish clerks needed to be competent singers, and some of them were top musical professionals (see Brygeman, below).[33] Did 'singing man' therefore mean someone else, or could the term have been used for the parish clerk?

After such a lengthy digression, it is time to test the purported picture, and particularly the network hypothesis, on the surviving west country evidence.

Let us return to All Saints Bristol. Here we can be sure that polyphony was practised, for some time after 1504 the church acquired as parish clerk the composer William Brygeman from Eton College, in whose great choirbook

---

[33] Temperley 1979, i: 7.

his music had been represented, though in portions of it now largely lost. Brygeman died in Bristol in 1524, leaving behind him 'three choirbooks, three sets of partbooks and some 50 smaller items providing music for use on all liturgical occasions throughout the church's year. The music was in up to five parts, and included such items as Fayrfax's Magnificat and Mass O bone Jesu, and a Mass Ascendo ad patrem by Brygeman.'[34] For Brygeman to have forsaken Eton for Bristol, he must surely have been paid a full-time salary to be in the city, and without further evidence it seems most likely that All Saints had the will, the economic means, and the persuasive power to have got him there. Long before Brygeman's appointment, in the 1470s and 1480s, All Saints made plenty of extra payments to 'priests and clerks', and to the 'choir', for festal performances – the Passion sung from the rood loft on Palm Sunday, a Jesus Mass sung several times a week, Christmas celebrations, Our Lady Mass during Lent[35] – but there are no unambiguous references to polyphonic practice until 1524–25; John Beech's pricking of the carol books is in fact the first. It is however quite possible that a small permanent choir was established in the later 1480s and that thereafter no extra payments were required. Child choristers are mentioned in 1518 and 1520 in connection with Corpus Christi, and from then on as though being trained regularly in some kind of choir school, which suggests that they were added to an otherwise all-adult musical texture (trebles and means are specifically mentioned), or that polyphony only began to be sung at this time. At first there were nine children, then six, paid a penny each per performance.[36] All in all, the most likely scenario is that polyphony came with Brygeman, and stayed, for there are plenty of references to it after his death, at least up until 1535–36.[37]

It is worth noting that in 1527 6s 8d was paid by All Saints 'to the clerk of St Thomas for 5 pricksong books containing 8 Masses', so perhaps St Thomas's also sang polyphony.[38] Bowers, indeed, points out that All Saints will not have been alone in its provision: 'Since the most important of the Bristol religious fraternities, the Gild of the Kalendars, was established in All Saints, ... [the Brygeman] inventory gives an impressive insight into the musical repertoire of the choirs widely maintained in parish churches throughout England by

---

[34] Bowers 2001b.
[35] Burgess 2000: 68, 72, 80, 88, 97, 98, 104, 108; Duffy 1992: 113, quoted Allinson 1998: 54.
[36] Burgess 2000: 238–9, 254, 262–3, 271, 331; Burgess 2004: 283–4; Bowers 2007: 22–3.
[37] Burgess 2000: 321, 340; Burgess and Wathey 2000: 44.
[38] Burgess 2000: 331.

such fraternities in the century before the Reformation.'[39] Anyone who has visited Spain during Holy Week will not find it difficult to imagine the pride and performance impact generated by such fraternities, nowadays expended on military bands and costumes as well as the elaborate floats and feats of endurance of their bearers. Each fraternity still attached to a parish, there are many within a single city: thirty-five in Córdoba.

Bristol also had an abbey, St Augustine's, already mentioned; one of its singers, presumably a lay clerk or at the most a secular clergyman, was paid to mend the organ at All Saints in 1478–79.[40] The abbey had had such singers, a small group of three or four, in its Lady Chapel choir since the 1370s or earlier, and Bowers thinks they were performing polyphony daily. From the 1490s we know who they were and how they were employed. The first clerk was cantor, teaching the six boys who had recently been added to the Lady Chapel ensemble, the second was *succentor capella*, given board and £2 per annum in 1491–92 and 1503–04, rising to £2 13s 4d by 1511–12, and the third, who got free board and £1 or £1 6s 8d, was a part-time singer, also acting as the almoner's servant. Ambitious men came and went in these positions. Henry Blackburn rose from third to second clerk; William Muldar went on to become a chaplain of the Chapel Royal; Richard Bramston came from Wells, where he had already been organist, around 1509–10, returning to Wells in disguise to kidnap a choirboy for Bristol, only to return there again five years later, this time in full and open view, and spend the remainder of a long and ultimately distinguished career in the cathedral's service.[41]

Monastic establishments elsewhere that had an opportunity to interact with an urban musical environment may have included Exeter's Franciscan friary, if as has been suggested it was there that the British Library's Ritson Manuscript originated, for that source contains the carols of Smert and Truelove, the former an Exeter Cathedral vicar choral, the latter probably in the chapel employment of Bishop Edmund Lacy of Exeter. Lacy was dead by the probable time of the manuscript's compilation, but Smert and Truelove were not, Smert having additionally become rector of Plymtree near Exeter, a covetable pluralistic privilege.[42] A more isolated establishment could also sustain a musician's career, however. Tavistock Abbey lost its 'maister of the singing children' (cantor), William Preston, to Cerne Abbey in 1517, 'lured

---

[39] Bowers 2001b.
[40] Burgess 2000: 93.
[41] Bowers 1975: 4084, 6045–6; Bowers 2007: 24–5, 29; Bowers et al 2006: 26.
[42] Hamm et al 2001: 903; Greer 2001c and d; Orme 1978: 401–3; Orme 2004; Orme 2013: 15–16, 249–50.

from secure employment' there to a similar post that must have seemed more attractive; Glastonbury Abbey's James Renynger was clearly a significant organist and choirmaster as well as 'singingman'; and 'it is possible that polyphony ... made its way into the four largest monasteries in Cornwall'.[43] One of the latter was Tywardreath, Thomas Rayne's duties there as cantor already having been described in chapter 4, the others being Launceston, Bodmin, and St German's.[44] Ralph Drake was cantor at Muchelney around 1520, Robert Derkeham at Buckland Abbey in 1522, John Elyott at Tavistock in 1529, Nicholas Hullande at Maiden Bradley Priory in 1534, Thomas Foxe at Taunton Priory in 1538, and John Dunster at Bruton Abbey from 1529 until its dissolution ten years later.[45] Launceston and Bodmin were relatively important towns, and in both we have evidence of some level of distinction in parish music. At Launceston, what John Davy, William Parker, and the 'other singers' were paid (in wine) to sing on the church's matronal feast of St Mary Magdalene in 1471 could have been polyphony.[46] (William Parker may have been a secondary – a broken-voice adolescent cathedral singer in preparatory minor orders – at Exeter, now thrown onto the open market.)[47] Sixty years later Launceston also had an organist, Richard Dingle, paid – or paid extra – on St Mary Magdalen's feast.[48] Bodmin was donated two books of polyphony in 1529–30, when it acquired its organ mentioned in chapter 2.[49] A more suggestive link between town and monastery is, however, that of Plymouth, where in 1487 'a shilling was paid "to the old man the singer" from St Andrew's to go to [neighbouring] Plympton to fetch songs for the mass'; Plympton had a priory, and the 'songs' were probably pricksong.[50] Still in south Devon, Dartmouth and Paignton were exchanging pricksong books in 1539, and Tavistock bought some in 1552–53 which will have come in handy with the return of the Roman Catholic rite.[51]

If the possibility of reciprocity or professional networking tended to aid the establishment of polyphony in an isolated small town, capital investment in Ashburton will have come with its bishop's palace, built in 1314 for Walter Stapledon of Exeter, whose chapel, St Lawrence's, home of a guild, was

[43] Burgess and Wathey 2000: 18; Bowers 2007: 31; Stokes 1996: 127; Orme 2010: 52.
[44] Rowse 1941: 190–1; Orme 1990.
[45] Bowers 2007: 28; Bowers et al 1983: 173.
[46] Joyce and Newlyn 1999: 585.
[47] Orme 2013: 210.
[48] Burgess and Wathey 2000: 31–2; Joyce and Newlyn 1999: 586.
[49] Orme 2010: 80.
[50] Gill 1979, i: 115.
[51] Waterfield 1946: 24; Worth 1887: 23.

endowed with a chantry priest who was to be 'master of the song school', i.e. teaching the town children.[52] This, seemingly (for there has been some scholarly uncertainty), was the moment of the foundation of Ashburton School, 'probably the oldest institution of the kind ... in the west', closed amid protest in 1938.[53] Again, throughout the fourteenth century and for much of the fifteenth the children may have sung nothing of any great consequence in the parish church, until the local merchant elite again facilitated the musical gradation to polyphony. 'Thomas Tankret's obit (instituted c. 1481) provided for payment to four men singers and four "scollers" [boys]; William Dolbear's for five of each, and John Ford's (c. 1534) for five men and six scholars.'[54] The boys, it is thought, were already on hand; the expert adult singers will have been bought in on an ad hoc or residential basis. Thus we find pricksong books being mended in 1493–94 and a '"rector coryys" (director of the choir)' mentioned five years later.[55]

Musicians' names then begin to appear in the Ashburton records. The Richard Davy who mended the pricksong books may have been the important Eton Choirbook composer, possibly then resident in Exeter, though there is no positive evidence to equate the two.[56] One John Predeaux was playing the organ and renting a house in Ashburton around 1510 (perhaps it was he who got them to buy a new organ eight or nine years later).[57] Richard Turpin, apparently a chorister, was paid 6s 8d as a liturgical singer in 1529–30, and he and two other 'lads', John Bartlet and Stephen Mayne, were again paid in 1531–33, though this would suggest monodic performance.[58] William Whyte's is the last name to be found: he was paid 3s 4d as 'cantor' from 1546 to 1552.[59]

When did it all end? Career musicians clearly hung on, and, at a time when in the new cathedrals provision was actually strengthened, it was not immediately lacking in parish churches. At Bristol, there seems to have been an arrangement whereby the cathedral's singing men toured the parish churches, or were hired piecemeal to supplement meagre choral resources: they turn up at Christ Church, St Ewen's, and St James's at various times between 1579 and 1597. Alan Smith, from whom this information comes,

---

[52] Pilkington 1978: 53–5; Cherry and Pevsner 1989: 132.
[53] Hanham 1970: xix; St Leger-Gordon 1950: 355.
[54] Hanham 1970: xix.
[55] Skinner 2001: 83, citing unpublished research by John Harper; Hanham 1970: xix.
[56] Skinner 2001: 83; Orme 1978: 404–5.
[57] Hanham 1970: xvi.
[58] ibid: xix.
[59] ibid.

believed that St Mary Redcliffe and other Bristol churches were running down their choirs in Elizabeth I's reign through natural wastage, which might explain the need to share resources for what became rarer choral occasions.[60] It may be that as choral worship disappeared in the parish churches, these singers turned to other ways of supplementing their income, for by 1634 not all of Bristol Cathedral's six singing men could be together for the 10am Sunday service, some of them being clerks of parishes or organists of parish churches.[61] At Lyme Regis, John Coke was salaried with £5 per annum in 1552 'in consideration of the good service that he hath performed in the church of King's Lyme from time to time, in singing and playing at organs, and which the said John Coke was to continue during his life in the best manner he could'.[62] Once again we can imagine him as a single retainer – though of course there could have been more, unrecorded – mustering whatever choir was still required amid rapidly changing conditions of worship; the salary was comparable with that of Dowell of Bristol. He could have been identical with the John Cooke who was a secondary at Exeter Cathedral from 1541 but whose name disappears from there after 1549.[63] There may well have been accomplished organist-singers such as Coke, some of them previously employed by monasteries, who travelled around the region in a network of mutual support. Lyme Regis had music in the church in 1568–69. St Andrew's, Plymouth, had no more than Ashburton been fazed by uncertain times: by 1547 its 'songs for the mass' were becoming obsolete, so 'English songs were bought for the choir; Latin may have gone but not music.'[64] As for the Ashburton choir, it survived the immediate effects of the Reformation: 'in 1576-7, the choir men were given 12d, and in 1577-8 "the singynge men" got 2s for their services at the annual celebration of the Queen's preservation'.[65] As with All Saints, Bristol, we can only guess whether these were supplementary payments to singers paid permanently from other funds, or whether one permanent retainer such as Whyte acted as a fixer, keeping his freelance singers sweet for when required. But Ashburton may have given up on liturgical splendour shortly after this, the latest generation of town merchants having been brought up on a different theological economy: as mentioned in chapter 2, it dismantled its rood loft and organ in 1579–80, a pattern repeated

[60] Smith 1967, i: 281–4.
[61] Bettey 2007: 58, 61–2.
[62] Roberts 1834: 213.
[63] Orme 2013: 89.
[64] Wanklyn 1944: 36; Gill 1979, i: 133 (see also Temperley 1979, i: 61).
[65] Hanham 1970: xix.

at this time throughout England.⁶⁶ The Corpus Christi plays and visiting players at Christmas had gone earlier.⁶⁷ Hartland, at the westward extremity of north Devon, may have been unique in its seeming imperviousness to the increasing constraints of parish liturgy, for it bought partbooks in 1598–99, was still paying singing boys until 1608, and, as mentioned in chapter 2, erected a new organ on a rood loft in 1637–38.⁶⁸

Other west country parishes in which there seem to have been pre-Reformation choirs include Barnstaple, in whose St Thomas chantry at some point in the later middle ages 'for those who contributed to the funds of the Bridge a "dirge" should be sung by the "Song men and boys"', and where Henry Redwin bequeathed funds for his choral obsequies in 1503.⁶⁹ St John the Baptist, Yeovil, appears to have had a choir school in the fifteenth century attached to the surviving chantry chapel, which is now physically separate from the church.⁷⁰ St Bartholomew's, Crewkerne, had a 'singing man' in 1585, which again probably indicates some element of continuity with pre-Reformation practice.⁷¹ In 1524, William Selake bequeathed £10 to St Peter's, Tiverton 'that a dayly masse of our blessed lady may be said and songe by note ... att a certyn howre wt. the pristes and clerks of the said churche for the tyme beying and wt the orgones'; this could have been plainsong or pricksong, but more likely was the latter.⁷²

As for the collegiate churches, they were parish churches endowed with a community of priests, and normally also with boys.⁷³ Their potential musical importance has already been suggested, but what of the documentary evidence? Wimborne Minster was declared a Royal Peculiar in 1318, and its choir wore scarlet robes like those of St George's, Windsor, and Westminster Abbey.⁷⁴ In subsequent centuries its musical establishment ran to 'four vicars choral, four secondaries (lay clerks), two chantry priests and five boy choristers', and it was re-established in 1563 after dissolution by Edward VI.⁷⁵ The collegiate foundation of Holy Cross, Crediton, included twelve

---

⁶⁶ Temperley 1979, i: 43–4.
⁶⁷ Hanham 1970: xi.
⁶⁸ Temperley 1979, i: 51.
⁶⁹ Edwards 1917: 1–2.
⁷⁰ Personal visit, 8 Feb 2010.
⁷¹ Dunning and Bush 1985: 31.
⁷² Curtis nd: [3].
⁷³ Harwood 2008.
⁷⁴ Wimborne 1998: 14.
⁷⁵ Williamson 2008: 191.

vicars choral, and 'a choir school existed from 1334 until 1545'.[76] In 1438 one of the canons of Glasney College, Penryn, James Michell, 'owned a booklet of "songs of music"' which was 'almost certainly works of polyphony'; and fragments of polyphony used to repair a Tywardreath Priory office book could have come from Glasney (or from Tywardreath itself).[77] The resources of Ottery St Mary make it likely that polyphony was regularly heard and valued in this otherwise sleepy Devon parish from, say, 1450 onwards.[78] John Hampton, probably he whose Salve Regina appears in the Eton Choirbook, was a clerk at Westbury-on-Trym collegiate church from 1474 to 1484 before moving to Worcester Cathedral.[79] Crantock College had four vicars choral, two clerks, and two or three boys from 1352 onwards and will have been musically 'unobtrusive', while of the pre-Conquest colleges of St Buryan and Chulmleigh no musical traces can be found, though the colourful recusant composer and theatrical impresario Sebastian Westcote, who taught Peter Phillips, was born in Chulmleigh and could conceivably have been trained there.[80]

It would be gratifying to be able to round out this picture in two further dimensions: by demonstrating that there was porosity between an ecclesiastical and a civic musical living, and by reference to surviving polyphonic repertoire. But no evidence has yet come to light that the two institutionally paid types of musician, singing men and waits, interacted in the west country. Elsewhere, we know that waits were paid to learn to read music (in Norwich in 1533–34) and that they doubled as church singers and an organist (in Coventry in the mid-sixteenth century).[81] It would be good to establish comparable connections in Bath, Exeter, Wells, or Bristol, but the most we know is that Bristol Cathedral hired the waits, presumably to play rather than sing, in 1582.[82] To take the second of these desiderata, it is sad, possibly perplexing, that no actual polyphonic music survives that can be associated with one of the west country collegiate churches even with the partial degree of confidence that attaches to the association of the *Ordinalia* with Glasney. Without it, we have no real picture of musical creativity's achievements across the region. What then does remain of pre-Reformation

---

[76] Crediton nd.
[77] Orme 2010: 55, 258; O'Connor 2007: 44–5.
[78] Whitham 1972: 9, 11; Harwood 2008: 231; Wasson 1986: 321; Williamson 2008: 190.
[79] Bowers 2001e.
[80] Orme 2010: 55; Bowers 1975: 2041, 2043; Bowers 2001f.
[81] Rastall 1996: 305–6.
[82] Smith 1967, i: 228.

west country polyphony, in terms of actual notated compositions? A healthy crop of carols has already been mentioned, and there are one or two other pieces by Smert. We have some of Brygeman's music, and Richard Hygons, organist and master of the choristers at Wells Cathedral throughout most of the second half of the fifteenth century and the early part of the sixteenth, is represented in the Eton Choirbook by an enormous Salve Regina.[83] Two antiphons by Bramston are also extant, and he had a broad reputation as a composer, perhaps not entirely justified on the basis of these pieces.[84] Robert Driffield, vicar choral of Salisbury Cathedral 1424–68, may have been the composer of pieces in the Trent codices (if he was, they furnish the unique example of west country polyphony surviving in Continental sources), and John Garnsey or Guernsey, vicar choral of Wells 1443–58, of a *Laudes deo* surviving in the Pepys 1236 Manuscript.[85] John Hampton and Richard Davy, further Eton Choirbook composers, have already been mentioned. The Ritson Manuscript contains works by other men from Exeter Cathedral, including Richard Mowere or Mawere (not a vicar choral) and the prolific Thomas Pack.[86] Yet another Exeter Cathedral man, John Darke, is represented elsewhere by a single surviving piece, a five-part Magnificat with one voice now missing, but appears to have been a composer 'of limited ability; the music is short-winded, aimless and clumsy'.[87]

Anonymous fragments date from much farther back and are in their way more intriguing. Half a century ago, a manuscript fragment was discovered walled up in the (later) clock chamber of Netherbury parish church in Dorset, and it included parts of a piece of two-part polyphony from the early thirteenth century. A later, fourteenth-century two-part fragment in the Bridport archives apparently went missing at the start of the twentieth century.[88] Traces of obsolete music reused in bindings include a tantalising example of fifteenth-century three-part composition found in a Luttrell family court book, which raises the possibility that Minehead or Dunster heard polyphony.[89] But more gratifying and at the same time more mysterious than all these local survivals against the odds is the Dartmouth Magnificat, a complete, sturdy work of four-part polyphony to be discussed further in the Epilogue. It heads the first of Dartmouth's borough court books, which

---

[83] Bowers et al 2006: 25.
[84] ibid: 26; Bowers 2001a.
[85] Bowers 2001c and d.
[86] Wathey 2001; Trowell 2001.
[87] Sandon 2001a: 23.
[88] Bent 1970: 227–30.
[89] Bowers et al 1983: 156–73.

came into use in 1484 and remains in its original binding.[90] Thurston Dart, still a teenager living with his parents across the river in Kingswear, viewed it in Exeter in 1940, and it may well have been the first ancient manuscript he seriously studied, though he was already an experienced musician.[91] Years later he speculated that the piece was composed for the opening of the town's new guildhall (John Hawley's old town house, for which St Saviour's parish church was now responsible) around 1480. One would not disagree with Dart's conclusion that John Kendall, senior chantry priest, appointed in 1480, and perhaps town clerk in Dartmouth, is its most likely composer.[92] But Dart missed one, possibly two things. First, the music is suffixed 'To his loveinge freinde Mr Roberte Smythe maior of Dartmouth'. Dart must have considered this inscription to be one of the scribblings that are 'no more than rough drafts of official correspondence' that 'certainly do not relate to the music itself', in which case one might disagree.[93] No Robert Smyth[e] of the period is mentioned in Watkins's compendious pre-Reformation history of the borough, which includes a list of its mayors, but the mayors for the years 1478 and 1482 are not known.[94] Second, both a John Kendale or Kendall and a Robert Smyth turn up as newly admitted vicars choral of Exeter Cathedral in Midsummer Term 1484. (Smyth remained on the Exeter books only two or three years, Kendall until some time before 1509.)[95] It would be foolish to conclude too much where England's most common surname is concerned, equally so to expect a mayor to turn cleric, and downright fanciful to imagine the loving friends somehow contriving to decamp to Exeter together. But stranger things happened in the middle ages, and it is at least reasonable to guess that Kendall was the same man, now furthering his career (and earnings) in a more distinguished environment while remaining within the county of euphoric living and leaving behind him his Magnificat in the otherwise still empty clerk's book, to be utilised by the borough.[96]

❧ Education and Music

Beyond the apprenticeship model, the chorister was for centuries the link between the institutional worlds of musical education and professional

---

[90] DeHC SM 1981.
[91] Holt.
[92] Dart 1958: 215–16.
[93] ibid: 216.
[94] Watkin 1935: 186.
[95] Orme 1980: 38.
[96] ibid: 5; Watkin 1935: 186.

musical culture, as to a certain extent he (and now sometimes she) still is in England. Many current and recent classical musicians in Britain, in the world of early music possibly a majority, began their musical life as choristers. So did Several British pop idols, west country examples including Chris Martin of Coldplay, an Exeter Cathedral chorister, and Roger Taylor, drummer of Queen, who in 1960 was briefly and reluctantly a member of Truro Cathedral Choir.[97] As we have seen, endowed foundations in the middle ages tended to make provision for the education of the young – as indeed with their almshouses for the decline of the old – and in addition to the churches, colleges, monasteries, and cathedrals of the previous section, we find choristers in places such as Gaunt's Hospital, Bristol (its chapel now St Mark's church), which from 1232 onwards supported twelve poor scholars, expected to sing when required, and the Hospital of St John the Baptist in Exeter, which a hundred years later was refounded by Grandisson with provision for 'eight boys to learn grammar'.[98]

All this amounts to evidence of certainly no fewer than 150 choristers across the region at any one time in the later pre-Reformation years. Nearly as many again were no doubt to be found in places where the evidence fails or has not been cited – towns such as Bideford, Bridgwater, Sherborne, and Totnes – so we might hazard a total of 250–300. This is a large number of male children being taught some degree of music and Latin, possibly not far off one in fifty of the eligible cohort, which would be getting on for twice as large as the estimate for the proportion of the regional cohort playing a musical instrument three hundred years later (see the opening of chapter 3). Just as with performers in bands, such a figure may have represented a relatively broad social spectrum, with one choirboy recruited from perhaps every dozen settlements. No wonder Erasmus singled out English choirboys in his criticisms of musical excess in church.[99] What we have to conclude is that a fair number of people will have known choirboys personally, as members of their family or parish, and had some experience not just of hearing them sing but also of witnessing in some measure their way of life and education, just as, according to the calculations of David Allinson, one person in eight (if we assume five sharing a copy) will have had access to a liturgical primer with which to personalise their devotions.[100] Of course one still wants to know

[97] Wikipedia: 'Chris Martin'; Queen.
[98] Bowers 1975: 2055.
[99] Miller 1966: 339.
[100] Allinson 1998, i: 41–2.

about the other seven people, but it seems clear that we can speak of a shared culture in which the choirboy and his music played a familiar role.

Thanks to the painstaking work of Nicholas Orme, we have a window onto the social background of the Exeter Cathedral choristers in the early sixteenth century. Of the thirty-seven choristers between 1527 and 1549 whose names he had found on record by 1980, demographic details are known for thirteen of them. Among their fathers, there were five farmers ('husbandman'), a weaver and a miller, and a merchant. One father was a 'yeoman', another a 'gentleman' (his boy a bastard son), three were of unspecified occupation. If anything, this weights the recruitment or selection bias towards the middling and lower end of the social spectrum. While it is possible that the boys (including the twenty-four with an undifferentiated record) for whom no parental occupation information is available were those with high-ranking parents, it seems more likely that the diocesan elite privately tutored their sons, and although some of them may have been sent to the royal chapels and colleges beyond the region, it was important for an upper-class elder son not to be embraced by the Church and adopt celibacy: his duty was to continue the family line. Lower down the social scale, then as later, two or more sons from the same family might keep each other company as choirboys – John and Walter de Alphington and Alfred and Walter Pistor ('Baker') in the early fourteenth century, Lewis and John Mugg in 1555.[101]

Equally helpful is Orme's logging of where the choristers came from. The diocese recruited boys for their good voices and good conduct, and was supposed to do so only from within its boundaries, though exceptions could be made and, as we have seen, there was a healthy market in trading and even kidnapping in the sixteenth century.[102] Adding a concentrated sample available from the early fourteenth century, we have choristers taken or sent from many places across Devon, as far away as Modbury and Tavistock, though with an apparent preponderance of boys from relatively nearby – Clyst, Larkbeare, Alphington, Bradninch, Ottery – or from Exeter itself, and with only one chorister (out of over eighty) known to have come from Cornwall, still part of the diocese of Exeter, and that not very far into the county. (We know what happened to this person, Robert de Egloshayle: he became vicar of St Paul's, Exeter.)[103] There will have been good reasons for this favouring of the nearer hinterland, among them perhaps parents' greater

---

[101] Orme 1980: 126–32; see also Orme 2013: 12, offering a marginally larger sample, and Orme 1986: 41.
[102] Bowers 1975: 2024.
[103] Orme 2013: 114.

willingness to relinquish their boys if they were not going too far away, or simply greater awareness of the cathedral and its musical establishment on the part of those accustomed to visit the city. But it does suggest that geography has played into the equation of sustained musicality: you were more likely to become a musician if you lived in or near the cathedral city.

How different the overall equation has been in more recent centuries is difficult to judge. It may not have changed radically. One notable element was added: the capacity of lay clerks (as opposed to vicars choral) to marry and produce a legitimate family, an early example of a lay clerk or organist father placing one or more chorister sons in the same establishment being the murderous John Farrant at Salisbury in the early 1580s.[104] Married staff rendered a diocese less the self-contained machine it had previously been, educating a selection of the county's young, sending them to university, and taking them back as clergy with parochial livings across the diocese, for by analogy with the younger sons of the aristocracy, multiple offspring would now need to look further afield for a livelihood regardless of aptitude and preference for a settled succession. Thus at Salisbury in the closing years of the eighteenth century we find its cathedral organist, Joseph Corfe, carefully preparing his son Arthur for taking over his position, while he spends huge amounts of money on assisting another son, John, to achieve a military commission.[105] It may also latterly have been the case that ambition propels a talented young musician out of the region for their education. Theophilus Willcocks, Barclays Bank manager in Newquay, sent his son David not to Truro or Exeter Cathedral but to Westminster Abbey as a chorister in 1929. (It was, however, within the region that David Willcocks undertook his secondary education, at Clifton College, enlisted for his immensely distinguished wartime military service, in the Duke of Cornwall's Light Infantry, and was appointed to his first professional position, as organist of Salisbury Cathedral in 1947.)[106] Nicolas Kynaston, similarly, was born in Morebath, Devon, but attended Westminster Cathedral as a chorister in the later 1940s; in this case one assumes that family religious allegiance propelled the decision, no Roman Catholic diocesan establishment within the region offering sufficient opportunity, a fact reminding us how religious dissenters have been musically disadvantaged as youngsters in the English provinces and may still be.[107]

---

[104] Robertson 1938: 146–56.
[105] WHC 1214/17–20; Banfield 2016: 13.
[106] *Guardian* online, 17 Sep 2015.
[107] Hale 2001.

A song school has often been portrayed as run incompetently or with virtually no settled resources. Dora Robertson's *Sarum Close* paints a picture of chronic inadequacy or unsustainability.[108] Abuse of choristers has taken many forms, including their physical assault by Sebastian Wesley at Exeter in 1840, their mercenary exploitation for the treble line in eighteenth- and early nineteenth-century glee clubs and madrigal societies at the expense of a safeguarded curriculum and regular hours, and a limited, neglectful horizon of training.[109] On the other hand, they got paid when hired out (unless their master pocketed the hire money, which may have happened with Joseph Corfe at Salisbury), and their early experience of the musical world, with its mixture of rigid discipline and confidence in professional performance, remains unparalleled.[110] So does their opportunity for excelling, already clear in Renynger's Glastonbury contract of 1534, which provided for two of his six boys to be additionally instructed in keyboard playing, the two admittedly chosen by the abbot, not Renynger.[111]

But what of girls? High-born daughters were frequently consigned to English convents before the Reformation. Most of the west country foundations were in Dorset and Wiltshire, perhaps because of the powerful exemplar of Shaftesbury Abbey, a house of Benedictine nuns founded by King Alfred around 888.[112] In the later middle ages, once numbers had recovered from the Black Death, there will have been two to three hundred nuns in the west country at any one time, roughly 20 per cent of the total of male religious in the region.[113] They had to learn to sing and memorise plainsong, just like monks and vicars choral, and were thus equally immersed in the spiritual demands and beauties of music; they were led and disciplined by a 'chantress'; and they will have composed their own monodic chant on occasions, such as when acting and singing the elaborate and moving Easter Sepulchre dramas, that of Wilton Abbey reproduced complete in a recent publication.[114] But of course for them there was no interface with the musical profession outside the convent walls. There is, moreover, little evidence of polyphonic practice by nuns in pre-Reformation England, though it is not entirely lacking, and polyphony could conceivably have been sung at Cannington Priory near Bridgwater when Dame Eleanor Hull (*ca* 1395–1460)

---

[108] Robertson 1938.
[109] Horton 2004: 117; Hobson 2015: 123, 125, 179.
[110] Hobson 2015: 128; Banfield 2016: 12–13.
[111] Stokes 1996: 127.
[112] Wikipedia: 'List of monastic houses in England'.
[113] Figures extrapolated from Yardley 2006: 4.
[114] Yardley 2008: 58–65; Yardley 2006: 146–55, 235–6, 243–54.

was resident there, for her name is associated with a manuscript in which five three-part polyphonic pieces appear. Hull, a learned noblewoman who one guesses retired to Cannington so as to be near her family's estate at Enmore (the next village), probably did not actually compose these pieces, but even that cannot be entirely out of the question.[115]

Male choristers continued to be educated, after a fashion, and produced as professional musicians by the cathedrals throughout the post-Reformation centuries, except for the period of the Civil War and Commonwealth, and there were heady opportunities for the exceptionally talented boy, offered to Arthur Corfe in the Salisbury Festivals of the 1780s and Sebastian Wesley in the Bath Festival of 1824, when they sang important oratorio and cantata numbers, solo and ensemble, alongside the likes of Tenducci, Rauzzini, and Catalani, though Wesley's participation in Bath was compromised through no fault of his own in what seem to have been one performance mishap after another under the conductorship of Sir George Smart.[116] But town and village churches, increasingly nonconformist as well as Anglican, mostly lacked this proto-professional dimension until the later nineteenth century, children's voices before then relegated to the gallery, where they comprised either the serried ranks of charity waifs or the treble line, or part of it, of a psalmody quire, both functions more tolerated than loved and both potentially unruly. Away from the cathedral close and outside the artisanal family or a military academy, it must have been easier for a girl to become a literate musician than a boy, and it seems that neither of the west country's most famous gentlemen amateurs, Claver Morris and John Marsh, had the opportunity to learn the violin in boyhood but only in their years of tertiary education or its equivalent, or even later.[117]

Girls rather suddenly found themselves expected to be musical when in the seventeenth century the burgeoning materiality of bourgeois England made domestic keyboard playing into a fashionable accomplishment for the marriageable female, and teaching it was what would sustain the average 'general practice' musical career right through the nineteenth century and even into the twentieth.[118] We have witnessed women keyboard players in chapter 4, but not yet the institutions that began to produce them. These were the ladies' schools or academies that sprang up like mushrooms in prosperous

---

[115] Yardley 2006: 109–10; Barratt 1995: xxiv–xl.
[116] Reid and Pritchard 1965: 60; Matthews 1970: 28; Smart 1824; Clarke 2007: 22–3.
[117] Johnstone 2008: 96, 104; Robins 2001: 895.
[118] Banfield 2016.

Georgian towns, above all in Bath but in most other places besides, especially from the 1730s onwards at least where Bristol was concerned.[119] Anne Rogers was advertising a dancing school in Blandford in 1737.[120] Young men as well as women will have needed to acquire that skill, and there was probably nothing to stop them learning music at the same establishment, but, as a standard combination, music and dance tuition applied predominantly to young women. Mrs Pearce's academy opened in Sherborne in 1778, and violinist John Tewkesbury served as its music and dancing master.[121] Dancing and music were taught at Mrs Sydenham's school in Blandford in 1779.[122] And at Salisbury in the early nineteenth century, Arthur Corfe from his cathedral organist's position was conducting an endless round of teaching visits to ladies' academies, namely Alford's, Beale's, Blandy's, Blatch's, Butler's, Mrs Davis's, Mrs Harris's, Miss Pinnock's, Saffery's, and Mrs Saph's schools, plus quite a few others, possibly beyond the city, including the odd one, such as Rev Hodgson's, that catered for young gentlemen.[123]

In most establishments, music, dancing, and sometimes languages were extras – hence the substantial freelance fee extracted by the peripatetic teacher – and music as an integral part of the male curriculum had to wait an inordinately long time to be established. The pre-Reformation free grammar schools such as Queen Elizabeth's in Wimborne, founded in 1497, and those of Dartmouth, Crediton, Crewkerne, and elsewhere, will have been staffed by chantry and collegiate priests who taught singing to the boys employed as choristers in the nearby church, but there is little if any evidence of music as a boy's educational accomplishment in the new schools of the sixteenth and seventeenth centuries such as Blundell's in Tiverton, founded in 1604, and Sherborne, founded as a grammar school in 1550.

Blundell's and Sherborne were two of what in the nineteenth century became the English 'public' schools (independent and fee-paying, though with scholarships), and within the region, probably with one exception, it was not until the founding of Clifton College in 1860 that music was sufficiently valued for provision to be properly thought through and money to be spent on it by the institution. The glaring exception was Downside, because it was a Catholic school, staffed by the Benedictine monks of the abbey on the same site. Immune from the social anxieties attendant upon the

---

[119] Borsay 1989: 138–9; Barry 1985: 46.
[120] *SM*, 26 Apr 1737: 4.
[121] *SM*, 25 May 1778: 3, 10 Jan 1780: 1.
[122] *SM*, 15 Feb 1779: 1.
[123] WHC 1214/19; Pigot 1822: 559.

Illus. 7.2 Clifton College, Frederick Bligh Bond's Music School (right)

performing arts within aspiring Protestant culture in Britain, it was staging musical productions by the 1870s, when it mounted a home-grown opera, *The Doge of Venice*, and once Richard Terry had been appointed organist of the abbey in 1896 the boys of the school choir found themselves pioneering the revival of Byrd and Tallis 'as composers of Catholic and not Anglican church music', as well as Italian renaissance music and such Catholic concert items as Pergolesi's Stabat Mater.[124] The point is perhaps underlined by the fact that a significant London theatre composer, Joseph Mazzinghi, who had written them a mass in 1823, actually died at Downside in 1844 while visiting his son there.[125]

Continental values apart, Clifton College marked a forward stride when it employed a professional musician almost from the start, the first postholder being W F Trimnell, brother of the Thomas Tallis Trimnell encountered earlier; he played the harmonium for the official opening in 1862 and took up the post of organist and choirmaster in 1864.[126] Trimnell, alongside the Roeckels, Riseley, and others, was an important cog in the musical

---

[124] Lowerson 2005: 47; Birt 1902: 272, 277; Andrews 1948: 33–54; BL Cat (Downside printed programmes).
[125] Jeboult 1923: 59; Fiske 2001b; DoHC D/WLC/MU/Boxes 2 and 3.
[126] *WDP*, 1 Oct 1862: 3; Fox and Lidell 1962: 96; *BTM*, 24 Dec 1864: 6.

mechanism of Bristol in the second half of the nineteenth century, a machine generating a certain amount of cultural capital, and it is to the college's credit that it made and sustained this link between downtown and uptown, local product and national provision. An apprentice of John Davis Corfe at Bristol Cathedral and an associate, possibly pupil, of S S Wesley who commissioned a late anthem from Wesley for Clifton, 'Let us now praise famous men' (which exists in two versions), Trimnell had national visibility, for he edited the Collegiate Series of anthems and partsongs and *Songs for Public Schools*, both collections privileging Bristol composers and topics. He stayed at Clifton for thirty-two years, retiring to Torquay in 1896 where he died five years later.[127]

In the days of Victorian autocracy, the prospects for music in a public school depended entirely on the disposition of the headmaster, and Clifton was lucky in its first, John Percival, who personally donated the chapel organ.[128] Still, there was only so much Trimnell could do at Clifton, and his salary at first was a paltry £30 (sixty-six years later, Douglas Fox would be appointed on a scale rising to £770).[129] The activities Trimnell directed were extra-curricular, and he had to work with the raw material of Britain's philistine gentry: complaining to the reporter John Graham in 1891, he asserted that 'eight out of sixteen' of his school's entrants 'had no ear or could not sing; four out of sixteen, and eleven out of thirty-one were the numbers of growlers on other similar occasions'.[130] Parker complained comparably about the Sherborne boys, while Barnby at Eton thought that only 10 per cent of public schoolboys 'had an ear'.[131] Nor did Clifton provide a music building in Trimnell's day, though it came soon afterwards, designed by Frederick Bligh Bond and opened in 1898, right next to the zoo.[132] This may have been the first institutional building in the west country erected solely for musical purposes in several hundred years (Illus. 7.2). Sherborne's followed in 1926, though thanks to a sympathetic headmaster the institution had already been 'one of the best equipped schools in England', musically speaking, early in Parker's time.[133] At Clifton, Trimnell's work was to begin with mostly a matter of organs, choirs, chapel services, and the interminable miscellany concerts that continue to plague school music today. He did what he could

---

[127] Graham 1891: 369, 371; Edwards 1905: 240; Horton 2009: 158–81; obituary, *WDP*, 8 Oct 1901: 7.
[128] Graham 1891: 369.
[129] Knighton 2012: 293, 318.
[130] Graham 1891: 368–9.
[131] Parker 1894: 101; Graham 1894: 137.
[132] Fox and Lidell 1962: 104; Edwards 1905: 238–9.
[133] DoHC S.235/D 1/22; Parker 1894: 103.

with an instrumental ensemble, though it would be a long time before British battles were won in public school orchestra pits.[134] Gradually the belief that music was a cultural good must have taken hold, for by 1905 Clifton was offering a music scholarship worth £25 a year, enough to cover the fees.[135]

When Louis Parker gave a talk to the Musical Association in 1894 on music at Sherborne, it was music appreciation and such matters as the understanding of orchestration that he began by highlighting, i.e. the beginnings of music as an academic study for 'the general cultivated public of a future day'; and he made a point of ignoring the chapel music: 'we are not educating choirboys, but musical audiences on the broadest basis'.[136] Arthur Peppin at Clifton emphasised something similar a decade later.[137] This was a huge cultural shift from the centuries-old norm of conceptualising group musical education as children singing, and we must follow it through. On the other hand, Parker could still pursue this ideal only through voluntary class performance, mostly singing (though there was a school orchestra), and the administering of individual instrumental or vocal lessons, for there were no curricular slots and he and Trimnell will have been second-class citizens among the staff, through lacking a university education and a degree. Trimnell appears to have had to convert a portion of his own house into a series of practice rooms prior to the building of Clifton's Music School.[138] Nevertheless, it seems remarkable that in 1888 over one-third of the boys at Sherborne, namely 110 out of 300, were involved in music-making.[139] And Parker or someone else had wisely negotiated music's status in relation to sport: he pointed out that 'the captain of the games is always a member of the choir, *ex-officio* if he cannot sing'.[140] Music's role at Sherborne was special, as later acknowledged by Graham, who had published a series of articles on music in public schools for the *Tonic Sol-fa Reporter* and its successor the *Musical Herald*.[141] Clifton, however, similarly relied on the musicality of several of the schoolmasters for the good standing of the choral society. Those 'eight or nine' who were members of it subscribed to give the boys an annual outing.[142]

---

[134] Graham 1891: 370; Fox and Lidell 1962: 97–9.
[135] Graham 1891: 371; Edwards 1905: 240.
[136] Parker 1894: 98–100.
[137] Edwards 1905: 240.
[138] Graham 1891: 369.
[139] Graham 1888: 467.
[140] ibid: 468.
[141] Parker 1894: 110; see also Graham 1888, 1891, and 1894.
[142] Graham 1891: 370.

Class singing as sufficient unto the day died hard in Britain. But the traditional emphasis on group vocal performance did ensure that by the end of the nineteenth century, mass singing for children had been sufficiently productive of literate musicians from the state education system (the board schools) that the lower far outshone the upper classes, who continued to regard active music-making as, at best, a suitable pursuit for those who could not afford to hunt.[143] Slowly this regrettable social equation changed, instrumental prowess becoming more highly prized in the public schools alongside other shifts in the musical economy of the nation. Public schools had already developed their equivalent of the competitive music festival, inter-house glee-singing competitions.[144] These were then extended to instrumental solos, each house (a residential unit) putting forward three boys to play an instrumental piece each for a prize, to be judged and awarded by a well-known musician engaged for the occasion. Already an established tradition at Clifton by 1905, in 1924 Basil Harwood adjudicated the nine competing houses from which fifty-two pieces were heard, mostly for solo piano. Some of them were quite difficult; there was a great deal of Chopin.[145]

While it must not be forgotten that one-third of the Clifton boys were local ('town') in Trimnell's time, public schools have always taken their pupils from across the nation and sent them out even more widely.[146] The same is true of English universities. Nevertheless, the relationship of such an institution to the town or city in which it is located bears pondering in terms of the added musical value it contributes and the resources it can draw upon. There is no doubt that at the time of Britain's industrial supremacy, music in a small town was at a disadvantage. For concerts at Sherborne, Parker had to bring down his orchestral extras from London, local players being insufficiently reliable, while his instrumental teaching seems to have been done by a sole assistant, Charles Regan, who led the local orchestras and was employed at Sherborne School for 37 years, until 1911.[147] Clifton, by contrast, enjoyed the teaching expertise of a team of Bristol professionals of standing rounded up by Trimnell, which will have made for a more efficient and settled pedagogic equation which in its turn helped sustain local livings and a local musical identity. These men included Frederick Maker, William Fear Dyer, organist of St Nicholas's and a published composer, a member of the Vowles family,

---

[143] Parker 1894: 109–11; Graham 1894: 136.
[144] Graham 1891: 371; Parker 1894: 105.
[145] Edwards 1905: 238–9; Peppin 1927: 194–6.
[146] Graham 1891: 372.
[147] Graham 1888: 467; *MT* xix (1878): 230 and lii (1911): 127; Sherborne 1950: 529; DoHC S.235/A 8/2.

and two who would become stalwarts of the Bristol Music Club, the pianist Fred Rootham (nephew of Daniel) and violinist Frank Gardner.[148]

Not only that, but Clifton's first headmaster, John Percival, became a prominent advocate, perhaps the leading one, for the establishment of universities in the larger English cities, Bristol included. He was just as concerned with the lack of opportunities for women – with his wife he founded the Clifton Association for the Higher Education of Women in 1868 – as with the fact that 'the great majority of young men of the middle classes … are absolutely and entirely precluded by pecuniary and other imperative considerations from seeking the advantages of higher education … unless the means are brought home to them in the busy centres of commercial life'.[149] Others were equally worried that denizens of the largest commercial centres no longer saw any need for a university education.[150] Percival's proposal, published in 1873, was that the rich colleges of Oxford and Cambridge should convert some of their non-resident fellowships into provincial chairs.[151] Benjamin Jowett, the influential master of Balliol College, Oxford, supported this idea, and when the move to establish a college at Bristol was under way he made sure that it would include the arts as well as the sciences.[152]

Inevitably, music was not yet classed alongside 'literature', even though the meeting of 11 June 1874 to establish University College, Bristol, which opened in 1876, took place in the city's best established concert venue, the Victoria Rooms. But over the succeeding decades, Clifton, on the fringes of which the university buildings were placed (and whither in due course Bristol Grammar School would also relocate), developed what must have been for England a unique musical triangulation between school, club, and university college. While this was nothing like the matrix of student music-making that, for example, Johann Sebastian Bach's Leipzig had already supported two hundred years earlier, and the university college's work in the early years was little more than what we would now think of as evening classes (it became the chartered University of Bristol only in 1909), it is clear that a critical mass of professional musicians and adult musical amateurs who enjoyed professional status in some other field was achieved by the early twentieth century and sustained thereafter.[153]

---

[148] Graham 1891: 369; Brown and Stratton 1897: 133; Dobson 1995: 29–31.
[149] Cottle and Sherborne 1959: 7; Percival 1873: 15–16; Sadler 2004: 673.
[150] Percival 1873: 22.
[151] ibid: 16–18.
[152] Cottle and Sherborne 1959: 8.
[153] ibid: 8, 12–17.

John Dobson's history of the Bristol Music Club, founded in 1903 and perhaps uniquely in England occupying from the start its own premises, which are in Clifton and include a tiny recital hall (previously a dance studio), describes and often amusingly illustrates the leading figures, to whom one or two more may be added. Confident enough to land as the club's first president the great Austro-Hungarian violinist Joseph Joachim, who dined there with his peerless Berlin Quartet in 1906 after a concert at the Victoria Rooms, these musicians, conservative in cast and devoted to chamber music, were by and large of professional performance standard, though some were 'gentlemen' (or ladies) rather than 'players'. They included the succession of music masters at Clifton College, namely Peppin (1896–1915), Richard Beachcroft (1915–26), William McKie (1926–30), later organist of Westminster Abbey, and Douglas Fox (1931–57), a keyboard virtuoso brought up in Bristol and educated at Clifton College who lost his right arm in the First World War and triumphed nevertheless on the organ and piano, twice playing the Ravel left-hand concerto at the Colston Hall, once under Sir Malcolm Sargent. Roeckel attended the founding meeting but played no major part thereafter. Fred, Dan, and various other Roothams, probably all three of Mabel, Helen, and Cyril, were all chronically involved, as were C S 'Beaker' Lang, another Clifton College music teacher, and Hubert Hunt, who unusually for an organist (recently appointed to Bristol Cathedral) also played violin to a professional standard and did so for many years in the Clifton Quintet. Bristol's university musicians included two physicists, Silvanus Thompson in the early years of the university college and Arthur Tyndall, professor at the university from 1919 and later acting vice-chancellor, and Cedric Bucknall, a micologist and (very) minor published composer who was organist of All Saints, Clifton, and founded the university orchestra around 1908; presumably he was related to Roger Le Duc Bucknall, who taught cello at Clifton College.[154]

Clifton College in the earlier decades of the twentieth century was a source of musical employment; the university was not, and the circulation of financial capital for musical purposes in Bristol, with the exception of Clifton and a few other private schools, was until after the Second World War in the hands of committed amateurs who were commercially and/or professionally resourceful in non-musical spheres. Charles Budgett, first chair of the music club, was a wholesale grocer who later became mayor of the city, while its first treasurer, Bernard Beilby, was a banker. Philip Napier Miles,

---

[154] Dobson 1995: 3–37; Cottle and Sherborne 1959: 10, 15, 20, 43; Carleton 1984: 87; Banfield 2010: 360.

Bristol's most empowered musical achiever, was a serious and by no means conservative composer who inherited a fortune based on West Indian trade and the Avonmouth Docks and lived in Vanbrugh's Kingsweston House. J W Arrowsmith, an original club member, had suddenly become one of the leading non-metropolitan book publishers in the 1890s with an astonishing scoop of best-sellers, notably *Three Men in a Boat*, *Diary of a Nobody*, and *Prisoner of Zenda*.[155] This was Bristol money, mostly old money, at its most resourceful, supporting the club, festivals, choral societies, and much else, but it was not a professional musical infrastructure in the sense of producing the region's audiences, performers, scholars, and creators and sustaining them without reference to London. Manchester had in the nineteenth century achieved this with the Hallé Orchestra and what is now the Royal Northern College of Music. Bristol never did.

What eventually changed was the intellectual embedding of music in the university syllabus. Tyndall managed to sneak the provision of a chair of music into the very last item of his very last Senate agenda as acting vice-chancellor, which speaks volumes about the continuing philistinism of Britain's elite.[156] It was established, at about the same time as Bristol's Drama department which was the first in the country, under Tyndall's successor in 1946, W K Stanton taking up the position the following year. (His successors have been Willis Grant, Raymond Warren, Jim Samson, the present author, Katharine Ellis, and Sarah Hibberd.) Yet even then there was no single honours undergraduate degree programme, as indeed there still was not at almost all English universities.[157] Music degrees were traditionally postgraduate, non-residential, or additional awards, mostly for composers. The story of music's eventual acceptance and development as a residential first degree subject in England has never been told, though this is probably true also of many other disciplines. At Bristol, three students graduating with a general arts BA in 1951 included music as one of their three subjects, and this might form a prerequisite to a BMus gained through a further year of postgraduate study: a number of male and female students followed this path in the 1950s. The BA in Music appears to have been inaugurated in 1960, with its first students graduating in 1963.[158]

---

[155] Dobson 1995: 3–4, 7, 10–11; Turner 2004b.
[156] Carleton 1984: 91–2.
[157] ibid; Cottle and Sherborne 1959: 55, 68–71.
[158] Kenneth Mobbs, Raymond Warren, and Ian Coates, personal communications, 29 Nov 2015, 2 Dec 2015, and 13 Dec 2016.

Yet even from here on it is difficult if not impossible to prove what difference the presence of a university music department has made to the cultural economy of a city and its hinterland. Bristol's employs about ten academics (two or three composers, seven or eight musicologists) whose presence will have given rise to various concerts, some of them containing adventurous repertoire, the odd stage production (of which Kenneth Mobbs's with Bristol Opera [School] stand out), and periodic conferences drawing in national and international delegates, that would not have taken place otherwise.[159] Some undergraduates and postgraduates, most of them brought up elsewhere, will have stayed and enriched the region as part-time performers or as music teachers, some supplementing their income as lay clerks at either the Anglican or the Roman Catholic (Clifton) cathedral or at St Mary Redcliffe, a provision offered to students who are good singers and attracting them to the department in the first place. Yet probably an equal number will have migrated out, by leaving home for university and not coming back, unless Bristol's relative proximity to the nation's best surfing beaches is by now making a permanent net difference. Increasingly, master's and doctoral candidates have been mature students whose local or regional profile as musical amateurs or professionals is enhanced by their university study rather than transmuted into something else entirely, which would not be true of those taking up law, for example, where a new career that could be pursued locally would open up on graduation. But rarely will Bristol music graduates remain in the region as professional composers, who turn disproportionately to London for their place of domicile.

The history of Exeter's university and its music offers a pointed example of something slightly different: how difficult it has been to sustain any kind of regional equation in Britain at least where the south-west is concerned. In parallel with Bristol though much later, Exeter turned a university college into a chartered university and not only added a music department but then lost it again. At the time of the department's closure in 2004, appeal was made to the difference its loss would mean for the amount, standard, and degree of enterprise of musical culture not just in the city but in the entire region; and with Dartington College also slated for closure not long afterwards, the lament was that nowhere further west than Bristol would have university music.[160] But the impossibility of establishing an institutional learning economy genuinely functioning at the regional level had already

---

[159] Bristol Opera; *MT* xcvi (1955): 39, xcvii (1956): 93, xcviii (1957): 685–6, cii (1961): 366, and ciii (1962): 324.

[160] Banfield 2005: 3.

been shown when an inter-war initiative stalled. No less a figure than the aged Thomas Hardy had been called upon to support this idea: 'the efficiency of our centres of learning is of the greatest moment if we are to hold our place in the world', he wrote, sounding for all the world like a present-day vice-chancellor.[161] 'The aim', Crispin Gill explains, 'was to create a full regional university with colleges at Exeter, Plymouth and Redruth. Lord and Lady Astor tried to force the pace by creating a hall of residence at Devonport and brought Bernard Shaw down to open it in 1929. But it was to be over twenty years before UCSW became a full university, and then it was concentrated at Exeter.'[162] Exeter City Council can be congratulated on having instituted higher education in the city as early as 1865; incorporated as the University College of the South West of England (UCSW) in 1922, this offered sufficient provision that the young Thurston Dart could become an expert mathematician – not musicologist – prior to his Second World War RAF service in operational research, for which he was mentioned in dispatches.[163] It became the University of Exeter in 1955, and Reginald Moore resigned his cathedral organistship in 1957 in order to work more fully there as director of music. A department was established in 1965 with Moore as lecturer and acting head, though the university did not inaugurate a chair until 1968, when on Moore's death it appointed Arthur Hutchings.[164] Moore's replacement at the cathedral, Lionel Dakers, distinguished himself there for fourteen years before moving to Surrey as director of the Royal School of Church Music and gave Exeter what must have been another musical golden era to match its earlier ones, drawing in the university among many other constituents.[165] For large-scale works such as Verdi's Requiem, Dakers could call on the 600 combined voices of the Exeter Festival Chorus, which he founded in 1961, the Exeter Musical Society, and the University Choral Society, as well as contingents from St Luke's and Dartington colleges, accompanied by the Bournemouth Symphony Orchestra, which the largest amateur choruses could in those days afford to hire.[166] The BBC broadcast a number of Dakers's performances.[167] Did anything in Bristol match this level of opportunity and community integration for music students?

---

[161] Richardson 2013: 4.
[162] Gill 1979, ii: 192.
[163] St Leger-Gordon 1950: 355; *Times*, 31 Oct 1955: 10; Holt.
[164] Shaw 1991: 117; anon 1970: 33; Clapp 1982: 152.
[165] Matthews Exe: 29.
[166] Dakers 1995: 120.
[167] ibid: 135.

Dartington until 2008 stood for what was probably the most distinctive higher education environment in the country where the creative arts are concerned, and although many other universities have since copied its multidisciplinary approach, none has the environment and the visionary history to match. Dartington Hall is a beautiful mediaeval manor house set in an estate on a curve of the River Dart two miles upstream from one of England's best-preserved small towns. Totnes, conveniently a stop on the main railway line from Cornwall to London, is accessible from Exeter and Plymouth and sits within peerless countryside with Dartmoor on the one side and south Devon's maritime attractions on the other. Like Haydn in his seclusion at Eszterháza, these factors will have forced any creative arts student to be original. At the same time, Dartington surely represented the final stage, the *ne plus ultra*, of the west country's destiny as privileged playground or retreat for the incomer. It was not quite of this world.

Around the Hall, purchased by Dorothy and Leonard Elmhirst who then formed a trust, sprang up first, in the 1930s, Dartington School with its highly progressive curricular approach and some leading modern architecture, and then a variety of other educational initiatives, including many for adults and the internationally famous summer schools for music held at Dartington Hall since the 1950s. One can imagine how various elements of the postwar economy – labour and fuel shortages, high taxation – will have driven private schools to maximise their occupancy during vacations, just as similar factors had turned aristocratic mansions into schools in the first place. Bryanston, near Blandford Forum, was a prime example, and William Glock first rented it in 1947 for his Bryanston Summer School, which would set the bar high when it boasted Nadia Boulanger, Paul Hindemith, George Enescu, and Artur Schnabel among its teachers and lecturers.[168] Dartington, whither Glock's enterprise migrated in 1953, aimed even higher, and Igor Stravinsky was in residence in the summer of 1957, when he might have been spotted taking time off at Tintagel, Exeter, Glastonbury, Bath, and Wells.[169] Another private school with well-known musical summer courses was Canford, near Wimborne, its proximity to Bournemouth giving its young performers access to BSO players and conductors, notably George Hurst, whose inexplicable eastern European accent caused perennial amusement. Founded in 1952, it moved to Sherborne School in 2004.[170] A third was Cranborne Chase School, once again in the depths of the countryside and not far from Bryanston. It

---

[168] Goodwin 2001; Dartington 1949: 192; Norris 1981: 330.
[169] Norris 1981: 316, 318, 320, 336.
[170] SSSM.

was in Wardour Castle, and here, in 1964 and 1965, while he was teaching at the school, Harrison Birtwistle with Peter Maxwell Davies and Alexander Goehr created a miniature British version of Darmstadt's radical *Ferienkurse* for avant-garde composers and performers. Davies came to live nearby, and during one of the summer schools Tippett was visited in Corsham, Birtwistle playing croquet on his lawn while Davies perched on the garden wall like a pixie.[171] Davies moved to the opposite end of the country – to Hoy, on Orkney – in 1969, but Birtwistle has returned to the region: he now lives in Mere, having written the prehistoric sites and downland of the area into some of his most memorable music, notably *Silbury Air* (1977) and the opera *Yan Tan Tethera* (1984).[172]

Dartington's year-round musical profile commenced during the Second World War. In 1938 Imogen Holst had been appointed a 'traveller' (and she must have looked like one, wearing the 'sackcloth clothes woven by her mother') covering the west country for CEMA, the Council for the Encouragement of Music and the Arts.[173] This was gruelling assessment work, and the Elmhirsts cushioned it by inviting her to live at Dartington Hall. She took up residence in 1942, and over time the CEMA position gave way to her appointment as director of music in what eventually became the College of Arts, founded as such in 1961 some years after her departure.[174] It is not entirely clear when adult education work such as her father's at Morley College in London began to turn into full-time student residencies and degrees, and how both then co-existed, though the same could be said of the metamorphosis of university colleges into chartered universities; but Holst's approach – creativity for all – will have permeated the transition.[175] In some respects she was curiously ahead of her time, taking a sabbatical early in 1951 to go to India to study its music, and presaging the 1970s educational revolution of John Paynter for composition in the classroom, based on the avant-garde idea of taking music right back to the raw materials of sound in whatever form. In others, her ideas were quaintly out of date, almost a caricature of the Arts and Crafts ideal that had never worked anyway, at least in socio-economic terms. She recognised this, and yearned increasingly for a professional environment. This she achieved in 1952, a year after her resignation, when Benjamin Britten appointed her his personal assistant.[176] But Dartington was in any case many worlds, and one cannot

[171] WCSS.
[172] Banfield 2009: 46, 50–1.
[173] Tinker 2009: 141.
[174] Tinker 2013: 6.
[175] Dartington 1982: 30.
[176] ibid.

Illus. 7.3 Concert by Imrat Khan and Latif Ahmed Khan in the Great Hall, Dartington, 1970

imagine her having played any role in Glock's summer schools there, though it is important to realise that she was on the staff of his Bryanston one in

1948.[177] Still, her influence lived on, and if there was any kind of a connection between the theosophical framework that had dominated attraction to the East in her father's period and the hippy culture of Dartington College's most flourishing years, around 1970, she embodied it. It will all have come together with Imrat Khan playing the sitar cross-legged in the Great Hall (Illus. 7.3) – Khan taught at Dartington from 1968 to 1970.

Dartington, above all the college, produced and achieved many things: a professional string quartet, professional training courses for county music staff, a couple of well-known saxophone players (Dick Heckstall-Smith at the school, Mornington Lockett at the college), an Institute of Traditional Arts which included documentary resources for Devon fiddling, a major Birtwistle commission (*The Fields of Sorrow*, 1971), the glassware company now relocated to Great Torrington, a rural educational outlier in the north Devon Beaford Centre, a travelling theatre company, the Roger Yates organ of 1969 (see chapter 2), and a Utopian ideal all too rarely followed through in the arts in Britain.[178] But by 1982 its establishment of 350 college students across three departments was reeling from the unprecedented, historic round of government cutbacks to university funding, and the tone of its publication of that year was becoming necessarily defensive. Recognising that Dartington's history 'has been as full of contradictions and failures as it has been of successes', and talking in terms of 'survival', it was keen to forestall criticisms of the enterprise having become 'a mausoleum to bygone ideals'. As for the school, one picture caption runs 'Individual bedroom at Aller Park School: guitar lesson, with David Gribble, headmaster' – the headmaster is a guitarist, the small boy has his own bedroom, the headmaster is in the bedroom (the boy on the bed), the floor is polished wooden planks. Again, self-criticism follows: 'the School remains keyed into the needs created by examinations and the value which society ascribes to them. Plans are being put into operation for a new programme of studies.'[179] But Dartington Hall School closed in 1987.

Our utilitarian age has seen the closure of Dartington's tertiary education campus in 2010, the College's identity having been merged in 2008 with that of University College Falmouth. The transformed institution became Falmouth University in 2012, which is one of various bodies, including the University of Exeter, sharing the CUC (Combined Universities in Cornwall)

---

[177] Grogan 2010: 155.
[178] PSAC; Fairweather 2002; Gilbert 2002; Dartington 1972 [np]; Dartington 1982: 25; BL Cat.
[179] Dartington 1982: 6–7.

campus at Penryn. So once again the idea of a federal, regional college system in the south-west has emerged. Let us see whether it really takes root this time. As for Falmouth, which already had a College of Art of its own, its robust and unique mixture of bohemian refuge, eccentric seaside resort, classic Cornish fishing town, and industrial shipyard ought to augur well for twenty-first-century creativity. As the song by Martin Shaw and W E Henley proclaims, its sheet music duly framed in de Wynn's coffee shop, 'Falmouth is a fine town'.

Totnes is a fine town too, and its aura of artisanal production and ecological living together with a lively performance calendar – at least in 2010 it was lively – will render the Dartington legacy palpable well into the future. One of the most obvious musical concomitants to the Dartington and Totnes mindset being the early music movement, it is both unsurprising that the professional orchestra Devon Baroque, founded in 2000 as the result of a workshop led by Margaret Faultless, now one of the world's leading 'period' violinists, should be based in the area, and gratifying that it has managed to survive playing only in Devon venues, bar the odd excursion into Somerset.[180] Composers, however, have not been permanently attracted to Devon, Dartington or other inducements notwithstanding. A statistical analysis of 186 composers with known addresses domiciled in England in 1972 revealed only eight of them living in the West Country – about 4 per cent, not the geographically proportional 10 or 12 per cent that might have been expected.[181] They still end up in and around London. Bruce Montgomery, composer of the earlier *Carry On* films and, as Edmund Crispin, author of a successful series of detective novels, was something of an exception. He lived first with his parents in Brixham and later in Week, near Dartington.[182]

But the essential measure of regional limitation, of what has prevented the west country from generating a truly distinctive musical story, is the fact that it has never produced a stable, nationally recognised conservatoire. Bournemouth, with its permanently established, professional symphony orchestra, might have been a more obvious place for it than Bristol, and both Bournemouth and Plymouth have reinvented themselves as university towns in the wake of their decline. Bournemouth University has no music department, however. (Plymouth University has a modest one.)

Small-scale enterprises came and went, as was not untypical of any larger town in the nineteenth century, including London. Most of these ventures

---

[180] DBPC.
[181] Jacobs 1972: 445–51 (A–H sampled).
[182] Whittle 2007.

will have consisted of a few freelance teachers giving their standard round of lessons, no doubt mostly on the piano, in rooms in the proprietor's dwelling or in rented premises. The Bristol guitar teacher Stephen Pratten lived in Park Street in the 1830s and designated his home a music academy.[183] A Mr F Norton Erith was running an Academy of Music in Taunton in 1843.[184] In the earlier 1840s Alfred Angel, organist of Exeter Cathedral, opened by subscription an Exeter School of Church Music; perhaps this was an early initiative aimed at consolidating what had been his controversial appointment as successor to Sebastian Wesley. The school's aim was to train up the clergy and some lay singing adults for the better performance of church music: Angel wanted 'to cultivate the taste for good sacred music, and to improve the character of congregational psalmody', clearly an anti-'west gallery' measure. By 1850 called the Exeter Church Choral Training School, it survived until at least 1868, and perhaps had some connection with the teacher training and theological seminary initiatives of the same period based at St Luke's college in Heavitree.[185] In 1914, when Boughton was living in Glastonbury, he started a year-round Festival School, but it did not take root.[186] Plymouth in the 1920s and '30s had its Bedford Park Music and Dancing Academy, its College of Music, and its Stoke School of Music in Devonport, none of them remotely approaching a seedbed for selective professional training.[187]

Bristol and Bournemouth came closest to developing a proper conservatoire. In the 1851 census Bristol had a population of about a hundred Germans, including eleven professional musicians, probably bandsmen.[188] One of them was the Bertram von der Mark already mentioned in chapter 3, who identified himself as director of the Bristol Conservatoire of Music. Here for once was a promising institution, founded in Portland Square in 1849, with at least marginal potential for training professionals, for Mark's 'Juvenile Band', featured in mid-performance on the cover of 'The Bristol Conservatoire polka', consisted of boys and male adolescents. Clearly it took a foreigner to aim beyond a female domestic clientele, and in 1857, when his band visited York, Mark's conservatoire was previewed as 'an entirely

---

[183] Britton 2010: 245, 349.
[184] *SCH*, 7 Oct 1843: 1.
[185] *WT*, 11 Jun 1842: 4; *EFP*, 7 Nov 1844: 7, 7 Aug 1845: 2, 21 Jan 1847: 3, 13 Jan 1848: 3, 22 Aug 1850: 8, and 29 Jul 1868: 3, all indexed EFPSCI; *The Parish Choir*, ii/22 (Oct 1847): 8; Little 1983: 70; Cherry and Pevsner 1989: 407.
[186] Benham 2006: 176.
[187] Lawer 2007: 154; Plym 1937: 5, 30; Plym 1932: 20.
[188] Dresser and Fleming 2007: 107.

new system of musical education ... the first musical conservatoire for the people in this country', a reminder that the Royal Academy of Music had in its earlier years been criticised for catering largely for the well-to-do, not for those who would need a livelihood. No doubt the puff was written by Mark himself, but it allows us to see what he was aiming at: an establishment of forty boys aged five to sixteen, apparently recruited well beyond the locality given that they were 'English, Scotch, and Irish', each one resident for three years, after which they were 'either apprenticed to a trade, or if they show a decided taste for music, educated as professors', though whether 'professors' was meant to include professional players is not clear.[189] It sounds as though Mark's establishment doubled as an orphanage or foundling school, which will have done nothing to promote music's suitability as a pursuit for the male gentry. Nevertheless, he must have invested hard in his venture, for a sizable number of his polkas and galops feature lavish cover illustrations of Bristol scenes and mottos, which cannot have been cheap to produce.[190] A modern youth orchestra being an unprecedented novelty in Britain, no doubt it aroused profitable audience curiosity on tour. But we hear no more of Mark's activities after 1857, and a stray reference to a young female singer studying at the Bristol Conservatoire more than fifty years later suggests either that it was a different institution with the same name or that the conservatoire's clientele had in due course reverted to British type.[191]

Bournemouth's attempts at a conservatoire came once the Municipal Orchestra had proved its eminence and value. The first pupils' concert of the Bournemouth School of Music was given in March 1914; the Bournemouth Conservatoire of Music was in existence in December 1926; and the Bournemouth Academy of Music promoted a pupils' concert in October 1950.[192] These may all have been the same institution, refounded or renamed for financial or other reasons. They were probably not of any professional consequence, for Dartington's 1949 report on the state of the arts in postwar Britain, out of which Bournemouth, in contrast to nearly everywhere else in the region, in general comes very well, specifically urged that local training schools were needed for players in towns where there was a professional orchestra: only Birmingham and Manchester had them.[193] But they never happened in Bournemouth or anywhere else in the west country, and the

---

[189] *Yorkshire Gazette*, 6 Jun 1857: 9.
[190] BL h.904, especially (2) and (10).
[191] *Gloucester Citizen*, 1 Jun 1910: 5.
[192] Watkins 1914: 56; *Monthly Pictorial*, BLMA; ADA.
[193] Dartington 1949: 32.

eventual siting of one of England's four specialist music schools for children in Wells had no follow-through effect on the region in terms of professional training. (The BBC based its Training Orchestra, later the Academy of the BBC, in Bristol, but it survived for only twelve years and was gone by 1977, not many years after Wells Cathedral School gained its specialist status.)[194] London's perennial pre-eminence had produced a 'National' Training School (1873) in the wake of the Great Exhibition and its follow-up South Kensington project, and when that failed, the soubriquet 'Royal' was what distinguished and guaranteed the brand of its successor, the RCM. Conservatoires in Cardiff, Glasgow, and Manchester eventually became royal too. No west country institution encompassing musical education has ever been able to boast that prefix, for the divisions of the Royal Marines Band that have served the naval establishments at Plymouth, Lympstone, and, until 2008, Dartmouth have been trained elsewhere.[195]

❧ Concert Life, Theatre Life, and Audiences

If conceptualised as a series of venues in which music has been heard as entertainment, as an incidental part of entertainment (which would include theatrical performances and social dancing), or as spiritual uplift, even quite small places in the west country have left evidence of spaces for music at least from early modern times, and sometimes earlier. Cornish playing places have already been mentioned. Acoustic jars set into an internal church wall, as found in Luppitt and Tarrant Rushton perhaps as early as the Norman period, were an architectural feature almost certainly introduced in order to assist musical intonation as well as preaching and the spoken liturgy.[196] Itinerant theatrical troupes will normally have included a minstrel or waits, and several towns had or still have a church house, built and maintained by the parish, which they were lent or rented. This was probably what visiting players paid 12d for in Morebath at Easter 1533; that same hamlet had a local harper, John Timewell, member of the village's most prominent family, who was paid to play at the annual church ale, the sum being eight groats on one occasion.[197] One imagines he would have positioned himself in the churchyard, retreating to the church house only in case of rain. Sherborne's church house, rented out normally for 4s, was built in 1534–35 and still

---

[194] BBCW; Langley and Small 1990: 74.
[195] Wikipedia: 'Royal Marines Band Service'.
[196] Benfield 1950: opposite 192; Newman and Pevsner 1972: 420; Lewcock 2001.
[197] Duffy 2001: 6, 210; Wasson 1986: 211.

survives, a long room above shops measuring 116ft by 19.[198] Wimborne's, converted from a church in the 1540s, has gone. Blandford rented out its guildhall between 1587 and 1621.[199] Church houses in other towns and villages will have hosted players without surviving record, because they were not charged.

Following England's long battle for and against public entertainment in the seventeenth century, concert life as we know it in western cultural history originated in London in the second decade of the Restoration, namely the 1670s, though the idea of 'lovers of musick', as the phrase began to be widely used, getting together to hear or perform it took root in Oxford somewhat before this. As Elizabeth Chevill has pointed out, the clergy across England had been trained largely at the universities of Oxford and Cambridge, so it was hardly surprising that they might attempt to reconstruct the elements of musical sociability in some out-of-the-way place to which their subsequent career had been assigned.[200] Lawyers from the Inns of Court presumably stimulated county and Assize towns similarly while temporarily resident in them during circuit duties, if they had taken part in concert gatherings in London.

The society active in Salisbury in 1700 and already referred to in chapter 3 appears to represent the earliest known usage of the locution 'lovers of musick' in the west country; Claver Morris from Wells, who had journeyed to Salisbury to participate in the music-making on that occasion, was himself using the phrase nine years later, both instances being in conjunction with St Cecilia's Day celebrations.[201] The idea of free association of like-minded gentlemen on some kind of institutional basis was the new element, one that would see clubs, societies, and charitable activities mushroom throughout the eighteenth and nineteenth centuries. Some early west country music clubs were mentioned in chapter 3, and they are best thought of as one of four manifestations of music as sociable entertainment or civic participation in Enlightenment England, the other three being concerts or festivals arranged on some other basis, balls, and theatrical performances. The identities of these four phenomena overlapped a good deal: a concert often *segued* into a ball, with which a two-day festival might end, and music clubs gave concerts or, in the case of madrigal societies, performed repertoire that might as it were be *over*heard by others (on Ladies' Nights). By the mid-eighteenth century, one

---

[198] Hays and McGee 1999: 40; Newman and Pevsner 1972: 382.
[199] Hays and McGee 1999: 40–1.
[200] Chevill 1993: 148–9.
[201] ibid: 10, 135, 215.

might pick up the local newspaper to see when the next attraction of one of these kinds would arise, mostly during the winter months when the gentry were not in London or on the grouse moors, though music societies can be difficult to trace because their meetings were not necessarily advertised.

What drove people to invest in concert activity was *taste*, and although the Restoration Court and the Restoration's major composer, Henry Purcell, took their cue primarily from French manners and styles, it was a taste for Italian music, exemplified above all in music for the violin and for the operatic solo voice, that soon won out, fruit of that country's perennial genius for exporting its cultural products and people. Corelli's sonatas and concertos, and then the compositions of Handel (German but master of the Italian style), who was resident in London from 1710 and pioneered Italian opera in the capital, led the field in terms of repertoire, immigrant or visiting Italian virtuosi and teachers for the best part of two centuries in terms of personnel, climaxing where the west country was concerned when Rauzzini retired to Bath. Already in the first quarter of the eighteenth century most of Claver Morris's musical library was Italian.[202] And it was mostly, though not exclusively, Italian string virtuosi whom the Herbert family patronised at Wilton House in the 1770s and early 1780s, this period something of a late 'golden age for the participation of the high aristocracy in chamber music'.[203]

Church music remained something of an exception to the Italianate imperative, and Purcell's Te Deum was habitually performed in earlier festival services, though later ones went for one or more of Handel's.[204] Nor did the operatic idiom of oratorios immediately permeate ecclesiastical buildings, for festival oratorio performances generally took place in town halls or assembly rooms, an early exception being the 1758 performance of Handel's *Messiah* in Bristol Cathedral, apparently its only performance in a church during the composer's lifetime.[205] (Salisbury heard *Messiah* in the cathedral from 1768, *Samson* and other oratorios being allowed in after 1772.[206]) Furthermore, the musical sounds of a social dance at a ball, of a song or a stage dance in the theatre, or one of the provincial pleasure gardens aping London's Vauxhall and Ranelagh, and of a drinking song, catch, or glee in a tavern gathering, were decidedly English, drawing for a large part upon repertoires such as the country dance tune collections published by John Playford and the sociable

---

[202] Johnstone 2008: 121–7.
[203] Holman 2012.
[204] Chevill 1993: 149; Reid and Pritchard 1965: 52ff.
[205] Barry 2010b: 151.
[206] Reid and Pritchard 1965: 52ff.

and theatre songs of playwright Thomas Durfey (who was probably born in Exeter).

By the end of the eighteenth century, this mixed equation of taste and activity amounted to a sturdy cultural machine for the middling and upper ranks. Nowhere was it as comprehensive and as well regulated as in Bath, Beau Nash's ideas about order and authority no doubt having helped bring about the achievement of a weekly evening calendar whereby there were plays (always with music) at the Theatre Royal on Tuesdays, Thursdays, and Saturdays, a dress ball at the New (Upper) Assembly Rooms (the building still in existence) on Mondays and a cotillon ball there on Thursdays, complemented at the Lower Assembly Rooms by a cotillon ball on Tuesdays and a dress ball on Fridays, with a subscription concert at the New Assembly Rooms on Wednesdays and the Catch Club at the White Hart tavern on Fridays. Thus there were never more than two events per evening, while the Abbey hosted occasional charity concerts and the Pump Room had its orchestra which played daily.[207]

The Bath formula is borne out, more or less, by sampling a newspaper. The issue of the *Bath Chronicle* for Thursday 11 March 1790 has the New Musical Society meeting at the White Lion (not Hart) 'on Friday evening', 'Catches and Glees to begin at Seven o'Clock', with a Ladies' Night promised for the 26th. The New Assembly Rooms Wednesday concert announced for 17 March is a benefit for Mr Brooks (James Brooks, 1760–1809, a violinist who led the Bath theatre orchestra and composed and arranged much music for it),[208] with Charles Incledon and two youngsters singing and Brooks playing, tickets costing 5s, not far off half a week's wages for a poor artisan but a drop in the ocean for a person of means, for whom four such outlays per week might still only amount to one-tenth of their weekly income. The music is by Haydn, Handel, Bertoni, Kozeluch, Pleyel, Rauzzini, Sarti, and Brooks, a broader Continental mixture than would have been the case earlier in the century but with nothing much from the English tradition. Saturday's Theatre Royal bill (it is the Orchard Street theatre) is highly musical, and this was completely typical of the Georgian period. A benefit for Mr Durravan junior, one of the actors, it begins with the comic opera *Lionel and Clarissa* (its music composed and assembled by Dibdin) and ends with James Townley's farce *High Life Below Stairs*, with star turns by Mr Ward (probably comic) between the two, by Incledon, singing 'The lass of Richmond Hill' between the acts of the farce, and by Mrs Didier, performing a 'mock minuet' with Ward in

---

[207] Clarke 2011: 10, citing Gillaspie 1986: xxv.
[208] James 2001.

its second act. Tuesday's theatre bill (15 March), mounted as a benefit by the New Musical Society, is not dissimilar (again Incledon is singing), though the first piece is a spoken comedy. The Bath balls are not being advertised, presumably because subscriptions have been purchased earlier in the season and maximising attendance numbers is less crucial than for a benefit concert. But a subscription ball in Warminster Town Hall on 25 March is announced; whether this deliberately borrows one of Bath's ball nights (Thursday) would be impossible to say. Spring Gardens are opening for Monday and Thursday breakfasts from 15 March, 'attended with Horns Clarionets, &c', and with Holy Week coming up at the end of March and start of April, Rauzzini is mounting a selection of items from Handel oratorios in the Abbey on Easter Saturday preceded by 'A Grand Miscellaneous Concert of Modern and Antient Musick' (roughly what we would call classical and baroque) at the New Assembly Rooms on the Tuesday, again costing 5s per concert.[209]

Bristol never quite managed to replicate this thoroughgoing cultural machine, though its own Theatre Royal (the Bristol Old Vic), operated at some periods under joint management with Bath's, has had its proud moments. Musically, the proudest was when Julian Slade's musical *Salad Days*, composed largely in the prop room in 1954, achieved the impossible dream, that goal to which all musical thespians in the provinces perennially aspire, and not only took the West End by storm but enriched the Bristol Old Vic and its theatre school by £40,000, a huge sum at the time.[210]

Other towns clutched at whatever isolated fragments of the formula they could grasp. We might take Barnstaple as an example. It was a regional centre and port of some importance in the mediaeval and early modern periods, and such places sometimes continued to punch above their weight following later decline or marginalisation, the latter due in Barnstaple's case to its comparatively increasing isolation in terms of road and then railway links, and to its not being a deep water port. Considering that its population was less than 4,000 in the early nineteenth century, it seems to have been doing well at the end of the Georgian period. *Pigot's Directory* for 1830 claimed that in addition to its three music teachers mentioned in chapter 4, it boasted 'indeed of some marks of a metropolis, having a theatre, ladies' ball every Thursday, gentlemen's every Friday night; a musical society once a fortnight, and a subscription news room'.[211] In addition to its long-serving parish church organist Christopher Huxtable (one of the three teachers), there

---

[209] *BC*, 11 Mar 1790: 1, 3–4.
[210] Norris 1981: 311; Barker 1974: 218.
[211] Pigot 1830: 47.

must have been a handful of active professional musicians making at least a partial living from these regular activities, plus a certain amount of concert repertoire old and new circulating thanks to the club. A successor to the subscription news room eventually appeared in the form of the North Devon Athenaeum, still in existence, but not until 1888.[212] Earlier 'urban renaissance' records are meagre, however. While Barnstaple was proud of having been the birthplace of John Gay in 1685, little to mirror the pre-Civil War era of travelling theatre companies, when visits to Barnstaple were plentiful, can be traced by way of professional entertainment after the Restoration. Gay spoke 'of singing at inns, from 1710 to 1720', and there is little else to go on.[213] Yet in 1760 a theatre in Honey Pot Lane was inaugurated.[214] This was six years ahead of Bristol's Theatre Royal, and since then Barnstaple appears always to have had a theatre, so there must have been some level of demand, enterprise, and infrastructure in the second half of the eighteenth century and it must have made a permanent difference. There was a professional violinist, John Collard, living in the town in 1794, perhaps the theatre's leader and arranger, and from around the same year the North Devon Militia was stationed there, its drum major a Mr Bridgman, though he will not have been directing harmonic wind musicians (if there were any).[215] The 29th (Worcestershire) Foot Regiment's black drummers must have made a stir when stationed in Barnstaple in 1797–98.[216]

The opening of a new Barnstaple venue, the Subscription Cassino [sic] Rooms, was reported in the *Exeter Flying Post* in 1801, but the nature of the 'evening's amusement' that gratified 'the most respectable families in the North of Devon' on that occasion was not specified.[217] It was another twenty years before the same paper had anything else of musical relevance to report from what it called 'the petite but elegant town'. This was a concert at an unnamed venue organised by John Day – not one of *Pigot's* 1830 teachers – who was clearly a versatile general practitioner of the sort one still had to be, for he played a Kalkbrenner piano concerto as well as singing bass in glees. The glees were performed by himself, three male associates, and a young female singer, Miss Syle (a local surname), who was already beginning 'a professional career of considerable promise', which in this town of some theatrical tradition was perhaps not looked down upon as much as it might

[212] Edwards 1917: 4–5; NDA.
[213] Edwards 1917: 7.
[214] Wikipedia: 'Queen's Theatre, Barnstaple'; Crane 1980: 47.
[215] Doane 1794: 14; Edwards 1917: 7.
[216] MacKeith 2003: 31–2.
[217] *EFP*, 1 Oct 1801: 4.

have been by (again) 'all the families of respectability and fashion in the town and vicinity' who were present. She must surely have been an actress, perhaps starting locally, and one can imagine Day, playing virtuoso music by the still up-and-coming Kalkbrenner, as her manager and musical mentor, just like Bows and his young Irish protégée in Thackeray's *Pendennis*. But apart from her status and possibly Day's, this was a celebration of amateur talents in the traditional sense of gentlemen of leisure who could afford to excel at music, and in this case two of the other glee singers were equally versatile, for one played the harp and another, together with Day himself, accompanied it on a pair of horns in a sonata by Petrides, a truly obscure item. One of the men performing was a colonel, another a clergyman.[218] One can have no idea of what the standard of performance may have been like, for almost certainly the review will have been supplied by Day himself.

Barnstaple acquired its own newspaper, the *North Devon Journal*, in 1824, and from then on it becomes easier to trace what was going on. Not coincidentally, this expansion of journalism was contemporaneous with the onset of a period of great social change, reflected in the very invention of mass music in the form of mass participation for performers and mass listening for audiences in a new range of paid-for entertainment: so there was more going on anyway. The former took shape in amateur bands and choirs, already treated in chapter 3 and further investigated below. The latter continued to include the theatre, which had always had its 'groundlings', later the denizens of the pit and the gallery, and also encompassed pleasure gardens, circuses, and music in zoos, but added to them the new commercial concept of the music hall, which eventually became 'variety' (vaudeville in North America).[219] Yet what all too soon would be separated off by the cultural pundits as proletarian vulgarity was not the only new entertainment in sound to arise through mass marketing. Something beginning to be called simply the public now flocked (or was expected to) to hear a new phenomenon, the touring virtuoso. Paganini and Liszt were the epitome of this, and Liszt toured the west country, though he never got to Barnstaple.

Liszt's summer visit in 1840, only three years into Queen Victoria's reign and part of a much longer tour of Britain and Ireland, preceded the region's railway network and was made by coach, though he was able to reach his final venue, Bristol, by train from Bath, since Brunel's line had opened two

---

[218] *EFP*, 29 Nov 1821: 4.
[219] Nourse 2012: 37–98.

days earlier on 31 August 1840.[220] This aside, we have perhaps underestimated the changes in Britain's infrastructure that had already occurred to make a tour such as Liszt's possible, above all the nation's network of turnpike roads created by mustering a vast malleable workforce, a professional surveyor class empowered to organise it, and a tradition of sound investment. The turnpikes' legacy can still be grasped topographically, for example between Bodmin and Wadebridge on either side of Dunmere Bridge, as can the speed and reliability of the mails they carried in addition to the passengers, responsible as they must have been for the machinery of concert organisation from this period that has now disappeared entirely from view, though we know that Liszt's impresario on this occasion was Louis Lavenu. But one marvels nonetheless at Liszt's schedule, young though he was (not quite twenty-nine). He entered the region via Salisbury and left it via Bristol, booked to give seventeen concerts in fifteen days, though his Torquay appearance had to be cancelled through illness, perhaps contracted in Teignmouth. There were four days on which he gave two concerts in different towns. On Thursday 20 August he gave a concert at Blandford's Assembly Rooms and another at those of Salisbury, and also managed to visit Stonehenge. The following day he was in Weymouth and the day after that in Lyme Regis and Sidmouth, where he performed at the London Hotel. On Sunday 23 August he rested, the following day taking in concerts at Ewen's Beacon Hotel in Exmouth and the Assembly Rooms in Teignmouth, presumably crossing the Exe estuary by boat between them. Torquay missed on the 25th, he was playing in Plymouth on the 26th, and had an unexpected free day on the 27th when a planned second concert was cancelled because only seven people had bought tickets. (Shame on Plymouth this may be, while perhaps confirming the nature of the travelling virtuoso's appeal in Britain and the tour's financial basis, unsatisfactory as it turned out: see and hear him once.) At the Royal Clarence Hotel in Exeter he then gave two concerts, on Friday evening 28 August and the following 'morning' (2pm). This is probably where he met Sebastian Wesley, who persuaded him to subscribe to the publication of his anthems, planned to appear imminently.[221] He seems to have remained in Exeter the night of the 29th as well, moving on to Taunton on the 30th for a concert the following day. From there he went to Bath, no doubt the climax of this leg of the tour, where he played at the Theatre Royal on Tuesday 1 and Wednesday 2 September, the latter a daytime engagement, for he was in Bristol by the evening, playing at the Royal Gloucester Hotel Assembly Rooms in Hotwells.

[220] GWR.
[221] Banfield and Temperley 2010: 216.

Up the hill at Ivatt's Hotel in Clifton he gave another concert on the evening of the 3rd.[222] Note that these were not yet piano recitals, though Liszt himself had invented that term in London earlier in the year, but 'miscellaneous' concerts, with Liszt as the main attraction backed up by operatic singers, a flautist, and John Orlando Parry as accompanist, all travelling with him.[223]

Experiencing a legend once may have been at the root of profit, but the public did not turn out – or fail to do so – only for Liszt: his slightly younger rival Sigismond Thalberg had toured the west country the previous year, penetrating further, to Ilminster, Chard, Bridgwater, Tiverton, and Truro, among other places.[224] He had recently performed at Court in Windsor, which interested the regional newspapers just as much as his appearance in their own midst. And he did visit Barnstaple, playing at the Assembly Rooms at 1pm on Saturday 30 November 1839.[225]

Advertisements for Thalberg's concerts were still wooing the 'nobility and gentry' on whose patronage the cathedral cities' festivals and events in county towns had always relied.[226] Indeed, at 6s a concert, or a whole guinea for a family ticket admitting four, which were the prices at Bridgwater and Barnstaple, who else could afford to attend?[227] By the time the showman conductor Louis Jullien visited Barnstaple and Bideford in 1850 with the *'elite'* of his band (fourteen players, comprising single strings, wind, and a drummer), the targeted clientele had increased to 'the Nobility, Gentry, and Inhabitants of Barnstaple', and prices had dropped to 3s 6d for a box, 2s for a seat in the pit, and, in the gallery, 1s for what was indeed beginning to be known as 'the shilling public', a phrase immortalised the following year when the Great Exhibition opened its doors to the unwashed at that price.[228] Jullien democratised what by then were the musical classics while creating the promenade concert and the cult of the conductor. The *North Devon Journal* critic – for concerts were at last being genuinely reviewed in retrospect as well as announced in advance – recognised this, asserting that 'no man has ever laboured so energetically or successfully as Mons Jullien to popularise the taste for music among the masses; and his visit to the North of Devon

---

[222] Norris 1981: 309, 322, 324, 329, 331–2, 338, 340; *EFP*, 13 Aug 1840: 2 and 20 Aug 1840: 1; *BM*, 22 Aug 1840: 5 and 29 Aug 1840: 8.
[223] Walker 2001: 762, 764.
[224] *SM*, 18 Nov 1839: 3; *DCC*, 21 Nov 1839: 4; *EFP*, 28 Nov 1839: 2; *RCG*, 22 Nov 1839: 3.
[225] *NDJ*, 28 Nov 1839: 1.
[226] *EPG*, 23 Nov 1839: 2.
[227] *NDJ*, 28 Nov 1839: 1; *DCC*, 21 Nov 1839: 4.
[228] *NDJ*, 28 Feb 1850: 4 and 4 Apr 1850: 5; *Daily News*, 27 May 1851: 4.

must have convinced him that his efforts have not been unappreciated'.[229] This was a pointed assertion: 'the masses' were now a fact of life, and it took 'labour' and 'efforts' to educate 'taste' on this broader front. Culture was work; 'successful' production.

Expectations, and a supposed dynamic, that have never quite left it thereby accrued to the urban audience for music. With the decline of agriculture and the growth of industry as well as the nation's overall population (not forgetting a good deal of immigration from Ireland), English towns, with certain exceptions such as Ottery St Mary, grew in size at unprecedented rates in the nineteenth century and into the twentieth. Infant mortality gradually declined, and it is generally believed that standards of living gradually rose, with the effect that by the 1930s almost anybody could be expected to find the money to go to the cinema two or three times a week. (The question of whether, a hundred or more years earlier, the relatively poor had any equivalent of this expenditure on entertainment – their evenings were just as long – with their pubs, pleasure gardens, circuses, and indeed the theatre gallery, is too difficult to answer here, though Nicholas Nourse's work makes us more aware of it.)[230]

On the one hand, provision of ever larger and smarter venues and the development of advertising, communications media, and long-distance transport industrialised entertainment into an efficient and relatively risk-free business. Gone were the endemic bankruptcies of artisanal musicians and traders when they turned concert impresario or dealer, replaced as these people were by companies and syndicates that built theatres and ran music halls across the country, some of the regional gentry no doubt investing in them as shareholders at the same time as going to see and hear their productions with their constant supply of travelling stars. Popular entertainment paid its way, so long as the public was given what it wanted, which was partly, though only partly, what it had been made to want by commercial enterprise. On the other hand, the Victorian culture of respectability, while by no means confined to urban living, produced an alliance of paternalistic interests – clergy, newspaper editors, mutual benefit associations, educators, town councils – concerned about what the public ought to want, which in aural terms was 'good' music. Good music was never fully defined, except perhaps in terms of cost to the consumer. The nobility and gentry had been able to afford their lessons and their festivals, and it was important to commit the expenditure,

---

[229] *NDJ*, 4 Apr 1850: 5.
[230] Nourse 2012: passim.

because it indicated very clearly what people and families were worth. Their successors, the 'inhabitants', would never be able to afford a symphony orchestra, let alone opera, in their town. It had to be subsidised. Up to a modest point, it was, and this chapter will conclude with observations on the twin poles of corporate provision that over various decades of the twentieth century lent the region now a hopeful identity, now a hopeless cultural balance sheet: broadcasting and professional orchestras.

ಜಿ *A Bristol Studio, a Bournemouth Orchestra, and the Variety Principle*

Listening to a day's radio offerings used to be rather like hearing a symphony with modular alternatives for second subjects, trio, coda, etc, or perhaps more like the performance options in Harrison Birtwistle's *Verses for Ensembles*. One could imagine the national news or weather as opening fanfares, after which you tuned to whatever suited you best, from the BBC or abroad, using the frequency bands and stations that appear on old radio sets. (It is important to realise that until the Second World War, when Nazi occupation closed them down, International Broadcasting Company relays from overseas stations in American-style commercial format attracted 80 per cent of British listening away from the BBC, a fact which any argument about the BBC as inescapable force for cultural cohesion has to acknowledge.[231]) The BBC itself offered choice, with regional stations such as Bournemouth's (6BM) on individual wavelengths; these stations had been set up in the 1920s as unnetworked local relays but were soon incorporated into the national matrix.[232] Once the matrix had been established, radio's symphony was modular not just between stations but within each one – or rather, switching stations was built into any one station's programming.

It sounds and was complex, and is best explained by giving an example. The *Bristol Evening Post*'s radio listings for Sunday 12 March 1939 began with those of the 'West of England' (285.7 metres), printed ahead of the 'National' (1,500 metres) and 'Regional' (342.1 metres).[233] The logic of channelling was not obvious, for it was the West of England Programme, not the National, that started with the coronation of Pope Pius XII relayed live (as everything then was unless a gramophone record was played). This finished at 1.15pm, when all West of England listening switched to

---

[231] Wikipedia: 'BBC Radio'.
[232] Street and Carpenter 1993: 32.
[233] *BEP*, 11 Mar 1939: 7.

the National Programme. The modules were not well co-ordinated, for the National was at this point into its last fifteen minutes of Callender's Senior Band. At 4pm it switched again, this time to the Regional, which had itself been with the National since 1.15. This had the virtue of allowing 'listeners-in' to miss Rev A C Deane's exposition of the Fourth Gospel and hear Peter Dawson instead, this time at the beginning of his programme. At 5.30pm one had the choice of staying with the Regional proper for 'Gramophone Records' – though this would mean changing wavelength: was the listener alerted? – or automatically returning to the West for its one musical item of the day that was truly regional, an organ recital by W Gordon Brewer relayed from St Mary Abbotsbury, Newton Abbot. If, however, you had opted for the gramophone records, you were returned to the West anyway at 6pm – for a news bulletin in French. One wonders how many people worked it all out in advance, or even on the spot with the newspaper or *Radio Times* open, and how many simply twiddled the knob to something more palatable when the moment of distaste arrived. Brewer, by the way, was an old hand at radio broadcasting, having two years earlier inaugurated the radio series *Organs of the West* with what was described as 'the first broadcast of its kind in South Devon'.[234]

The postwar regime was simpler. On the Home Service, simply labelled 'West of England' in a newspaper listing such as that of the *Torbay Express* (which on weekdays gave only the evening broadcasts), the regional element was close to the format still familiar from television today, that is, starting the evening with national news followed by regional news and weather. Thereafter, genuinely regional items were interspersed with those produced and syndicated nationally. Of the former, on Wednesday 10 March 1948 there were only two that could have been identified in advance by listeners: a half-hour programme, *Songs of the Westcountry*, at 6.40pm, and what must have been a drama, '"The Widow Woman" (adapted from the Cornish story)', running from 9.15 until 10.35pm. Not everybody would have realised that a third item, Kathleen Frazier's ten-minute piano recital that followed *The Widow Woman*, was also regional. She was one of the BBC West of England's regular pianists, presumably broadcasting on this occasion from the Bristol studios in Whiteladies Road, Clifton.[235] Helpfully, the *Torbay Express* ran a weekly column, 'Next week's West radio features', that highlighted regional contributions in advance. On Friday 6 August 1948 it gave a useful biography of Bryan Little, who would be giving a talk about west country

[234] NA Boxes, from *WMN*.
[235] *TE*, 10 Mar 1948: 3; anon 1948: [25].

holidays the following Tuesday, and pointed out that the *Songs and Piano Music* programme two days later would be given by a pianist (Daphne Spottiswoode) and a singer (Marjorie Mason) from Bournemouth, plus a singer from Eastleigh, Hampshire.[236] This was in the middle of Torbay's hosting of the yachting races in the first postwar Olympic Games, a section which began on 2 August and may have constituted 'South Devon's greatest day' but whose separate opening ceremony, including the Hallelujah Chorus and the Olympic Hymn conducted by Ernest Goss, apparently did not warrant scheduled broadcasting.[237]

The BBC could be peculiar about such things but nevertheless took its regional broadcasting very seriously. Around 1948 it published a 48-page booklet, *Broadcasting in the West*, which presented its position and is an important primary source. The account began by trying to untangle the technicalities of regional broadcasting:

> As the 'national' programme spreads out from London ... it is modified and adapted to local audiences ... And so through the day the Control Room engineers switch to and fro, from the London 'pipe-line' to local studios in Bristol or Plymouth, or to outside points where West Region engineers have set up temporary microphones. The transmitters at Start Point and Clevedon and Bartley take up the result and spread it from Portsmouth to the Scillies. And what comes out of your radio when you tune to 307 or 217 is the West of England Home Service, addressed to you as a Briton and a westcountryman – as both.[238]

The booklet proceeded to identify three elements in regional broadcasting: news, views ('the sauce of opinion'), and 'the not very attractive word' culture.[239] It was confident that with such programmes as *The West in Westminster*, which reported on the Government's and MPs' handling of west country matters, 'not since Wessex ceased to be a kingdom ... has the West had the means of forming any unified opinion about its own affairs'.[240] Where culture was concerned, it lauded the new postwar broadcasting regime as eminently fit for regional purpose:

> During the war the resources of local culture were so uprooted and diffused, so generalized in the national pool, that the return of regional broadcasting in 1945 amounted almost to a new venture. The pre-war fabric had largely

---

[236] *TE*, 6 Aug 1948: 3.
[237] *TE*, 5 Aug 1948: 3 and 3 Aug 1948: 3.
[238] anon 1948: [2].
[239] ibid: [2–20].
[240] ibid: [18–19].

collapsed. Choirs and orchestras had disbanded, broadcasters of every kind had moved or died or lost touch. The programme staff of West Region were mainly newcomers with no pre-war recollections to guide them, so there was much to be done.

A few experienced radio stalwarts were available ... but in the main the first need was to make a new survey of the region's resources; to find more actors and dramatists, singers, choirs, bands, and orchestras, whose work was up to broadcasting standards.

This meant, of course, a great deal of auditioning ... In nine months over two hundred and thirty musicians and singers were heard at auditions, and thirty-five of these broadcast shortly afterwards. There was also considerable auditioning of bands, choirs, and light orchestras, and this search for new talent still, of course, goes on ...

Regional broadcasting has the obligation to foster local talent for two reasons: because the opportunities it offers can resist the draining into London of provincial talent (and the consequent impoverishment of local life), and because each region is best fitted to provide its own distinctive style of performance ... The primacy of London as the focus of our national culture is indisputable and right; but it has been becoming too strong a magnet. One of the proudest objectives of regional broadcasting is to restore vigour and abundance and exacting standards to local forms of culture.[241]

The author(s) believed that two areas of culture exhibited regional particularities. One of them might be summed up as landscape and rurality – 'the westcountryman is more interested in gale warnings than the Midlander' – and extended to building styles. The other, despite the arts being 'no great respecters of frontiers' and their leading practitioners such as authors needing and attaining national or international fame, was a west country set of 'characteristic traditions' in music and drama; it singled out folksongs and 'the Cornish style of choral singing'.[242] Respecting the first particularity, nature programmes were privileged – there was even a programme called *Bird Song of the Month*, produced in Bristol – and they survive today as a Whiteladies Road production speciality amid mere remnants of the BBC's once powerful regional mission.[243] Paying more than lip-service to the second manifestation of regional culture entailed the formation and maintenance of the BBC West of England (sometimes West-Country) Singers and the West-Country Studio Orchestra; these were founded by Reginald Redman (1892–1972), who as BBC Director of Music, Western Region, from

[241] ibid: [23–7].
[242] ibid: [20–3].
[243] ibid: [32].

1936 to 1952 must have accomplished a great deal, though the story of this prolific conductor and composer who was also an expert on Chinese music has never been told.[244]

The dream of a regional culture unified through radio must have seemed quite close in the 1930s and '40s. The first performance of Redman's own male-voice partsong 'On Newlyn Hill' offers evidence:

> Newlyn is in the news again. The controversy over the housing question there has died down somewhat, but this week people all over the country have heard of Newlyn again, for on Tuesday night [21 December 1937] its excellent male voice choir broadcast on the West Regional wavelength.
>
> What is more, the choir sang a song about Newlyn, and it was the first time the radio or any other listeners had heard it. 'On Newlyn Hill' was the title of this new work and it was very appropriate that its first performance should be by the Newlyn choir.
>
> 'On Newlyn Hill' is a delightful little poem from the pen of the late Crosbie Garstin, the well-known author, who lived at Lamorna for many years, and who wrote 'The Owl's House' and other novels which have added to the district's literary fame. It has now been set to music by Mr Reginald Redman, the West Regional director, who is also a well-known composer. He has written some exquisite melodies in this song and the choir sang it beautifully. Their rendering was expressive, with a very light touch, and their chording was fine.[245]

The partsong itself, published in London in 1937, is a slight composition, only thirty-eight bars long and in ABA form, but it is not trivial in technique, and would have challenged listeners with no awareness of fugal imitation or current British art music styles, a certain pandiatonicism emerging from its mixture of tonal and modal features. There is no apology for these attributes, no talking down, in this reasonably specific and authoritative review of the occasion for a general readership in Cornwall's leading weekly newspaper. We are not told why the premiere of a piece whose score is dedicated 'to Leonard Collins and the Mousehole Choir' was given by a neighbouring ensemble, but we might reasonably hope that the linking of three contiguous villages, Newlyn, Mousehole, and Lamorna, through this poem, musical setting, and first performance was viewed proudly rather than jealously by their inhabitants. Garstin's name at one extreme of the west country and Redman's at the other would both remain familiar to radio listeners over the coming years, and the sense of belonging that radio early on learnt to

---

[244] ibid: [27]; Wikipedia: 'Reginald Redman'; ASSL: DM489.
[245] C, 23 Dec 1937: 5.

maximise will have been enhanced thereby. The review, perhaps drawing on a press release, is careful to explain how these names represent the region. Under what merging or redirecting of channels the nation, as opposed to the region, would have automatically heard the broadcast is not now clear, but interested parties could presumably have tuned to it anyway.

One of the most important benefits of radio culture in its regional guise was the promotion of both amateur and professional music, equal in front of the microphone's and the Corporation's exacting standards. Those standards were monitored and maintained by freelance assessors as well as BBC staff, and one of them was the composer Robin Milford. He was living near Bristol in the period of *Broadcasting in the West* and got to know Redman, who made use of his critical skills after Milford had moved to Lyme Regis. Writing to his friend Gerald Finzi from there in 1955, Milford attested: 'In the course of one of my "Listening" programmes for the BBC recently I heard a male voice choir from a village somewhere near Helston; called Trever[v]a, evidently all "locals" + conducted by someone who sounded like the village carpenter + handyman – they gave some astonishingly good performances, better than anything I remember at Leith Hill or Newbury festivals, + some of them were by no means bad!'[246] The Treverva Choir remains in Cornwall's front rank.[247]

As for the professionals, there were two main beneficiaries of the BBC's regional patronage: organists, and the city of Bristol. Examples of the former, Dom Gregory Murray at Downside and Percy Whitlock in Bournemouth, were discussed in chapter 2. Concerning the latter, Bristol had suddenly shot to prominence as a place where more than a handful of professional musicians lived when the BBC was evacuated there at the start of the Second World War. The BBC's head of music, Adrian Boult, and the composer Sir Henry Walford Davies, whose talks were extraordinarily popular, came to live in the city, Walford Davies dying in nearby Wrington in 1941 (he is buried in the Bristol Cathedral cloister garden).[248] The BBC Symphony Orchestra and the BBC Theatre Orchestra, totalling presumably not far short of a hundred musicians, had also relocated to Bristol in 1939, only to be moved on again two years later to Bedford once Bristol had proved just as much a target of enemy destruction as London.[249] Three old railway tunnels in Clifton, one of them funicular, were earmarked by the BBC with the help

---

[246] FL, 12 Dec 1955.
[247] Skinner 2013: passim.
[248] Norris 1981: 313.
[249] BBCB.

of Bristol Corporation for equipment and bunkered studio broadcasting: they would become lifelines in the event of Nazi occupation, and the funicular tunnel was actually used.[250] The permanent difference made by the BBC's wartime sojourn was 'what you might call the Bohemianisation of Clifton' accomplished by the Corporation's 'pipe-smoking artistic types',[251] and possibly the sense of an obligation to keep Bristol a professionally resourced broadcasting centre for music after the war, though it would eventually lose out to Cardiff, a much smaller city but a national capital which today enjoys a resident symphony orchestra, a leading opera company with its own orchestra, and a conservatoire, Bristol having none of these.

The history of music broadcasting in the west country would benefit from a comprehensive study of its own, though as with all spheres of radio in earlier days it would be difficult to prove statistically its influence on listeners. Anecdotal evidence abounds, a memorable example occurring in H V Morton's *In Search of England*, where the author, having fallen in love with the idyllic St Anthony in Roseland on the St Mawes peninsula, where he is spending the night, is invited up the road to a cottage where the family and their guest sit listening to tangos and 'The blue Danube' broadcast from a dance band at the Savoy.[252] The implication is that the owners of the radio were proud to be connected with the metropolis in such a remote spot, shared its tastes, and wanted those facts to be known to their visitor. It may be that, conversely, when items were broadcast with a west country badge, it was as a siren call to visitors that they made most impact.

From the 1930s to the 1950s the amount of such branding was enormous: there were the West of England Folk Song Singers (a different group from the West-Country Singers?); features such as the 1940–41 series *Britain and Its Music*, which with programmes devised and produced by Redman and Douglas Cleverdon covered all of the south-western counties individually as well as in episodes such as 'The Looe fishermen' and 'A west-country miscellany'; and *Radio Times* commentaries that left the listener in no doubt about regional identity when they asserted that 'in no part of England have the music and folk songs of the old village life been more carefully recorded and preserved than in the West' (*Folk Song Almanack*, 1 January 1938, Regional Programme).[253] The BBC West of England Singers appear to

---

[250] BBCCR; Reid 1992: 117–19.
[251] Reid 1992: 118.
[252] Morton 1936: 83–4.
[253] BBCG.

have survived until 1979, conducted latterly by Philip Moore.[254] As for the orchestra, there were further combinations nested within the main pool of players, but they too succumbed to the rationalisations and cuts of the 1960s and '70s that eventually saw no more professional musicians employed by the BBC in Bristol.[255]

The BBC's greatest service to the region was probably to its traditional music. Cleverdon and Redman seem to have incorporated traditional performers into their county programmes, and it was Cleverdon who made two of the four west country field recordings that appear on Reg Hall's *Dance Music of the South of England* compact disc compilation, although they cannot be matched up with actual broadcast programmes.[256] One of these recordings was of the Dorset Trio (Charlie Pond, Bill Hooper, and Perce Damer), which also undertook a BBC studio recording session in Bristol in 1941.[257] Cleverdon and Redman adventurously combined folk musicians with their studio forces in early episodes of the programme *Dance Them Around* (1948–51), the former led by Peter Kennedy with his Haymakers Square Dance Band (he played melodeon). Kennedy, son of the president of the EFDSS and nephew of Maud Karpeles, was the single most important figure in the dissemination and preservation of British traditional music through field recordings, and although he worked throughout the British Isles, he achieved a staggering body of work in the west country, where his band lives on, though he himself lived beyond its boundaries as defined in the present book, in Gloucestershire, apart from a period at Dartington College.[258] A detailed account of how one folksinger of the Dorset/Somerset border, Charlie Wills, was discovered in the 1950s is given in the memoir of an admiring local singer of a much younger generation, Robbie Teague.[259] Chief among later radio programmes with which Kennedy was associated was *As I Roved Out* (1953–58), whose second episode focused on the west country, still with professional classical musicians playing song arrangements in the studio alongside the field recordings.[260] It is only fair to add that Kennedy has aroused passion both positive and negative, the latter because, like Sharp, he made a living through his work, which meant copyrighting materials.[261]

[254] ibid.
[255] BBCW.
[256] Hall 1998, tracks 5 and 19; BBCG.
[257] Hall 1998, tracks 8 and 25.
[258] Schofield 2006; Davies 2008.
[259] Teague 2008: 79–90.
[260] BBCG.
[261] Stradling 2006.

A more devastating criticism, from inside, of the BBC's and Kennedy's documentary earnestness overlapped by a couple of months with *As I Roved Out*; this was *Beyond Our Ken*, which introduced Kenneth Williams's rural character Arthur Fallowfield. In the enormously successful sequel to the series, *Round the Horne*, Williams substituted for Fallowfield the more outrageously suggestive Rambling Syd Rumpo in folksong burlesques such as 'The terrible tale of the Somerset nog', sung to the tune of 'Widdecombe Fair' and like all Rumpo's immortal contributions delivered in a thick west country accent.

In a democracy, corporate authority accrues to bodies supported by law and the taxpayer. The BBC still levies a licence fee, and local councils spend according to revenue raised from householders. The later nineteenth-century 'civic gospel' driven forward by figures such as Joseph Chamberlain in Birmingham certainly encompassed entertainment and leisure activities, especially those seen as healthy and improving, but until 1907 it required a specific local bill in Parliament for a council to be able to trade in music, and a resort was not supposed to spend public money on self-promotion. Given that petty local interests, then as now, were bound to make municipal outlay on music a contested endeavour in any case, Bournemouth's successful Parliamentary application for power to provide a pavilion and a band in 1892 becomes all the more significant. (Bristol's 1898 proposal to support a band for its parks was roundly defeated before even leaving the local council chamber.)[262] It is equally remarkable that what became Bournemouth's professional symphony orchestra still, against the odds, retains the town's name, long after the region's family resort economy and the range of activities originally associated with it have foundered and the orchestra's home has moved to neighbouring Poole. It cannot quite claim to have been the only orchestra in the south-west and the only resort orchestra in the UK ever to have provided year-round salaried employment for its players, for Torquay's municipal orchestra appears to have done this too (see below), though after 1912, Bournemouth's players no longer had to double up on military band and theatrical duties, which may not have been true in Torquay.[263] (Nor must Bath's Pump Room band be forgotten; it still plays every day, though now only as a trio.[264]) Although the Second World War severely curtailed the Bournemouth orchestra's size and scope, bringing back some of the players' unwelcome duties, from 1947 it flourished again, having not just survived

---

[262] Szreter 2002; May 1983: 200; Roberts 1983: 138–40; Latimer 1902: 76.
[263] Watkins 1914: 17, 52; Roberts 1983: 149.
[264] Hyman and Hyman 2011.

the war but played through it, which it is said no other British municipal orchestra did (or could Torquay again claim that distinction?).[265]

The cultivation of permanent, institutionalised orchestras was motivated on two fronts in Britain, in contrast to their *raisons d'être* in the princely states of the Continent. The first was indeed that of guaranteed public entertainment in a resort, a model stemming from Bath. The second was the voluntary association of expert players, and originally singers as well, in a harmonic or philharmonic society. London's Philharmonic Society dates from 1813; other harmonic societies might be no more than glee-singing clubs, which Bath's, established in 1779, definitely was. However, most of the west country's harmonic societies of the early nineteenth century – Camborne, Falmouth (as noted in chapter 3), Truro, Helston, Penzance (this one *phil*harmonic), Exeter, Totnes, and Plymouth furnish characteristic examples – appear to have had sufficient instrumental personnel to attempt at least an overture or two and some solos.[266] The more musicianly they were, the more democratic in feeling they might be. A titled aristocrat was ejected from the front seats when he presumed upon his position in the Exeter Harmonic Society in 1802, and cancelled his subscription, though not many societies will have gone as far as Plymouth in 1830, which included a street singer in one of its concerts because of her musicality.[267]

The Bath Philharmonic Society was established by John David Loder in 1815 on the London model.[268] Both the London and the Bath Philharmonic programmed singers and vocal ensembles in their concerts alongside instrumental works, but by the later 1830s the need for the rapidly self-canonising repertoire of classical symphonies and overtures to be presented by a balanced orchestral ensemble was becoming tantamount, even though glees and solo songs would still be interspersed and church singers might be the fallback component, as with the Barnstaple Harmonic Society.[269]

Harmonic societies came and went, and may not have expected to survive as named institutions any longer than the perennially insecure subscription seasons of earlier periods. Yeovil had one in 1826, and lent its name to a scratch orchestra for a charity concert in 1840. It gave a concert in 1842, but an 1843

---

[265] Exon 2004: 176–7; Ashley 2006: 29, 47; Street and Carpenter 1993: 44; Dartington 1949: 22.
[266] Robins 2006: 90; Kollmann 1812: 140–1; McGrady 1991: 10, 41, 45–7, 68–76; O'Connor and Ashbee 2009: 88; *EFP*, 18 Nov 1802: 4 and 17 Mar 1803: 4, both indexed EFPSCI; *NDJ*, 4 Dec 1824: 4.
[267] *Kentish Weekly Post*, 28 Dec 1802: 4 and 7 Jan 1803: 2; *EPG*, 27 Nov 1830: 3.
[268] *BC*, 4 May 1815: 3; Andrew Clarke, personal communication, 13 Nov 2013.
[269] Edwards 1917: 6–7; *EFP*, 11 Jan 1838: 3; *NDJ*, 4 Jul 1839: 3.

concert was reported as though given by a new body.²⁷⁰ Chard Harmonic Society was active in 1843, reviewed like its Yeovil equivalent as if new.²⁷¹ But a quite different Chard Harmonic Society started in 1857, the old one apparently forgotten, and the contrast in reportage of its two incarnations is notable and instructive. The earlier was an old-style presentation of professionals and their pupils, the later a modest attempt at that more promising equation, already mentioned in chapter 3, a *sacred* harmonic society of raw amateurs, in this case unctuously patronised though quite severely criticised – parts of the opening concert must have been grim indeed.²⁷² A sacred harmonic society, nowadays called a choral society, would ideally mean a large-scale amateur oratorio choir. Here, as discussed in chapter 3, singing members' subscriptions and the presence of their friends in the audience would, and still do, cover the cost of an accompanying 'scratch' orchestra (meaning one assembled for a particular concert or festival). For purely orchestral music, however, longer-term patronage on a business model was the only solution, and this is where the resort municipalities came in. True, aristocrats invested in seaside resorts when they owned the land on which they were growing, and the Duke of Devonshire created his own orchestra in Eastbourne, but even before the First World War he was keen to sell it to the Corporation, which took it over in 1922, and in any case the west country nobility and gentry appear to have been moved by no such largesse.²⁷³

Aspirations towards modern symphonic repertoire were those of ambitious conductors, not their paymasters or the larger public, at least until after the Second World War, when the Bournemouth Municipal Orchestra was renamed the Bournemouth Symphony Orchestra. Dan Godfrey's achievement at Bournemouth, discussed in chapter 5 along with something of its municipal context, was matched by that of no other resort conductor. His nearest thing to a competitor in the south-west was Basil Hindenberg in Torquay. Appointed in 1912 with suitably Germanic credentials (though born in Reading, he came from an immigrant family), Hindenberg was given a total budget of up to £85 a week for twenty-five musicians by the town council.²⁷⁴ We might conclude that they were not paid particularly well but could have survived on this employment alone, for if, say, Hindenberg's salary was £750 and another £250 went in overheads, each player will have

---

[270] *BC*, 18 May 1826: 2; *DCC*, 8 Jun 1826: 4; *SM*, 23 Mar 1840: 2, 31 Jan 1842: 3, and 18 Nov 1843: 3.
[271] *SCH*, 7 Oct 1843: 4 and 18 Nov 1843: 4; *EPG*, 7 Oct 1843: 3.
[272] *TC*, 11 Mar 1857: 4.
[273] Roberts 1983: 141, 155; Cannadine 1980: 348–51; Lloyd 1995: 165.
[274] Free BMD; TTC Min 8879, 19 Apr 1912.

earned on average £137 per annum (more than an engine driver but less than the lowest-paid dentist), and the band's engagement appears from earlier negotiations with other parties to have been envisaged as an all-year-round presence for three years.[275] Hindenberg, more ambitious than Godfrey, and with a surname changed to Cameron at the outbreak of hostilities in 1914, moved on to Hastings in 1923 and to the San Francisco and Seattle Symphony Orchestras in the 1930s, though he returned to Britain in 1938.[276]

Torquay could not sustain what Cameron and his successor Ernest Goss had built up. In 1950, the Torquay Labour Party forced the council to acknowledge that the orchestra was responsible for the Pavilion Theatre's huge annual losses of £3,871 in 1948–49 and £5,857 in 1949–50. Goss resigned the following year, and the number of full-time musicians in the orchestra, which had risen to thirty in 1919, was reduced to fourteen, supplemented by eleven part-timers.[277] This was roughly the number that Bournemouth had maintained in the depths of the war, some of its twenty-four players, reduced from sixty-one, probably being part-time.[278] But the Torquay orchestra disbanded permanently in 1953, having been, more or less since its inauguration, the political football that such bodies always are.[279] The demise of Ilfracombe's seasonal orchestra occurred in the same year.[280] Bournemouth, meanwhile, achieved the spectacular in 1947 when it appointed Rudolf Schwarz its first postwar conductor. This was national front-page news, for Schwarz was a survivor of the Nazis' concentration camps at Auschwitz, Sachsenhausen, and Bergen-Belsen, so ill at the moment of Belsen's liberation by the British in 1945 that he lay unconscious. 'Man from Belsen gets £1,500 post', ran one national headline, among many others.[281]

Both Torquay and Bournemouth had suffered badly in the 'Baedeker' raids in the later years of the war. In full daylight, Torquay's St Marychurch suburb lost a whole Sunday school class to a bomb on 30 May 1943.[282] The previous Sunday morning it had been Bournemouth's turn, when the town experienced its worst air raid on the very day of the orchestra's fiftieth anniversary (did they know?). The following account makes abundantly clear what a municipal orchestra could mean for citizens and do for morale under

---

[275] Ehrlich 1985: 178; TTC Min 8279 and 8280, 14 Feb 1912.
[276] Wikipedia: 'Basil Cameron'.
[277] TTC Min 1309, 22 Dec 1950, and 1415 A and B, 19 Jan 1951; Morgan 1991, ii: 294.
[278] Street and Carpenter 1993: 43–4.
[279] Morgan 1991, ii: 294–8.
[280] ibid, i: 186.
[281] Exon 2004: 217, 245.
[282] Bainbridge 2005: 96–7.

such circumstances. Gwen Chapman and a friend, audience members, were coming in for the concert from Parkstone:

> Earlier in the day, bombs had been dropped on the centre of Bournemouth ... This was long before instant news and local radio, so we knew nothing about the bombing, although we had heard distant explosions. I suppose we realised that something was wrong, but we did what most people would do – went to see! When we arrived at the Square, it was visually evident that something terrible had happened. The streets were packed with fire engines, Punshon Church was in ruins at the bottom of Richmond Hill, and the whole area was a mess. We made our way to Old Christchurch Road, stepping over fire hoses and pavements melting in the heat and then we saw our lovely Beales shop in total devastation. I remember having a most peculiar feeling; there was still the concert to go to, or would it have been cancelled? That all mingled with the horror that such dreadful things could happen, and we feared that another bomb might drop on the Pavilion. But we walked on, thinking that the musicians would already have arrived. Quite honestly, our minds were in terrible torment. I can't remember if the concert hall was full or not, but I know that the conductor of the Bournemouth Municipal Orchestra was Sir Adrian Boult. As he reached the rostrum, he picked up his baton, solemnly turned to the audience and said that he had changed the programme slightly. 'Cockaigne Overture' by Elgar was replaced by 'Nimrod' in honour of the people who had just suffered so much. It was a great moment, bringing tears to our eyes. Somehow, all the people there and the orchestra playing on as if nothing had happened was like an act of defiance, and we were proud to be there.[283]

That day's conductor was an inspired choice. Never was an upper lip stiffer.

Schwarz's appointment four years later caused a different kind of storm, not because of his concentration camp credentials (although some people questioned his physical stamina), but because he was foreign. The Musicians' Union objected to the appointment, made from a pool of seventy-three applicants, as did the Director of the RCM, and questions were asked in Parliament. But Bournemouth Corporation knew whom it wanted. Schwarz had contacts there (his nephew had been at school with the son of the Borough Council Treasurer), and the town's extensive Jewish community will have been able and keen to vouch for his Continental standing and musical superiority to British applicants, which nobody doubted in any case. The town stuck to its guns, the government approved the appointment, and media interest died down, having given Bournemouth a timely boost: 'not

---

[283] Ashley 2006: 102–3.

every orchestra enjoys the splendid publicity of having its name dragged nationally through the mud', as the *Bournemouth Times* commented.[284] Today, alas, it no longer seems extraordinary that a nationalist mindset could have been so categorical, only thirty-five years after Hindenberg had accumulated cachet in Torquay for quite the opposite reason. The BSO's subsequent roster of conductors fully reflects the postwar trajectory of internationalism in classical music performance: after Charles Groves (English) came Constantin Silvestri (Romanian), Paavo Berglund (Finnish), Uri Segal (Israeli), Rudolf Barshai (Russian), Andrew Litton (American), Yakov Kreizberg (Russian), Marin Alsop (American), and Kirill Karabits (Ukrainian).[285] Alsop was the first woman to become principal conductor of a major British symphony orchestra and the first woman to conduct the Last Night of the Proms, breaking through a notorious glass ceiling.

Schwarz stayed four years, by the end of which time a period of generally noisy strife between town councils, trade unions, orchestral players, and the listening habits of the public had become part of the British soundscape. If the financial figures spoke for themselves in Torquay in 1950, so did they in Bournemouth. The orchestra's subsequent history has been a massive series of ups and downs: a new home, the much-loved second Winter Gardens, from 1947, abandoned for the Lighthouse, Poole, when the latter opened as the Poole Arts Centre in 1978; a second associated ensemble, the Bournemouth Sinfonietta, active from 1968 until funding difficulties put an end to it in 1999 (though its amateur choir continues); and, above all, the long-drawn out debate about whether the orchestra should remain based in Bournemouth and Poole or move to the region's largest city, Bristol. The Winter Gardens was demolished in 2006, only for its site to remain a car park. As with Simon Rattle in Birmingham (and now London), a new concert hall symbolic, indeed productive, of urban rejuvenation, which Bournemouth desperately needs, would probably keep a star conductor in post.[286] Will Karabits achieve it?

Should the orchestra have moved to Bristol? Full examination of the historic debate would no doubt uncover much about audience demographics, local authority mindsets, and national funding imperatives, and it is an undoubted fact that the players' lives are not made easier by substandard road networks from Bournemouth: from there it takes a long time to get to Exeter or to Bristol, though going east is easier. But the life of an orchestral player is nowadays a complicated portfolio in any case. In addition to a

---

[284] Exon 2004: 178, 192, 195–8, 200, 202–3, 282; *BT*, 20 June 1947: 3.
[285] Wikipedia: 'Bournemouth Symphony Orchestra'.
[286] *BDE*, 24 Feb 2015: 3.

bewildering variety of educational and community initiatives no doubt involving many of the players, the BSO's website showed, at the time of writing, its public concert schedule for February 2016. It covered fifteen of the twenty-nine days in the month and ranged geographically from the western half of Cornwall to Brighton on the south coast. With five of its string players appearing in the remotest of Cornish villages (Gwinear and Constantine), its regional commitment surely could not be faulted. Karabits appeared five times, though this represented a minority of the orchestra's engagements. A film music programme, not conducted by Karabits, was taken to Exeter, Portsmouth, and Brighton on successive nights in a Thursday-to-Saturday sequence, and appeared in Poole on the following Saturday (these were 'prime-time' slots). Youth was courted in a programme that included a James MacMillan premiere deploying 'a special choir of young people from Bristol, Bournemouth and Poole', performed, again on successive nights, at the Lighthouse in Poole and the Colston Hall in Bristol. A young star violinist, Agustin Hadelich, played the Tchaikovsky concerto in a not unenterprising programme across a further three-day touring sequence, this time from Poole to Exeter and thence to Cheltenham between Wednesday and Friday. The following week, again from Wednesday to Friday, a programme of Berlioz, Mussorgsky, and Scriabin was played in Poole, Portsmouth, and Basingstoke with another young soloist, the pianist Yevgeny Sudbin. The orchestra's only appearance in Bournemouth was a Sunday afternoon concert with a popular programme at the Pavilion at the end of the month. This was with a female guest conductor, the Polish Marzena Diakun. Curiously, Bristol featured no more frequently than Bournemouth, though in general the orchestra plays there about once a month. None of the names mentioned in this paragraph is English, though it is a fair guess that those of the great majority of the audience were.[287] We can be equally sure that the average age of the soloists and conductors will have been half that of their public. Over a hundred years ago, Cecil Sharp discovered that nobody under sixty still sang a folksong. Now, nobody under sixty goes to a 'real' classical music concert. A film music concert is different: Ludovico Einaudi's appearance at the Colston Hall, Bristol, in March 2016 sold out well beforehand.[288]

What in the end strikes one most about the unwinnable struggle for 'flagship' musical institutions, be they broadcasting corporations or symphony orchestras in concert halls, is that what may seem to be the polar opposite of their cultural elevation and sanctity of taste, namely the principle

[287] BSO.
[288] CH.

of a miscellany that mixes or compromises tastes or simply takes them as they come, will always win out in a democracy. The proprietors of the BSO, like those of any orchestra or large-scale venue, know that an anthology of film music or the Grieg piano concerto (an outstandingly original work, be it said) will fill a hall. Radio and TV inherited the variety show format: a concatenation of short slots, or slots of varying length, with contrasting content, some of it musical, some of it not. Theatre bills, as we have seen, in the eighteenth century contained a fair amount of music interspersed with speech; concerts at that period were divided into 'acts' and contrasted solo and ensemble, vocal and instrumental turns. In the nineteenth century, even the Church was exploring forms of variety entertainment. One could argue that, within a liturgical context, that is what the Service of Nine Lessons and Carols represents: a variety of performers for the readings, and a pleasing mixture of choral and congregational music, familiar and unfamiliar numbers, for the carols. *Songs of Praise*, the BBC1 television programme that until the 1990s was attracting 25 per cent of Britain's population as viewers on Sunday evenings, was no doubt mindful of the Nine Lessons and Carols precedent when it created its own formula of interspersed music, documentary commentary, interview features, and changing topography in 1961.[289] One internet site classified it as 'Variety. Genre: family / music'.[290] Fifty years later it was continuing to recognise traditional tropes of geography when, for example, it was broadcast from Padstow harbour on 19 August 2001,[291] but the programme has finally declined to do so, for since late 2014 its format for each episode is no longer place-specific.

The Nine Lessons and Carols and *Songs of Praise* are still very much with us, but easily forgotten now is the hugely widespread parish and especially nonconformist function of which they must be considered offshoots: the service of song. This was a way of harnessing variety in order to keep people within the fold, a local clergyman acting as impresario. One church historian defined it as consisting of 'songs and recitations built around a theme, often mawkish in sentiment and trivial in music – a product probably of the "seventies" or "eighties"', and another paid tribute to its 'unique way of conveying a moral message'.[292] Its precursor seems to have been the penny reading, a two-hour format of local, home-grown entertainment (spoken recitations, glees, duets, and comic songs) amounting to a veritable craze

---

[289] Wikipedia: 'Songs of Praise'.
[290] *SoP*.
[291] ibid.
[292] Shaw 1967: 103; Quick 2000: 8.

in 1866–67.[293] The service of song may have been invented for temperance meetings, and certainly the Band of Hope regularly hosted services of song. Such were 'Bart's joy', given by the youth of Withycombe in Roadwater Temperance Hall on 11 March 1879, and 'Caleb's curse', given by the Band of Hope Choir in St Austell's Bible Christian schoolroom ten years later, on 19 April, a day which saw not one but two temperance services of song performed in that town, the other being the Bethesda Band of Hope's annual festival, its entertainment entitled 'Father come home'.[294] Gnomic titles were common; sometimes the theme was homage to an upright Christian man ('Billy Bray' at St Ives, as late as 1925; 'Uncle Tom' at Minehead in 1879; 'John Tredgenoweth, his mark' at Williton Baptist Chapel, also in 1879).[295] Often all the music was sung by the church or association choir, but 'Father come home' had solos and duets sung by six different people, accompanied on the harmonium by Mr E Pascoe, who had trained them up, whereas its readings were all performed by one person.

The village concert also, perforce, adopted the variety principle, and again the clergyman might be the master of ceremonies, drawing on his flock's growing access to performance material – books they had been reading, pieces of music they had been learning, school lessons they had been reciting. A classic description of a village concert in the Widecombe schoolroom appears as chapter 50 of the 1913 novel *Widecombe Fair* by the Devon writer Eden Phillpotts. It is an old-fashioned benefit, given in aid of the blind accordion player Nicky Glubb and his wife, the latter having recovered from a serious illness. It adopts the commercial variety format of a dozen or more turns, in this case fourteen: overture (piano and banjo), comic recitation, coon song, sacred song, 'eastern' juggler, song of pathos, medley (piano and banjo again), handbell ringers, comic recitation, piano solo (Beethoven), serious recitation ('Excelsior'), handbell ringers, banjo, and finally Glubb singing two songs to the accordion, announcing the proceeds, and thanking people for them. In fact this running order is not vastly different from that of an eighteenth-century miscellaneous concert, elements of the format being perennial. Phillpotts cleverly sets up the cultural drama through the necessity of Glubb's wife describing to him the arrival of each party of the audience, including which seats they are sitting in (1s, 6d, and 3d). Glubb comments with rustic bluntness on each performer and item in advance, to which Phillpotts adds the observations of a detached and omniscient narrator.

---

[293] *LH*, 5 Jan 1867: 4–5 and 12 Jan 1867: 5; Sutton 1973: 100.
[294] *WSFP*, 15 Mar 1879: 5; *SAS*, 26 Apr 1889: 4; ibid.
[295] *SIT*, 17 Apr 1925: 4; *WSFP*, 8 Mar 1879: 4 and 1 Mar 1879: 2.

The banjo player is the young doctor, who commands the programme, not only by the degree of insertion of his own performances and those of his friends the reciter and conjuror, but by being desired by both of the young female performers, one of them his duettist, who consequently fudge their contributions. None of this tension is helped when a third girl, this time in the audience, faints due to over-tight corsetting, which the doctor has to undo. The music is merely the vehicle for the social comedy: afterwards, 'the real pleasure of that evening's work circled round fifty supper-tables, where the unconscious humours of the concert were weighed and measured to accompaniment of laughter both deep and shrill'.[296]

Nor was traditional entertainment in village pubs anything different from a series of variety turns. Edmund Blunden, writing around 1940, referred to 'the queer selection of the songs ... not a matter of what are officially called folk-songs ... but of a drifting element of popular pieces, one can hardly guess whence' that he recalled from his previous visit to his local (in Kent, not the west country). He went on to mention a non-musical turn from 'Banjo Bert'; recitations, ghost stories, and the spoons no doubt fitted a comparable slot.[297]

Nowadays the variety principle manifests itself most obviously in the administrative arrangements and programming for venues, including some ecclesiastically functioning churches as well as redundant ones. The idea is that a town building, especially an older one expensive to maintain and perhaps listed (i.e. not allowed to be pulled down), must maximise its usage and be hired out, just like the church house will have been half a millennium ago, to whomever can hope to fill it. It becomes an arts centre, with co-ordinated programming, advertising, fundraising, and outreach done by a professional arts administrator or executive team including an artistic director, perhaps paid from government funds by the town, which will have had to compete for them. Variety can be at a premium in order to encourage the same limited group of people to come to as much as possible, or in order to reach different catchments for different types of event.

Decommissioned nonconformist churches make for good arts centres, and two of the best must be Bridport's and Ilminster's. The former took over a fine Wesleyan chapel of 1838, with galleries on three sides in the auditorium, giant Corinthian columns at the back of what is now the stage, and the schoolroom converted into an exhibition gallery.[298] Its summer programme for 2010 included a good deal of inventive theatre (much of it

---

[296] Trewin 1981: 75.
[297] Blunden 1941: 36–8.
[298] Newman and Pevsner 1972: 112; Burton-Page 2010; personal visit, 30 Apr 2010.

for children), talks, stand-up comedy, art exhibitions, and dance, plus a number of participatory activities. Of music there was plenty, fourteen items so labelled (solely or in conjunction with another) out of a total of twenty-eight. Identification by genre included folk, roots, jazz, big band, opera, traditional, musical comedy, drum 'n' bass, folk and acoustic, alternative pop rock, African drumming, and comic songs, with not a single concert of classical music.[299] The Ilminster Arts Centre 'at the Meeting House', one of the loveliest and proudest nonconformist buildings in Somerset, built in 1719 for a congregation dating back to 1662, was in 2010 labelling its musical offerings during the same four summer months as 'performances' (there was no theatre) and subdividing them into seven 'jazz', six 'classical', and three 'music' events.[300] Penzance, meanwhile, was in 2009–10 aligning its parish church with art music of an enterprisingly pure kind, Concerts Penzance ('Classical Music for everyone') mounting its series 'Four Quartets' there, each of the four concerts featuring not only different repertoire (including recent works) but a different professional string quartet.[301] The cultural spheres of religion and entertainment that over several centuries had remained not only separate but in some cases irreconcilable have thus found themselves in twenty-first-century alliance. Even together, their socio-economic leverage is fragile: nobody gets rich on this model. Such alliances may too become history, while the stuff of musical entertainment gets passed to some further norm of transmission.

---

[299] Bridport Arts Centre, programme booklet.
[300] Ilminster Arts Centre, programme brochure; anon nd.
[301] Concerts Penzance, 'Four Quartets 2009–2010' leaflet.

EPILOGUE

The Measure of a Region

Britain's EU membership referendum of June 2016, discussed in the Preface, measured something decisively, and while the interpretation of the figures is open to question, the result was not, and it will have changed Britain for ever. Other things about the west country could be or have been similarly measured: its GDP, for example, for purposes of comparison with those of other regions and the ensuing balance of trade. (The GDP per capita of the West of England, which ranks fourth of the nine official regions, is less than a 9 per cent share of the English total: London has nearly 26 per cent.)[1] But has anyone ever tried to measure music?

The sum total of all musical production and consumption in a region could in theory be calculated in similar ways to GDP, and for similar purposes. This would include net export and import balances in relation to the metropolis, other regions, and other countries. It would, however, soon lead to the desire to put a figure on qualities not habitually turned into quantities, such as the value of personal skills produced within the region but consumed outside it, or vice versa. (Fanny Moody would be an example of the former, the current Glastonbury Festival of the latter.) It would also quickly lead to an attempt at calculating value in terms somewhat akin to the measurement of half-life in radioactive substances: how great has been the resonance over time of a particular musical product, centre of production, type of activity, or person? Given that this question of resonance or, to return to Bourdieu, *distinction*, is precisely what universities' Research Evaluation Framework submissions are now having to wrestle with under the name of 'impact', does anyone have the stomach for this?

Perhaps not. Yet it is difficult to conclude a comprehensive study of musicking within a region over six or seven centuries without wanting to know what it has all amounted to. Has activity ebbed and flowed? Was there a golden age? Or is there some kind of a formula for the amount of music a

---

[1] Wikipedia: 'Economy of England'.

community or a network of communities needs that does not vary much with time? Within such a formula, do some places create or represent more value than others (which gets us back to the perceptions underlying the results of the EU referendum)? And are some activities more valuable than others? Solely from the worn-out state of the manuscripts, one might measure the decades of intense pleasure, week in, week out, experienced by the users of the Cruwys Morchard psalmody volumes, but from this index of value one would need to subtract the annoyance factor represented by all those who disliked hearing their efforts.

The human person, according to Friedrich Nietzsche, 'describes himself as a being which assesses values', and since very early times has developed 'the habit of comparing power with power, of measuring, of calculating'.[2] Economics has taught us to conceive of all social interaction as essentially monetary, that is, in terms of exchange, reciprocity, and balancing value, and while some commentators question this, it is a mode of thought and belief that informs our motivation and value systems very deeply indeed. Percy Grainger understood that the sea shanties of John Perring of Bayard's Cove, Dartmouth – the man who sang the magnificent 'Shallow Brown' to him – had their commercial value, for sea captains would vie for the best shantyman because of his effect on the crew's labours.[3] Even the folksong sung in the pub has its exchange value, which is not just that of the pints of beer stood by its audience or by other singers but also that of its meaning as an individual asset, as a contributor to identity and status, for the person who has taken the considerable effort to learn and perfect it as a performance, and that of its meaning for the community, including outsiders and incomers, in terms of how its words and story and perhaps its antique musical mode resonate with their dreams and reinforce their identities as people living within, or yearning for, some kind of a tradition. If it accomplishes this role powerfully, it will have a long and perhaps unpredictable half-life or a high index of distinction: it will get passed on, from one singer to another, in print, in broadcasting, on disc, or, in the case of 'Widdecombe Fair', on postcards, notation included. If it does not, it will be dropped, which is not to say that it may not unexpectedly return later, for posterity never arrives.

How then to measure musical exchange value? Finnegan found it 'really impossible to quantify', and discussed the grey areas between costs and benefits, for example where performances in pubs were concerned, with some sensitivity, while pointing out that 'the idea of "music" as something

---

[2] quoted Graeber 2014: 76.
[3] Waterfield 1946: 42.

valuable in itself seems to be deeply embedded' in human societies.[4] Various measurements of musical activity have, however, arisen in the course of this book. At the start of chapter 3 it was suggested that more than one in a hundred of the eligible cohort (males beyond childhood, or at least early childhood) may have been playing in bands in Devon at the time of Queen Victoria's coronation, and in chapter 7 it was calculated that nearly twice this proportion (one in fifty of the eligible cohort) could have been educated as choristers in the decades before the Reformation. Again in chapter 3, an even higher participation rate, one in twenty-nine, was observed in the parish psalmody of Clovelly in the early nineteenth century, while almost all of Falmouth's children seem to have attended Sunday school, with its singing activities, in 1861. Against these estimates, the participation rate for present-day Cornish male voice choirs, perhaps one in two hundred of the gender cohort (see again chapter 3), may be high against the national average but seems less impressive than the musical inclusivity of earlier times. On the other hand, the incidence of music teachers towards the end of the nineteenth century – elsewhere I have estimated this at 'one ... per 1,000–2,000 population in the smaller towns' – suggests a high density of musical experience at that time.[5] The difficulty in this case is in estimating the size of the eligible cohort: it may have been a quarter of the overall population, if one assumes that most pupils were still female and that most lessons were given to younger people. That being the case, if a teacher had on average thirty to forty pupils (Arthur Corfe seems to have had around thirty at any one time while organist of Salisbury Cathedral), the cohort participation rate could have been as high as one in ten.[6]

Then, as now, the chasm between early tuition in music and lifelong participation in it was probably unbridgeable, and of those forty pupils most will have given up music at a relatively early age. Thus, in order to compare like with like not just across time but across place, the sum total of musicking in any one location at a particular time – what the young were doing, what the old were doing, as well as the rich and the poor – would need to be calculated. Finnegan was very tentative in her estimates for musical participation in Milton Keynes in the 1980s: possibly more than 1 per cent of the population involved in choirs (I would guess far more, perhaps 2 per cent), and a broader participation rate, which seems to include adjunct, non-performing roles,

---

[4] Finnegan 2007: 252, 286, 292, 333.
[5] Banfield 2016: 16.
[6] WHC 1214/17–20.

of 5 to 6 per cent, again of the total population.[7] As already urged in the Preface, one might try to measure the sum of musical activity for a village or a small town within a certain time frame, say a decade, by a combination of gathering together every material scrap of information – parish records, references in newspapers, collections of sheet music (and signs of their use) in country houses, and so on – with calculations based on patterns of investment, production, and consumption. To give an example of the latter, if a town produced a prominent musician such as Cecilia Summerhayes (see chapter 4), it would be possible to estimate the amount of time she had devoted to music while growing up in that place: algorithms for how many hours' practice, and how much peer or family support, make for a robust professional have already been worked out by music psychologists.[8] How much that cost the community would be a factor of the number of person-hours and what else those hours might have been devoted to, for example on the part of a poor child sent out to work instead. (As we have seen, the artisanal family model of professional music-making already implied an economic equation of this sort.)

Putting a figure on the production costs of a Cecilia Summerhayes would in itself contribute to an index of distinction; putting a figure on the return on the investment as far as the region or the locality was concerned would be much more difficult. The same will be true if we start not with a person but with a piece of music produced within the region. Let us further consider the Dartmouth Magnificat of the early 1480s.

How might we measure the work's sonic distinction? The simplest way of answering the question would be to estimate how much it cost to produce. Table 8.1 samples the cost of musical sounds, with one non-musical one added for comparison at the end, across a spectrum of time, place, and function within its general period.[9] While no allowance has been made for fluctuations in the value of money, many of the types of payment have been

---

[7] Finnegan 2007: 40, 198–200, 298.
[8] Sloboda 2005: 269, 279–83, 293.
[9] Sources for the rows of data are as follows, in order: Burgess 2000: 72; Gill 1979, i: 115; Duffy 2001: 6, 210; Joyce and Newlyn 1999: 580–1 (the years actually 1514–39); Duffy 2001: 143; Wasson 1986: 174; Stokes 1996: 401; Joyce and Newlyn 1999: 470; ibid: 212; Stokes 1996: 402; Burgess 2000: 331; Stokes 1996: 402; ibid: 128; ibid; Bulleid 1891: 35; Dilks 1948: 57; Wasson 1986: 346; ibid: 140–1; Burgess 2000: 70; ibid: 67; Orme 2010: 292; Wasson 1986: 249; ibid: 177–8; Burgess 2004: 356; ibid: 51; Burgess 2000: 360; Joyce and Newlyn 1999: 138; Stokes 1996: 128; Joyce and Newlyn 1999: 258; Burgess 2000: 70–1; Matthews Exe: 1; Clark 2002: 14.

Table 8.1 Economic investment in sonic stimulus in the west country parish, 1366–1602

Place	Year	Item	Cost	Cost (£ decimal-ised)
Bristol, All Saints	1473	Pottle of osey for singers of the Passion	5d	0.025
Plymouth, All Saints	1487	Old singer to go to Plympton to fetch book of songs for mass	1s	0.05
Morebath	1533	Players – hire of church house?	1s	0.05
Bodmin	1514	Dancer(s) from Lanivet	1s 4d	0.067
Morebath	1549	Sale of leather bindings of mass books	1s 6d	0.075
Bath waits	1596	Unspecified appearance in Exeter	2s	0.1
Yatton, St Mary	1531	One Whitsun minstrel	2s 8d	0.133
Bodmin	1506	Visit of Lord Devonshire's minstrels	3s 8d	0.183
Lyme Regis	1553	Visit of the King's players	5s 2d	0.258
Yatton, St Mary	1537	Two minstrels	6s 8d	0.33
Bristol, All Saints	1527	Pricksong copying	8s 10d	0.442
Yatton, St Mary	1538	Minstrels	10s 1d	0.504
Glastonbury Abbey	1534	Organist's clothing allowance	13s 4d	0.67
Glastonbury Abbey	1534	Organist's housing allowance	14s 4d	0.712
Glastonbury, St John	1439	Repairs to organ	15s	0.75
Bridgwater, St Mary	1448	Two bellows for the organ	18s	0.9
Exeter waits	1366	Annual payment	£1 6s 8d	1.33
Exeter	1547	John Yeo's six-year apprenticeship fee to organist T Wyncote	£2	2
Bristol, All Saints	1473	Rood loft	£2 13s 4d	2.67
Bristol, All Saints	1473	Old organ (received)	£2 13s 4d	2.67
Tywardreath Priory	1522	Salary and board for director of music	£2 13s 4d	2.67
Plymouth waits	1582	Annual payment	£4	4
Exeter waits	1602	New double curtal	£5	5

Place (cont.)	Year	Item	Cost	Cost (£ decimal-ised)
Bristol, All Saints	1548	Singing priest's chantry stipend (David Dowell)	£5 13s 4d	5.67
Bristol, All Saints	1534	Singing priest's obit stipend (Joan Pernaunt will)	£6	6
Bristol, All Saints	1530	Musician's (singer's?) salary	£6 13s 4d	6.67
Bridport	1555	Robin Hood ale, overall profit	£9 3s	9.15
Glastonbury Abbey	1534	Organist's salary (James Renynger)	£10	10
Sherborne, All Hallows	1537	Profit received from the 'king' of the church ale	£17 6s 8d	17.33
Bristol, All Saints	1473	New organ	£22 15s	22.75
Exeter Cathedral	1514	New organ	£165 15s 7¼d	164.78
Tavistock Abbey	1520	(ca) Mining income per annum	£900	900

discussed earlier in this book, thus the reader will know how tentatively to contextualise the areas of musical activity and meaning they represent, which go beyond the immediate ones of the Dartmouth Magnificat. One element of distinction seems clear enough: Exeter Cathedral paid about seven times as much for its organ in 1514 as All Saints, Bristol, had done forty years earlier. But this amount, exceptional by any standards, can pertinently be turned around into an observation that a rich urban parish such as All Saints could apparently pay not such a great deal less for its church music in the 1520s and '30s – singers' salaries, copying of polyphony – than the mighty Glastonbury Abbey was paying its last organist, James Renynger, though Renynger got generous allowances besides. As for secular livelihoods, minstrels were no doubt in short supply for church ales and crucial to the considerable fundraising effort if a single appearance could earn a pair of them three times as much at Yatton in 1537 as the Bath waits earnt in some unspecified appearance in Exeter in 1596. Yatton was paying increasingly more for its Whitsun minstrels throughout the 1530s; it was worth it if Sherborne's overall profit of over £17 from its ale in 1537 is typical. As for the cost of secular musical instruments, a new double curtal for the Exeter waits in 1602 appears to have cost more than the group of Plymouth waits was paid annually. Today a top-of-the-range grand piano could easily cost the equivalent of four salaries – so should we therefore calibrate the social and aesthetic value of the waits as equivalent to today's expenditure on, say, the setting up of a small-town arts centre equipped to host national or international concert performers?

Plotting the possible expense of the Dartmouth Magnificat against Table 8.1 might be done as follows. Composition and rehearsal could easily have represented two or three months' work on the part of a single singing priest or lay singer – say £1. Add another 8s for copying, 18d for paper and/or bindings, and two weeks' work each for two other singers and a schoolmaster to teach the treble line to the grammar school boys – that is, a further six weeks of very highly skilled manpower: say 10s. Altogether that makes for an investment of nearly £2. All Saints, Bristol, had commissioned a rood loft for not a great deal more than this at the same period, and it will have lasted a long time. This makes the Magnificat, which as a sonic stimulus was unique to the moment or heard only rarely and only by those in that particular place, an individual building, for a few minutes, a very rare and particular thing indeed.

As for the return on the investment, even how the Dartmouth Magnificat worked as a sonic event at the time is unclear. We know or can assume that it happened in a particular place at a particular moment. We do not actually know what it sounded like – whether it was performed coherently (there are ambiguities and at least one glaring error in the manuscript), whether it was sung at something like modern written pitch or down a 4th, how fast or loud it was, what manner of voice production and pronunciation were used, whether it was memorised, whether there was more than one voice on each part, whether any instruments accompanied it, whether people in the audience shuffled and muttered or chatted or sat or stood or moved while it was proceeding, and so on. Nor do we know how it was received: how much it had been looked forward to, how much it was remembered as an achievement afterwards, and by which and how many people. Did its performance become an annual event, at least for a few years? There is no evidence.

The Magnificat will have disappeared largely from view after the performance or performances in its own time. It is conceivable that it was performed in Exeter Cathedral, if Kendall had composed it and then moved there (see chapter 7), though this is unlikely. Yet its presence as a historical quantum over the succeeding centuries never reduced quite to nil. One may not be able to estimate how much it affected how many people over what period of time, by comparison, say, with the ongoing presence and use of a building. But some people would have remembered the performance and talked about it, and there the notation stood, at the head of the borough court book, for scribes and civic officials to see every time the volume was opened, with some iota of pride in what had once taken place. Once the volume was archived, eventually in Exeter, perhaps only one person at a time over decades, even centuries, was aware of its contents, though showing them to a visitor or a colleague or friend will have kept the tiny thread of value alive: it was like a piece of latent energy, a store of value ready to spring up once the moment was ripe. Henry Davey somehow knew about the Magnificat when he published the second edition of his *History of English Music* in 1921. Nineteen years later, having read about it in that book, the young Thurston Dart viewed the manuscript, and, as suggested in the previous chapter, this may well have been the exercise that gave the first, decisive impetus to what would become a stellar career in the early music revival.[10] Dart had more influence on scholars and performers of historical performance practice and early repertoires than any other single person in England at the time of that movement's greatest currency, which was probably in the 1960s and 1970s, and England arguably made as great a contribution to the movement overall as any other country, perhaps more in certain respects.

In terms of indirect influence, then, one might measure this particular musical object at a high value, just as one would the moment of John England singing 'The seeds of love' to Cecil Sharp in 1903. True, there has been no recording of the Dartmouth Magnificat, and its published sheet music, edited by Dart, will have sold very few copies. But its historical trajectory, like that of every other identifiable or recreatable element of music in the west country over all the centuries, is by no means over. Perhaps someone reading this book will be inspired to make a recording of the piece. That might offer the people of Dartmouth some way of minutely enhancing the borough's and their own value through publicity, memorability of place and occasion for visitors, and pride, while recuperating that of the Magnificat itself. Ultimately, the value of music in the west country will be what we make it.

---

[10] Dart 1958: 209.

Bibliography

Bibliographical Abbreviations

The abbreviations listed below feature throughout both the footnotes and the Bibliography. For guidance through the Bibliography please see the Author's Note.

Add	Additional
ASCAP	American Society of Composers, Authors and Publishers
ASSL	University of Bristol, Arts and Social Sciences Library, Special Collections
BA (BRO)	Bristol Archives (formerly Bristol Record Office)
BL	British Library
BLMA	Bournemouth Library Music Archive
BM	*British Music*
BMS	British Music Society
CE	*Cork Examiner*
comp	compiled, compiler
DeHC	Devon Heritage Centre, Sowton, Exeter (formerly Devon Record Office)
diss	dissertation
DoHC	Dorset History Centre, Dorchester (formerly Dorset Record Office)
EM	*Early Music*
ET	*Early Theatre*
ExeLWSL	Westcountry Studies Library (formerly in Exeter Central Library; remnants now in DeHC)
ExmL	Exmouth Library
GDAM	*The Grove Dictionary of American Music* ed Charles Hiroshi Garrett (2nd edn, 8 vols, New York, 2013)
GHR	*Gainsborough's House Review 1996/7* (William Jackson special issue, ed Amal Asfour and Paul Williamson)
GSJ	*Galpin Society Journal*
HTV	Harlech Television
IlfM	Ilfracombe Museum
JAMS	*Journal of the American Musicological Society*
JRMA	*Journal of the Royal Musical Association*

LG	*London Gazette*
ms	manuscript
MB	*Musica Britannica*
MH	*Musical Herald*
ML	*Music & Letters*
MM	*Melody Maker*
MO	*Musical Opinion*
MS	*Musical Standard*
MT	*Musical Times*
MW	*Musical World*
NAMHE	National Association for Music in Higher Education
nd	no date
NDRO	North Devon Record Office, Barnstaple
NewL	Newton Abbot Library, Local Studies Collection
NG	*The New Grove Dictionary of Music and Musicians*, ed Stanley Sadie and John Tyrrell (2nd edn, 29 vols, London and New York, 2001)
NGJ	*The New Grove Dictionary of Jazz*, ed Barry Kernfeld (2nd edn, 3 vols, London and New York, 2002)
np	no place, no page
NSLS	Weston-super-Mare Library, North Somerset Local Studies room
ODNB	*Oxford Dictionary of National Biography*, ed H C G Matthew and Brian Harrison (60 vols, Oxford, 2004)
PlymL	Plymouth Public Library, Local and Naval Studies Library
PMA	*Proceedings of the Musical Association* (later *JRMA*)
pp	privately printed
qv	*quod vide* (which see)
R/	revised edition
RAM	Royal Academy of Music, London
RC	Roman Catholic
RCM	Royal College of Music, London
refs	references
repr	reprinted
rev	revised
RMARC	*Royal Musical Association Research Chronicle*
RT	*Radio Times*
s	supplement
SHC	Somerset Heritage Centre, Norton Fitzwarren, Taunton (formerly Somerset Record Office)
SMR	*School Music Review*
SOED	*Shorter Oxford English Dictionary*, ed C T Onions (rev edn, 2 vols, Oxford, 1973)
TAPA	Taunton Association of Performing Arts
TLS	*Times Literary Supplement*
Univ	University
v	verso (reverse side)

WHC   Wiltshire and Swindon History Centre, Chippenham
WHS   Wesley Historical Society

1 *Manuscripts, Archives, and Collections*

ADA. Austin Dewdney Archive, BLMA

ASSL. Bristol Madrigal Society Archive; Pinney Music Collection; Reginald Ernest Redman Collection

BA (BRO). All Saints' church, churchwardens' accounts and other documents; postcard in Vaughan Collection; scrapbook of William Sidney Pratten; will of Joseph Robinson of Weymouth

Barry 2010a. Jonathan Barry (Univ of Exeter): personal research materials

Bevan 2013. 'A family affair', concert programme, St John's RC Church, Bath, 10 Nov (copy in private possession)

BMP. Betty Matthews Papers, RCM Library

Cann 1977. I G Cann, comp: *Exmouth History: extracts from … The Alfred 1820–1831* (typescript, ExeLWSL, ExmL)

Cann 2001. I G Cann, comp: *Exmouth History: extracts from Woolmer's Plymouth & Exeter Gazette. 1813–1844* (typescript, ExeLWSL, ExmL)

Cann and Bush 1967. I G Cann and R J E Bush, comps: *Exmouth History: extracts from Trewman's Exeter Flying Post from 1763. Volume 1: 1763 to June 1809* (typescript, ExmL)

Census. Census Records. *Via* Ancestry

DeHC. Archive of Paish and Co, Torquay; Ashburton, Cruwys Morchard, and Otterton psalmody volumes; Dartmouth Borough Court Book 1484–1511; Modbury Band papers

DeHCSCI. Devon Heritage Centre subject card index

Devon Celeb. *Celebrations in Devon* (Devon Library Services Theme Packs, Exeter, 1989, photocopies NewL)

DoHC. Sherborne School archive; Weld family papers; Yetminster parish records

EFPSCI. *Exeter Flying Post* subject card index, ExeLWSL

ExeterVC. *Catalogue of the Records of the Custos and College of Vicars Choral of Exeter Cathedral,* Exeter Cathedral Archives

ExmLSCI. Exmouth Library subject card index to local newspapers

Fashion 1989. Handbill for fashion show, Octagon Theatre, Yeovil, 11 Nov 1989, Tite Collection, Yeovil Library

FL. Letters to and from Gerald Finzi, Bodleian Library, Oxford

Flight nd. Madelaine Flight: *Westbury Under the Plain* (typescript, nd, Westbury Library)

Glastonbury LS. Somerset County Council Local Studies pack, Glastonbury Library

Gugan 2006. Donald Gugan: *Bristol Madrigal Society* (typescript guide to the archive, 8 vols, ASSL)

Herbert 2010. Trevor Herbert (Open University): personal research information

Hird 1995. Ernest Hird: *A History of the Old Corsham Choral Society* (typescript, March 1995, in the possession of Nicholas Nourse)

Holman 2012. Peter Holman: 'New light on music at Wilton House in the 1770s', unpublished paper

Hutchinson 1870–80. Peter Orlando Hutchinson: *A History of Sidmouth* (ms, 5 vols, photocopy, ExeLWSL)

NA Boxes. Newton Abbot and Devon newspaper clippings, 3 box files, NewL

NDRO. Parish and town records

NSLS. 'Bands' file; Weston-super-Mare Orpheus Glee Society programmes

PCMAG. Plymouth City Museum and Art Gallery, collections on display

PFSFSC. Clippings file, 'Folk songs and folk song clubs', PlymL P.784.4

PRGDB. Clippings file, 'Rock group & dance bands + rock festivals (include Plymouth Musicians Co-operatives)', PlymL P.785.12

PSAC. Clippings file, 'Concerts and recitals', PlymL P.780.73

PSJ extracts. Extracts from the parish records inscribed on boards in the church vestibule, St James's parish church, Poole

SdeB. *Somerset Directories (excluding Bath): 1784 to 1852–3*, Somerset Studies Library, Taunton Library

SHC. Dunster, Sampford Brett, and South Petherton psalmody volumes; Clapton-in-Gordano parish records; Croscombe churchwardens' accounts

Shepherd 1907. William Shepherd: 'Reminiscences of 54 years with 1st Devon Militia'. See Cultures of Brass (internet site)

Smart 1824. Sir George Smart: annotated programmes of the Bath and Somersetshire First Triennial Grand Musical Festival (BL, C.61g.2)

StMaryMus. Isles of Scilly Museum, Hugh Town, St Mary's: photographs and artefacts on display, with captions

Tatham. Research files from the *Sherborne Mercury* compiled by George Tatham, Yeovil

Temperley 1971–76. Nicholas Temperley: Dorset research notes (in the possession of the present author)

TTC Min. Torquay Town Council Minute Books, Local Studies Collection, Torquay Central Library

USSC. University of Southampton Special Collections

Venn 1955. Major T W Venn MBE: *Crediton als Critton, als Kirton, and Thereabouts* (typescript, Crediton Library)

WHC. Papers relating to the Wiltshire Militia; Joseph and Arthur Corfe account books, 1793–1834; Richard White autobiography
WHCSCI. Wiltshire History Centre subject card index
White 1903. Richard White: 'Account of his life … ' (ms, WHC 2841/1)

2 Regional Newspapers, Periodicals, and Series

(Definite articles omitted)
Alf. Alfred or West of England Journal and General Advertiser (Exeter)
BA. *Bridgwater Almanack*
BC. *Bath Chronicle*
BDE. *Bournemouth Daily Echo*
BEP. *Bristol Evening Post*
BG. *Bournemouth Guardian*
BH. *Bath History*
BM. *Bristol Mercury*
BPM. *Bideford Parish Magazine*
BRS. *Bristol Record Society*
BT. *Bournemouth Times*
BTM. *Bristol Times and Mirror*
C. *Cornishman* (Penzance)
CL. *Clifton Life*
CM. *Conduit Magazine* (Yeovil)
CN. *CHOMBEC News*
CRT. *Cornubian and Redruth Times*
CS. *Cornish Studies* (2nd series)
DCC. *Dorset County Chronicle* (Dorchester)
DCNQ. *Devon and Cornwall Notes and Queries*
DCRS. *Devon and Cornwall Record Society* (New Series)
DH. *Devon Historian: Journal of the Devon History Society*
DHN. *Dartington Hall News*
DL. *Dorset Life*
DLHGN. *Dawlish Local History Group Newsletter*
DYB. *Dorset Year Book*
EFP. *Exeter Flying Post* (earlier *Exeter Evening Post*)
EH. *Exmouth Herald*
EJ. *Exmouth Journal*
EL. *Exmouth Leader*
EPG. *Exeter and Plymouth Gazette*

EPJ. *Exeter Pocket Journal* (directory)
FFBJ. *Felix Farley's Bristol Journal*
FPWT. *Falmouth and Penryn Weekly Times*
FSYB. *Frome Society Year Book*
HC. *Hartland Chronicle*
JRIC. *Journal of the Royal Institution of Cornwall*
Kelly. *Kelly's City and County [Post Office] Directories*
LH. *Langport Herald*
Mercury. *Mercury: a review of the arts in Wessex*
NDJ. *North Devon Journal* (Barnstaple)
OGA. *Okehampton Gazette and Advertiser*
PDNHAS. *Proceedings of the Dorset Natural History & Archaeological Society*
Pennant. *Pennant: the local history journal of Nailsea, Backwell, Tickenham and Wraxhall*
PevsBE. *The Buildings of England* (Harmondsworth, later New Haven and London)
RCG. *Royal Cornwall Gazette* (Falmouth, then Truro)
REED. *Records of Early English Drama* (Toronto)
SAS. *St Austell Star*
SCG. *Somerset County Gazette* (Taunton)
SCH. *Somerset County Herald [and Taunton Courier]*
SDNQ. *Somerset & Dorset Notes and Queries*
SIT. *St Ives Times*
SJ. *Sherborne Journal*
SM. *Sherborne Mercury* (from 1749 *Western Flying Post or Sherborne and Yeovil Mercury*)
SRS. *Somerset Record Society*
ST. *Swanage Times*
SWJ. *Salisbury Journal* (at times *Salisbury and Winchester Journal*)
TC. *Taunton Courier*
TDA. *Transactions of the Devonshire Association*
TE. *Torbay [Herald] Express and South Devon Echo*
TT. *Totnes Times*
VCH. *Victoria County History* (London, later Oxford, then Woodbridge)
WB. *West Briton* (Truro)
WBExt. *Life in Cornwall ... being extracts from the* West Briton *newspaper* (Truro)
WDP. *Western Daily Press* (Bristol)
WEH. *Western Evening Herald* (Plymouth)

WellsM. *Wells Miscellany*
WEPG. *Woolmer's Exeter and Plymouth Gazette*
WG. *Western Gazette* (Yeovil)
WM. *Weston Mercury* (Weston-super-Mare)
WMN. *Western Morning News* (Plymouth)
WR. *Warminster, Wylye Valley and District Recorder*
WSFP. *West Somerset Free Press* (Williton)
WSMG. *Weston-super-Mare Gazette*
WT. *Western Times* (Exeter)
WTTA. *Wiltshire Times and Trowbridge Advertiser*
WWJ. *Warminster and Westbury Journal*
YY. *Yatton Yesterday* [and *More Yatton Yesterdays*]: journal of the Yatton Local History Society

3 Internet Sites

(all accessed 1 April 2017, unless listed as no longer available)

Ah. Archives hub (archiveshub.ac.uk)
Ancestry (www.ancestry.co.uk)
Anderson 2012. Ian Anderson: 'The Bristol Troubadour', *CL* 146 (Aug) (www.ianaanderson.com/bristol-troubadour)
Australharmony. Graeme Skinner: 'Biographical register', *Australharmony: an online resource toward the history of music in colonial and early Federation Australia* (sydney.edu.au/paradisec/australharmony)
BBCB. Colin Day: 'The BBC in Bedford' (www.colindaylinks.com/dayspast/bbcbedford.html)
BBCCR. Gerald Daly: 'The Clifton Rocks Railway Tunnel', *Old BBC Radio Broadcasting Equipment and Memories* (www.orbem.co.uk/clifton/clifton.htm)
BBCG. BBC Genome beta: *Radio Times* 1923–2009 (genome.ch.bbc.co.uk)
BBCN. BBC News (www.bbc.co.uk/news)
BBCW. Brian Reynolds: 'BBC orchestras in the West of England' (www.turnipnet.com/mom/bbcwest.htm)
Bearman and Staelens 2006. C J Bearman and Y Staelens: 'The Somerset folk map', *Bournemouth University Research Online* (eprints.bournemouth.ac.uk)
Beer CCW. Beer Congregational Church Wurlitzer (www.beerwurlitzer.org.uk)
BL Cat. British Library catalogue, 'Explore the British Library' (explore.bl.uk)
BLB. British Listed Buildings (www.britishlistedbuildings.co.uk)
Blue plaques. Bristol City Council, 'List of blue plaques in Bristol' (www.bristol.gov.uk)

Bristol Opera (www.bristolopera.co.uk/pastoperas.html)

BSO. Bournemouth Symphony Orchestra website (www.bsolive.com)

Butimba. Butimba Teachers' Training College blog (en-gb.facebook.com/pages/CHUO-CHA-UALIMU-BUTIMBA/118781671548036)

CFMVC. Cornish Federation of Male Voice Choirs (www.fed-cornishchoirs.org.uk)

CH. Colston Hall, Bristol (www.colstonhall.org)

ChoralWiki (www1.cpdl.org)

Clegg nd. Brian Clegg: 'Caleb Simper: 1856–1942' (www.cul.co.uk/music/compx.htm)

COPAC (copac.ac.uk)

CPH. Royal College of Music, Centre for Performance History. Concert Programmes, 1790–1914: case studies by William Weber (www.cph.rcm.ac.uk/Programmes1/Pages/Index.htm) [no longer available]

Cultures of Brass. Trevor Herbert and Helen Barlow: *Cultures of Brass Project* (Open University) (www.open.ac.uk/Arts/cultures-of-brass)

DBPC. Devon Baroque: past concerts (www.devonbaroque.co.uk/pastconcerts.html)

eBLJ. Electronic British Library Journal (www.bl.uk/eblj)

Elec Comm. Electoral Commission: 'EU referendum results' (www.electoralcommission.org.uk)

Endelienta. 'Who was St Endelienta?' (www.endelienta.org.uk/appeal-who-was-endelienta.html) [no longer available]

FF. Fisherman's [Fishermen's] Friends (www.thefishermansfriends.com)

Free BMD. Free Births, Marriages, and Deaths civil registration indices (GRO index) (www.freebmd.org.uk)

Full English. Vaughan Williams Memorial Library, The Full English Digital Archive (www.vwml.org/vwml-projects/vwml-the-full-english)

GP. Gwennap Pit (www.gwennappit.co.uk)

Gracyk 2006. Tim Gracyk: 'Richard Jose – America's great countertenor' (www.gracyk.com/dickjose.shtml)

Greenaway 2007. Richard L N Greenaway: 'St Paul's Anglican cemetery tour, Papanui' (christchurchcitylibraries.com/heritage/cemeteries/papanui/stpaulspapanuicemetery.pdf)

Guardian **online.** *The Guardian* (www.theguardian.com)

GWR. 'Great Western Railway (1835–1948)' (www.networkrail.co.uk/VirtualArchive/great-western) [no longer available]

Holt. Greg Holt: 'Thurston Dart – a biography' (gregholt.co.uk/rtd-biog.htm)

HTI. *The Hymn Tune Index* (hymntune.library.uiuc.edu)

Intermusic (www.intermusic.com)

International Musicians' Seminar. 'Steven Isserlis on Sándor Végh and IMS' (www.i-m-s.org.uk/about/isserlisonvegh)

JCR-UK. Jewish Communities and Records United Kingdom: Exeter Synagogue Archive (www.jewishgen.org/jcr-uk/community/exe/history.htm)

Loosemore 2006. W R Loosemore (1923–2007): *Loosemore of Devon: an outline family history* (www.loosemore.co.uk)

MacCann. Concertina Library: John Hill MacCann (www.concertina.com/maccann and www.concertina.com/maccann-duet)

Mackenzie 2006. Clayton G Mackenzie: 'Ideas of landscape in John Keats' Teignmouth poems' (www.thefreelibrary.com)

Mail **online.** *Daily Mail* (www.dailymail.co.uk)

Marazion AMC. Marazion Apollo Male Choir (marazion-apollo.com)

MCII. Male Choir International Index (kvam.est.is/choirlink)

Mellstock. The Mellstock Band (www.davetownsendmusic.com/mellstockband)

Mickleburgh. Mickleburgh Musical Instruments (www.mickleburgh.co.uk)

Mousehole MVC. Mousehole Male Voice Choir (www.mouseholemalevoicechoir.com)

NA online. National Archives online (www.nationalarchives.gov.uk)

NDA. North Devon Athenaeum (www.northdevonathenaeum.org.uk)

NLA. National Library of Australia, catalogue, including digitised material (catalogue.nla.gov.au)

NPOR. The National Pipe Organ Register (www.npor.org.uk)

Papers Past. Digitised New Zealand newspapers (paperspast.natlib.govt.nz)

Pathé. British Pathé (www.britishpathe.com)

PFB 2011. Poole Festival of Busking 2011 (www.poolerunners.com/PFOR/PFOB.aspx) [no longer available]

Plymouth Data (www.plymouthdata.info)

Queen. Official International Queen Fan Club: Roger Taylor (www.queenworld.com/about_queen_roger.php)

Real World Studios (realworldstudios.com)

Rhodes 1999. Julian Rhodes: 'The rise and fall of the Octopod: an essay in memoriam' (cdmnet.org/Julian/essays/octopod.htm)

RM. *Radical Musicology* (www.radical-musicology.org.uk)

Rose nd. 'jon rose web: the emidy violin concerto' (www.jonroseweb.com/f_projects_emidy.html)

Royal Marines Band Service (www.royalmarinesbands.co.uk/reference/index.htm) [no longer available]

St Endellion Festivals (www.endellionfestivals.org.uk)

SBG. Sabine Baring-Gould Manuscript Collection. In Full English (see above)

Sherborne Pageant. The redress of the past: historical pageants in Britain. The Sherborne Pageant 1905 (www.historicalpageants.ac.uk/featured-pageants/sherborne-pageant–1905 and histpag.dighum.kcl.ac.uk/pageants/1193)

Small 1995. Chris[topher] Small: 'Musicking: a ritual in social space' (www.musekids.org/musicking.html)

SoP. Songs of Praise episode list (www.tvrage.com/Songs_of_Praise/episode_list/all) [no longer available]

SSSM. Sherborne Summer School of Music (www.sherbornemusicsummerschool.co.uk)

Stradling 2006. Rod Stradling: 'Peter Kennedy', *Enthusiasms no 53* (www.mustrad.org.uk/enth53.htm)

Szreter 2002. Simon Szreter: 'A central role for local government? The example of late Victorian Britain', *Policy Papers*, 2 May (www.historyandpolicy.org/policy-papers)

Telegraph **online.** *The Telegraph* (www.telegraph.co.uk)

Thomson 2010. Mike Thomson: 'How to play the piano in Russ Conway's honky-tonk style' (www.russconway.co.uk)

Trove. Digitised Australian newspapers (trove.nla.gov.au)

V&A. Victoria and Albert Museum (collections.vam.ac.uk)

VBT. A Vision of Britain through Time (www.visionofbritain.org.uk)

VC. Village Carols (www.villagecarols.org.uk)

Vinnicombe. 'Mr Vinnicombe at St Peter's' (www.stpetersudbury.co.uk/vinni.htm)

Wade. Harry E Wade: 'Peters, William Smalling', Texas State Historical Association (www.tshaonline.org/handbook/online/articles/fpe65)

Warburton blog (groups.google.com/forum/#!topic/rec.music.theory/oWgQVVcwNHc)

WCSS. Michael Hooper: 'Wardour Castle Summer School' (wardourcastlesummerschool.wordpress.com)

WGMA. West Gallery Music Association (www.wgma.org.uk)

Wikipedia (en.wikipedia.org)

William Drake (www.williamdrake.co.uk)

YouTube (www.youtube.com)

4 Films, Broadcasts, and Recordings

(see Author's note)

Bevan family 1976. *Harmony at Parsonage Farm* (HTV West documentary, viewable on YouTube)

FF 2002. *'Fishermen's Friends' Are 'Home from the Sea'* (Clovelly Recordings Ltd, CLCD12702)

MAC 2006. *Massive Attack Collected* (Virgin Records Ltd, CDV3017)

Minstrelsy 2006. *Monarchs of Minstrelsy* (Archeophone Records, ARCH1106, St Joseph IL)

Hall 1998. Reg Hall, ed: *Rig-a-Jig-Jig: dance music of the south of England. The Voice of the People*, vol 9 (Topic Records, TSCD 659)

Whitlock 1997. *Percy Whitlock: organist & composer. Recorded 1926–1951* (Amphion CD, PHI CD 147)

Wurzels TW nd. The Wurzels: *A Taste of the West* (Absolute CD, CIA001, nd)

5 Scores and Musical Editions

(see Author's note)

Baring-Gould and Sheppard 1889–91. S Baring-Gould and H Fleetwood Sheppard, eds: *Songs and Ballads of the West: a collection made from the mouths of the people*, series 1–4 (London, notes added 1891)

Baring-Gould et al 1905. S Baring-Gould, H Fleetwood Sheppard, and F W Bussell, eds: *Songs of the West: folk songs of Devon and Cornwall collected from the mouths of the people* (London, 5th edn)

Barrett 1887. George S Barrett, ed: *Congregational Church Hymnal* (London)

Brett 1967. Philip Brett, ed: *Consort Songs* (*MB* xxii, London)

Brocklebank 1977. Joan Brocklebank, ed: *The Dorchester Hornpipe: thirty four country dance tunes from the manuscript music books of Thomas Hardy I, II and [III]* (Dorchester)

Caldwell 2011. John Caldwell, ed: *The Mulliner Book* (*MB* i, London, 1951, ed Denis Stevens; rev edn)

Davey 2009. Merv, Alison, and Jowdy Davey: *Scoot Dances, Troyls, Furrys and Tea Treats: the Cornish dance tradition* (London)

Davey and O'Connor 2006. Alison Davey and Mike O'Connor, eds: *Dancing above Par: dances of John Old, dancing master of Par* (Wadebridge)

Heath 1889. R H Heath, ed: *Cornish Carols* (Redruth)

Horton 1993. Peter Horton, ed: *Samuel Sebastian Wesley: Anthems: II* (*MB* lxiii, London)

Horton 2009. Peter Horton, ed: *Samuel Sebastian Wesley: Anthems: III* (*MB* lxxxix, London)

Knapp 1738. William Knapp: *A Set of New Psalm-Tunes* (Poole)

Morehen and Mateer 2012. John Morehen and David Mateer, eds: *Thomas Ravenscroft: rounds, canons and songs from printed sources* (*MB* xciii, London)

O'Connor 2002. Mike O'Connor, ed: *No Song, No Supper! the music of John Old, dancing master of Par* (Wadebridge)

O'Connor 2005. Mike O'Connor, ed: *Dons an Garrow: tunes from the music book of William Allen* (Wadebridge)

O'Connor 2006. Mike O'Connor, ed: *Petticoats Tight, Petticoats Loose! tunes and dances from the Morval music book, 1770* (Wadebridge)

Percival nd. John Percival: 'The Bristol Volunteer troop' (London, *ca* 1797)

Playford 1669. John Playford: *Apollo's Banquet* (London, 1st edn, date not certain)

Sharp and Marson 1904–09. Cecil J Sharp and Charles L Marson, eds: *Folk Songs from Somerset*, series 1–5 (London and Taunton)

Stevens 1952. John Stevens, ed: *Mediaeval Carols* (MB iv, London)

Temperley and Drage 2007. Nicholas Temperley and Sally Drage, eds: *Eighteenth-Century Psalmody* (MB lxxxv, London)

Tester et al 1905. Archibald F Tester, F C S Carey, and Louis N Parker: *The Complete Choral Music in the Sherborne Pageant* (Sherborne)

Verne 1920. H Verne: 'Dear old Ilfracombe', *Song of Devon no. 2* (Barnstaple and London)

Woods 2009. Rollo G Woods, ed: *Never on Sunday: marches, dances, song tunes and party pieces as played by a 19th century village church band* (Swanage)

Woolfe 2007. Geoff Woolfe, ed: *William Winter's Quantocks Tune Book* (Halsway Manor Society: Crocombe)

6 Books, Articles, Dissertations, and Pamphlets

Adams 1808. T Adams: *A History of the Ancient Town of Shaftesbury* (Shaftesbury)

Adams 1986. Richard Adams: *A Book of British Music Festivals* (London)

Alford 1952. Violet Alford: *Introduction to English Folklore* (London)

Allinson 1998. David Allinson: *The Rhetoric of Devotion: some neglected elements in the context of the early Tudor votive antiphon* (2 vols, PhD diss, Univ of Exeter)

Alsbury 2006. Rev Colin Alsbury, ed: *Frome Vestry Minutes of the Eighteenth Century: the parish church of St John the Baptist Frome Selwood* (pp)

Andrew 1993. Simon Andrew: *St Bartholomew's Church, Crewkerne: a guide for visitors* (Crewkerne)

Andrews 1948. Hilda Andrews: *Westminster Retrospect: a memoir of Sir Richard Terry* (London)

anon 1820. 'Mr Clementi', *Quarterly Musical Magazine and Review* ii: 308–16

anon 1821. *George the Third: his court and family* (2 vols, London)

anon 1824a. 'Mr Davy, the composer', *Somerset House Gazette* i: 350

anon 1824b. 'Mr John Davy', *Gentleman's Magazine* (Mar): 280–1

anon 1824c. 'Mr John Davy', *The Harmonicon* ii: 54

anon 1904–05. 'Sherborne Pageant', *DYB* i: 35–6

anon 1948. *Broadcasting in the West* (Wembley, nd [1948?])

anon 1970. *Exeter University Register 1893–1962* (Exeter)

anon 1975. 'Focus on the South-West and South Wales', *Beat Instrumental and International Recording Studio* 145 (Jun): 47–55

anon nd. 'Ilminster Arts Centre at the Meeting House', leaflet (np)

Appledore nd. Anon, ed: *A Band for All Seasons: the story of the Appledore Band* (pp [Exeter])

Asfour and Williamson 1996/97. anon [Amal Asfour and Paul Williamson?]: 'Appendix: "Rogues tricks" – the problem of Gainsborough's portrait of Jackson', *GHR*: 140–2

Ashley 2006. Hugh Ashley: *Bournemouth Pavilion: a celebration, 1929–2006* (np [Bournemouth])

Aspden 2004. Suzanne Aspden: 'Linley, Elizabeth Ann' and 'Linley, Thomas', *ODNB*, xxxiii: 923–5, 926–30

Badcock 1837. John Badcock: 'Music-seller', in N Whittock et al: *The Complete Book of Trades* (London): 336–44

Bainbridge 2005. John Bainbridge: *Torquay: a history and celebration of the town* (Teffont)

Baker 1978. C Jane Baker, comp: *Catalogue of Oil Paintings, Watercolours, Drawings and Sculpture in the Permanent Collection 1978* (Exeter, Royal Albert Memorial Museum)

Baker 2008. Geoffrey Baker: *Imposing Harmony: music and society in colonial Cuzco* (Durham, NC)

Baldwin and Wilson 2001. Olive Baldwin and Thelma Wilson: 'Incledon, Charles', *NG*, xii: 146

Baldwin and Wilson 2004. Olive Baldwin and Thelma Wilson: 'Rauzzini, Venanzio', *ODNB*, xlvi: 117–18

Balls nd. Ivan Balls: *Buccas' Song: Newlyn Male Choir: a short history* (np)

Banfield 2005. Stephen Banfield: 'Department closures: Reading and Exeter', *NAMHE Newsletter* (spring): 2–3

Banfield 2006. Stephen Banfield: 'Bristol's music and musicians in region, nation and empire', *BM* xxviii: 30–55

Banfield 2009. Stephen Banfield: 'Megaliths in English art music', in *The Sounds of Stonehenge*, ed Banfield (Oxford): 46–55

Banfield 2010. Stephen Banfield: 'They came, they stayed and they went: musicians and Bristol in the nineteenth century', in *'A Grand City' – 'life, movement and work': Bristol in the Eighteenth and Nineteenth Centuries*, ed M J Crossley Evans (Bristol and Gloucestershire Archaeological Society): 355–64

Banfield 2015. Stephen Banfield: 'Nonconformist singing in Devon', *DH* lxxxiv: 69–81

Banfield 2016. Stephen Banfield: 'Earning a musical living: the Loders' career choices', in Temperley 2016: 8–23

Banfield and Temperley 2010. Stephen Banfield and Nicholas Temperley: 'The legacy of Sebastian Wesley', in Temperley and Banfield 2010: 216–29

Barber 1980. Graeme Barber: *Bournemouth Winters Gardens: 1882 to 1908* (Bournemouth)

Barclay Squire 2001. William Barclay Squire, rev James Deaville: 'Röckel', *NG*, xxi: 487

Baring-Gould 1891. 'Preface' and 'Notes on the songs', in Baring-Gould and Sheppard 1889–91: vii–xliii

Baring-Gould 1899. Sabine Baring-Gould: *A Book of the West: Cornwall* (London, repr 1981 with an introduction by Charles Causley)

Baring-Gould 1905a. 'Introduction', in Baring-Gould et al 1905: vi–xii

Baring-Gould 1905b. 'Notes on the songs', in Baring-Gould et al 1905: [new page sequence] 1–33

Barker 1974. Kathleen Barker: *The Theatre Royal, Bristol: 1766–1966* (London)

Barlow 2004. Helen Barlow: 'Bevin, Elway', *ODNB*, v: 603

Baron 1858. John Baron: *Scudamore Organs, or practical hints respecting organs for village churches and small chancels, on improved principles* (London)

Barratt 1995. Alexandra Barratt, ed: *The Seven Psalms: a commentary on the penitential psalms translated from the French into English by Dame Eleanor Hull* (Oxford)

Barry 1985. Jonathan Barry: *The Cultural Life of Bristol 1640–1775* (DPhil diss, Univ of Oxford)

Barry 2010b. Jonathan Barry: 'Charles Wesley's family and the musical life of Bristol', in Temperley and Banfield 2010: 141–53

Bartlett 1995. Tom Bartlett: *Ilfracombe: postcard views* (np [Tiverton?])

Barton 1970. R M Barton, ed: *Life in Cornwall: in the early nineteenth century* (*WBExt*, i)

Bath 1792. *The New Bath Directory* (Bath)

Beacham and Pevsner 2014. Peter Beacham and Nikolaus Pevsner: *Cornwall* (*PevsBE*, 2nd edn)

Bearman 2004. C J Bearman: 'Overd, Emma', *ODNB*, xlii: 156–7

Beckett and Windsor 2003. John Beckett and David Windsor: 'Truro: diocese and city', *CS* xi: 220–7

Beeson 2009. Anthony Beeson: *Bristol in 1807: impressions of the city at the time of Abolition* (Bristol)

Bell nd. Ian Bell: *The Organs of Bristol Cathedral* (np)

Bellich 2009. James Bellich: *Replenishing the Earth: the settler revolution and the rise of the Anglo-world, 1783–1939* (Oxford)

Benfield 1950. Eric Benfield: *Dorset* (London)

Benham 2006. Patrick Benham: *The Avalonians* (Glastonbury, 2nd edn)

Bent 1970. Ian Bent: 'A new polyphonic "Verbum bonum et suave"', *ML* li: 227–41

Berry 1949. Claude Berry: *Cornwall* (London)

Bettey 2007. Joseph Bettey, ed: *Records of Bristol Cathedral* (*BRS* lix)

Bevan 1984. Cecilia Bevan: *Against All Advice: an autobiography* (Wells)

Bevan 1995. Roger Bevan: *A Quiver Full: memoirs of a family man* (Wells)

Bideford 1890. *Wilson's [Illustrated Commercial] Almanack*

Birt 1902. Dom Henry Norbert Birt: *Downside: the history of St Gregory's School from its commencement at Douay to the present time* (London)

Black 1926. Clementina Black: *The Linleys of Bath* (London, 1911; rev edn)

Blackstone 1988. Mary A Blackstone: 'Patrons and Elizabethan dramatic companies', *Elizabethan Theatre* x: 112–32

Blezzard 1979. Judith Blezzard: 'The Wells musical slates', *MT* cxx: 26–7, 29–30

Blunden 1941. Edmund Blunden: *English Villages* (London)

Boalch 1956. Donald Howard Boalch: *Makers of the Harpsichord and Clavichord 1440 to 1840* (London)

Boeringer 1983–89. James Boeringer: *Organa Britannica: organs in Great Britain 1660–1860* (3 vols, Lewisburg, PA)

Boggis 1930. R J E Boggis: *History of St John's, Torquay* (Torquay)

Boosey 1931. William Boosey: *Fifty Years of Music* (London)

Borsay 1989. Peter Borsay: *The English Urban Renaissance: culture and society in the provincial town 1660–1770* (Oxford)

Bourdieu 1984. Pierre Bourdieu, trans Richard Nice: *Distinction: a social critique of the judgement of taste* (London)

Bowers 1975. Roger Bowers: *Choral Institutions within the English Church: their constitution and development 1340–1500* (PhD diss, Univ of East Anglia)

Bowers 2001a, b, c, d, e, and f. Roger Bowers: (a) 'Bramston [Smyth], Richard' (b) 'Brygeman, William' (c) 'Driffelde [?Robert]' (d) 'Garnesey [?John]' (e) 'Hampton, John', and (f) 'Westcote [Westcott], Sebastian', *NG*, iv: 233, iv: 526, vii: 595, ix: 547, x: 741, xxvii: 323

Bowers 2004. Roger Bowers: 'Taverner, John', *ODNB*, liii: 836–40

Bowers 2007. Roger Bowers: 'An early Tudor monastic enterprise: choral polyphony for the liturgical service', in *The Culture of Medieval English Monasticism*, ed James G Clark (Woodbridge): 21–54

Bowers et al 1983. Roger Bowers, Andrew Wathey, and Susan Rankin: 'New sources of English fourteenth- and fifteenth-century polyphony', *Early Music History* iii: 123–73

Bowers et al 2006. Roger Bowers, L S Colchester, and Anthony Crossland: *Organs and Organists of Wells Cathedral* (Wells, 1951; rev edn)

Braggs and Harris 2006. Steven Braggs and Diane Harris: *Sun, Sea and Sand: the great British seaside holiday* (Stroud, 2nd edn)

Brain 1995. John Brain: 'Memories of Backwell schooldays in the 1930's', *Pennant* 13 (Dec): 15–18

Brett 2008. R L Brett, ed: *Barclay Fox's Journal* (Fowey, 2nd edn)

Brewer 1997. John Brewer: 'The English provinces' and '"The harmony of heaven": John Marsh and provincial music', *The Pleasures of the Imagination: English culture in the eighteenth century* (London): 493–8 and 531–72

Bridge 1928. Joseph C Bridge: 'Town waits and their tunes', *PMA* liv: 63–92

Briggs nd. David Briggs MA, FRCO, ARCM: *The Great Organs of Truro Cathedral* (np, nd)

Bristol 1883. *Work in Bristol: a series of sketches of the chief manufactories in the city, reprinted from the Bristol Times and Mirror* (Bristol)

Bristol 1924. *Bristol Pageant*, programme book (Bristol and London)

Britton 2010. Andrew Britton: *The Guitar in the Romantic Period: its musical and social development, with special reference to Bristol and Bath* (PhD diss, Royal Holloway, 2010)

Brooks 1988. Dr Chris Brooks: 'The Victorian restorations of Uffculme church', *Uffculme: a Culm Valley parish*, ed Gordon A Payne (Uffculme [Local History Group]): 48–57

Brown 1969. Miss Theo Brown (Recorder): '66th report on folklore', *TDA* ci: 281–90

Brown 1982. Theo Brown: 'The haunted organ', *Devon Ghosts* (Norwich): 18–19

Brown 1988. Martyn Brown: *Australia Bound! The story of West Country connection 1688–1888* (Bradford on Avon)

Brown 1994. Robert W Brown: 'The Bristol residences of Charles Wesley', *WHS Bristol Branch Bulletin* 67: 2–6

Brown 2009. Dr June Brown: *The Church of Lady St Mary Wareham* (pp, nd [2009?])

Brown and Samuel 1986. Malcolm Brown and Judith Samuel: 'The Jews of Bath', *BH* i: 150–72

Brown and Stratton 1897. James D Brown and Stephen S Stratton: *British Musical Biography* (Birmingham)

Browne 2005. Nigel Browne: *Organs, Organ Builders and Organists in Nineteenth Century Devon* (PhD diss, Univ of Exeter)

Bulleid 1891. J G L Bulleid: 'The benefice and parish church of Saint John the Baptist, Glastonbury', *Glastonbury Antiquarian Society: Second Series of Papers and Lectures* (Bridgwater): 19–50

Burgess 2000. Clive Burgess: *The Pre-Reformation Records of All Saints', Bristol. Part 2: The Churchwardens' Accounts* (BRS liii)

Burgess 2004. Clive Burgess: *The Pre-Reformation Records of All Saints', Bristol. Part 3: Wills, The Halleway Chantry Records and Deeds* (BRS lvi)

Burgess and Wathey 2000. Clive Burgess and Andrew Wathey: 'Mapping the soundscape: church music in English towns, 1450–1550', *Early Music History* xix: 1–46

Burnett 1969. John Burnett: *A History of the Cost of Living* (Harmondsworth)

Burrows and Dunhill 2002. Donald Burrows and Rosemary Dunhill: *Music and Theatre in Handel's World: the family papers of James Harris 1732–1780* (Oxford)

Burton-Page 2010. Tony Burton-Page: 'Bridport's arts hub', *DL* 377 (Aug): 53–6

Bush 1983. Robin Bush: *Jeboult's Taunton* (Buckingham)

Bwye-Turner 2010. Beshley Bwye-Turner: *Psalmody vs Folk-Song: vernacular music of the west country in the nineteenth century* (BA diss, Univ of Bristol)

Byard 1966. Herbert Byard: *The Bristol Madrigal Society* (Bristol)

Caldwell 1991. John Caldwell: *The Oxford History of English Music. Volume I: from the beginnings to c.1715* (Oxford)

Campbell 1992. Jennet Campbell: 'Radford', *The New Grove Dictionary of Opera*, ed Stanley Sadie (4 vols, London, 1992), iii: 1211

Cannadine 1980. David Cannadine: *Lords and Landlords: the aristocracy and the towns, 1774–1967* (Leicester)

Carew 1602. Richard Carew: *The Survey of Cornwall* (London)

Carleton 1984. Don Carleton: *A University for Bristol* (Bristol)

Carnall 2004. Geoffrey Carnall: 'Moore, Thomas', *ODNB*, xxxviii: 1001–4

Cawley 1956. A C Cawley, ed: *Everyman and Medieval Miracle Plays* (London)

Chambers 1923. E K Chambers: *The Elizabethan Stage* (4 vols, Oxford)

Chappell 1992. David Chappell: 'Henry Burgum of Bristol and Tickenham', *Pennant* i/1 (summer 1992): 10–11 and i/2 (autumn 1992): 8–9, with postscript by Phyllis Horman, i/3 (winter 1993): 6

Chatterton 1842. *The Poetical Works of Thomas Chatterton* (2 vols, Cambridge)

Chedzoy 2003. Alan Chedzoy: *Seaside Sovereign: King George III at Weymouth* (Wimborne)

Cherry and Pevsner 1989. Bridget Cherry and Nikolaus Pevsner: *Devon* (PevsBE, 2nd edn of *North Devon* and *South Devon*)

Chevill 1993. Elizabeth Jane Chevill: *Music Societies and Musical Life in Old Foundation Cathedral Cities 1700–60* (PhD diss, King's College, Univ of London)

Christie and Grant 2005. Peter Christie and Alison Grant: *The Book of Bideford: the development of a Devonian market town* (Tiverton)

Clapp 1982. B W Clapp: *The University of Exeter: a history* (Exeter)

Clark 2002. James G Clark, ed: *The Religious Orders in Pre-Reformation England* (Woodbridge)

Clarke 2007. Andrew Clarke: *The Bath Messiah: the celebration of 250 years of a provincial choral tradition* (Bath)

Clarke 2009. Norma Clarke: review of *Eighteenth-Century Women: studies in their lives, work, and culture* vol 5, *TLS*, 30 Oct: 27–8

Clarke 2011. Andrew Clarke: *Bath and Its Musical Diaspora, 1788–1868: three case studies* (MPhil diss, Univ of Bristol)

Clegg 1972. A Lindsay Clegg: *A History of Dorchester, Dorset* (London, nd [1972?])

Clegg 2006. Brian Clegg: *Studying Using the Web: the student's guide to using the ultimate information resource* (London)

Cobbett 1967. William Cobbett: *Rural Rides*, ed George Woodcock (London, 1830; Penguin edn)

Colley 1992. Linda Colley: *Britons: forging the nation 1707–1837* (New Haven, CT)

Cook 1982. Beryl Cook: *One Man Show* (Penguin edn, Harmondsworth)

Cooper 1895. T Cooper: *The Abbotsbury Guide* (np [Abbotsbury], nd [2nd edn])

Cooper 1989. Albert W Cooper: *Benjamin Banks 1727–1795: the Salisbury violin maker* (Haslemere)

Cooper 2003. Victoria Cooper: *The House of Novello: the practice and policy of a Victorian music publisher, 1829–1866* (Aldershot)

Corbin 1998. Alain Corbin, trans Martin Thom: *Village Bells: sound and meaning in the 19th-century French countryside* (New York)

Cottle and Sherborne 1959. Basil Cottle and J W Sherborne: *The Life of a University* (Bristol, 1951; rev edn)

Cowgill and Holman 2007. Rachel Cowgill and Peter Holman: 'Introduction: centres and peripheries', *Music in the British Provinces, 1690–1914* (Aldershot): 1–7

Cox 1913. J Charles Cox: 'Organs – other music – singing men', *Churchwardens' Accounts: from the fourteenth century to the close of the seventeenth century* (London): 195–210

Cox 2000. Delwyn Cox: *Holy Trinity Church Nailsea: the story of a parish church* (np [Nailsea])

Crane 1980. Harvey Crane: *Playbill: a history of the theatre in the West Country* (Plymouth)

Crediton nd. Crediton, Holy Cross parish church, Music Endowment Fund leaflet

Crittall 1965. Elizabeth Crittall, ed: *Wiltshire*, vol 8: *Warminster, Westbury and Whorwellsdown* (VCH)

Crosland 1996. Connie Crosland: 'Close harmony', *Tiz oll Accordin: miscellaneous tales of the parishes of Stocklinch Magdalen and Stocklinch Ottersey, in the county of Somerset* (pp): 30–1

Cunnack nd. Edward M Cunnack: *The Helston Furry Dance* (Helston, nd [ca 1955])

Curry 1965. Kenneth Curry, ed: *New Letters of Robert Southey* (2 vols, New York and London)

Curtis nd. F V Curtis, with A E Welsford: *Notes on the Organ of St Peter's Church Tiverton* (leaflet, np)

Dakers 1995. Lionel Dakers: *Places Where They Sing: memoirs of a church musician* (Norwich)

Dart 1958. R Thurston Dart: 'The Dartmouth Magnificat', *ML* xxxix: 209–17

Dartington 1949. anon [Peter Crossley-Holland and Peter Cox]: *Music: a report on musical life in England sponsored by The Dartington Hall Trustees* (London)

Dartington 1972. *Dartington Hall and Its Work* (Dartington)

Dartington 1982. anon: *Dartington* (Exeter)

Davey 2006. Merv Davey: '"Guizing": ancient traditions and modern sensitivities', *CS* xiv: 229–44

Davie 2004. Peter Davie: 'Bennett, William James Early', *ODNB*, v: 156–8

Davies 2008. Gwilym Davies: 'Peter Kennedy (1922–2006)', *Folk Music Journal* ix: 483–4

Davis 1754. James Davis: *Origines Divisianae. Or the Antiquities of the Devizes* (London)

DCPRG 1985. Dorchester Community Play Research Group: *Dorchester 1854: a year in the life of a county town seen through its local newspaper* (Dorchester)

de Vries 2008. Jan de Vries: *The Industrious Revolution: consumer behavior and the household economy, 1650 to the present* (Cambridge)

Debus 2006. Allen Debus, 'Monarchs of minstrelsy', sleeve note to Minstrelsy 2006: 3–22

Denny 2009. Allan Denny: *A Guide and History of the Parish Church of St Mary the Virgin, Yatton* (Yatton [Moor Parochial Church Council])

Dilks 1948. Thomas Bruce Dilks BA, FRHistS, ed: *Bridgwater Borough Archives: 1445–1468* (SRS lx)

Doane 1794. Joseph Doane: *A Musical Directory for the Year 1794* (London)

Dobson 1995. John Dobson: *Bristol Music Club: the first 90 years* (Bristol)

Doggett 2006. Anne Doggett: *'And for Harmony Most Ardently We Long': musical life in Ballarat, 1851–1871* (2 vols, PhD diss, Univ of Ballarat)

Donnelly 1978. Joyce Donnelly: *The First Sixty Years of the CFWI: 1918–1978* (Truro)

Douglas 1996. Audrey Douglas: '"Owre thanssynge day": parish dance and procession in Salisbury', *English Parish Drama*, ed Alexandra F Johnston and Wim Hüsten (Amsterdam): 41–63

Douglas 2003. Audrey Douglas: '"Parish" and "city" – a shifting identity: Salisbury 1440–1600', *ET* vi/1: 67–91

Drage 2000. Sally Drage: 'A reappraisal of provincial church music', *Music in Eighteenth-Century Britain*, ed David Wyn Jones (Aldershot): 172–90

Drage 2009. Sally Drage: *The Performance of Provincial Psalmody c.1690–c.1840* (PhD diss, Univ of Leeds)

Draisey 1996. John Draisey: 'Discordant notes or a broken consort; Exeter's waits in 1631', in Gray 1996: 62–6

Draper 2001. Jo Draper: *Dorchester Past* (Chichester)

Dresser and Fleming 2007. Madge Dresser and Peter Fleming: *Bristol: ethnic minorities and the city 1000–2001* (Chichester)

Driscoll 2008. Patrick Driscoll: *A Cultural History of Wiltshire, 1750–1800* (PhD diss, University of Cambridge)

Drummond 2011. Pippa Drummond: *The Provincial Music Festival in England, 1784–1914* (Farnham)

Duffy 1992. Eamon Duffy: *The Stripping of the Altars: traditional religion in England, c.1400–c.1580* (New Haven and London)

Duffy 2001. Eamon Duffy: *The Voices of Morebath: reformation and rebellion in an English village* (New Haven, CT)

Duncan 1966. Ronald Duncan: *Devon and Cornwall* (London)

Dunhill 2004. Rosemary Dunhill: 'Harris, James', *ODNB*, xxv: 430–1

Dunning 2006. R W Dunning, ed: *Somerset*, vol 9: *Glastonbury and Street* (VCH)

Dunning and Bush 1985. R W Dunning and R J E Bush, eds: *Somerset*, vol 4 (VCH, 1978, repr Bridgwater 1985 as an extract for Crewkerne)

Eastcott 1793. Richard Eastcott: *Sketches of the Origin, Progress and Effects of Music* (Bath)

Edwards 1905. 'Dotted crotchet' [F G Edwards]: 'Clifton College and its music', *MT* xlvi: 237–41

Edwards 1917. Henry J Edwards MusD Oxon, Hon RAM: 'Notes on the musical history of Barnstaple', *TDA* xlix: 283–95

Edwards 2002. Elisabeth Jane Edwards: *Observations and Interpretations of Musical Life in Bristol in the Mid to Late Nineteenth Century* (MA diss, Univ of Bristol)

Ehrlich 1985. Cyril Ehrlich: *The Music Profession in Britain since the Eighteenth Century: a social history* (Oxford)

Ehrlich 1990. Cyril Ehrlich: *The Piano: a history* (London, rev edn)
Eliason and Farrar 2001. Robert E Eliason and Lloyd P Farrar: 'Distin', *NG*, vii: 381–2
Ellsworth 2016. Therese Ellsworth: '"A magnificent musician": the career of Kate Fanny Loder (1825–1904)', in Temperley 2016: 167–90
Elvin 1995. Laurence Elvin: *Pipes and Actions: some organ builders in the Midlands and beyond* (pp [Lincoln])
Emidy 2000. Marjorie A Emidy: *The Emidy Family* (pp [Viroqua, WI])
Ensor and Banerji 2004. R C K Ensor, rev Nilanjana Banerji: 'Parker, Louis Napoleon', *ODNB*, xlii: 703–4
Evans 1969. Rev H R Evans, MC, MA (ed Thomas Paynter): 'Harpford', *TDA* ci: 45–81
Exhibition Catalogue 1862. *International Exhibition: Official Catalogue, industrial department* (London)
Exon 2004. Charlotte Exon: *The Role and Reception of Rudolf Schwarz (1905–1994) within the Musical Life of Nazi Germany and Post-War Britain up to 1962* (PhD diss, Univ of Birmingham)
Fairweather 2002. Digby Fairweather: 'Heckstall-Smith, Dick', *NGJ*, ii: 209–10
Falconer 1964. David Falconer: *Notes on the Organs of Bath Abbey* (np [Bath], nd [1964])
Farbrother 1872. John E Farbrother: *Shepton Mallet* (Shepton Mallet, 1860; facsimile of 1872 edn, Bridgwater, 1977)
Farmer 1950. Henry George Farmer: *Music Making in the Olden Days: the story of the Aberdeen concerts 1748–1801* (Leipzig, London, and New York)
Farquharson-Coe 1976. A Farquharson-Coe: *Mostly Ghostly* (Plymouth)
Fawcett 1979. Trevor Fawcett: *Music in Eighteenth-Century Norwich and Norfolk* (Norwich)
Fawcett 1988. Trevor Fawcett: 'Dance and teachers of dance in eighteenth century Bath', *BH* ii: 27–48
Fawcett 2001. Trevor Fawcett: *Bath Administer'd: corporation affairs at the 18th-century spa* (Bath)
Field 2001. Christopher D S Field: 'Coprario [Coperario, Cooper, Cowper], John [Giovanni]', *NG*, vi: 408–11
Finnegan 2007. Ruth Finnegan: *The Hidden Musicians: music-making in an English town* (Cambridge, 1989; 2nd edn, Middletown, CT)
Fiske 1973. Roger Fiske: *English Theatre Music in the Eighteenth Century* (London)
Fiske 2001a. Roger Fiske, rev: 'Davy, John', *NG*, vii: 82–3
Fiske 2001b. Roger Fiske, rev Gabriella Dideriksen: 'Mazzinghi, Joseph', *NG*, xvi: 192–4

Fleming 2003. Peter Fleming: 'Performance, politics, and culture in the southwest of Britain, 1350–1642: historian's response', *ET* vi/2: 97–102

Fort 2012. Tom Fort: *The A303: highway to the sun* (London)

Fox and Lidell 1962. D A G Fox and Y P Lidell: 'Music at Clifton', in *Centenary Essays on Clifton College*, ed N G L Hammond (Bristol): 95–127

Foyle and Pevsner 2011. Andrew Foyle and Nikolaus Pevsner: *North Somerset and Bristol* (*PevsBE*, 2nd edn)

Frame 1999. Pete Frame's *Rockin' Around Britain: rock 'n' roll landmarks of the UK and Ireland* (London)

Freeman 2007. Ray Freeman: *Dartmouth and Its Neighbours: a history of the port and its people* (Chichester, 1990; Dartmouth, 2nd edn)

French 2001. Katherine L French: *The People of the Parish: community life in a late medieval English diocese* (Philadelphia, PA)

Gainsborough 1882. Thomas Gainsborough: 'Gainsborough's letters to William Jackson', *Leisure Hour* xxxi: 718–20

Galpin 1893. F W Galpin: 'The village church band: an interesting survival', *Musical News* v: 31–2, 56–8

Galpin 1906. F W Galpin: 'Notes on the old church bands and village choirs of the past century', *The Antiquary* xlii: 101–6

Gammon 1985. Vic Gammon: *Popular Music in Rural Society: Sussex 1815–1914* (PhD diss, Univ of Sussex)

Gammon 2006. Vic Gammon: 'Problems in the performances and historiography of English popular church music', *RM* i (see internet site)

Gardiner 1838–53. William Gardiner: *Music and Friends* (3 vols, London)

George 1979. Eric A George: *Music in Bournemouth: a brief survey of professional music* (Bournemouth)

Gibson 1969. Tom Gibson: *The Wiltshire Regiment (The 62nd and 99th Regiments of Foot)* (London)

Gilbert 2002. Mark Gilbert: 'Lockett, Mornington (Edward)', *NGJ*, ii: 619

Gill 1979. Crispin Gill: *Plymouth: a new history* (2 vols, Newton Abbot; rev edn)

Gill nd. Crispin Gill et al: *A Walk Around the Church of St Andrew, Plymouth* (Plymouth)

Gillaspie 1986. Jon Gillaspie, ed: *The Catalogue of Music in the Bath Reference Library to 1985*, vol 1 (London)

Girling 1998. Roy Girling: 'Percy Daniel & Co Ltd: organ builders', *Clevedon's Social and Industrial Heritage: further studies in the history of Clevedon*, various edns (Clevedon [Civic Society]): 37–9

Glennie and Woodhouse 1996. Christiane Glennie and the Revd Patrick Woodhouse: *The Parish Church of St Andrew, Chippenham* (np [Chippenham])

Godfrey 1924. Sir Dan Godfrey: *Memories and Music* (London)

Godfrey 1969. Mrs Elsa Godfrey: 'Notes on Dawlish parish and its churchwardens' accounts', *TDA* ci: 17–43

Goodman 1974. W L Goodman: 'Musical instruments and their makers in Bristol Apprentice Register, 1536–1643', *GSJ* xxvii: 9–14

Goodwin 2001. Noël Goodwin: 'Dartington International Summer School', *NG*, vii: 28

Gosling and Huddy 1992. Gerald Gosling and Frank Huddy, comps: *Chard and Ilminster in Old Photographs* (Stroud)

Götz 2006. Thomas Götz: *Stadt und Sound: das Beispiel Bristol* (Berlin)

Graeber 2014. David Graeber: *Debt: the first 5,000 years* (rev edn, Brooklyn and London)

Graham 1888. anon [John Graham]: 'Music in the public schools: I. – Sherborne', *Tonic Sol-fa Reporter* (later *MH*) 485 (Aug): 466–8

Graham 1891. anon [John Graham]: 'Music in great schools. – Clifton', *MH* 525 (Dec): 368–72

Graham 1894. anon [John Graham]: 'Music in the public schools', *MH* 554 (May): 136–7

Grant 2001. Kerry S Grant: 'Burney, Charles', *NG*, iv: 639–44

Graves 1958. Perceval Graves: 'The Moody-Manners partnership', *Opera* ix: 558–64

Gray 1996. Todd Gray, ed: *Devon Documents* (*DCNQ* special issue, Tiverton)

Green 1988. Lucy Green: *Music on Deaf Ears* (Manchester)

Greenacre and Stoddard 1988. Francis Greenacre and Sheena Stoddard: *The Bristol Landscape: the watercolours of Samuel Jackson 1794–1869* (Bristol, 2nd edn)

Greer 2001a, b, c, and d. David Greer (c and d with Nicholas Orme): (a) 'Childe' (b) 'Phelyppis [Phillips, Phillipps], Thomas' (c) 'Smert, Richard', and (d) 'Trouluffe [Truelove, Treloff], John', *NG*, v: 611, xix: 550, xxiii: 537, and xxv: 820

Greer 2004. David Greer: 'Daniel, John', *ODNB*, xv: 69–70

Gregory and Chamberlain 2003. Jeremy Gregory and Jeffrey S Chamberlain, eds: *The National Church in Local Perspective: the Church of England and the regions, 1660–1800* (Woodbridge)

Griffiths 2001. Ann Griffiths: 'Parish Alvars, Elias', *NG*, xix: 126

Griggs 1956–71. Earl Leslie Griggs, ed: *Collected Letters of Samuel Taylor Coleridge* (6 vols, Oxford)

Grogan 2010. Christopher Grogan, ed: *Imogen Holst: a life in music* (rev edn, Woodbridge)

HaHa 1862. [Harrison, Harrod and Co's] *Postal Directory and Gazateer* [sic] *of Devonshire and Cornwall* (London)

Haines 2006. John Haines: 'Anonymous IV as an informant on the craft of music writing', *Journal of Musicology* xxiii: 375-425

Hale 2001. Paul Hale: 'Kynaston, Nicolas', *NG*, xiv: 66-7

Hamm et al 2001. Charles Hamm, Jerry Call, and David Fallows: 'Sources, MS, §IX, 4: Carol manuscripts', *NG*, xxiii: 902-3

Hampson 2012. Peter Hampson: 'Medieval vicars choral – choristers and property dealers', *Ex Historia* iv: 55-79

Hancock 1911. F Hancock MA, SCL, FSA: *Wifela's Combe: a history of the parish of Wiveliscombe* (Taunton)

Handford 2006. Margaret Handford: *Sounds Unlikely: music in Birmingham* (Birmingham, 1992; rev and expanded edn, Studley)

Hands 1992. Timothy Hands: *Thomas Hardy and Stinsford Church* (Stinsford)

Hands 2000. Timothy Hands: 'Hymns and metrical psalms' and 'Music', in *Oxford Reader's Companion to Hardy*, ed Norman Page (Oxford): 195-6, 284-6

Hanham 1970. Alison Hanham MA, PhD: *Churchwardens' Accounts of Ashburton, 1479-1580* (*DCRS* xv, Torquay)

Hannay 2004. Margaret Patterson Hannay: 'Herbert [née Sidney], Mary, countess of Pembroke', *ODNB*, xxvi: 708-12

Hardie 1992. Melissa Hardie, ed: *A Mere Interlude: some literary visitors in Lyonnesse* (Newmill [Penzance])

Harding 1986. John Anthony Harding: *The Re-Birth of the Roman Catholic Community in Frome (1850-1927)* (MLitt diss, Univ of Bristol)

Hardy 1873. Thomas Hardy: *A Pair of Blue Eyes* (3 vols, London)

Hardy 1930. *The Collected Poems of Thomas Hardy* (London, 4th edn)

Harker 1985. Dave Harker: *Fakesong: the manufacture of British 'folksong' 1700 to the present day* (Milton Keynes and Philadelphia, PA)

Harper 2001. John Harper, with Peter le Huray: 'Gibbons, Orlando', *NG*, ix: 832-6

Harper 2010. John Harper: 'Continuity, discontinuity, fragments and connections: the organ in church, c. 1500-1640', in *Essays on the History of English Music in Honour of John Caldwell: sources, style, performance, historiography*, ed Emma Hornby and David Maw (Woodbridge): 215-31

Harrison 1963. Frank Ll Harrison: *Music in Medieval Britain* (London, 2nd edn)

Harvey 1926. F Pedrick Harvey, ed: *[A Manual Designed to Justify the Claims of] Musical Plymouth[: giving some account of Plymouth's musical societies and their programmes for 1926-1927]* (Plymouth)

Harwood 2004. Ian Harwood: 'Holborne, Antony', *ODNB*, xxvii: 591-2

Harwood 2008. Winifred A Harwood: 'The college as school: the case of Winchester College', in *The Late Medieval English College and Its Context*, ed Clive Burgess and Martin Heale (York and Woodbridge): 230–52

Haslam 1996. Fiona Haslam: *From Hogarth to Rowlandson: medicine in art in eighteenth-century Britain* (Liverpool)

Hayasaka 2016. Makiko Hayasaka: *Organ Music as Popular Culture: evolving secularisation in Britain's organ recitals, 1850–1945* (PhD diss, Univ of Bristol)

Haycock 1991. Lorna Haycock: *John Anstie of Devizes 1743–1830: an eighteenth-century Wiltshire clothier* (Stroud)

Haycock 2001. Lorna Haycock: *'In the Newest Manner': the economy and society of Devizes, Wiltshire 1760–1820* (PhD diss, Univ of Portsmouth)

Hays and McGee 1999. Rosalind Conklin Hays and C E McGee, eds: *REED: Dorset* [with *Cornwall*]

Hayward 2009. Philip Hayward: 'Jynweythek ylow Kernow: the significance of Cornish techno music', *CS* xvii: 173–86

Heaney 2004. Michael Heaney: 'Sharp, Cecil James', *ODNB*, l: 4–8

Hedges 2002. Isobel Hedges: *The Story of Truo Choral Society (former Truro Singers): 1962–2002* (Truro)

Henderson 1964. Charles Henderson: *The Cornish Church Guide* (Truro)

Herbert 2000. Trevor Herbert: *The British Brass Band: a musical and social history* (Oxford)

Herbert and Barlow 2013. Trevor Herbert and Helen Barlow: *Music and the British Military in the Long Nineteenth Century* (New York)

Hicks 1978. C E Hicks AIB: 'Nineteenth-century nonconformity in Tavistock', *TDA* cx: 9–18

Highfill et al 1973–93. Philip H Highfill, Kalman A Burnim, and Edward A Langhans, eds: *A Biographical Dictionary of Actors, Actresses, Musicians, Dancers, Managers & Other Stage Personnel in London, 1660–1800* (16 vols, Carbondale and Edwardsville Il)

Hill 1942. W Thomson Hill: *St Saviour's, Dartmouth through the Centuries* (Gloucester, nd [1942?])

Hill 2007. William Hill: *A Short History of Allington and Its Church* (Bridport, rev edn)

Hobhouse 1934. Edmund Hobhouse, ed: *The Diary of a West Country Physician AD 1684–1726* (London)

Hobson 2008: James Hobson: 'Austin Phillips', *CN* 5 (summer): 11–13

Hobson 2010. James Hobson: 'Bristol and the foundation of its Madrigal Society', in Crossley Evans 2010: 277–93

Hobson 2012. James Hobson: 'Three madrigal societies in early nineteenth-century England', in *Music and Institutions in Nineteenth-Century Britain*, ed Paul Rodmell (Farnham): 33–53

Hobson 2015. James Hobson: *Musical Antiquarianism and the Madrigal Revival in England, 1726-1851* (PhD diss, Univ of Bristol)

Holman 1993. Peter Holman: *Four and Twenty Fiddlers: the violin at the English court 1540-1690* (Oxford)

Holman 2000. Peter Holman: 'Eighteenth-century English music: past, present, future', *Music in Eighteenth-Century Britain*, ed David Wyn Jones (Aldershot, 2000): 1-13

Holman 2001a. Peter Holman: 'Locke [Lock], Matthew', *NG*, xv: 44-52

Holman 2001b. Peter Holman: 'Mell, Davis', *NG*, xvi: 348-9

Hook 1838. [Theodore Hook?]: 'The manager's note-book – no 8: Charles Benjamin Incledon', *New Monthly Magazine and Humorist* liii/210: 216-29

Hooper 1963. Graham Hooper: *A Survey of Music in Bristol: with special reference to the eighteenth century* (MA diss, Univ of Bristol)

Hooper 2001. Graham Hooper: 'Bevin, Elway', *NG*, iii: 497-8

Hornsey 1994. Brian Hornsey: *Ninety Years of Cinema in Plymouth* ([Plymouth], rev edn)

Horton 2004. Peter Horton: *Samuel Sebastian Wesley* (Oxford)

Hoskin 2004. Michael Hoskin: 'Herschel, Caroline Lucretia' and 'Herschel, Sir William', *ODNB*, xxvi: 822-5, 831-7

Howell 1989. Chris Howell: *Wells in Old Photographs* (Gloucester)

Hudson 2002. Hazel Hudson: *The New Wedmore Chronicles* (pp [Wedmore])

Hughes 2001. Rosemary Hughes: 'Novello', *NG*, xviii: 214-17

Humphries and Smith 1970. Charles Humphries and William C Smith: *Music Publishing in the British Isles: from the beginning until the middle of the nineteenth century* (Oxford, 2nd edn)

Hunt 1977. Edgar Hunt: *Robert Lucas Pearsall: the 'compleat gentleman' and his music (1795-1856)* (pp, Chesham Bois)

Hurd 1962. Michael Hurd: *Immortal Hour: the life and period of Rutland Boughton* (London)

Hutton 1994. Ronald Hutton: 'The ritual year in England c.1490-c.1540', *The Rise and Fall of Merry England: the ritual year 1400-1700*: 5-48 (Oxford)

Hyman and Hyman 2011. Robert and Nicola Hyman: *The Pump Room Orchestra Bath: three centuries of music and social history* (East Knoyle)

Irving 2005. David R M Irving: 'The Pacific in the minds and music of Enlightenment Europe', *Eighteenth-Century Music* ii: 205-29

Irving 2010. David R M Irving: *Colonial Counterpoint: music in early modern Manila* (Oxford)

Jackson 1783-1802. William Jackson: 'Twenty letters', *GHR*: 113-39

Jackson 1791. William Jackson: *Observations on the Present State of Music in London* (London)

Jackson 1795. William Jackson: *Thirty Letters on Various Subjects* (London, 3rd edn)

Jackson 1798. William Jackson: *The Four Ages; together with essays on various subjects* (London)

Jackson 1802. William Jackson: 'A short sketch of my own life', *GHR*: 57–112

Jackson 1882. William Jackson: 'Character of Gainsborough' and 'Character of Sir Joshua Reynolds', in Jackson 1798: 147–61, 162–84, repr as 'Personal remembrances of Gainsborough' and 'Sir Joshua Reynolds', *Leisure Hour* xxxi: 620–5

Jackson 1971. Gertrude Jackson: 'Studien zur Biographie und zum literarischen Nachlass des William Jackson, of Exeter. 1730–1803', *English Miscellany* [Rome] xxii: 269–332

Jacobs 1972. Arthur Jacobs, ed: 'Composers', *The Music Yearbook 1972-3* (London): 445–57

James 1987. Kenneth James: *Concert Life in Eighteenth-Century Bath* (PhD diss, Royal Holloway, Univ of London)

James 1990. Kenneth James: 'Venanzio Rauzzini and the search for musical perfection', *BH* iii: 90–113

James 2001. Kenneth James: 'Brooks, James', *NG*, iv: 428

Jeans 2001. Susi Jeans: 'Facy [Facye, Facey, Facie, Facio], Hugh', *NG*, viii: 508

Jeboult 1923. H A Jeboult: *Somerset Composers, Musicians & Music* (Somerset Folk Series, no 10: London)

Johnson 1996. Phil Johnson: *Straight Outa Bristol: Massive Attack, Portishead, Tricky and the roots of trip hop* (London)

Johnston 2003. Alexandra F Johnston: 'The feast of Corpus Christi in the west country', *ET* vi/1: 15–34

Johnstone 2008. H Diack Johnstone, 'Claver Morris, an early eighteenth-century English physician and amateur musician *extraordinaire*', *JRMA* cxxxiii, 93–127

Jones 2006. Kelvin I Jones, ed: *Cornwall's May Folk Festivals* (np)

Jones 2009. Mark Jones: *Bristol Folk: a discographical history of Bristol folk music in the 1960s and 1970s* (Bristol)

Joslin 1987. John Joslin: *Old Posset: Portishead people and places* (Bristol)

Joyce and Newlyn 1999. Sally L Joyce and Evelyn S Newlyn, eds: *REED: Cornwall* [with *Dorset*]

Julian 1988. Hubert Julian: 'Music in Cornish Methodism: the first 250 years', in *Methodist Celebration: a Cornish contribution*, ed Sarah Foot (Redruth): 61–7

Jusserand 1905. J J Jusserand: *English Wayfaring Life in the Middle Ages (XIVth Century)* trans Lucy Toulmin Smith (London, 1888; 8th edn)

Karpeles 1967. Maud Karpeles: *Cecil Sharp: his life and work* (London)

Karpeles 1973. Maud Karpeles: *An Introduction to English Folk Song* (London)

Keep 1977. David J Keep MA, PhD: 'Nonconformity in Woodbury and Lympstone', *TDA* cix: 51–7

Kent 2007a. Alan M Kent: 'Alex Parks, punks and pipers: towards a history of popular music in Cornwall, 1967–2007', *CS* xv: 209–47

Kent 2007b. Christopher Kent: 'Music of rural byway and rotten borough: a study of musical life in mid-Wiltshire *c.* 1750–1830', in Cowgill and Holman 2007: 163–81

King 2010. Emma King, ed: *Chippenham Official Guide and Map* (Chippenham)

Knighton 2012. C S Knighton, ed: 'Section XV: music', *Clifton College: foundation to evacuation* (*BRS* lxv)

Kollmann 1812. anon: 'On the origin, progress, and present state of music in Bath, 1812', and 'Abstract from a letter to the editor, dated Bristol, Feb 14, 1812', *Quarterly Musical Register* i: 131–43 and 145–8, repr in Michael Kassler: *A F C Kollmann's Quarterly Musical Register (1812): an annotated edition with an introduction to his life and works* (Aldershot, 2008)

Krummel 1981. D W Krummel: 'Music publishing', in *The Romantic Age: 1800–1914*, ed Nicholas Temperley (*The Athlone* [later *Blackwell*] *History of Music in Britain*, vol 5, London): 46–59

Ladle 1994. Lilian Ladle: *Wareham: a pictorial history* (Chichester)

Lamb 2001. Andrew Lamb: 'Lancers', *NG*, xiv: 206

Lambert 1948. Constant Lambert: *Music Ho! A study of music in decline* (London, 1932; Penguin edn)

Lancaster 1936. Osbert Lancaster: *Progress at Pelvis Bay* (London)

Lancaster 1949. Osbert Lancaster: *Drayneflete Revealed* (London)

Langley 2013. Leanne Langley: 'A place for music: John Nash, Regent Street and the Philharmonic Society of London', *eBLJ*

Langley and Small 1990. Martin Langley and Edwina Small: *Wells: an historical guide* (Bradford on Avon)

Lansdown 1997. M J Lansdown: *The Trowbridge Chartists: 1838–1848* (Trowbridge [Museum and West Wiltshire Branch of the Historical Association])

Lasocki 1983. David Lasocki: *Professional Recorder Players in England, 1540–1740* (2 vols, PhD diss, Univ of Iowa)

Lasocki 1992. David Lasocki: 'The Levashers and the Le Vachers', *GSJ* xlv: 111–14

Latimer 1887. John Latimer: *The Annals of Bristol in the Nineteenth Century* (Bristol)

Latimer 1893. John Latimer: *The Annals of Bristol in the Eighteenth Century* (pp)

Latimer 1900. John Latimer: *The Annals of Bristol in the Seventeenth Century* (Bristol)

Latimer 1902. John Latimer: *The Annals of Bristol in the Nineteenth Century (concluded): 1887–1900* (Bristol)

Laurence 1981. Dan H Laurence, ed: *Shaw's Music* (3 vols, London)

Lawer 2007. Diana Lawer: *'Get Your Skates On': a history of Plymouth's roller skating rinks 1874–1989* (Plymouth)

le Fleming 1982. Christopher le Fleming: *Journey into Music (by the slow train)* (Bristol)

le Huray and Morehen 2001. Peter le Huray, rev John Morehen: 'Holmes, John', *NG*, xi: 644–5

Leaver 2010. Robin Leaver: '*Psalms and Hymns* and *Hymns and Sacred Poems*: two strands of Wesleyan hymn collections', in Temperley and Banfield 2010: 41–51

Leech 1850. [Joseph Leech:] *The Church-Goer: rural rides; or, Calls at Country Churches*, 2nd series [vol 3 of 4 overall] (Bristol, 2nd edn)

Leech 1995. John Leech: *Inside-Out: the view from the Asylum* (pp [Devizes])

Lefkowitz 1960. Murray Lefkowitz: *William Lawes* (London)

Lefkowitz 1965. Murray Lefkowitz: 'The Longleat papers of Bulstrode Whitelocke: new light on Shirley's *Triumph of Peace*', *JAMS* xviii: 42–60

Legg 1983. Rodney Legg: *Old Swanage: quarry port to seaside spa* (Sherborne)

Lever and Jeyes 2005. Ted Lever and Nigel Jeyes: *Memories of Wartime St Ives* (St Ives [Trust Archive Study Centre])

Lewcock 2001. Ronald Lewcock et al: 'Acoustics, §I: room acoustics. 8. Medieval times', *NG* i: 82–6

Lewis 1988. Tony and Freddie Lewis: *Keynsham Past and Present: an illustrated history of Keynsham* (pp, nd [1988?])

Lilly 1990. Jane Lilly: *Clevedon in Old Photographs* (Stroud)

Lilly 1999. Jane Lilly: *[Volume 1:] The Shops of the Old Village* (Clevedon History Series, [Clevedon])

Lilly 2002. Jane Lilly: *[Volume 2:] The Shops on the Hill* (Clevedon History Series, [Clevedon])

Little 1983. Bryan Little: *Portrait of Exeter* (London)

Little 1996. Bryan Little: *A History of the Victoria Rooms* (np, nd [1996?])

Lloyd 1969. A L Lloyd: *Folk Song in England* (London)

Lloyd 1995. Stephen Lloyd: *Sir Dan Godfrey: champion of British composers* (London)

Loder 1858. [George Loder:] 'Recollections of California & Australia: by a musician', *MW* xxxvi: 199, 236, 259–61, 276–8, 293–4, 332–3, 347–8, 365–6, 380–1, 404–5, 419–20, 436–8, 454–5, 468–9, 486–7, 499–500, 515–16, 531–2, 547–8, 563–4

Loesser 1990. Arthur Loesser: *Men, Women and Pianos: a social history* (Mineola, NY; repr from 1954)

Lomas 1990. Michael John Lomas: *Amateur Brass and Wind Bands in Southern England between the Late Eighteenth Century and circa 1900* (2 vols, PhD diss, Open Univ)

Lorigan 2009. Catherine Lorigan: *Connections: aspects of the history of north Cornwall* (Caversham)

Lowerson 2005. John Lowerson: *Amateur Operatics: a social and cultural history* (Manchester)

Lumbard 1998. Ray Lumbard: 'A boyhood on the beach: recollections of Clevedon and life in the 20s to 30s', *Clevedon's Social and Industrial Heritage: further studies in the history of Clevedon*, various eds (Clevedon [Civic Society]): 71–6

Lynan 2004. Peter Lynan: 'Broderip, William', *ODNB*, vii: 769

MacDermott 1948. K H MacDermott: *The Old Church Gallery Minstrels* (London)

McGrady 1991. Richard McGrady: *Music and Musicians in early nineteenth-century Cornwall: the world of Joseph Emidy – slave, violinist and composer* (Exeter)

McGrady 2001a. Richard McGrady: 'Emidy, Joseph Antonia', *NG*, viii: 185

McGrady 2001b. Richard McGrady: 'Jackson, William (i) [Jackson of Exeter]', *NG*, xii: 724–6

McGrath 1983. Patrick McGrath, ed: *The Religious Buildings of Keynsham* (Keynsham)

MacKeith 2003. Lucy MacKeith: *Local Black History: a beginning in Devon* (London)

MacLean 2003. Sally-Beth MacLean: 'At the end of the road: an overview of southwestern touring circuits', *ET* vi/2: 17–32

Malan 1986. Jacques P Malan: 'Searelle, Luscombe (Isaac Israel)', in *South African Music Encyclopedia*, ed Malan (Cape Town), iv: 223–5

Malcolm 1807. James P Malcolm: *First Impressions or Sketches from Art and Nature. Animate and Inanimate* (London)

Manning-Sanders 1949. Ruth Manning-Sanders: *The West of England* (London)

Manns 1948. Albert E Manns: *One Hundred Years of Music: a short history of Duck, Son and Pinker* (London)

Mansell 2005. Tony Mansell: *Camborne Town Band* (St Agnes)

Marín 2002. Miguel Ángel Marín: *Music on the margin: urban musical life in eighteenth-century Jaca (Spain)* (Kassel)

Marshall 2003. Ian Marshall: *The Amazing Story of 'The Floral Dance' in Words, Music & Pictures* (Liskeard)

Marson 1904. Charles L Marson: 'Introduction', in *Folk Songs from Somerset*, first series ed Cecil J Sharp and Marson (London and Taunton): xi–xvii

Martin 2003. Darryl Martin: *The English Virginal* (2 vols, PhD diss, Univ of Edinburgh)

Maslen 1988. Geoffrey Maslen: *Burnham-on-Sea and Highbridge in Old Photographs* (Gloucester)

Matthews 1967. Betty Matthews: 'J C Bach in the West Country', *MT* cviii: 702–4

Matthews 1969. Betty Matthews: 'The organs of Lulworth Castle', *Organ* xlix: 156–60

Matthews 1970. Betty Matthews: addenda and corrigenda to Reid and Pritchard 1965, *RMARC* 8: 23–33

Matthews 1985. Betty Matthews, comp: *The Royal Society of Musicians of Great Britain List of Members 1738–1984* (London)

Matthews 1989. Betty Matthews: 'The ghosts of St John's, Torquay', *Organ* lxviii/267 (Jan): 25–30

Matthews 2001a. Betty Matthews: 'Broderip', *NG*, iv: 416–17

Matthews 2001b. Betty Matthews: 'Corfe', *NG*, xi: 463–4

Matthews Exe. Betty Matthews: *The Organs and Organists of Exeter Cathedral* (Exeter, nd)

Matthews Sal. Betty Matthews: *The Organs and Organists of Salisbury Cathedral* (Salisbury, nd)

Matthews Wim(a). Betty Matthews: *The Organs and Organists of Wimborne Minster 1408–1972* (Bournemouth, nd [1972?])

Matthews Wim(b). Betty Matthews: *The Organs and Organists of Wimborne Minster from 1408* (Bournemouth, nd [after 1977])

Matthews and Spink 2001. Betty Matthews and Ian Spink: 'Silver, John', *NG*, xxiii: 393

Matthews et al 2001. Betty Matthews, Ian Stephens, Jill Tucker, and John Snelson: 'Bristol', *NG*, iv: 360

May 1983. F B May: 'Victorian and Edwardian Ilfracombe', in *Leisure in Britain 1780–1939*, ed John K Walton and James Walvin (Manchester): 187–205

Means 1972. Andrew Means: 'Focus on folk: Bristol's cream', *Melody Maker*, 1 Jan: 32

Michell 1985. Frank Michell: *Annals of an Ancient Cornish Town – Redruth* (Redruth, 2nd edn)

Middleton 1995. Richard Middleton: 'The rock revolution', in *The Twentieth Century* (*The Blackwell History of Music in Britain*, vol 6; Oxford): 79–106

Milestone 2009. Rachel Milestone: *'A New Impetus to the Love of Music': the role of the town hall in nineteenth-century English musical culture* (PhD diss, Univ of Leeds)

Miller 1966. Clement A Miller: 'Erasmus on music', *Musical Quarterly* lii: 332–49
Millington 2008. Barry Millington: 'Richard Hickox', *Guardian*, 25 Nov: 32
Milton 1993. Christine Milton: '150 years of education at Christ Church/Four Oaks School', *Pennant* i/4 (summer): 3–8
Mitchell 2004. Rosemary Mitchell: 'Weld, Thomas', *ODNB*, lvii: 979–80
Mitroulia and Myers 2011. Eugenia Mitroulia and Arnold Myers: 'The Distin family as instrument makers and dealers 1845–1874', *Scottish Music Review* ii/1: 1–20
Money 2010. John Money, ed: *The Chronicles of John Cannon, Excise Officer and Writing Master* (2 vols, London)
Montague-Smith 2004. Helen Montague-Smith: *Isaac Pitman: a Trowbridge man* (Trowbridge)
Moody and Nash 2007. Frogg Moody and Richard Nash: *Hold Tight! Voices of the Sarum sound 1945–1969* (Salisbury)
Morgan 1991. Nigel John Morgan: *Perceptions, Patterns and Policies of Tourism: the development of the Devon seaside resorts during the twentieth century with special reference to Torquay and Ilfracombe* (2 vols, PhD diss, Univ of Exeter)
Morris 1872. *Morris's Directory of Somerset & Bristol* (Clevedon pages photocopied in Clevedon Library)
Morton 1936. H V Morton: *In Search of England* (London, 23rd edn)
Mowl and Mako 2010. Timothy Mowl and Marion Mako: *Historic Gardens of Somerset* (Bristol)
Murray 2001. D J S Murray: 'Military music. §3. Britain', *NG*, xvi: 686–7
Newman and Pevsner 1972. John Newman and Nikolaus Pevsner: *Dorset* (PevsBE)
Newton 1978. Jill Newton: *Helston Flora Day* (St Teath)
Nicholas 1991. D M Nicholas: 'Yatton Women's Institute 1941–1991', *YY* 8: 5–9
Nightingale 2010. John Nightingale: 'Catalogue of compositions by Charles Wesley the younger', in Temperley and Banfield 2010: 231–41
Norris 1981. Gerald Norris: *A Musical Gazetteer of Great Britain and Ireland* (Newton Abbot)
Norvall 1991. Colin J Norvall: *The Story of the Organ and Organists of Frome Parish Church* (Frome)
Nourse 2008. Nicholas Nourse: *An Independent Folk Scene: Oxford, c.1945–c.1970* (MA diss, Univ of Bristol)
Nourse 2012. Nicholas Nourse: *The Transformation of the Music of the British Poor, 1789–1864, with special reference to two second cities* (PhD diss, Univ of Bristol)
Nourse 2014. Nicholas Nourse: 'Musical migrations: the origins of the portable street barrel piano', *GSJ* lxvii: 33, 49–57

O'Connor 2007. Mike O'Connor: 'Recent discoveries in Cornish music', *JRIC*: 38–47

O'Connor and Ashbee 2009. Mike O'Connor OBE and Andrew Ashbee: 'A Jacobean bass viol book in Cornwall', *Viola da Gamba Society Journal* iii: 83–92

Ogasapian 1994. John Ogasapian: *English Cathedral Music in New York: Edward Hodges of Trinity Church* (Richmond, VA)

Ogden 2001. Nigel Ogden: 'Foort, Reginald', *NG*, ix: 81

Olivier 1951. Edith Olivier: *Wiltshire* (London)

Olleson 2003. Philip Olleson: *Samuel Wesley: the man and his music* (Woodbridge)

Opie 1988. June Opie: *'Come and Listen to the Stars Singing'. Priaulx Rainier: a pictorial biography* (Penzance)

Orme 1978. Nicholas Orme: 'The early musicians of Exeter Cathedral', *ML* lix: 395–410

Orme 1980. Nicholas Orme: *The Minor Clergy of Exeter Cathedral, 1300–1548: a list of the minor officers, vicars choral, annuellars, secondaries and choristers* (Exeter)

Orme 1986. Nicholas Orme: *Exeter Cathedral As It Was 1050–1550* (Newton Abbot)

Orme 1989. Prof Nicholas Orme MA, DPhil, DLitt, FSA, FRHistS: 'The history of Brampford Speke', *TDA* cxxi: 53–86

Orme 1990. Nicholas Orme: 'Music and teaching at Tywardreath Priory, 1522–1536', *DCNQ* xxxvi: 277–80

Orme 2004. Nicholas Orme: 'Lacy, Edmund', *ODNB*, xxxii: 179–80

Orme 2010. Nicholas Orme, with Oliver Padel: *Cornwall*, vol 2: *Religious History to 1560* (VCH)

Orme 2013. Nicholas Orme: *The Minor Clergy of Exeter Cathedral: biographies, 1250–1548* (DCRS liv, Exeter)

Osborne 2013. William Osborne: 'Florio, Caryl [Robjohn, W(illiam) J(ames)]', *GDAM*, iii: 321

Oswald 1988. Neville C Oswald TD, MD, FRCP: 'Life in the South Hams in World War II', *TDA* cxx: 97–113

O'Toole 2011. Hanna O'Toole: *Julius Harrison (1885–1963): unjustly neglected?* (MA diss, Univ of Bristol)

Palmer 1996. Roy Palmer: *The Sound of History: songs and social comment* (London, reissue)

Parke 1830. W T Parke: *Musical Memoirs* (2 vols, London)

Parker 1894. Louis Napoleon Parker: 'Music in our public schools', *PMA* xx: 97–113

Parker 1918. Louis Napoleon Parker: 'Provincial memories', *PMA* xlv: 13–28

Parker 1928. Louis Napoleon Parker: *Several of My Lives* (London)
Parker 2016. Peter Parker: *Housman Country* (London)
Parsloe 1932. Guy Parsloe: *The English Country Town* (English Heritage series: London)
Patten 2016. Bob Patten: 'Study day report: West Gallery Musical Association – research group meeting', *CN* 21 (summer): 2–4
Patterson 1952. C H Patterson: *The History of Paignton: reprinted from the* Paignton Observer (Paignton, nd [1952?])
Payne 1988. Gordon A Payne, ed: *Uffculme: a Culm Valley parish* (Uffculme [Local History Group])
Payne 2003. Ian Payne: 'The will and probate inventory of John Holmes (d 1629): instrumental music at Salisbury and Winchester Cathedrals revisited', *The Antiquaries Journal* lxxxiii: 369–96
Payne 2004. Ian Payne: 'Lugge, John', *ODNB*, xxxiv: 733
Payne 2009. John Payne: *The West Country: a cultural history* (Oxford)
Payton 2004. Philip Payton: *Cornwall: a history* (Fowey, 2nd edn)
Payton 2005. Philip Payton: *The Cornish Overseas* (Fowey, rev edn)
Pazdírek nd. Franz Pazdírek, ed: *Universal-Handbuch der Musikliteratur aller Zeiten und Völker, I. Teil* (Vienna)
Peach 1987. Victor Peach: *Patriots All! a study of the Totnes Volunteers* (Totnes [Community Archive])
Pengelly 1886. W Pengelly: 'Prince's "Worthies of Devon" and the *Dictionary of National Biography*. Part II', *TDA* xviii: 269–369
PenStM leaflet. 'The organ in St Mary's, Penzance' (nd)
Penwill 1953. F Ralph Penwill FRICS, FRSA: *Paignton in Six Reigns: being the history of local government in Paignton ... 1863 to 1952* (Paignton [Coronation Celebrations])
Peppin 1927. Arthur H Peppin: *Public Schools and Their Music* (London)
Percival 1873. John Percival: *The Connection of the Universities and the Great Towns* (London)
Perry 2009. Seamus Perry: review of *Thomas Hardy's 'Poetical Matter' Notebook*, ed Pamela Dalziel and Michael Millgate, *TLS*, 20 Nov: 7–8
Pevsner and Cherry 1975. Nikolaus Pevsner, rev Bridget Cherry: *Wiltshire* (*PevsBE*, rev edn)
Pevsner and Lloyd 1967. Nikolaus Pevsner and David Lloyd: *Hampshire and the Isle of Wight* (*PevsBE*)
Pigot 1822. *Pigot & Co's London and Provincial New Commercial Directory for 1822–3* (Manchester)
Pigot 1823. *Pigot & Co's London and Provincial New Commercial Directory, for 1823–4* (London)

Pigot 1830. *Pigot & Co's National Commercial Directory ... [for] Cornwall, Dorsetshire, Devonshire, Somersetshire, Wiltshire* (facsimile edn, Castle Rising, 1993)

Pilkington 1978. Francis Pilkington: *Ashburton: the Dartmoor town* (np)

Pilkinton 1997. Mark C Pilkinton, ed: *REED: Bristol*

Pinel 2006. Stephen L Pinel: 'Robjohn, Thomas (1809–1874)', *The Organ: an encyclopedia*, ed Douglas E Bush and Richard Kassel (New York): 468

Pinner 2011. Mark Pinner: 'Racial stereoptypes as comedic mechanism: Luscombe Searelle and Walter Parke', *Grainger Studies* i: 35–54

Pinto 2004. David Pinto: 'Lawes, William', *ODNB* xxxii: 778–80

Plantinga and Tyson 2001. Leon Plantinga (with Alan Tyson, work-list): 'Clementi, Muzio', *NG*, vi: 39–46

Plym 1923. Plymouth & District Trades & Labour Council: *Souvenir of the Trades Union Congress: Plymouth 1923* (np)

Plym 1932. *The British Music Society (Plymouth Centre): 10th Musical Competition Festival*, programme (np)

Plym 1937. *City of Plymouth Musical Festival: programme for 1937* (np)

Poole 2009. Sharon Poole: *The Grand Pier Weston-super-Mare* (Stroud)

Porter 1984. J H Porter BA, PhD: 'The incidence of industrial conflict in Devon 1860–1900', *TDA* cxvi: 63–75

Powell 2008. Christopher Powell: *Henry Bennett Junior (1813–1868): organist – composer – hymnwriter* (pp [Cardiff])

Price 1981. David C Price: *Patrons and Musicians of the English Renaissance* (Cambridge)

Probyn 1991. Clive T Probyn: *The Sociable Humanist: the life and works of James Harris 1709–1780* (Oxford)

Pulman 1875. George P R Pulman: *The Book of the Axe* (1844–5, ?2/1854, 4/1875, facsimile edn Bath, 1969)

Quick 2000. Mary Quick: 'Music: a golden thread woven through our Cornish lives', *Changing Times in Old St Ives* vol 3 (St Ives [Trust Archive Study Centre], nd): 7–17 (repr from *St Ives Times & Echo*, 22 Sep and 6 Oct 2000)

Radford 1950. Cecily Radford: 'Three centuries of playgoing in Exeter', *TDA* lxxxii: 241–69

Radford 1965. Maisie and Evelyn Radford: *Musical Adventures in Cornwall* (Dawlish)

Rainbow 1970. Bernarr Rainbow: 'W J E Bennett and the Pimlico riots', *The Choral Revival in the Anglican Church (1839–1872)* (Oxford): 143–61

Rastall 1968. Richard Rastall: *Secular Musicians in Late Medieval England* (2 vols, PhD diss, Univ of Manchester)

Rastall 1996. Richard Rastall: *The Heaven Singing: music in early English religious drama I* (Cambridge)

Rastall 2001a. Richard Rastall: *Minstrels Playing: music in early English religious drama II* (Cambridge)
Rastall 2001b. Richard Rastall: 'Wait', *NG*, xxvii: 4–5
Reay 1899. Samuel Reay: 'Mendelssohn's wedding march', *MT* xl: 194
Reeve 2000. David C Reeve: *Wimborne Minster, Dorset: a study of a small town 1620 to 1690* (PhD diss, Univ of Exeter)
Rehrig 2013. William H Rehrig: 'Brockenshire, James Opie', *GDAM* i: 638
Reid 1992. Helen Reid: *A Chronicle of Clifton and Hotwells* (Bristol)
Reid and Pritchard 1965. Douglas J Reid, with Brian Pritchard: 'Some festival programmes of the eighteenth and nineteenth centuries. 1. Salisbury and Winchester', *RMARC* 5: 51–79
Richards 1923. Charles G Richards: *Scenes from the Life of Drake* (np [Plymouth])
Richards 2000. Fiona Richards: *The Music of John Ireland* (Aldershot)
Richardson 1972. Alan A Richardson: 'Salisbury's super cinema[s]', *Wessex Life* (Dec): 28–30
Richardson 1981. Alan A Richardson: *The Cinema Theatres of Salisbury: 50th anniversary special, Odeon, Salisbury. September 7th, 1981* (Salisbury)
Richardson 2013. Angelique Richardson: review of *The Collected Letters of Thomas Hardy* vol 8, ed M Millgate and K Wilson, *TLS*, 12 Jul: 3–4
Riley 2003. Malcom Riley: *Percy Whitlock: organist and composer* (London, 1998; York, 2nd edn)
Riley 2004. Malcolm Riley: 'Whitlock, Percy William', *ODNB*, lviii: 741–2
Riley 2007. Malcolm Riley, ed: *The Percy Whitlock Companion* (Staplehurst)
Roberts 1834. George Roberts: *The History and Antiquities of the Borough of Lyme Regis and Charmouth* (London; facsimile edn Lyme Regis, 1996)
Roberts 1983. Richard Roberts: 'The Corporation as impresario: the municipal provision of entertainment in Victorian and Edwardian Bournemouth', in *Leisure in Britain 1780–1939*, ed John K Walton and James Walvin (Manchester): 137–57
Robertson 1938. Dora H Robertson: *Sarum Close: a history of the life and education of the Cathedral choristers for 700 years* (London)
Robins 1998. Brian Robins, ed: *The John Marsh Journals: the life and times of a gentleman composer (1752–1828)* (Stuyvesant, NY)
Robins 2001. Brian Robins: 'Marsh, John', *NG*, xv: 895–6
Robins 2006. Brian Robins: 'Provincial catch and glee clubs', in *Catch and Glee Culture in Eighteenth-Century England* (Woodbridge)
Robinson 1999a. Chris Robinson: 'Dance days with the White Notes', *WEH*, 14 Dec 1999, in PRGDB
Robinson 1999b. Chris Robinson: 'Playing sax in the band', *WEH*, 15 Jun 1999, in PRGDB

Robinson 2004. Chris Robinson: 'Theirs was a very musical marriage', *WEH*, 10 Jul 2004, in PRGDB

Robinson 2011. Jane Robinson: *A Force to Be Reckoned With: a history of the Women's Institute* (London)

Rosselli 2004. John Rosselli: 'Incledon, Charles', *ODNB*, xxix: 227–8

Rowntree 1987. John P Rowntree: 'Lulworth Chapel and a missing Arne mass', *MT* cxxviii: 347–9

Rowse 1941. A L Rowse: *Tudor Cornwall* (London)

Rowse 1949. A L Rowse: 'The stone that liked company', in *West Country Short Stories*, ed Lewis Wilshere (London): 77–94

Rowse 1950. A L Rowse: *The England of Elizabeth* (London)

Russell 2000. Dave Russell: 'Musicians in the English provincial city: Manchester, *ca* 1860–1914', in *Music and British Culture, 1785–1914: essays in honour of Cyril Ehrlich*, ed Christina Bashford and Leanne Langley (Oxford): 233–55

Sacchi 1999. Floraleda Sacchi: *Elias Parish Alvars: life, music, documents* (Dornach)

Sadler 2004. John Sadler: 'Percival, John', *ODNB*, xliii: 673–4

St Leger-Gordon 1950. D St Leger-Gordon: *Devonshire* (London)

Salisbury 1897–98. *Langmead & Evans' Directory of Salisbury & District* (Salisbury)

Sandon 2001a. Nicholas Sandon: 'Dark [Darke], John', *NG*, vii: 22–3

Sandon 2001b. Nicholas Sandon: 'Salisbury ["Sarum"], Use of', *NG*, xxii: 158–63

Schafer 1977. R Murray Schafer: *The Tuning of the World* (New York)

Schofield 2006. Derek Schofield: 'Peter Kennedy', obituary, *Guardian*, 19 Jun: 35

Scholes 1947. Percy A Scholes: *The Mirror of Music 1844–1944: a century of musical life in Britain as reflected in the pages of the* Musical Times (2 vols, London)

Scholes 1954. Percy A Scholes: *God Save the Queen! The history and romance of the world's first national anthem* (London)

SDNQ Morris. 'Dr Claver Morris' accounts', *SDNQ* xxii (1936–8): 78–81, 100–2, 147–51, 172–5, 199–203, 230–2 and 263, and xxiii (1939–42): 40–1, 100–3, 134–40, 164–6 and 345–7

Self 1997. Geoffrey Self: *Music in West Cornwall: a twentieth century mirror* (pp [Camborne])

Sharp 1907. Cecil J Sharp: *English Folk Song: some conclusions* (London and Taunton)

Shaw 1967. Thomas Shaw: *A History of Cornish Methodism* (Truro)

Shaw 1991. Watkins Shaw: *The Succession of Organists of the Chapel Royal and the Cathedrals of England and Wales from c.1538* (Oxford)

Sherborne 1950. anon: 'School music', in *The Sherborne Register: 1550–1950*, ed B Pickering Pick (Winchester, 4th edn): 528–31

Shuttleworth 1700. John Shuttleworth: *A Sermon Preached at Bridgwater in Somersetshire, July the 17th, 1700: at the opening of the organ lately erected there* (London)

Simkins 1939. Cyril Frank Simkins: *West Country Musicians of the Days of Old* (Dawlish)

Sketchley 1775. *Sketchley's Bristol Directory* (Bristol)

Skinner 2001. David Skinner: 'Davy [Davys], Richard', *NG*, vii: 83–4

Skinner 2011. Gavin Skinner: 'Inter-Varsity Folk Dance Festival: 25–27 February 2011, Bristol', *CN* 10 (winter 2010–11): 12–13

Skinner 2013. Susan Margaret Skinner: *A History of the Cornish Male Voice Choir: the relationship between music, place and culture* (PhD diss, Univ of Plymouth)

Slatter 1965. Doreen Slatter, ed: *The Diary of Thomas Naish* (Devizes)

Slaytor 2013. Michael Slaytor: 'Frances Joan Singleton (1886–1975): pianist and accompanist', *BM* xxxv: 35–51

Sloboda 2005. John Sloboda: *Exploring the Musical Mind: cognition, emotion, ability, function* (Oxford and New York)

Smith 1892. George Smith: *Henry Martyn, Saint and Scholar* (London)

Smith 1948. R A L Smith: *Bath* (London, 3rd edn)

Smith 1967. Alan Smith: *The Practice of Music in English Cathedrals and Churches, and at the Court, during the Reign of Elizabeth I* (3 vols, PhD diss, Univ of Birmingham)

Smith 1968. Peter Smith: *Blandford* (Blandford)

Smith 1989–90. Stanley G Smith: 'Growing up in Frome in the 1930s', *FSYB* iii: 2–14

Smith 1990. Chris Smith: *Village Profiles: a personal view of some of Devon's villages based on the BBC Radio Devon Series* (Exeter)

Smith 1999a. Bruce R Smith: *The Acoustic World of Early Modern England* (Chicago)

Smith 1999b. John Wilson Smith: *Elias Parish Alvars, 1808–49: king of harpists* (Teignmouth)

Smith 2001a. James G Smith, with Percy M Young: 'Chorus (i)', *NG*, v: 767–86

Smith 2001b. Michael Smith: 'Edwards [Edwardes], Richard', *NG*, vii: 902–3

Smith et al 2001. Ruth Smith, Michael Smith, and Jeremy Maule: 'Herbert [Harbert], George', *NG*, xi: 401–2

Smollett 1771. Tobias Smollett: *The Expedition of Humphry Clinker* (3 vols, London and Salisbury)

Southern 1925. H Southern: 'Clementi in the Dorset park-country, *DYB* xxi: 78–86

Southey 2006. Roz Southey: *Music-Making in North-East England during the Eighteenth Century* (Aldershot)

Sowden 2002. Barry Sowden: *Oh No! It's Local Rock and Roll ... but I Like It! A fond look back at the roots of rock and roll in Mid Devon, 1954-1979* (Tiverton)

Sowden 2003. Barry Sowden: *Oh No! It's Local Rock and Roll ... but I Like It! A fond look back at the roots of rock and roll in Exeter and East Devon* (Tiverton)

Sowden 2004. Barry Sowden: *Oh No! It's Local Rock and Roll ... but I Like It! A fond look back at the roots of rock and roll in Taunton and South Somerset 1959-1979* (Tiverton)

Spaeth 2003. Donald Spaeth: '"The enemy within": the failure of reform in the diocese of Salisbury in the eighteenth century', in Gregory and Chamberlain 2003: 121-44

Spark 1888. William Spark: *Musical Memories* (London)

Spink 1992. Ian Spink: 'Music and society', in *Music in Britain: the seventeenth century*, ed Spink (Oxford): 1-65

Spink 2000. Ian Spink: *Henry Lawes: Cavalier songwriter* (Oxford)

Spink 2004a. Ian Spink: 'Child, William', *ODNB*, xi: 435-6

Spink 2004b. Ian Spink: 'Lawes, Henry', *ODNB*, xxxii: 772-5

Spinke 1877-79. *Spinke's Directory of Chippenham*

Spinney 1954. L M Spinney et al: *'These 150 Years': being a brief history of Poole Baptists, 1804-1954* (np, nd)

Spring 2001. Matthew Spring: *The Lute in Britain* (Oxford)

Squire and Golby 2004. W Barclay Squire, rev David J Golby: 'Bridgetower, George Augustus Polgreen', *ODNB*, vii: 596-7

Staelens 2002. Yvette Staelens: *Girls Rock ON! Chard Foundation for Women in Music's groundbreaking Young Womens' Band Project* (Chard)

Stally and Woods nd. Brian Stally and John Woods, illus A P Thompson: *The Medieval Bench Ends at St Nonna's Altarnun* (pp [Altarnun])

Stater 2004. Victor Stater: 'Herbert, William, third earl of Pembroke', *ODNB*, xxvi: 738-44

Steele 2001. John Steele: 'Lugge, John', *NG*, xv: 287-8

Stéphan 1948. Dom John Stéphan OSB: *Historical Guide to Buckfast Abbey* (np, rev edn)

Sternfeld and Greer 1967. E H Fellowes, rev Frederick W Sternfeld and David Greer: *English Madrigal Verse 1588-1632* (Oxford, 3rd edn)

Stevens 1961. John Stevens: *Music and Poetry in the Early Tudor Court* (London)

Stevens 1969. John Stevens, ed: *Music at the Court of Henry VIII* (MB xviii, London, 1962; rev edn)

Stevens 1976. Robin S Stevens, 'Joseph Summers, 1839-1917, Musician', in *Australian Dictionary of Biography*, vi, ed Bede Nairn (Melbourne): 220-1

Stokes 1996. James Stokes, with Robert J Alexander, ed: *REED: Somerset, including Bath* (2 vols)

Stokes 2003. James Stokes: 'Landscape, movement, and civic mimesis in the west of England', *ET* vi/1: 35–49

Street and Carpenter 1993. Sean Street and Ray Carpenter: *The Bournemouth Symphony Orchestra: a centenary celebration* (Wimborne)

Strohm 1985. Reinhard Strohm: *Music in Late Medieval Bruges* (Oxford)

Strong 2007. Roy Strong: *A Little History of the English Country Church* (London)

Summers 1910. Joseph Summers, *Music and Musicians: personal reminiscences, 1865–1910* (Perth, Western Australia)

Summers 2006. Vivian Summers, incorporating material by David Cook: *Church of the Holy Cross, Crediton* (London)

Sutcliffe Smith 1945. J Sutcliffe Smith: *The Story of Music in Birmingham* (Birmingham)

Sutton 1973. Anna Sutton: *A Story of Sidmouth: and the villages of Salcombe Regis, Branscombe, Sidbury and Sidford* (1953; Chichester, 2nd edn)

Swift and Elliott 2009. Andrew Swift and Kirsten Elliott: *The Year of the Pageant* (Bath)

Taunton 1951. *Official Souvenir Programme of the Borough of Taunton Celebrations of the Festival of Britain, 1951* (Taunton)

Teague 2008. Robbie Teague: *The Strummings of a Long Distance Folk Singer* (pp [Bridport])

Temperley 1979. Nicholas Temperley: *The Music of the English Parish Church* (2 vols, Cambridge)

Temperley 2001a. Nicholas Temperley: 'Knapp, William', *NG*, xiii: 688

Temperley 2001b. Nicholas Temperley: 'Loder', *NG*, xv: 56–9

Temperley 2001c. Nicholas Temperley: 'Psalmody (ii). I. England', *NG*, xx: 472–80

Temperley 2009. Nicholas Temperley: *Studies in English Church Music, 1550–1900* (Farnham)

Temperley 2016. Nicholas Temperley, ed: *Musicians of Bath and Beyond: Edward Loder (1809–1865) and his family* (Woodbridge)

Temperley and Banfield 2010. Nicholas Temperley and Stephen Banfield, eds: *Music and the Wesleys* (Urbana, IL)

Temperley et al 2001. Nicholas Temperley, David Charlton, Trevor Fawcett, and Christopher Smith: 'Norwich', *NG*, xviii: 66–70

Thackeray 1848–50. William Makepeace Thackeray: *The History of Pendennis* (*The Oxford Thackeray*: London, 1908)

Thicknesse 2012. Robert Thicknesse: 'Starting on high notes', *The Tablet*, 11 Feb: 24

Thomas 1904. A[lfred?] G T[homas?]: *Counterslip Baptist Church, Bristol: centenary souvenir* (pp)

Thomas 1993. Margaret Thomas: *The Heritage Book of Nailsea* (Buckingham, 1984 as *The Book of Nailsea*, rev edn np)

Thomas 1996. Gavin Thomas: 'Beam me up, Scotty', *MT* cxxxvii (Jul): 19–21

Thomas 2008. Matthew Thomas: 'New light on Andrew Ashe', *Traverso* x/4 (Oct): 13–15

Thomas 2009a. Matthew Thomas: *Andrew Ashe, Performer, Conductor, Composer: an assessment of the Irish flute player* (MA diss, Univ of Bristol, 2008; rev typescript)

Thomas 2009b. Matthew Thomas: 'William Wrenn: Bristol's forgotten flute-player', *CN* 7 (summer): 8–9

Thompson 2004. Robert Thompson: 'Locke, Matthew', *ODNB*, xxxiv: 231–4

Tinker 2009. Christopher Tinker: 'Imogen Holst: biographical sketch', *BMS News* 122 (Jun): 138–43

Tinker 2013. Christopher Tinker: 'Imogen Holst, Benjamin Britten, and related activity', *BM* xxxv: 5–17

Tooley 2004. John Tooley, rev: 'Turner, Dame Eva', *ODNB*, lv: 613–14

Torrens 2015. Hugh S Torrens: '"Gone for a Burton": Thomas Arthur Burton (1842–1936), musician & composer, and his family (from Leicestershire, Derbyshire, Cotswolds, Hampshire & Dorset)', *PDNHAS* cxxxvi: 38–56

Toulmin 1791. Joshua Toulmin: *The History of the Town of Taunton* (Taunton)

Trewin 1981. J C Trewin, ed: *The West Country Book* (Exeter)

Troost 2001. Linda Troost: 'Reeve, William', *NG*, xxi: 75–6

Trowell 2001. Brian Trowell: 'Pack [Packe, Pakke, Parke], Thomas', *NG*, xviii: 867–8

Tudsbery-Turner 2002. Stephen Tudsbery-Turner: *Wells in Old Picture Postcards* (Zaltbommel, Netherlands)

Tunstall-Behrens 2007. Hilary Tunstall-Behrens: 'The virtuoso violinist Sándor Végh in Cornwall', *JRIC*: 19–37

Turner 1949. M Lovett Turner: *Somerset* (London)

Turner 2004a. F J Turner: 'Weld, Thomas', *ODNB*, lvii: 979

Turner 2004b. John R Turner: 'Arrowsmith, James Williams', *ODNB*, ii: 525–6

Universal 1799. *The Universal British Directory* (London)

Varcoe nd. Stephen Varcoe: 'Richard Hickox – an appreciation', in 'St Endellion Festivals' [qv]: Richard Hickox

Vecsey 1931. Armand Vecsey: *The Fiddler of the Ritz, etc* (New York)

Verey 1976. David Verey: *Gloucestershire. 2: The Vale and the Forest of Dean* (*PevsBE*, rev edn)

W R 1829. W R: 'Recollections of an old favourite', *Blackwood's Edinburgh Magazine* xxvi: 567–70

Walker 2001. Alan Walker: 'Liszt, Franz [Ferenc]', *NG*, xiv: 755–85, 872–7

Walker 2008. Trevor Walker: *150 Years of Music Making: Penzance Choral Society 1858–2008* (pp, np, nd)

Walker and Walker 1995. Gordon and Ailsa Walker: 'The Brockley elephant', *Pennant* 13: 12–13

Walrond 1897. *Historical records of the 1st Devon Militia (4th Battalion the Devonshire Regiment)* (London)

Wanklyn 1944. Cyril Wanklyn: *Lyme Leaflets* (pp)

Wardell 2011. Francis Wardell: 'Queen Elizabeth I's progress to Bristol in 1574: an examination of expenses', *ET* xiv/1: 101–20

Warne 1969. Arthur Warne: *Church and Society in Eighteenth-Century Devon* (Newton Abbot)

Warrack 2001. John Warrack: 'Moore, Thomas', *NG*, xvii: 80–2

Warrack 2004. John Warrack: 'Davy, John', *ODNB*, xv: 513

Warren 1938. C Henry Warren: *West Country (Somerset, Devon and Cornwall)* (London)

Wasson 1986. John M Wasson, ed: *REED: Devon*

Waterfield 1946. R Waterfield BA: 'Address of the President: Music in Devon; the historical aspect', *TDA* lxxviii: 23–48

Waterhouse 1993. William Waterhouse: *The New Langwill Index: a dictionary of musical wind-instrument makers and inventors* (London)

Wathey 2001. Andrew Wathey: 'Mowere [Mawere], Richard', *NG*, xvii: 253

Watkin 1917. Hugh R Watkin: *The History of Totnes Priory & Medieval Town* (2 vols, Torquay)

Watkin 1935. Hugh R Watkin: *Dartmouth. Vol 1: pre-Reformation* (Exeter)

Watkin 1950. Dom Aelred Watkin: 'Glastonbury's last Christmas', *Catholic Herald*, 8 Dec: 7

Watkins 1792. John Watkins: *An Essay Towards a History of Bideford, in the County of Devon* (Exeter)

Watkins 1914. Hadley Watkins: *Twenty-One Years of Municipal Music. 1893–1914* (Bournemouth)

Watkins 1993. Dr John Watkins: *An Essay Towards the History of Bideford* (rev edn of Watkins 1792)

Weatherly 1926. Fred E Weatherly: *Piano and Gown: recollections* (London and New York)

Webb 2007. Peter Webb: 'Interrogating the production of sound and place: Bristol as a site of music production, from lunatic fringe to worldwide massive', *Exploring the Networked Worlds of Popular Music* (New York and Abingdon): 41–59

Wetzel 1983. Richard D Wetzel: 'The search for William Cumming Peters', *American Music* i: 27–41

Wetzel 2001. Richard D Wetzel: 'Peters, W(illiam) C(umming)', *NG*, xix: 492–3

Whistler 1947. Laurence Whistler: *The English Festivals* (London)

White 1850. William White: *History, Gazetteer, and Directory of Devonshire* (Sheffield)

Whitham 1972. John A Whitham: *The Church of St Mary of Ottery in the Country of Devon: a short history and guide* (Gloucester, 5th edn)

Whitlock 1936. Percy Whitlock: 'Organs in and around Bournemouth', Part 1, *MO* (Jun 1936): 792–3, repr in Riley 2007: 55–63

Whittel 1689. John Whittel: *An Exact Diary of the Late Expedition of the Prince of Orange* (London)

Whittle 2007. David Whittle: *Bruce Montgomery/Edmund Crispin: a life in music and books* (Aldershot)

Wickens 2001. David C Wickens: 'Crang & Hancock', *NG*, vi: 646

Wilcox 2004. Helen Wilcox: 'Herbert, George', *ODNB*, xxvi: 677–85

Williams 1979. David Williams: *Genesis and Exodus: a portrait of the Benson family* (London)

Williams 2001. Peter Williams, with Nicholas Thistlethwaite: 'Swell, §1', *NG*, xxiv: 779–80

Williams nd. Douglas Williams, ed: *A Century of Song: the story of Mousehole and its famed Male Voice Choir* (np [2009])

Williamson 1996/97. Paul Williamson: 'Realising Jackson', *GHR*: 39–43

Williamson 2004. Paul Williamson: 'Jackson, William', *ODNB*, xxix: 533–4

Williamson 2008. Magnus Williamson: 'The will of John Boraston: musicians within collegiate and parochial communities', in *The Late Medieval English College and Its Context*, ed Clive Burgess and Martin Heale (York and Woodbridge): 180–95

Wilshire 1949. Lewis Wilshire: *West Country Short Stories* (London)

Wilson 1959. John Wilson, ed: *Roger North on Music* (London)

Wilson 2012. Paul Wilson: 'Come sing for the season', *English Dance and Song* lxxiv/4 (winter): 12–13

Wiltshire 1993. Christopher Robin Wiltshire: *The British Male Voice Choir: a history and contemporary assessment* (PhD diss, Goldsmiths, Univ of London)

Wimborne 1998. anon: *Wimborne Minster* (Derby)

Wollenberg 2001. Susan Wollenberg: *Music at Oxford in the Eighteenth and Nineteenth Centuries* (Oxford)

Wolpowitz 1982. Lily Wolpowitz: 'Heath, Robert Hainsworth', in *South African Music Encyclopedia*, ed Jacques P Malan (4 vols, 1979–86), ii: 179

Woodcock 2010. G Woodcock: 'The Town Band', *Tavistock's Yesterdays: episodes from her history*, vol 19 (pp [Tavistock]): 93–6

Woodfield 1995. Ian Woodfield: *English Musicians in the Age of Exploration* (Stuyvesant, NY)

Woodfill 1953. Walter Woodfill: *Musicians in English Society: from Elizabeth to Charles I* (Princeton, NJ)

Woodhouse 1994. Harry Woodhouse: *Cornish Bagpipes: fact or fiction?* (Trewirgie [Redruth])

Woodhouse 1997. Harry Woodhouse: *Face the Music: church and chapel bands in Cornwall* (St Austell)

Woolrich nd. Tony Woolrich: *A History of the Organs of Saint Mary's Church, Bridgwater* (Bridgwater)

Wormleighton 1996. Tim Wormleighton: 'An eighteenth-century tour of Plymouth', in Gray 1996: 207–10

Worth 1887. R N Worth FGS: *Calendar of the Tavistock Parish Records* (Plymouth)

Wright 2013. David C H Wright: *The Associated Board of the Royal Schools of Music: a social and cultural history* (Woodbridge)

Wrigley 1998. V J Wrigley: *A History of Burnham-on-Sea and Highbridge* (Taunton)

Wylie 1916. J H Wylie, ed: *Report on the Records of the City of Exeter* (London)

Yardley 2006. Anne Bagnall Yardley: *Performing Piety: musical culture in medieval English nunneries* (Basingstoke)

Yardley 2008. Anne Bagnall Yardley: 'The musical education of young girls in medieval English nunneries', in *Young Choristers, 650–1700*, ed Susan Boynton and Eric Rice (Woodbridge): 49–67

Yeovil VE/VJ 2005. *Yeovil Town Council Presents ... Music in the Park: marking [the] 60th anniversary of VE & VJ Day* (commemorative programme booklet, WG)

Yetties 1986. *A Little Bit of Dorset: the Yetties* (Bridport)

Young 1968. Kenneth Young: *Music's Great Days in the Spas and Watering-Places* (London)

Index

abbeys *see* monasteries and abbeys
Abbots Leigh 84
Abbotsbury
    parish church 41
Abel, Carl Friedrich 232
Academy of the BBC *see* BBC Training Orchestra
accents, regional 14, 18, 145, 206, 255, 260, 357
accordionists 132-3, 137, 273-4, 365
Acland family 165, 299
    Sir John 159
acoustic jars 339
actors 99, 141, 276-7, 342-3
Adams, Aubrey 53
Addison, Joseph 181
admission prices *see* economics
agriculture *see* industry
Alcock, John 31
Aldeburgh Festival 281, 297
Alfonso 154
Alfred, King 320
Alice ? 191
Allen, John 16
Allen, William 137
Allington
    parish church 125
Alphington 318
Alphington, John and Walter de 318
Alsop, Marin 362
Altarnun
    parish church 66-8
amateurs 183, 207, 277, 284, 330
    competitive festivals 282
    emigrant 205
    gentlemen 74-8, 112, 264, 321, 328-9, 345
    in choirs and bands 104-26, 295, 331, 354
    women 43, 114-15, 174
    see also psalmody
Amesbury 161
    Abbey 160
Amyand, Sir George 32
Anderson, Ian 148
Anderson, Lucy 192
Andrews, Edward 260
Anelli, Giuseppe (Joseph) 193, 209
Angel, Alfred 337
Anglicanism 40, 113, 161, 199, 212 *see also* politics
Anne, Edward 74
Anne of Denmark 289
Anonymous IV 1
Appledore
    town band 120
apprenticeships 124, 154, 166-70, 184, 316
    and class 230
    and families 189-91, 223
    cost 372
    of particular individuals 218, 226, 257
    of women 222

post-conservatoire 338
to singing men 194
to waits 73, 191, 299
architects and architecture 9, 45, 231, 332, 339
    choirs 67
    organs as architecture 23, 29
    see also G E Street, venues
Arditi, Luigi 216
aristocracy 33, 41, 75, 100, 153-4, 197, 319, 358
    as patrons 158-66, 218, 282, 341, 347-9, 359
    see also country houses and estates
armed forces 92-7, 131-2, 145
    county regiments 264, 268
    officers 77-8, 101
    volunteer corps 268
    see also field musicians, military music, regiments and their bands, Royal Navy, volunteer bands
Arne, Thomas 232-3
Arnold, Malcolm 89
Arnold, Samuel 233
Arrowsmith, J W 329
Arthur, King 289, 292
    depicted in music dramas 295-6
artisans
    and artistic production 292, 336
    and family economics 371
    as musical multitraders 195, 348
    as performers 95, 105, 136, 246
    emigrant 206
    fishermen 110-12
    values and their erosion 124, 189
    see also Thomas Shoel
arts, visual *see* iconography
Arts and Crafts movement 60, 268, 294, 333
arts centres *see* venues
Arundell family 195
Ash Priors 67-8
Ashburton xiv, 122
    choral polyphony 311-13
    hymn tune 83-6
    organist 34, 85, 311
    psalmody 85-7
    St Andrew's church 25-7, 87, 311-12
    St Lawrence's chapel 310
    song school 310
    teachers 174, 184
Ashburton School 311
Ashe family 191, 222
    Andrew 220-3
    see also Comer family
Ashley, John 173, 192
Ashley, Josiah 95
Associated Board (ABRSM) 183, 187, 282
Astor, Lord and Lady 331
Attwater, Mr 102
    Attwater's Quadrille Band 100
Attwood, William 173

Aubrey, John 18
audiences 252, 288, 298, 339–49, 366, 374
  local 280
  supporting performers 359
  village 365–6
Austen, Jane 63, 292
Austin, Richard 130
Australia 92
  as market 211, 247
  emigrants and convicts 5, 51, 129, 201–7, 215
  Opera Australia 285
  psalmody 91
  reverse migration 246
  see also Peter Dawson
Avonmouth Docks 329
Axford, Mr 172
Axminster
  parish church 102
Aylward family 192

Bach family
  Johann Christian 163, 174–5, 198, 232
  Johann Sebastian 41, 327
Backwell 19
  parish church 125
Bacon, Roger 1
Badminton 218
bagpipers 66–8
Bailey, Charles and John 192
Bairstow, Edward 282
Baker, Gordon 142
ballads
  and class 134
  genteel 257–64
  hunting 261
  popular 211–12, 217–18, 266–8
  traditional 256, 260
  see also folk music
ballrooms 134
Bampfield [Bampfylde] family 299
  Sir Amos 159
  John 232
Bampton 124
Band of Hope 365
bandleaders 102, 128–31
bandmasters 94, 97, 103, 119, 124–8
  as martinets 127
  circus 237
  German 178
  in families 207, 224, 240
bands 64–8, 102–4, 120–7, 152, 159, 352
  brass 65, 104, 118–23, 128, 176
  circus 120, 237
  dance 56, 128–33, 141–2
  folk 133–4, 139–40
  German 97, 126
  Hungarian 126
  in church 58, 80–1, 85, 91–2, 102–3, 135–6
  Italian 126
  jazz 100, 129–30, 141, 144
  jug 100
  juvenile 337–8
  military 65, 77–80, 92–9, 102, 120, 131, 207, 220, 240

municipal 120, 240–1
on piers 53, 126–7
performance practice 101–3, 125–6
pop groups 72
punk 100
quadrille 99–102, 126, 237
rates of participation 64–5, 317
resort 127
rock 65, 100, 138–50
Salvation Army 122–5
seaside 120
swing 100
theatre 120
town 102
volunteer 123–5
works 98, 120–2, 125
  see also fiddlers, orchestras, psalmody, regiments and their bands, waits
bandstands 127–8
banjo players 365–6
bankrupts 168, 175, 192–3, 205, 256, 348
Banks, Benjamin and family 170–1
Banksy 145, 288
Banwell
  parish church 26
Barber, Chris 141
Barber, Mrs 100
Barford St Martin 246
Baring and Baring-Gould families 231
  Baring, Miss 32
  Baring-Gould, Sabine 9, 261, 266–9, 271, 279
Barnard, James 135
Barnicott and Pearce 269
Barnstaple 9, 64, 72, 159, 191, 313
  Assembly Rooms 105, 347
  balls 343
  choral society 116, 158
  composers 246–8
  concert life 343–8
  dealers 176, 246, 258
  Emmanuel Church 247
  music halls 246
  musical society 343–4
  North Devon Athenaeum 344
  parish church 24–5, 31–2, 63, 343
  politics 116
  professionals 343–4
  Puritanism 2
  St Thomas chantry 313
  Subscription Cassino Rooms 344
  teachers 186, 247, 343
  theatres 343–4
Barnstaple Harmonic Society 105, 358
Baron, Rev John 47–8, 61–3
Barons 141
barrel organs 32, 37, 195
  grinders 197
Barrett, George and Slater 155
Barrow, Geoff 150
Barshai, Rudolf 362
Bartlet, John 311
Bartlett, Mary 230, 236
Bartlett, Master 123
Bartlett, Rev Thomas 87

INDEX 423

Bartley 351
Basingstoke 363
Basset family 158
Bath xvi, 8, 75–6, 79, 202, 230, 332
   as microcosm of London 300
   as place of employment 133
   as place of publication 87
   as resort 300–1, 358
   Assembly Room (1708) 76
   bands 126
   bankrupts 192
   Buff Club 191
   Catch Club 342
   choral societies 118
   composers 86, 214–15
   concert life 197, 216–25, 300, 342–3, 346
   Countess of Huntingdon's chapel 86
   dancing 99
   dealers 95, 171–7, 192
   decline 43, 50, 200, 223
   diocese 8
   families 191–2, 218–25
   festivals 287
   fiddlers 137
   guitarists 2, 196, 209
   instrument makers 173
   introduction of pianos 175
   Jewish musicians 195
   Kensington proprietary chapel 222
   ladies' schools 322
   Lower Assembly Rooms 222, 342
   Mrs Wiltshire's Assembly Rooms 79
   multitraders 195
   New Musical Society 342–3
   New (Upper) Assembly Rooms 222, 342–3
   Octagon Chapel 221
   Orchard Street theatre 342
   orchestras 231
   organ builders 31, 60
     see also Robert Hayward, William Sweetland
   organs 50
   pianists 214–15
     see also Lucy Anderson, Kate Loder
   professionals 197–8, 314
   Pump Room Orchestra 76–8, 342, 357
   St Michael's church 41
   soundscape 16–17
   Spring Gardens 343
   teachers 184, 186, 196, 215, 222
   Theatre Royal 99, 342–3, 346
   theatres 300
   violinists 97, 195, 198
   waits 17, 71–4, 372, 373
   White Hart and White Lion taverns 342
   see also Hamswell Farm
Bath Abbey 298, 301, 342–3
   bells 17–18
   organ 25, 59
   organist 155, 218
Bath Choral Society 118
Bath Festival 287, 321
   chorus 118
Bath Folk Festival 286
Bath Harmonic Society 105, 220, 358

Bath Pageant 290
Bath Philharmonic Society 358
Bath Volunteers' march 95
Bayton, William 195
BBC 281, 331, 349–57
   and folk music 134, 136, 271
   The Archers 243
   as institutional force 8
   organ broadcasts 55–6, 179, 244–6
BBC Symphony Orchestra 354
BBC Theatre Orchestra 354
BBC Training Orchestra 339
BBC West of England Singers 352, 355
Beachcroft, Richard 328
Beaford Centre 335
Beale's (department store) 58, 130, 361
Beare, John 69
Beaufort, Duke of 218
Beaumont, Robert 154
Beckford family
   Peter 162–3, 175
   William 163
Bedford 354
Bedminster 95, 169
   Ebenezer Methodist Church 49
Beech, John 304, 308
Beecham, Sir Thomas 109
Beer
   Congregational Church 54
Beethoven, Ludwig van 214
Beilby, Bernard 328
Bellamarsh Barton 206
bells 12, 16–18, 24, 98
   bell ringers 85, 138–9
   change ringing 12, 81, 138
   handbell ringers 365
   zone of attraction 275
Bemerton 160–1
benefit concerts see concert life
Bennet, John 255
Bennett, Henry 86
Bennett, James Sterndale 290
Bennett, John 137
Bennett, W E 196
Bennett, Rev W J E 43–4
Bennett, William (of Combeinteignhead) 86–7
Bennett, William (of Plymouth) 32, 86, 175, 192
Bennett, William Sterndale 290
Benson, Bishop Edward 287
Bentinck, Colonel 220
Berglund, Paavo 362
Berlin Quartet 328
Berlioz, Hector 256
Bertini, Ernesto 126, 242–4
Betjeman, John 285
Betts, Mr 240
Bevan family 224–5
Bevin, Elway 156–7
Biddick family 135
Biddlecombe, William 198
Bideford 9, 317
   concert life 347–8
   Corporation 32
   dealers 176, 258

    Hungarian Military Season Band 126
    ladies' school 33
    pageant 291
    parish church 23, 31–4, 125
    singing men 181
    teachers 186
Bilk, Acker 143–6
Birch, Montague 130
Birmingham 49–50, 184–5, 190, 201, 338, 357, 362
Birtwistle, Harrison 332–5, 349
Bishops Lydeard
    parish church 81
Bishopsteignton 289
Bitton
    parish church 43
Black, William 35
black musicians 17, 94, 344
    see also Samuel Coleridge-Taylor, Joseph Emidy, Massive Attack, Tricky
Blackburn, Henry 309
blackface minstrelsy 64, 138, 206, 266, 273
    see also Padstow: darkie day festival
Blackmore, Brian 141
Blackmore Vale 18
Blagdon 168
Blagrove, Henry 185
Blandford Forum 75, 162–3, 332
    Assembly Rooms 346
    bells 119
    concert life 346
    cornopean band 118–19
    dancing school 322
    dealers 172
    mayor 119
    Mrs Sydenham's school 322
    parish church 36, 81
    racecourse 93
    Yeomanry Waltz 100
Blewett's Garages 129
Blue Vinney Folk Band 146
Blundell's School see Tiverton
Blunden, Edmund 366
Bobby's (department store) 130
Bodmin 61, 372
    bands 94
    organ builders see Roger Yates
    St Petroc's church 22, 34, 310
    waits 68
Bodmin Moor
    the Hurlers 274
Bodmin Priory 310
Boeringer, James 59–60, 189
Bonaparte, Napoleon 39, 94–9
    see also wars
Bond, Frederick Bligh 324
Boon, John and Robert 103
Boosey, John 211
    Boosey & Co 263
Boscastle 12–13, 135
Boscombe 56
Boskednan
    Nine Maidens stone circle 274
Boston 199
Boughton, Rutland 166, 294–7, 337

Boulanger, Nadia 332
Boult, Adrian 354, 361
Boulton, Harold 262
Bourchier, Fulk see Lord FitzWarin
Bourdieu, Pierre 253, 368
Bournemouth xix, 10, 58–9, 200, 237, 332, 354
    'Baedeker' raids 360–1
    BBC station 349
    borough organists 51, 246
    Bright's Restaurant 131
    choirs 363
    composers 242
    concert life 240–6, 360–4
    conservatoires 336–8
    Corporation 54, 241–4, 361
    dance bands and salon orchestras 130–1
    dealers 142, 176–7
    department stores 58, 130–1
    Geraldo salon orchestra 130
    Gli amici della musica 284
    Holdenhurst Road Methodist Church 54
    Holy Trinity church 243
    mayor 241
    municipal band 120
    musical distinction 51, 240–6
    opera 296
    pageants 291
    pianos 177–8
    Punshon Memorial Methodist Church 42, 361
    Regent Cinema, Westover Road 56–7
    Richmond Hill Congregational Church 42
    Rosebery Park Baptist Church 58
    Royal Bath Hotel 130
    Royal Italian Band 126, 244
    St Andrew's Presbyterian Church 42
    St Michael's church 42
    St Peter's church 42, 45, 243
    St Stephen's church 42, 45, 52, 56
    singers 351
    town churches 42
    venues 362
    Westover Ballroom 130
    Westover Cinema 57
    Winter Gardens (first) 243–4, 291, 296
    Winter Gardens (second) 362
    see also Boscombe, Charminster, Dan Godfrey, Percy Whitlock, Winton
Bournemouth Academy of Music 338
Bournemouth Conservatoire of Music 338
Bournemouth Corporation Military Band 126
Bournemouth Municipal Orchestra 54–6, 120, 130, 240–4, 291, 296, 338, 357–61
Bournemouth Pavilion 51–6, 130, 141, 244–6, 361–3
Bournemouth School of Music 338
Bournemouth Sinfonietta and choir 362
Bournemouth Symphony Orchestra 280–1, 298, 331–2, 336, 357–64
    see also Bournemouth Municipal Orchestra
Bournemouth University 336
Bowcher, Katherine 174
Bowen, Samuel 120
Bowen, York 263
Bowood House 164
Box

parish church 84, 104
Boy Scouts 139–40
    Cubs 125
Boyce, William 233
Boys' Brigade 132–3, 139–40
Boyter, Mr 195
Brace, Richard 159
Bradford 50
Bradford on Avon 75, 121
    Wiltshire Music Centre 287
Bradninch 318
Bradock
    parish church 68
Bradstone
    pageant 291
Brampford Speke
    parish church 37–9
Bramston, Richard 309, 315
Brantingham, Bishop Thomas de 276
brass bands *see* bands
brass quintets 115, 118, 223
Bray, Billy 365
Brazil 239
Brendon 260
Brenner, J G 131
Brewer, W Gordon 350
Brexit xvi–xvii, 368–9
Brian, Humphrey and Isaac 169
Bridge, Richard 190
Bridges family 32
Bridgetower, George 240
Bridgetown *see* Totnes
Bridgwater 43, 72, 75, 317
    concert life 347
    Corpus Christi 67–8
    dance bands 141
    dealers 172, 177
    instrument makers 192
    organists 188
    St Mary's church 22, 25, 31, 372
    Song of the Bridgwater men 292
    teachers 188
    Tudor Restaurant 188
Bridgwater Grammar School for Girls 188
Bridgwater Pageant 290–2
Bridgwater String Orchestra 188
Bridgwater Studio of Music and Dramatic Art 188
Bridgwater Youth Orchestra 188
Bridport 33, 168, 315, 373
    arts centre 366–7
    parish church 36
    Wesleyan chapel 366
    see also Allington
Bridport, La 100
Brighouse and Rastrick Brass Band 271
Bright family, alias Lucas 157
Brighton 200, 363
Bristol xvi, 97, 150, 202–3, 354
    accent 145
    All Saints' church 95, 301–4, 307–9, 371–4
    amateurs 328–9
    and the Bournemouth Symphony Orchestra 362–3
    apprenticeships 162, 166–9, 191, 194, 324

artists 2
as gateway xi, 7, 346
as hub 9, 167–8, 184
as musical centre 300
as place of employment 279
Ashton Court 291
bands 357
bankrupts 192–3, 205
BBC broadcasting 9, 84, 350–6
bibliography 4
choirs 363
choral societies 116
Christ Church 31, 311
city churches 28, 31, 311–12
clubs and societies 76, 105–9, 134, 146–9
Colston Hall 50–1, 328, 363
composers 86, 105, 198–9, 209–18, 324, 326–30, 353
concert halls 300
concert life 118, 220–4, 328–9, 341–3, 345–7, 355, 362–3
conservatoires 300, 337–8
Corporation 355
Countership Baptist Church 33
dealers 95, 172–7, 192–3
decline 170, 201
diocese 7–8
Dug Out Club 146–9
Empire Theatre 130
families 83, 155, 184–5, 327–8
folk music 134, 147–8
Free Port Day 100
Gaunt's Hospital *see* Lord Mayor's Chapel
Gild of the Kalendars 308
Gordon Baker Orchestra 142
guitarists 2, 209, 337
hinterland 113
hymn tune 83
immigrants 197
industry 146
instrument makers 38, 169, 192, 195, 201
Jews 300
ladies' schools 322
lay clerks and singing men 194, 311–12, 330
Lord Mayor's Chapel (St Mark's church) 16, 105, 317
mayor 68
migration patterns 157, 199–205, 329–30
military music 92–7
nonconformists 300
organ builders 35, 44, 59–60, 190, 196
organists 195, 198–9
patronage 159, 297
pianos 175–7
pre-Reformation polyphony 301–9
Prince's Street Assembly Room 16
printers 172
professionals 186, 198, 220, 230, 301–9, 314, 323, 326, 354
publishing 205
royal progresses 7, 288–9
St Ewen's church 311
St James's church 16, 31, 311
St James's Fair 197
St John's Gate 289

St Mary Redcliffe church 35–6, 288
    choir 312
    choristers 145
    hymn tune 83
    lay clerks 330
    organ 21-2, 31, 35–6, 49, 220
    organist 16, 184
St Michael's church 105, 205
St Nicholas's church 31, 326
St Paul's (district) 143, 148
St Peter's parish 194
St Stephen's church 31
St Thomas's church 31, 308
soundscape 15–16, 32
Stanshawe Band 120
street musicians 197
subculture 146–9
suburban churches 42
suburbs 145, 300
taverns 134, 145
teachers 172–4, 184–5, 205, 326, 337–8
Temple Church 31
Theatre Royal (Bristol Old Vic) 95, 99, 343–4
theatres 300
trumpeters 195
University College 327
venues 327
waits 68–77, 95, 154, 167–9, 191, 195, 197, 302, 314
wealth 31–2, 59
Whitefield Tabernacle 38
women musicians 174
see also Bedminster, Clifton, Horfield, Hotwells, Knowle West, Redland, Shirehampton, Southville
Bristol Abbey 298, 309
Bristol Æolian Male Voice Choir 109
Bristol Catch Club 105–6
Bristol Cathedral 156–7, 314, 341, 354
    apprenticeships 166–7, 324
    choristers 108, 205
    lay clerks 107, 155, 168, 184, 194–5, 311–12, 330
    organ 31, 48
    organist 34, 45, 155–7, 199, 291, 328
Bristol Cathedral School 145
Bristol Cecilian Society 105
Bristol Chamber Choir *see* Bristol Madrigal Society
Bristol Channel 149
Bristol Conservatoire of Music 100, 337–8
Bristol Conservatoire polka, The 337
Bristol Grammar School 327
Bristol Hippodrome 141
Bristol Madrigal Society 108, 150, 205
Bristol Mercury 177, 184
Bristol Music Club 217, 327–9
Bristol Opera [School] 330
Bristol Orpheus Glee Society 107–9
Bristol Pageant 290–1
Bristol Paramount Jazz Band 146
    see also Acker Bilk
Bristol quadrilles, The 100
Bristol sound 2, 143–6
Bristol Times 42
Bristol Troubadour 147
Bristol Tune-Book 33, 83–4

Bristol University 147, 225, 300, 327–31
    CHOMBEC xi
    folk revival 134
    organs 50, 63
    student demography 293
Bristol University Morris and Long-Swords Men 134
Bristol Volunteer Band 95
Bristol Volunteer troop, The 96–7
Bristol waits (tune) 73
British Empire 77, 174, 211
    emigration to 198–208
    Jamaica 163
    Menorca 220
    settler colonies 250
    see also Australia, Canada, India, New Zealand, overseas territories, Singapore, South Africa, Tanzania, West Indies
Britten, Benjamin 2, 37, 281, 284, 295, 333
    Noyes Fludde 297
Britton, Andrew 209
Brixham 29, 336
Brixham Band 64
Brixham town (song) 268
Broadbent, Derek 271
broadcasting 112, 133, 247, 253, 298, 349–57, 363–4
    from overseas stations 349
    from resorts 130
    see also BBC
Broadchalke 18
Broadwood, John 174
    Broadwood & Sons 175, 237
Brockenshire *see* Brokenshire
Brockley Combe 19
Brockman, Nigel 111
Broderip family
    Edmund 15–16
    John 15–16, 86–7, 105, 172
    Robert 105
Brokenshire, James Opie 206
Bromham 164
Brooks, James 342
Brown, Antony and Fiona 187
Brunel, Isambard Kingdom 5
Bruton
    Abbey 310
    Gilcombe Farm festival 286
    parish church 26–8
Bruton town (song) 268
Bryan, Cornelius 83, 86–7
Bryanston 332–5
Bryant, A W 60
Bryceson Brothers 51
Brygeman, William 307–8, 315
Bryne *see* Brian
Bucca 190
Buckfast Abbey 49
Buckfastleigh
    organ builders *see* William Drake
    textile factory 122
Buckingham, James Silk 239–40
Buckland, Jacob 196
Buckland Abbey 289, 310
Buckland Filleigh 183
    parish church 83

INDEX 427

Buckland Monachorum 190
Buckland Newton 27
Buckley, Reginald 295
Bucknall, Cedric 328
Bucknall, Roger Le Duc 328
Buckner, J A 94–5
Buckton, Alice 291
Bude 5
Budgett, Charles 328
Budleigh Salterton
    organ builders *see* Michael Farley
Bugle 176
Buller family 137
    Margaret 174
Burch, John 169
Burgat, Mr 164–5
Burgoyne, General John 92, 232
Burgum, Henry 193
Burney family
    Charles 232–5
    Fanny 79, 219, 232, 235
Burnham-on-Sea 188
    Methodist Chapel 38
Burton, Thomas Arthur 243
Bussell family 191
    Aldred and John 299
Butt, Clara 176, 185
Butterfield, William 42
Butterworth, George 246
Byfield *see* Harris family (organ builders)
Bylewyne, Peter 69
Byron, Lord George 228

C, H and W 166
Cade, Rowena 278
cafés and restaurants 130–1, 148, 212
Cahusac, Thomas 260
Caldwell, John 163
Camborne 286
    barrel organ 37
    Beunans Meriasek 276
    celebrations 98
Camborne Harmonic Society 358
Camborne Town Band 120
Camborne Volunteers 98
Cambridge 106
    King's College 306
    University 39, 61, 284, 327, 340
    University Press 188
Cameron *see* Hindenberg
Canada 92, 115, 207–8, 247
    Yukon 204
Candler, Alfred 187
Canford (Magna) 332
Cannington Priory 320
Cannon, Philip 284
Cannon family
    John 138–41, 181–3
    William 139
Carbis Bay Motor Garage 129
Cardiff 339, 355
Carew, Richard 110, 277–8
Carey, F C S 290
Carey, Henry 171

Carhampton 167
Carlyon Bay
    Cornwall Coliseum 147
carnivals 132–3
carols and carol singing 89–91, 115, 205, 274, 304, 308–9, 315
Carse, Adam 242
Carton, B 260
Caruso, Enrico 110, 166, 176
Castle Cary
    parish church 181
Catalani, Angelica 280, 321
catch singing *see* clubs and societies
cathedral cities 8, 33, 299–301
    and names of hymn tunes 83
    and their parishes 31
    culture 75, 106
    failure to industrialise 200
    festivals 279–81, 293, 347
    organ builders 60
    organs 28
    teachers 186
    see also Bath, Bristol, Exeter, Salisbury, Truro, Wells
cathedral music 8, 298–300
    pre-Reformation 303–6
    with sackbuts and cornetts 80, 300
    see also choristers, individual cathedrals, lay clerks (lay vicars)
Cecil, Sir Robert 159
Cellars, J 97
Celtic topics 4, 67–8, 261, 274, 296
Cerne Abbey 309
Chagford
    St Michael's church 25
chamber music 328, 341, 367
Chambercombe 260
Chamberlain, John Joseph 25
Chamberlain, Joseph 357
Chambers, Peter 299
Champernowne, Sir Richard 159–60
Chancellor, John and Edith 302
chantries and their priests 26, 302–4, 310–16, 322, 373
Chapman, Elizabeth and John 39–40
Chapman, Gwen 361
Chapman, Shadrach 86, 91
Chappington family 60, 189, 300
    Hugh 27, 189
Chapple, Samuel 85–6
Chard xv, 195
    concert life 347
    Perry Street Works Band 125
    St Mary's church 21, 36
    Young Women's Band Project 140
Chard Harmonic Society 359
Chard Volunteer Band 125
charity 24, 64, 98, 124, 143, 227, 280, 293
    see also fundraising
charity children 44, 64–5, 84, 104, 112–14, 304, 321, 338
Charles I 160
Charlton Mackrell 204, 271
Charlton Park 286
Charminster
    St Francis of Assisi church 58

428   INDEX

Charmouth
  hymn tune 83
Chartists 120–2
Chatterton, Thomas 15–16, 193, 227
Chauklin, Mrs 172
chaunting 43
Cheddar
  parish church 24, 28
Chelston 178
Cheltenham 221, 363
Chester 276
Chester, Henry, John, and Alice 302
Chew Magna
  parish church 114
Chideock
  Baptist Chapel 39
Chilcot, Thomas 172, 218
Child, William (of Bristol) 168, 200
Child, William? (of West Lydford) 304
Chippenham 8, 75, 268
  concert life 223
  dealers 176, 196
  festivals 287
  High Bailiff 167
  St Andrew's church 21, 31, 167
  town band 102
  see also Eddie Cochran
choir schools *see* education
choirmasters 116–17, 196
choirs 27, 65–7, 104–18, 247, 352, 365
  broadcasting 331, 352–4
  carol singing 89–91
  children's 43, 112–14
  choral societies 22, 65, 104, 112–18, 125, 158, 283, 359
  festival 280–1, 284
  in galleries 44, 81, 84–5
  large-scale 36, 51, 98, 104
  nonconformist 42, 212
  pre-Reformation 301–14
  psalmody 92, 139
  size of 104–5
  surpliced 41, 44, 65, 113, 265
  temperance 104
  works 125
  youth 287, 363
  see also charity children, male voice choirs
Chopin, Frédéric 257–8
choral societies *see* choirs
choristers 145, 167, 316–21, 370, 374
  as viol players 80, 300
  education 316–25
  female 317, 320
  in glee clubs and madrigal societies 105, 108
  in pre-Reformation liturgy 301–14
  in royal progresses 288
  recruitment and payment 125
  Roman Catholic 323
  training 104
Christchurch xix, 10
Christchurch Priory 58
Christmas 102, 304, 308, 313
  festivals 287
  see also carols and carol singing

Chudleigh 165
  bands 64
  Clifford Arms 64
Chudleigh Knighton 206
Chulmleigh
  band 64
  college of priests 314
  Congregational Church xi
church ales *see* festivals and celebrations
church houses *see* venues
church music 298–316, 337, 341
  Roman Catholic 323
  see also cathedral music, choirs, choristers, individual churches, organs, organists, psalmody, services of song
Church Organ Co *see* A W Bryant
Churchill, William 174
cinemas 53
  orchestras in 57
  organs in 53–4, 56–7
  see also screen media
circuses 345, 348
  see also bands
civic identity 128, 298, 340, 375
  municipal spending 127, 357, 359–62
  see also drummers, municipal orchestras, town bands, town halls, trumpeters, waits
Civil War *see* wars
Clapton-in-Gordano
  parish church 84, 104
clarinets 97, 114, 125, 145
Clark, John 60
Clark family
  Roger 295
  shoe company 292
Clarke Brown, T S 57
Clarke, Andrew 191
Clarke, Dick 141
Clarke, James 35, 196
Clarke, William 35
class
  public schools
  and betterment 104, 116, 348
  and salaries 360
  and status 179, 228–30
  distinctions 129, 164–5, 265–7, 325, 338
  lower 134, 144–5, 246, 265, 326
  middle 142, 171, 229, 327
  mixture 318
  porosity 137, 142
  upper 104, 326
  women musicians 43
  see also education
Clemens, Matthew 155
Clementi, Muzio 162–3, 175
clergy 247, 319, 337, 348
  and organs 22, 32, 35–48
  and psalmody 85, 113, 266–7
  as antiquaries 268
  as participants 67, 84, 87, 104, 106, 136, 284, 337, 364–5
  as playwrights 276
  as pre-Reformation singing men 302–7, 373
  purchasing pianos 178–9

recruiting choristers 125
stipends 32
see also colleges of priests
Clevedon 149, 351
 Curzon Cinema 53, 129
 dealers 129, 176-7, 196
 organ builders *see* Percy Daniel
 SA band 123
 St John's church 23
 Whitsun festivities 151
Clevedon Silver Band 126
Cleverdon, Douglas 355-6
Clifford, Lord and Lady 165
Clifton 108, 147-8, 184, 186, 216, 220, 327, 354-5
 All Saints' church 42, 45, 328
 Assembly Rooms 99
 Christ Church 42
 concert life 214
 conservatism 328
 dealers 129, 193
 Emmanuel church 42
 Ivatt's Hotel 347
 organ builders 190
 St Paul's church 42
 teachers 99
 Victoria Methodist Church 42
 Victoria Rooms 50, 53, 63, 106-8, 129, 134, 327-8
 zoo 300, 324
 see also Bristol Music Club
Clifton Association for the Higher Education of Women 327
Clifton Cinema 53
Clifton College 319, 322-8
 organ 33, 324
Clifton Glee Singers 107
Clifton quadrilles, The 99-100
Clifton Quintet 328
Clovelly
 idea of 257-9, 262
 parish church 104-5, 370
clubs and societies 105-9, 143, 340-1
 catch clubs 105-7, 109, 341-2
 folk clubs 134, 147-8
 glee clubs 114, 143, 320, 358
 harmonic societies 105, 114, 358-9
 madrigal societies 105, 108-9, 320
 music clubs 75-7, 80
 nightclubs 146-7
 sacred harmonic societies 114-15, 359
 song-and-supper clubs 65
 youth clubs 139-40, 142
 see also Women's Institute
Clyst 318
Coalpit Heath
 parish church 42
Cobley, Uncle Tom 269
Cochran, Eddie 142, 287
Coke, John 312
Colby, Theodore 34
Coldplay 317
Cole, John 192
Cole[, Mr] 70
Coleford 202
Coleridge, Samuel Taylor 237

Coleridge-Taylor, Samuel 243
Collard, John 344
colleges of priests 304, 306-7, 313-14
Collier, William 121
Collins, Benjamin 172
Collins, Leonard 353
Collyer, Giles and John 169
Colyton Female Friendly Society 78
Combeinteignhead 86
Comer family 222
Common, Bob and Pam 140
Commonwealth (period) 21, 74, 155, 169, 298, 321
composers 252, 353
 and patronage 159-66, 299-300
 and soundscapes 14, 17-19
 and the metropolis 234-5, 237-40
 and their livelihoods 154, 174, 181, 209-18
 demography 336
 emigrant 202-3, 206
 of madrigals 158
 of pageants 290-2
 of psalmody and carols 85-91, 129
 regional premieres 115, 241-3
 romantic 256-7
 success beyond the region 246-8
Compton, John 49, 54-8
concert life 109, 191-2, 223-4, 339-49, 357-67
 and dealers 176
 benefit concerts 77, 240, 342-3, 365
 choirs 114-18
 classical music 52, 280-5, 287, 363, 367
 gramophone concerts 129
 in Bournemouth 241-6
 in Cornwall 281
 in Devon 336
 introduction of pianos 174-5
 music clubs 76-8
 organists 49-52
 programming 77, 198, 344-5, 363-7
 promenade concerts 118
 rock concerts 141
 subscription concerts 77, 109, 164-5, 192, 222-3, 342, 358
 touring professionals 197-8
 village concerts 135, 365-6
 see also entertainment, festivals and celebrations, oratorio performances, organ recitals, piano recitals, visitors: star performers
concertinas 38, 135-7, 170
conductors
 as trainers 116-17
 of choirs 107, 112, 115-18, 284-5, 354
 of orchestras 130, 240-4, 284-5, 359-63
 visiting 347-8
 see also bandleaders, bandmasters
conservatoires *see* education
Constantine 363
convents *see* monasteries and abbeys
Conway, Russ 144-6
Cook, Beryl 123
Cook, John and Joshua 172
Cook, Mary 223
Cook, Percy 131
Cooke, Benjamin 184

Cooke, John 312
Cooke family 223
Coombes, Thomas 168
Coombs, Harold 56
Coombs, James 167
Cooper ('Coprario'), John 160
Cooper, Margaret 258
Copplestone's music warehouse 246
Córdoba 309
Corelli, Arcangelo 341
Corfe family
　Arthur 155, 319-22, 370
　John 319
　John Davis 155, 167, 199, 324
　Joseph 165, 198, 319-20
Corfe Mullen
　hymn tune 83
Cork 215-16
Cornelius, Joseph 269
Cornish (language) 276
Cornish Federation of Women's Institutes 115
Cornwall xix, 167
　as lifestyle choice 61
　as separate entity 5
　bagpipes 68
　bibliography 4
　brass bands 2, 119-20
　carols 82, 89-90, 205
　choral singing 352
　concert life 281, 363
　County Music Adviser 115, 280
　County Music Festival 282
　dealers 176
　diocese 8, 300
　emigrants 201-7, 261, 279
　Federation of Male Voice Choirs 111
　festivals and celebrations 67, 98, 270-86
　fishermen 258, 292
　folk music 190, 269
　gentry 282
　idea of 260-1, 263
　male voice choirs 2, 104, 110-12, 353-4, 370
　miners 51, 90, 200, 203-6, 258, 279
　monasteries 310
　newspapers 172
　Ordinalia and other plays 66-7, 276-8, 290, 293, 307, 314
　organs 50, 62
　patronage 158
　professionals 71, 237-8
　psalmody 87
　rebellion of 1549 26
　recusants 195
　remoteness 41, 254-5, 257, 318
　rock 'n' roll 140
　stone circles and stone rows 274
　subculture 147
　tourism 279
　tune books 137-8
　venues 147, 281-2
　weather 118
　see also Celtic topics, regiments and their bands
Cornwall Coliseum *see* Carlyon Bay
Cornwall Rural Music School 281

Corpus Christi 26, 67-8, 276-8, 304, 308, 313
Corsham 196, 333
　Baptist Church 38
Corum, Alfred 131
Coster, Henry 60
Council for the Encouragement of Music and the Arts 333
counterculture 286
country and western 133
country houses and estates 101, 158-66
　as venues 124, 134, 282, 286
　music archives 137-8, 371
　used for summer schools 332-3
　see also individual houses
county
　boundaries 8
　identities 263-4, 267-70
　society 268, 280
　towns 268, 340, 347
Court *see* London, Windsor
Cove, Robert 103
Coventry 314
Cox, Charles 81
Cox, Mary 174
Cox, Victor 53
Crabb, Henry 40, 60
Cranborne Chase 108
　School 332-3
Crang, John 31, 60, 63, 189-90
　Crang & Hancock 60
Crantock
　college of priests 306, 314
Crediton 93, 227
　college of priests 25, 306, 313
　grammar school 322
　Holy Cross church 25, 27, 186, 226
　Penton House 124
　SA band 122
　see also Shobrooke Park
Crewkerne xv
　grammar school 322
　music club 76
　Nag's Head tavern 76
　St Bartholomew's church 21, 36, 66-8, 81, 84, 102, 313
Crewkerne Town Band 102
crime 107-8, 145, 148, 177
　and transportation 201-3
　drugs 7
　kidnapping 309, 318
　piracy 262
　political 121, 215
　smuggling 257
　see also bankrupts
Crispin *see* Montgomery
Crook, Noah 121
Crook, T H 107
Croscombe
　Parsonage Farm 224-5
Crosse, John 26
Crouch, Frederick 192
Cruikshank, Robert 191
Crump, Charles and Isabella 173
Crute, Francis 47

INDEX 431

Cruwys Morchard
    parish church 86, 369
Cuff, Mary 84
cultural capital 180
Cummins, Charles 99
Curry Rivel
    parish church 68
Curzon, Miss 100
Cutler, Adge 142-3

Daddy G *see* Grant Marshall
Dad's Army 271
Dakers, Lionel 331
Dallam, Thomas 190
Damer, Perce 356
dancing, display 134, 367, 372
    see also morris dancing, step dancing
dancing, social 134-8
    ballroom 131
    balls 17, 339-43
    country 135-7, 262
    folk 132-4
    jitterbugging 131-2
    processional 273
    quadrilles 99-102, 137-8
    square 134
    tuition 322
    waltzes 97-101, 130-1, 138, 140
dancing masters 17, 137, 164, 198, 322
Daniel, John 162
Daniel, Percy 53, 58-60
Daniel, Peter 195
Darewski, Herman 130
Dark, Mr 129
Darke, Harold 49
Darke, John 315
Dart, R Thurston 316, 331, 375
Dart, River 332
Dartington
    educational and cultural institutions 63, 135, 330-6, 338, 356
Dartington Crystal 335
Dartington String Quartet 335
Dartmoor 263, 283, 332
    depicted in music 242
    Two Moors Festival 286
Dartmouth 64, 72, 375
    Bayard's Cove 369
    composers 174, 316
    grammar school 322
    guildhall 316
    mayor 316
    Royal Marines 339
    Royal Naval College 63
    St Saviour's church 25-7, 44, 81, 310, 316
Dartmouth Artillery Corps Band 123
Dartmouth Magnificat 315-16, 371-5
Davey, Henry 375
Davey family 190
Davidstow
    parish church 68
Davies, Alex 63
Davies, Arthur, Charlie, and Harry 128-9
Davies, Henry Walford 107, 354

Davies, Peter Maxwell 333
Davis, Thomas Henry 185-6
Davy, John (of Launceston) 310
Davy, John (of Upton Hellions) 93, 225-9, 232-3, 237, 240
Davy, Richard 311, 315
Daw, Benjamin 113
Dawe, John 154
Dawlish 102
    parish church 27
    teachers 256
Dawlish Quadrille Band 100
Dawson, Peter 271, 350
Day, George 133
Day, John 344-5
Day, T and Sons 129
de Vries, Jan 43, 186
dealers 38, 95, 100-103, 171-80, 246-7, 348
    bankrupts 192-3
    multitraders 195-6
    of gramophones and radios 128-9
    of records 142
    warehouses and repositories 173-4
Dear, James Richard 262
Debussy, Claude 272
Delamotte, Mrs 43, 195
demographics 110-11, 167-8
department stores 58, 130-1
Dering, Richard 14, 19
Derkeham, Robert 310
Devizes 17, 74, 268
    Bear Club 76
    concert life 198
    parish church 125
    rough music 121
    Scout Cubs 125
    social strife 121
    soundscape 17
    theatre 17
Devon 5, 157-8
    as catchment area for choristers 318-19
    Assizes 202
    bands 64-5, 370
    bibliography 4
    change ringing 12
    County Music Festival 282
    county town 268
    dealers 176
    diocese 8
    emigrants 206-7
    festivals 280
    fiddle music 135, 335
    glee clubs 107
    idea of 257-64
    Irish immigrants 134
    migration out 250
    north Devon 9, 186, 257-8, 335, 348
    organ builders 60-3, 189
    rebellion of 1549 26
    rock 'n' roll 140
    south Devon 73, 100, 103, 174, 286, 310, 332, 351
    teachers 186
    touring groups 126
    venues 336

villages 64–5, 179, 257–60, 365–6
  west Devon 190, 269
  see also regiments and their bands
Devon, Earl of *see* Powderham Castle
Devon [and Exeter Catch and] Glee Club 106–8
Devon Baroque 336
Devon Madrigal Society 108, 231
Devonport 64, 179
  celebrations 98
  choral society 116
  hall of residence 331
  Stoke School of Music 337
  teachers 186–7
Devonport Choral Society 64
Devonshire
  Duke of 359
  Lord 372
Devoran
  WI choir 115
Diakun, Marzena 363
Dibdin, Charles 175, 232–3, 342
Dicker, H P 32, 60
Didier, Mrs 342
Dinder 161
Dingle, Richard 310
Dinglestadt, John Friedrich 77
Dinton 160
dioceses 7–9, 318–19
Diptford 167
discant 303–4
  see also faburden
Distin family 223–4
  Henry 119
  John Henry 94, 118, 223–4
Ditton Newman, Henry 45–7
Dock *see* Devonport
Dodd, Ken 271
Doddridge, Humphrey 299
Dolbear, William 311
Dolby, Charlotte 185
domestic music 74–5, 107
  barrel organs 37
  organs 21–23
  see also country houses and estates, lutenists, pianos, radios
Dorchester
  All Saints' church 113
  Antelope Hotel 119
  dealers 172
  Franciscan Friary 25
  Holy Trinity church 37
  Maiden Castle 252
  military music 92
  National School 113
  Robinson's Music Repository 38
  St Peter's church 36
Dorchester, La 100
Dorchester Barracks 135
Dore, James 103
Dore, Philip 51, 55, 244
Dorn *see* Roeckel
Dorset 5, 162–3, 168, 223, 252
  bands 79
  cider 261
  convents 320
  diocese 8
  folk music 140, 265, 356
  idea of 263
  licensing authorities 166
  organs 36–7
  psalmody 37, 83
  singing masters 181
  titled dances 100–1
  see also regiments and their bands
Dorset Rangers
  band 79
Dorset Trio 356
Dorsetshire march, Royal 95
Dort, James 82
Douglas, Capt Charles 47
Dow, John *see* John Dawe
Dowell, David 302, 373
Downside Abbey 49, 354
  organ 55
  school 322–3
Drage, Sally 106
Drake, Sir Francis 71, 99, 157, 262, 289, 291
Drake, Ralph 310
Drake, William 62–3
Draycott 86, 91
Driffield, Robert 315
drummers 70, 73, 191, 195, 300, 317, 344
  African drumming 367
  rock 138
  see also fifers and drummers
Dublin 221
Duck, Son and Pinker 129, 176–7, 180
Dudeney, T J 40
Duncan, Ronald 5, 157–8
Dundry
  parish church 114
Dunmere Bridge 346
Dunster 87, 162, 167, 315
Dunster, John 310
Durfey, Thomas 342
Durravan, Mr 342
Durston, B 188
Dyer, Reg 141
Dyer, William Fear 326

early music movement 281, 317, 336, 375
  organs 60–3
East Lulworth *see* Lulworth Castle
East Lydford 182
Eastbourne 359
Eastcott, Richard 113, 174, 226–7, 231
Easter Sepulchre dramas 320
Easton-in-Gordano
  parish church 26
Eavis, Michael 286
economics 279, 367
  admission prices 132–3, 177, 278, 342–3, 347–9, 365
  exchange value 369–70
  fees and piecemeal income 24, 52, 123–5, 162, 177, 181–2, 186, 197, 219, 228, 268, 280, 322, 372
  hire purchase 103, 177–8
  of choral societies 118
  of festivals 280–1

parish accounts 275
poverty 64-5, 98, 286
regional decline 200-1, 223, 257-8
regional productivity 368
remittances 51, 203
salaries 32-5, 52, 68-73, 224, 240, 244, 295, 302-3, 307, 309, 324, 359-60, 371-4
unsustainable enterprises 280-1, 294, 320
see also bankrupts, livelihoods, patronage
Edinburgh 186
education 51, 124-5, 183, 298, 316-39
  adult 333
  board schools 326
  choir schools 47, 308, 313-14
  competitive festivals 282
  conservatoires 2, 187, 336-9, 355
  costs 225
  educational music 212, 268
  elementary schools and schoolchildren 104, 112-14
  examination systems 188
    see also Associated Board (ABRSM), Trinity College of Music
  grammar schools 84, 142, 305, 311, 322, 374
  instrumental classes 117
  military 95, 97
  musical training 128, 144-5, 338-9
  National Schools 113
  nonconformist 110
  of boys 322, 337-8
  of girls 320-2, 337-8, 370
  of women 327
  public schools xvii, 200, 322-8, 332-3
  scholarships 325
  secondary modern schools 142
  singing classes 116-18
  song schools 304-5, 310, 320
  state schools 200
  summer schools 293, 296, 332-3
  see also apprenticeships, charity children, Sunday schools, universities
Education Act (1870) 38, 212
Edward IV 288
Edwards, Henry 247
Edwards, John 116
Edwards, Richard 288-9
Eget, John 69
Egloshayle, Robert de 318
Eiffe, Mrs 215
Einaudi, Ludovico 363
Elgar family 246
  Edward 2, 118, 230, 282, 361
Elizabeth I 7, 160, 288-9
Elizabeth II
  coronation 281
Ellis, Katharine 329
Ellis, Paul 290
Elmhirst, Dorothy and Leonard 332-3
Elton, Richard 259
Elyott, John 310
Emidy family
  Joseph 237-40
  Thomas 237
emigrants 108, 198-208

and gold rushes 204-5, 240
ballads 261
Cornish 51, 90, 260
nostalgia 84, 257
remittances 203
reverse migration 241, 246
to British Empire destinations 129, 167
to other English regions 111, 179, 199
to the Continent 150, 256-7
to the USA 54, 237
employment *see* livelihoods
Endellion String Quartet *see* St Endellion
Enescu, George 332
England, John 207-8, 265-7, 375
England, Mrs 266
England family (organ builders) 190
Enmore 321
entertainment 52-8, 348, 358
  see also variety
entrepreneurs 53
  see also impresarios
Erasmus, Desiderius 317
Erith, F Norton 337
Eton College 306, 324
  choirbook 307, 311, 314-15
Eulenstein, Karl (Charles) 196, 209
Eustace and Aldridge 63
Evans, Charles 182
Evans, General 77
Evans, William 162
Everdell, James 199
Evershot
  music club 76
Eves, Miss 188
Exe, River 346
Exeter 8, 168, 332, 342, 371-5
  as musical centre 299-300, 315, 331
  bands 64
  bankrupts 192
  bishops *see* Thomas de Brantingham, John Grandisson, Edmund Lacy, Walter Stapledon
  brass band contests 119, 125
  choral society 116
  city churches 27, 31-2
  City Council 331
  composers 165, 225-37, 299-300, 309, 311, 315
  concert life 225-6, 231, 346, 363
  Cowley Place 231
  dealers 142, 171-6, 192
  decline 108, 200
  diocese 8
  drummers 300
  emigrants 205
  Franciscan Friary 309
  Globe Inn 31
  Hospital of St John the Baptist 317
  incoming musicians 73, 197, 372
  instrument makers 169, 192
  mayor and Corporation 299-300
  military music 92-4
  music club 231
  music society 76
  musicians 94, 304
  New London Inn 64

orchestras 231
organ builders 60, 63, 300
pianos 174, 179
professionals 198, 314
rebellion of 1549 26
Ritson Manuscript 309, 315
Royal Albert Memorial Museum 169
Royal Clarence Hotel 346
St Luke's College 331, 337
St Mary Arches church 31
St Mary Major church 19
St Mary Steps church 64
St Olave's parish 31
St Paul's church 318
St Petrock's church 25
Society of Exeter Gentlemen 237
song school 305
street musicians 197
teachers 186
theatre 228
trumpeters 154, 300
Victoria Hall 50-1
waits 69-77, 154, 159, 191, 197, 299, 371-4
Westcountry Studies Library xii
see also Alphington, Devon [and Exeter Catch and] Glee Club, Devon Madrigal Society, Richard Eastcott, Heavitree, William Jackson
Exeter Cathedral 64, 169, 374
    apprenticeships 257
    choir 231
    choristers 22, 108, 226, 299-300, 317-20
    clergy 239
    lay clerks and vicars choral 155, 186, 195, 227, 299, 303, 309, 315-16
    musicians and patronage 299-300
    organ 22, 24-5, 27-32, 371-3
    organist 22, 25, 29-30, 34, 40, 50, 155-6, 165, 203, 228-35, 299, 331, 337
    politics 29-30
    secondaries 299-300, 310, 312-13
    use of instruments 80
Exeter Church Choral Training School *see* Exeter School of Church Music
Exeter Festival 223, 280
    chorus 331
    see also Devon: County Music Festival
Exeter Harmonic Society 105, 358
Exeter Musical Society 331
Exeter School of Church Music 337
Exeter Trainband (militia) 300
Exeter University 331, 335
    choral society 331
Exminster Hundred
    band 94
Exmoor
    carols 82
    Two Moors Festival 286
Exmoor Stag Hunt 260
Exmouth 155, 255
    aristocracy 100
    bands 64
    bandstand (Performance Stage) 127
    Baring family 32, 231
    choral society 116

concert life 102, 346
dealers 173, 176
Ewen's Beacon Hotel 346
Sir Digory Forrest's ball 100
instrument makers 192
Exonian Quadrille Band 100
Eyers, Robert 119

faburden 277, 303, 305
Facy, Hugh 299
fairs 137, 197
Fallowfield, Arthur 357
Falmouth 336
    Carrick Roads 283
    composers 237
    de Wynn's coffee shop 336
    dealers 196
    newspapers 34
    singing class 117
    Sunday schools 114, 370
    University College 335
    WI pageant 291
    Wynn's Hotel 98
Falmouth College of Art 336
Falmouth Harmonic Society 98, 358
Falmouth Opera Singers 283-4
Falmouth Sax-Tuba Band 119
Falmouth University 335
families 102, 154, 184-5, 189-93, 214-25, 319
    bandsmen 102-3, 125-6
    emigrant 207
    fiddlers 157
    instrument makers 170
    migrant 199-201
    mixed-race 237
    organ builders 60
    psalmodists 83, 181
    siblings 318
    travelling ensembles 223-4
Faning, Roger 186
Farley, Michael 62-3
Farrant, John 319
Faultless, Margaret 336
Festival of Britain 115
festivals and celebrations 7, 66-8, 152, 270-97, 348
    adjudicators 282
    church ales 152-3, 275, 339, 373
    competitive festivals 119-20, 280-2, 287, 293, 326
    festivals in cathedral cities and county towns 114, 223, 268, 340, 341, 347
    for peace 97-9, 123, 132-3
    liturgical 304
    Midsummer's Eve 300
    Nine Lessons and Carols 287, 364
    of orchestral music 242
    parades 119
    royalty 64-5, 127
    travellers 147
    triennial festivals 2, 49
    WI 115
    see also carnivals, Christmas, Corpus Christi, Easter Sepulchre dramas, Festival of Britain, May Day, Palm Sunday, St Cecilia's Day, Whitsun

Fframpton, Ambrose 139
fiddlers 65, 134-8, 191, 195, 205, 275
    Devon fiddling 335
    family 157
    in psalmody quires 81, 136-7
    Irish 197
    on ships 237
    or violinists 79, 161
    see also violinists
field musicians 93
fifers and drummers 93-5, 98, 119, 123
Filleigh 64
Finnegan, Ruth 10, 146, 218, 371
Finnimor's band 64
Finzi, Gerald 354
fishermen *see* artisans, Cornwall
Fishermen's Friends 111-12, 288, 292
Fiske, Roger 227
FitzWarin, Lord 158
Flashman, George and William 103
flautists 99, 174, 220-3, 237, 243, 347
    in bands 97, 103, 125, 271
    rural and psalmody 64-5, 85, 136-7
Fleming, Francis 137, 220
Florio *see* Robjohn
flowers and music 287
flute players *see* flautists
Fogwill, N 123
folk, the 270
folk music 89-90, 143-8, 355-7, 367
    and copyright 356
    English Folk Dance and Song Society 134
    families of performers 190-1
    festivals 286-7
    first revival 207, 264-70
    folksingers 265-7, 356-7, 363, 375
    folksong 250-2, 261-73, 282, 298, 352, 369
    folksong collectors 265, 267-9, 272
    performance practice 112
    second revival 134, 147-8, 280, 355-7
    shanties 111, 369
    see also dancing, Sabine Baring-Gould, Charles Marson, Cecil Sharp
folklore 255, 264, 268
Fonthill 163
Foort, Reginald 56-8
Ford, John 311
foreigners 77, 97, 154, 233
    conductors 359-63
    Germans 178
    see also immigrants, professionals
Forester, C S 237
Forster, William 170
Foster, Rev Priestley 44
Fovant Hut 107-8
Fowens, Sara 174
Fowey 22, 71
Fowles, John 63, 292
Fox, Douglas 324, 328
Foxe, Thomas 310
Foy, Lance 62-3
fraternities *see* guilds
Frazier, Kathleen 350
Freemasons 102, 143

French Revolution 79, 98
friaries 25, 309
Fripp, E B 83
Frome 35, 43-4, 75, 191, 195, 200, 202
    bells 18
    Bluecoat School 113
    organ builders 196
    St John's church 23-4, 27, 31, 35-6, 43-44, 113
    see also Selwood
Frome Festival 288
Fry family 122
Fryer, William 95
Fudge, Leslie 180
fundraising
    by professionals 366
    by subscription 81, 91, 337
    church ales 373
    concerts 38, 124, 365-6
    for bands 102-3, 124
    for charities 280, 293
    for individuals 40, 240
    for organs 23, 32-3, 38
Fury, Billy 141

Gabriel, Virginia 258
Gadgecombe, John 71
Gainsborough, Thomas 230-2, 235-6
Gale, Henry 70
Gale, Thomas 299
Galhampton
    Party in the Park 286
Gammon, Vic 12
Gandy, William 230
Gardiner, William 197
Gardner, Frank 327
Garland, Miss G 188
Garnsey, John 315
Garstin, Crosbie 353-4
Gasworkers' Brass Band (Plymouth?) 122
Gaunt, Roger 284
Gay, George 196
Gay, John 181, 344
gentlemen *see* amateurs
    scholars and collectors 267-9
gentry 33, 75, 101, 153, 268-9, 324, 341
    as patrons 158-9, 165-6, 269, 347-9, 359
    philistinism 33, 324-6, 338
    see also country houses and estates, county
George III 7, 79, 221
George V 127, 263
Georgian values
    free association 75
    psalmody style 87
    urban culture 15-17, 75
German, Edward
    Glorious Devon (song) 262, 271
Germany
    emulation of 60, 109, 290, 294
    military detachments 97
    see also immigrants
Gershwin, George 272
ghosts 45-7
Gibbons, Beth 150
Gibbons, Grinling 23

Gibbons family
    Edward 299
    Orlando 14
Giddy, John 137
Gifford, Emma 12, 251
Gifford, William 86
Gilbert, John 93
Gilbert and Sullivan
    The Pirates of Penzance 278
Gill, Radford and Thomas 300
Gillingham 199
Girardet, Jules 99
Glasgow 184, 339
Glasney
    college of priests 276, 306, 314
Glastonbury 137, 166, 292, 332
    Assembly Rooms 296–7
    choir singers 182
    George Inn 182
    hymn tune 83
    pageants 291
    St Benedict's church 84
    St John the Baptist church 25–7, 36, 81, 114, 287, 372
    singing competition 182
Glastonbury Abbey 25–6, 194, 291–2, 372–3
    organ 25
    organist 310, 320, 373
Glastonbury Festival (first) 293–7
    School 337
Glastonbury Festival (second) 2, 274, 286, 292–3, 368
Glastonbury Festival Players 297
glee singing 64–5, 76, 105–9, 116, 341–5, 358, 364
    in public schools 326
    see also clubs and societies
Glen[, Mr] 24
Glendoning, William 173
Glock, William 332–5
Gloucestershire 5–7
Glover, Hurst 172
Glover's (dealer) 129
Gluck, Christoph Willibald von 284, 295–6
God save the King 79, 98
Goddard, Arabella 211
Godfrey, Dan 56, 126, 237, 240–4, 296, 359–60
Godwin, Matthew 156–7
Godwin family 125
Goehr, Alexander 333
Goetze, Willy 127
Goldsithney and District Male Voice Choir 110
Goldsmith, Oliver 232
Goode, Henry 107
Goodman, ? 302
Gorham, George 37–9
Goss, Ernest 351, 360
Gossington
    gypsy festival 286
Gould, Mr 172
Graham, Elsie 187
Graham-Jones, Ian 281
Grainger, Percy 369
grammar schools *see* education
gramophones and record players 129, 138, 180
    HMV 147
    recordings 132, 144, 148, 271, 349–50, 355–6, 375

see also hits, popular
Grandisson, Bishop John 276, 317
Grant, Willis 329
Gray of London 39, 186, 207
Great Torrington *see* Torrington
Green, Charles 60
Green, Samuel 7
Greene, Harry Plunket 262
Greenhalgh, Bill 142
Greenstone, Jack 131
Greethead, Robert 222–3
Grenville, Sir Richard 157
Greville, Thomas 191
Greville, William 158–9, 191
Gribble, David 335
Griffen and Stroud 60
Grove, Chafyn 32
Groves, Charles 362
Guernsey *see* Garnsey
Guildhall School of Music and Drama 184
guilds
    Ashburton 311
    Bristol 308–9
    London 166
guitarists 163, 175, 180, 196, 209, 335
    folk 144
    rock 138
    skiffle 140
guitars, electric 58, 180
Gulliford Meeting House 32
Gundry, Inglis
    The Tinners of Cornwall 19
Gunnell, Robert 168
Gunning, Alexis 242
Gunnislake 5
Gurney, Ivor 246
Gwennap Pit 279
Gwinear 363
gypsies 286

Hadelich, Agustin 363
Hake, John 195
Hale, Alfred 263
Hale, Robert 264
Hall, Marie 214
Hall, Nelson 47–8, 63
Hallé, Charles 185
Halleway, Thomas and Joan 302
Ham, Elizabeth 97
Hambridge 207, 265–8
    parish church choir 265
    village school 268
Hambridge and Westport Band 266
Hamilton-White, Reginald 51
Hammond organs 58
Hampreston
    hymn tune 83
Hampton, John 314–15
Hamswell Farm
    festival 286
Hancock, Mary 174
Hancock family (organ builders) 189
Handel, George Frideric 164, 198, 232, 234, 341–2
    influence of 87, 89

oratorio performances 341
Hardwich, Richard 24
Hardwick, Sarah 84
Hardy, Thomas (poet) 261, 331
   Far from the Madding Crowd 251
   'The fiddler' 135
   'Her song' 249-54
   A Pair of Blue Eyes 12-14
   The Queen of Cornwall 295-96
   soundscapes 12-14
   'To my father's violin' 136
   Under the Greenwood Tree 37
   The Woodlanders 267
Hardy family (poet's) 82-3, 136-8
   see also Emma Gifford
Hargreaves, Walter 120
Harker, Dave 265
harmonic societies *see* clubs and societies
harmoniums 37-8, 53, 56, 90, 246, 323, 365
Harpford
   parish church 81
harpists 126, 137, 222, 235, 256, 345
   in bands 126
   pre-modern 66-7, 72, 151, 159, 191, 339
harpsichords and virginals 75, 159, 169, 174-5, 194, 226-7
Harris, Michael 137
Harris family (of Salisbury) 174
   James 164-5, 170
Harris family (organ builders)
   Harris and Byfield 35, 60, 190
   Renatus 31, 44, 48, 59-60, 190
   Thomas 31, 190
Harrison, Julius 263, 282
Harrison & Harrison 33, 49
Harry ?, 'Happy' 122
Hartland 181
   parish church 27-8, 313
Harvey, Simon 182
Harvey, William 86
Harwood, Basil 326
Harwood, Blanche 53
Hawker, Rev Robert 261-2
Hawkes, Thomas 86
Hawkins, Robert H 188
Hawkins family
   Sir John 71
   Sir Richard 70-1, 157
Hawley, John 316
Hawley, Stanley 166
Haydn, Franz Joseph 221, 234, 240, 332, 342
Hayle Choral Society 116-17
Haymakers Square Dance Band 356
Haynes, Battison 262
Hayter family 199
Hayward, John 168
Hayward, Robert 31
Head, Janet Hardwick 155
Heale, Richard 73
Heard, John 172-3
   Heard & Sons 172
Heath, Paul 34
Heavitree 337
Heckstall-Smith, Dick 335

Hele & Co 45, 53, 60
Hellier, Geoffrey 162
Helston 186, 354
   Flora Day 270-4
   Floral dance, The (song) 270-3
   Hal an Tow 273-4
Helston Harmonic Society 358
Helston Town Band 271-2
Hempel, Charles William 197
Henley, W E 336
Henman, Richard 156
Henry VII 288
Henry VIII 291
Hepworth, Barbara 281
Herbert, George 160-1, 187
Herbert family *see* earls of Pembroke
heritage movement 289
Herschel family 191, 221
   William 220-1, 232-3
Hertford, Earl of 160
Hewett, Mr 42
Hewitt, William 34
Hibberd, Sarah 329
Hibberd, Widow 24
Hickox, Richard 284-5
Hicks, Mrs 56
Hicks family 195
   Joseph 201
Higgins, R L 131
High Ham 38
Highbridge
   SA band 125
Hill, Percy 132-3
Hill & Son 45, 50-1, 53
Hilliar, Mr 102
Hindemith, Paul 233, 332
Hindenberg, Basil 178, 359-62
Hinge and Bracket 283
Hinton St George Festival 287
hip-hop 143, 145, 149-50
hits, popular 144, 271
Hobbs, C E 188
Hobby, John and Mabel 191
Hockin, William 135
Hodges, Edward 83-4, 198-9, 203, 207
Holborne, Antony 160
Holbrook, John 196
Holcombe Burnell 64
Holden, Nicholas 191, 195
Holland 247
Hollyman family 84
Holman, Peter 75
Holmes, John 158
Holst family
   Gustav 126, 243, 335
   Imogen 188, 333-5
Holsworthy 261
Holt 157
Holwell 223
homosexuality 239, 256
homosociality 105-9, 114
Honey, Henry 201-2
Honiton
   choral society 116

parish church 31, 34, 43
Honiton Glee Club 107
Hook, James 233
Hooper, Bill 356
Hooper, Stephen 181
Hop, T 25
Hope-Jones, Robert 53-4
Horfield
　parish church 114
　Rifle Brigade quadrilles, The 101
Horn, Charles Edward 233
horn players 17, 345
hotels 130, 133, 142, 346-7
Hotwells 220
　Holy Trinity church 155
　Royal Gloucester Hotel Assembly Rooms 347
Housman, Laurence 295
Howell, Thomas (father and son) 173, 175
Hubner, bandmaster 126
Huguenots 200
Huish Episcopi
　parish church 39
Hull, Dame Eleanor 320
Hullah, John 113
Hullande, Nicholas 310
Humboldt, Alexander von 221
Hummel, Johann Nepomuk 214
Humphries, Phil 92
Hunt, Hubert 291, 328
Hurst, George 332
Hutchins, Jennifer 237
Huttoft, William 170
Hutton, Gena 56
Hutton, Ronald 274-5
Huxtable, Christopher 343
Huxtable, Mary 43
Hyde, Thomas 155
Hygons, Richard 315
hymns
　hymnals 172
　singing 110, 113-14
　tunes 83-4, 138, 212
　see also Bristol Tune-Book, psalmody, singing

iconography 66-8
　photographs 125-6
Ilchester, Count and Countess of 41
Ilfracombe 101, 150
　Baptist Chapel 58-9
　dealers 258
　pier 126
　resort orchestra 360
　song about 258-60
Ilfracombe Band Concerts 258
Ilfracombe quadrilles 101
Ilfracombe Town Band 126
Illogan 87
Illogan Highway
　choral society 90
　Methodist churches 90
Ilminster xv, 179
　concert life 347
　Harmony Restored pub 196
　Meeting House 367

　parish church 23-4
Ilminster Arts Centre 367
Ilminster Flower Festival 287
immigrants 197
　Afro-Caribbean 142-3
　French 200
　German and Austrian 94, 126-7, 196-7, 207, 209, 214-15, 220-1, 337, 359
　Hungarian 126
　Irish 16, 134, 137-40, 197, 220, 338
　Italian 126, 145, 197, 209, 244, 341
　Scottish 338
　see also incomers
impresarios 105, 231, 252, 346, 364-5
　and eighteenth-century concerts 191-3, 198, 231
　arts administrators 366
　entertainment industry 141, 348
　metropolitan 240, 314
　see also Ashe family: Andrew
Incledon, Charles 225-8, 232, 237, 239, 342-3
incomers 83, 188, 250, 293, 297, 332, 369
　in Cornwall 111, 279
　students 326
India 123, 247, 333-5
industry 2, 7, 50-1, 98, 111, 279, 336, 348
　agricultural workers 205, 246, 265
　anti-industrial feeling 60-1
　lack of xvi, 110, 170-1, 200
　mining 373
　music industry 141-2
　post-agricultural society 286, 293
　see also artisans, brass bands, Clark family, Cornwall, dealers, factory bands, TUC Congress
instrument makers 154, 168-71, 191, 252
　bankrupts 192
　pianos 175
　violins 170-1
　see also organ builders
instrumentalists 65-8
　see accordionists, bagpipers, banjo players, fiddlers, fifers and drummers, flautists, guitarists, harpists, horn players, melodeon players, pianists, serpents and their players, trumpeters, viol players, violinists
Intermusic *see* Minns
Ireland, John 251-3, 261
Irish 163
　see also immigrants
Isserlis, Steven 281
Ivybridge
　Ivy Live 286
Iwerne *see* Stepleton House

Jackson, Ada 209
Jackson, Enderby 119
Jackson, Jane 186, 209-17
Jackson, Mrs *see* Mary Bartlett
Jackson, Samuel 209
Jackson, William (of Brampford Speke) 37
Jackson, William (of Oxford) 232
Jackson family 229, 231
　William (composer 'of Exeter') 164, 226, 228-37
Jacques, Reginald 283
Jake ? 161

James I 160, 289
James, Kenneth 191
James, Leslie 57
jazz 122, 129–30, 147, 252, 367
  see also bands
Jeboult family 175
Jeffcoat, Miss 188
Jeffery, Stephen 35
Jenkins, William 87
Jennens, Charles 164, 232
Jews 121, 195, 256, 300, 361
Joachim, Joseph 328
John, Samuel 71
Johns, Master 123
Johnson, Samuel 164
Johnson, William 72–3, 154, 167–9
  and family 191
Joint, 'Jimmy' 129
Jones, Josiah 192
Jones, Mr 186
Jones & Co 38
Jordan, Abraham 35, 59
Jose, Richard 206
Jowett, Benjamin 327
Jullien, Louis 347–8
Jupp, Alfred 131

Kahlen, Mrs 43
Kandt, Julian 178
Kaps, Karl 178
Karabits, Kirill 362–3
Karpeles, Maud 267, 356
Katherine of Aragon 19
Kea 137
  see also St Kea
Keats, John and Tom 255–6
Keele, William 168
Keen, Percy W 258
Kellow, W 123
Kelly, Bill 132
Kelston 75
Kendall, John 316, 374
Kennedy family 190
  Peter 356–7
Kennerleigh 86
Kenwyn 238
Ketèlbey, Albert W 19, 52
Keynsham 75
  parish church 31–2
Khan, Imrat and Latif Ahmed 334–5
Kilkhampton
  parish church 61, 287
Killerton House 165
King, [Mr] 161
King's Lynn 233
Kingsbridge 179
Kingsdon 182–3
Kingsley, Charles 262
Kingswear 316
Kingsweston House 329
Knapp, William 83, 172, 181
Kneller Hall 120, 240
knighthoods 241
Knowle West 145

Kreisler, Fritz 109
Kreizberg, Yakov 362
Kretzschmar, Hermann 186
Kynance Cove 38
Kynaston, Nicholas 319

Lacock Abbey 21
Lacy, Bishop Edmund 68, 309
Lake, Harold 242
Lakeman, Seth 190–1
Lambert, Constant 263
Lamorna 353
Lamotte, Franz 43
Lancaster, Osbert xvi, 10
Landon, Letitia Elizabeth 256
landscapes 253–4
  as inspiration 283, 289
  musical depiction of 242
  prehistoric 274–5, 333
  see also Stonehenge
Lang, C S 328
Langdon, Richard 231
Langport 267
  dealers 196
Lanivet 372
Lanner 206
Lansdowne, Lord 164
Lanza, Gesualdo 221–2
Larkbeare 318
Laud, Archbishop William 156
Launceston 5, 261
  minstrels 68
  St Mary Magdalene church 28, 66, 310
  Wesleyan Church 54
Launceston Priory 310
Lavasher see Levasher
Lavenu, Louis 346
Laverton, William Henry 166
Lawes family 160–1
Lawrence, D H 285
Lawrence, T E 295
lawyers 340
lay clerks (lay vicars) 106–8, 161, 186–7, 194–5, 306, 319
  apprenticeships 168
  longevity 155
  male altos 109
  see also singing men, vicars choral
le Fleming, Christopher 17–18, 252
Leake, Mr (James?) 171–2
Leech, Joseph 42–3, 113–14
Leeds 50, 257
Legg, John 77
Leipzig 185–6, 327
Leke, William 302
Leno, Dan 166
Levasher family 169, 200
Levy, Pauline 133
Lewis, C S 274
Lewtrenchard 269
Leyton, John 141
libraries xi–xii, xv
Ling, James 192
Linley family 191, 193, 198, 218–24, 230, 232
Lintern, James and Walter 173

440 INDEX

Liszt, Franz 345-7
Little, Bryan 350
Littlehempston 64
Litton, Andrew 362
livelihoods 8, 42, 60, 151-248, 324
    and status 227
    band musicians 128
    general practitioners xiv, 33, 268, 344
    in Exeter 299-300
    monopolies 189
    multitraders 80, 111, 137, 154, 167-8, 172-3, 193-7
    pensions and legacies 155, 227, 231, 247, 267
    see also bankrupts, economics
Livermead 179
Liverpool 2, 50, 170, 201
Lizard, the 278
Lloyd, A L 267
Lloyd, Edward 176
Lloyd, George 242
    Iernin 19
Loader *see* Loder
Locke, Matthew 300
Lockestone, Roger 168
Lockett, Mornington 335
Loder family 191, 201, 203-4, 220, 223-4
    Andrew III 173-4, 192, 223
    Edward James 201, 223
    George II 201, 203-4, 223
    John David 99, 118, 173-4, 201, 222-3, 280, 358
    Kate 192, 201, 203, 223
    see also Bathsheba Cantelo, Mary Cook
London 4, 34, 43, 130, 362
    adjudicators from 280
    Almack's 93
    and cultural cringe 282
    as career destination 16, 84, 146-8, 185-6, 192, 198-203, 219-23, 225-9, 330, 352
    as hub 141-2, 184, 220
    as market 62, 176, 194, 255, 343
    as paradigm 10, 74, 106, 113-15, 148, 164, 170-1, 231, 234, 341, 355, 358
    as place of employment 279, 290
    as place of performance 115, 119, 174, 211, 240, 290, 295
    as place of publication 85-7, 172, 211, 246-7, 258, 263, 269
    as place of residence 56, 163, 271, 336, 341
    as place of training 158, 289, 319, 339
    Chapel Royal 306, 309
    connections with 170
    conservatoires 183-4, 201, 336
    Court 74, 161, 221, 288, 341
    Covent Garden Theatre 225-6, 296
    Drury Lane Theatre 79, 219, 232, 255
    exports to region 22, 174-6, 181
    finance 53
    Great Exhibition 48, 339, 347
    Hampstead Conservatoire 268
    Madrigal Society 108
    national broadcasting 349-50
    organ builders 22, 45, 48, 60, 189-90
    origins of concert life 340
    Parliament 21, 26, 357, 361
    performers from 76, 79, 130, 165-6, 197, 280, 326
    Philharmonic Society 222, 358
    pleasure gardens 341
    professionals 240
    refugees from 283
    Richmond Hill 294
    Royal Albert Hall 50, 115
    St James's Hall 211
    St Paul's Cathedral 112-13
    the season 341
    theatres and their music 171-2, 184, 225-8, 234-5, 271, 290, 323
    West End 225, 230, 271, 343
    Westminster Abbey 313, 319, 328
    Westminster Cathedral 319
    see also Kneller Hall, National Training School, Royal Academy of Music, Royal College of Music, Windsor
London Dance Band 130
London Symphony Orchestra 109
Longfleet
    hymn tune 83
Longleat House 7, 161-2
Looe 137
    fishermen 355
Loosemore family
    John 27-9, 60, 62, 169, 189
    Samuel 189
Lostwithiel 22
    hymn tune 84
Lott, Felicity 109
Lovegrove, John 196
Lovett, Sydney H 187
Lowther, Aimée 165
Loxton, Henry (father and son) 73
Luard-Selby, Bertram 45
Lucas, Alexander and Charles 170
Lucas family *see* Bright
Luccombe
    parish church xi, 81
Lucette, Mrs 43
Lugg, John 22, 155, 299
Lukins, Bill 131
Lulworth Castle 49
    Camp Bestival 286
Luppitt 339
    Buddhist community 19
lute songs 158
lutenists 159-62, 299
Luttrell family 315
Luxon, Benjamin 109
Lygon *see* Trefusis
Lyme Regis 86, 292, 372
    Assembly Rooms 137
    composers 354
    concert life 346
    parish church 27, 63, 137, 312
Lympstone
    quadrilles 137
    Royal Marines 339
Lynde, John 154
Lyne, Hannibal Lugg 87
Lynton 23, 150

MacCann, John Hill 170
McGrady, Richard 233
McGregor, Dr 179
Mackenzie, Alexander 243
McKie, William 328
MacMillan, James 363
Madge, William 161
madrigal singing 187
 see also clubs and societies
Magge, John 159
Mahon, John 79
Maiden Bradley Priory 310
Maiden Castle see Dorchester
Maker, Frederick Charles 209–12, 326
Makin, J J 58
Málaga 205
male voice choirs 109–12, 115, 353–4, 370
Manchester 50, 184, 188, 201, 329, 338–9
Maniford, Thomas 168
Manning-Sanders, Ruth 29, 278
Mantovani, Annunzio 131
Marazion Apollo Male Voice Choir 110
March, John 171
Mark, Bertram von der 100, 192, 337–8
Market Lavington 86
Markham, Ernest 263
Markordt, J 174
Marks & Spencer 281
Marsh, John 78, 170, 174, 321
Marsh, 'Old' 137
Marsh, Stephen 192
Marshall, Ian 271
Marson, Charles 265–9, 297
Martin, Chris 317
Martin, James 256
Martyn and Turner 98
Mary, Queen (consort of George V) 291
Masefield, John 187
Masland, William 177
Mason, Marjorie 351
Mason, Thomas 192
Massive Attack 143–5
Mathews, James 173
Matthews, Betty 228
Matthews, James 95
Matthews, 'Nibs' 134
Maunder, J H 247
Mawde, Hugh 24
Mawere see Mowere
May Day 70, 121
Maybrick, Michael 218
Mayne, Stephen 311
Mazzinghi, Joseph 323
Medland, John 71–3, 154, 299
Mee, Arthur 264
Melba, Nellie 109, 166
Melhuish, Mr 100
Melhuish, William 102
Melksham 86
 concert life 223
Mell, Davis 160
Meller, Clara 186
Mells
 fair 137
 schoolchildren 113
Mellstock see Stinsford
Mellstock Band 92
melodeon players 356
Melody Maker 141–2
Mendelssohn, Felix 23
 influence of 90
Mere 333
 choir singers 182
 parish church 182, 199
Merritt, Thomas 89–90
Merry, Roland 260
Methodists 202–3, 220, 279, 292
 and male voice choirs 110–12
 and organs 36, 38
 and psalmody 86
 carols 89–90
Mevagissey 146
Mevagissey Male Choir 111
Michaelstow 61
Micheau, Paul 60, 192
Michell, James 314
Mickleburgh 176–7
migration
 regional and seasonal 133, 197–9
 students 330
 to London 250
 see also immigrants, London: as career destination
Miles, Mrs 222
Miles, Philip Napier 297, 328
Milford, Robin 354
Milgrove, Benjamin 86–7
military music 298
 see also fifers and drummers, bands
militia see regiments and their bands
Miller, Arthur 252
Mills, Henry 115, 280
Milton Keynes 10, 218, 370
Minack Theatre see Porthcurno
Minehead 150, 315
 Butlins holiday camp 279
 parish church 31, 172
 service of song 365
miners see Cornwall
Miners Sax-Tuba Band 119
Minns 142, 176–7, 180
minstrels 99, 132, 141, 168, 277, 339, 372–3
 as spies 195
 domestic 158–9
 family groups 191
 licensed 166
 see also blackface minstrelsy, waits
Mobbs, Kenneth 330
Modbury 318
 aristocratic patronage 159–60
 band 104
modernism 297
Molloy, J L 218
monasteries and abbeys 298–9, 302–10
 convents 320–1
 organs 26
 see also friaries
Montacute 86
Montgomery, Bruce 336

Montrie, James 192
Moody, Fanny 158, 368
Moody and Sankey 89
Moon & Sons 176-7
Moore, Edna 187
Moore, Philip 356
Moore, Reginald 331
Moore, Thomas 163-4
   Irish Melodies 89
Moore, William 159, 299
Morebath 319, 339, 372
   parish church 26
Moreton family
   Ethel 52
   Harry 51-2, 155
Moretonhampstead
   town band 102
Morgan, Frederick 33
Morris, Margaret 296
Morris, William 62
morris dancing 134, 289
Morris family
   Betty 75
   Claver 74-7, 321, 340-1
Mortimore, T 24
Morton, H V 29, 262, 283, 355
Morval House 137, 174
Morwenstow 261
   Coombe 135
Mosley, Grace 174
Moss, Katie 270-3
Mount's Bay 110
Mousehole 353
   SA Corps 123
Mousehole Male Voice Choir 109-12, 288, 353
Mowere, Richard 315
Mozart, Wolfgang Amadeus 162-3, 284
Muchelney Abbey 310
Mugg, Lewis and John 318
Muldar, William 309
multitraders *see* livelihoods
municipal spending *see* civic identity
Murray, Dom Gregory 55, 354
Mushroom *see* Andrew Vowles
music hall 138, 250, 266, 345, 348
   see also variety
musicals 343, 367
Musicians' Union 361
musicking 252-3, 368, 370
Mylor
   St Mylor Festival 281
myth-making 254
   folk music, invention of 264-73
   west country, invention of 254-64

Nailsea
   Adge Cutler 143
   brass bands 120
   cider factory 145
   minstrels 151-2
   parish church 41-2
Nailsea Glassworks 120
Nailsea Volunteers 124
Naish, Thomas 76, 173, 175

Naja, Robert del 145
Nash, John (architect) 201
Nash, John (wait) 73
Nash, Richard 'Beau' 76, 342
National Training School 339
National Trust 289, 291
nationalism 362
Nempnett Thrubwell 146
Netherbury 315
networks 8, 189, 195, 298
   and polyphonic practice 302, 307
   church singers 84
   gentlemen amateurs 75
   professional performers 197-8
   singing masters 181-3
   waits 71
New, Albert Edward 155
New York 101, 198-9, 203-4, 207
New Zealand 167, 206-7, 211
Newbolt, Henry 187
Newcombe, John 186
Newlyn 110
   On Newlyn Hill (song) 353-4
Newlyn Male Choir 110, 353
Newman, Eldridge 263
Newquay 115, 319
   Methodist Church 49
newspapers 107, 172, 177, 341, 381-3
   see also *Bristol Mercury*, *Bristol Times*, *Melody Maker*, *Salisbury Journal*, *Torbay Express*, *West Briton*, *Western Times*
Newte, Rev John, 32 104
Newton Abbot 29, 123
   Quest 286
   racecourse 286
   St Mary Abbotsbury church 350
   South Devon Festival 286
Nicholas, Stephen 129
Nicholls, Alfred 205
Nicks, John 173
Nietzsche, Friedrich 369
Nine Lessons and Carols, Service of
   see festivals and celebrations
Nixon, John 65, 79
nobility *see* aristocracy
nonconformists xix, 2, 44, 114, 212, 246
   and hymn singing 36
   and organs 38-9, 42, 49, 58
   and psalmody 85
   church choirs 212
   decommissioned churches 366-7
   lack of preferment 198-9, 319
   services of song 364
   set pieces 87
   see also Methodists, Puritans, individual churches
Norris, Thomas 198
North, Roger 234
North Curry
   Methodist Chapel 38
north Devon *see* Devon
North Perrott
   parish church 68
North Petherton
   parish church 34

teachers 175
North Tawton 266
Norvall, Mr 24
Norwich 3-4, 60, 71, 314
Norwood, Andrew 77
Nourse, Nicholas 348
Novello, Ivor 131, 133
Novello family
    Clara 185
    Novello & Co 115
    Vincent and J Alfred 211
Nunn, John H 116-17
Nunney 168
Nynehead Court waltzes 101

observer-participation 272, 289
O'Connor, Feargus
    National Land Scheme 121
Odcombe
    carol singing 82
Okehampton xiv
    as resort 127
    bandstand 127
    Chagstock Festival 286
    dealers 129, 176
Old, John 137, 257, 262
old way of singing 37, 104, 181
Oliver, Herbert 263
open-air and camp meetings 279
opera 166, 214, 349, 355, 367
    amateur operatics 187
    arias in tune books 138, 266
    composers 19, 256-7
    first performances 284
    in and about Cornwall 19, 283-5, 291
    singers 158
    stars 280
    see also Bristol Opera [School], Gilbert and Sullivan, Glastonbury Festival (first)
Oram, Ernest G 131
oratorio performances 17, 115, 117-18, 341, 359
orchestras 114, 117, 231, 352, 357-64
    amateur 75
    dance 141
    municipal and resort 120, 240, 246, 298, 357-60
    professional 2, 10, 280-1, 336, 338, 349, 355, 360-3
    salon 126-8
    school 324-5
    student 284
    theatre 240, 342
    university 328
    visiting 347
    youth 188, 287, 338
Ordinalia and other Cornish plays *see* Cornwall
organ blowers (human and mechanical) 23-5, 35
organ builders 22, 29-31, 45-9, 59-63, 169, 189-90, 207
    see also Hugh Chappington, John Clark, Henry Crabb, John Crang, Percy Daniel, H P Dicker, William Drake, Eustace and Aldridge, Michael Farley, Lance Foy, Griffen and Stroud, Harris family (organ builders), Robert Hayward, Heard & Sons, Hele & Co, John Loosemore, George Osmond, Seede family, John Smith, William Sweetland, Robert Taunton, W G Vowles, Roger Yates
    festivals 287
    multitraders 196
organ builders (from London and other regions) 60
    see also Bryceson Brothers, John Compton, Gray of London, Samuel Green, Hammond, Thomas Harris, Harrison & Harrison, Hill & Son, Robert Hope-Jones, Abraham Jordan, J J Makin, Anthony Parsons, Schmidt (Smith) family, Anton Skrabl, John Snetzler, Thomas Swarbrick, J W Walker & Sons, Henry Willis, Wurlitzer
organ music
    voluntaries 16, 27, 246, 299
organ recitals 50-2, 55-6, 63, 350
organists 45-7, 55-6, 61, 87, 105, 247
    apprenticeships 166-7
    borough 51-2, 244-6
    broadcasting 354
    cathedral 25, 306
    cinema 53, 56-7
    concert 50
    financial arrangements 33-5, 372-3
    longevity 155
    migration 200
    performance practice 55
    recruiting choristers 125
    women 39-40, 42-3
    see also individual cathedrals and churches
organs 7, 15-17, 21-63, 87, 114, 335, 372-3
    electronic 57-9, 63, 180
    in chancels and choirs 48
    in church galleries 27-8, 36, 41-2, 44, 59, 84
    in cinemas 23, 53-7
    neoclassical trends 60-3
    on seaside piers 53
    secularisation 52-9
    see also barrel organs, harmoniums, individual churches
organum 1
Orme, Nicholas 305, 318
Osmond, George 60
Otterton
    parish church 86
Ottery Glee Club 107
Ottery St Mary 171, 237, 318, 348
    carnival 18, 132-3
    college of priests 306, 314
    parish church 63, 102
Ottery St Mary Institute 132
Ottery St Mary Silver Band 132-3
Ouseley, Sir Frederick Gore 43-4
Overd, Emma 267
overseas territories 92-3, 248, 315
    New Caledonia 216-17
    South America 201, 206
    see also British Empire
Oxford 106, 340
    Balliol College 327
    New College 306
    University 39, 61, 134, 231, 327, 340

Pachmann, Vladimir de 109
Pack, Thomas 315

Paddon, James 226, 228, 232
Padstow 297, 364
    accordion band 19, 274
    carol singing 82
    darkie day festival 279, 287
    Obby Oss festival 19, 273, 279
    Prideaux Place 137
    St Petroc's church 23
Paganini, Niccolò 345
pageants xvi, 115, 288–92
Paignton 179
    parish church 310
    pier 53, 128
    SA band 122
Paish & Co 176–80
Palm Sunday 308
Palmer, George 24
pantomimes 141
Par 137
Parfet, Robert 139
Parfitt, James 155
Paris 214–17
parish clerks 70, 81, 265, 307
Parish family
    Benjamin 256
    Eli[as] Parish Alvars 256–7
    Joseph 33, 192, 256
Parke, W T 239
Parker, Louis Napoleon 25, 289–90, 324–7
Parker, Master 139
Parker, Nathaniel 182–3
Parker, William 310
Parkes, David 109
Parkhouse, Master 123
Parkstone 361
    St Osmund's church 55
Parratt, Walter 50, 56
Parry, Hubert 212, 243
Parry, John 165
Parry, John Orlando 347
Parry, Robert 175
Parsloe, Guy 70, 132–5
Parsons, Anthony 60
Partridge, R 86
Pascoe, E 365
Pascoe's Sax-Tuba Band 119
Pasmore, Peter 29–30
Pathfinders 140
patronage 154, 157–66, 230, 252, 298
    aristocratic 41, 49, 81, 94, 170, 218, 282
    BBC 354
    bequests and endowments 26, 302–3, 306, 310–14
    by the gentry 32–3, 101, 113, 239
    by women 32–3, 84
    church livings 23
    civic 300
    commercial sponsorship 281
    in cathedral cities 299–300
    industrial 295
    military 77, 94, 220
    monastic 26
    municipal 243–4, 359–62
    new churches 42–3
    of amateurs 124
    of emigrants 203
    organs 32–3, 39, 324
    privateers 70–1
    royal 7
    subsidisation 349, 366
    see also charity
Paynter, John 333
Payton, Philip 201, 261, 279
Pearce, Mrs 322
Pearce, Percy 130
Pearsall, Robert Lucas 108–9, 150
Pearson, J L 45
Pellew, Admiral 237–9
Pembroke, earls of 160, 187, 341
Penke, John 302
Penlee Lifeboat disaster 111
Penryn 276, 314
    Combined Universities in Cornwall campus 336
    Temperance Hall 38
    see also Glasney
Pensford 143–5, 195
    parish church 114
Penzance 40
    Chapel Street Methodist Church 40, 49
    Concerts Penzance 367
    Golowan festival 67
    Methodist chapel 38
    Morrab Library xii
    SA Corps 123
    St John's Hall 51
    St Mary's Arts Festival 284
    St Mary's church 40–1, 207, 367
    venues 117
Penzance Choral Society 117–18
Penzance Festival 283
Penzance Philharmonic Society 358
Peppin, Arthur 325, 328
Pepys, Samuel 74
Perceval, Spencer 39
Percival, John (of Bristol) 95–7
Percival, John (of Clifton College) 324, 327
performance practice
    bands 101–3
    changing 273
    congregation 81
    Cornish drama 276–8
    double-handedness 120
    dress 65, 117
    folk music 269
    minstrels 151–2
    pre-Reformation church music 303–7
    rehearsals 115–17
    virtuoso 222, 281
    vocal 91–2, 112, 206, 352, 374
    see also old way of singing
performers 252, 298
    actresses 344–5
    virtuoso 256, 321, 345–8
    see also instrumentalists, visitors
Perkins, Dodd and William 155
Pernaunt, Joan 302, 373
Perranporth 205
Perring, John 369
Perry, Robert 194, 302

Peters, Thomas 195
Peters, W C and William S 207
Pevsner, Nikolaus 264
Philips, Thomas 304
Phillips, Austin 205
Phillips, Elizabeth 167
Phillips, Mr 198
Phillips, Peter 314
Phillips, W H 188
Phillpotts, Eden
    Widecombe Fair 365-6
pianists 137, 183, 214, 283
    leading bands 102
    women 174, 185-6
    see also education
piano recitals 347, 350
piano tuners 171, 174-5, 196, 201, 237
pianos 174-80, 291, 373
    barrel 195
    in church 59
Picton, Arthur and Harry 128-9
Pidgeon, Fred 135
piers 53, 126-7, 131
Pilbrow, Tycho 173-5
Pill 146
Pilton 293
    Worthy Farm 286
Pindar, Peter *see* John Wolcot
Pine, William 172
Pinney family (of Exeter) 94
Pinto, Thomas 195
Pinwill sisters 29
Piper, John 209
pipers 275, 278
    see also bagpipers
Pistor, Alfred and Walter 318
Pitman, Isaac 176
plainsong 303-5, 320
Playford, John 15-16, 341
playing places *see* theatres and theatrical
        entertainment
pleasure gardens 341, 345, 348
Plomer, Richard Haynes 172
Plummer Roddis 130-1
Plymouth xvi, 8, 29, 60, 332
    4th Boys' Brigade 133
    ABC Cinema 57
    Andrews' Picture House 53
    bands 93, 100
    bankrupts 192
    Bedford Park Music and Dancing Academy 337
    British Music Society centre 187
    broadcasting 351
    Cinedrome 53
    cinemas 53
    concert life 110, 346
    conservatoires 337
    Corporation 52
    dance bands 133
    dealers 142, 176-7, 192
    Drill Hall 109, 291
    festivals 282
    Gaumont Palace 57
    Guildhall 50-2, 130
    Hoe 289
    instrument makers 170
    introduction of pianos 175
    organ builders 60
    organ culture 51
    organists 155, 242
    pageant 291
    Palladium 53
    Paramount Dance Band 133
    piano tuners 201
    plans for a university college 331
    Puritanism 3
    Raleigh Dance Orchestra 133
    Royal Marines 93, 133, 339
    SA convention 123
    St Andrew's church 31-2, 51-2, 175, 310, 312, 372
    St Peter's church 44-5
    teachers 186-7
    Theatre Royal 141
    theatres 177
    trumpeters and drummers 73
    Victory Revellers Dance Band 133
    visit of Bristol waits 72
    waits 70-2, 99, 373
    White Notes Dance Band 133-4, 138-9
    see also Devonport, Gasworkers' Brass Band,
        Stonehouse
Plymouth College of Music 337
Plymouth Folk Song Club 147-8
Plymouth Harmonic Society 358
Plymouth Orpheus Society 109
Plymouth Sound 70-1, 99
Plymouth University 336
Plympton 94, 372
    Priory 310
Plymtree 309
politics 23, 29-30, 50, 116, 134, 362
    and newspapers 64, 172
    and social solidarity 121-2
    Anglican ritualism 39-48
    imperialism 262
    municipal 357, 360
    national 361-2
    socialism 294
    see also Chartists, class
Polperro
    Ship Inn 98
Polperro Fishermen's Choir 111
polyphony 301-16, 320-1
Pond, Charlie 356
Ponthieu, Prince de 100
Poole 10, 75, 177, 357
    choirs 363
    composers 86
    dealers 172, 177
    Festival of Busking 69
    Hill Street Baptist Church 39
    Lighthouse 362-3
    minstrels 68-9
    St James's church 34-6
    see also Parkstone
Poole, La 100
Poole Arts Centre 362
pop groups *see* bands

pop music 280, 317
   see also bands, rock, youth culture
Pope, Alexander 181
popular classics 51-2, 214
Porlock
   carols 82, 91
Port Isaac 292
   see also Fishermen's Friends
Porter-Brown, Reginald 57
Porthcurno
   Minack Theatre 278
Porthgwarra 283
Porthoustock 283
Portishead (town) 149-50, 217
   bandleaders 128-9
   town band 102
   We Three dance band 128-9
Portishead (trip hop band) 144, 148-50
Portsmouth 363
Portugal
   Lisbon 238-40
Potter, Joseph 155
Powderham Castle
   band 94
Pratten, Stephen 209, 337
Predeaux, John 311
prehistoric sites *see* landscapes
Preston 179
Preston, William 309
Prickett, Reynold 195
pricksong *see* polyphony
Prince, Thomas 168
Prisk, Thomas 87
professionals 123-4, 371
   and amateurs 105, 112, 183, 197, 284, 330
   and retirement 241
   cost of hiring 117
   elite 233
   folk groups 140
   foreign 337, 363
   from London 165-6, 326
   immigrants 126-7
   in Exeter 299-300
   institutional employment 241-4, 354-6
   instrumentalists 75-8, 95, 99-102
   masterclasses 281
   minstrels 152, 277
   on tour 197-8
   pre-Reformation singing men 104, 301-16
   professional conditions 296, 333
   training as choristers 316-17
   women 43
   see also livelihoods
professors of music *see* teachers
provincial values 234
Prowse, Samuel 123
Prussia Cove
   International Musicians' Seminar 281-2
Prynne, G H Fellowes 45
psalm tunes *see* hymns: tunes
psalmody 36, 80-92, 196, 247, 321
   and folk singing 266-7
   and tune books 137-8
   choirs and singing masters 181-3

dealers 172
opposed and superseded 36-9, 43, 113-14, 116, 124
participation 104-5, 370
performance practice 84, 87, 91-2
value 369
see also hymns
public schools *see* education
publishers and agents 171-2, 211-12, 252
   see also dealers
pubs *see* taverns
Pucklechurch
   parish church 81
Pugin, A W 48
Purcell, Henry 295, 341
Puritans 2-3, 21-3, 28
Pusey, Les 141
Pye, Kellow 231
Pyne, James Kendrick 155

Qatar 247
quadrille bands *see* bands
Quakers 38
Quantock Hills 137, 200
Queen 317
quires *see* psalmody

race 149, 237-40
   see also immigrants
Rachmaninov, Sergei 130
Radford, Evelyn and Maisie 282-4, 286, 291
Radford, Shadrach 77
radios 129, 138, 180, 349, 355
Raikes, Robert 114
railways xi, 7-8, 17-18, 332, 346
   tunnels in wartime 354-5
Rainier, Priaulx 281
Raleigh, Sir Walter 157, 262
Rancock, Thomas 72, 169
Randell, Greenwood 299
Rattle, Simon 362
Rauzzini, Venanzio 184, 186, 192, 221-2, 321, 341-3
rave 143, 147
Ravenscroft, Thomas 14, 255
Rawlings, Charles *see* H Verne
Raybould, Clarence 295
Rayne, Thomas 194, 310
Reade, C J 178
recordings *see* gramophones and record players
Redland
   Redland Park Congregational Church 42, 209
   Tyndale Baptist Church 42
Redman, Reginald 352-6
Redruth 203-6, 279
   Bible Christian Chapel 90
   carols 82, 89-90, 129
   dealers 129
   Fore St Methodist Church 155
   parish church 38, 81
   plans for a university college 331
   Wesleyan Chapel 90
   see also Fanny Moody
Redwin, Henry 313
reed organs *see* harmoniums
Reed, Doris 188

Rees, Mr 110
Reeve, William 184
Reeves, Sims 185, 211
Reformation 26–8, 298
Regan, Charles 326
regiments and their bands 92–3, 120
    1st Devon Militia 94
    4th Dragoons 77
    17th Devon (Dart Vale Rifle Volunteers) 123–4
    22nd Regiment of Foot 93
    29th (Worcestershire) Foot Regiment 344
    Devon Rifle Volunteers 11 Battalion 124
    Dorset Militia 79, 119
    Duke of Cornwall's Light Infantry 319
    North Devon Militia 344
    Royal Cornwall Militia 98
    Royal Marines *see* Plymouth
    Somerset Light Infantry (Band of the 3rd Battalion) 125
    Somerset Militia 94
    South Devon Militia 94
    Wiltshire Militia 94, 95
religion *see* Anglicanism, Huguenots, nonconformists, open-air and camp meetings, organs, politics: Anglican ritualism, Puritans, Quakers, Roman Catholics, sabbatarianism
Renynger, James 194, 310, 320, 373
Reprazent 148
resorts *see* Bath, Okehampton, seaside resorts
Restoration 21, 28, 74–5, 340–2
Réunion, La 247
Rewallin, Charles 169
Reynolds, Joshua 230–2
Rhodes, Harold 179
rhythm 'n' blues 133
Rhythm Arcadians 132
Richards, A 123
Richards, 'Fiddler Jim' 205
Richards, John 71
Rickard, Jimmy 132
Righton, Henry 121–2
Rio, J 195
riots *see* strife and unrest
Risdon, John 195
Riseley, George 45, 51, 107, 167, 211, 323
ritualism *see* politics
roadies 252
Roadwater Temperance Hall 365
Roberton, Hugh 282
Robertson, Dora 320
Robinson, Joseph 196
Robjohn family 207
Roborough Down 283
rock 138, 274, 286, 367
    pop videos 144
    rock 'n' roll 138, 140, 287
    see also bands
Rockstro, W S 45
Roeckel (Röckel) family 214–18, 323
    Jane *see* Jane Jackson
    Joseph Leopold 209–18, 261, 328
Rogers, Anne 322
Rogers, Nelme 174, 184
Rogers, Sir John Leman 231

roller-skating rinks 53
Roman Catholics 44, 163
    and organs 49
    education 145, 319, 322–3
    immigrants 145, 323
    recusants 156, 195, 314
romanticism
    in composition 256–7
    in organ design and repertoire 41, 48–52, 53
Rootham family 184, 327–8
Ross, Craigie 242
Rossini, Gioachino 284
rough music (charivari) 121
Rowe, Peter 111
Rowe, Thomas 192
Roy, Harry 130
Royal Academy of Music (RAM) 183–4, 201–3, 289, 338
Royal College of Music (RCM) 184, 240, 339, 361
Royal Navy 51, 98, 145, 177, 201, 237–9
    dockyard workers 98
    fiddlers 237
    see also Dartmouth: Royal Naval College, Plymouth: Royal Marines
royalty 95, 107, 160, 173, 288–9, 339
    see also Alfred, Arthur, Charles I, Edward IV, Elizabeth I, Elizabeth II, George III, George V, Henry VII, Henry VIII, James I, Katherine of Aragon, London: Court, Victoria, William of Orange, Windsor
Ruan Major and Minor 278
Rumpo, Rambling Syd 357
rural culture 249–53, 264–7, 274–6, 352, 365–6
    organ building 47–8
    see also fiddlers, folk music, psalmody
Russell, Rev Jack 261
Russell, Peter 142
Russell, W 64
Rutter, John 247

sabbatarianism 53, 250
St Agnes Male Voice Choir 110
St Anthony in Roseland 283–4, 355
St Austell 71, 196
    Band of Hope Choir 365
    Bethesda Band of Hope 365
    Bible Christian schoolroom 365
    hymn tune 83
    parish church 68
    WI choir 115
St Austell Amateur Brass Band 118
St Austell Sax Horn Band 119
St Blazey
    brass band 118
St Buryan
    college of priests 314
    Merry Maidens stone circle 274
St Cecilia's Day 76–7, 164, 340
St Columb Major
    Nine Maidens stone row 274
    parish church 68
St Dennis 137
St Endellion
    Endellion String Quartet 284

Festival 284-5
parish church 29
St Enodoc 285
St German's Priory 310
St Ives 63, 137, 242, 292, 297
   American forces bands and dancing 131-2
   as artists' colony 281
   Bedford Road Methodist Church 49
   civic plays 277-8
   dealers 129
   Drill Hall 129
   parish church 28-9
   SA bands 123
   September Festival 288
   service of song 365
   teachers 181
   see also Carbis Bay
St Ives Jazz Band 129-30
St Juliot 12-13
St Just 277
St Kea
   Beunans Ke 276
St Keverne 226
St Marychurch *see* Torquay
St Mary's (Isles of Scilly)
   bugle signal 19
   town band 102
St Mawes 283
   castle pageant 291
St Mawgan 87
St Michael's Mount 25
St Mylor Festival *see* Mylor
Sainton, Prosper 185
salaries and fees *see* economics
Salisbury 8, 77, 121, 160-1, 200, 268
   as gateway 7, 346
   as musical centre 299-300
   Assembly Rooms 346
   concert life 164-5, 170, 340, 346
   dancing days 273
   dealers 170-2
   diocese 8
   families 192
   Rev Hodgson's academy 322
   instrument makers 170-1
   introduction of pianos 174
   ladies' academies 322
   light opera 187
   Malmesbury House 164
   military music 92
   orchestras 187
   organ builders 60
   origin of Salvation Army 122
   Pathfinders 140
   professionals 198, 230
   Regal Cinema 57
   rock 'n' roll 140
   St Edmund's church 27, 76, 187, 192-4
   St Martin's church 28, 192
   St Thomas's church 27, 192, 195
   Serenaders Concert Party 187
   Society of Lovers of Musick 76
   teachers 187-8, 282
   women musicians 174
Salisbury Catch Club 106
Salisbury Cathedral 7, 160-1, 170, 299, 305, 319
   authorities 57, 76
   bells 24
   choir school 320
   choristers 167, 199, 304
   close 77
   composers 158
   lay clerks and vicars choral 187, 303-4, 306, 315
   oratorio performances 341
   organ 7, 21, 24-5, 31-3, 48
   organ blower 24
   organist 45, 155, 165, 319, 322
   Sarum Rite 1-2
   use of instruments 80
Salisbury Festival 164-5, 170, 223, 280, 321, 341
Salisbury Journal 172
Salisbury Musical Society 187, 246
Salomon, Johann Peter 221, 238-40
Saltash 5
Salvation Army 139-40
   see also bands
Sampford Brett 87
Sampford Courtenay 26
Samson, Jim 329
Sanderson, Wilfrid 263
Sandwich *see* Swanage
Sarum Rite *see* Salisbury Cathedral
Saunders, Misses or Mrs 32
Sax, Adolphe 103
Schafer, R Murray 11
Schmidt (Smith) family
   Christian 23
   'Father' Bernard 23, 61
Schnabel, Artur 332
Schwarz, Rudolf 360-2
Scilly, Isles of xvi, 351
   see also St Mary's, Tresco
Scott, Sir Walter 100
screen media
   Brassed Off (film) 271
   Carry On films 336
   concerts of film music 363
   documentary xvi, 272
   newsreels 273
   silent films 290-1
   see also television
Searelle, William Luscombe 206-7
seaside resorts
   bands 95, 100, 123, 126-7
   concert life 197
   dealers 173
   growth and demise 200-1, 288
   orchestras 130-1, 357-62
   organ builders 60
   organs 44-7, 49-53
   see also individual resorts, piers
Seatown 146
secondaries *see* Exeter Cathedral
Seede family 60, 196
   Bryce 34, 60
   Richard 49, 60
Seeger family 190
Seeley's (dealer) 129

INDEX 449

Segal, Uri 362
Selake, William 313
Self, Geoffrey 4, 89, 280
Selley, Charley 24
Selwood
    parish church 26
serpents and their players 81, 85, 92, 94–7, 103
services of song 364–5
Seymour, Edward *see* Earl of Hertford
Shaftesbury
    concert life 198
    Holy Trinity church 36
Shaftesbury, La 100
Shaftesbury Abbey 320
Shaldon Festival 287
shanties *see* folk music
Sharp, Cecil 9, 207, 270, 289, 356, 363, 375
Sharp, Mr 174, 184
Shaw, George Bernard 183, 294–6, 331
Shaw, Martin 336
Shaw, Mr 116–17
Shearme, John 189
Shepherd, William 94
Sheppard, H Fleetwood 269
Shepton Beauchamp 269
Shepton Mallet
    matadors 146
    parish church 21, 27, 31-2, 155
Sherborne 317
    All Hallows church 373
    balls 102
    church house 339
    concert life 198
    dealers 172
    Mrs Pearce's academy 322
    town band 102
Sherborne, La 100
Sherborne Abbey 36
    festival 287
    organ 31
    organist 155, 198
Sherborne Chamber Choir 290
Sherborne Pageant 289–91
Sherborne School 25, 289–90, 322–6, 332
Sherborne Town Band 290
Sheridan, Richard Brinsley 219, 232
Shield, William 232–3
Shirehampton 214
Shobrooke Park
    Aeon Festival 286
Shoel, Thomas 86-7
Shrewsbury 233
Sidbury
    parish church 28
Sidmouth 135
    All Saints' church 24
    concert life 346
    London Hotel 346
    parish church 24, 32, 63, 81
Sidmouth Choral Society 116
Sidmouth Folk Week 286
Sidmouth Town Band 132
Sidney [Herbert], Mary 160
Silberman, L 259

Silbury Hill 333
Silver, John 155
Silvestri, Constantin 362
Simper family 246
    Caleb 246–8, 258
Singapore 84, 247
singers 109–10, 221, 352
    amateur 359, 364–6
    amplified vocalists 131, 138, 150
    children 325–6
    church 358
    contraltos 109, 258
    from London 280, 321
    male altos 107, 109
    operatic 341, 347
    street 358
    tenors 109–10
    see also charity children, choirs, clubs and societies, folk music, lay clerks (lay vicars), opera, psalmody, singing men, vicars choral, visitors
singing
    congregational 22, 32, 36, 104, 181
    in schools 112–14, 118, 325–6
    see also old way of singing
singing masters, itinerant *see* teachers
singing men 26, 161, 194, 306–7, 314, 373–4
    see also lay clerks (lay vicars), professionals
Singleton, Joan 185–6
Siprutini, Emanuel 195
Sivrai, Jules de *see* Jane Jackson
skiffle 140
Skrabl, Anton 63
Slade, Julian 343
Slapton Sands 132
Slater, Ernest 203
slavery 163, 239
Small, Christopher 252–3
Smart, George 321
Smert, Richard 304, 309, 315
Smith, Bruce 162
Smith, Glades 187
Smith, John (impresario) 141
Smith, John (of Bristol) 38, 60, 196
Smith, John (of Market Lavington) 86
Smith family (organ builders of London) *see* Schmidt (Smith) family
Smollett, Tobias 16–17
Smyth, Ethel 19, 242
Smyth, Sir John Hugh 81
Smythe, Robert 316
Snetzler, John 49
Snygge, John 302
societies *see* clubs and societies
Sodbury, Adam de 25
Somerset 1, 5, 8, 68, 188, 336, 356
    folk music 2, 267–9
    idea of 263
    organs 26
    rock 'n' roll 140
    South Somerset Youth Choir 287
    see also regiments and their bands, Taunton and Somerset Music and Drama Festival
Somerset Federation of Women's Institutes 115

Somerset nog, The terrible tale of the (song) 357
Somersetshire march, The new 95
Somerton 182
song schools *see* education
Songs of Praise see television
sonic distinction 371-4
Sontag, Henriette 214
Sorge, H P 100, 102
soundscapes 3-4, 11-19, 22, 58, 71, 93, 162, 272-3, 362
South Africa 51, 90, 92, 204, 207, 240-1
south Devon *see* Devon
South Hams 132
South Petherton 86
Southey, Robert 232, 237
Southville 145
Southworth, Wilfrid 57
Spagnoletti, Paolo
    'La Dorset' 100
Spain-Dunk, Susan 242
Spark, William 257
Spaxton
    Village Hall 141
Spittle or Spittel, Augustus 77
sport and games 264, 268, 277, 325
Spottiswoode, Daphne 351
Spreyton 269
Staelens, Yvette 140
Stainer, John 203
Stanford, Charles Villiers 243, 290
Stanford, Trevor *see* Russ Conway
Stansbury, Joseph 95
Stanton, W K 329
Stanton Drew 146
    stone circles 274-5
Stapledon, Bishop Walter 310
Starcross 95
Starling, George 70
Start Point 351
statistics 177
    concerts 242
    datasets 371
    examination entrants 183
    migration 199-200
    musicians in Bath and Exeter 186, 300
    organ installation and provision 36, 42
    piano sales 178-80
    rates of participation 65, 104-5, 111, 114, 317-18, 370-1
    regional disaffection xvi-xvii
    teachers 186-7
    west country composers 336
    see also sonic distinction
Stein, Rick 297
step dancing 134-5
Stephens, John 165
Stephenson, J H 269
Stephenson, Joseph 86
Stepleton House 162-3, 175
Sternhold, Thomas 15-16
Stevens, John and Richard 113
Stiby, W 76
Sticklepath 269
Stinsford
    parish church 83, 136
Stinsford House 136

Stockham, Mr 93, 100
Stockham, Thomas 103
Stockland 135
Stocklinch Ottersey
    parish church 24
Stockton Glee Choir 107
Stogursey 200
Stoke Climsland
    Whiteford Festival 286
Stoke St Michael 202
Stone 85
Stone, Alfred 107
Stone, G H 258
Stone, G R 123-4
Stonehenge 8, 346
    depicted in music 242
Stonehouse (Plymouth)
    dealers 103
    teachers 186-7
Stopes, Marie 295
Storace family 192
    Stephen 232-3
Stravinsky, Igor 332
Streating *see* Stretting
Street 292-5
    see also Clark family
street music and musicians 197, 200, 358
    see also bands
Street, G E 45
Stretting, John 151-3
strife and unrest 26, 37-40, 43, 103, 110, 148, 177, 202
    hooliganism 122
    see also Chartists
Stucley, Sir Lewis 23
Sturge, Joseph 95
Sturminster Newton, La 100
subculture 142-3, 180
    see also counterculture
Sudbin, Yevgeny 363
Suggia, Guilhermina 109
Sullivan, Arthur 272
    see also Gilbert and Sullivan
summer schools *see* education
Summerhayes family
    Cecilia 185, 201, 371
    Robert 102
    Samuel 101, 102
Summers, Charles and Joseph 204-5
Sun Life Band *see* Bristol: Stanshawe Band
Sunday schools 104, 112-14, 360, 370
Sutton, Raymond 263
Swaffield, Bennett 196
Swanage 87
    hymn tune 83
Swanage Jazz Festival 286
Swanage Town Band 125
Swarbrick, Thomas 59-60, 190
Swayne-Hall, Una 187
Sweden 247
Sweetland, William 49, 60, 287
Swindon 7
Sydenham, Mrs 322
Syle, Miss 344
Symons, William 194

Tamar, River 5
Tankret, Thomas 311
Tanzania 189
Tape, Fred 135
Tapp, John Charles 202-3, 206
Tapper, Ivy 187
Tarrant Rushton 339
taste 92, 122, 143, 247, 355, 363
    English 342
    French 341
    Italian 74, 164, 232-4, 342
        see also bands
    popular 117
    Victorian 212
Taunton 10, 185, 201-3, 222
    Academy of Music 337
    Assizes 202
    Buddhafield Festival 286
    concert life 346
    dance bands 141
    dealers 101-2, 172, 192
    Gaumont Theatre 141
    military music 92
    organ builders 60
    publishers 269
    SA band 122
    St James's church 39-40
    St Mary Magdalene church 31, 44
    teachers 175
    Temple Methodist Chapel 40
    Tone Ballroom Orchestra 141
    Young Musician of the Year award 287
Taunton, Robert 31
Taunton and Somerset Music and Drama Festival 287
Taunton Castle
    Museum of Somerset 169
Taunton Priory 310
Taunton Sacred Harmonic Society 115
Taunton School
    fife and drum band 125
taverns 72, 131, 146, 267, 298, 369-70
    city 134
    entertainment 366
    expenditure in 348
    landlords 119, 195-6
    patriotic singing 98
    rehearsing in 112
    singing groups 341-2
    subculture 146-7
    see also clubs and societies, individual villages, towns and cities
Tavistock 5, 33, 207, 318
    choral society 116
    Devon Great Consols Miners' Band 120
    St Eustachius's church 24-5, 68, 310
    waits 72
    Wesleyan Chapel 38
Tavistock Abbey 309-10, 373
Tawney, Cyril 147-8
Tawstock Court 169
Taylor, A 196
Taylor, Cyril 84
Taylor, Gilbert 103
Taylor, Roger 317

Taylor family 192
teachers 112, 181-9, 230, 237, 330, 337-8
    and job creation 200
    emigrant 199, 206
    Italian 341
    of women 321
    part-time livelihood 52, 102, 154, 196, 209-11
    professors of music 121-2, 129, 171, 183, 186
    singing masters, itinerant 81, 85, 139, 181-3
    statistics 370
    see also dancing masters
Teague, Robin 146, 356
Tebay, J 95
technology 22, 28, 48, 57, 65, 195
    telephones 117, 133
    see also broadcasting, gramophones and record players, radios, screen media, television
Tehidy 158
Teignmouth 255-7, 261
    Assembly Rooms 346
    concert life 346
    instrument makers 192
    The Legend of Teignmouth 256-7
    see also West Teignmouth
television 144, 146, 350, 364
    Songs of Praise 364
temperance movement see Band of Hope, choirs, services of song
Temperance Seven 141
Temperley, Nicholas 36, 87, 90
Temple, John 195
Tenducci, Giusto 321
Terry, Richard Runciman 323
Teschemacher, Edward 263
Tester, Archibald F 290
Tetcott 261
Tewkesbury, John 164-5, 198, 322
Thackeray, William Makepeace
    The History of Pendennis 171, 345
Thalberg, Sigismond 185, 347
theatres and theatrical entertainment 5, 56, 141, 335, 339-49, 364, 366-7
    concert parties 65, 187
    in country houses 165-6
    playing places 277-8, 339
    travelling players 2, 68, 153, 159, 166, 197, 339-40
    see also actors, Cornwall: *Ordinalia* and other plays, Easter Sepulchre dramas, individual towns and cities, music hall, opera, Porthcurno: Minack Theatre
Thomas, Ilva 115
Thomas, Michael 107
Thompson, G A 188
Thompson, Silvanus 328
Thompson, William 198
Thoms, William 264
Three Choirs Festival 185, 280
Thynne family 161-2
Tidderleigh, William 162
Tiddy, David 103
Tietjens, Thérèse 185, 216
Tilley, Rev 178
Timewell, John 339
tin horns 121

Tintagel 135, 289, 332
  castle 296
  pageant 291
Tippett, Michael 281, 297, 333
Tiverton
  Blundell's School 322
  brass band 118
  concert life 347
  Congregational Church 114
  first performance of Mendelssohn's wedding march at a church wedding 23, 117
  hymn tune 83
  St Peter's church 23, 25–7, 31, 36, 104, 257, 313
  Sunday schools 114
Toby, James 81
Tolhurst, George 246
Tomkins, Giles 155
Tomkins, Richard 77
tonic sol-fa 113–16
Tope, Gordon 133
Topsham Glee Club 107
Torbay 99
  Olympic Games 351
  Torbay Express 350–1
Torbuck, George 172
Torch, Sidney 56
Torquay xvi, 90, 257, 324, 362
  bandleaders 102
  bandmasters 178
  bandstand 127
  choral society 116
  concert life 346
  dealers 102, 176–80
  Pavilion Theatre 360
  Royal Italian Band 126
  SA band 122
  St John's church 45–7, 179
  St Marychurch 65, 360
  teachers 102
  see also Torbay
Torquay Labour Party 360
Torquay Municipal Orchestra 357–60
Torquay Pavilion 141
Torquay Quadrille Band 100
Torrington 335
Torrington Glee Union 107
Torrington Sacred Harmonic Society 115
Totnes 63, 72, 124, 256, 317, 332, 336
  Guildhall 123
  St John's church, Bridgetown 62
  St Mary's church 25, 31, 155
Totnes and Bridgetown Fife and Drum Subscription Band 124
Totnes Harmonic Society 358
town bands *see* bands
town halls 56–7
  organs in 49–52
Townley, James 342
Townsend, Roger 186
traditional music *see* folk music
transport *see* travel
Trathan, J J 196
travel 345–6
  abroad 230–1

  artefacts (folksongs) 267
  cars named after counties 264
  from London 165–6
  road deaths 142
  to other English regions 72
  tourism 262–4, 268, 272
  transport 22, 41, 171, 348
  turnpikes 346
  zone of hearsay 275–9
  see also emigrants, migration, railways
travellers *see* festivals and celebrations
travelling players *see* theatres and theatrical entertainment
Travers, John 229
Tredgenoweth, John 365
Trefusis, Lady Mary 282
Tregarthen, William 45
Tregian, Francis 195
Tregoning's Repository 173, 177
Trehern, Mr 101
Trenwith, Henry and Vic 19
Tresco (Isles of Scilly)
  band 125
Trethosa
  WI choir 115
Treverva Choir 354
Treviscoe
  WI choir 115
Trevisone, Alfonso 244
Tricky 144–5, 148
Trimnell family
  Thomas 155, 195
  Thomas Tallis 167
  William Frederick 323–7
Trinity College of Music 184
  examination system 183, 282
trip hop *see* Bristol sound
Trowbridge 75, 92, 175–6, 268
  bands 120–2
  Baptist church 176
  Chartists 120–2
  parish church 121
Trowbridge Choral Society 116, 121
Trowbridge Working Men's Association 121
Trudoxhill 168
Truelove, John 304, 309
trumpeters 70–1, 73, 161, 191, 198
Truro 239
  as musical centre 299–300
  celebrations 98
  choral societies 118
  composers 237
  concert life 347
  dancing 99
  dealers 173, 177
  diocese 8, 45
  Methodist Church 282
  military music 92
  organ builders *see* Lance Foy
  parish church 31, 35, 197
  social dancing 137
  street musicians 197
  Three Spires Festival 281
  Three Spires Singers 281

Truro Amateur Sax-Tuba Band 119
Truro Cathedral 45, 89, 115, 319
  choir 317
  Festival of Nine Lessons and Carols 287
  organ 48
Truro Concert Room 51
Truro Festival 223, 280
Truro Harmonic Society 358
TUC 52
Tucker, Isaac 83
Tuckwell, Kerwin 'Jack' 128–9
tune books 85, 87, 136–8, 266
Tunmore, Thomas A 187
Tunstall-Behrens, Hilary 281
Turin 231
Turle, James 83–4
Turner, Austin and George 205
Turner, Eva 185
Turner, Will 81
Turpin, Richard 311
Twigges, ? 195
Tyndall, Arthur 329
Tyrolese Minstrels 126
Tywardreath Priory 194, 310, 314, 372

Uffculme
  parish church 27
Uffculme Band 125
Ugbrooke House 165
Ulrico, Signor 126
Ulster 247
universities 61–3, 145, 200, 327–36, 368
  Inter-Varsity Folk Dance Festival 134
  music degree courses 63, 184, 329
  students on vacation 284
  see also Bristol University, Cambridge, Dartington: educational and cultural institutions, Exeter University, Oxford
University College of the South West of England 330–1
  see also Exeter University
Upjohn, John 100–2
  Upjohn & Drake 173
Upton Hellions 226
Upton Scudamore 63
urban culture 348–9
  Georgian renaissance 75
  symbiosis 170
USA 131–2, 147, 212, 247, 254, 262
  American Forces Military Band 131
  as destination 54, 84, 198–9, 203–7
  influence of its music 64, 89, 122, 131–5, 144, 146, 268
  see also blackface minstrelsy, Boston, country and western, New York, rhythm 'n' blues, jazz
Utley, Adrian 150

Vageler, Walter 25
value 19–20, 91, 368–75
vamphorns *see* tin horns
variety 141, 144, 363–7
Vaughan, Lady 100
Vaughan, Winifred 260
Vaughan Williams, Ralph 115, 214, 243, 247

Veale, H C 123
Vecsey, Armand 179
Vecsey, Franz von 179
Végh, Sándor 281
venues 117, 147–8, 173, 281–2, 294, 341–3, 348
  arts centres 366–7, 374
  church houses 138, 339–40, 366, 372
Verne, H 258–60
Viardot, Pauline 216
vicars choral 168, 194, 303, 306
  see also lay clerks (lay vicars)
Victoria 192
  coronation 64, 370
village halls 131, 141, 146
Village Thing 148
Viner family
  Frederick 207
  William Litton 41, 207, 222
Vinnicombe brothers 192
viol players 74–5, 300
violin makers *see* instrument makers
violinists 43, 174, 187, 283, 327–8, 341–4
  amateur 246
  dancing masters 164–5
  early music 336
  gentlemen amateurs 74–5, 321
  in country houses 160–1
  leading bands 102, 130–1
  musical leadership 102, 237–9, 326
  virtuosi 179
  see also dancing masters, fiddlers, Loder family: John David, Marie Hall, Sándor Vegh
virginals *see* harpsichords and virginals
Visick, Clarence 205
visitors 285–6, 355
  players 372
  royalty 288–9
  star performers 109–10, 130, 141–2, 166, 176, 179, 280, 286–8, 321, 341, 345–8
  see also incomers
volunteer bands *see* bands
Vowles family 327
  W G 44–9, 58–60

Wagner, Richard 215, 284
  Bayreuth Festival 294
Wainwright, Alex 130
Waite, Andrew Winpenny 95
waits 14, 65, 68–74, 153, 191, 314, 339, 372–3
  see also Bath, Bristol, Exeter, Plymouth, Wells
Wakefield 276
Wales 2, 109, 111, 118, 247
Walker, J W & Sons 49
Walker, Trevor 118
Waller, Fats 146
Walmisley, Thomas Attwood 184
Walshe, Christina 296–7
Walton 183, 199
Warburton, Annie O 188–9
Ward, Mr 342–3
Wardour Castle 332–3
Ware family 125
Wareham
  hymn tune 83

454 INDEX

Lady St Mary church 44
town band 102, 125
Wareham, La 100
warehouses and repositories *see* dealers
Warlock, Peter 246
Warminster 47
    St Denys parish church 21–3, 27, 186
    St Lawrence's chapel 48
    town hall 343
Warren, Raymond 329
Warren and Ninnes 129
wars
    Civil War 21–2, 74, 298, 321
    First World War 115, 117, 125–8, 130, 135–6, 187, 290–5, 328, 360
    Franco-Prussian War 126
    Napoleonic wars 68, 93–9, 207
    Second World War 52, 117, 123, 131–2, 331, 333, 349–55, 357–8, 360–2
    see also festivals and celebrations: for peace
    Seven Years' War 92
Watchet 86, 150
Watchet Music Festival 286
Watermouth Castle 158
Watersmeet 258
Watkins, Hadley 242
Wayte, Thomas [the] 69
Weatherly, Fred E 217–18, 261, 263
Webbe, John 168
Webber, Mr 100, 102
Webber, Thomas Nichols 102
Wedlock, Fred 144–7
Wedmore
    bands 98
    Methodist Chapel 38
    parish church 131
Wedmore, Charles 77
Weedon, Bert 141
Week 336
Weekes (publisher) 247
Welcombe
    Mead Barn 135
Weld, Thomas (father and son) 49
Wellington 101
    Baptish Church 85
Wellington, Francis 77
Wellington Sacred Harmonic Society 115
Wells 39, 60, 73, 77, 195, 201, 301, 33
    almshouses 168
    Bishop's Palace 18
    composers 86
    concert life 185, 340
    diocese 8
    education 301
    long dances 273
    musical slates 305
    professionals 314
    scandal of 1607 162
    St Cuthbert's church 25
    teachers 162, 175
    visit of James I 289
    waits 73, 197
    see also Claver Morris
Wells, Mary 79

Wells Brush Works Band 125
Wells Cathedral 299
    hall of the vicars choral 304
    organ 27, 31–2
    organist 16, 25, 35, 155, 172, 175, 185, 309, 315
    vicars choral 303, 315
Wells Cathedral School 301, 338–9
Wells Music Club 76–7
Wesley family 220
    Charles (composer) 177, 220
    John 7, 172, 279
    Samuel 95, 170, 177, 220
    Samuel Sebastian 24, 40, 45, 50, 165, 231, 257, 320–1, 324, 337, 346
Wessex 250, 254, 291, 351
West, Henry 192
West, Jock 133
West Briton 172
west country xi, 5
    as holiday destination 242, 253–5, 264
    as lifestyle choice 5, 61–3, 255
    as paradigm 254–97, 355–7
    bibliography xiii, 3–5
    boundaries 5–8
    musical individuality 1, 59–60
    pre-Reformation compositions 314–16
    see also Wessex
west gallery music *see* psalmody
West Indies 239, 329
West Lydford 138–9, 181–3, 304
    parish church 139
West of England Folk Centre *see* Plymouth Folk Song Club
West of England Folk Song Singers 355
West Teignmouth
    St James's church 33
Westbury
    as gateway 8
    Leighton House 166
Westbury-on-Trym
    college of priests 306, 314
Westcote, Sebastian 314
West-Country Singers 355
    see also BBC West of England Singers
West-Country Studio Orchestra 352, 356
Western Times 64–5
Weston-in-Gordano 84, 287
Weston-super-Mare 129, 146, 149, 200
    Dismaland 288
    Grand Pier band (or orchestra) 53, 127, 131
    Holy Trinity church 204
    Italian Band 126
    Knightstone Pier 127
    Odeon Cinema 57
    Old Pier 126–7
    Skeleton Army 122
    T4 on the Beach 287
    Worlebury Camp 19
Weston-super-Mare Orpheus Glee Society 107
Westonzoyland 43
Westward Ho! 262
Weymouth 7, 43, 79–80, 95, 97, 261
    concert life 346
    dealers 100, 173, 196

St Mary's church 36, 43, 80, 195
Wheatstone, Charles 38
Whippie, Miss 114
Whistler, Laurence 274
Whitby, John & Son 177
Whitchurch
  parish church 114
White, Ann 99
White, James 230
White, John T 246, 258, 260
White, Richard 113
White, Thomas 72
Whiting, Abbot 26
Whitlock, Percy 45, 49, 52, 55-7, 244-6, 354
  Bridgwater Pageant 290-2
  Plymouth Suite 71, 263
Whitsun 151-3, 276, 279, 372-3
Whyte, William 311
Widdecombe Fair (song) 258, 260, 269-70, 357, 369
Widecombe Fair (novel) 365-6
Widecombe in the Moor 137, 270
  concert 365-6
Wilcox, Ella Wheeler 207
Wilde, Oscar 109
Wilkey, Taverner 195
Willcocks, David 319
William of Orange 29-30
Williams, David 95
Williams, J W 196
Williams, Jack 134
Williams, John 87
Williams, Kenneth 356-7
Willis, Henry 23, 32, 45, 48, 50
Williton 86
  Baptist Chapel 365
  dealers 196
  service of song 365
Wills, Charlie 356
Wills family
  H H 33
  tobacco factory 145
Wilson, John 205
Wilton 160, 246, 268
Wilton Abbey 320
Wilton House 7, 160-1, 341
Wiltshire 5-8, 47, 84, 107-8, 320
  County Music Festival 282
  County Record Office 268
  county town 268
  idea of 263
  youth ensembles 287
  see also regiments and their bands
Wiltshire march, The 93
Wiltshire Music Centre *see* Bradford on Avon
Wimborne 332
  church house 340
  dealers 172
  Gaunts House Summer Gathering 286
  Queen Elizabeth's School 322
  SA citadel 18
  soundscape 17-18
Wimborne, La 100
Wimborne Folk Festival 287
Wimborne Minster 313

  as college of priests 306
  bells 18
  organ 21, 25, 31, 36
  organ blower 24
  organist 35, 155
Wincanton 198
Winchester College 306
Windsor 232
  Castle 221
  Court 347
  St George's Chapel 168, 199, 313
Wingrove, Mrs 222
Winscombe
  nonconformist chapel 53
Winsham 195
Winter, William 137
Winton 242
Withers, Nathaniel 139
Withycombe
  service of song 365
Witton, Henry James 202
Witton, J 202
Wiveliscombe
  Congregational Church 39
Wogan, Terry 271
Wolcot, John 232
Womad *see* world music
women
  amateur pianists 174
  apprenticeships 167
  as audience 108, 340-2
  as dedicatees 100
  as patrons 32-3
  at university 134
  clubs and societies 78
  composers 100-1, 209-14, 242, 271, 320-1
  conductors 362-3
  entrepreneurs 282-4
  folksingers 265
  in bands 100, 140
  in choirs 44, 84, 105, 109, 114-18
  in glee performances 105
  in SA bands 122
  lute pupils 162
  minstrels 191
  musicians' wives 191
  nuns 320-1
  performers 223
  professional pianists 185-6, 192
  purchasing pianos 179
  subscribers 81
  teachers 185-9, 242
  violinists 75
  see also education, organists
Women's Institute 115, 291
Wood, Arthur 243
Wood, Daniel 50-1
Wood, Fred and May 188
Wood, John 161-2, 168
Woodbury 207
Woodhouse, Harry 87, 92
Woods, Samuel 202
Woodward, Thomas 173
Wookey

parish church 185
Woolwich
   Royal Military Academy 220
Worcester 223, 246, 314
Wordsworth, William 283
workers and labourers *see* industry
workhouses 64
works bands *see* bands
world music 286
Worth, Bill 133
Worth, Herbert 155
Woulds, James 99
Wrenn, William 99–100
Wright and Round 125
Wright, David 187
Wright, Julian 259
Wrington 354
   parish church 114
Wurlitzer 54, 56
Wurm, Stanislaus 178
Wurzels 142–6, 271
Wyatt, Catherine 256
Wylie, Peter 161
Wyncote, T 372

Yates, Mrs M 101
Yates, Roger 61–2, 335
Yatton
   St Mary's church 26, 59, 114, 155, 372–3
   WI choir 115

Yealmpton Hotel 133
Yeo, John 372
Yeomanry Cavalry quadrilles, The 100
Yeovil
   Boys' Brigade band 132
   Brass at the Octagon festival 287
   dealers 172
   Girls' Brigade band 132
   Masonic Ball 102
   quadrille band disaster 101–2
   SA Band 123, 132
   St John the Baptist church 313
   VE Day celebrations 132
Yeovil Harmonic Society 358–9
Yerbary, Mrs 100
Yetminster 140
Yetminster Irish Dancers 140
Yetties 140
York 214, 218, 276, 282, 337
youth culture 138–40, 142–3, 180, 274
   festivals 287
   see also subculture

Zennor 285
   Mermaid of 284
zone of hearsay *see* travel
zoos 345
   see also Clifton

Titles listed here were originally published
under the series title *Music in Britain, 1600–1900*
ISSN 1752-1904

Lectures on Musical Life:
William Sterndale Bennett
edited by Nicholas Temperley, with Yunchung Yang

John Stainer: A Life in Music
Jeremy Dibble

The Pursuit of High Culture: John Ella and
Chamber Music in Victorian London
Christina Bashford

Thomas Tallis and his Music in Victorian England
Suzanne Cole

The Consort Music of William Lawes, 1602–1645
John Cunningham

Life After Death: The Viola da Gamba
in Britain from Purcell to Dolmetsch
Peter Holman

The Musical Salvationist: The World of Richard Slater
(1854–1939) 'Father of Salvation Army Music'
Gordon Cox

British Music and Literary Context:
Artistic Connections in the Long Nineteenth Century
Michael Allis

New titles published under the series title
Music in Britain, 1600–2000
ISSN 2053-3217

≥≥

Hamilton Harty: Musical Polymath
Jeremy Dibble

Thomas Morley: Elizabethan Music Publisher
Tessa Murray

*The Advancement of Music in Enlightenment England:
Benjamin Cooke and the Academy of Ancient Music*
Tim Eggington

George Smart and Nineteenth-Century London Concert Life
John Carnelley

The Lives of George Frideric Handel
David Hunter

*Musicians of Bath and Beyond:
Edward Loder (1809–1865) and his Family*
edited by Nicholas Temperley

*Conductors in Britain, 1870–1914:
Wielding the Baton at the Height of Empire*
Fiona M. Palmer

Ernest Newman: A Critical Biography
Paul Watt

*The Well-Travelled Musician: John Sigismond Cousser and
Musical Exchange in Baroque Europe*
Samantha Owens

≥≥